The Economic Way of Thinking

The Economic Way of Thinking

SIXTH EDITION

Paul Heyne
University of Washington

Macmillan Publishing Company

New York

Collier Macmillan Canada

Toronto

Maxwell Macmillan International

New York   Oxford   Singapore   Sydney

Acknowledgments

Credits for photographs: facing page 1: Elliott Erwitt/Magnum Photos; p. 14: M. Durrance/ Photo Researchers; p. 46: Harvey Stein; p. 68: Bruce Davidson/Magnum Photos; p. 98: H. Cartier-Bresson/Magnum Photos; p. 128: H. Cartier-Bresson/Magnum Photos; p. 152: Kosti Ruohomaa/Black Star; p. 178: Paul Sequeira/Photo Researchers; p. 198: Burk Uzzle/Picture Group; p. 224: Bruce Davidson/Magnum Photos; p. 252: Jeff Albertson/Picture Cube; p. 294: H. Cartier-Bresson/Magnum Photos; p. 328: DisFarmer/Miller/Magnum Photos; p. 362: Elliott Erwitt/Magnum Photos; p. 396: Charles Harbutt; p. 422: Harvey Stein; p. 436: H. Cartier-Bresson/Magnum Photos; p. 460: Elliott Erwitt/Magnum Photos; p. 484: Bruce Roberts/Photo Researchers; p. 510: Gordon Baer/Black Starr; p. 534: Harvey Stein; p. 560: Inge Moratti/Magnum Photos; p. 576: H. Cartier-Bresson/Magnum Photos.

Editor: Caroline Carney
Production Supervisor: John Travis
Production Manager: Richard C. Fischer
Text and cover designed by Patricia Smythe
Cover illustration by Juliana Heyne, oil painting "Temple".
Main illustrations by Vantage Art, Inc.
Marginal illustrations by V & M Graphics.

This book was set in Trump Mediaeval type by V & M Graphics and printed and bound by Halliday Lithograph.
The cover was printed by New England Book Components.

Macmillan Publishing Company
866 Third Avenue, New York, New York 10022

Collier Macmillan Canada, Inc.
1200 Eglinton Avenue, E.
Suite 200
Don Mills, Ontario, M3C 3N1

Library of Congress Cataloging in Publication Data

Heyne, Paul T.
    The economic way of thinking / Paul Heyne. — 6th ed.
        p.   cm.
    ISBN 0-02-354181-4
    1. Economics.   I. Title.
    HB171.5.H46 1990
    330 — dc20   90-34668
                                                                        CIP

Printing: 1 2 3 4 5 6 7 8 9 0   Year: 1 2 3 4 5 6 7 8 9 0

With gratitude to my joint authors,
Wallie and Ruth

Preface_____

Introductory economics has long been an easy subject to
teach. It's been a hard subject to *take*, but that's another
matter. Moreover, the amount of learning that comes out of
principles courses bears no reasonable relationship to the
amount of teaching that goes in.

Principles of economics has been an easy course to teach
because we have used it largely to regurgitate the bits of
technique acquired during our own training in economics.
There are so many such bits and pieces, and they are so hard
for students to grasp, that principles teachers need never
worry about what to do today. They can always introduce a
new complication or spend the hour clarifying the complication introduced yesterday. And they don't even have to
prepare the complications. A single phrase — elasticity, total-
average-marginal revenue, long-run competitive equilibrium,
marginal-value product, IS-LM, the multiplier — will serve as
an adequate text for an entire class session.

What Are We After?

What should be the learning goal in the beginning economics
course? It is clear from what has already been said that I
have little use for what I take to be the usual learning goal:
introducing the student to bits and pieces of technique. Why
should we want a beginning student to be familiar with the
concepts of average variable, average total, and marginal
cost, their downward then upward shapes, the necessary intersection of marginal cost at the low point of average cost,
and everything else contributing to the demonstration that
in the long run, under perfectly competitive conditions, price
will be equal to average total and marginal cost for all firms
after quasi-rents have been capitalized? To ask the question
is to answer it. We have no good reason for wanting a beginning student to know all this. Then why have we continued
to teach it?

Part of the explanation lies in our commendable concern
to teach *theory*. It is economic theory that gives to economics almost all its predictive or clarifying power. Without
theory, we must grope our way blindly through economic
problems, conflicting opinions, and opposing policy proposals.

But economic theory has proved itself unusually difficult to communicate. So those responsible for teaching undergraduate economics, struck by the apparent failure of theory-oriented principles courses, have sometimes opted instead for a problems and issues course. In such a course, students typically read and discuss statements by labor leaders, industry representatives, agricultural lobbyists, politicians, and a few domestic radicals or foreign socialists. They look at figures on income distribution, gross national product, employment, prices, and rates of economic growth. They read and discuss the arguments for guaranteed incomes and against planned obsolescence, for free enterprise and against unregulated competition, for nuclear power and against uncontrolled economic growth. And when it is all over, what have they learned? They have learned that opinions abound, with data to support every one of them, that "it's all relative," that every American is entitled to an opinion, and that economics is not a science and is probably a waste of time.

The insistence on teaching theory is correct insofar as it is a denial of the significance of facts without theories. Theory is essential! But what theory? Economic theory, of course. But that begs the real question. What *kind* of economic theory? And in what *context*? Before we can answer, we must know what we're after.

Concepts and Applications

I want beginning students to master a set of concepts that will help them think more coherently and consistently about the wide range of social problems that economic theory illuminates. The principles of economics make sense out of buzzing confusion. They clarify, systematize, and correct the daily assertions of newspapers, political figures, ax grinders, and barroom pontiffs. And the applicability of the economist's thought tools is practically unlimited. Students should come to appreciate all of this in a beginning course.

But they won't unless we, the teachers and textbook writers, persuade them. And we can persuade them only by showing them. *The principles of economics must therefore be taught as tools of analysis.* The teaching of a concept must take place in the context of application. Better, the potential application should be taught first, then the tool. There is so much evidence from pedagogy to support this approach that it's hard at first to understand how any other approach could ever have conquered the field.

"Here is a problem. You recognize it as a problem. What can we say about it?" That's step one.

"Here is how economists think about the problem. They employ the concept of such and such." Step two entails the exposition of some concept of economic theory.

After the applicability of the concept to the original problem has been demonstrated and some of the implications examined, the concept should be applied to additional problems. That's step three.

It isn't as easy as one-two-three, of course, and I don't mean to imply that it is. The teaching of economic principles requires imagination, insight, a knowledge of current events, and a sense of perspective, as well as familiarity with the formal techniques of economic analysis. Those are all scarce goods. And it presupposes a conviction on the part of the teacher that economic theory really is useful for something more than answering artificial questions and passing equally artificial examinations.

The Virtue of Restraint

Perhaps no one would disagree in principle with any of the foregoing statements. If so, our practice has been far out of step with our precept. One reason is undoubtedly the obsession with formal technique that characterizes so much teaching of economic theory at all levels. The disciple will very rarely rise above the master. And if the masters in our profession are more concerned with form than content, the effects will be felt at the principles level. We need not debate here the question of how much of the material taught in intermediate and advanced theory texts really belongs there, or what balance should be struck in graduate theory courses between the logic-mathematics and the economics of theory. For the question of what should go into a beginning course can be answered without resolving the other questions. And that answer is: *very little*.

For very little indeed of what might go into a complete and current compendium of economic theory is actually useful in enabling us to make sense of the real world and to evaluate policy proposals. Almost all the genuinely important things that economics has to teach are elementary concepts of relationship that people could almost figure out for themselves if they were willing to think carefully.[1]

The challenge is getting people to *appreciate* these few, simple concepts. To do that, we must practice the virtue of

---

[1]A compelling statement of this view was provided by Ely Devons in the first two of his *Essays in Economics* (London: George Allen and Unwin, 1961), pp. 13–46.

restraint. We must attempt less and thereby accomplish more. An introductory course should distinguish itself as much by what it excludes as by what it incorporates. Unless it is our aim to impress students with the esoteric quality of economists' knowledge, we should teach no theory in the introductory course that cannot be put to work immediately. Otherwise we drown beginning students; they are made to thrash about so desperately that they don't learn to swim a single stroke. Our aim should be to get them swimming and to instill in them the confidence that through practice they can learn to swim better.

Every introductory economics teacher ought to read a short essay by Noel McInnis, entitled "Teaching More with Less." Here are three excerpts:

> I dare say that all of us who teach have been guilty of telling our students much more than they cared — or needed — to know. In fact, I would theorize that we have probably been telling them more about our subjects than *we* care to know. That is one reason why we feel compelled to rely on notes to deliver lectures.
>
> Our present methods of communicating often obscure meaning rather than reveal it. . . . We often see the tragic results of this in our "best" students, who can repeat what we have told them but cannot apply it in a new context so that it means something. Their learning may have been comprehensive, but it has not been comprehending.
>
> Survey courses in almost all disciplines are becoming increasingly impractical because of their compulsive attempt to cover all relevant information. They could be made highly practical once again — or perhaps for the first time — if they were organized to convey the five or six most fundamental organizing and conceptual principles of the discipline, utilizing only the most immediately relevant information to bring the principles to life.[2]

I agree wholeheartedly with McInnis. My implementation of this vision will undoubtedly be found far from perfect. But the teacher who wonders why this or that topic is not treated in the book, or why there is no complete exposition of some familiar portion of theory, should remember that knowledge is imparted by what is left out as well as by what is included. Judgments on relevance and relative importance will, of course, vary. But the argument of McInnis should be faced every time we are tempted to add another jot or tittle

2. *Change: The Magazine of Higher Education* (January–February 1971), pp. 49, 50, 51.

to the corpus of what we teach in beginning principles courses.

One Term or Two?

Every economics teacher, whether of graduates or under-graduates, knows how disconcertingly little most students bring with them from principles courses into subsequent studies. Sometimes they don't seem to remember anything except that they've "heard of it." Is the solution more credit hours of introduction? Should we detain them longer so that we can drill them more thoroughly in the fundamentals of our discipline? In my judgment the solution lies rather in the direction of fewer hours spent in the introductory course.

What is true and relevant tends to get lost when a begin-ning course is extended over two quarters or semesters. The student gets many fuzzy ideas of what the subject is *about*, but little grasp of what it *is*.

Moreoever, there are too many pedagogical and adminis-trative problems associated with the truncated unity of a two-term single course. Teachers change, textbooks change, micro comes before macro and then macro is put before micro, students drop out after the first term and return two years later for the second term. Why have we nonetheless persisted? It sometimes seems as if we're afraid to teach it all in one term for fear that we'll cut our demand in half. If we can persuade the curriculum makers, especially in the business schools, that two terms is the absolute minimum, we can better maintain the demand for our services.

But a single *worthwhile* term can leave the beginning student eager for more. And economic education doesn't have to end with the introductory course. It won't, at least for many of the students whom we want to continue, if we do a better job of getting them started. The demand for eco-nomic principles may even prove to be elastic: if we cut the hourly cost in half, the number of customers may more than double.

Some economists feel that, although a one-term course may be adequate for the general student, two terms are the essential minimum for economics or business majors. But isn't a brief and lively introduction to economics the best start for everyone, for those who plan never to take another course and for those who intend to go on to graduate school in economics? After all, a one-term principles course does not preclude subsequent courses in theory, courses that could be required or strongly recommended for majors. And more students might enroll in the theory courses if the introductory course managed to persuade them that economic theory is a worthwhile and occasionally even an exciting study.

Changes in the Sixth Edition

Important changes have been made for this edition in Chapters 7, 11, and 13. The data in the chapters on macroeconomics have, of course, been brought up-to-date, or as up-to-date as is possible given all the leads and lags of both data publishing and book publishing. There are also some substantive changes in the macroeconomics chapters, including a few notable omissions, all with the aim of telling a simpler and more cogent story.

Many users have recommended inclusion of a glossary. I don't like glossaries because they present terms out of context, and context is vital in teaching the basic concepts of economic theory. So I have compromised. A list of glossary terms is presented just prior to the index. The reader can then find these terms defined on the page or pages printed in **bold type** in the index.

I have also been urged to include answers to some of the questions at the end of the book. Again I have compromised. The Instructors' Guide to the sixth edition will print *all* the answers in a separate section on perforated pages that instructors can then tear out, if they wish, and make available to students for photocopying.

Acknowledgments

My thinking continues to be challenged, clarified, and corrected by interactions with students, graduate assistants, and faculty at the University of Washington, and by conversations and correspondence with colleagues at other schools. I am grateful to them all. Special thanks go to P.J. Hill of Wheaton College; John Eggers of Towson State University; Mary L. Eysenbach of Knox College; Robert Higgs of Seattle University; Charles Lave of the University of California, Irvine; Ian Laxer of Concordia University; Potluri Rao and Stephen J. Turnovsky of the University of Washington; and Constance Spangler, Michelle Donohue and S. Lauren Heyne, all of whom contributed in significant ways to changes in this edition. Since I usually followed their advice, you may give them credit for the improvements you find. Since I sometimes refused to heed their counsel — at least once in a blatant way — lay the blame for all that is wrong-headed at my door.

Once again I want to acknowledge the pioneering role of Armen A. Alchian and William R. Allen, whose *University Economics* first showed me how to make introductory economics a useful and exciting course. And for the forms and colors whose primacy I so easily forget in the pale and amorphous world of academia, I am grateful to my wife, Juliana.

Paul Heyne

Contents

The Theory of Economics does not furnish a body of settled conclusions immediately applicable to policy. It is a method rather than a doctrine, an apparatus of the mind, a technique of thinking which helps its possessor to draw correct conclusions.

John Maynard Keynes

Chapter 1

The Economic Way of Thinking

Good mechanics can locate the problem in your car because they know how your car functions when it *isn't having any problems*. A lot of people find economic problems baffling because they do not have a clear notion of how an economic system works when it's working well. They are like mechanics whose training has been limited entirely to the study of malfunctioning engines.

When we have long taken something for granted, it's hard even to see what it is that we've grown accustomed to. That's why we rarely notice the existence of order in society and cannot recognize the mechanisms of social coordination upon which we depend every day. A good way to begin the study of economics, therefore, might be with astonishment at the feats of social cooperation in which we daily engage. Rush-hour traffic is an excellent example.

Recognizing Order

You are supposed to gasp at that suggestion. "Rush-hour traffic as an example of social *cooperation*? Shouldn't that be used to illustrate the law of the jungle or the *breakdown* of social cooperation?" Not at all. If the association that pops into your mind when someone says "rush-hour traffic" is "traffic jam," you are neatly supporting the thesis that we notice only failures and take success so much for granted we aren't even aware of it. The dominant characteristic of rush-hour traffic is not jam but movement, which is why people venture into it day after day and almost always reach their destinations. It doesn't work perfectly, of course. (Name one thing that does.) But the remarkable fact at which we should learn to marvel is that it works at all.

Thousands of people leave their homes at about eight in the morning, slide into their automobiles, and head for work. They all choose their own routes without any consultation.

They have diverse skills, differing attitudes toward risk, and varying degrees of courtesy. As these passenger automobiles in their wide assortment of sizes and shapes enter, move along, and exit from the intersecting corridors that make up the city's traffic veins and arteries, they are joined by an even more heterogeneous mixture of trucks, buses, motorcycles, and taxicabs. The drivers all pursue their separate objectives, with an almost single-minded devotion to their own interests, not necessarily because they are selfish but simply because none of them knows anything about the objectives of the others. What each one does know about the others is confined to a few observations on the position, direction, and velocity of a changing handful of vehicles in the immediate environment. To this they add the important assumption that other drivers are about as eager to avoid an accident as they themselves are. There are general rules, of course, which everyone is expected to obey, such as stopping for red lights and staying close to the speed limit. That's about it, however. The entire arrangement as just described could be a prescription for chaos. It ought to end in heaps of mangled steel.

What ensues instead is a smoothly coordinated flow, a flow so smooth, in fact, that an aerial view from a distance can almost be a source of aesthetic pleasure. There they are — all those independently operated vehicles down below, inserting themselves into the momentary spaces between other vehicles, staying so close and yet rarely touching, cutting across one another's paths with only a second or two separating a safe passage from a jarring collision, accelerating when space opens before them and slowing down when it contracts. The movement of rush-hour traffic, or indeed of urban traffic at any time of day, really is an astounding feat of social cooperation.

The Importance of Social Cooperation

The traffic example is particularly effective in making us see how much social cooperation we totally fail to notice, because everyone is familiar with traffic but almost no one thinks of it as a cooperative endeavor. But the example is also useful in making the point that we depend on mechanisms of coordination for far more than what we usually think of as "economic" goods. If we had no working procedures to induce cooperation, we could enjoy none of the benefits of civilization. "In such a condition," as Thomas Hobbes (1588–1679) observed in an often-quoted passage of his *Leviathan:*

. . . there is no place for industry, because the fruit thereof is uncertain; and consequently no culture of the earth; no navigation, nor use of the commodities that may be imported by sea; no commodious building; no instruments of moving and removing such things as require much force; no knowledge of the face of the earth; no account of time; no arts; no letters; no society; and, which is worst of all, continual fear, and danger of violent death; and the life of man, solitary, poor, nasty, brutish, and short.[1]

Because Hobbes believed that people were so committed to self-preservation and personal satisfaction that only force (or the threat of it) could keep them from constantly assaulting one another, his writings emphasize only the most basic form of social cooperation: abstention from violence and robbery. He seems to have supposed that if people could be induced not to attack one another's persons or property, then positive cooperation — the kind that actually produces industry, agriculture, knowledge, and art — would develop of its own accord. But will it? Why should it?

How Does It Happen?

By what means do the members of a society induce one another to take precisely those complexly interconnected actions that will eventually produce the multitude of goods, tangible and intangible, that we all enjoy? Even a society of saints must use some procedures for inducing positive cooperation *of the right kind* if the life of each saint is to be more than "solitary, poor, nasty, brutish, and short." Saints must, after all, somehow find out exactly what ought to be done and when and where it ought to be done before they can play an effective part in helping others.

Hobbes probably failed to see the importance of this question for understanding life in the "commonwealth," because the society he knew was far simpler, more bound by custom and tradition, and less subject to rapid and disruptive change than the societies in which we have grown up. Not until late in the eighteenth century, as a matter of fact, did any significant number of thinkers begin to wonder why it was that society "worked" — that individuals pursuing their own interests on the basis of extremely limited information nonetheless managed to produce not chaos but a remarkably ordered society.

One of the most perceptive and surely the most influen-

[1]Hobbes, *Leviathan, or the Matter, Forme and Power of a Commonwealth Ecclesiastical and Civil,* 1651.

tial of these eighteenth-century thinkers was Adam Smith (1723–1790). Smith lived in an age when most educated people believed that only the diligent attentions of political rulers could prevent a society from degenerating into disorder and poverty. Smith did not agree. But in order to refute the accepted opinion of his day, he had to describe the mechanism of social coordination that he saw operating in society — a mechanism that not only functioned, in his judgment, without the constant attention of government, but worked so powerfully that it often canceled the effects of contrary governmental policies. Adam Smith published his analysis in 1776 as *An Inquiry into the Nature and Causes of the Wealth of Nations* and thereby established his claim to the title, Founder of Economics. He did not *invent* "the economic way of thinking." But he developed it more extensively than any of his predecessors had done, and he was the first writer to use it in a comprehensive analysis of social change and social cooperation.

An Apparatus of the Mind

What exactly do we mean by *the economic way of thinking*? To begin with, it is exactly what the term suggests: an approach, rather than a set of conclusions. John Maynard Keynes phrased it aptly in the statement quoted in the front of this book:

> The Theory of Economics does not furnish a body of settled conclusions immediately applicable to policy. It is a method rather than a doctrine, an apparatus of the mind, a technique of thinking which helps its possessor to draw correct conclusions.

But what is this "technique of thinking"? It is, most fundamentally, an assumption about what guides human behavior. The theories of economics, with surprisingly few exceptions, are simple extensions of the assumption that individuals take those actions they think will yield them the largest net advantage. Everyone, it is assumed, acts in accordance with that rule: miser or spendthrift, saint or sinner, consumer or seller, politician or business executive, cautious calculator or spontaneous improviser.

Self-interested (not "selfish"!) actions.

But don't misunderstand. Economic theory does not assume that people are selfish, or materialistic, or shortsighted, or irresponsible, or interested exclusively in money. None of these is implied by the statement that people try to secure for themselves the largest possible net advantage. Everything depends on what, in fact, people find in their own interest.

As we know, some derive enormous satisfaction from helping people. A few, unfortunately, seem to derive satisfaction from actually hurting others. Some find their keenest pleasure in the sight of roses blooming. Others would far rather speculate on urban real estate.

But if people are all that different, how can economic theory explain or predict anything about their behavior merely by assuming that they all act in what they think will be their own best interests? What does the assumption imply except that people do what they want to do, whatever that is?

Matters aren't that hopeless, however, for people don't really seem to be as different in their interests as the preceding contrasts would suggest. All of us regularly and successfully predict the behavior of people whom we have never even met, and we could not function effectively in society without the ability to do so. Rush-hour traffic flow, for example, would be impossible if we could not predict the actions of others who are usually complete strangers. Moreover, in any society that uses money extensively, just about everybody prefers more money to less, because money offers a general command over the resources that can be used to advance one's interests, whatever they may be. This is a most useful fact to know when we are trying to predict the behavior of others.

It is also a useful piece of information when we want to *influence* the behavior of others. And that brings us back to the issue of social cooperation and to a second prominent characteristic of the economic way of thinking. Economic theory asserts that the actions people take in the pursuit of their own interests create the alternatives available to others, and that social coordination is a process of continuing mutual adjustment to the changing net advantages that their interactions generate. That is a very abstract argument. We can make it more concrete by referring once more to traffic flow.

Even Mother Teresa does better with more money.

Cooperation Through Mutual Adjustment

Picture a freeway with four lanes in each direction and with all the entrances and exits on the right. Why don't all the drivers stay in the far-right lane? Why do some of them go to the trouble of driving all the way over to the far left when they know they'll have to come back to the right lane to exit? Anyone who has driven on a freeway knows the answer: the traffic flow is impeded in the far-right lane by slow-moving vehicles entering and exiting, so people in a hurry get out of the right lane as quickly as possible.

Which of the other lanes will they choose? Although we can't predict the action of any single driver, we know that the drivers will disperse themselves quite evenly among the three other lanes. But why does this happen? How does it happen? The answer is also the explanation of what we meant just now by *a process of continuing mutual adjustment to the changing net advantages that their actions generate.* Drivers are alert to the net advantages of each lane and therefore try to move out of any lanes that are moving slowly and into those that are moving faster. This speeds up the slow lanes and slows down the fast lanes until all lanes are moving at the same rate, or, more accurately, until no driver perceives any net advantage to be gained by changing lanes. It all happens quickly, continuously, and far more effectively than if someone at the entrances passed out tickets *assigning* each vehicle to a particular lane.

That, according to the economic way of thinking, is how the social world works. Individuals choose their actions on the basis of the net advantages they expect. Their actions alter, however minutely, the relative benefits and costs of the options that others perceive. When the ratio of expected benefit to expected cost for any action increases, people do more of it. When the ratio falls, they do less. The fact that almost everyone prefers more money to less is an enormous aid in this process, an extremely important lubricant, if you will, in the mechanism of social coordination. Modest changes in the monetary cost and monetary benefit of particular options can induce large numbers of people to alter their behavior in directions more consistent with what other people are concurrently doing. And this is the primary system by which we obtain cooperation among the members of society in using what is available to provide what people want.

How Much Does Economic Theory Explain?

Some might object that the preceding paragraph claims too much. "You haven't given a description of 'how the social world works' but only of how the economic part of it works. You've described the market system. But that's not the whole of society. In addition to the market or economic sector, we have other institutions (such as the government sector) that operate by different principles and procedures."

That sounds like a reasonable objection, or at least one consistent with the traditional ways in which we've learned to divide up the world. But the economic way of thinking is subversive when it comes to those traditional distinctions. If it makes sense to explain the output of the Bethlehem Steel Company and the Chrysler Corporation as the product of competing interests mutually adjusted, why won't it make sense to explain the output of the United States Congress or the Department of Agriculture in the same way? Why draw a line between "the economy" and "the government"? Isn't every branch and agency of government made up, just like any other social group, of ordinary mortals with a wide variety of interests? The necessity of inducing others to cooperate doesn't stop when the capital city is reached! Or if it does, someone has failed to communicate that fact to the lobbyists, legislative leaders, staff assistants, and executive agents who struggle daily to shape the directions of government action.

To tell the embarrassing truth, economic theorists are highly imperialistic. They tend to think that their way of looking at society explains everything, or at least explains more occurrences more adequately than does any other approach. And so economists have been venturing out in recent years to raid territories traditionally occupied by sociologists, political scientists, historians, and others. Economists don't all agree (and representatives of the raided disciplines *surely* do not all agree) that these excursions have always captured valuable terrain. Some critics of the imperialistic ambitions of economics have even accused it of saying nothing about everything. We won't try to resolve those disputes at this point. But you should be aware in advance that this book will draw no clear lines to mark the boundaries of economics. Instead, we shall fall back on the vague but sensible principle that economic theory should be used wherever it successfully explains or predicts and abandoned for something else whenever it sheds no light.

The Biases of Economic Theory

The admission that economics has imperialistic ambitions may not disturb you as much as our admission now that *the economic way of thinking is a biased perspective*. It does not offer an unprejudiced view of society, in which all the facts are presented and all interests are given the same weight. It operates rather with a firm presupposition that *all social phenomena emerge from the choices individuals make in response to expected benefits and costs to themselves*. It rules out anything that cannot be reconciled with this basic presupposition.

Is that a biased perspective or is it not? Consider the emphasis on *choice*. Economic theory is so preoccupied with

Is there actually a separate, distinguishable "economic sector" in our society? Where could we observe it?

choice that some critics have accused it of assuming people choose to be poor or choose to be unemployed. When we come to the issues of poverty and unemployment, you can decide for yourself whether this is a fair criticism or a misunderstanding. But there can be no doubt that economic theory attempts to explain the social world by assuming that events are the product of people's choices.

People choose.

Closely related to this focus on choice is the emphasis economic theory gives to the *individual*. Because only individuals actually choose, economists try to dissect the decisions of such collectives as governments, universities, or corporations until they locate the choices of individual persons who make them up. Does economic theory miss the significance of group action and social bonds by unduly emphasizing the individual? Whatever the merit in this charge, the economic way of thinking definitely does make the individual the ultimate unit of explanation.

Only individuals choose.

Economic thinking is also criticized by some as false or misleading because of its emphasis on calculation and consistency of ends and means. Economists assume that people do not act capriciously, that they compare the expected costs and benefits of available opportunities before they act, and that they learn from and therefore do not repeat their mistakes. But are people really that calculating? Aren't our actions guided more by unconscious urges and unexamined impulses than all this would admit? And is every action really a means to some end? Although economists do not claim that people know everything or never make mistakes, the economic way of thinking does indeed assume that people's actions follow from calculations of costs and benefits. And it does emphasize the instrumental character of human action while neglecting the fact that many important activities — a spirited conversation, perhaps, or a friendly game of tennis — are not engaged in as a means to some end.

Individuals choose after calculating benefits and costs.

Another charge often leveled against the economic way of thinking is that it harbors a *promarket* bias. This criticism, too, calls attention to a genuine and significant characteristic of economic theory, although a characteristic that may not be altogether what it seems to be. Economic theory does not really assume that markets work better than alternative institutions, notably government. Rather it assumes, as we have already indicated, that however poorly or well *any* institution functions, its functioning can best be understood as a consequence of market processes. Exaggerating somewhat for emphasis, we could say that economic theory does not find market solutions better (or worse) than government solutions, because it insists that government solutions

All social interactions can be viewed as market processes.

are market solutions. The actions of government are the outcomes of market processes: individuals pursuing their own interests and mutually adjusting to one another's behavior, but doing so in the context of the special "rules of the game" that apply to the institutions we call government.

Rules of the Game

That's a term you're going to meet repeatedly in this book: the *rules of the game*. Whether the "game" is business, government, science, family, school, traffic, basketball, or chess, it can't be played satisfactorily unless the players know what the rules are and generally agree to follow them. Most social interaction is directed and coordinated by the rules that participants know and follow.

The rules of a game such as basketball or chess determine who gets to make what moves under which circumstances. So do the rules of the other "games" mentioned above. As we shall discover, property rights form a large and important part of the rules governing most of the social interactions in which we regularly engage; by deciding *what is whose,* they determine, just as with games in the ordinary sense, who gets to make what moves under which circumstances. In this manner property rights and other rules of the game help determine exactly what individuals will choose to do in the pursuit of their interests.

Biases or Conclusions?

Let's go back to those four prominent (and interrelated) biases inherent in the economic way of thinking. Are they really biases or prejudices? Why couldn't we call them convictions (or even conclusions) and simply say that economists explain social phenomena by postulating interaction among the calculated choices of individuals, because this enables them to understand those phenomena? Do we say that astronomers are biased because they assume that all the light they observe has traveled toward them at 186,000 miles per second, or that biologists are biased because they assume that DNA molecules control the development of organisms?

The questions we're raising now are important and interesting.[2] But we cannot follow them further without push-

[2]The thoughtful student who would like to pursue these issues further should be sure to read *The Structure of Scientific Revolutions* by Thomas S. Kuhn (Chicago: University of Chicago Press, 1962). This highly readable essay on the history and philosophy of science has had an enormous influence on the thinking of social scientists about the respective roles of assumption and evidence in their investigations.

ing this chapter to an intolerable length. It has long seemed obvious to the author (a prejudice or a conclusion?) that the search for knowledge of any kind necessarily begins with some *commitments* on the part of the inquirer. We cannot approach the world with a completely open mind, because we weren't born yesterday. And completely open minds would in any event be completely empty minds, which can learn nothing at all. All discussion, every inquiry, and even each act of observation are rooted in and grow out of convictions. We cannot begin everywhere or with everything. We must begin somewhere with something. We proceed from where we find ourselves and on the basis of what we believe to be true, important, useful, or enlightening. We may, of course, be wrong in any of these judgments. Indeed, we are always wrong to some extent, since every "true" statement necessarily leaves out a great deal that is also true and thus errs by omission.

We cannot avoid this risk, as some people suppose, by steering clear of theory. People who sneer at "fancy theories" and prefer to rely on common sense and everyday experience are often in fact the victims of extremely vague and sweeping hypotheses. Consider this actual letter to a newspaper from a young person in Pennsylvania who was once "one of a group of teenage pot smokers. Then a girl in the crowd got pregnant. Her baby was premature and deformed and needed two operations." The newspaper's adviser to the teenage lovelorn printed that letter approvingly, as evidence that the price of smoking marijuana is high.

Perhaps it is. But suppose the writer of that letter had written: "Then the Pittsburgh Steelers won the Super Bowl, and the Philadelphia Flyers took the Stanley Cup." Everyone would object that those events had nothing to do with the group's pot smoking. *But how do we know that?* If the mere fact that the young girl's misfortunes followed her pot smoking is evidence of a causal relationship, why can't we also infer a causal relationship in the case of the Steelers and the Flyers?

No Theory Means *Poor* Theory

The point is a simple but important one. We cannot discover, prove, or even suspect any kind of causal relationship without having a theory in mind. Our observations of the world are in fact drenched with theory, which is why we can usually make sense out of the buzzing confusion that assaults our eyes and ears. Actually we observe only a small fraction of what we "know," a hint here and a suggestion there. The rest we fill in from the theories we hold: small ones and broad ones, vague and precise ones, well tested and poorly tested, widely held and sometimes peculiar, carefully reasoned and dimly recognized.

I.M.D. Little is a distinguished British economist who worked for a time as an adviser to the British treasury. He later wrote an article describing his experiences and discussing the usefulness of economic theory in the world of policymaking. Here is an interesting paragraph:

> Economic theory teaches one how economic magnitudes are related, and how very complex and involved these relationships are. Noneconomists tend to be too academic. They abstract too much from the real world. No one can think about economic issues without some theory, for the facts and relationships are too involved to organize themselves: they do not simply fall into place. But if the theorist is untutored, he is apt to construct a very partial theory which blinds him to some of the possibilities. Or he falls back on some old and over-simple theory, picked up from somewhere or other. He is also, I believe, apt to interpret the past naively. *Post hoc ergo propter hoc*[3] is seldom an adequate economic explanation. I was sometimes shocked by the naive sureness with which very questionable bits of economic analysis were advanced in Whitehall. Of course, economists may be too academic in another sense: they may not appreciate administrative difficulties, or may lack a sense of political possibility. But, then, there is no danger of these things being overlooked.[4]

"*Noneconomists* tend to be too academic. They abstract too much from the real world." That isn't the way you usually hear it. But Little is probably correct. "I don't know anything about fancy economic theory," the confident amateur begins, "but I do know this. . . . " And what he says next demonstrates all too often that he was quite right in denying any knowledge of economic theory, but quite wrong in supposing that this preserved him from error. Those who try to reason about complex economic interrelationships without theory usually manage only to reason with very poor theory.

None of this should be interpreted as a wholesale defense of economists, who sometimes like to dazzle the public with complex theorems and exercises in pure logic instead of addressing the questions people are actually asking. Even in the teaching of economics, we have often behaved as

[3]Literally, "After this, therefore because of this"; the logical fallacy of assuming that A must have caused B if A preceded B in time. The argument of the penitent Pennsylvania pot smoker is an example.
[4]I.M.D. Little, "The Economist in Whitehall," *Lloyds Bank Review* (April 1957).

if all the students enrolled in an introductory course were aiming at a Ph.D. in the subject, and that it was our duty to begin their preparation for the doctoral exams. That's probably why introductory courses typically offer so many more ideas than students can possibly digest.

This textbook developed out of a growing suspicion that when students found economic theory mystifying and tedious, it was largely because we economists were trying to teach them too much. This book very consciously sets out, therefore, to achieve more by attempting less. It is organized around a set of concepts that collectively make up the economist's basic kit of intellectual tools. The tools are all related to the fundamental assumptions we have discussed and are surprisingly few in number. But they are extraordinarily versatile. They unlock such mysteries as foreign exchange rates, business firms that make profits by accepting losses, the nature of money, and different prices charged for "identical" goods — mysteries that are generally conceded to be in the economist's province. But they also shed light on a wide range of issues that are not ordinarily thought of as economic at all — traffic congestion, environmental pollution, the workings of government, and the behavior of college adminstrators — to mention just a few that you will encounter in the chapters ahead.

The primary goal of this book is to start you thinking the way economists think, in the belief that once you start you will never stop. Economic thinking is addictive. Once you get inside some principle of economic reasoning and make it your own, opportunities to use it pop up everywhere. You begin to notice that much of what is said or written about economic and social issues is a mixture of sense and nonsense. You get in the habit of sorting the sense from the nonsense by applying the basic concepts of economic analysis. You may even, unfortunately, acquire the reputation of being a cynic, for people who habitually talk nonsense like to cry "cynic" at anyone who points out what they are doing.

Questions for Discussion

1. How much do people have to know about one another in order to cooperate effectively? Contrast the situation of two family members who are planning to take a vacation together with the situation of motorists who are simultaneously using intersecting streets. How are "collisions" avoided in each case? What do you know about the interests, the personality, or

the character of the people whose cooperation supplied your breakfast this morning?

2. What do you predict would happen if Los Angeles decided to reserve one lane on each of its freeways for "urgent vehicles," with an urgent vehicle defined as any vehicle whose driver might be late for an important event if the vehicle were to be delayed by congestion in the regular lanes? Do you think drivers would stay out of the urgent vehicle lane? Or would it become just as congested as all the other lanes? Would such an idea be more likely to succeed in practice if drivers were generally less selfish and more considerate?

3. When Mother Teresa accepted the Nobel Prize for Peace in October 1979 and decided to use the $190,000 award to construct a leprosarium, was she acting in her own interest? Was she behaving selfishly?

4. What happens when the rules of the game (written or unwritten) decree that important meetings won't start until everyone is present and that late arrivals will incur no penalty? Is it in anyone's interest to be punctual? Are these rules of the game likely to prove satisfactory over time?

5. What are some of the more important rules that coordinate the actions of all those playing the "game" of this economics course? Who decided where and when the class would meet, who would teach it, who would enroll as students, what the textbook would be, when the exams would be given, and so on? Who decides where each student will sit? Do you find it odd that two students rarely try to occupy the same seat?

6. In the early 1980s, when the Polish people had to stand in long lines in order to purchase most consumer goods, the government ordered that every third place in line be reserved for pregnant women or disabled persons. This was presumably done to reduce their discomfort. Do you think it resulted in less standing in line by pregnant women? Do you suppose any women became pregnant in order to be able to cut into the long lines?

7. What do we mean when we say, "That's just a coincidence; it doesn't prove anything"? How does theory enable us to distinguish relevant evidence from mere coincidence?

8. Would you say that physicians who don't believe acupuncture works are biased if they reject it without trying it? If someone told you that you can get a perfect grade in this course without studying just by regularly chanting the mantra "invisible hand," would you believe him? Would it be a sign of bias or prejudice on your part if you totally ignored this advice even though you are extremely eager for a high grade in the course?

9. Char Cole bought four steaks at the butcher shop on Friday afternoon. Later that evening three friends came over for a barbecue. Do you suppose her purchase of the steaks *caused* the friends to come over? How can you decide which event was more likely the cause and which the effect? If you read that the crime rate increased in a certain city during a time when the purchase of handguns had also increased, would you suspect a causal connection? Which would more likely be the cause and which the effect? How does *theory* shape your answer?

Chapter 2

Substitutes Everywhere: The Concept of Demand

You must have heard or read statements like these many times in your life:

- Fire safety requires that there be two exits from each apartment unit.
- We need a new car.
- Our state will need large amounts of additional water in the coming decade.
- Traffic surveys have established the need for a new expressway.
- All citizens should be able to obtain the medical care they need regardless of ability to pay.
- There is no substitute for victory.

Fire safety, water, the smooth and rapid movement of traffic, medical care, victory, and even automobiles are all "goods." We say "even" automobiles because some doubts have begun to be expressed about the goodness of automobiles in our congested cities. But you can ask the man who owns one, and a lot of young people who don't. They will assure you that a new car is very much a good. Then what's wrong with those statements?

The element common to all six is the notion of *necessity*. And that is what makes each statement seriously misleading.

Take the first one. Will apartment dwellers who live with only one exit all be injured or killed by fires? Of course not. It's just that the risk is greater with one exit than with two. But then why not three exits? Or four? Why not go the whole route and make the outside walls nothing but doors? The answer is that, although fire safety is a good, it isn't the only good apartment dwellers are interested in. Low rental costs and low heating and cooling costs are also goods, to say nothing of protection from burglars who notice that multiple exits are also multiple entrances. Moreover, there are other

and perhaps better ways to increase fire safety. Extin-
guishers, alarm sprinklers, and large ashtrays also reduce the
risk to apartment dwellers of injury or death from fire. If
more than one exit is required, why not also require a fire
extinguisher on every wall?

That sensible-sounding statement about apartment exits
overlooks three interrelated facts: (1) Most goods are not free
but can be obtained only by sacrificing something else that
is also a good. (2) There are substitutes for anything. (3) Intelligent choice among substitutes requires a balancing of
additional costs against additional benefits.

Costs and Substitutes

Now go back and look at the five other statements. "We
need a new car." Who *needs* a new car? Obviously only
those who value a new car more than what they must sacrifice to obtain one. That might be a vacation trip this year,
new clothes, a lot of movies, and a stereo set. Is it worth it?
There are, after all, plenty of substitutes for a new car: an
overhaul of the present one, a used car, a bicycle, a car pool,
public transportation, moving closer to work, or staying
home more often. Intelligent consumers determine their
preferences after considering these various costs and benefits.
(Of course, once a man has made up his mind, he might still
want to say "We *need* a new car" in the hope that the de-
finitive tone of his statement will dissuade his wife from
making her own comparison of the costs and benefits of a
new one.)

Consider the third statement: "Our state will need large
amounts of additional water in the coming decade." Does
any state really need large amounts of additional water?
Dams and reservoirs, pipelines, and desalinization plants are
ways of obtaining more water. But they have costs. Do the
benefits justify the costs? If you think there are no substitutes for water, then you're thinking too academically. You
have abstracted in a seriously misleading way from the real
world. Probably you're assuming that water is used primarily
for drinking, whereas in fact the overwhelming bulk of the
water consumed in the United States goes for other uses.
Since we shall use the case of water a bit later as an extended working exercise, we can pass this problem by for
now. You might want to begin thinking, though, about the
substitutes for water in such places of chronic scarcity as
Arizona and southern California.

You'll be able to make much more sense out of the

water problem and the expressway issue we take up next if you keep in mind that entities like *states* or *cities* never really want anything. Wants and goals are always attached ultimately to individuals. What does the person who says "The people want . . . " really mean? That all the people want it? A majority? Those who count? It is usually a good rule in analyzing statements like those opening this chapter to ask: *Who* wants more water, or more expressways, or more fire safety?

Only
individuals
choose!

> Things are seldom what they seem.
> Skim milk masquerades as cream.

The fourth of our misleading propositions — "Traffic surveys have established the need for a new expressway" — leads into one of the vexing issues in city planning. Perhaps it would never have become such a troublesome issue if we had admitted all along that expressways entail costs as well as benefits, that there are excellent substitutes for more expressways, and that intelligent city planning calls for the weighing of additional benefits against additional costs. Those who hope to derive most of the benefits from a new expressway while paying only a small percentage of the costs will not want others to notice the full costs of the expressway or how many substitutes there really are. That's why they pretend that a traffic survey can establish "needs." But a traffic survey only shows how many cars travel given routes *at existing costs to the drivers,* including such non-monetary costs as delay, danger, and ulcers. Suppose that the cost of downtown parking increased 500%. What do you think would happen to rush-hour traffic? Commuters would form car pools and begin using public transportation. If the cost *to drivers* of commuting were made high enough, through parking charges, toll fees, or some other device, the need for a new expressway could turn overnight into a "need" for an improved public transportation system. It's a strange kind of need that can vanish so quickly in the face of a price change.

The fifth statement sounds humanitarian and liberal. "All citizens should be able to obtain the medical care they need regardless of ability to pay." But how much medical care does any person need? We might all agree that a woman with an inflamed appendix and no money should have an appendectomy completely at the taxpayers' expense if she is unable to meet any of the costs herself. But what of the man with a splinter in his finger? The services of physicians are not free goods, and they would not become free goods even if every physician treated patients without charging a fee. There just would not be enough physicians to go around if everyone consulted a doctor for every minor ill. The lower the price of visiting a physician, the more frequently will people substitute a trip to the doctor for such other remedies as going to bed, taking it easy, or waiting and hoping. One could rather confidently predict that lower monetary fees would result in higher fees of other sorts, like waiting in line for many hours.

What about the sixth statement: "There is no substitute for victory"? It just isn't so. That may be a good battle cry, but it's unrealistic political analysis. Victory is usually obtained by making sacrifices. If the sacrifices reach a certain intensity, people choose compromise or even defeat, although they are then inclined to *say* that they have "no choice." Once again we notice that the intelligent formulation of policy, including foreign policy, flows from a careful balancing of additional expected costs and additional expected benefits.

The word *expected* should be stressed. We live in a world of uncertainty, forced to make choices that will affect our future without knowing for sure just how they will do so. A common mistake in reasoning about economic problems is to assume that there is no uncertainty or that economic decision makers are omniscient. At last report, omniscience was still a virtue denied to mortals. Condemned as we are to living with uncertainty, we can at least keep from making matters worse by pretending otherwise. Be alert for statements, in this book and elsewhere, which assume that completely adequate information is always available. You might even notice that information, too, is a good that has costs of acquisition and for which there are substitutes available.

The Concept of Demand

The concept of "needs" encourages all-or-nothing thinking. That's why economists prefer the concept of *demand*. Demand is a concept that *relates amounts people want to obtain to the sacrifices they must make to obtain these amounts.*

Ask yourself the following questions: How many records do you want to own? How many times do you want to go out to dinner in a year? What grade do you want from this course?

If you can answer any of those questions, it is because

you have assumed some cost in each case. Suppose you said you want an A from this course and plan to get one. What difference would it make if the price of an A went up? The teacher isn't taking bribes; the price of an A *to you* (that's what counts) is the sacrifice you must make to obtain it. Would you still want an A if it required twenty hours of study a week, whereas a B could be had for just one hour a week? You might still want it, but you would probably not be willing to buy it at such a high price when a fairly good subsitute, a B, is so much cheaper. And that is what counts. Human wants seem to be insatiable. But when a want can only be satisfied at some cost — that is, by giving up the satisfying of some other wants to obtain it — we all moderate our desires and accept less than we would like to have.

Course grade	Cost of earning it
A	20 hours per week
B	1 hour per week
C	3/4 hour per week

The phenomenon of which we're speaking is so fundamental that some economists have been willing to assign it the status of a law: *the law of demand*. This law asserts that there is a negative relation between the amount of anything that people will want to purchase and the price (sacrifice) they must pay to obtain it. At higher prices, they will want to purchase less; at lower prices they will want to purchase more.

Would you agree that this generalization can be called a *law*? Or can you think of exceptions? Genuine exceptions, if they exist at all, are rare. Why would people be indifferent to the sacrifices they must make? Or prefer more sacrifice to less? That is what a person would be doing who took *more* of something as the cost of obtaining it *increased*.

Alleged exceptions to the law of demand are usually based on a misinterpretation of the evidence. Consider the familiar case where the price of something rises and people increase their purchases in anticipation of further price rises. If you think about it carefully you will see that this is not an exception to the law of demand. The expectation of higher prices in the future, created by the initial price rise, has increased people's current demand for the item. They want to buy more now so they can buy less later. It isn't the higher price but the changed *expectations* that have caused people to buy more at the present time. We would observe something quite different if the initial price increase did *not* create those changed expectations. Moreover, those whose expectation of further price increases has prompted them to purchase sooner than they otherwise would have done will still consider the sacrifice they must make in deciding how much to buy.

"Let's stock up before the price goes even higher."

It has sometimes been argued that certain prestige goods

are exceptions to the law of demand. For example, people supposedly buy mink coats because the price is high, not low. No doubt there are people who buy some items largely to impress others with how much they can afford to pay. And people sometimes, in the absence of better information, judge quality by price, so that over a limited range at least, their willingness to purchase may be positively rather than negatively related to price. But these seeming exceptions can readily be explained in a way consistent with the law of demand. People are purchasing prestige rather than mere mink, or judging quality by price because they have no better information.

Cases such as these, however, are rare curiosities at most. Whether or not you are willing to call it a law, the fact is undeniable and extremely important: increases in the price of goods will characteristically be accompanied by decreases in the total amount people want to purchase, and decreases in price will characteristically be accompanied by increases in the amount they want to purchase. It is a serious mistake to overlook this relationship.

Misperceptions Caused by Inflation

One major reason why many people today think that the law of demand doesn't operate is that they have forgotten to take the effects of inflation into account. In an era of rapid inflation, such as the United States and much of the rest of the world have experienced in recent years, most apparent price increases are not real price increases at all. The nature, causes, and consequences of inflation will be examined in detail later in this book (beginning with Chapter 15), but inflation so distorts our perceptions of relative price and cost changes that we'd better think about it before going any further. An ounce of anticipation may prevent a pound of confusion.

Inflation means an increase in the average *money* price of goods. But because we're accustomed to think of the price of anything as the quantity of money we have to sacrifice to get it, we easily conclude that twice as much money means twice as large a cost or sacrifice. That isn't the case, however, if twice as many dollars have only half as much purchasing power. If the money price of each and every good, including human labor and whatever else people sell or rent to obtain money, were to double, then *no* good would have changed in real price — except money, of course, which would have fallen by one-half. And so a doubling of the price of gasoline won't necessarily induce people to use any less gasoline — *if* at the same time their incomes and the prices of all the other goods they use have also doubled.

All money prices do not, in fact, change in equal proportion as a result of inflation — which is one of the reasons inflation is a problem. But they do tend to move together. Consequently, if we want to examine the effect of a particular price increase, we must first abstract from the effects of a general increase in prices. Suppose, for example, that a college which had been charging its students $2000 per year tuition in 1975 was charging $4000 in 1985. By how much had it raised tuition over this ten-year period? The answer is that it hadn't really raised its tuition at all. Because the purchasing power of money was cut in half between 1975 and 1985, a $4000 tuition in 1985 was equivalent to a $2000 tuition in 1975.

Demand and Quality Demanded

There is a general lesson to be drawn from all of this. In using the concept of demand, you must remain alert for the possibility that something else has changed in addition to the price. Your best protection is a clear grasp of the distinction between *demand* and *quantity demanded*. Commentators on economic events often use the word *demand* as a shorthand term for *quantity demanded*. That can and often does lead to error, as we shall see in a moment.

Demand in economic theory is a relationship between two specific variables: price and quantity demanded. You can't state the demand for any good simply as an amount. Demand is always a series of prices and a series of quantities (or amounts) that people would want to purchase at each of those prices. We express that fact by saying that demand is a schedule. A movement from one row of the schedule to another should always be called a change in the quantity demanded, not a change in the demand.

Demand is a schedule

Price	Quantity demanded
50¢	125,000
40¢	160,000
30¢	175,000

Making It Graphic

Many of the concepts economists use can be most easily expressed and understood by means of graphs. The troublesome but important distinction between demand and quantity demanded becomes clear immediately when it's presented on a graph. We can illustrate with the demand for water, as shown in Figure 2A.

(If you happen to be one of that considerable number of

otherwise able people whose insides knot up at the sight of a graph, you ought to slow down at this point. Discover for yourself that graphs are not fatal by following carefully to see exactly what Figure 2A is asserting.)

The vertical axis shows possible prices that might be charged for water, in cents per 1000 gallons. The horizontal axis shows the quantity of water that would be demanded, or that people would want to purchase, at some of those prices.[1] The quantities are expressed in billions of gallons per year for whatever population the graph is summarizing.

Figure 2A yields the following demand schedule:

Price per 1000 Gallons	Billions of Gallons per Year
74¢	9
50	13
36	18
28	29

If the price happened to be 74 cents per 1000 gallons to begin with and was then lowered to 50 cents, the *quantity demanded* would increase from 9 to 13 billion gallons per year. At a price of 28 cents, the *quantity demanded* would be more than three times as great as at 74 cents. But the *demand* would be unchanged through all this, because the demand is the whole curve or schedule.

For the demand to increase, something would have to occur that made these people want to purchase more water than before *at each price*. A drought, for example, might induce people to water their lawns more frequently. Population growth in the area would also be likely to increase the demand; that is, move the whole curve upward and to the right. A campaign to conserve water, if successful, would decrease the demand, causing the curve or schedule to shift downward and to the left to reflect the fact that, at unchanged prices, people now want to purchase less water than previously.

If you would like to graph an increase in the demand for water, plot the quantities in the second column below on

---

[1] It's unfortunate that economists ever chose the word "demand" to describe the desire to purchase; but they've been using it in this way for several centuries and it's too late to change now. The economist's concept of demand carries absolutely none of the word's ordinary connotations of authority or threat, as in "non-negotiable demand." Demand as the economist thinks of it is preeminently negotiable.

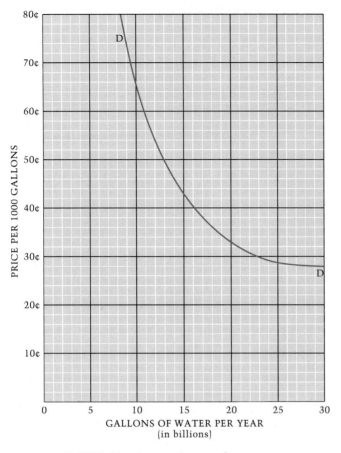

FIGURE 2A   Demand curve for water

Figure 2A. If you prefer to graph a decrease in demand, practice with the third column.

Price per 1000 Gallons	Billions of Gallons Demanded per Year	Billions of Gallons Demanded per Year
70¢	15	5
60	16	7
50	18	10
40	22	13

The Difference It Makes

A short editorial in *The Wall Street Journal* in November 1977 revealed the perils awaiting those who think such verbal distinctions are too trifling to bother with. The editorial

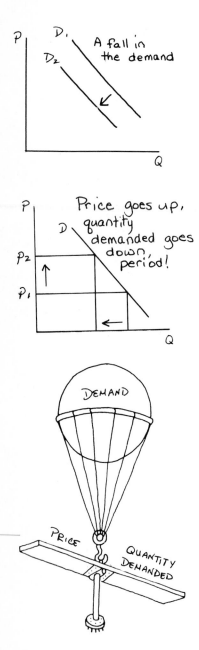

writer wanted to chide an Agriculture Department econo-mist for his ignorance of economics, an ignorance supposedly revealed by his stating that "the power of the U.S. consumer movement" had brought the price of coffee down again after it had hit a high of $4.42 a pound. Not so, said the *Journal's* editorial writer: "The coffee market is behaving the way the basic textbooks say a market behaves: Prices go up, demand falls, and prices come down."

The basic textbooks say nothing of the sort. On the con-trary, they say that the editorial writer has confused the quantity demanded and the demand. When the price of coffee went up, the quantity demanded fell. Period. If the consumer movement managed to change people's attitudes toward serving and drinking coffee (some people got so angry about the price rises that they wouldn't drink coffee for a while at *any* price), then the consumer movement did succeed in changing the demand. And if the demand falls, *then* the price comes down. The *Journal's* mistaken logic implies, if you think about it carefully, that the price will bob up and down indefinitely, since when the price comes down again, demand ought to increase once more, causing the price to go up, whereupon the demand will fall, causing the price to go down. . . .

But it's all just a confusion of thought introduced by a careless use of terms. Think of price and quantity demanded as objects on the opposite ends of a seesaw, and demand as a large, lighter-than-air balloon to which the seesaw is at-tached. When price goes one way, quantity demanded goes the opposite way. Changes in the demand (movements of the balloon up or down) will exert simultaneous pressure in the same direction on both the price and the quantity demanded. The demand for any good is the product of biological realities, social relationships, psychological factors, and a broad assortment of economic variables, such as income and the price, quality, and general availability of substitutes. All these forces combine to create the demand for a particular good, the relationship that will exist between changes in its money price and changes in the quantity people will try to obtain. Unless the demand is changing (the balloon is as-cending or descending), price and quantity demanded will always move in opposite directions.

To put it most simply: the one change that will *not* cause a change in the demand for bicycles is a change in the price of bicycles. If a combination of rising incomes, environ-mental concern, and new interest in outdoor exercise induces more people to want bicycles, the demand for them will increase. And both the price and quantity demanded may well increase as a consequence. Something like this happens frequently. You have grasped the distinction between demand and quantity demanded if you see clearly why this in no way contradicts the law of demand. An increase in demand may pull up both price and quantity demanded. But it will still be as true with the high demand as with the low demand that a smaller quantity will be demanded at higher than at lower prices. And this is what the law of demand asserts. Economic theory isolates the money price of goods for special attention because of the exceptionally important role that money prices play in adjusting and coordinating people's behavior.

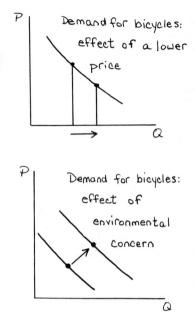

Money Costs and Other Costs

None of this implies, however, that the price in money that must be paid for something is a complete measure of its cost to the purchaser. Indeed, sometimes it is a very inadequate measure (as in the case of the student who wanted an A). Economists know this at least as well as anyone else. The concept of demand definitely does not suggest that money is the only thing that matters to people. Confusion about this point has done so much to create misunderstanding that we might profitably take a moment to clarify the matter.

Consider the case of a woman buying soft drinks. Assume that she can purchase them in either returnable or throwaway bottles, and that a liter of her favorite drink is priced at $1.80 in the throwaway bottle, whereas a liter in a returnable bottle is $1.60 plus 40 cents deposit. Which will she buy? Which is cheaper? It depends on the cost to her, of which the retailer's price is only one element. If she doesn't mind saving and returning bottles — that is, if the cost to her of doing so is low — she will probably find the returnable bottles cheaper and will buy them. On the other hand, if she lives in an apartment with very limited storage space, gets to the store rarely, consumes large quantities of soft drinks, and has a waste-disposal chute a few steps from her door, she may well find the throwaway bottles cheaper and will purchase them in preference to returnable bottles.

Now suppose that our hypothetical apartment dweller with a passion for pop attends an ecology conference and comes away convinced that we must recycle to survive. The cost to her of using throwaway bottles suddenly jumps, for

Is a 20-cent saving worth the trouble?

now she suffers pangs of guilt each time she tosses a bottle in the waste-disposal chute. The added cost in moral regret may be sufficient to induce her to switch to returnable bottles.

Or it may not. Suppose that she is going on a camping trip and wants to take along a dozen bottles of pop. She must backpack them in to her campsite, and backpack the empties out again if she returns the bottles. The added cost of carrying a dozen empties may be enough to overcome the added cost of an uneasy conscience, so that in this case, at least, she reverts to throwaway bottles. (Of course, she will throw them in a trash can.)

But let's change the last situation. Suppose the price of throwaways is not $1.80 per liter but $2.20, with the price of the returnable bottle still $1.60 but the deposit now raised to 80 cents. She can now save 60 cents, not just 20 cents, if she buys (and returns!) the returnable bottle. At *some* price we may confidently predict that the cost of transporting empties will become less than the combined cost of buying throwaway bottles and living with guilt.

Is a 60-cent saving worth the trouble?

There are several lessons to be drawn from this tale of the pop bottles. To assert that people purchase less of anything as the cost to them increases does *not* imply that people pay attention only to money, or that people are selfish, or that concern for social welfare does not influence economic behavior. It *does* imply that people respond to changes in cost and — a crucial implication — that a sufficiently large change in price can be counted on to tip almost any balance. Those who say that Americans won't give up the convenience of throwaway bottles and cans unless the government outlaws them are overlooking several possibilities. A widespread change in attitude toward the environment could overcome the cost of being inconvenienced. And a sufficiently large tax on throwaway containers (call it a deposit if you wish) would make convenience a luxury too expensive to enjoy very frequently.

The essential point in all this is that the money price of obtaining something is only one part, and occasionally even a very small part, of its cost. What the law of demand asserts is that people will do less of what they want to do as the cost to them of doing it increases, and will try to do more as the cost decreases. But at the same time we want to remember that money is a common denominator, and therefore a most useful device for securing widespread changes in behavior. That's why economists give it so much of their attention.

Who Needs Water?

People are creatures of habit, in what they think as well as what they do. Perhaps this also explains why so many have trouble recognizing the significance of substitutes and hence such difficulty appreciating the law of demand. Water provides an excellent example.

Back in the mid-1960s the first of a string of serious water shortages hit New York City. Several years of less than normal rainfall had depleted the city's reservoirs, and there was great fear that New York would run short of water during the summer unless consumption could be sharply reduced. A few brave souls suggested that the city should install more water meters and raise the price of water. The suggestion was not taken very seriously because, as everyone supposedly knows, water is a necessity. "People won't go thirsty just because the price of water goes up a little, or even a lot," said the critics. And so New York launched a massive campaign of education plus legal threat to try to get its citizens to be more sparing in their use of water.

Lawn sprinkling and car washing were condemned. Restaurants were told not to give customers a glass of water with their meals unless they specifically asked for it. The ornamental fountains of the city were turned off—largely as a symbolic gesture, since the water in the fountains is recirculated. Citizens were asked to refrain from keeping their beer cool by letting the shower drip on it. One of the more amusing aspects of the campaign was a set of ads for a particular Scotch whiskey that urged people to drink their Scotch with water. The word *water* was crossed out in the advertisement and *soda* was written above it, with an appended admonition to save water by drinking soda.

The water shortage was relieved not by any of these trivial measures but by a providential end to the drought. New Yorkers thereupon went back to their old familiar habits to await the next drought. It came in 1980, and in January of 1981 the mayor of New York City, warning that "there will be a calamity" unless residents conserve water, signed a law imposing fines of up to $1000 on "water wasters." Fortunately, the rains came soon thereafter, enabling New Yorkers to return to their dangerous conviction that the forces of Nature, not human beings, cause water crises. Unfortunately, that conviction may soon make water crises a chronic condition in New York City.

The best way to turn a drought into a calamity is to pretend that water is a necessity. The truth is that there are many substitutes for water, a fact that becomes glaringly obvious as soon as we break loose from the habit of assuming that people do nothing with water except drink it.

Here are just a few of the substitutes for water in New York City: dirty automobiles, brown lawns, plumbers, migration, deodorant, larger refrigerators (to hold the beer that would otherwise be cooled in the shower), plus a host of small inconveniences. The trick is to persuade people to *use* these substitutes: To call the plumber, for example, and have that leaky toilet repaired rather than allow it to continue wasting fifty gallons of water a day. To spend money on a larger refrigerator. To tolerate a dirty automobile. To put an ice cube in their glass of drinking water, rather than let the tap run for several minutes to cool it. In the case of industries using huge quantities of water, to sacrifice the advantages of a New York location in favor of locating near more plentiful water supplies. Or to install recycling equipment.

But what is the best way to induce the use of substitutes? Educational campaigns and moral exhortation can help. But how much? Most people are expert rationalizers when their own interest is involved, and it is all too easy to put off calling the plumber until the end of the month, or next month, or the month after that, always fully intending, of course, to do one's civic duty and get that leak repaired.

What about criminal penalties for wasting water? Enforcement becomes a problem here. Are the police to stage surprise raids to catch people cooling their beer in the shower? Shall we fine a person for rinsing a glass too many times before taking a drink? What constitutes *criminal* waste?

A quite different approach is available. Is there any way to enlist almost everyone in a conscientious effort to seek out and use substitutes for water? A sizable increase in the price of water just might do the job. Wouldn't the careless householder call the plumber more quickly if that leaky toilet cost more per month than the plumber would charge to fix it? Wouldn't people accept dirty automobiles more readily, or at least not let the hose run the whole time they were washing the car, if water became very expensive? There is some price for water at which it becomes cheaper to buy a new refrigerator than to use the shower as a cooler. Industries that use large quantities of water will tend to locate elsewhere if the price of water is high in their area of first choice.

And so it goes. There are substitutes for anything. A higher money price will induce some people to find and use some of those substitutes. And the higher the price, the more will substitutes be used.

Time Is on Our Side

If you are at all the suspicious sort of person, you will have wondered whether all these changes might not take too much time to be helpful. That is a healthy suspicion. Changes in the amount purchased will be greater for any given price change the longer the time period allowed for adjustment.

Check this out for yourself with a mental experiment. Suppose the price of water has been 30 cents per 1000 gallons for twenty years and it is raised overnight to 60 cents. What subsitutions for water will be made *right away*? What substitutions would you expect to observe after a month or two had passed? What substitutions would you expect to observe over the next ten years — assuming that everyone expects the price to remain at the higher level?

An even better example is gasoline. How high will the price of gasoline have to go before Americans reduce their consumption? Don't answer without first noting that the price hasn't gone up by nearly as much as the newspaper headlines suggest. It's the *relative* price that matters, and much of the increase in the price of gasoline since 1972 is merely an inflation-induced rise in its *money* price. The 1972 price of 38 cents per gallon for regular would have been about $1.10 by 1990 *if gasoline prices had merely gone up at the rate of inflation.* The question is nonetheless a good one: How large a relative price increase will it take to cut gasoline consumption by 10 percent or 25 percent or even 50 percent? The answer clearly depends on the time allowed for adjustments. People will buy cars that use less fuel, will move closer to work, and will arrange car pools if the price of gasoline rises far enough, but they won't do so at once. It will also take time for automotive engineers to increase the fuel efficiency of cars and for buses and airlines to expand their schedules.

By taking our examples almost entirely from the area of household decisions, we may have obscured the important fact that customers include producers as well as consumers. Business firms use water and gasoline, too, and they sometimes use so much that they are exceptionally sensitive to price changes. You'll be neglecting some of the major factors that cause demand curves to slope downward if you overlook the contribution producers make to the demand for many goods. In the case of water, location decisions are often made on the basis of the expected price of water, and those decisions then affect the quantities demanded in different geographic areas.

But it takes time for customers to find and begin to use substitutes. It also takes time for producers to devise, produce, and publicize substitutes. As a result, the amount by which people increase or decrease their purchases when prices change depends very much on the time period over which we are observing the adjustment. Occasionally, even a rather large price increase (or decrease) will lead to no significant decrease (or increase) in consumption — *at first*. And this sometimes causes people to conclude that price has no effect on consumption. A very mistaken conclusion! Nothing in this world happens instantly. People, creatures of habit that they are, must be allowed time to prove that there are substitutes for anything.

Price Elasticity of Demand

It is extremely cumbersome to talk about "the amount by which people increase or decrease their purchases when the price changes." But this is an important relationship with many useful applications. So economists have invented a special concept that summarizes the relationship. The formal title of the concept is *price elasticity of demand*.

That's an appropriate name. Elasticity means responsiveness. If the amount of any good that people purchase changes substantially in response to a small change in price, demand is said to be elastic. If even a very large price change results in little change in the amount purchased, demand is said to be inelastic.

Price elasticity of demand is defined precisely as *the percentage change in quantity demanded divided by the percentage change in price*. Thus, if a 10 percent increase in the price of eggs leads to a 5 percent reduction in the number of eggs sold, the elasticity of demand is 5 percent divided by 10 percent, or 0.5. To be completely accurate, it is *minus* 0.5, since price and amount purchased vary inversely. But for simplicity we shall ignore the minus sign and treat all coefficients of elasticity as if they were positive.

Whenever the coefficient of elasticity is greater than 1.0 (ignoring the sign) — that is, whenever the percentage change in quantity purchased is *greater* than the percentage change in price — demand is said to be elastic. Whenever the coefficient of elasticity is less than 1.0, which means whenever the percentage change in quantity purchased is *less* than the percentage change in price, demand is said to be inelastic. Compulsive learners will want to know what is said when the percentage change in quantity is exactly equal to the percentage change in price, so that the coefficient of demand elasticity is exactly 1.0. You may file away the information that demand is then *unit elastic*. (Economics is a very systematic discipline.)

You can begin to familiarize yourself with the uses of this concept by asking whether demand is elastic or inelastic in each case below. Each case is discussed in the subsequent paragraphs.

- "People aren't going to buy much more no matter how far we cut the price."
- "This is a competitive business. We would lose half our customers if we raised our prices by as little as 2 percent."
- The demand for salt.
- The demand for Morton's salt.
- The demand for Morton's salt at the Kroger store at Fifth and Main.
- "The university's total receipts from tuition would actually increase if tuition rates were cut by 20 percent."
- "It's odd but true. Wheat farmers would gross more money if they all got together and burned one-quarter of this year's crop."

Thinking About Elasticity

"People aren't going to buy much more no matter how far we cut the price." If a businessman doubts that even a very large price decrease will do much to increase his sales, he believes that his demand is highly inelastic. He will obviously not want to lower his price under such circumstances, for he will lose more through the lower price than he will gain through the larger volume. But if people don't respond very much to a price cut, will they also be relatively insensitive to a price hike? If they are, a businessman out to increase his income will want to raise his price. Businessmen typically complain that prices are too low. Then why don't they raise their prices? The answer, of course, is that they would usually lose too many customers if they did so. It is the elasticity of demand that determines whether or not a businessman can add to his money receipts by raising his prices.

"This is a competitive business. We would lose half our

Inelastic demand for table salt

customers if we raised our prices by as little as 2 percent." The businesswoman making this statement is saying in effect that she faces a highly elastic demand: a 50 percent decline in quantity demanded would follow a mere 2 percent increase in price. The coefficient of elasticity is 25. The demand is very elastic indeed. Another way of putting it would be to say that her customers are extremely sensitive to any price change. And that makes it difficult for her to raise her prices, however eager she might be to do so.

The demand for salt. What makes demand curves elastic or inelastic? The availability of good substitutes is the most important factor. Another is the significance of the item in the budget of purchasers. If the expenditure on some good is large relative to the income or wealth of purchasers, they will be more sensitive to any change in its price.

Apply this to table salt. One pound of salt lasts a long time and costs a penny or two an ounce. So who cares? Shoppers will be relatively insensitive to any change in the price of salt. Moreover, salt has few good substitutes. You would not be inclined to put sugar on your eggs if the price of salt rose dramatically, just as you would not cut the pepper and double the salt if the price of salt fell substantially.

Adam Smith observed in *The Wealth of Nations* that "salt is a very ancient and very universal subject of taxation. . . . The quantity annually consumed by any individual is so small, and may be purchased so gradually, that nobody, it seems to have been thought, could feel very sensibly even a pretty heavy tax upon it." Moreover, salt was one of "the necessaries of life" in Smith's terminology. We can object to the term *necessary* and express Smith's meaning more accurately: salt has few good substitutes. The result is a highly inelastic demand and an apparently irresistible temptation to some governments to levy taxes on salt.

But it's possible to exaggerate the inelasticity of even the demand for salt. Householders in wintry regions sometimes sprinkle table salt on their sidewalks or porch steps to melt the ice. If salt were ten times as expensive, many would substitute chopping and scraping for salt.

The demand for Morton's salt. Why would the demand for Morton's salt be less inelastic than the demand for salt? Because there are good substitutes — namely, other brands of salt. The Morton Salt Company is not in the privileged position of ancient governments, which could raise the price of *all* salt. If someone in the marketing department at Morton chanced to read Adam Smith and was inspired by him to

double the price, the grocery stores that are Morton's customers would purchase from other salt manufacturers.

*The demand for Morton's salt at the Kroger store at
Fifth and Main.* If there are more good substitutes for Morton's salt than for salt, there are even more good substitutes
for Morton's salt sold at the local Kroger store. We have
moved from a very inelastic to what is probably a highly
elastic demand for the same quantity. And that is why you
aren't victimized when you purchase salt. You might be
willing to pay $5 a pound if salt were not available at a
lower price. But fortunately for you, there are many options.
Sellers who tried to take advantage of the fact that the total
demand for salt is highly inelastic would lose customers.
The demand for *the salt they sell* will be quite elastic.

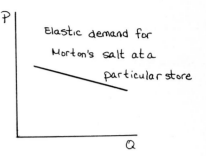

People often make the mistake of assuming that those
who sell "vital necessities" can get away with charging almost any price they choose. We have learned to be suspicious of the phrase *vital necessities.* Now we see again the
grounds for this suspicion. Food has as good a claim as anything to the title "vital necessity." But the relevant fact is
that *no one buys food.* Shoppers do not purchase a pound of
"food"; they buy a pound of hamburger, or bacon, or calf's
liver. And there are many sellers selling many kinds of food.
All of which means that there are excellent substitutes for
specific food commodities, and hence the demand curves are
highly elastic. So sellers are for the most part closely constrained in the prices they can charge.

Elasticity and Total Receipts

*"The university's total receipts from tuition would actually
increase if tuition rates were cut by 20 percent."* The university's total receipts from tuition are the product of the
tuition rate and the number of students who enroll. If a 20
percent decrease in the tuition rate results in an increase in
tuition receipts, then there must have been a more than 20
percent increase in enrollment. The percentage change in
quantity demanded is greater than the percentage change in
price, so demand is elastic.

This suggests a simple way of thinking about elasticity.
Keep in mind that the quantity demanded will always move
in the opposite direction from the price. *If the price change
causes total receipts to move in the* opposite *direction from
the price change, demand must be elastic.* The change in
the quantity purchased has to be larger in percentage terms

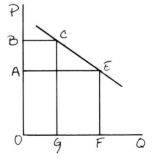

*Demand is
elastic between
C and E, because
OBCG < OAEF.*

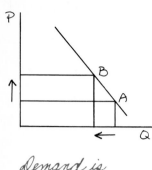

Demand is inelastic between points A and B.

than the price change because total receipts are nothing but the product of price and quantity. And that is the definition of an elastic demand. *If a price change causes total receipts to move in the* same *direction as the price change, demand must be inelastic.* The change in amount purchased was not large enough to outweigh the change in price. And that is the meaning of an inelastic demand.

Don't jump to the conclusion that the university will always be in a better financial position, given an elastic demand, if it lowers its tuition. True, lower tuition charges will mean larger receipts whenever demand is elastic; but a larger enrollment probably also means larger costs. The university must decide in such a case whether the addition to total receipts will be larger than the addition to total costs. (But problems of pricing strategy must be deferred until we reach Chapter 9.)

"It's odd but true. Wheat farmers would gross more money if they all got together and burned one-quarter of this year's crop." The logic of the preceding case also applies here. Farmers can gross more money while selling less wheat only if the percentage change in price is greater than the percentage change in the amount sold. Demand would have to be inelastic. The only difference is that we have reversed the causal relationship assumed till now. We have been tacitly assuming that sellers set the price and buyers respond. This is not always the best way to look at the price–quantity relationship. In some industries, such as agriculture for the most part, it is more useful to assume that the quantity available for sale will determine the price. We'll be talking a lot about this later. For now it is only important to notice that the relationship between changes in total sales and changes in price depends on the elasticity of demand.

Farmers may never have heard about elastic or inelastic demands. But when they lobby for government controls on production, they are usually very much aware of the relation between price and the amount that is sold. Like Molière's famous Monsieur Jourdain, who spoke prose for forty years without knowing it, you can make good use of demand elasticities without ever having heard the term.

The Myth of Vertical Demand

Let's go back to the beginning. In the six statements with which we began this chapter, what was implicitly assumed about the elasticity of demand? Our objection to each statement, you recall, was that it ignored the fact that all goods have substitutes and that substitution does occur when prices change. In other words, demand curves are *not* completely inelastic. A completely inelastic demand curve would graph as a vertical line. You would be wise not to look for such demand curves in the real world.

The law of demand can now be expressed in the language of elasticity: *there is no such thing as a completely inelastic demand* over the entire range of possible prices. Most purchasers will respond at least a little to changes in the cost to them, and all purchasers will respond to a sufficiently large change. If this seems too obvious to bother mentioning, consult your daily newspaper for evidence that it is by no means obvious to everyone. Well-intentioned people and some not so well-intentioned talk constantly of basic needs, mininum requirements, and absolute necessities.

Demand curves are rarely as inelastic as orators suppose. This does not imply, of course, that they are always elastic. That is a more difficult question, to be answered by looking at each case. But as we shall subsequently discover, it is a very important question for anyone who wants to decide how well our economic system functions.

A mythical creature

Once Over Lightly

Every good has substitutes: other goods that will be used in its stead when the cost of using the original good rises, goods for which the original good will become a substitute when their cost rises. Pork replaces beef when the price of beef goes up, and a restaurant beefsteak takes the place of a movie when theater tickets become more expensive.

By talking about "needs" we can sometimes win arguments we might otherwise lose. Needs are actually wants of many different urgencies.

People want more or less of a good as the cost those people must pay decreases or increases.

The concept of *demand* is preferable to the concept of *need*, because demand relates the amounts that people want to purchase to the sacrifices that must be made to obtain these amounts.

The "law of demand" asserts that people will want to purchase more at lower prices, less at higher prices — assuming that something in addition to the price has not changed to offset this consequence.

The money cost of a good is only one part of the cost that affects people's decisions.

A sufficiently large change in money cost (price) can usually overcome the effects that nonmoney costs exert on people's decisions.

A change in price will usually induce a larger change in amounts purchased when more time is allowed for consumers and producers to learn about and invent new substitutes.

Price elasticity of demand is a measure of the percentage change in the quantity of a good demanded relative to the percentage change in its price.

Demand is (price) elastic when the percentage change in quantity demanded is greater than the percentage change in price. Demand is inelastic when the percentage change in quantity demanded is smaller than the percentage change in price.

Price elasticity of demand depends on the importance of the price relative to one's income, but even more on the quality and price of available substitutes.

More separate sources of supply for a good imply better substitutes for any particular good and hence a more elastic demand.

Total receipts or expenditures move in the opposite direction from price when demand is elastic and in the same direction as price when it is inelastic.

The concept of "needs" implies a perfectly inelastic demand curve — an extremely rare phenomenon.

The demand for a good refers to the *schedule of relationships* between price and quantity demanded and must be distinguished from the quantity or amount that is demanded. The quantity of a good demanded changes with its price. But a true change in demand will alter both price and quantity demanded.

Questions for Discussion

1. A Gallup Report quoted by *The Wall Street Journal* in January 1985 found that the average U.S. family says it needs at least $252 per week after taxes "to get by." College graduates reportedly needed $301 a week on the average, but high-school graduates needed only $250 a week. While Democrats said they could get by on $251 a week, Republicans needed $298. Do you think college graduates and Republicans really have more needs, or more expensive needs, than high-school graduates and Democrats? What explains these differences?

2. According to a National Automobile Safety Study conducted by Northeastern University and reported on by *The Wall Street Journal* in February 1986, 16 percent of all surveyed consumers said they would "definitely buy" an air-bag safety system for their automobiles if one were available for $500. Only 5 percent of them would "definitely buy," however, at a price of $1000. What does this imply about the "need" for air-bags on the part of those people who are convinced that air-bags will work? What does the study suggest in general about the "need" for life-saving goods?

3. U.S. courts decided in 1977 that prohibitions on advertising by lawyers were illegal. Since that time many legal "clinics" have sprung up, advertising standard legal services at lower than ordinary fees. Would you agree with the results of a survey showing that about 60 percent of all middle-income Americans have "unmet legal needs"? What are some "legal needs" that many people will only have if they can hire a lawyer cheaply?

4. Most systems of hospitalization insurance substantially reduce the cost to the patient of hospitalization, sometimes to zero. How does this affect hospital use? Why? Evaluate the argument that it does not affect hospital use since "no one gets sick just because hospitals are cheap or avoids getting sick because they're expensive."

5. In 1967 the president of the American Medical Association was quoted as saying that medical care was a privilege and not a right. Today the AMA officially proclaims that "health care is the right of everyone." What quantity and quality of health care do you suppose they're talking about? Is a liver transplant, for example, the right of everyone with a diseased liver?

6. Here is a paragraph from a front-page story that was published in August 1988 in *Workers World* during a record-breaking heat wave in the midwestern United States:

> Shouldn't air conditioning be a right? Why should it only be accessible to those who can afford it? Only a system which defines human worth based on how much money you have would reject the simple solution that in these crisis weeks everyone who needs air conditioning must have it.

Who "needs" air conditioning? Do people in wealthy nations like the United States "need" air conditioning more than people in much hotter but also much poorer nations, such as Bangladesh or Niger? Did anyone "need" air conditioning before it had been invented?

7. The contention that certain goods are "basic human needs" carries a strong suggestion that access to those goods should be a matter of right, not of privilege. But the assertion of rights logically entails the assertion of obligations. Your right to vote, for example, entails the obligation of election officials to accept and count your ballot; your right to use your own umbrella implies an obligation on the part of others not to borrow it without your permission. If "health care is the right of everyone," who has the obligation to provide health care to everyone? Who currently accepts the obligation to provide people with health care? How are they persuaded to accept these obligations?

8. According to a 1983 report by the American Planning Association, the average four-member household uses about 345 gallons of water daily. The report broke that down into 235 gallons for inside use and 110 for outside use. Of the "inside" water, about 95 gallons per day went to flush toilets. Drinking and cooking used 9 to 10 gallons per day. Water rates vary; but they are rarely higher than 0.1¢ (that's $0.001) per gallon. Would a doubling or even a quadrupling of water rates work a serious hardship on poor people?

9. On June 18, 1985, *The Wall Street Journal* ran an article entitled "Denver Turns on to Xeriscape," describing efforts to persuade Denver residents to avoid "a consumer water crunch" by growing lawns that require little irrigation. (*Xeriscape* is the technique of gardening in dry climates.) The predominant grass in Denver lawns is currently Kentucky bluegrass, which requires about 18 gallons of added water per square foot each summer to thrive in the arid climate. Buffalo grass, by contrast, will do well on half as much water.

   (a) How much extra would a homeowner with a typical 5000 square-foot lawn pay in water costs to enjoy Kentucky blue rather than buffalo grass at a price of 60¢ per 1000 gallons? Is this likely to affect the decisions of many homeowners?

   (b) The schedule of water prices for Denver users with a ¾-inch main in June 1985 was actually 74¢ per 1000 gallons for the first 15,000 gallons per month, 60¢ per 1000 for the next 35,000, 46¢ per 1000 for the next 650,000, and 42¢ per 1000 gallons for all consumption beyond 700,000 gallons per month, with a minimum charge of $2.65 per month. How much does the first 4000 gallons cost under this pricing scheme?

10. A 1980 drought in the northeastern United States produced, early in 1981, numerous water-rationing schemes in the states, cities, and towns of the region. The following bits of information were gleaned from a *Wall Street Journal* feature of February 25, 1981:

   (a) Greenwich, Connecticut, limited users to 45 gallons of water per day. One resident predicted they would soon be drinking Perrier. Is that likely?

   (b) In Randolph, Massachusetts, people were paying 10 cents per gallon for deep-well water, because the low level of the town's reservoirs had given the water from them an offensive taste. What would have been a cheaper way for the citizens of Randolph to obtain good-tasting drinking water?

   (c) Many cities and towns banned "nonessential uses of water." Which of these uses, in your opinion, is nonessential: macaroni manufacture, beer brewing, lawn sprinkling, filling of swimming pools, ordinary household use (cooking, cleaning, showering, flushing)?

   (d) When New Jersey imposed rationing on about 200 communities, it limited each resident to 50 gallons per day. How many people have "essential uses" for 50 gallons of water per day?

(e) Per-capita water use in New York City at the onset of the drought was 190 gallons. How much of that do you think went for "essential uses"?

11. A front-page article in *The Wall Street Journal* of May 13, 1980, was headlined: "Europe's Drivers Don't Reduce Gasoline Use Despite Soaring Prices." In the continuation of the story on a back page, the reporter revealed that pump prices had increased 120 percent in Great Britain from 1973 to 1979 while the general price level had risen by about 140 percent. How would you criticize that headline?

12. If the government forbids motorists to drive more than 55 miles per hour, does everyone stay within the 55-mile limit? What are the costs of going faster? What are some of the costs of going faster that do not fall on the speeding motorist? Do these later costs affect motorists' decisions? Why might the fact that faster driving uses up more of the nation's scarce petroleum reduce the speed of some drivers but not others?

13. Why do people live in New York City if the costs of doing so — high rents, noise, dirt, congestion, the risks of being robbed or assaulted — are so high? Is it true that most of them "have no choice"? What do you think would happen if the costs mentioned were significantly reduced?

14. Here is a question from a letter to the editor of a Seattle newspaper protesting a proposal to reduce gasoline consumption by imposing a tax of 50 cents per gallon. "How could you or anyone think that such a tax would reduce gas consumption when a doubling of the price, consisting of considerably more than 50 cents a gallon over the past two years, has not reduced consumption one iota?"

(a) What does this letter writer think the demand curve for gasoline looks like?

(b) Do we have any evidence on whether or not he is correct?

(c) The writer recommends the elimination by law of nonessential uses and mentions as an example rural mail deliveries six days a week. Would we be eliminating a nonessential use of gasoline if all rural carriers took Saturdays off? Why don't we eliminate Tuesday and Thursday deliveries as well and save even more gasoline?

15. "Coffee Prices Sink as Demand Wanes." Does that newspaper headline use the word *demand* correctly? Would you expect those falling prices to be associated with more or with less coffee consumption?

16. Higher prices for beef, automobiles, or television sets will lead to a reduction in the *amount of each demanded.* Think of some specific changes (such as in tastes, prices of substitutes, quality of complementary goods) that would cause the *demand* for each to increase so that more might actually be demanded at higher prices. Why is this completely consistent with the law of demand?

17. Does the graph in Figure 2B, employed by some medical organizations to predict a "doctor glut," use the concept of demand in the same way that economists use it?

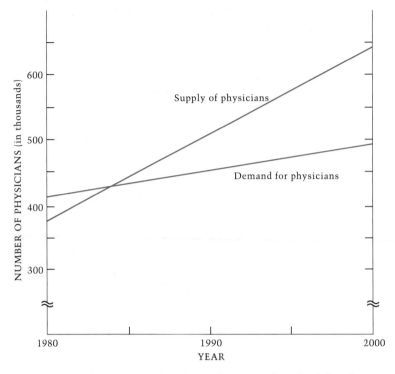

FIGURE 2B   Demand and supply curves for physicians?

18. Do the following statements use the word *demand* correctly? Or should the term *quantity demanded* be substituted?

   (a) When OPEC raised the price of oil in the 1970s, the demand for oil fell.
   (b) Inflation has increased the demand for oil.
   (c) When the Iran–Iraq war broke out, oil refiners panicked, and their panic increased the demand for oil and sharply raised its price.
   (d) The 55-mile-per-hour speed limit has reduced the demand for oil.
   (e) Price controls imposed by the United States in the 1970s on domestic oil producers, by keeping down the price of U.S.-produced oil, increased our demand for OPEC oil.

19. A change in expectations can cause a change in demand. Explain how this could lead to a situation in which a price decline was followed by a decrease in the amount purchased.

20. Is it strictly true that a change in the price of a good causes a change in the quantity of that good demanded but *not* a shift in the demand curve for the good?

   (a) What effect did the large increases in the price of gasoline in the 1970s have on the demand (curve) for fuel-efficient cars?

(b) What effect did this have after several years on the original demand (curve) for gasoline?

(c) How did the increase in the price of heating oil in the 1970s affect the demand for housing insulation? How did this eventually shift the demand for heating oil?

(d) Can you think of similar processes through which changes in the price of other goods would lead over time to shifts in the demand for those goods?

(e) If the price of a good returned to its previous level after a time but the quantity demanded did not, would this be evidence that the demand had changed in the interim?

21. The graphs in Figure 2C show the demand for bus service (left) and the demand for downtown parking space (right) in an imaginary city. If the city raises bus fares from p_1 to p_2, the demand curve will not change, but the quantity demanded will fall. With fewer people riding the bus, what will happen to the demand for downtown parking? What effect will this have on downtown parking rates? With higher parking rates, more people will want to ride the bus. So what effect will the higher bus fare have after all on the demand for bus service?

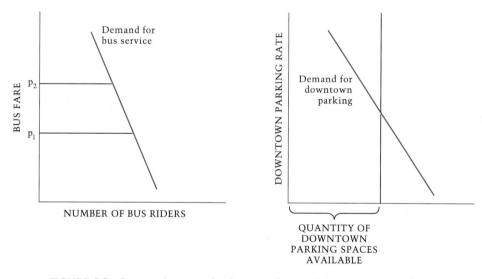

FIGURE 2C Demand curves for bus service and downtown parking

22. Here is a classroom exercise that might be fun and also sharpen your ability to recognize substitution possibilities. Let one person come up with two goods that seem to have no connection and challenge others to construct a plausible set of circumstances in which one would be a substitute for the other. (Avoid the easy, though correct, answer that all goods are in the last analysis substitutes inasmuch as the acquisition of each uses up scarce time or income.)

23. John loves butter and thinks that margarine tastes like soap. George can't tell the difference. Whose demand for butter is likely to be more elastic?

24. Would the elasticity of a crowd's demand for cold lemonade be affected by the proximity of a drinking fountain?

25. How do you think the development of other copying machines affected the elasticity of demand for Xerox machines?

26. Is the demand for prescription drugs elastic or inelastic? Why? Do you agree with the statement sometimes made that the prices charged for prescription drugs can be freely set by the manufacturers, since people must buy whatever the doctor prescribes?

27. How does ignorance affect elasticities of demand?

28. How might the development of science and technology affect demand elasticities?

29. Does a society's transportation system in any way affect elasticities of demand? How?

30. The demand for aspirin at currently prevailing prices seems to be highly inelastic. What do you think would happen to the elasticity of demand if the price of aspirin relative to everything else were five times as high? Fifty times as high? Why?

31. In 1977 Brazil was supplying about one-third of the world's coffee exports. When a frost wiped out about 75 percent of Brazil's 1976–77 crop, the price of green (unroasted) coffee rose 400 percent. What was the approximate price elasticity of demand for coffee? Why was it so low?

32. Harvest-time rains in California in the spring of 1978 destroyed a portion of the lettuce crop. As a result, the price for a 24-head carton loaded in California hit a record of $18 on May 1, 1978. On June 29, after new crops had come in, the price was $2.75. What does all this suggest about the demand for lettuce? What attitudes and practices on the part of households and restaurants contribute toward making the demand for lettuce very inelastic with respect to price?

33. In a January 1984 *Wall Street Journal* article on Chicago's attempt to attract more transit riders with lower fares, Joseph L. Schofer, research director at Northwestern University's Transportation Center, was quoted as saying that "lower fares never make up for loss of revenues. Even when losing riders by increasing fares, revenue usually goes up. It's a law of economics." What exactly is the "law of economics" Mr. Schofer seems to be defending? Would you agree in calling it a "law of economics"?

34. The Congressional Budget Office concluded in 1984 that adding access charges of $2 to $6 per month to the bills of phone subscribers would not induce many users to give up their phones — as some critics of the charges had maintained. "Demand for local telephone service is quite inelastic," according to the CBO report.

(a) If the cost of local phone service rose from $12 to $18 per month, what percentage of telephone subscribers would have to give up their phones for the demand to be described as elastic?

(b) What percentage do you estimate would actually do so? What is the coefficient of elasticity that you are estimating?

35. Price elasticity of demand can be calculated by dividing the percentage change in the quantity demanded by the percentage change in the price.

(a) What is the coefficient of elasticity between the two points of the demand schedule in each of the cases shown below?

Price per Ticket	Tickets Demanded	Price per Cup of Coffee	Cups of Coffee Demanded
$2	200	35¢	600
$1	400	70¢	300

(b) If you divided 100% by 50% in the ticket case, and 50% by 100% in the coffee case, you got very different coefficients (2 and 0.5, respectively) for what are actually identical relative changes. The different results come from using the larger price and the smaller quantity as the base from which to calculate the percentage change in the first case, and using the smaller price and the larger quantity as the base in the second case. But the coefficient of elasticity should be the same between two points regardless of the direction in which the change is measured. How can this problem be handled?

(c) What is the coefficient of elasticity in each of these cases if you use the *average* of the prices and quantities between which the change is occurring as the base for calculating the percentage changes?

(d) In both cases, total expenditure (price times quantity) does not change when the price changes. What does this imply about the elasticity of demand between the prices given? Does this implication agree with your answer in (c)? (It should.)

36. Figure 2D shows a hypothetical demand curve for strawberries.

(a) What price per case would maximize the gross receipts of strawberry growers? [Peek at part (d) of this question rather than waste too much time trying all sorts of different prices. The price that maximizes gross receipts will be found at the midpoint of a straight-line demand curve when the curve is extended to the axes. If you see why, good. If not, it's a bit of knowledge with only academic usefulness anyway.]

(b) If the price of strawberries is determined by the total quantity harvested in conjunction with the demand, what size crop will result in the price quoted in part (d)?

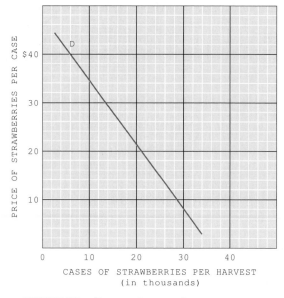

FIGURE 2D   Demand curve for strawberries

(c) What would the gross receipts of strawberry growers be if the crop turned out to be 30,000 cases?

(d) Can you prove that the demand for strawberries is elastic above a price of $24 per case and inelastic below that price?

(e) If strawberry growers can make more money by selling fewer than 30,000 cases, why would they ever market that much? Why wouldn't they destroy some of the crop rather than "spoil the market"?

37. See if you can clarify this analysis: "If half of our forests were destroyed in a fire, the value of the remaining lumber would be greater than the value of all the lumber in the country before the fire. This absurdity — that the whole is worth less than a half — shows that values are distorted in a market economy."

38. The advertising slogan of Maker's Mark whiskey is: "It tastes expensive . . . and is."

(a) Isn't the seller foolish to advertise the high price? Or will people buy more at higher prices? Does this contradict the law of demand?

(b) A waiter at Jean-Louis, a restaurant in Washington, DC, often patronized by eminent politicians, says, "It is good to be known as expensive. People know they can impress their guests here." What does he think people are purchasing when they go to Jean-Louis for dinner?

39. Here's a question for those who wondered why price was graphed along the vertical axis in Figure 2A, which is the standard procedure in economics, rather than along the horizontal axis, where the independent variable usually goes. Is price in fact the independent and quantity the dependent variable? If quantity depends on price, on what does price depend? Who or what determines prices?

Chapter 3 _____

Opportunity Cost and the Supply of Goods

You have already been introduced to the central concept of this chapter. If you failed to notice, that's because we didn't call it by its proper name. But several times in the preceding chapter, in talking about the relationship between price and quantity demanded, we pointed out that the amount of any good that a person will want to purchase is determined by the good's cost to that person, or the value of the sacrifice required to obtain it. That is the definition of *opportunity cost*, a concept that ties together the law of demand and the principles governing supply. We shall try to convince you in this chapter that it makes sense to think of cost as *the value of sacrificed opportunities.*

Costs Are Valuations

Everyone will concede that demand reflects people's values. But supply, many believe, is the material side of economics, governed by costs of production that are objective realities, in contrast with such subjective factors as people's values and preferences. That belief is in error. Supply and cost are also based on valuations. To help you see this, we shall detour through a college dormitory on a Monday night in the fall, where the following exchange takes place.

"Hey, Jack, do you want to go see the new Wim Wenders movie? It closes after tonight."

"I'd like to, but I can't. We've got a Russian test tomorrow, and I'll flunk if I don't cram some vocabulary."

"Forget it. You can borrow my vocabulary cards in your free period tomorrow. An hour with the cards right before class is a B for sure."

"Well — trouble is, the Redskins and Miami are on TV tonight and I'd rather watch the game if I don't have to study."

"We'll go at six and be back for the kickoff."

"All right. Just let me see how much money I've got — five, six, seven, eight dollars — to last until I get paid on Thursday. And I'm out of meal tickets!"

"Eat peanut butter sandwiches! I thought you wanted to see the movie."

"I do. O.K., I'll let my stomach shrink until Thursday. Should we leave at quarter to six?"

The cost of any action is the value of the opportunity forgone by taking that action.

The real cost of any action (going to a movie, buying a pair of jeans, manufacturing a lawnmower, moving to Halifax, raising beef cattle, building a hardware store, taking out an insurance policy) is the value of the alternative opportunity that must be sacrificed in order to take the action. The cost for Jack of going to the movie was at first calculated as a passing grade (given up!) in Russian. When his friend showed him how to reduce that cost, Jack looked at the next most valuable opportunity he would have to sacrifice if he went to the movie: watching the Monday night football game, a game he particularly wanted to see. His friend eliminated that cost for him, and Jack turned to the money cost. But money wasn't the real cost. The real cost that dollars and cents represent are the opportunities given up when the money is spent in one way rather than another. The four or five dollars Jack will spend for the movie represent some meals he would have liked to eat but is willing to sacrifice in order to see the film.

Producers' Costs as Opportunity Costs

The theory of supply in economics is not essentially different from the theory of demand. Both assume that decision-makers face alternatives and choose among them, and that their choices reflect a comparison of benefits and costs. The logic of the economizing process is the same for producers as it is for consumers.

When we think about producers' costs — asking ourselves, for example, why it costs more to manufacture a ten-speed bicycle than a redwood picnic table — we tend to think first of what goes into the production of each. We think of the raw materials, of the labor time required, perhaps also of the machinery or tools that must be used. We express the value of the inputs in monetary terms and assume that the cost of the bicycle or the table is the sum of these values. That isn't wrong, but it leaves unanswered the question of why the inputs had those particular monetary values. The concept of opportunity cost asserts that those values reflect the value of the inputs in their next-best uses, or the value of the opportunities forgone by using the inputs in the production of bicycles and picnic tables.

The manufacturer's cost of producing a bicycle will be determined by what he must pay to obtain the appropriate resources. And, because these resources have other opportunities for employment, he must pay a price that matches the "best opportunity" value. The value of forgone opportunities thus becomes the cost of manufacturing a bicycle. This makes excellent sense, for the meaningful cost of obtaining one more bicycle is the value of what must be given up or sacrificed or forgone in order to obtain that bicycle.

Consider the example of the picnic table. Part of its cost of production is the price of redwood. Assume that the demand for new housing has increased recently and that building contractors have consequently been purchasing a lot more redwood lumber. If this causes the price of lumber to rise, the cost of manufacturing a picnic table will go up. Nothing has happened to affect the physical inputs that go into the table, but its cost of production has risen. Because houses containing redwood lumber are now more valuable than formerly, the table manufacturer must pay a higher opportunity cost for the lumber he wants to put into his picnic tables.

The concept of opportunity cost also explains how labor enters into production costs. Workers must receive from their employers a wage that persuades them to turn down all other opportunities. A skilled worker will be paid more than an unskilled worker because and only insofar as those skills make the skilled worker more valuable somewhere else. Workers who can install wheel spokes while standing on their heads and whistling "Dixie" are marvelously skilled. But our bicycle manufacturer will not have to pay them additional compensation for that skill unless their unusual talent makes them more valuable somewhere else. That could happen. A circus might bid for their talents. If the circus offers them more than they can obtain as bicycle producers, their opportunity cost to the manufacturer rises. In that case the manufacturer will probably wish them goodbye and good luck and replace them with other workers whose opportunity cost is lower.

When the National Basketball Association and the American Basketball Association merged into one league, what happened to the opportunity cost of hiring physically coordinated seven-footers? With two leagues, each player had two teams bidding for his services. What either team was compelled to pay to get him was determined by what the other team was willing to pay, and both were willing to pay a lot if they thought he would make a big difference in ticket sales. When the leagues merged, however, the right to hire a particular player was assigned to a single team, and the opportunity cost of a well-coordinated seven-footer fell. It's not surprising that owners of professional basketball teams prefer one league to two.

Let's take a more common case. If a large firm employing many people moves into a small town, the cost of hiring grocery clerks, bank tellers, secretaries, and gasoline station attendants in the town will tend to go up. Why? Because grocery stores , banks, offices, and gasoline stations must all pay the opportunity cost of the people they employ, and these people may now find better opportunities for employment in the new firm. Suppose the new firm is interested in hiring women exclusively; then only the opportunity cost of hiring women will increase at first. But that will pull women out of some jobs, thereby creating additional opportunities for men and causing the opportunity cost of male workers to rise.

The resource that most clearly illustrates the opportunity-cost concept is probably land. Suppose you want to purchase an acre of land to build a house. What will you have to pay for the land? It will depend on the value of that land in alternative uses. Do other people view the acre as a choice residential site? Does it have commercial or industrial potentialities? Would it be used for pasture if you did not purchase it? The cost you pay for the land will be determined by the alternative opportunities that people perceive for its use.

Case Studies in Opportunity Cost

Let's examine some other cases of varying costs to see how the concept of opportunity cost explains familiar but often misunderstood phenomena.

Why, in the last fifty years, has the cost of getting a haircut gone up so much more than the cost of goods generally? It's because people who want barbers to cut their hair must be willing to pay them enough to keep them in the trade. If productivity in haircutting had kept pace over the last fifty years with productivity in manufacturing, barbers would have been able to maintain their incomes by trimming more heads per hour. But with productivity virtually unchanged, only a higher price per head could keep them working in the barber shop. We who want our hair cut by professionals have bid up the price of haircuts to meet the

If a barber can give 2 haircuts in an hour, what price must he charge to earn $10 an hour? What price would yield $10 an hour if he could give 10 haircuts in an hour?

rising opportunity cost to barbers of working at a job in which productivity never increases.

Why is it often so much harder to find a teenage babysitter in a wealthy residential area than in a low-income area? The frustrated couple unable to find a babysitter may complain that all the kids in the neighborhood are lazy. But that is a needlessly harsh explanation. Teenage babysitters can be found by any couple willing to pay the opportunity cost. That means bidding the babysitters away from their otherwise most valued opportunity. If the demand for babysitters in the area is large because wealthy people go out more often, and if the local teenagers receive such generous allowances that they value a date or leisure more than the ordinary income from babysitting, why be surprised to find that the opportunity cost of hiring a babysitter is high?

Why did the cost of obtaining a college education rise so steeply during the 1960s? A very large part of the explanation lies in sharply increased instructional costs, made up partly of higher faculty salaries and partly of reduced teaching loads. But how did these developments come about? Ask your friendly neighborhood professor and she will probably tell you about the long years that must be spent getting a Ph.D. and the impossibility of doing research while teaching twelve hours. Any good member of the professorial guild will assent to the virtues of those arguments. But no good economics professor will be much impressed with their cogency as an explanation of why professors earned more and taught less at the end of the decade than at the beginning.

The rapidly rising demand for professors provides the explanation. State legislatures poured money into building new colleges and expanding old ones; the federal government responded to the fear of Soviet scientific superiority by appropriating vast sums for higher education and for research, which gave teachers new opportunities; the World War II baby boom became a college-student boom in the 1960s; and a larger percentage of the population became persuaded that a college degree was a passport to the good life. The government and private industry meanwhile increased their demand for the services of highly trained persons, widening the range of opportunities for people with extensive education. The net result was a vastly increased demand for the services of college professors. College professors, too, are scarce resources with opportunity costs. A larger number of them were obtained by bidding them away from alternative employments with the offer of higher salaries and reduced teaching loads. (All college professors know that it is easier

to raise their incomes by finding a better opportunity elsewhere than by reciting their virtues to their current deans.
Deans are more attentive to the recitals of professors with
alternative opportunties.)

If you have grasped the argument, you should see why
the salaries of many college professors declined in the 1980s.
Inflation partially concealed that decline; but once we have
adjusted for changes in the value of the dollar, we can see
the same factors that pulled faculty salaries up in the 1960s
pulling them down in the 1980s.

Why does the high-school dropout rate decrease during a
recession? The opportunity cost of remaining in high school
varies with the job market for teenagers. A decline in job
opportunities reduces the opportunity cost of remaining in
school for some young people; therefore fewer drop out.

Why are poor people more likely to travel between cities
by bus and wealthy people more likely to travel by air? A
simple answer would be that taking the bus is cheaper. But
it isn't. It's a very expensive mode of transportation for
people for whom the opportunity cost of time is high; and
the opportunity cost of time is typically much lower for poor
people than for those with a high income from working.

Do you have the idea? Figure out for yourself the cost of
going to college. If you include in your calculations the value
to yourself of whatever you would be doing if you were not
in college, you have grasped the principle of opportunity cost.

A final example. Consider the case of a woman who
runs a small grocery store all by herself. She says that she
does pretty well because she has no labor cost. Is she right?
The cost of her own labor is not a monetary outlay, but it
certainly is a cost. And that cost can be measured by the
value of the opportunities she forgoes by working for herself.

Costs and Actions

The economic way of thinking recognizes *no* objective costs.
That offends common sense, which teaches that things do
have "real" costs, costs that depend on the laws of physics
rather than the vagaries of the human psyche. It's hard to
win a battle against common sense, but we must try.

Perhaps we can disarm common sense most quickly by
pointing out that "things" have no costs at all. We are talking about costs relevant to supply, of course — costs that
have an effect on people's decisions to make goods available.
"Things" cannot have costs in that sense. Only actions can.
If you think that things do indeed have costs and are ready

with an example to prove it, you are almost certainly smuggling in an unnoticed action to give your item a cost.

For example: What is the cost of a baseball? "Five dollars," you say. But you mean that the cost of *purchasing* a baseball at the local sporting goods store is five dollars. Since purchasing is an action, it can entail sacrificed opportunities and thereby have a cost. But note the smuggled-in action. With other actions, the cost of a baseball changes. The cost of *manufacturing* a baseball is quite different. *Selling* one has yet another cost. And what about the cost of *catching* one at the ball park by spearing a line-drive foul with your bare hand, where the sacrifice may be the opportunity to wear an unbroken nose the rest of your life?

Let's return to the case of a college education. What does it cost? The answer is that "it" cannot have a cost. We must first distinguish the cost of *obtaining* a college education from the cost of *providing* one. As soon as we make that distinction, we should also notice something that has been implicit in everything we've said so far about costs, either in this or the preceding chapter: costs are always cost *to someone.* The cost of obtaining an education usually means the cost to the student. But it could mean the cost to the student's parents, which is not the same. Or, if that student's admission entailed the rejection of some other applicant, it could even mean the cost to John (who was refused admission) of Marsha's obtaining entrance to the first-year class. Those will all be different.

A great deal of fruitless argument about the "true cost" of things stems from a failure to recognize that only actions have costs, and that actions can entail different costs for different people. The ongoing debate about reinstituting the military draft is an excellent example. Let's take a look.

The Cost of a Volunteer Military Force

Selective service, as it is euphemistically called, has been around for a long time. Although almost everyone regards it as undesirable in itself, many Americans still seem to think of it as the only way to secure an adequate supply of military personnel at an acceptable cost.

There may be good arguments for the draft, but the familiar argument that an adequate volunteer army[1] would

[1]In some contexts, a volunteer means someone who works without pay (volunteer firefighters, hospital volunteers). That is *not* the case with the volunteer military force, where payment of an attractive wage is the key to success.

cost too much is not one of them. The Department of Defense and others who worry about the relative costs of a conscripted and a volunteer military are conveniently bypassing the question of cost to whom. Are we talking about the cost to taxpayers, enlisted personnel, Congress, or the Pentagon? They are very different.

What is the cost to a young person of becoming a soldier? The best way to find out would be to offer a bribe and to keep raising it until it was accepted. If Marshall would enlist for $5000 per year, Carol for $8000, and Philip for no less than $60,000, these represent the opportunity costs of Marshall, Carol, and Philip. The cost of drafting all three, *to them*, would then be $73,000, even though the government can conceal this fact by offering far less in wages and then compelling each to serve.

The opportunity cost is a function of forgone alternative employment opportunities and all sorts of other values: preferences with respect to life-style, attitude toward war, degrees of cowardice or bravery, and so on. When the government bids for military personnel, raising its offer until it can attract just the desired number of enlistments, the government in an important sense actually minimizes the cost of its program. For it pulls in those with the lowest opportunity costs of service — everyone like Marshall but no one like Philip. Under a draft, this could occur only through the most unlikely of coincidences. Figure 3A provides a simple way to grasp the argument.

There is a supply curve of military volunteers. The argument that people won't voluntarily risk their lives is refuted by the fact that people do — not only military volunteers but also police, steeplejacks, and even skiers. Whatever its precise position and slope, the supply curve will certainly incline upward to the right. Some people (those who assign low value to their available alternatives) will volunteer at a very low wage. But three million volunteers can be secured, on our assumptions, only if the wage offer is at least $16,000 per year. That would mean a wage bill of $48 billion annually. But because taxpayers don't like to have their taxes raised, Congress is reluctant to approve such a huge appropriation. And the people in the Department of Defense care very much about the likes and dislikes of the people in Congress. They can cut that upsetting bill in half by offering only $8000 and compelling enlistments. The published cost will now be only $24 billion. Hurrah for cost savings!

But what of the costs to those who make up the armed

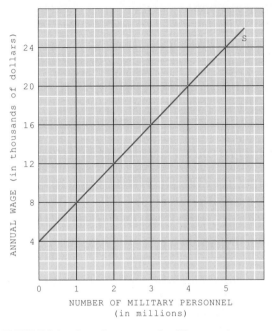

FIGURE 3A Supply curve of military volunteers

forces? The cost of the *volunteer* army (to the volunteers) under our assumptions would be $30 billion. That is the value of the area under the supply curve up to three million men and women, or the sum of the values of the opportunities forgone by those who enlisted. The other $18 billion paid out by the government is a transfer of wealth from taxpayers to members of the military who would have enlisted at a lower wage but who nonetheless receive the higher wage that is required to induce the enlistment of the three-millionth volunteer.

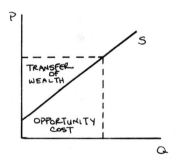

What will be the cost of a *conscripted* army to those who are drafted? We can't say, except that it will certainly be larger. Only if the draft happened to hit exactly those and only those who would have enlisted under a volunteer system would the cost be as low as $30 billion. That is most unlikely. The more draftees who are grabbed from the upper, rather that the lower, end of the supply curve, the higher will be the cost to the conscripts. For example, a man who would have volunteered at a wage of $9000 is offered only $8000. He rejects the offer, and he is subsequently not drafted. Instead, a person who would only have volunteered at $24,000 is drafted—and paid $8000. The net result is that taxpayers save $8000 by obtaining for only $8000 services for which they would have had to pay $16,000 under an all-volunteer system. But someone whose opportunity cost is $24,000 has been substituted for someone whose opportunity cost was only $9000. That's a $15,000 increase in cost from the standpoint of those who serve.

The military draft does *not* reduce the cost of maintaining a military establishment. It rather transfers that cost from the shoulders of taxpayers to the shoulders of the draftees. That may in your judgment be one of the least of its faults, or it may be outweighed in your mind by presumed advantages. But at least it's a consequence that economists can point out.

Costs and Ownership

Everyone who has been in the armed forces know horror stories about the inefficient ways the military makes use of its personnel. A highly skilled accountant is put to work painting barracks, and the commissary books are kept by someone who counts on his fingers. The stories are probably exaggerated. Nonetheless, we have grounds for predicting that personnel will tend to be used in such wasteful ways in the military more often than in civilian life.

Why? Because, in civilian life, those who employ people are usually compelled to pay them their opportunity cost. When you have to pay accountants the wages of accountants, you don't have them paint barracks — at least not if you're an employer with regard for the profitablilty of your enterprise. On the other hand, what is the cost to a sergeant of assigning a highly skilled recruit to a task that requires no skill at all? If the sergeant happens to resent the recruit for his air of superiority, real or imagined, then transferring him to a job more suited to his abilities might actually entail the sacrifice of a valuable opportunity for the sergeant — the opportunity to humiliate someone he dislikes.

Two conclusions emerge from the foregoing analysis. First, resources tend to be utilized thoughtlessly and carelessly when users don't have to pay the opportunity cost, or the value of the resources in their next-best use. Second, users are most often compelled to pay the opportunity cost of resources when those resources are clearly and definitely owned by someone. A man who is drafted does not "own his own labor," because the law has deprived him of the power to decide where and for whom and on what terms he will work. And so he can't insist on receiving his opportunity cost when Uncle Sam beckons—as he can when United Soapchips wants his services.

The point also applies, of course, to nonhuman resources. If no one owns a resource, there is no one to insist that potential users of the resource pay the value of the opportunities sacrificed by their use. The resource will consequently tend to be underpriced. And underpriced resources, as we shall see time and again in a variety of situations, tend to be used with little care or thought for the consequences. The incentive to economize is weak when the cost of using is low.

A Note on Alternative Systems

Don't fail to notice that the concept of opportunity cost is fully applicable to a socialist society in which resources are allocated by government planners. To economic planners in the Soviet Union, the cost of building a railway from Lubny to Mirgorod is the value of whatever could otherwise have been done with the resources. But if government officials have the power to obtain valuable resources without having to bid for them, how will they discover the value of the resources in alternative uses? Recall the remarkable workers who could install spokes in bicycle wheels while standing on their heads and whistling "Dixie." In the absence of circus owners willing to bid for their services, how would central planners ever find out that they were too valuable to be assigned to bicycle production?

A distinguishing characteristic of different economic systems is the way in which they assign costs to alternative actions. Where resources are privately owned, competing bids and offers generate prices that approximate opportunity costs to resource owners. Where resources are not clearly owned by anyone, this process cannot operate. What takes its place? Who determines the relative value of this railway line and that one, or of using steel for railroad tracks versus using it to build trucks, or of improving transportation versus improving the quality of what is transported, or of more and better consumer goods versus additional leisure? In the absence of the information that competing bids and offers create, the economic planners are fairly free to impose their own, private evaluations on the alternatives before them. Remember that intelligent choices presuppose good information. An effective economic system will be one that transmits reliable information to decisionmakers and gives them strong incentives to use the information so provided.

Do Costs Determine Prices?

When sellers announce a price increase to the public, they like to point out that the increase was compelled by rising costs. The business press publishes frequent announcements of this kind, and it's rare indeed when the announcement fails to include an expression of regret that higher costs made this unfortunate step necessary. In Chapter 9 we'll explore more fully the principles that guide sellers when they're setting prices. All we want to do now is use the concept of opportunity cost to examine critcally the basic notion that prices are determined by costs. We want to show you that it makes as much sense to assert that costs are determined by prices. More accurately, we shall argue here that *costs always depend on demand.*

Demand and Cost

We can begin with an example discussed earlier in this chapter. Does it make sense to claim that the price of getting a haircut has gone up because barbers' wages have risen? If people weren't willing to pay high prices for haircuts, how could barbers' wages rise? The price people are willing to pay to have their hair cut professionally is one important factor that causes costs — that is, wages — to be what they are.

Plastic surgeons receive high wages for their services. Is this why it costs so much to have a face lift? Not exactly. The causal relationship also runs in the opposite direction. It's the fact that people are willing to pay a high price for cosmetic surgery that makes the cost of hiring a plastic surgeon so high. Few people have the requisite skills, of course, and their acquisition is difficult and time consuming. That's why the demand for cosmetic surgery raises the income of the surgeons rather than merely increasing the number of people willing and able to provide the service. But the cost to any one person of the services of a plastic surgeon is obviously not independent of the demand of others for plastic surgery.

When the owners of professional football teams announce in the summer that ticket prices will be raised in the fall, they like to blame the increase on rising costs, especially the high wages that must be paid to the players. But why do the players receive such high wages? It can't be that their work is so dangerous and grueling, because it was just as dangerous and grueling in the days when players received only a few hundred dollars for the season. It's the demand, the willingness of many people to pay high prices to watch, that has made football players such valuable resources. Soccer players in the United States receive far less, not because they work less hard, but because soccer isn't that popular in this country.

One of the most interesting cases of the relationship we're stressing is found in agriculture. The average price per acre of farm real estate in the United States rose 267 percent from 1971 to 1981, more than twice as fast as the general price level increased over the same period. Consequently, anyone who decided to go into farming in 1981 found that he had to pay a high price to obtain productive land. It would clearly be misleading to assert that the high cost of land was the cause of high food prices. It was the demand for land, determined in large part by the demand for agricultural products, that pulled up the cost of farming land. When farmers argue for higher government support prices for their crops because land costs so much, they are ignoring the fact that higher support prices will tend to pull up the price of the land on which those crops can be grown. It will do so by enhancing the value of the opportunities available to one who owns the land.

How demand affects the cost of buying land

Similarly, the sharp declines in agricultural land prices in the 1980s were the result, not the cause, of lower farm commodity prices.

Consider the case of a farmer whose land lies near a large city. As the suburbs expand, residential developers offer to buy the land for a price that is three or four times higher than the price it can command as agricultural property. If the farmer refuses to sell because he wants to stay in farming, it is very unlikely that he will complain about the rising cost of land. But farmers who *rent* land near large cities often do just that. The landowner will understandably want to sell the land to developers unless the tenant farmer is willing to pay three or four times more rent. We can certainly sympathize with the tenant farmer dispossessed by the growth of the suburbs. But it's important that we see why he's being asked to pay a rent so much higher than before: it is the demand for the land that is raising its cost.

Note that if *tax assessments* are based on what is called "highest and best use," then the owner who wants to remain in farming can legitimately complain that he can't afford *not* to sell. In those circumstances he is required to pay taxes based not on his own use of the land, but on the use to which the land would be put by the highest bidder.

But let's push the analysis a bit further. Suppose the

farmer himself owns the land he's cultivating, and that the county does not raise the assessed value of the land when suburban developers bid up its price because public officials want to keep the land in farming. Will the policy succeed?

The cost to the farmer of maintaining the land in agriculture is the net value of the opportunities he thereby forgoes. By rejecting an opportunity to sell, he gives up the income he could obtain from investing the sales proceeds. If his annual net income from the farming operation is $5000 per year, he will be losing a large sum each year if he refuses to sell the land for $300,000, since $300,000 can earn far more than $5000 per year in such low-risk investments as U.S. government bonds.

What about the value to the farmer of remaining a farmer? Might he not, in selling his land, be giving up a valuable opportunity to lead a good, simple, honest, and satisfying life? Probably not. If he really does value farm living so highly, he can buy a replacement farm in some location where suburbanites aren't competing for the land. If he chooses not to do this, we have evidence that he doesn't place all that high a value on the agricultural life. In either event, the cost to him of continuing to farm on the land that the developers want goes up as soon as the developers bid up the price. That means he is less likely to continue farming that land, which means in turn that he is more likely to increase the supply of land available for suburban development.

Consumer Prices as Opportunity Cost

In all these examples we've tried to show that the costs of productive resources like labor and land are prices determined by demand. That, in fact, is what's meant by calling them opportunity costs. We can just as easily argue that the prices of consumer goods are, in reality, costs — opportunity costs that measure the value of the goods in alternative uses.

Take, for example, the case of lobster. Sad to relate, so few lobsters come to market that it just isn't possible for all of us to have as many as we could enjoy. More are brought to market as higher prices offer larger incentives to lobster fishermen; but the demand in recent years has increased considerably faster than the supply, and the price has consequently risen sharply.

The higher price can be viewed as the opportunity cost of the resources engaged in bringing lobsters to market. But when the lobsters have all been brought to market on a given day, so that the quantity is, for that day at least, completely fixed, then the price should be viewed as the opportunity cost of the last potential purchaser who was persuaded by the high price to do without lobster. Think of it as follows: lobsters have many alternative uses, at least as many as there are potential lobster eaters. Lobsters have only one function, it is true, from the aggregate point of view. (We're notorious for ignoring the values and preferences of the lobster.) But the consumption of a lobster by one gourmet prevents its consumption by another. Lobster lovers in effect bid against one another for the limited supply. As the price rises, more and more potential consumers are reluctantly persuaded to do without. The price that clears the market, that makes the quantity demanded equal to the quantity supplied, will be the price that just barely persuades the most reluctant of the disappointed lobster lovers to go home from the seafood market with ocean perch or flounder fillets. It is *that person's* opportunity cost that is expressed by the market clearing price.

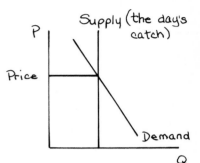

The demand for lobster determines the cost (price) of bringing one home.

The point of all this is that people don't pay what lobster is worth to them, but rather what lobster is worth in its most valued alternative use: as food for the consumer who was just barely deterred by the price from making a purchase. It's the opportunity cost of this disappointed lobster lover that the price reflects, as well as the opportunity costs of the resources that might have been used to bring additional lobsters to market.

How many coffee drinkers realize that when the price of coffee soars because of a freeze in Brazil, they are continuing to pay a price based on cost? It's not the cost of *growing* the coffee that determines the new, much higher price; it's the opportunity cost of those coffee lovers who must be persuaded (by a rising price) to sacrifice the caffeine they covet to others who are less willing to give it up and therefore willing to pay more.

But now we have moved into the question of scarcity and its social management. That is the topic for Chapter 4.

Once Over Lightly

Supply curves, as well as demand curves, reflect people's estimates of the value of alternative opportunities. Both the quantities of any good that are supplied and the quantities that are demanded depend on the choices people make after assessing the opportunities available to them.

Supply depends on cost. But the cost of supplying is the

value of the opportunities forgone by the act of supplying. This concept of cost is expressed in economic theory by the assertion that all costs relevant to decisions are opportunity costs — the value of the opportunities forsaken in choosing one course of action rather than another.

Insofar as the resources utilized in producing goods can be obtained only through competitive bidding, costs of production will reflect the value to the resource owners of the alternative uses of those resources. This implies that producers will want to suppress competitive bidding for the resources they use, if they can find an effective way to do so.

The value of a human being may be infinite, but the wages of human beings in any task will be much closer to the value of their services in alternative employments than to infinity.

Many disagreements about what something or the other "really costs" could be resolved by the recognition that "things" cannot have costs. Only actions entail sacrificed opportunities, and therefore only actions can have costs.

Costs are always the value of the opportunities that particular people sacrifice. Conflicting assertions about the costs of alternative decisions can often be reconciled by agreement on whose costs are under consideration.

Prices rise to the level of opportunity costs insofar as the owners of resources insist on being paid their value in the next-best use. This discourages a careless use of resources and assigns resources to those uses on which people place the highest monetary value.

Supply curves slope upward to the right because higher prices must be offered to resource owners to persuade them to transform a current activity into an opportunity they are willing to sacrifice.

Demand curves slope upward to the left because higher prices persuade resource users to sacrifice a current activity for their next-best opportunity.

Demand helps determine costs. Costs contribute to the determination of prices. The prices of goods affect the demand for other goods that they complement or for which they can substitute. From the perpective of opportunity cost, everything depends on everything else.

Questions for Discussion

1. A prominent hospital in New England decided in 1980 to turn down a request by staff surgeons to perform heart transplants. The general director of the hospital objected to the statement that this decision was "based

largely on cost considerations." On the contrary, he insisted, "the decision was based largely on the limited physical resources and highly trained personnel of the hospital. For each heart transplantation operation," he pointed out, the hospital "would have to turn away a number of other patients who receive less resource-draining open-heart surgery that is much more predictably beneficial to them than heart transplants currently are." Do you agree that the decision was not based on cost considerations?

(a) What is the valuable opportunity forgone when the hospital performs a transplant operation?

(b) Why didn't the hospital simply hire more surgeons and buy more physical resources if "cost considerations" were not the reason for the hospital's decision?

(c) What do you suppose prompted the hospital's general director to insist that the decision was *not* based on cost considerations?

2. Here is a statement from the economics textbook most widely used in American colleges before 1860: "The qualities and relations of natural agents are the *gift* of God, and, being His gift, they *cost us nothing.* Thus, in order to avail ourselves of the momentum produced by a water-fall, we have only to construct the water-wheel and its necessary appendages, and place them in a proper position. We then have the use of the falling water, without further expense. As, therefore, our only outlay is *the cost of the instrument* by which the natural agent is rendered available, *this* is the only expenditure which demands the attention of the political economist." Why do modern "political economists" disagree with Francis Wayland and pay attention to the cost of using "natural agents"?

(a) What was the cost to a nineteenth century mill owner of using a waterfall to power his mill if he owned the site of the waterfall?

(b) What was the cost to the mill owner if someone else owned the site?

(c) Under what circumstances would use of a waterfall to power a mill actually have cost nothing?

3. The acres of grass surrounding the Taj Mahal in Agra, India, are often cut by young women who slice off handfuls with short kitchen blades. Is this a low- or high-cost way to keep a lawn mowed?

4. By taking an airplane one can go from D to H in one hour. The same trip takes five hours by bus. If the air fare is $30 and the bus fare is $10, which would be the cheaper mode of transportation for someone who could earn $2 an hour during this time? For someone who could earn $10 an hour? Five dollars an hour?

5. At a sufficiently high price for gasoline, almost everyone would choose to leave the car at home and use public transportation to commute to and from work. But that price will differ vastly from one person to another. Why might it be higher for self-employed than for salaried people? For executives than for clerks?

6. What would be the effect on the cost to students of completing high school if legislation denied drivers' licenses to anyone under the age of 18?

7. Why did the cost of hiring domestic servants increase dramatically during World War II? What would you have replied to people who said that servants "just weren't available"?

8. Explain the following statement by a military recruiter: "There's nothing like a good recession to cure our recruiting problems."

9. Are hand-carved redwood flamingos that sell for $150 valuable because they take so many hours to carve? Or do people spend many hours carving redwood flamingos because they are valuable? Does the value of an object ever depend on what people know about how it was produced? Would a flamingo be more valuable if people thought it had been carved by Pope John XXIII than if they thought you had carved it?

10. Smith, Ricardo, Marx, and Keynes are potential tutors for students in introductory economics. Each wants to work 8 hours a day at his best available monetary opportunity. Students regard their services as perfect substitutes: as far as students are concerned, as hour of tutoring is equally valuable whichever of the four provides it.

    Marx is willing to tutor 8 hours a day for $4 an hour, because his next-best opportunity, fomenting revolution, currently pays only $3.99 an hour. Ricardo can work 4 hours a day at Merrill Lynch for $13.99 an hour; after that he's reduced to selling shoes for $4.99 an hour. Smith's best alternative is teaching moral philosophy at the local college for $7.99 an hour, 8 hours a day. Keynes has an 8-hour per day job, paying $11.99 an hour, raising money for the local symphony.

    (a) Construct the supply curve of tutoring services from these data on the graph in Figure 3B.
    (b) Show how the supply curve would change if Merrill Lynch hired Ricardo full time.
    (c) Show the change that would occur if someone offered Marx a job as a newspaper reporter at $9.99 an hour.

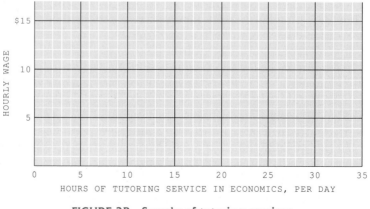

FIGURE 3B   Supply of tutoring services

(d) How would the supply curve change if the public suddenly became much more interested in learning something about moral philosophy?

11. The supply curve on the graph in Figure 3C shows the wage rates that would have to be offered by business firms to obtain various quantities of hours of envelope stuffing on any given day.

(a) What wage rate will firms have to offer if they want to hire 400 hours of envelope stuffing?

(b) What will be the firms' total expenditure on the wages of envelope stuffers?

(c) What will be the total opportunity cost to the envelope stuffers of stuffing envelopes? (Hint: Each square represents $20: 20 hours times $1.)

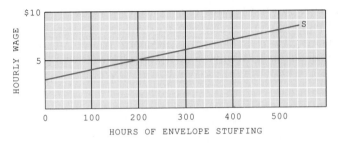

FIGURE 3C   Supply curve for envelope stuffing

12. (a) It has been argued that a volunteer army would discriminate against poor people, because they tend to have the lowest-value alternatives to military service and hence would dominate the ranks of volunteers. Do you agree with the analysis and the objection?

(b) Some critics have argued that if the military relied exclusively on volunteers, the armed forces would be filled with people of such low intelligence and skills that they could not operate sophisticated weapons. International Business Machines relies exclusively on "volunteers," and *its* employees are not predominantly people of low intelligence and skills. What's the difference between the armed forces and IBM? How would you reply to the argument of these critics?

(c) Another frequent criticism of a volunteer military is that we don't want "an army of mercenaries." How high does the military wage have to be before the recipient becomes a mercenary? Are officers compelled to remain in the armed services? Why do they stay in? Are they mercenaries? Is your teacher a mercenary? Your physician? Your minister?

13. Why might a multinational corporation with identical plants in different countries pay different wage rates to workers in the two countries even though their skill levels are the same? Does this strike you as unjust? Why might the *higher-paid* workers object?

14. If people are offering to pay $100 for $10 (face-value) tickets to the Big Game, and someone gives you a ticket, what does it cost you to attend the game? Would you be more likely to attend if someone gave you a ticket than if you had to purchase one for $100? Would you be more likely to attend if someone gave you a ticket than if you had to purchase one that you could buy (through an inside source) for $10?

15. Rising commercial rents in San Francisco in recent years have induced many corporations to move their offices out of the city. Can a San Francisco firm that owns its own office building simply ignore rising rents?

16. Henrietta George bought her large, old house 48 years ago for $2000. She could get $200,000 for it today if she chose to sell it. About how much do you suppose it's costing her per month to continue living in her large, old house?

17. What is the cost per ticket to a professional baseball club that offers 50 free tickets to an orphanage? Does it matter for what game the tickets are offered? Why would it probably cost the ball club more to give the tickets to college students than to poor orphans?

18. Think about the cost of television commercials. What enters into the cost of a 30-second commercial plugging Friendly Fred's Ford Dealership? How do you explain the fact that the same commerical will cost $90 on Wednesday morning but $1600 right before a big football game? Local television stations are often asked to donate time for public-service spots. Does this cost the station anything? Do you think that station owners' religious beliefs make them more willing to donate time on Sunday mornings than on weekday mornings?

19. The network advertising fee per 30-second spot during Super Bowl XVIII was $484,000. Did that reflect the network's estimate of the cost of providing a 30-second advertising spot? What made the cost so high?

20. Why do parking lot fees vary so widely from city to city in the United States? The all-day rate in Manhattan, for example, is often $20. In Atlanta, it is likely to be less than $5. Does this difference reflect the greater greed of New York City parking-garage owners?

21. In 1977 a Seventh Day Adventist congregation in Manhattan purchased a former synagogue for $400,000. Several years later the congregation decided to sell it because the maintenance costs were running $100,000 per year, too much for the 80-family congregation to pay. In 1982 a developer paid the congregation $2.4 million cash for the property. (The information is taken from a *Wall Street Journal* article of September 27, 1982.)

    (a) What would it have cost the congregation to continue using the building?
    (b) Would you say that it is greed that prompts congregations to sell large, old churches in downtown areas to commercial developers?

22. Most mobile-home owners own their homes but pay rent for the land on which the home sits. Some municipalities have recently begun to impose legal limits on the amount by which the owners of mobile-home parks can increase the rent they charge for their sites. One argument given in

defense of such rent controls was that zoning regulations against mobile-home parks made it difficult for mobile-home owners to move to a new site when faced with a huge rent increase.

(a) What determines the rent a mobile-park owner can charge for a site?
(b) To what cost, if any, is this charge related?
(c) How do zoning regulations against mobile-home parks affect the rents park owners can charge?
(d) Do you agree with the mobile-home owner who, when faced with a large increase, protested indignantly, "my home gives value to that pad of dirt"?

23. A number of American cities have passed rent-control ordinances in recent years. These ordinances often try to restrict rent increases to the amount of the owners' cost increases. Use the analysis of this chapter in thinking about these questions:

(a) What is the cost to a landlord of renting an apartment to you for $150 if someone else is willing to pay $250?
(b) What determines the cost to a potential landlord of purchasing an apartment building?
(c) What effect will a rent-control ordinance have on the cost of purchasing an apartment building?
(d) What effect will a rent-control ordinance have on the cost to landlords of letting an apartment unit stand idle, or of using it themselves, or of allowing relatives to live in it rent-free?
(e) What concept of cost do you think supporters of rent controls have in mind when they speak of basing maximum rents on landlords' costs?

24. Many Americans today seem to be much more "pressed for time" than were their grandparents. This is rather odd in view of the fact that today's homes and workplaces are full of so many time-saving devices to which our grandparents had no access. How would you account for this? If you can't think of an explanation, ask yourself what causes anyone to feel "pressed for time." What happens to the cost of engaging in an activity, whether it's for business or for pleasure, when attractive alternative opportunities suddenly present themselves?

25. "In the Middle Ages people believed in a just price for goods, not determined by supply and demand, but by the cost of raw material and labor." Assume that the author of that statement is accurate in his historical facts, and correct his economic analysis.

Chapter 4_____

Supply and Demand: A Process of Coordination

In every functioning society, large or small, tasks must be assigned and benefits distributed.

"Who takes out the garbage?"

"Who gets the last slice of pumpkin pie?"

The above questions represent two common kinds of allocation issues that arise in the family, the smallest functioning society we know.

"Who will live in the White House?"

This is a recurring allocation question in the largest functioning society in which we participate, the nation. The answer we give simultaneously assigns some very important tasks and distributes some intensely coveted benefits.

One way for a society to assign tasks and distribute benefits is by the principle: "from each according to ability, to each according to need." That seems to be a sensible principle; but in order for it to become workable, it must be attached to an acceptable system for assessing both abilities and needs. That's where the problems begin.

Allocating Tasks and Benefits

In one sense, individuals are the best judges of their own abilities and needs: I know better than anyone else what I can and cannot do and what will satisfy my particular wants. But in another sense, I am the person *least* qualified to judge, because of my obvious partiality toward my own interests. It is well and wisely established that people ought not to be judges in their own cases. Societies commonly compromise, therefore, by making the allocation of tasks and benefits a matter for negotiation among the interested parties.

These negotiations rarely take the form of committee meetings. They are rather the daily bids and offers that we make in the many societies in which we participate, bids

69

and offers that are based on well-defined rules of the game, and in which 99 percent of the relevant rights and obligations are taken for granted. "Will you do this for me, if I agree to do that for you?" Usually we don't even have to ask. We just walk uninvited into the pizzeria and tell an attendant to prepare us a medium pizza with green peppers, black olives, and extra cheese. The attendant doesn't ask what we're willing to do in return, but simply assumes we will pay the posted money price.

The Coordinating Role of Prices

These continual negotiations are what the economist refers to as supply and demand. Money prices play a crucial role in the process.

It is nowhere decreed in the laws of nature that tasks and benefits have to be allocated on the basis of monetary bids and offers. But it is undeniably the case that a whole lot of allocation and reallocation will have to occur before most goods get where they're going. Consider a gallon of gasoline. People and machinery have to be precisely assigned to explore, drill, pump, pipe, truck, and store before we can fill our tanks at the self-service island. That intricate system is coordinated by means of adjustments in money prices. The right number of people, equipped with the necessary knowledge and skills and accompanied by the appropriate tools, showed up at the correct times and places, so that we could eventually buy our fifteen gallons of unleaded regular. They did not accomplish this spectacular feat of coordination because they love us and know how much we need gasoline. They did it to further their own interests. Their efforts meshed because those efforts were coordinated by the ever-changing signals emitted by money prices.

We must insist again that the crucial importance of money prices to the working of our society implies nothing about the character or morality of our citizens. People pay attention to money prices insofar as they want to economize, that is, to get as much as possible of what they value from the resources they command. They don't pay attention *exclusively* to money prices, of course; that wouldn't make sense. They do, however, change their behavior when prices change, in order to "take advantage" of the new situation signaled by the new prices. This is what causes markets to clear and self-interested behavior to become cooperative action.

Try thinking of supply and demand as a process of

A process of mutual accommodation

mutual accommodation. When any good becomes more scarce — less is supplied relative to how much is demanded — its price rises. The higher price persuades demanders to take less, thus leaving more for others, and persuades suppliers to produce more. A lower price signals that a good has become less scarce than before; the lower price induces demanders to substitute this good for other goods and prompts suppliers to shift their efforts toward the production of alternative, more highly valued goods.

In a society as wealthy and specialized as ours — and it is wealthy *because* it is so extensively specialized — the coordination of activities is an enormously complex task. Its successful performance requires, above all else, a social system that facilitates the rapid exchange of accurate information about relative scarcities and induces people to act appropriately on the basis of that information. If economists are obsessed with money prices, it's because they see that prices provide such indispensable information and incentives.

The Urge to Fix Prices

To a demander, the price of a good is its cost. Demanders consequently tend to look on rising prices as an imposition. To a supplier, prices represent income. So suppliers see falling prices as a threat. That's probably why so many people don't appreciate the coordinating role that price changes play and why they often try to get government to prevent the changes from occurring. The consequences will usually be quite different from what was intended, however, because price fixing amounts to suspending the mechanism of social coordination.

Figure 4A presents a hypothetical demand curve for gasoline in the United States, labeled DD, with the price per gallon on the vertical axis and the number of gallons demanded per month on the horizontal axis. The demand is very inelastic within the range shown: a large percentage increase in the price will lead to a much smaller percentage decrease in the quantity demanded. That's a reasonable assumption, well supported by experience. The substitutes for gasoline are not very attractive to most of the people who use it.

But there *are* substitutes for gasoline: joining a car pool, moving closer to work, buying a smaller car, taking the bus, planning ahead, getting more frequent tune-ups, or staying at home. As the price of gasoline rises, so do the sacrifices people must make in order to buy it. As a result, although a

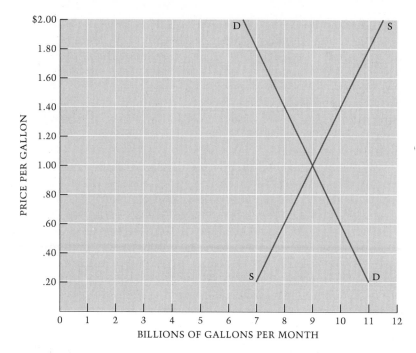

FIGURE 4A   Hypothetical demand and supply curve for gasoline

few may choose not to reduce their consumption at all, most people will find ways to economize at least a little, and some will decide to curtail their purchases substantially as the price goes up. The demand for gasoline is not totally inelastic.

Figure 4A also shows a relatively inelastic supply curve of gasoline, labeled SS.[1] The element of time, which plays such a large role in determining the responses of users to price changes, performs an even larger part in determining the responses of suppliers. Gasoline in storage can be quickly released for sale if a higher price makes selling more attractive than storing. But time is required to import gasoline from abroad in response to a higher price. Still more time is required to increase the flow of gasoline from the refineries by switching over from the production of other refined products, such as heating oil. And far more time will necessarily elapse before additional refinery capacity can be created in response to the higher price of gasoline.

What about the availability of crude oil? Weren't the

[1]Price elasticity of supply is analogous to price elasticity of demand: the percentage change in quantity supplied divided by the percentage change in price.

gasoline shortages of 1973-74 and 1979 the result of inadequate supplies of the basic raw material? We must answer carefully if we are to avoid begging the question. Iran's
political turmoil in 1978 and 1979 certainly disrupted the
flow of oil imports into the United States. But other OPEC
countries had the capacity to step up their rate of production
and thereby compensate for the Iranian cutbacks. They did
not do so, because they wanted the price of crude oil to rise.
But that is precisely our point. More than enough oil could
have been supplied in 1979 to keep the refineries running at
100 percent of capacity if the refineries — and ultimately the
consumers of refined products — had been willing and able
to pay the price. We must add the word *able*, because the
ability of consumers and refiners to offer more money for
gasoline and for crude petroleum was deliberately restricted
by law in the United States.

Why was it restricted? Why did the U.S. government
impose ceiling prices on the sale of petroleum and petroleum
products in the 1970s? Judging by the statements made at the
time, the price controls were designed to prevent "oil companies" from obtaining large, unearned profits at the expense
of low-income consumers. Proponents of the controls failed
to point out, however, perhaps because they didn't realize,
that by freezing prices the government was disconnecting a
crucial link in society's system of mutual adjustment and
cooperation.

The "Popular Perspective"

That raises yet another question. Why don't advocates of
price controls recognize the consequences of what they are
calling for? Some of them probably know very well but expect to benefit personally from price controls. The majority
of those who support price controls in such situations, however, are quite likely sincere in their belief that freezing
prices by law protects vulnerable people while doing little
harm. They probably hold what we shall call the Popular
Perspective on supply and demand.

According to the Popular Perspective, those who supply
particular goods won't supply any at all below some
minimum price but will supply "all they can" once the price
rises above that minimum. Those who purchase will purchase "what they need," regardless of the price, until some
upper limit is reached, above which they will do without the
good entirely. The supply and demand curves in Figure 4B
portray the world according to the Popular Perspective. The

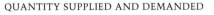

FIGURE 4B   The popular perspective on supply and demand

vertical segment of the supply curve is drawn slightly to the right of the demand curve to reflect the common belief that suppliers typically want to sell more than demanders are willing to buy.

In this way of thinking, prices do not coordinate decisions; they merely redistribute wealth. Price controls on gasoline, therefore, will only keep oil companies from exploiting a crisis to get rich at the expense of helpless motorists. Who but an oil company executive or stockholder could reasonably object to emergency price controls if supply and demand conform to the Popular Perspective?

How many people actually hold the Popular Perspective? Probably no one holds it clearly and consciously. It's one of those views that make little sense when thought through carefully but that may nonetheless be widely held because so few people take the pains to think carefully, especially when they know in advance what they want to believe. We'll come back a number of times to the Popular Perspective in the pages ahead. It's one way of accounting for some of the most perverse but persistent public policies.

What Causes Shortages?

The economist's perspective is quite different. Go back to Figure 4A. If the price of gasoline in this situation is $1 per gallon, demanders will want to purchase precisely as much as suppliers want to sell. The market clears at a price of $1.

Now suppose that the price of gasoline is fixed by law so that it cannot exceed 60 cents a gallon. At 60 cents the quantity demanded per month will be 10 billion gallons. But the quantity supplied will be only 8 billion gallons. That is what we mean by a shortage: the quantity demanded exceeds the quantity supplied, in this case by 2 billion gallons per month.

On the graph of Figure 4A, the shortage appears as a gap between the demand curve and the supply curve at the 60-cents-per-gallon price. People cannot obtain as much as they want even though they are willing to pay the money price that's being asked. The price fixing is the *cause* of the shortage.

Scarcity and Competition

No one blames the thermometer for low temperatures or seriously proposes to warm up the house on a cold day by holding a candle under the furnace thermostat. People do, however, often blame high prices for the scarcity of certain goods and act as if scarcity could be eliminated by enforcing price controls. That just isn't so.

Scarcity is a relationship between desirability and availability, or between demand and supply. In a society where everyone is terrified of snakes, snakes may be rare but they cannot be scarce. In another society, where snakes are valued as food, they could be quite common but nonetheless scarce. *A good is scarce whenever people cannot obtain as much of it as they would like without being required to sacrifice something else of value.*

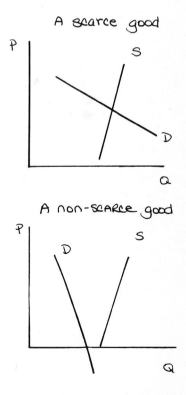

Now it follows immediately that if a good is scarce, it must be rationed. In other words, a criterion of some kind must be established for discriminating among claimants to determine who will get how much. The criterion could be age, eloquence, swiftness, public esteem, willingness to pay money, or almost anything else. We characteristically ration scarce goods in our society on the basis of willingness to pay money. But sometimes we use other criteria in order to discriminate.

Harvard University each year has many more applicants than it can place in the freshman class, so Harvard must ration the scarce places. It discriminates on the basis of high-school grades, test scores, recommendations, and other criteria.

Only one person at a time can be president of the United States. Since many more people than one want the position, we have evolved an elaborate system of discrimination in the form of conventions and elections. Although there is considerable doubt about just what the criteria for discrimination are, the system does discriminate. We end up every fourth year with only one satisfied candidate.

Joe College is the most popular man on campus and has young women clamoring for his favor. He must therefore ration his attentions. Whether he employs the criterion of beauty, intelligence, geniality, or something else, he must and will discriminate in some fashion.

The other side of discrimination is competition. Once Harvard announces its criteria for discrimination, freshman applicants will compete to meet them. The criteria for selecting a president are studied carefully by the hopefuls who begin competing to satisfy those criteria long before the election year. If the women eager to date Joe College believe that beauty is his main criterion, they will compete with one another to seem more beautiful.

Competition is obviously not confined to capitalist societies or to societies that use money. The point is of fundamental importance: *competition results from scarcity* and can be eliminated only with the elimination of scarcity. Whenever there is scarcity, there must be rationing. Rationing is allocation in accord with some criteria for discrimination. Competition is merely what occurs when people strive to meet the criteria that are being used.

Of course, the criteria used do make a difference. If a society rations on the basis of willingness to pay money, members of that society will strive to make money. If it uses physical strength as a primary criterion, members of the society will do body-building exercises. And if the better colleges and universities use high-school grades as an important criterion for selection, high-school students will compete for grades. They might be competing for grades to acquire other goods as well (status among classmates, compliments from teachers, use of the family car), but it is odd for colleges to complain of grade grubbers when their own rationing criteria promote grade grubbing.

Competition When Prices Are Fixed

What is going to happen, then, when a good like gasoline becomes more scarce but its money price is not allowed to rise? We will certainly see increases in the nonmonetary costs of purchasing it, for gasoline is scarce and therefore *must* be rationed. If by law we suppress the rationing device of monetary price, other rationing criteria will have to be used, whether by drift or by design. Potential purchasers of gasoline will attempt to discover the new criteria being used to discriminate among buyers, and they will compete against one another in trying to satisfy those criteria. Their competition will raise the total cost — price plus nonmonetary costs — and will continue raising it until the quantity demanded no longer exceeds the quantity supplied.

The gas line is probably the best example. When people think they may be unable to purchase as much gasoline as they would like to buy at 60 cents a gallon, they try to get to the station early before the stocks have all been sold. But others have the same idea, so that the lines form earlier and grow longer. Waiting in line is unquestionably a cost. As this cost rises, the law of demand comes into play: consumers drive less when they expect to have to pay $12 plus half an hour's wait for a fill-up than when they can fill their tanks for a straight $12.

Some drivers may decide to hunt around rather than wait in line. They will pay their additional cost in time and gasoline spent on searching. Others will strike deals: a fill-up out of reserved supplies in return for a tip to the station operator, or the payment of a special fee for parking at the station, or an agreement to have service work performed there, or maybe tickets to the theater for the station owner. All these ways of competing for gasoline raise the cost of obtaining it. And the cost will continue rising until it finally reduces the quantity demanded to match the quantity supplied.

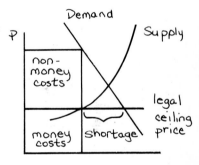

Competition among people — whose combined desires to purchase a good cannot all be fully satisfied at the prevailing money price — will bid up the cost of purchasing it. Usually it is the money price that rises in such a situation. Whenever other components of the cost of purchasing a good start to climb, we can be fairly certain that some kind of social pressure (such as legislated price controls) is holding down the money price. And when that occurs — that is, when lengthening lines, longer searching, or special arrangements come into play to ration a good (because the quantity demanded is greater than the quantity supplied *at the prevailing money price* — we have a shortage of that good.

The economist's concept of shortage zeroes in on the money price. Shortages exist only when money prices are not able to perform the function of rationing scarce goods to competing demanders. *We spot a shortage in real life whenever we find the nonmoney costs of acquisition rising to ration scarce goods.*

The Supplier's Role in Rationing

We expect to see the money price of a good rise when the good becomes scarcer. Why? Because it is almost always in the interest of suppliers to raise the money price rather than see some other component of the acquisition cost increase. What does the owner of a gas station gain, after all, when customers wait in line for 30 minutes? Nothing (and maybe less than nothing if they are all less pleasant people by the time they get to the pump). But an increase of 20 cents in the money price of a gallon of gasoline is simultaneously an addition of 20 cents per gallon to the station owner's wealth. An increase in nonmoney costs usually entails an increase in what the economist calls *deadweight costs.* These are *costs to the purchaser that are not simultaneously benefits to the seller.* The cost of waiting in line is a perfect example.

If sellers have it in their power to transform a dead-weight cost into a benefit for themselves, they will want to do so. And whenever sellers are free to raise the money price of the good they are supplying, they have ready at hand a simple tool for making that transformation. Notice what a handy and versatile tool it is. Everyone values money because its possession confers command over a whole universe of other goods. Everyone is accustomed to paying money for goods. The seller is usually the owner or agent of the owner with an acknowledged right to change the money price. The money price can be minutely adjusted, up or down, in a search for the price that most completely converts the buyer's cost of acquisition into the seller's benefit from supplying.

All of this explains why changes in money prices are the usual response to changes in relative scarcities, and why economists view changing money prices as such a crucial means for securing social coordination. No doubt there are goods that *cannot* and other goods — most people would agree — that *should not* be rationed by means of changing money prices.[2] But it is a fact well worth noting that where

---

[2]It would be difficult to assign all residents on a city block the precise amount of street illumination for which each is willing to pay. And we apply a variety of derogatory terms to people who ration their affections by the criterion of money price.

this mechanism for achieving social coordination is not available, cooperation on any extensive scale becomes much more difficult to achieve.

Appropriate and Inappropriate Signals

What will suppliers do if the law prevents them from raising their prices in a situation of obvious shortage? They will probably look for alternative ways to turn the situation to their advantage. Gasoline retailers may decide to lower the cost *to themselves* of selling by reducing their daily hours of operation and closing altogether on weekends. If they can sell their entire weekly allocations in 20 hours, why should they bother to stay open for 120 hours a week? This response to the shortage will tend further to increase the cost to *buyers* of purchasing gasoline: they will face even longer lines, will be forced to cancel or curtail weekend traveling, will more frequently find themselves stranded because of the inability to obtain fuel, and will pay additional costs through searching, worrying, and even endangering their lives by improperly siphoning and storing gasoline.

FRED'S FRIENDLY SERVICE
Open for ~~your~~ my convenience
~~24~~ 3 hours daily

    Those who supply or demand gasoline are not peculiarly selfish or inconsiderate. The costly chaos that we actually witnessed in recent years at the gasoline pumps simply demonstrated how dependent we are on changing money prices to secure effective cooperation in our complex, interdependent society and economy. When prices are not permitted to signal a change in relative scarcities, suppliers and demanders receive inappropriate signals. They do not find, because they have no incentive to look for, ways to accommodate one another more effectively. It is important that people receive some such incentive, because there are so many little ways and big ways in which people *can* accommodate — ways that no central planner can possibly anticipate, but which in their combined effect make the difference between chaos and coordination. Changing money prices, continuously responding to changing conditions of demand or supply, provide just such an incentive, because, contrary to the Popular Perspective, supply curves slope upward to the right and demand curves slope downward.

Is There a *Better* System?

To say that money prices perform this function is not to say that they perform it perfectly. They certainly don't. In subsequent chapters we'll be looking at the limitations of social coordination through a price system as well as at its accomplishments. We'll ask under what circumstances money prices are less likely to reflect people's preferences in an adequate way, and we'll discover that ignorance, market power, collusive arrangements, disagreements about property rights, and inequalities in society all interfere with the "ideal" operation of the price system. But we do not discard the first law of motion (which says that bodies in motion tend to remain in motion) just because there is friction in the actual world. It would be a similar mistake to overlook the achievements of the price system just because it fails to coordinate flawlessly.

A system that rations scarce goods by means of money prices will, of course, allocate the goods to those who are willing to pay. Consequently, when rationing occurs by means of price, poor people tend to get less than rich people. That, in fact, is the very meaning of *rich* and *poor* when used in an economic context. But it is not the whole picture. Price rationing accommodates all sorts of other differences among people as well, differences that will prove extremely difficult to handle fairly under any other form of rationing.

Suppose we decide to ration gasoline by means of specially issued coupons. How will the government allocate those coupons? It would not be fair to allocate the same number to a single person as to a family of seven, but neither would it be fair to give seven times as many coupons to the family. It wouldn't be fair to allocate an equal number of coupons to each licensed driver, and it wouldn't be fair to assign coupons to each owner of an automobile. (This would encourage people to stock their driveways with clunkers.) People who live in dense metropolitan areas probably travel shorter distances on average and also are more likely to have access to public transportation. Fairness therefore suggests that they should receive fewer coupons than those who live in thinly populated regions of the country. But some people in New York City regularly drive farther than some people in Silverton, Colorado. Would a system that ignored the special circumstances of individuals be fair? How could coupons be awarded fairly to a traveling sales representative in west Texas and an elderly woman in Cedar Rapids who drives only to church? Should the person who hates to drive receive as many coupons as someone who enjoys driving?

And what about business users? (An adequate rationing system must take account of the fact that diesel fuel and gasoline compete for scarce petroleum and scarce refinery capacity.) If farms, taxicab companies, commercial fisheries, and trucking firms – to mention just a handful of businesses that use large amounts of motor fuel – are allotted "all that they need," they will turn out to "need" more than anyone had anticipated. If we therefore create a government agency charged with determining the specific quantities to which each individual firm is entitled, what criteria will it use to make its decisions? Past consumption? Probably. But in an economy where new firms are continually born and old ones die, where some businesses expand and others decline, where technology is constantly changing and so is demand, how can past consumption be an adequate guide to current allocation?

The unfairness of its decisions might be the least of the agency's worries. Because business firms supply inputs to other business firms, as well as final goods to consumers, mistakes that were not quickly caught and corrected could have a domino effect. An error in allocation could close down an entire industry by inadvertently preventing the manufacture or transportation of some seemingly minor but actually crucial input. The intricate interdependence of a modern, industrialized economy could not long be maintained in the face of arbitrary allocations of motor fuel among business firms.

Inflation and Rent Controls

Popular hostility to rationing by means of money prices grows in periods of inflation, because people mistakenly assume that an increase in money prices means a decline in their level of living. It's hard for most of us to see that our money incomes tend to rise right along with the prices of the goods we buy. When expenditures on a particular good take up a large percentage of our monthly budget, we become especially sensitive to increases in that good's price. If in addition the price of the good changes infrequently, and therefore by large jumps when it does change, we grow even more indignant about increases in its price. And popular indignation is fertile ground for the growth of legislative interference with the movement of money prices.

Rent controls are far and away the best example. Although grocery and clothing prices creep slowly upward in a period of inflation and are therefore commonly ignored, rents tend to remain fixed for longer periods of time — and then to do their advancing with a bound. A rent increase from $150 to $225 also makes a big dent in the budget and seems unreasonably steep, even when the average prices of the other goods we buy have increased by more than 50 percent since the last rent increase. People look for scapegoats in such circumstances, and landlords (the word itself stirs resentment) are prime candidates.

There is an unusual irony in the case of residential rents, an irony that greatly aggravates the problem. Because residential rents are exceptionally "sticky" prices, tending to lag behind the rate of change in other prices, the average level of rents tends actually to fall during rapid inflations. Thus, whereas the average level of prices paid by consumers more than doubled from 1967 to the end of 1978, rents increased slightly less than 70 percent. So rents actually declined by about 15 percent.[3]

But this fall in rental prices was caused by a malfunction of the price system, not by any change in underlying conditions of demand or supply. The result in one American city after another was *declining vacancy rates*. These low vacancy rates, themselves a result of underpriced housing, then became a further argument for rent controls. "We cannot permit rent gouging when the vacancy rate is less than 1 percent." Or even better: "We must impose rent controls until the vacancy rate rises to an acceptable 3 percent." Since the low vacancy rate is the product of low rents, that is an argument, whether recognized or not, for permanent rent controls. Note that the suppliers who are thus singled out and specifically forbidden to raise their prices are suppliers whose prices are already failing to keep pace with inflation.

When law or custom keeps money rents below the level at which the quantity demanded equals the quantity supplied, other ways of rationing will evolve. Landlords might discriminate on the basis of age, sexual preference, personal habits, family size, letters of reference, pet ownership, length of residence in the community, or willingness to abide by petty regulations. Tenants who were lucky enough to be in a rent-controlled apartment when the controls were imposed will hang on to as much space as possible for as long as they can and will try to pass the unit on to a friend or to sublease when they do vacate. Landlords will lower the quality of the services they provide, since they know that there is long line of tenants waiting to move in if any current tenant becomes dissatisfied.

---

[3]The ratio of rents to all consumer prices, which by definition was 100/100 in 1967, had become 170/200 in 1978; so rents in 1978 were at only 85 percent of their 1967 levels when measured in relative prices. That constitutes a 15 percent decline.

All these responses will lead to demands for costly administrative review boards and for additional legislation prohibiting particular landlord responses. The long-term result may be the eventual disappearance of landlords, as existing buildings are allowed to deteriorate or are turned into condominiums, and new rental units are not constructed. But even the most unrelenting foe of landlords must concede that it will be hard to find an apartment to rent when none is being offered.

Surpluses and Scarcity

Many people use the word *surplus* to suggest that a particular good is not scarce. But this doesn't make a lot of sense. Let's consider the much discussed problem of farm surpluses.

Agricultural surpluses have been a continuing concern in the United States for many years. Farmers and their supporters maintain that the prices of agricultural products should go up at about the same rate as the prices of other goods. They have persuaded Congress to establish parity prices: prices that preserve the ratio that farmers had enjoyed from 1910 to 1914 (prosperous years for farmers generally) between the prices they received for their crops and the prices they paid for the goods they bought. A common policy goal was 90 percent of parity.

Through the Commodity Credit Corporation, an agency of the Department of Agriculture, the federal government offers to store for farmers, free of charge, any crops for which they cannot find a market at the established parity price, meanwhile lending the farmers the value of the crops they choose to store. These are nonrecourse loans, which means that farmers can simply pocket the loan and let the Commodity Credit Corporation keep the stored produce. In effect farmers use the government as a buyer of last resort in order to be sure of receiving the target price for any "supported" crop. The resulting surpluses do not mean that wheat, corn, cotton, and other supported crops are not scarce. They simply mean that Congress is unwilling to let key farm prices fall to the level at which the quantity demanded for current consumption will match the quantity farmers want to produce.

The American Medical Association has long been warning about an imminent surplus of physicians. If we don't stop training so many physicians, says the AMA, we will soon be burdened with more than we need. But there is no

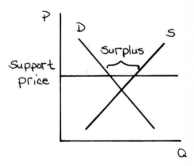

precise number of physicians "needed" by any population. When members of a profession talk about the number "needed," they almost always mean the quantity demanded *at the current price*. Of course, a lower price for their services is precisely what they don't want to see. And that makes them reluctant to admit that lower prices would also produce lower incomes for physicians and an eventual reduction in the number of physicians practicing. Do you detect the Popular Perspective at work?

Surpluses of teachers also became a problem in recent years, at least for the teachers. From the standpoint of school boards and local taxpayers, the problem looked more like an opportunity. At lower wage rates, school districts would be willing to hire more teachers. And at lower wage rates, some of those now offering to teach would decide to seek careers elsewhere. If salary scales cannot be reduced, either because of union contracts or just because it "wouldn't be right" to lower the pay of those to whom we entrust the hearts and minds of our youth, other ways are usually found to balance the quantity supplied and the quantity demanded. Salary scale increases that are less than the rate of inflation reduce the real wage. School boards can also add to the duties of teachers, lowering the wage per unit of product by getting more product for a given salary.

If these measures are insufficient to balance quantity supplied with quantity demanded, other criteria will of necessity be used to ration out the scarce supply of teaching positions. (A surplus of teachers is a shortage of teaching positions.) Seniority is an obvious and common rationing criterion. It's one that appeals to long-established teachers, but not one that younger or prospective teachers find very attractive. And certainly it does little to promote a situation in which those most eager to teach are also most likely to end up in the classroom.

Suppliers Who Don't Care About the Price

When a good becomes more scarce, competition from demanders tends to bid up its price. Suppliers are usually happy to cooperate in letting this occur, because they benefit from higher prices. What will happen, however, when a good becomes more scarce but those who supply the good have nothing to gain from letting its price rise?

A good example is landing space at some of the nation's busiest airports. The Federal Aviation Administration predicts that as many as 50 U.S. airports will face serious congestion problems by the end of the century. Why is this occurring?

An increase in demand, even a huge, rapid increase in demand, won't necessarily create a shortage. There is no current shortage of personal computers, to take a dramatic example. And when more people want to fly, the airlines simply offer more flights. They hire more people and buy more airplanes, if they must. That costs them money, of course, but those are expenses the airlines are happy to incur, because they expect their additional revenue to exceed their additional costs.

The bottleneck appears at the airports because the airports and the airspace surrounding them are not privately owned and hence are not priced to earn a profit. The additional travelers who bring joy to the heart of the airline managers are a pain in the neck to those who manage the airports, because those who "own" the airports and the airspace around them have no interest in charging higher prices when the goods they supply become more scarce.

Your Very Own Airport

The easiest way to grasp the essential point might be to suppose that you owned National Airport in Washington, DC, one of the most crowded in the country, and that you were free to operate as you saw fit. The "congestion problem" would disappear immediately, transformed into "full-capacity operation." (Do theater owners worrry about congestion when they've sold all the tickets?)

The various airlines would still be eager to schedule more flights into National, because it's just a few minutes from the Capitol and hence the airport preferred by most travelers to Washington. But you would make them bid for the scarce landing slots, because you (money-grubbing rascal that you are) want to squeeze as much revenue as you can out of the landing fees. In the resulting competition, the price would rise to reflect the opportunity cost of the first *excluded* bidder. You would make a mint. But you would also have allocated the available landing slots to those who valued them most highly, as measured by their willingness to pay a landing fee that clears the market.

Won't travelers suffer, however, from your mercenary maneuver? It's quite likely that the airlines would tack a little extra onto the ticket price under this system for flights into National Airport. But that would in effect ration the scarce landing space at National to those passengers who placed a high value on the convenience of landing close to downtown rather that an hour away at Dulles Airport far out in Virginia.

In fact, many passengers would be better off if passengers flying into National had to pay a premium. That would induce the airlines to divert more flights to the uncrowded, almost deserted runways of Dulles. As a result, many passengers who didn't want to go to downtown Washington in the first place, or who were merely making a connection in Washington, would be able to enjoy the convenience and greater safety of Dulles Airport.

Moreover, if there is any way for you to expand the capacity of your airport, you will investigate it carefully. And if the cost of the expansion is less than the value of the expansion, as measured by the willingness of the airlines and ultimately of travelers to pay for landing, you will quickly and expeditiously carry through the expansion. You won't behave like the FAA, which cries "crisis" but announces a program to upgrade air-traffic-control equipment only *over a ten-year period.*

Flight delays, near collisions, and other evidence of a shortage of airspace can be traced directly to our system of airspace ownership. The rules of the game make it next to impossible for those who value scarce airspace most highly to bid it away from those who value it far less. A slow, small, propeller-driven plane carrying half a dozen passengers will be allowed to land at Washington's National Airport or Chicago's O'Hare at a peak hour, thereby delaying two jumbo jets with 600 passengers, because the rules of the game make it almost impossible for the 600 passengers to bid the landing slot away from the six. Supply and demand are still at work, but they don't produce a great deal of mutual accommodation in cases like this.

Prices, Committees, and Dictators

The central economic task for a society is to secure cooperation among people in using what is available to obtain what is wanted. Effective cooperation among large numbers of people who barely know each other requires that the terms of exchange be clear, simple, and standardized.

Money prices are a device of extraordinary effectiveness for simplifying, clarifying, and standardizing. Have you ever wondered why committees achieve so little while consuming so much of their members' time and energy? It's because committees are such poor devices for simplifying, clarifying,

Information about Scarcity

and standardizing the available options. If a committee does manage to evolve procedures for performing these tasks, it ceases to behave like a committee — instead it becomes a cooperative venture.

There's another method for getting work done through committees, of course: by letting one person make all the decisions. Dictators do get things done quickly. And dictatorial decisionmaking can also perform, in the larger society, many of the simplifying, clarifying, and standardizing functions of the price system.

The other side of the coin is that the price system makes social cooperation possible in the absence of dictators. That's a definite plus for all those who don't care much for dictators.

Once Over Lightly

Scarcity is a relationship between availability and desirability, or between supply and demand. A good ceases to be scarce only when people can obtain all that they want at no cost.

Money prices provide information about relative scarcities.

Changes in relative prices create incentives to change behavior: to use less and provide more when prices have risen, to use more and provide less when prices have fallen.

Supply and demand is the process of interaction through which relative prices are determined. It is a process of mutual adjustment and coordination.

A system of money prices that change readily in response to changing conditions of demand and supply is an essential mechanism for coordinating behavior in highly specialized economic systems.

Scarce goods must be rationed in some fashion. Rationing entails the use of discriminatory criteria to determine who gets how much. Competition is the attempt to satisfy whatever discriminatory criteria are being used to ration scarce goods.

When a good becomes more scarce, but prices are prevented from rising, a shortage develops: the quantity demanded at the prevailing price is greater than the quantity supplied.

A surplus is a situation in which the quantity of a good supplied exceeds the quantity demanded at the prevailing money price. Any good, whatever its scarcity, will exist in surplus supply if its price is fixed at a high enough level.

When competition is prevented from raising prices, it

will raise other components of the cost of acquisition. These are often deadweight costs: costs to demanders that, unlike money payments, are not benefits to suppliers.

Suppliers usually have an incentive to convert deadweight costs into benefits for themselves by raising money prices when a shortage appears.

When suppliers do not benefit from higher prices, perhaps because the scarce resources are not privately owned, money prices will be less responsive to changing conditions of scarcity, and cooperation in the use of scarce resources will be more difficult to secure.

Allocating rights and obligations by means of monetary prices discriminates in favor of those with high monetary incomes. But it also allows individuals to obtain special consideration for their particular wants and abilities in social assignments of benefits and tasks.

Questions for Discussion

1. Here is a problem of social coordination you might want to think about. Millions of Americans change their residences each year, many moving long distances to new and strange areas. How do they all find places to live? Who sees to it that almost every individual or family moving to a new state finds someone in that state willing to sell or rent them a house or apartment that suits their tastes and circumstances? Who oversees new construction so that those states which are growing most rapidly manage to expand their stock of housing at a rate that matches their population growth?

2. A *Wall Street Journal* article of January 3, 1983 was headed, "Moving House Isn't Easy to Do in China, Where Government Is the Only Landlord." Government not only owns all housing in China; it also keeps rents down to a level equal to about 3% of an average worker's income.

   (a) What effect would you expect such low rents to have on the vacancy rate? Would you expect to have trouble locating housing in an American city where rents were limited by law to $100 a month?

   (b) How could a Chinese family that wanted to move to another city persuade anyone in that city to vacate housing space for them? Think about what they would have to do.

   (c) The Chinese government maintains housing-exchange stations in all the major cities. Why is a housing exchange so much less effective than a system of changing prices when it comes to facilitating trades among millions of people who want to move?

3. Should parents with one television set and three children allocate program choice to the sibling who submits the highest bid? How do parents ration

scarce strawberries, served as dessert at dinner, among competing children? If it is better for parents to allocate these scarce goods according to their sense of justice and fairness, wouldn't it also be better if the Department of Energy allocated scarce energy resources among competing citizens according to the Department's sense of justice and fairness? What is the difference between the two cases?

4. The text maintains that the price system is an institution that secures social cooperation in large part by simplifying options. Another institution that does this effectively is the traffic light. Are traffic lights fair? How much attention do they pay to the special circumstances of the drivers who approach them? Would you prefer a system of traffic control that always gave the right of way to the motorist on the more urgent errand?

5. If the distribution of income were completely equalized, would everyone purchase the same quality automobile? Against whom do automobile prices discriminate? Under an equal income distribution, would all families of the same size want to own or rent the same quantity and quality of housing space? Against whom do rental prices discriminate?

6. When federal environmental rulings forced stricter limits on street parking in midtown New York, parking-garage rates rose. Why? New York's consumer affairs commissioner called for a crackdown on parking-garage "gougers." What would happen if parking-garage rates were held down by law?

7. The city of Seattle decided to "give downtown parkers a break" on Monday, February 22, 1982, because so many had put money into the parking meters when they didn't legally have to on the previous Monday, a legal holiday. Did downtown parkers really benefit from not having to pay the meters on February 22? Who benefited from this decision, and who was made worse off?

8. Many ceiling prices were fixed by law in World War II. How were scarce goods rationed?

9. State colleges and universities set very low tuition. How do they ration scarce facilities? Who do you think gains from this system? Why might professors and administrators of state schools prefer *not* to have scarce facilities rationed by means of higher prices (tuition)?

10. There are no toll charges for driving on many urban expressways during the rush hour. How is the scarce space rationed?

11. Parking space is often sold on college campuses at a zero price. How is the scarce space rationed? If all students who bring cars onto the campus are charged $100 a year by the college as an automobile registration fee, is that fee a rationing device?

12. A parking space in the 1500-car garage under the Boston Common cost $110 a month in 1988, according to a November 7 article in *The New York Times.* Those who want to rent a space could expect a seven-year wait, according to the state agency that runs the garage. Is the rate too high, too low, or about right, in your judgment? What do you think would happen to the monthly parking rate if the garage were privately owned? Why doesn't the state raise the rate?

13. If you travel through the western states in the summer, you are much more likely to encounter a shortage of camping spaces than of motel rooms. Why?

14. When motels raise their rates "during the season" and reduce them "off season," are they exploiting customers or promoting a better allocation of resources?

15. The government did not impose controls on sugar prices in 1974, and the price per pound rose about 600 percent. Did the high price cause any more sugar to be available in 1974 than would have been available at a lower, controlled price? Do you think there would have been any refined sugar available on grocers' shelves if the government had frozen the price near its original level? Where would it have gone?

16. What do you think would have happened had the government imposed price ceilings in 1977 when the price of coffee increased about 400 percent? What do you think would have happened had the government imposed price controls in 1978 when lettuce prices increased by about the same percentage?

17. If a ceiling of $1 per pound were placed on lobster sold at retail, where could you go to eat a lobster?

18. A May 1979 wire-service story reported that a San Diego Chargers' football player got so upset waiting in line to buy gasoline for his Rolls Royce that he purchased a gas station. "I bought it for my friends' convenience, too," Johnny Rodgers said. Do price controls keep the wealthy from obtaining more than the poor?

19. One reason that local governments sometimes impose rent controls is precisely to prevent money prices from rationing scarce residential space. Do the controls succeed in doing this? How has it happened, do you suppose, that most of New York City's rent-controlled apartments are occupied by relatively wealthy people?

20. Suppose the Department of Defense decides to close a military base along the seashore and to turn the land over to private citizens. The land is close to heavily populated areas and offers choice view lots.

   (a) If the lots are allocated by means of a lottery, who will end up building on them?

   (b) Some lots are clearly more desirable than others. Will more expensive houses tend to be constructed on the more desirable lots if the lots are allocated by lottery?

   (c) Were you assuming in the answers above that the government places no restrictions on reselling? What difference will it make if the rules of the lottery declare that lottery winners cannot sell their lots for 5 years after acquisition, on penalty of forfeiture?

   (d) Is it fairer to allocate the lots by a lottery than on the basis of willingness to pay?

21. Help the Federal Communications Commission decide how to award scarce broadcast licenses for low-power television stations among the 5000

competing applicants by indicating the principal advantages and disadvantages of the following systems. Award the licenses:

(a) to the highest bidders.
(b) to the most qualified applicants.
(c) by lottery.
(d) by a lottery that favors groups currently underrepresented in the ranks of broadcast license holders as long as the lottery winners are qualified.

Can you understand why the FCC, when instructed by Congress to use method (d) above, replied that it lacked the ability to devise a system that would withstand lawsuits from disappointed applicants?

22. Utah annually sells 27 licenses to hunt buffalo in a 1500-square-mile area of the state. The fee is $200 for residents and $1000 for nonresidents. Because the state receives more than a thousand applicants each year, it holds a lottery to decide who will get the 27 licenses.

(a) Why do you suppose Utah doesn't sell the licenses to the highest bidder?
(b) Do you think people who receive a license should be allowed to sell it to someone else?
(c) What effects do you think a lottery system *with freely transferable licenses* would have?

23. A letter to the editor recommends: "Gasoline should be rationed, if it becomes necessary, according to need — real need." How will the rationing authorities determine *real need*?

24. Evaluate for their fairness toward single-car and multiple-car families the following proposed systems for rationing gasoline:

(a) People whose license plates end in odd numerals can buy only on odd-numbered days; people whose plates end in even numbers buy on even-numbered days.
(b) People are required to choose one day of the week on which each car will *not* be driven. They are assigned numbers (1 through 7) that they must display. Any car being driven on the prohibited day is ticketed by police.
(c) No one may buy gas on Sundays.
(d) No one may buy less than $10 worth of gasoline.

25. A well-known college basketball coach has urged high-school stars not to accept summer jobs, jobs for family members, or cash payments from college recruiters because this would violate National Collegiate Athletic Association rules that narrowly limit what a college can offer a star athlete by way of inducement to enroll. The famous coach urges high-school stars not to "sell their souls."

(a) Are the high-school stars selling their souls or their skills?
(b) Why do college recruiters secretly offer larger monetary inducements than the NCAA rules allow?

(c) If recruiters are prevented from offering high-school athletes as much money as the recruiters think the athletes are worth to the college, how will competition among colleges for the athletes' services nonetheless raise the cost to colleges of acquiring the athletes?

26. Far fewer babies are currently offered for adoption in the United States than couples want to adopt. Would you call this a shortage? Why doesn't the price of an adopted baby rise? By what criteria are the scarce babies rationed to demanders?

27. If the supply of turkeys in a particular November turned out to be unusually small, do you think a turkey shortage would result? Why or why not?

28. (a) There is currently some concern about a surplus of college teachers. How could the surplus be reduced or eliminated? Do you think this will happen? Why or why not?

    (b) Note that a surplus of college teachers can be viewed as a shortage of college teaching positions. How will the scarce supply of positions be rationed if price (salary of teachers) is not allowed to perform this function?

29. The summer of 1988 saw a record-breaking drought in the U.S. agricultural heartland. In the autumn of 1988, experts were predicting the largest jump in U.S crop acreage since World War II. What prompted farmers to undertake such a public-spirited response to the situation created by the drought?

30. The state with the highest ratio of physicians to population in 1985 was Massachusetts, with 277 physicians per 100,000 people. Idaho had the lowest ratio: 107 physicians for every 100,000 people. Does Massachusetts have a surplus of physicians? Does Idaho have a shortage? Or do people in Massachusetts need more doctors than people in Idaho? Why might people receive more medical services relative to the population of the state in Massachusetts than in Idaho even if people in Idaho were to receive exactly as much medical care per capita as people in Massachusetts?

31. Think about a registration scheme under which students would have to pay higher tuition for 10 o'clock classes and would receive discounts for taking 8 o'clock classes. Would you favor such a plan? Why do colleges *not* charge higher prices for the hours in greater demand? A student willing to pay a friend $5 to stand in line for him and grab a 10 o'clock section might protest vigorously if he were charged an extra $3 to take a 10 o'clock class — even though the $3 fee gets rid of the line that he was willing to pay $5 to avoid. If you think these apparently inconsistent responses are plausible, how would you explain the contradiction?

32. In an article in *Energy* (Vol. 8, No. 8-9, 1983) economist Charles Lave has written:

> Perhaps a virtue of price-oriented solutions (in the energy sector) is that people already know how to solve problems that way; there is continuity with the past. And perhaps the drawback of bureaucratic solutions is that

they lack this continuity and instead require people to learn and understand a new set of behaviors.

We vastly underestimate the complexity of the familiar. The distribution and sale of gasoline seemed a trivial thing until the government tried to manage it in 1973 and 1979.

(a) Does this explain in any way the "contradiction" pointed out in the preceding question — that we are *familiar* with bureaucratic solutions in school systems?

(b) Does Lave's suggestion explain why something like the system discussed in the the text for allocating scarce airspace is unlikely to be implemented? Would such a system require a sharp break with familiar patterns of behavior?

(c) How do complex systems ever become familiar? Who introduces them? Why does anyone ever try to introduce a new and complex system to replace an old and familiar but less "efficient" one?

(d) No one would want to open a gasoline station unless a large number of people owned and drove automobiles. But few people would be willing to invest in an automobile if gasoline stations were not readily available. It's easy to think of similar conundrums, but surprisingly hard to find a real-world example of one. How are such chicken-and-egg dilemmas resolved in practice? Why did people buy television sets before there were television stations or create stations before people owned sets?

33. The sign in the cafeteria says: "Please conserve napkins during the paper strike." Suggest some ways in which the cafeteria could ration paper napkins to its customers by raising the cost of taking one (in addition to charging for them). Who will conserve if the cafeteria does nothing except post the above sign?

34. Why do restaurants have such different pricing policies for different items? With napkins, for example, the policy usually is to charge no price and let customers have as many as they want. With beverages, a price may be charged with additional servings available at no fee or a reduced fee. With other items, customers pay a set price for each unit consumed. If your answer is that napkins don't cost very much, how do you account for the fact that grocery stores don't let their customers take as many napkins as they want free of charge? And why do cafeterias typically charge per pat of butter while sit-down restaurants will usually provide additional butter at no extra charge if the customer requests it? What accounts for these differences?

35. In many cities, tennis players can reserve municipal courts by phoning early in the week for a reservation. What will occur if there is no charge for reservations? If you think you might want to play later in the week, will you make a reservation? What will you do if you later change your mind and decide not to play? Why do people "waste" free goods? Who bears the cost of such waste?

FIGURE 4C Hypothetical demand and supply curves for economics tutoring

36. The graph in Figure 4C reproduces the original data of question 10 in Chapter 3 in the form of an opportunity cost curve, or supply curve. It adds to those data a demand curve, showing how many hours of tutoring students would want to buy at various prices.

   (a) What will students have to pay for an hour of tutoring in economics? How many hours will they buy?
   (b) The opportunity cost to Marx of tutoring was given as $3.99 — the wage he could get for fomenting revolution. If you know this fact and consequently ask Marx to tutor you for $5 an hour, he will tell you that the opportunity cost to himself of tutoring you is $8. Is he right? Or is he just trying to exploit you?
   (c) If Merrill Lynch offers Ricardo full-time work at $13.99 an hour, he will no longer be willing to supply 4 hours of tutoring per day for $5 an hour. What will happen to the price of tutoring service as a result?
   (d) If the demand for tutoring service doubled (i.e., twice as many hours were demanded at each price as previously), what would happen to the price of tutoring services and to the number of hours supplied?
   (e) If the demand tripled, what would be the price and the number of hours supplied?

37. The graph in Figure 4D presents a hypothetical demand curve for wheat labeled D, and the aggregated opportunity-cost curves of all wheat farmers, labeled S for supply.

   (a) Why will the price of wheat move toward $2.50? What would occur if the price were $2.75? If it were $2.25?
   (b) Suppose wheat farmers persuade the government to "support" the price of wheat at a "fair" price of $3.75 per bushel, by itself purchasing for

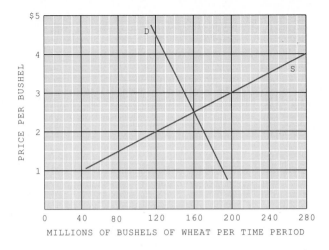

FIGURE 4D   Hypothetical demand and supply curves for wheat

$3.75 a bushel any wheat farmers can't sell at that price or higher. What will this do to the total demand for wheat?

(c) How many bushels of wheat will the government have to buy and store? (Why can't the government simply buy the wheat and then resell it?) Is this properly called a *surplus*?

(d) What would happen, under the supply and demand conditions depicted, if the government told wheat farmers they should sell their wheat for whatever they can get on the market, and then collect from the government a subsidy of $1.25 for every bushel sold? What will be the price of wheat? How many bushels will be exchanged?

(e) What will be the cost to the taxpayer of the support program? Of the subsidy system? Are there any other advantages that one method of aiding wheat farmers has over the other?

38. How do taxes imposed on the purchase or sale of a good affect its price? Does it matter whether the government requires the purchaser or the seller to remit the tax?

   Figure 4E presents a supply curve and a demand curve for soybean oil. The market-clearing price is 20 cents per pound.

(a) Suppose the government levies a tax on all soybean oil sold, requiring sellers to remit 5 cents for every pound they sell. How will this affect the cost of supplying soybean oil and hence the supply curve?

(b) When the supply curve rises by 5 cents a pound, what does the market-clearing price become?

(c) How much *more* do demanders pay per pound as a result of the tax? How much *less* do suppliers receive (after payment of the tax)?

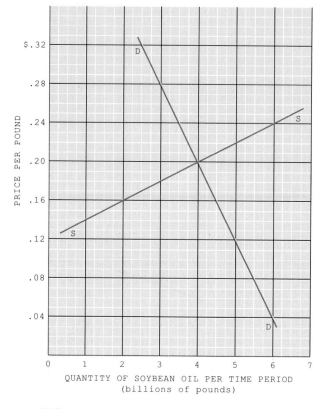

FIGURE 4E   Supply and demand for soybean oil

(d) The government ordinarily requires sellers rather than buyers to remit sales taxes in order to simplify the task of enforcing and collecting the tax. (Think about what would happen if consumers in states with sales taxes had to keep track of their purchases and send monthly checks to the government.) You can get some practice in reasoning with the aid of supply and demand concepts by figuring out what the market-clearing price would be and who would ultimately bear the burden of the tax in the soybean oil case if the government required purchasers to remit the tax. (Assume away all problems of enforcement.)

(e) What would be the effects if the government offered a 5-cent-per-pound subsidy to suppliers in order to boost their incomes?

(f) What would be the outcome if the 5-cent-per-pound subsidy were offered to demanders rather than to suppliers?

(g) Will suppliers always obtain most of the benefit from a subsidy and bear a smaller part of the burden of a sales tax? What features of the supply and demand curves produce those results in this case?

39. Is smallpox virus rare today? Is it scarce? What's the difference?

Chapter 5 ———————————

Marginal Costs, Sunk Costs, and Economic Decisions

Supply is the more interesting side of the demand and supply interaction. It is on the supply side that farmers rotate crops, wildcatters drill for oil, electricians wire houses, pharmacists compound prescriptions, semiconductor companies design digital circuits, and colleges hire faculty to teach economics.

Supply is limited by cost. In order to obtain a larger quantity of any good, we must offer potential suppliers some inducement to move resources from their current use into the production of the good we want. We must make the benefit of doing so greater than the cost — that is, greater than the value to potential suppliers of the opportunities they will have to forgo.

But what counts as cost? More precisely, what are the costs that influence the decisions of suppliers? The theme of this chapter is that the costs that influence supply are always *marginal* costs, or *expected additions* to the potential suppliers' costs. That turns out to have a lot of interesting implications that aren't always seen by people who haven't yet learned the marginal way of thinking.

Decisions at the Margin

Economic analysis is basically marginal analysis. Many economists even use the word *marginalism* to refer to what we have called "the economic way of thinking." *Marginal* means *additional*. Economic theory is marginal analysis because it assumes that decisions are always reached by weighing additional costs against additional benefits. Nothing matters in decisionmaking except marginal costs and marginal benefits.

Suppose that the love of your life phones you at 9 p.m., while you're studying desperately for your physics exam the next day. He wants to come over for a couple of hours. You

Marginal = Additional

tell him you have to study. He pleads. You say no. He asks plaintively, "Is physics more important than me?" And if you've grasped the economic way of thinking, you respond without hesitation: "Only at the margin."

If that doesn't stop his whining, tell him to enroll next term in an economics class, and go back to your studies. The issue of *his value* versus the *value of physics* just doesn't arise in this situation. The question, rather, is whether an additional two hours with him is worth more than an additional two hours with your physics text.

Since you don't want to alienate him, you might explain a little further. Ask him which is more important to him, water or toothpaste. If he answers, "Water," you've got him. For he undoubtedly *uses* water as if it had no value at all. And he would probably refuse indignantly to pay as little as 5 cents for a drink of water if someone tried to charge him that price in a restaurant. Why? Because it is the value and importance of *additional* water in his actual situation that affects his behavior, not the value of water in the abstract. What he and you are each willing to give up to obtain a drink of water is *not* what you would be willing to pay if you were dying of thirst in a desert; it is what you are willing to pay when you're surrounded by faucets and fountains that offer virtually unlimited quantities of water at the turn of your wrist.

He is thinking in terms of "all or nothing." But that just isn't the choice when he phones on the evening before your exam. In fact, that is rarely the choice we face when we're called upon to make decisions. It's usually more of this and less of that versus more of that and less this. The economic way of thinking rejects the all-or-nothing approach in favor of attention to marginal costs and marginal benefits.

Decisions are usually about a little more or a little less.

The Irrelevance of "Sunk Costs"

When you pass through the cafeteria line, pick up the tuna lasagna, and pay the cashier $1.90, you incur a cost: the value of whatever opportunity you will have to forgo because you've spent $1.90. Then you take your first bite and suddenly wish you hadn't selected this item. What will be the cost to you of leaving the lasagna on your plate?

It will *not* be $1.90 — or $1.80 if we assume your first bite consumed about ten cents worth of tuna lasagna. That cost is history. The cost of leaving the lasagna on your plate will be the value of whatever opportunity you forgo by doing so. Do you have a dog that would enjoy pasta with tuna, cheese, and spicy tomato sauce? If so, the cost of leaving the lasagna is the opportunity you forgo (by not asking for a doggie bag) to see your dog's eyes light up and its tail wag.

The price you paid is what economists dismiss as a *sunk cost*. Sunk costs are irrelevant to economic decisions. Bygones are bygones.

> The Moving Finger writes; and, having writ,
> Moves on; nor all your Piety nor Wit
> Shall lure it back to cancel half a Line,
> Nor all your Tears wash out a Word of it.

Of course, we must be certain that a cost is really sunk, or fully sunk, before we decide to regard it as irrelevant to decisionmaking. If you were to purchase a new motorcycle and immediately afterward regret your decision, what would be the cost to you of continuing to own the motorcycle? Clearly, you would not be forced to say, "I did it and now I'm stuck." You could resell the motorcycle. By not doing so you would incur a cost (a benefit forgone) equal to its resale value. The genuine sunk cost would therefore be only the difference between what you paid for it and what you can get by selling it. That is the irrelevant part of your cost. *In the economist's way of thinking it is no cost at all, for it represents no opportunity for choice.* It may be cause for bitter regret and the occasion of some education in the dangers of impulse buying, but it is no longer a cost in any sense relevant to the economics of present decisions.

Yet we all know that people do not consistently reason things out in this way. Many people who made such a purchase and then regretted it would be tempted to retain possession of the motorcycle rather than sell it for substantially less than the original price. They might justify this action by saying "I can't afford to take the loss." But they already took the loss! They made a mistake, and their full loss occurred when they made it. If they nonetheless choose to keep the motorcycle, they are probably practicing self-deception. They persuade themselves that a motorcycle gathering cobwebs in the garage has the same value as the money they paid to put it there, and more value than the opportunities forgone by keeping it there. But the only relevant cost now is the opportunity forgone *by not selling.*

The Case of the Las Vegas Caper

Let's practice this approach. Suppose you own a television retail store, and one of your suppliers is sponsoring a gigantic

price you paid = Sunk Cost (irrelevant)

all genuine costs reflect an opportunity to choose.

Dealers Contest. For every television set you buy (no returns allowed), you receive one day in Las Vegas with all expenses paid. You gleefully order 28 sets, and your wife starts planning your two-week holiday together.

Upon your return from Las Vegas you begin wondering how you will sell all those television sets. One month later you're still wondering. It seems that none of your customers is interested in that brand or model. You are about ready to give up and store the whole lot in the back workroom.

Then you get an offer from an orphanage in some distant city to take all those sets off your hands for $2000. You know that a businessman can't make money by selling below cost, so you sit down to figure out the cost of the sets. You paid $70 apiece to the supplier. Moreover, you have had them in your store for a month tying up valuable floor space. You borrowed the money to buy them at 12 percent annual interest. You also had various handling costs that you estimate at $200. And you spent $80 on advertising in a vain effort to move the sets. By estimating $140 as the cost of display space tied up for a month, you arrive at a figure of $2400. You write back to the orphanage that you would be willing to sell the lot at cost for $2400, forgoing any profit on the transaction in the interest of charity. The orphanage replies that $2000 is their top price, since they can get the sets they want somewhere else for that price. But you are a good businessman, you know that losses don't make profits, and you refuse.

You were actually a rather poor businessman. Every one of the "costs" you enumerated in arriving at your total of $2400 was a *past expenditure* and hence no cost at all. *The proper stance for making cost calculations is not looking back to the past, but forward to the future.* Your costs, if you sell, will be the opportunities thereby forgone, or what you can get for the sets if you do not sell to the orphanage. You know the market fairly well and you estimate you could get $560 by selling them for junk. The marginal cost of selling to the orphanage is therefore $560. Your gain from selling to the orphanage is consequently $1440. Any loss that you're worrying about should be assigned to experience and the glorious memories of Las Vegas. It is irrelevant for decisionmaking purposes.

Marginal Effects Guide Decisions

The word *marginal* means in economics exactly what it means in everyday speech: situated on the border or edge.

Margin notes:

$1960.00   Wholesale Costs
19.60   Interest for 1 month
200.00   Handling Costs
80.00   Advertising Costs
140.00   Display Space
$2399.60   Total Costs?

all genuine costs lie in the future.

The concept is of fundamental importance in economic thinking, because economic decisions, like all effective decisions, always involve *marginal* comparisons. That is, they always have to do with movements at the border, with positive or negative *additions*. What will be the *additional*, or *marginal*, cost that results from this decision? And how does it compare with the marginal cost of alternative decisions? If you think about it for a moment, you will discover that opportunity costs are always expected marginal costs. The term *marginal cost* does no more than bring into strong relief an aspect of opportunity-cost thinking.

all decisions are made "at the margin."

It's important not to get the marginal concept mixed up with the notion of *average*. You may have no intention of confusing marginal with average; if so, what follows may only plant in your head the seeds of a bad idea. Let's hope it doesn't. A simple production schedule of a hypothetical zerc manufacturer will illustrate the distinction.

Number of Zercs Produced	Total Cost of Producing Zercs
42	$4200
43	4257
44	4312
45	4365

A little long division reveals that 42 zercs can be produced at an average cost (total cost per unit) of $100; the average cost is $99 for 43 zercs, $98 for 44, and $97 for 45. A little subtraction reveals, however, that the cost of producing the 43d zerc is not $99 but $57. The incremental expenditure, or the extra cost, incurred by producing the 43d zerc, is its marginal cost. The marginal costs of the 44th and 45th zercs are $55 and $53, respectively. It is clear that marginal cost can be more or less than average cost and can even differ substantially from average cost. It should also be clear that for a zerc manufacturer trying to make production decisions, it is the marginal costs that should guide him. Shall we produce more? Or less? Marginal cost is the consequence of action; it should therefore be the guide to action.

Average costs:
$$\frac{\$4200}{42} = \$100 \qquad \frac{\$4257}{43} = \$99$$

Marginal cost:
$$\begin{array}{r} \$4257 \\ -\ 4200 \\ \hline \$\ 57 \end{array}$$

Marginal cost is the consequence of action.

Are business people then not interested in average costs? Unless they receive sufficient revenue to cover all their costs they will sustain a loss. They won't willingly commit themselves to any course of action unless they anticipate being able to cover their total costs. They might therefore set up the problem in terms of anticipated production cost per unit against anticipated selling price per unit. But notice that the *anticipated* costs of any decision are really *marginal* costs. Marginal cost need not refer to the additional cost of a single unit of output. It could also refer to the additional cost of a batch of output, or the addition to cost expected from a decision regarding an entire process. Decisions are often made in this "lumpy" way.

For example, no one plans to build a soda-bottling factory expecting to bottle only one case of soda. There are important economies of size in most business operations, so that unless business people see their way clear to producing a large number of units, they won't produce any. They won't enter the business. They won't build the bottling factory at all. The entire decision — build or don't build, build this size plant or that, build in this way or some other way — is a *marginal* decision at the time it is made. Remember that additions can be very large as well as very small.

Whether or not business people cast their thinking in terms of averages, it is expected marginal costs that guide their decisions. Averages can be looked at after the fact to see how well or poorly things went, and maybe even to learn something about the future if the future can be expected to resemble the past. But this is history again — admittedly an instructive study — whereas economic decisions are always made in the present with an eye to the future.

The Cost of Driving

The Hertz Corporation conducts an annual study of automobile operating costs to determine how much it costs motorists per mile to drive the cars they own. Hertz takes into account depreciation over the life of the car, license fees, insurance premiums, interest on the automobile loan, maintenance, and of course gas and oil. They then announce that it costs so many cents per mile to drive an intermediate-size car if the car is owned four years and driven 10,000 miles per year.

But what does this really tell us? Does it offer any guidance to someone who is trying to decide whether to drive or to take the bus to work each day? Or to someone weighing a commercial airplane against the family car for a vacation trip? Let's suppose you have been asked by your college to drive your car to a conference. You plan to attend the conference whether you drive your own car or not. The college offers you 25 cents a mile. Will it pay you to drive, or should you say no and hitch a ride with someone else? If you go about deciding by trying to calculate whether the cost to you of owning and operating a car is less than 25 cents a mile, you're being foolish. It makes no more sense to speak of the cost per mile of owning a car than to speak of the cost per mile of owning a house. Neither houses nor cars are *owned per mile*. They're owned per month or per year, but not per mile. If you nonetheless decide to divide the cost of owning by the miles driven, you will come up with numbers that tell you the more you drive, the less it costs. That just isn't so. Each time you drive, you *add* something to your costs. In order to decide whether or not to drive, you must know the marginal cost of driving.

Costs of purchase, license, insurance, borrowing, plus maintenance and depreciation not due to operation are all unrelated to your decision whether or not to drive. That is why they are irrelevant. The relevant cost is the marginal cost: How much extra will you be out of pocket if you drive? Be sure to include not only the cost of gas but also the costs of oil, tire wear, and mileage-induced repairs. Insofar as cost can be expected to vary proportionately with mileage driven, it can properly be expressed as so many cents per mile. If it is less than 25 cents, as it probably would be, you make money by driving your car. As long as the marginal cost remains less than the price paid by the college, you gain from every additional mile "produced" and "sold."

Are the costs of purchase, license, insurance, borrowing, and time-related depreciation *completely* irrelevant? Shouldn't you be allowed to cover these costs, too? After all, you have to pay them even if they are not related to the trip you've been asked to undertake.

You are certainly free to ask the college for as high a mileage rate as you choose. And if you have no scruples, you are even free to trot out all your sunk costs and wave them righteously. There is ample precedent for such action. But the one person you don't want to confuse is yourself. Only marginal costs are relevant to your decision, whatever price the college finally agrees to pay you.

Perhaps you've begun to suspect that it's our example that is irrelevant. We're interested, after all, in ordinary business decisions, and whatever may be true of the student driver as entrepreneur, businesses surely have to cover *all* their costs, not just marginal costs. It would seem so. But it isn't so. There is no more necessity to cover sunk costs in the business world than there is in our case study.

The plain fact is that each year many businesses fail to cover sunk costs. But most of them don't stop operating. We can illustrate by supposing that you bought your car with the intention of driving it for the college. When you made up your mind to become a sort of taxi operator, you hoped to make enough money to pay your way through college. So you purchased a car, the license, and insurance. You probably would not have done so had you expected the college to offer only 25 cents a mile. Maybe you had reason to believe they would pay you 50 cents. Your calculations in these circumstances might have run as follows:

Purchase price: $8000.00
License: $200.00
Insurance: $500.00
Gas and oil: $0.08 per mile
Maintenance: $0.04 per mile
Chauffeur service: $6.00 per hour

Your problem now is the familiar one of adding apples and oranges. Or even worse, adding apples and velocity. How can you add $8000 to 8 cents per mile and $6 per hour? Obviously you can't.

You could, however, turn all these figures into costs per year, much as Hertz does. The license and insurance are annual costs. The purchase price could be converted into an annual figure by estimating annual depreciation and adding the annual interest charge on your initial outlay of $8000. But you can't state the other costs on an annual basis without knowing how far and how long you'll be driving. You must anticipate. Remember what we said earlier: the significant costs and benefits in economics are *expected* costs and benefits. That means they're uncertain. But uncertainty is a fact of life, and if you want to be a student entrepreneur, you'll have to live with it. So you estimate that you'll obtain so many miles and so many hours of business per year. You can then plug in your estimate and obtain numbers for gas and oil, maintenance, and chauffeur services per year.

Now you can do your addition and come up with a figure for the annual cost of doing business. You can then take the mileage estimate you used to calculate gas, oil, and charges for wear and tear, multiply by the rate you expect to be paid, and thereby calculate prospective revenue per year. If the anticipated annual revenue exceeds the anticipated annual cost, you take the plunge and buy a car. If it doesn't, you don't.

So sunk costs are relevant? Of course not. Until you

(assuming 10,000 miles)

Expected Annual Costs

License	$200
Insurance	500
Interest at 10%	800
Depreciation	1000
Gas and oil	800
Maintenance	400
Chauffer service	1500
	$5200

Expected Annual Revenue

Rental fees	$2500

take the plunge they aren't sunk. They are marginal. They are additions to cost that you are thinking about incurring. That's the essence of being marginal. And as long as they're marginal, they are relevant. But only that long! Until you commit yourself in some way to a business operation, *all* your costs are marginal. Once you have committed yourself, the situation has obviously changed. If you want to maximize your profits (or minimize your losses, which comes to the same thing), you must produce and sell all those units of output whose anticipated marginal cost is less than the anticipated price to be set by the college.

Who Pays Sunk Costs?

But if a business firm doesn't cover its sunk costs, who does? Who pays the bill for mistaken decisions in the past? The general answer is *investors:* those who provided the means by which the mistakes were made. They had hoped to profit; but matters failed to turn out as expected, and so they take a loss.

Consider a simple case. Amber Crombie and her husband Fitch pay $250,000 to buy a lot and build a home overlooking beautiful Lake Lilypad. They expect to receive more than $250,000 worth of benefits from living in their comfortable new home with its breathtaking view. Soon after moving in, however, they notice that Lake Lilypad supplies an odor as well as a view. The smell gets progressively worse. Finally, Amber and Fitch decide they can't stand it any longer and will have to move. When they put their house on the market, however, the best offer they get is $60,000, from a couple with chronic nasal congestion. What will happen next?

Amber and Fitch must weigh the odor-reduced benefits from continuing to live in their house against the cost of doing so, which is $60,000 forgone. In other words, would they choose to buy this house, knowing what they now know, if the total price were $60,000? If not, they should sell.

What about the other $190,000 they've invested? That's the loss they incurred by paying $250,000 for something that has turned out to be worth only $60,000. They can't avoid that loss by staying in the house, at least not if they themselves place a lower value on the house than what the congested couple is willing to pay. They have sustained a $190,000 reduction in their wealth. And their loss will be even greater, under our assumptions, if they try to avoid the loss by not selling.

$75,000 down payment
+175,000 bank loan
$250,000 purchase price
-60,000 resale price
$190,000 total loss
-75,000 Crombie's loss
$115,000 bank's loss

Suppose, however, that the Crombies had put up only $75,000 of the original cost, and had taken out a bank mortgage for the remaining $175,000. Who bears the loss in this case? The bank will want the mortgage paid off when the sale goes through; but the sale proceeds of $60,000 won't come close to meeting the Crombies' indebtedness. If they have no other assets with which to satisfy the bank, the bank might decide to prevent the sale. But what is there then to stop the Crombies from defaulting on the mortgage and turning the house over to the bank? Whereupon the bank will sell the house to recover its investment, and get . . . $60,000 from the nonsmelling couple. In that case the Crombies will have lost $75,000, their original investment, and the bank will have lost $115,000, the difference between what it loaned and what it recovered by foreclosing on the mortgage and selling the property.

There are other possibilities, of course. The Crombies may decide that the (expected future!) loss of honor and credit worthiness is a cost too high to accept, in which case they won't default, but will faithfully continue to pay the bank long after they have abandoned the house on Lake Lilypad. There is a good chance that the Crombies or the bank will try to shift the loss to whoever can be found responsible for the odor, or, if no villain can be located, whoever should have warned the Crombies about the fumes from Lake Lilypad.

Whatever ultimately occurs, the cost of buying the lot and building the house were incurred when these steps were taken. All but $60,000 of that is a sunk cost and a loss. Mortgage payments in this case are the marginal cost of retaining possession, or, if the Crombies sell but continue paying, the marginal cost of retaining their credit rating and their honor.

The Rising Cost of Medical Care

Let's use this way of looking at costs and decisions to see if it can clarify the controversy over rising medical costs and how to contain them. We will look first at physicians' fees.

People often assert that physicians charge high prices in order to recover the cost of their education. Could this be true? The argument implies that dullards who take an extra year to finish medical school will set higher-than-average fees, and geniuses who breeze through in less than the normal time will set lower-than-average fees. We don't see that occurring. The argument also implies that physicians who went through college and medical school on full scholarships will establish lower fee schedules than those who had to pay their own way. That implication is not confirmed by observation either. Suppose a recent medical school graduate learns that she has only two years to live. Could she raise her fees enough to recover the full cost of her education in her two remaining years of practice? The argument makes no sense. To a practicing physician, the cost of a medical education is entirely in the past and consequently irrelevant to current decisions.

Does the cost of acquiring a medical education have no effect, then, on physicians' fees? The answer is that it affects fees indirectly by influencing the supply of physicians' services. The prospect of many arduous years in preparation deters people from premedical programs. The necessity of forgoing income for all those years and of borrowing money to live and to pay tuition decrease the anticipated attractiveness of a physician's life. The expected future cost of going through medical school thus restricts the number that will eventually supply physicians' services. (This restriction is in addition to others, of course: not everyone who wants to graduate from medical school is able to do so.) All of this ultimately affects the prices physicians charge. But to see exactly how it does so, we must push our analysis further.

The fees that physicians charge for seeing patients are indeed related to costs, but the relevant costs are *the costs of seeing patients*. What is the cost to physician X of seeing patient A? What opportunity does physician X thereby sacrifice? In the common case today it will probably be an opportunity to care for patient B. What determines the value to the physician of that opportunity? It will be the fee that patient B is prepared to pay.

In other words, people bid for the scarce time of physicians on the basis of their demand for physician care. This demand interacts with the supply of physicians' services to determine the cost of a visit to the doctor, or the price that physicians will be able to charge. The more that physician X can get from seeing other patients, the higher is the cost of tending patient A. Note that this is not determined by the value of the time the physician spent in school, but by the value of the physicians' time *to patients*. The point is a most important one. If the demand for physicians' services increases but there is no increase in the amount of such services supplied, demanders will simply raise the cost of medical care, essentially by trying to bid it away from other

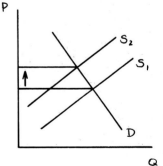

a higher expected cost of acquiring a medical education eventually reduces the supply of physicians' services (shifts the supply curve to the left.)

With a reduced supply of medical services, demanders bid up their prices.

people. In short, we who call for appointments determine the cost of physicians' services.

Physicians are not required to raise their fees when demand increases faster than supply, and many do not. They can instead allow other elements of the cost to rise. "I can't get you in before Thursday." "You can come into the office and wait, if you want to, but the doctor may not be able to see you." The less that fees rise in response to increased demand, the more queuing costs tend to rise. As a result, those who would have been willing to pay more money will tend to surrender some portion of available medical services to those willing to sit for hours reading old magazines.

The reasons for the large increases in recent years in the demand for physicians' services are many. People are living longer, and older people have more ailments. Our expectations of what physicians are able to do have gone up, and so we consult them more often. And increasingly, the people who visit physicians are not required to pay the marginal cost of that visit. The last reason is an especially important one, because it contains a warning against a popular "solution" to the problem of rising medical costs that is really no solution at all.

Costs and Insurance

Any system of medical insurance that pays for physicians' services lowers the cost to patients of obtaining those services — and thereby increases the amount people will want to purchase. It doesn't much matter for the present argument whether the insurance system is a public one financed wholly out of taxes or a private system under which the beneficiary pays all the premiums. So long as patient A's decision to visit the doctor has no discernible effect on the amount patient A must pay, the relevant price is zero. It's true enough that if beneficiaries go to the doctor more often, premiums (or taxes) will have to be increased. But those additional payments will be made by the policyholders (or taxpayers) whether they decide to see their physicians or, alternatively, to stay at home, get plenty of rest, and drink lots of liquids. The additional payments are sunk costs, and so they cannot affect decisions.

Here is the catch in the insurance approach to the problem of medical costs. If we respond to higher costs by offering larger insurance benefits, we subsidize the use of these scarce services. But that increases the demand, bids up the cost, and necessitates yet another increase in benefits. It also

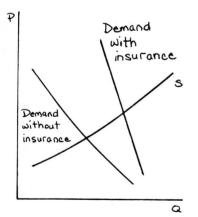

makes people ask why we don't do something to keep medical costs down! We will certainly not keep them down as long as our response to the problem is one that pulls them up by increasing the demand for medical services faster than the supply is increasing.

Hospital Costs

The question of *who pays* is also important in the case of another, even more important, contributor to rising medical care costs — hospital services. The average cost of a hospital room in 1985 was more than seven times what it was in 1965. It is almost certain that an increase this large would not have happened if the people using the rooms had been the ones who paid the bills. But under a system in which patients' payments for medical service are exactly the same whether they enter the hospital or receive only outpatient care, patients are much more likely to enter the hospital. The care is usually better in the hospital than outside it, and physicians can more easily monitor patients' progress in the hospital. On top of that, insurance often covers the full cost of hospital care, while paying only a part of outpatient care. That's a direct invitation to people to increase the demand for scarce hospital services, and it quite predictably produces a steadily mounting level of room charges.

Hospital administration also demonstrates that sunk costs do have their uses. Suppose a particular hospital adds a 200-bed wing and purchases a lot of sophisticated new laboratory equipment. Once these decisions have been taken, the costs associated with them are sunk costs. But that doesn't mean they can't be useful to the hospital's administrators. If the government and private insurance companies have agreed to make payments to the hospital based on the hospital's cost of providing service to patients, and if the hospital gets to decide what counts as cost, every dollar of those sunk costs will be used. The sunk costs will be "spread over" each patient, according to whatever formula enables the hospital to recover them as quickly as possible without unduly antagonizing those who must pay.

Cost *to whom*? Benefit *to whom*? That's always the best way to pose the question of costs and benefits if you want to find out why some policy is being followed. If the benefits from a hospital's ownership of all the most modern equipment accrue largely to its medical staff, if the cost of not pleasing the medical staff falls primarily on the hospital's administrators, if the cost of acquiring that equipment is borne entirely and uncomplainingly by government, insurance companies, or philanthropists, then hospital administrators will purchase expensive equipment even if it is rarely used — and the cost of hospital-care services will soar. In recent years insurers and government have started to pay hospitals a fixed fee for particular services rather than just reimburse the hospitals for whatever costs they claim to have incurred. Hospital administrators as a consequence now have more reason to control costs and less reason to pretend that sunk costs are costs of providing particular services.

Cost as Justification

The economic analysis of costs is an especially treacherous enterprise for the unwary, because costs often have an ethical and political as well as an economic dimension. Many people seem to believe that sellers have a right to cover their costs, have no right to any price that is significantly above their costs, and are almost surely pursuing some unfair advantage if they price below cost. This way of thinking, in which cost functions as *justification*, has even infiltrated our laws. Legislated price controls, for example, usually allow for price increases when costs go up but refuse to permit any price hikes that are not justified by higher costs. And foreign firms selling in the United States can be penalized for "dumping," if a government agency determines that they sold in this country at prices "below cost." In circumstances such as these, when costs become a rationalization rather than a genuine reason for decisions, all statements about costs must be inspected for evidence of special pleading.

Prices *ought* to be closely related to costs, in popular thought, because costs supposedly represent something real and unavoidable. The most enthusiastic advocates of rent control will agree, at least in principle, that landlords should be allowed to increase their rents when the cost of heating fuel goes up. They will never agree — if they did, they wouldn't advocate rent controls — that landlords should be allowed to raise rents merely because the demand for apartments has increased faster than the supply. That would be "gouging," "profiteering," or "a rip-off," because it is unrelated to cost. But such a rental increase is just as surely related to cost as is an increase in response to higher heating bills. When the demand for rental apartments increases, tenants bid against one another for available space, thereby raising the cost to the landlord of renting to any particular tenant. What another tenant would be willing to pay for the third-floor corner apartment in the Hillcrest Arms is the landlord's marginal cost of continuing to rent to the present occupant. The case seems to be different with higher heating-fuel prices but really is not. The cost of fuel oil is also determined ultimately by the bids of competing users in relationship to the offers of suppliers. Cost is always the product of demand and supply.

When you grumble to your butcher about the high price of hamburger, the butcher will deny all responsibility. "They keep raising the cost to me," he will say. If you were to investigate further to find out who "they" are and why "they" keep raising the butcher's cost, you would eventually discover that "they" are "we" — we who like hamburger and bid against one another for it. To see exactly how this works, imagine a sudden and unexpected increase in the demand for hamburger, occasioned perhaps by splendid summer weather and a surge of backyard cookouts. The first effect will be a depletion of butchers' hamburger inventories. When butchers find their hamburger inventories low and the demand continuing strong, they will increase their orders for beef suitable for grinding. With this happening all over the country, meat packers will in turn find their inventories of beef reduced and will try to buy more cattle. But the increased demand for cattle will encounter a relatively inelastic supply curve, and the price of cattle will rise. The packers who must consequently pay more for cattle will increase the price to the butcher, who can then honestly say "they raised the cost," without for a moment suspecting that "they" are in front of the checkout stand, not back at the wholesale meat market. The cost of hamburger in the supermarket is determined by the interactions of demanders and suppliers.

Price, Cost, and Suppliers' Responses

We can easily imagine circumstances under which such a surge in the demand for hamburger would *not* increase its cost to the butcher. Suppose that the increased demand for hamburger is accompanied by a *decreased* demand for round steak, chuck roast, and other beef cuts that can be used to make hamburger. The meat packers and the butchers may be able, under those circumstances, to produce the additional hamburger being demanded without increasing their demand for cattle. In that case, there would be no additional bidding for cattle to raise their price, create higher costs for the butcher, and hence produce a higher price for hamburger at the meat counter.

The passage of time can have a similar effect. Suppose the increased demand for hamburger is part of a general, widespread increase in the demand for beef. The demand for cattle will increase at the livestock market, the price per pound will rise, and consumers will end up paying more for beef.[1] The competitive bidding of consumers will have increased the price.

But that will trigger a new kind of competitive bidding, some of which will go on within the mind of single livestock growers. The higher price for cattle will make resources more valuable in cattle production than they were previously and will consequently "bid" some resources away from other uses — growing hogs, raising soybeans, feeding chickens, or working less at the business of feeding cattle. The more effective the higher price is in pulling additional resources into cattle growing, the less will the price of cattle (and hence the price of beef) increase as a result of the original increase in its demand. But the supply adjustments that we're now describing take time. That's why supply curves are typically more elastic in the long run than in the short run.

Let's summarize what we've been trying to say in this section. An increase in the demand for any good (hamburger, medical care, rental apartments) will bid up the cost of acquiring the good (its price) to the extent that it does *not* cause a larger quantity to be supplied. Or looked at from the other side, an increased demand for any good will *not* raise its price to the extent that suppliers respond by making larger quantities available. The responses of suppliers will depend on the marginal cost of transferring resources out of their current uses into the production of the good for which the demand has increased.

If resources can be shifted at marginal costs only slightly above those already prevailing, the increased demand will lead to a larger output rather than a higher price. But as the supply of such resources is used up, progressively higher prices will have to be offered to cover the rising marginal cost of shifting less suitable resources. Since resources are more mobile, or less rigidly specialized to one use, in the long run than in the short run, the marginal cost of additional output will usually rise less when adequate time has been allowed for adjustments than when suppliers are re-

The effect on price of a change in demand depends on the marginal cost to suppliers of responding.

---

[1]Don't forget that this higher price will also have the effect of decreasing the quantity demanded. Consumers will end up increasing their monthly beef consumption by less than they had originally intended — before their increased demand raised the price.

stricted entirely to those responses that are immediately available to them.

Summaries tend to be both abstract and obscure. You can make the preceding paragraph more concrete and thus more comprehensible by testing each step of the argument against some real-life situation with which you're familiar. (The case of rental housing in the vicinity of your college might be an excellent example on which to practice.)

Another Note on Alternative Systems

Is all this just the economics of capitalist societies? Or does it also apply to communist and socialist societies? The principles we have described are the general principles of economizing, applicable wherever resources are scarce. The central planners in a socialist state also operate within the constraints imposed by scarcity: the resources available to them have alternative uses; substitution possibilities are pervasive; one good can usually be achieved only by giving up some other good. Rational planners will calculate the opportunity cost of contemplated actions, treating sunk costs as irrelevant and paying attention only to marginal costs.

There will nonetheless be important differences. Suppose that the minister of coal production in a socialist state is trying to decide how much coal should be mined this month. He can increase coal production by using more workers or employing them for longer hours, or by using more machinery or better machinery. The relevant cost to the society of doing so is the value of whatever is given up through his decision, or the marginal (opportunity) cost. If he obtains new machinery in order to increase coal output, society loses what could otherwise have been produced with the aid of that machinery, or what could have been produced with the resources employed in the construction of the new machinery. The real cost to the larger society of increased coal production is therefore decreased production of locomotives, or cement, or farm tractors.

If the minister can expand coal production by using machinery already in place that would otherwise stand idle, the opportunity cost is much lower and may even be zero. The sunk cost of the equipment is irrelevant. Notice, though, that the marginal cost will be greater than zero if the machinery has any alternative use, including use as scrap metal.

The differences emerge when we ask how all these costs are calculated. In a society where workers own their own labor and must therefore be induced through monetary bribes (wages) to work in particular ways, the wage measures the opportunity cost to workers. The wage must be sufficient to attract them from their (subjectively) next-best alternative. But if workers can be compelled to do what the state dictates, the wage need not bear any relation to the opportunity cost as determined by the workers. (We saw in Chapter 3 how that occurs under a military draft.) In moving from an eight- to a ten-hour day, the miners might be sacrificing two hours of leisure. Whether this is worthwhile would depend on the *planners'* valuation of the extra coal produced in relation to the *planners'* valuation of the leisure forgone.

It would be clearly wrong under any circumstances to suppose that the cost of producing the extra coal can be determined from the *average* cost of coal production. Some have argued that marginal cost considerations are relevant only in an economy guided by the pursuit of private profit. It is true that in a capitalist society entrepreneurs will not choose to produce anything whose marginal cost of production to them exceeds its value to the consumer as measured by its price. But is is just as true that in a socialist society the central planners and enterprise directors will want to produce nothing whose marginal cost exceeds its value.

The major difference lies in the different rules of the game under which opportunity costs and prices are calculated. In a system characterized by substantial private ownership and control of resources, competitive offers to buy and sell resources interact to establish scarcity prices and opportunity costs expressed in monetary units. An enormous quantity of information summarizing a vast range of alternatives is thus distilled into the prices that in turn guide the choices of decisionmakers.

In no economic system past or present have prices ever summarized perfectly the available range of opportunities. And under certain circumstances, as we shall see later, they may do so in a fashion so inadequate as to be politically unacceptable. The relevance of all this for making a choice between alternative economic systems is a complex issue that cannot be resolved exclusively by economic arguments.

In any economic system, however, the following general principles will be applicable:

- Real costs are opportunity costs, the value of opportunities forgone.
- Sunk costs are irrelevant, because they are costs that the decision cannot affect.

- Opportunity costs are always additional or marginal costs, the costs expected to result from the decision under consideration.
- Some method of assigning indexes of value to alternative opportunities must be used in any economic system, or decisionmakers will be operating blindly.
- Supply and demand, or the market process of competing bids and offers, create indexes of value for decisionmakers by placing price tags on available resources.

The supply and demand process also operates in socialist societies. But where the rules of the game do not clearly assign to particular persons rights to control and exchange specific resources, this process will not generate indexes of scarcity to guide allocation and coordinate activity.

Once Over Lightly

The economic way of thinking is a marginal way of thinking. It assumes that demanders and suppliers pay attention to the marginal (additional) benefits and costs of the actions they are considering: How much extra benefit or extra cost will this decision entail?

Supply curves reflect costs. All costs capable of influencing supply will have three interrelated characteristics that should be watched for: they will belong to actions, not to things; they will be opportunities forgone by particular decisionmakers; and they will be the expected, not-yet incurred consequences of decisions at the margin.

Past expenditures cannot be affected by present decisons: they are sunk costs and hence irrelevant to decisionmaking.

Opportunity costs are necessarily marginal costs: they are the additional costs that a decision entails.

If costs per unit are to be used in making supply decisions, the units must be related to the decisions. The cost per mile of owning a car or the cost per bushel of owning a farm are both meaningless, because "owning" is not a decision that produces either miles or bushels (although it may be a precondition for such decisions).

Because economic decisions are based on future or expected consequences, they always entail some degree of uncertainty. The expectation that future revenue will cover future costs is often frustrated in experience.

The common notion that prices ought to be related to costs generates a substantial amount of confusing rhetoric among suppliers who want to justify (or others who want to condemn) a particular price.

Costs are not something independent of demand. The demand for goods helps to determine the cost of supplying them.

Increases in demand for a good will result in higher prices, rather than additional output, to the extent that resources cannot be shifted into production of that good. To the extent that resources can be shifted with no significant rise in marginal cost, the increased demand will result in additional output rather than higher prices.

Under a system characterized by private ownership and control of resources, the forces of supply and demand will establish relative prices that function as indexes of scarcity. It will ordinarily be in the interest of private decisionmakers to be guided by these indexes in their decisions to demand or to supply.

Questions for Discussion

1. Test your understanding of the marginal principle by helping Paul Behrer decide how much fertilizer to apply to his parsnip patch. We'll keep the problem simple by assuming that, as Paul applies additional fertilizer, the only cost that changes is the cost of purchasing fertilizer. Here is how yields increase as fertilizer is added:

Bags of Fertilizer Applied	Parsnip Yield in Tons
1	12
2	22
3	28
4	32
5	35
6	37

Paul can sell all the parsnips he raises for $2 a ton. Fertilizer costs $10 per bag, but Paul receives quantity discounts: 2 bags for $18, 3 for $24, 4 for $30, 5 for $35, and 6 for $42.

(a) What is the marginal benefit to Paul, in dollars, of applying fertilizer? In other words, how many dollars does Paul add to his receipts from parsnip sales each time he applies an additional bag of fertilizer?

(b) What is the marginal cost of applying additional bags of fertilizer? In other words, by how much do Paul's costs change each time he adds a bag of fertilizer?

(c) How many bags should Paul apply if he wants to make as much money as possible from parsnip production?

2. The photocopy machine in the library costs $295 per month to rent. The rental fee covers repair service, toner, developer, and 20,000 copies per month. The library also pays 1 cent for every copy beyond 20,000, plus one-half cent for every sheet of paper used.

   Harriet Martineau has to read a 20-page journal article for tomorrow's class. She is willing to pay 50 cents for a photocopy of the article; but she will read it in the library if she has to pay more than that.

   (a) What is the highest price per page Harriet will be willing to pay to use the copier?
   (b) What is the lowest price per page the library should be willing to accept? What additional information must you have in order to answer?
   (c) Harriet just found out she is supposed to read a second article for tomorrow's class, an article full of complex graphs. Harriet badly wants her own copy of this article and will pay whatever she has to pay to get one. What is now the highest price Harriet will be willing to pay to use the library copier? (You must supply some information from your own experience to answer.)
   (d) How does the $295 monthly rental fee affect the price the library will want to charge users of its copier?

3. In 1981, when AT&T was the exclusive provider of long-distance telephone service in the United States, a cost specialist for the company estimated the cost of a daytime telephone call from New York to Los Angeles at 68.9 cents for the initial period and 33 cents for each additional minute. The 68.9 cents included 11.3 cents for maintenance, 3.3 cents for operator services, 4.4 cents for business services such as sales and advertising, 2.7 cents for pricing and billing, 8.2 cents for depreciation and amortization, 10.6 cents for general purposes, 12.9 cents for taxes, and 15.5 cents for earnings.

   (a) When these calculations were made, AT&T was charging less than 25 cents for a one-minute call from New York to Los Angeles. Was the phone company losing money at that rate? Or don't some of those costs have to be met at night and on weekends?
   (b) AT&T presented these data to the Federal Communications Commission, which oversees long-distance rates, and asked for permission to set a fee of 74 cents. Does that fact help explain which items the cost specialist included?
   (c) Does it actually cost the phone company less when people place long-distance calls at night or on weekends? What is the marginal cost to the phone company of a call from New York to Los Angeles? Why might it differ with time of day and day of the week?
   (d) An AT&T advertisement in 1989 said: "AT&T's daytime prices are so low, you can call anywhere in the U.S. for 28¢ per minute or less." A

footnote explained that this was the average price per minute for a 10-minute call, dialed direct. Do you think the cost of providing long-distance telephone service fell by that much in the 1980s?

4. *The Wall Street Journal* headlined a story in January 1982: "Ford Offers Incentives on Subcompacts That Are Unprofitable Despite Hot Sales."

   (a) Why would a company offer incentives that were unprofitable?
   (b) The story reveals that Ford executives, convinced the subcompacts would be a big success, had spent $2 billion to convert four assembly plants that would be capable of producing 950,000 of these models per year. Sales were running at a rate below 400,000 when the "unprofitable" promotion was announced. Use the concept of *expected marginal cost* to explain both Ford's decision to invest $2 billion and its decision to cut prices "below cost."

5. How long will you search for a $20 bill that you lost if you value your time at $5 an hour? Suppose you know that you lost it somewhere in your bedroom. Would it ever be rational for you to search more than four hours? Use the concepts of sunk cost and expected marginal cost to explain how a rational person who values time at $5 an hour could *search indefinitely* for a lost $20 bill.

6. An airline is thinking about adding a daily flight from Denver to Billings. It has estimates of the number of passengers who would use the flight. What costs should and should not be considered in deciding whether the anticipated revenue is sufficient to make the flight profitable?

7. The city of Seattle owns a marina and rents space to boat owners. City officials decided in 1981 to set rental rates that would yield a 5 percent profit on the estimated cost of replacing the facility. They said this would call for an approximate doubling of moorage fees over the next three years.

   (a) What does the estimated cost of replacing the facility have to do with the cost of renting out moorage space?
   (b) The most important part of the facility is the ocean water that fills Puget Sound, on which the marina was constructed. Should the estimated cost of replacing the ocean be included in the price? (If you argue that it should *not* be included because the ocean is a free gift of Nature, go back and check your answer to question 2 at the end of Chapter 3.)
   (c) At the time they announced their intention to raise the fees, city officials estimated the waiting time for a space at 17 to 20 years. What does this have to do with the cost of renting out moorage space?

8. According to an article by economist Terry Anderson in *The Wall Street Journal* of September 30, 1983, farmers in the Imperial Irrigation District of California are required to pay only $6.50 an acre-foot for water that may cost taxpayers as much as $300 an acre-foot to deliver.

   (a) At which number — $6.50 or $300 — will Imperial Valley farmers look when deciding whether to irrigate a little more or a little less?

(b) Do these figures demonstrate that irrigation is not really worthwhile in the Imperial Valley?

(c) Why would anyone pay $300 to supply an acre-foot of water that is worth only $6.50 to the demander?

(d) What do you think the demand curve for water in the IID looks like? What about the opportunity-cost curve of supplying water to the IID?

9. Suppose that taxicabs raised their fares during rainstorms and lowered them again when the sun came out. How would these different prices be related to cost? Whose cost? Of doing what?

10. "Tuition covers only 43 percent of the cost of educating your son or daughter. We're counting on your annual gift to sustain operations that are fundamental to the kind of education for which our university is noted." Those sentences are from a letter sent to parents by a prestigious university whose tuition is currently close to $10,000. Do you think that a student paying $10,000 per year in tuition is really paying only 43 percent of the education's cost? Would the university find its total costs reduced by $23,256 if the student dropped out?

11. In order to decide whether or not to drop intercollegiate football, your school undertakes a study of the program's cost. To what extent do you think the following budget items represent genuine costs?

(a) Tuition scholarships to players.
(b) Payments on the stadium mortgage.
(c) Free tickets to all full-time students.
(d) Salaries of the athletic director, ticket manager, and trainer.

12. What determines the cost to a university of providing parking spaces on campus for faculty, staff, and students? Why would a parking facility probably cost an urban university more than it would cost a university located in a small town? If monthly parking fees are higher for students than for faculty, does this mean it costs the university more to provide parking for students?

13. The American Society of Internal Medicine is not happy with the schedule of relative fees that insurers use to compensate for different kinds of medical service. The ASIM maintains that internists are grossly underpaid relative to surgeons. It wants fees set by taking into account the time and effort required to learn the particular skill (e.g., cardiac surgery or diagnosis of an infection) and the time it takes to perform the service. (See "Doctors Debate How to Split the Fees" by Harry Schwartz, *The Wall Street Journal*, January 15, 1985.)

(a) Does the ASIM proposal violate the maxim that sunk costs are irrelevant?

(b) What consequences would you predict from implementation of this proposal? If surgeons' fees fell and internists' fees rose, would a shortage of surgeons and a surplus of internists develop?

(c) If an internist and a surgeon are both necessary to the successful com-

pletion of a particular medical procedure, how can the relative importance of each one's contribution be assessed?

14. Pan American Airways has complained to the British government that
flights between the United States and Britain on the supersonic Concorde
are priced too low. The Concorde flies for British Airways, which is subsidized by the British government. That enables Concorde fares to be set
below cost, according to Pan Am.

(a) Is the cost of developing the Concorde supersonic plane part of the
cost of flying it from New York to London?
(b) If there are empty seats on a Concorde flight, what is the cost to British
Airways of carrying an additional passenger?

15. What does it cost you to sleep through one of 30 lectures in a course for
which you paid $300 in tuition?

16. Do students put more effort into courses when they have to pay higher
tuition to take the courses?

17. Do hot dogs taste better at the ball park where they cost twice as much
as they ordinarily cost? Do they taste better *because* they cost more?

18. Would you expect to find any people who don't particularly like Ingmar
Bergman's movies attending a Bergman film festival if the price of the
festival ticket is $5 for 10 movies? Would you expect to find many people
who aren't enthusiastic about Bergman attending a Bergman festival where
the price is $50 for 10 movies? Does your answer to this question change
your answer to the preceding question about hot dogs at the ball park?

19. "We regret that rising costs have compelled us to raise our prices." That's
a very common statement made by sellers who are raising their prices.
But is it true? Do increases in suppliers' costs always compel them (or
even allow them) to raise their prices? Think carefully about each of the
following cost-increase scenarios. In which cases would you expect higher
prices to follow from the higher costs? In which cases would you expect
to see the sellers absorb the cost increases rather than raise their prices?

(a) Physicians are forced to pay higher malpractice insurance premiums.
(b) Only some physicians — those with poor records or credentials — have
their malpractice insurance premiums raised.
(c) A taxi driver pays high insurance rates because he has a poor driving
record.
(d) A grocery store in a high-crime area must pay extra for store security.
(Would its customers pay higher prices rather than shift their patronage
to stores in low-crime areas?)
(e) Landlords' expenses rise due to a general increase in property taxes.

20. When the price of coffee quadrupled in 1977, many cafés and restaurants
doubled the price they charged for a cup of coffee. Sometimes they accompanied the price increase with a statement to the effect that, although
they were willing to absorb most of the price increase, harsh reality com-

pelled them to pass along a portion of the increase to their valued customers. How many cents worth of ground coffee goes into a restaurant cupful? Why do restaurants and other businesses make such statements?

21. **(a)** What differences would you expect to observe in the fees set by three young physicians just setting up practice if one financed her education by borrowing and must now make payments of $4000 per year for 15 years, another had his entire education paid for by his parents, and the third went all the way through on government-provided scholarships and grants?

(b) Evaluate the argument, put forward in a *Newsweek* column of March 19, 1979, that the government could lower our doctor bills by paying for the entire education of physicians, thus making it unnecessary for physicians to recover the costs of their education (plus interest) by raising their fees.

(c) The author of the *Newsweek* article asserts that "you and I" will have to cover the cost of the doctors' loan repayments in our fees because these payments "are a legitimate cost of doing business." What difference does it make whether particular payments are or are not "a legitimate cost of doing business"? Suppose all physicians practicing in an area were required to pay $5000 a year to the local crime syndicate as protection money. Would these payments be "a legitimate cost of doing business"? Would they affect doctors' fees?

22. In June of 1988 the Canadian Horticultural Council filed a petition with the Canadian Revenue Department claiming that U.S. apple growers were selling American red and golden delicious apples in Canada at prices below cost.

(a) U.S. growers admitted that they had sometimes sold below cost, but they blamed this on the huge harvest. Do you agree that a huge harvest could push prices down *below cost*? Cost to whom of doing what?

(b) In response to the petition, the Canadian government sent long questionnaires to U.S. packing houses, seeking information on the cost of planting new orchards and building new packing plants and cold-storage warehouses. The head of a U.S. apple growers association objected on the grounds that the cost of orchards and plants many years old is lower than the cost of new ones. Can you resolve this dispute?

23. The Department of Defense awards you a cost-plus-10% contract to build missiles in your garage. Which of the following may you legitimately include in your costs?

(a) Original cost of constructing the garage, adjusted for inflation and depreciation.

(b) Weather damage to your car from parking it outside because your garage is full of missile-making machinery.

(c) Cost of lengthening the garage by four feet so the missiles don't extend into your driveway where neighborhood children might accidentally set one off.

(d) Cost of the course you took at the community college to qualify as a missile maker so you could win the government contract.

(e) Cost of the math courses you took years ago which turned out to be prerequisites for the course on missile making.

(f) Cost of your elementary school education, since you wouldn't be able to manufacture missiles if you didn't know how to read.

(g) Cost of the tetanus shot you received when you were three years old, which saved your life and thereby enabled you to become a successful defense contractor.

(h) Cost of psychological counseling whereby you seek to overcome depression when your children scorn you as a member of the military–industrial complex?

24. Your boss tells you in an angry voice, "I don't care what you learned in economics. If you don't include all our sunk costs in your report and recommendation, I'll fire you." Are the sunk costs now irrelevant to your decisionmaking?

25. Should the casualities already incurred in a war be taken into account by a government in deciding whether it is in the national interest to continue the war? This is obviously not a trivial question. And it is a much more difficult question than you might at first suppose, especially for a government depending on popular support.

26. The *American Economic Review* published in its September 1986 issue a fascinating article by Daniel Kahneman, Jack L. Knetsch, and Richard Thaler that bears on the relevance of costs. It is titled "Fairness as a Constraint on Profit Seeking: Entitlements in the Market." The authors report on and interpret the results of a public opinion survey designed to determine the rules of fairness people use in evaluating actions by business firms.

Here is one hypothetical situation that was described in the survey and the respondents' evaluations:

> A grocery store has several months' supply of peanut butter in stock which it has on the shelves and in the storeroom. The owner hears that the wholesale price of peanut butter has increased and immediately raises the price on the current stock of peanut butter.

Of the 147 respondents surveyed, only 21% thought this was acceptable behavior while 79% deemed it unfair.

(a) The wholesale price of peanut butter in stock is a sunk cost. Is it relevant to pricing decisions for a seller who shares the majority view on fairness in pricing?

(b) How could it be relevant to a seller who personally holds the minority view but also knows that his customers will find out what he has done if he raises the price on "old" stock?

(c) The economist does not distinguish a sum of money *paid out* from a sum of money *not received*: both are equally costs. The majority of the public apparently does distinguish, because it holds that sellers may raise their prices to cover higher wholesale cost payments but may not do so merely because consumers are willing to pay the higher prices. Can you defend the popular distinction, or do you think it is simply the product of failure to understand what's going on?

27. The economist's rule, "sunk costs are irrelevant," is like a string around your finger. It reminds you to consider only marginal costs, but it cannot identify the marginal costs. That requires informed judgment. You could sharpen your judgment by trying to enumerate and assess the marginal costs of retaining or not retaining your college apartment over the summer vacation. Try to calculate the minimum rental from subleasing that would persuade you to retain it for fall reoccupancy.

28. Here is what it would cost you to fulfill your long-time ambition to own and operate a small ski resort:

• To acquire the land	$200,000
• To acquire the ski lift	100,000
• To acquire a shelter	20,000
• To operate the lift and sell tickets	50 per hour

You plan to be open 50 hours a week for 20 weeks in the year. You therefore anticipate operating costs of $50,000 per year. You will be able to borrow the $320,000 you need to get started under a 20-year loan. Your annual payments on the loan (principal and interest) will come to $43,000 per year.

(a) What is the minimum amount of annual revenue from the sale of lift tickets that you will have to anticipate in order to take the plunge and invest $320,000?

(b) Suppose your actual revenue in the first year of operation turns out to be $60,000. Should you go out of business?

(c) You can occasionally earn $600 by opening your resort for 8 hours on weekdays (when you would ordinarily be closed) for the benefit of special charter groups. This revenue will cover your operating costs of $400 for the day; but since your operating costs are only 54 percent of your total costs, you would need about $750 in revenue to make it worth your while to open. Or would you?

(d) If you spend $10,000 a year on advertising in your second year, and as a result increase your total revenue to $75,000, was the decision to advertise a good one?

(e) What are your options if it turns out after several years that you cannot do any better financially than you did in your second year of operation? Should you go out of business? If you decide you can't afford to lose $28,000 a year on a ski resort, what are your options? Suppose the best offer you get when you put the facility up for sale is $100,000 for land, lift, and shelter. Should you sell?

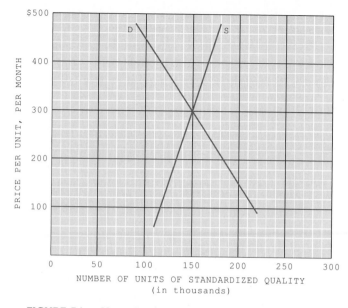

FIGURE 5A   Hypothetical demand and supply curves for residential rental space

(f) If the lender forecloses because you default on your payments, what will he do with the property? Should the lender foreclose or allow you to spread out the length of your loan so that your payments are reduced to an amount you can meet out of your revenue?

29. The graph in Figure 5A shows the demand for and the supply of residential rental space in an imaginary city. The market-clearing rent is $300 per month.

    Then two events occur: (1) Inflation causes the value of money to fall by one-third; (2) the city and state dramatically lower the property-tax rate, so that landlords' net income from residential rental property rises by one-third.

    (a) How would you expect these two events to affect the demand for and supply of residential rentals? What would happen to rents? Distinguish between short-run and long-run effects.
    (b) What difference would it make if the property-tax reduction were confined exclusively to residential property?
    (c) If rents rise in the short run as a consequence of these occurrences and the city responds by imposing rent controls, what will be the longer-run effect?

30. Figure 5B portrays a supply curve of physicians' services and a demand curve for those services. The market-clearing fee is $30.00.

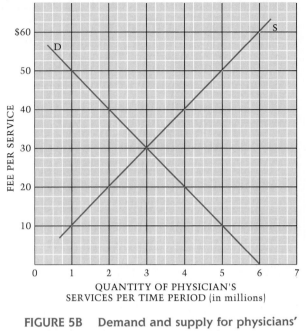

FIGURE 5B   Demand and supply for physicians' services

(a) To what position will the demand curve shift if the government agrees to pay the entire fee charged by physicians? What will consequently happen to the market-clearing price? (Hint: What quantity will people demand at a zero price?)

(b) What will happen to the demand curve and to the market-clearing price if the government commits itself to pay one-half of physicians' fees? (Hint: When the fee *charged* is $30, what is the fee *paid* by consumers? What quantity will they want to purchase at this price?)

(c) What will be the market-clearing price if the government pays 80 percent of the fee charged by physicians?

Chapter 6——————————

Efficiency, Exchange, and Comparative Advantage

Efficiency is the virtue most consistently praised by economists. That should occasion no surprise, since efficiency and
economy are practically synonyms. Both terms refer to the
effectiveness with which means are used to achieve ends.
Getting as much as possible out of the scarce resources available — that's what we mean by efficiency and by economy.

Voices have begun to appear in our society in recent
years suggesting that we place too high a value on efficiency;
that we sometimes sacrifice more valuable goals to achieve
an efficiency that isn't worth what it costs us. Could this be
true? Anyone who thinks about it carefully will discover
that there is something logically odd about this critique of
efficiency. While the critics may have valid and important
points to make, it cannot be true that we are paying too high
a price for efficiency.

Technological Efficiency?

If efficiency is to have any useful meaning, it must be understood as a ratio of one thing to another. Engineers use a definition of efficiency that seems to satisfy this test. They define efficiency as the ratio of the work done by a machine to
the energy supplied to it, and that ratio is usually expressed
as a percentage. From the engineering standpoint, a diesel
locomotive is more efficient than a steam locomotive because, per unit of potential energy contained in its fuel, the
diesel does more work.

This definition is unsatisfactory, however, when we
think about it more critically. Efficiency cannot be measured
by the ratio of energy output to energy input because, by the
laws of thermodynamics, that ratio is always unity for any
process. The engineer's efficiency is rather a measure of
work done in relation to energy input. But what constitutes
"work done"? Doesn't that depend on what is wanted? What

$$\frac{\text{Energy output}}{\text{Energy input}} = \text{One}$$

qualifies as "work"? Engineers actually call a steam engine less efficient than a diesel because with a steam engine a higher percentage of the energy input is *wasted*. Strictly speaking, however, even wasted energy does work. It just doesn't do any *useful* work. That means it doesn't do work that anybody wants done. All of which implies that efficiency is not a purely objective or technological matter but depends inevitably on valuations.

Efficiency and Values

Efficiency is inescapably an evaluative term. That's the first point to be grasped. It always has to do with the ratio of the *value* of output to the *value* of input. Efficiency will always have an objective component, of course; our likes and dislikes don't determine the potential heat in a pound of fuel. But physical facts by themselves can never determine efficiency. It follows that the efficiency of any process can change with changes in valuations, and because everything depends on everything else, any change at all in any subjective preference is in principle capable of altering the efficiency of any process.

$$\frac{\text{Value of output}}{\text{Value of input}} = \frac{\text{Measure}}{\text{of efficiency}}$$

Let's go back to the question of the relative efficiency of diesel and steam locomotives. Each can be put into operation only with the use of a large number of inputs; not only coal or oil and locomotive operators but also all the inputs used in manufacturing the locomotives, the inputs that went into the fabrication of these inputs, the inputs that went into the fabrication of the products that were inputs in the process of producing the products that were inputs in the manufacture of the locomotives, and so on, without any discernible limit. Anything that changes the value of anything that contributes to a locomotive's operation can in principle alter its efficiency.

We don't need any farfetched illustrations to make the essential point. An increase in the value of oil relative to coal, if it is large enough, can by itself transform their relative efficiences so that a coal-fired steam locomotive becomes more efficient than a diesel. It follows that these relative efficiencies depend on the demand for and supply of oil and coal, and hence on such factors as the motoring habits of the general public, the political situation in oil-producing countries, and the value placed on the environmental effects of strip-mining coal. Perhaps it never occurred to you that the relative efficiency of the old steam locomotive was affected by the efforts of the United Mine Workers!

"Wait a minute," says a voice from the rear of the room.

"Aren't you talking now about something other than efficiency? I'll grant you that it costs a railroad less per ton-mile
of freight to use diesels than to use coal-fired steam locomotives. But that's not the same as being more efficient. If coal
became cheap enough, some railroads might go back to using
their old steam locomotives. But that would be because the
old locomotives were cheaper, not because they had become
more efficient."

From the standpoint of the railroad, however, cheaper *is*
more efficient, because the relevant values are monetary
values. The illusion of a purely technological efficiency dies
hard, but it deserves to be stomped until it's dead. No
machine, no process, no arrangement is so efficient that it
cannot be rendered inefficient (or so inefficient that it cannot
be made efficient) by an appropriate change in values.

The Myth of Material Wealth

In emphasizing the essential role of valuations in any measure of efficiency, we are also rejecting the common belief
that economics has to do peculiarly with the "material":
with material wealth, material well-being, or material pur-
suits. It just isn't so, and the word *material* actually makes
no sense when attached to such words as *wealth* or *well-
being*.

Of what does wealth consist? What constitutes your
own wealth? Many people have drifted into the habit of supposing that an economic system produces "material wealth,"
like cars, houses, basketballs, breakfast cereals, and ball-
point pens. But none of these things is wealth unless it is
available to someone who values it. Additional water is additional wealth to a farmer who wants to irrigate; it is not
wealth to a farmer caught in a Missisippi River flood. A food
freezer may be wealth to an American housewife but not to
an Eskimo. The crate in which the freezer was delivered is
trash to the housewife but a treasure to her small son, who
sees it as a playhouse.

Economic growth consists not in increasing the production of *things* but in the production of *wealth*. And wealth is
whatever people value. Material things can contribute to
wealth, obviously, and are in some sense essential to the
production of wealth. (Even such "nonmaterial" goods as
love and peace of mind do, after all, have some material em-
bodiment.) But there is no necessary relation between the
growth of wealth and an increase in the volume or weight or
quantity of material objects. The indefensible identification

of wealth with material objects must be rejected at root. It makes no sense. And it blocks understanding of many aspects of economic life. Trade (or exchange) is the best example.

Trade Creates Wealth

Trading has long had an unsavory reputation in the Western world. This is probably the result of a deep-seated human conviction that nothing can *really* be gained through mere exchange. Agriculture and manufacturing are believed to be genuinely productive: they seem to create something genuinely new, something additional. But trade only exchanges one thing for another. It follows that the merchant, who profits from trading, must be imposing some kind of tax on the community. The wages or other profit of the farmer and artisan can be obtained from the alleged real product of their efforts, so that they are entitled in some sense to their income; they reap what they have sown. But merchants seem to reap without sowing; their activity does not appear to create anything and yet they are rewarded for their efforts. Trading, some have thought, is therefore social waste, the epitome of inefficiency.

This line of argument strikes a deeply responsive chord in many people who still retain the old hostility toward the merchant in the form of a distrust of the "middleman." Everybody want to bypass the middleman, who is pictured as a kind of legal bandit on the highways of trade, authorized to exact a percentage from everyone foolish or unlucky enough to come his way.

However ancient or deep-seated this conviction of the unproductiveness of trade, it is completely erroneous. There is no defensible sense of the word *productive* that can be applied to agriculture or manufacturing but not to trading. Exchange is productive! It is productive because it promotes greater efficiency in resource use.

Many have taken a fatal wrong turn at the very beginning in considering this question by assuming that exchange, unless it is fraudulent or coerced, is always the exchange of *equal values.* The exact reverse is true: exchange is never an exchange of equal values. *If it were, it would not occur.* In an informed and uncoerced exchange (and this is what we mean by genuine exchange), both parties gain by giving up something of lesser for something of greater value. If Jack swaps his basketball for Jim's baseball glove, Jack values the glove more than the ball, and Jim values the ball more than the glove. Viewed from either side, the exchange was unequal. And that is precisely the source of its productivity. Jack now has greater wealth than he had before, and so does Jim. The exchange was productive because it increased the wealth of both parties.

"Not really," says that contentious voice from the rear. "There was no real increase in wealth. Jack and Jim feel better off, it's true; they may be happier and all that. But the exchange didn't really produce anything. There is still just one baseball glove and one basketball."

But the manufacturers of the baseball glove and the basketball didn't "really" produce anything either; they just rearranged materials into more valuable patterns. And isn't that essentially what occurs when people trade? Our suspicion of exchange is evidence of our material bias, a bias obviously shared by that voice from the rear. Both Jack and Jim do have greater wealth after their exchange.

Recall what we concluded earlier about efficiency: it is measured by the ratio of one *value* to another, not by physical ratios of any sort. You can think of Jack's and Jim's exchange as an act of production. Jack used the basketball as an input to obtain the output of a baseball glove. For Jim the glove was the input and the ball the output. The result of the productive process (the exchange) was an output value greater than input value for both parties. Nothing further is required to make an activity productive. The exchange expanded real output.

For Jack:
$$\frac{Value\ of\ glove}{Value\ of\ ball} > One$$

For Jim:
$$\frac{Value\ of\ ball}{Value\ of\ glove} > One$$

Efficiency and Opportunity Cost

Perhaps we can clarify all this and link it up with earlier chapters if we work our way through a simplified case study. Imagine a society with only two goods and three producers. We shall call the goods M and S, which you may think of, if you wish, as material goods and spiritual goods, respectively. The producers we'll call Ann, Ben, and Cal. In a given period of time (e.g., a day), each is capable of producing the following quantities of M or S:

- Ann can produce 8 Ms or 4 Ss or any linear combination between, such as 6 Ms plus 1 S, or 5 Ms plus 1½ Ss, or 2 Ms plus 3 Ss, and so on.
- Ben can produce 3 Ms or 3 Ss or any linear combination in between.
- Cal can produce 1 M or 2 Ss or any intermediate linear combination.

Ready for the question? Who would you say is the most

Cost of producing one unit
   of spiritual good

Cal	½ unit of material good
Ben	1 unit of material good
Ann	2 units of material good

efficient producer of spiritual goods in this drastically simplified economy? Check the data before answering.

Do you agree that it's Cal? Or did you mistakenly suppose it was Ann, who is in fact the *least* efficient producer of Ss in this society? If you failed to identify Cal correctly as the most efficient producer of Ss, you weren't using the concept of opportunity cost in your calculations.

What does it cost when Cal produces an S? The cost of an action is the sacrifice that action entails. Since Ms and Ss are the only goods in this society, the only way we can state the cost of producing an S is in terms of forgone Ms. Now look at the data. Cal forgoes the production of ½ M to make an S. Ben sacrifices 1 M when he makes an S. And Ann, who is such a prolific maker of Ms, gives up 2 Ms for each S she produces. The conclusion is obvious. Cal is the lowest-cost producer of Ss, and Ann is the highest-cost producer of Ss.

Suppose you are the commissar of production in this little society, and you want to produce the maximum quantity of Ss that can be obtained consistent with producing the minimum quantity of Ms required to keep the society going. Let's further assume that 1 M per day is enough to keep everyone alive and functioning; your production plan therefore calls for 1 M plus as many Ss as can be turned out with the resources that remain.

If you order Cal to produce that required 1 M, in the mistaken belief that he's an inefficient S producer, while instructing Ann and Ben to concentrate exclusively on Ss, you'll find yourself at the end of the day with the 1 M you ordered plus 7 Ss: 4 from Ann and 3 from Ben.

If, however, you recognize that Cal is your most efficient S producer, who must therefore be kept exclusively on S production, and that Ann should produce the single M you want because she's your most *in*efficient S producer—then you'll end up with 2 Ss from Cal, 3 from Ben, and 3½ from Ann, for a total of 8½ Ss, along with the required single unit of M. If more is better than less, you're better off by 1½ Ss per day when you assign Ann rather than Cal to M production.

What would the output have been if you had told Ben to produce the 1 M? Then you would have gotten 4 Ss from Ann, 2 from Ben, and 2 from Cal, for a total of only 8 (plus the 1 M).

What's going on here? Nothing at all strange if you remember to wear the spectacles of opportunity cost. What it costs you, as commissar, to have any person produce an M or an S is the value of what you thereby forgo. When Ann produces an S, you give up 2 Ms. When Ben produces an S, you lose 1 M. But when Cal produces an S, only ½ M is sacrificed. From you point of view, therefore, Cal is clearly the lowest-cost producer of Ss and Ann is the highest-cost producer.

When we look at the costs of M production, we see that it costs you ½ S when Ann produces an M, 1 S when Ben produces an M, and 2 Ss when Cal produces an M. Ann is therefore the lowest-cost producer of Ms, which is why you got the most of what you wanted by assigning Ann to M production.

Cost of producing one unit of material good

Ann	½ unit of spiritual good
Ben	1 unit of spiritual good
Cal	2 units of spiritual good

Efficiency and the Gains from Trade

Does this counterintuitive result — namely, that fumble-fingered Cal, who can't turn out much of anything, is nonetheless the most efficient producer of spiritual goods — does this affront to common sense perhaps arise from the fact that we put a dictator in charge? Not at all. It is entirely a result of the logic of opportunity cost.

Let's stage a coup, get rid of the commissar of production, and allow Ann, Ben, and Cal to decide individually what they want to produce.

They would presumably begin by deciding what each preferred to consume. Let's suppose that Cal, a well-balanced person, wants 1 M and 1 S. He's got a problem. There's no way he can produce that much. If he produces the M he wants, he'll have to go without S altogether. If he produces the 1 S he wants, he'll have to get along with only ½ M.

Now let's further suppose that Ben is an equally well-balanced person and wants to consume 1½ Ms and 1½ Ss, which is exactly what he's capable of producing. If Ben and Cal know and trust one another well enough, they can arrange an exchange that will be advantageous to Cal without making Ben any worse off. Cal could agree to specialize exclusively in S production. He would then keep one of his Ss for his own use and give the other to Ben. That would enable Ben to produce 2½ Ms, since he would now have to produce only ½ S for his own use. Keeping 1½ Ms for himself and giving the other to Cal would leave Ben no worse off than before. But Cal would now have obtained, through specialization and trade, the greater wealth that he wanted but hadn't been able to achieve on his own.

Does it look like a trick? Perhaps it is, but not in the sense of an illusion or something deceptive. It's the trick that all of us perform every day in order to supply ourselves with the goods that we want but can't even begin to produce for ourselves. We all specialize in the production of those goods in which we think we have the greatest *comparative advantage* and then exchange our products for the goods we really want. Just as Jack found that he could use a basketball as an input to produce a baseball glove that he wanted more than the basketball, so Cal found he could use an extra S as an input to obtain the M he wanted. That in essence is what we all do.

In a world where people can arrange and carry out exchanges with one another at low cost, people will find it in their interest to specialize and trade. They'll discover that specialization can bring them more of what they want, whether they want material goods, spiritual goods, leisure, or even a chance to make more of everything available to others. If Michael Jordan, a basketball player of extraordinary ability, had decided it was his primary aim in life to make more food available to the destitute in Chicago, he would still have worked as a professional basketball player. That's where his comparative advantage lay. He could "grow" far more food by playing basketball for pay and using the proceeds to "hire" farmers than he could ever have grown by sitting on a tractor. And the farmers of northern Illinois "grow" entertainment for themselves by specializing in grain production and using the proceeds to buy a color television set on which to watch Michael Jordan play.

You don't have to be "better than others" to pull this trick off. Cal can benefit from trading with Ben even though he's less productive than Ben in both spiritual and material goods. He can even gain from trade with Ann, who has the ability to turn out in a day twice as many Ss and eight times as many Ms as Cal. The important fact is that Ann has a *greater* advantage over Cal in Ms than in Ss. That means Cal has a *lesser disadvantage* with respect to Ann in Ss than in Ms. And that in turn implies that both Ann and Cal may be able to benefit from trading with each other after specializing in that good in which each has the *comparative advantage*.

How much food can be produced on a basketball court?

Comparative Advantage in International Trade

Popular thinking hangs on tenaciously to the notion that some countries may be able to produce almost everything at a lower cost. If wages in Mexico or Italy are lower than in the United States, won't Mexican and Italian manufacturers be able to produce just about anything more cheaply than U.S. manufacturers can do it? How can the United States compete with countries that tolerate wage rates, even for

skilled workers, below our legal minimum? In Mexico and
Italy, however, you could find workers arguing that they
can't compete with America's low-cost techniques of mass
production. And the suspicion would properly arise that
something is wrong with the argument.

The basic flaw in such arguments is their neglect of opportunity cost. It is *logically* impossible for one country to
be more efficient than another in the production of everything. And that becomes apparent as soon as you remember
to calculate efficiency as a ratio between what is produced
and what is consequently *not* produced. The real cost of producing anything is the value of what is given up in order to
produce it. Calculations in dollars, yen, pesos, and francs
(or working hours) all too easily obscure these real costs of
production.

Suppose that Japan and the United States each produced
only three goods: grain, textiles, and radios. Suppose further
that competition had moved prices in both countries to
levels that reflected the opportunity costs of each good, with
these results:

Prices per unit of good (identical
quantity and quality)

	United States	Japan
Grain	30 dollars	9,000 yen
Textiles	20 dollars	4,500 yen
Radios	50 dollars	13,500 yen

Which country is the more efficient or lower-cost producer of these goods? Before we can answer, we must find
some way of comparing costs. What measure is available?

Dollars and yen clearly won't do. It's obviously absurd
to suggest that the United States is more efficient in producing all three goods simply because the dollar prices are lower
than the yen prices. That would be true only if a yen had the
same value as a dollar. We shall see in the later chapter on
international exchange how the relative values of national
currencies are established. It's enough for now to note that
this is a blind alley because currency exchange rates only
reflect the value of currencies; they indicate nothing about
costs of production.

Some people might want to use the labor time invested
in the production of these goods as the ultimate measure of
their relative costs. To do that we would first have to find
some common denominator for labor of different skill and

effectiveness plus some way of translating such other inputs as machinery and land into units of labor time. And even if we could find a satisfactory way to do this, we would still be forced to adopt the arbitrary assumption that an hour of labor in Japan is as valuable as an hour of labor in the United States. But is it? Attitudes toward work and leisure are culturally determined, and there is no good reason to assume that an hour of working time is exactly as "costly" in one country as in another.

Then how can we decide which country is the lower-cost producer of these goods? The answer is: *There is no way at all to do so.* All we can do is determine that one country or the other is the more efficient producer of a particular good *relative to some other good or goods.* This is the meaning of comparative advantage.

Take radios, for example. The price ratios show that in the United States, a unit of radios costs either 1⅔ units of grain or 2½ units of textiles. It costs that much because that's what is given up in obtaining one unit of radios. In Japan, a unit of radios costs 1½ units of grain or 3 units of textiles. Those are the quantities of grain and textiles that are given up in Japan when additional radios are produced. It follows, then, that Japan is more efficient than the United States in producing radios *relative to grain,* but less efficient *relative to textiles.*

Which country is the more efficient textile producer? If you've gotten the idea by now, you will immediately ask: relative to what? A unit of textiles costs ⅔ unit of grain and ⅖ unit of radios in the United States, and ½ unit of grain and ⅓ unit of radios in Japan. So Japan is the more efficient (lower-cost) producer of textiles relative to both grain and radios.

The United States in turn is the lower-cost producer of grain relative to textiles: 1½ units of textiles are given up to produce a unit of grain, versus 2 units of textiles given up in Japan. The United States is also the lower-cost producer of grain relative to radios: ⅗ unit of radios is the cost of a U.S. unit of grain; ⅔ unit of radios is the Japanese cost.

Don't lose the point in all the fractions. *A nation can become an inefficient producer of good X simply by becoming a fabulously prolific producer of good Y.* When you become extraordinarily good at one thing, it is costly for you to do anything else. If Japan starts to produce radios and television sets at a lower cost than they can be produced in the United States, that does not imply that U.S. radio and TV manufacturers have failed in some fashion. It could just as

In the U.S.,
  1 unit of radio costs:
    1⅔ units of grain, or
    2½ units of textiles

In Japan,
  1 unit of radios costs:
    1½ units of grain, or
    3 units of textiles

well mean that U.S. productivity has been increasing rapidly in other industries.

The Pursuit of Comparative Advantage

No one except economists ever goes through these kinds of calculations, and even economists do it only in order to explain to students the logic of comparative advantage. In the real world people pursue comparative advantage, as distinct from merely talking about it, simply by choosing the option that seems most advantageous to them. Cal produces spiritual goods, Michael Jordan plays basketball, American apparel makers buy Japanese textiles, and Japanese millers purchase grain from the United States because, in each case, they believe that is the best way to obtain what they want. In all these decisions relative prices provide fundamental information. Given his various abilities and the price his work commands, Cal discovers that he can earn more income producing Ss than producing Ms. Americans looking for textiles find Japanese products less expensive than domestically produced textiles of similar quality. Japanese farmers choose not to raise wheat because they know that they could not raise enough to earn a satisfactory living, given the fact that they could not sell it above the price at which U.S.-grown wheat was available to Japanese millers. In short, they all behave as if the least costly way to achieve a given objective was the most efficient way. And in doing so they continuously coordinate these processes of cooperative interaction and mutual accommodation that comprise the economy.

None of this implies that they pay attention exclusively to prices, which would be an absurd and impossible way to behave. It means rather that relative prices guide their decisions when other things are equal. The other things that must be equal — or to be quite accurate, must be *thought* to be equal — include an enormous array of factors from the technological to the psychological. Consider a homeowner, for example, who wants to eliminate broad-leaved weeds from a lawn. Would it be more efficient to dig them out with a hand tool or to spray them with a herbicide? The homeowner's decision will reflect a judgment on the effectiveness of each procedure in killing the root, on likely damage to ornamental shrubs, on the desirability of exercise, and on the joys of yard work, and not just the relative prices of herbicide and hand tools. But those relative prices play a crucial coordinating role.

Disagreements on Values

If efficiency is finally an evaluative concept, expressing the ratio of output value to input value, anything at all can be inefficient to a person who holds the appropriate values. There are people to whom exercise is a total waste of energy. There are also people to whom a grassy knoll by the side of the road is a waste of space unless it displays a billboard. A person who neither visits wilderness areas nor derives satisfaction from knowing that they exist will correctly condemn as inefficient every legislative decision to create new wilderness perserves. Flying between cities rather than driving is a much more efficient travel arrangement for someone who gets car sickness than for someone who enjoys the scenery. And someone somewhere may even believe that Rembrandt wasted time by not painting with a six-inch-wide brush.

We could multiply such examples indefinitely, but the point is surely clear. *What we value determines what we will consider efficient or inefficient.* It follows that disagreements in society about the relative efficiency of particular projects will usually be disagreements about the relative value to be assigned to particular goods — or the relative disvalue of particular nongoods. Knowing this won't settle any controversial issue. But failing even to recognize what we're arguing about surely makes the resolution of controversy more difficult.

The question is not, "What is *really* more efficient?" but rather, "Who has the *right* to make particular decisions?" Crawling out of a sleeping bag to climb a mountain is atrociously inefficient to someone who plans to crawl back into that sleeping bag in the evening and is merely looking for the shortest distance between those two points. Fans of mountain climbing strenuously disagree, of course. But that creates no social conflict, because we all agree that individuals should have the right to decide for themselves whether it's more valuable to put their bodies on mountain peaks or to keep them in bed during vacations. When we do *not* agree on who has which rights, that's when we get into vehement arguments about whether it is "really" efficient, for example, to clear-cut forests or to stip-mine coal.

Efficiency, Values, and Property Rights

You should be able to see now why we insisted at the beginning of this chapter that the common critique of efficiency is logically confused. A society that placed "too high a value on efficiency" would be one that placed too high a value on using its resources in the most valuable way. That's an odd notion at best. The real target of the critics has to be either the values people hold or the rights they exercise.

Suppose a mineral exploration company came to the conclusion that there were large quantities of chrome, vanadium, and manganese under the ground in Yellowstone National Park and requested permission from Congress to search for them. Can you imagine the cries of outrage that would greet such a request? "Profiteers with no respect for nature!" "Greedy materialists willing to destroy an irreplaceable national heritage!" And someone would surely say: "Efficiency and economic growth are not worth pursuing if they deprive us of everything that makes life worth living."

The issue in such a case, however, would not be efficiency and economic growth versus Nature, wilderness, or anything else that makes life worth living. The issue would rather be *what is efficient,* or what constitutes genuine economic growth. There is nothing intrinsically more efficient about mining than about meditating. It is not necessarily the case that economic growth proceeds faster when manganese is extracted from the mountain than when trout are extracted from a stream. To decide whether it would be efficient to mine in Yellowstone Park, we must set the expected value of what would be obtained from mining against the expected value of what would thereby be lost. Chrome, vanadium, and manganese have no value that we can talk about apart from the purposes to which people intend to put them. And the same is true of the vistas, the tranquility, or the unblemished land and water that mining would destroy.

The issue comes down to this: *By what process should the prospective benefits and costs of mining in Yellowstone Park be evaluated?*

When the rules of the game establish clear and secure property rights, they implicitly decide by what process prospective benefits and costs are to be evaluated for decision-making purposes. If I decide to open my windows and turn up the thermostat on a cold winter day, I am using resources efficiently as long as I have an uncontested right to allocate all the resources I'm using. If, on the other hand, I am cooling off someone else's living space, or if someone else is paying the heating bills, my property rights are likely to be challenged. Then the issue becomes *not* the efficiency of my preferred arrangements but rather my exclusive right to value the inputs and the outputs in what I am doing.

When property rights are clear, stable, and exchangeable,

arguments about efficiency are almost always arguments about property rights.

scarce resources tend to acquire money prices that reflect their relative scarcity. Decisionmakers then pursue efficiency by using these prices as information. To say that the prices are "wrong" because they don't reflect the *real* value of certain costs or benefits amounts to rejecting the process by which those prices were determined. It is a critique not of efficiency but of the existing system of property rights, and of the rules of the game of which they form a part.

Comparative Advantage: The Economist's Umbrella

The term with which economists summarize almost everything we have been discussing in this chapter is *comparative advantage.* It might even be thought of as a term to summarize the entire collection of concepts presented thus far. To pursue comparative advantage means simply to sacrifice that which is less valuable for the sake of something more valuable.

Why do demand curves slope downward to the right? Because people pursue their comparative advantage. A rise in the price of any good means that its users will now be able to obtain the satisfaction it provides at a *relatively lower cost* by using some substitute.

How is the opportunity cost of any resource established? Through the pursuit of comparative advantage. People bid for a resource after estimating the potentiality of that resource *relative to other resources* for providing whatever they're after.

Why are only expected marginal costs and not sunk costs relevant to decisionmaking? Because expected marginal costs reflect the *comparative advantages of alternative decisions,* whereas sunk costs can never do more than reflect the comparative advantages of past decisions. But no one makes decisions with the hope of affecting what happened yesterday.

It is comparative advantage – the advantage resources have over other resources in particular uses relative to other uses – that determines the most efficient way to employ one's resources.

Once Over Lightly

Efficiency depends on valuations. Although physical or technological facts are certainly relevant to the determination of efficiency, they can never by themselves determine the relative efficiency of alternative processes. Efficiency depends on the ratio of output *value* to input *value*.

Exchange creates wealth, because voluntary exchange always involves the sacrifice of what is less valued (input) for what is more valued (output). Exchange is as much a wealth-creating transformation as is manufacturing or agriculture.

People specialize in order to exchange and thereby increase their wealth. They specialize in activities in which they believe themselves to have a comparative advantage.

Comparative advantage is determined by opportunity costs. No person, no group, no nation can be more efficient than another in every activity, for even the most highly productive agents must have some activities in which they are less highly productive. If you're four times as intelligent, three times as strong, and twice as beautiful as another person, then that person has a comparative advantage in beauty — and you, handsome as you are, have a comparative disadvantage in beauty.

A social system with clear property rights and few restrictions on exchange generates money prices that help people who are pursuing their comparative advantage to discover in exactly which direction their advantage lies.

Disagreements about whether some process or arrangement is or is not efficient are at root disagreements about the relative weights that should be given to different people's evaluations. They are therefore disagreements about the rules of the game, or about who should have what rights over which resources.

Questions for Discussion_____

1. Here is a criticism of shopkeepers and other middlemen written several centuries ago that still finds echoes today. "Their meer handing of Goods one to another, no more increases any Wealth in the Province, than Persons at a Fire increase the Water in a Pail, by passing it thro' Twenty or Forty hands."

   (a) Why would persons at a fire bother to pass a pail of water through forty hands if doing so increased no one's wealth?
   (b) It's true that the physical quantity of water is not increased when the water changes hands (some will even be spilled), just as the physical quantity of goods is not increased by the transactions of middlemen. But what about the *value* of the water and of the middleman's goods?
   (c) Does wealth depend on physical quantities or on valuations?

2. Many people enjoy the sight and sounds of a steam locomotive.

   (a) Should these aesthetic pleasures be included in the valuable output of a steam locomotive, right along with the value of the freight that is hauled?
   (b) If the owners of railroads could somehow collect a fee from all those who enjoyed seeing and hearing steam locomotives, would they include aesthetic pleasures in the value of a steam locomotive's output?
   (c) Would the efficiency of steam locomotives increase if a low-cost way were found to extract from steam-locomotive buffs a fee proportioned to the pleasure they derive from seeing and hearing them?

3. Is it efficient to feed a family using large quantities of frozen "convenience" foods? Under what circumstances could these expensive grocery items provide the lowest-cost inputs for producing the output of family dinner? What questionable premise is being used by someone who says that shoppers are wasting money by paying twice as much for convenience foods as they would have to pay for dinner items they prepare themselves?

4. Many Americans regularly drive their own cars to work rather than use public transportation or form a car pool.

   (a) How do you know that each person in a single-passenger vehicle during the rush hour is behaving efficiently?
   (b) The people riding the bus are also behaving efficiently. How can (a) and (b) both be true simultaneously?
   (c) What is actually being asserted by someone who says that it's inefficient for so many commuters to take their own cars to work?

5. The United States used wood as a fuel in metallurgy long after the British had changed to coal. Was this evidence of technological backwardness in the United States? If the United States was technologically backward, how would you explain the fact that all sorts of machines for woodworking were perfected in the United States in the first half of the nineteenth century? Fireplaces are often said to be inefficient ways to heat a room. Why then were they so widely used in the United States in the nineteenth century in preference to stoves? (Hint: Larger logs can be used in fireplaces.) Why did stoves become more popular as wood prices increased?

6. Is it more efficient to build dams with lots of direct labor and little machinery or with lots of machinery and little labor? Why will the answer vary from one country to another?

7. Which is more efficient: Japanese agriculture with its carefully terraced hillsides or American agriculture with far more "wasteful" use of land? How have relative prices in the two countries brought about these different methods of farming? How have opportunity costs entered into the formation of these relative prices?

8. Attorney Fudd is the most highly sought-after lawyer in the state. He is also a phenomenal typist who can do 120 words per minute. Should Fudd do his own typing if the fastest secretary he can obtain does only 60 words

per minute? Prove that Fudd is *not* twice as efficient as his secretary at typing, that he is in fact *less* efficient at typing, and that he should therefore retain a secretary.

9. The dean knows that Professor Svelte is the most capable administrator in his department, far more capable than Professor Klunk. Can you think of any reasons (related to efficiency rather than nepotism) for nonetheless appointing Klunk over Svelte as department chairperson?

10. The Boeing 767 uses less than 110 pounds of jet fuel per seat per 1000 miles. The older 727 uses about 155 pounds of jet fuel per seat per 1000 miles. But the 767 costs far more per seat to purchase. Which of the planes should an airline purchase if it is interested in efficiency? Does the price of jet fuel affect the answer? How might the decision to purchase a used 727 rather than a new 767 turn out to be not only more economical but also more conserving of natural resources?

11. It has often been claimed that under a capitalist system business firms will sometimes continue to use obsolete equipment rather than the new, "most efficient" equipment because they have a lot of money tied up in the old equipment. Does this make sense? What is the relevance to such decisions of "money tied up"? When would an airline that has "money tied up" in 727s elect to replace them with 767s?

12. You own and occupy a large brick house in an old residential neighborhood. The area is being rezoned to allow multiple-family occupancy and apartment buildings. How would you go about deciding whether to (a) continue to occupy the house as a single-family dwelling, (b) divide the house into several apartments, or (c) tear down the house and erect a new apartment complex? If you were to choose (b), could you be accused of retarding the economy by failing to adopt the most up-to-date equipment because of your vested interest in obsolete equipment? Does this differ from question 11?

13. A May 1979 letter to the editor of *The Wall Street Journal* wondered why, in view of the gasoline shortage, such "utterly wasteful uses of gasoline" as auto racing were still permitted. The writer also urged that such "obvious waste" be curtailed in the public interest. Is auto racing an utter and obvious waste of gasoline? Try to construct a clear and defensible definition of *waste* that would indict auto racing but exonerate other uses of automotive gasoline at a time when there might be a gasoline shortage.

14. Grain farmers have many options when it comes to preparing the soil. They can plow and then thoroughly harrow a field before planting, they can practice minimum tillage, or they can go so far as to plant without preparing the ground at all. Heavy tilling buries and thus kills weeds and insects. No-till farming requires careful and extensive use of herbicides and pesticides and also produces slightly lower yields. Explain how each of the following will affect the relative efficiency of maximum tillage and no-till farming:

(a) Higher prices for diesel fuel.
(b) Improved herbicides and pesticides.

(c) Tougher government controls on stream and lake pollution caused by chemicals used in agriculture. (Note: Untilled ground is more likely to retain the chemicals put into it.)

(d) Farmers adopt the same attitude toward their fields that some suburban homeowners have toward their lawns: they find satisfaction in looking at a broad, well-tended expanse of land.

(e) Higher prices for land.

15. Some critics of U.S. agriculture argue that highly mechanized production techniques in farming are inefficient because the energy consumed by the machinery used to grow food exceeds the amount of potential energy available in the food that is grown. Does this argument make any sense? Is energy the ultimate measure of value?

16. In recent years millions of acres of barley- and rye-growing land have been kept out of production in the Soviet Union to save scarce fertilizer. Nonetheless, Soviet farmers sometimes burn fertilizer to conceal the fact that they haven't spread it on the soil, and there are regions in which it is common to see huge mounds of unused, years-old, and now thoroughly hardened fertilizer. Can you account for this anomaly: the deliberate nonuse of a critically scarce resource? Why would U.S. farmers not behave in this way?

17. The Sevier River in Utah has been used for about a century to irrigate farm land in central Utah. Recently, a 3000-megawatt, coal-fired electrical generating plant was proposed for this area. The generating plant would require about 40,000 acre-feet of water per year from the Sevier River. Operation of the generating plant would mean less water for agriculture.

(a) Is the water of the Sevier River used more efficiently when it grows food or when it generates electricity?

(b) Can you answer this question by comparing the value of food with the value of electricity? (Hint: Value is determined at the margin.)

(c) If farmers who own rights to Sevier River water sell their rights to the power company, is the water allocated to its most valuable use?

(d) Who are some of the parties who might be adversely affected by the farmers' decision to sell their water rights?

18. Have you ever noticed how few gasoline stations are found in the center of large cities? With such heavy traffic one ought to be able to do an excellent business. Why then are there so few?

19. The key to question 18 is the high price of land in the center of large cities. Would it make sense for the city government, which has the right of eminent domain, to take over some of this land in order to provide "vitally needed service stations"?

20. Land has become so expensive in Beverly Hills and Westwood, California, that developers estimate it would require more than $25 million to construct a supermarket with adequate parking space in these communities, according to *Parade Magazine*, January 20, 1985.

(a) Why has the land become so expensive?

(b) There is only one supermarket in all of Beverly Hills and central Westwood. Why?

(c) At these land prices, supermarket construction is not a profitable investment project. Might it nonetheless be efficient to have another supermarket or two in the area?

21. In a June 6, 1985 article titled "On the Waterfront: Tugs, Barges Battling Quiche and Fern Bars," *The Wall Street Journal* discussed the gentrification of waterfront property.

(a) A Seattle land-use specialist who wants to halt this development said, "A condominium can be built anywhere, but the shipyard it replaces can't move two miles inland." Why is that not a conclusive argument?

(b) Maritime interests in Boston have objected to a plan to turn unused piers into housing and parkland on the grounds that the now vacant piers may be needed someday. Why is this an inconclusive argument?

(c) Maritime businesses complain that they cannot outbid developers for waterfront land and so need zoning help and other protection from local government in order to keep down the price of goods that move by water. Why should the cost of water carriage be kept down by government action?

22. Is it efficient for cars to have bumpers so strong and heavy that the car will sustain no damage in collisions at speeds up to 5 miles per hour? How would you answer such a question if you were a car buyer? If you were an automobile manufacturer? If you were a federal official charged with setting minimum standards for automobile bumpers?

23. In view of the high cost of transporting milk from the mainland United States, is it efficient for Hawaii to produce within its own borders all the milk its citizens consume? What difference does it make to your answer to know that Hawaiian dairy farmers import all their cattle feed? If it is inefficent to import milk into Hawaii, why does the state's Milk Control Board receive requests to import milk from other states? Is it efficient for the Milk Control Board to deny these requests, as it has regularly done?

24. A 1984 study issued by the Congressional Office of Technology Assessment concluded that a high-speed rail system capable of moving passengers between U.S. cities would probably not be able to attract enough riders to stay in the black. Does this imply that it would be inefficient to construct such a system?

25. Bonneville Dam is the oldest dam on the Columbia River, and its navigation lock is much smaller than the locks on the seven dams farther up the river. As a result, Bonneville is a bottleneck for Columbia River barge traffic, with barges sometimes compelled to wait 10 hours for passage.

(a) By what process could the federal government, which owns and operates the dam, decide whether it would be efficient to construct a new lock at Bonneville?

(b) The Burlington Northern and Union Pacific railroads operate tracks along the northern and southern banks of the Columbia River. They argue that a new lock should be constructed only if barge owners and towboat operators are willing to pay for it. Barge and towboat people respond that the benefits of the lock would extend far beyond themselves, and that this justifies a government subsidy for the proposed new lock. Would other beneficiaries be able to avoid paying for the benefits they receive if the federal government financed the new lock through a fee paid by the towboats and barges that use it?

26. Should the government build a $520-million network of dams, reservoirs, and irrigation canals near Durango, Colorado, to capture the spring runoff in the Animas and La Plata rivers? Would this be an efficient use of taxpayer funds? How could we decide?

27. Chapter 4 discussed the problem of increasing airport congestion, using Washington, DC's crowded National Airport and the near-deserted Dulles Airport as a case study. Airlines prefer to fly into National because it's only 10 minutes away from downtown Washington; Dulles is almost an hour away.

   (a) Is it efficient for airlines to choose National over Dulles when scheduling their flights? Would that efficiency change if the government charged a higher landing fee at National?

   (b) Is it efficient for passengers to choose a flight into National over one into Dulles? Would their relative efficiencies change if ticket prices for flights landing at National rose by twice the price of a cab from Dulles to the Capitol?

   (c) In 1966 the FAA decreed that flights coming into Washington from any city more than 650 miles away had to land at Dulles. Was this an efficient order? What effects do you think it had?

   (d) The Transportation Department has been floating proposals recently to buy and sell landing rights at National and other busy airports. Some critics of this proposal object that the larger airlines would buy all the slots. Do you think this would occur? What sort of factors would determine how much any airline was willing to pay for a particular landing slot?

28. Airlines are willing to overbook flights because they know that some people who make reservations will not show up. Sometimes, however, this results in more people holding reservations at the gate than there are seats on the flight.

   (a) Is overbooking efficient from the airlines' standpoint?

   (b) If the airlines are required by law to pay huge sums as compensation to passengers who are "bumped" because of overbooking, does this change the efficiency of overbooking?

   (c) Is overbooking efficient from the standpoint of passengers?

   (d) How would you recommend that airlines handle situations in which, because of overbooking, they are required to deny boarding to some passengers? Which passengers should be "bumped"?

(e) In recent years airlines have adopted the practice of "bumping" volunteers from overbooked flights. Volunteers are obtained by offers of money or free trips as inducements to surrender confirmed reservations. Who gets "bumped" under this system? Does the system discriminate against poorer people?

(f) If passengers can sell their confirmed reservations when a seat shortage arises, why can't passengers sell their right to land at a crowded airport when a shortage of landing slots arises?

(g) Compare your analysis here with your analysis in the question that follows, especially part (b).

29. Bent Grasz spent $100,000 to plant grass, flowers, shrubs, and trees and make his home a landscaping showplace. The city is suffering from a drought this summer and has prohibited all watering of lawns and gardens. Bent would be willing to pay several thousand dollars if necessary to obtain the water he needs to irrigate adequately. Many of Bent's fellow citizens would be willing to conserve the amount of water Bent wants in return for a payment far less than Bent is willing to offer.

(a) Is there room here for everyone to become better off through exchange?

(b) Why can't people ordinarily sell the water they conserve in a drought to someone else who wants it more than they do?

(c) Suppose the city responded to the drought not by prohibiting watering but by tripling the price of water. Would this make Bent happy?

(d) If the city distributed the extra revenue from higher water prices to water users, an equal amount going to each customer, would this cancel out the effect of the price increase? Who would be better off and who would be worse off under such a system (better or worse than under the system of restrictions on use but no price increase)?

30. During the 1970s the federal government maintained extensive and complex controls on the prices of petroleum and petroleum products.

(a) Why would you expect these controls to lead eventually to greater scarcity of petroleum products in some areas than in others, or to what were called "supply imbalances"?

(b) When the U.S. Department of Energy authorized oil companies to move as much as 5 percent of their supply among and within the states to "relieve imbalances," the companies generally declined to do so. How could the oil companies know where to move oil and how much to reallocate with prices fixed by law?

(c) The Department of Energy authorized the governors of states to move this 5 percent of supply when the oil companies declined the invitation. How were the governors able to allocate petroleum products efficiently when the oil companies could not do so?

(d) In a March 16, 1981, letter to the editor of *The Wall Street Journal*, the Commissioner of the New Jersey Department of Energy argued that the oil companies' refusal to accept the authority granted to them and their decision to hide "timidly behind government controls" demonstrates the inadequacy of "the free-market philosophy." Is this a sound argument?

31. Is it possible to assess the efficiency of the federal government's 55-mile-per-hour speed limit?

(a) What is the output or desired result whose value would go in the numerator of the efficiency ratio? What is the input or cost or forgone opportunity whose value would go in the denominator? How would you choose appropriate values once you had decided on the appropriate output and input?

(b) Suppose we use fuel saved as the output of the 55-mph limit and time lost as the input. What might we use as appropriate value weights so that we can decide whether the value of the output is greater than the value of the input?

(c) If we include in the output not only fuel saved but also the lives saved, won't our assessment inevitably conclude that the 55-mph speed limit is efficient? How can we set a finite value on a human life?

(d) Economist Charles Lave has calculated that the 55-mph speed limit causes Americans to spend 102 extra years driving in order to "save one life" and suggests that 102 years traveling in an automobile rather closely fits his personal notion of hell (*Newsweek*, October 23, 1978). List a few ways in which 102 years could be used to "save" far more lives than one.

(e) Far more lives would be saved if we required that all motorists be preceded by a person on foot carrying an orange flag. Would such an arrangement consequently be even more efficient than a 55-mph speed limit?

(f) Who gains from the 55-mph speed limit? Who loses the most?

32. A pumped-storage reservoir is a reservoir that an electrical utility drains during hours of peak demand in order to generate electricity, then refills during hours of slack demand by pumping water back up into it.

(a) The electricity generated by the falling water is inevitably far less than the electricity used to refill the reservoir. Does this mean the practice of using pumped-storage reservoirs is inefficient?

(b) If you think it's inefficient or wasteful to use two watts of electricity to create one watt, why do you suppose the utilities do it? Can it be profitable to behave inefficiently?

(c) If you believe that inefficient behavior can sometimes be profitable, would you ever want to condemn such behavior as not in the general or long-term interest of society? Why or why not? Under what circumstances?

33. If you saw a bumper sticker that said "Eliminate Government Waste — At Any Cost," would you laugh, cry, or cheer?

34. Construct the supply curve of Ms from the data in the text on Ann, Ben, and Cal. The quantity of Ms will go on the horizontal axis. What will you put on the vertical axis? Then construct the supply curve of Ss.

35. Efficiency is a relationship between ends and means. When we decide that a process is inefficient, we seem to be concluding that inappropriate means are being used to achieve some end.

(a) Can ends or goals be inefficient?

(b) Can you think of any ends or goals that are not also means to further ends?

(c) The chairman of a government committee studying manned space flight in the late 1950s said that they chose to send men to the moon because this "represented a true end objective which was self-justifying and did not have to be supported on the basis that it led to a subsequently more useful end." Do you agree that putting astronauts on the moon was a pure end and not a means to some further ends?

Chapter 7

Information, Middlemen, and Speculators

The costs and benefits that affect decisions to demand or to supply are always *expected* costs and benefits. Producers decide to supply so many units of X because they expect to pay no more than a certain amount for the required resources and to receive at least some larger amount than that from selling X. Consumers decide to purchase a product because they expect to receive some benefit from its possession greater than what they expect to pay for it. But the future is uncertain, so expectations are often frustrated by events. Decisions turn out to be mistaken. And mistakes are costly.

Because of all the interdependencies that characterize our highly specialized economic system, mistaken decisions will often have costly consequences for many more people than the ones who made the decision. If refiners don't build up adequate inventories of crude oil, motorists may have to wait in line for gasoline. If physicians don't anticipate the adverse side effects of a drug, a patient may die. And if manufacturers overestimate the demand for their product, employees who sacrificed other opportunities to work for those manufacturers may find themselves unemployed.

Since mistakes are costly, people try to avoid making them. Unfortunately, avoiding mistakes is costly, too. The way to eliminate mistakes is to acquire more information before acting. But information is a scarce good with its own costs of acquisition. It may be less costly, as a result, to accept some mistakes than to acquire the information that could have prevented them. One mistake we can all avoid is the mistake of assuming that information is a free good. We shall see as we proceed through this chapter just how often that mistaken assumption seems to influence our attitudes and actions.

Real Estate Agents Are Information Producers

"How to save about $900 and lose $3000 . . . right on your own home."

That was the headline under which the National Association of Real Estate Boards ran an advertisement urging people to use the services of a realtor in selling their homes. The ad continued:

> Don't laugh. It could happen. For instance, suppose you decide to sell your house. Yourself. You decide it's worth $15,000, and you sell it for $15,000. Great. But how did you arrive at that price? By guesswork. It takes a lot more than that to determine a property's value. It takes a Realtor who knows houses and what they're worth. Suppose he said your house was worth $3000 more. A fair price to buyer and seller. It could happen. Of course, you'd save the Realtor's fee. But at quite a cost.
>
> So when you decide to sell a house, use your Realtor. He's not just anyone in real estate. He's the professional who is pledged to a strict code of ethics. That's good. Especially if you want to make the best sale you can. Or for that matter, the best buy.

That ad is eloquent testimony to something mentioned in Chapter 6: the public's deep-rooted suspicion of middlemen.[1] The fact that the realtors' association thought the ad worth running is strong evidence that such a suspicion exists, and the argument used in the ad is further evidence. For the ad seems designed to obscure the realtor's function while defending it, almost as if the truth is more than the public would tolerate.

Suppose, we might ask, that the realtor said your house was worth $3000 *less*: "A fair price to buyer and seller." Isn't it just as likely that homeowners selling their own houses will guess too high as too low? Or even more likely in view of the hopeful optimism typical of so many homeowners? Then the use of a realtor will cost the owner twice over. And just what constitutes a "fair price"? Moreover, if the realtors obtain higher prices for sellers, how can they simultaneously obtain better buys for purchasers, as the last paragraph asserts? Something is wrong with the argument.

Don't criticize the realtors' association too harshly. The plight of middlemen forced to explain their function is not

---

[1]It is also testimony to the inflation and the relative increase in housing prices that have occurred since the early 1970s. While $15,000 today may buy a garage, it won't buy much of a house.

an easy one, because most people don't see that *information
is a scarce good* or what this fact implies. If you want to sell
your house for as much as you can get, the appropriate buyer
is the one person in the world willing to pay the highest
price. That seems obvious. What isn't obvious is how you
find that person. You presumably are not omniscient, so you
will never even discover the existence of many potential
purchasers. It is almost a certainty, therefore, that when you
finally do sell, you will not have found that one buyer willing to pay the very top price. Does this imply that you
should keep searching indefinitely?

Information is a scarce good with its own costs of production, including all the costs of postponing action. It simply does not pay to go on acquiring information forever before acting. A sensible seller will continue acquiring information, therefore, only as long as the anticipated marginal
gain from doing so is greater than the anticipated marginal
cost of acquiring information. A sensible buyer will behave
in the same way. The reason that both can gain from using
the services of a realtor is that the realtor enables each to
obtain additional information at low cost. When you think
about it, this seems in fact to be the primary function of
middlemen: they promote efficiency and hence increase
wealth by acting as low-cost producers of valuable information. Real estate agents provide sellers and buyers with better opportunities than they would otherwise have by putting
them in possession of additional information. That is a valuable service. Although it's true that only the seller actually
"hires" the agent, the fact that buyers go to them and make
use of their multiple-listing services shows that real estate
agents provide a service to buyers, too.

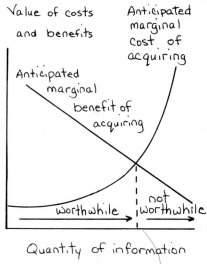

Reducing Search Costs

Suppose you own ten shares of General Electric stock and
want to sell. You could go around to your friends and try to
peddle it or you could put an ad in the newspaper. But it is
very likely that you would obtain a higher net price by using
the services of a middleman, in this case a stockbroker. No
doubt if you advertised long enough you could find a buyer
willing to pay the price the stockbroker obtained for you.
But it is most improbable that the cost of your search would
be less than the broker's fee.

"Getting it wholesale" is a popular pastime for many
people who think that they're economizing. Perhaps they
are. If they enjoy searching for bargains (and many people

do), then they may well gain from their activities. But for most people, retailers are an important low-cost source of valuable information. The retailer's inventory reveals something of the range of opportunities available, information that is often difficult to obtain in any other fashion. How many times have you gone shopping without knowing what you were looking for, hoping to discover what you want by finding out what retailers have for sale?

Much the same is true of job-placement agencies. People frequently resent the fee charged by private agencies for finding them a job. Unless they had expected the information obtained through the agency to be worth more than the fee, they presumably would not have used the agency's services. But as soon as they have established contact with a suitable employer, the agency seems useless — as it now is, of course — and its fee begins to look like an unwarranted imposition.

A large part of the middleman's bad press stems from our habit of comparing actual situations with better but nonexistent ones. The exchanges we make are rarely as advantageous as the exchanges we could make if we knew everything. So we conclude that the middleman takes advantage of our ignorance. But why look at it in that way? Using the same argument, you could say that doctors take advantage of your illnesses, and that they should receive no return for their services because they would be unable to obtain a return if you were always healthy. That is both true and irrelevant. We are neither always healthy nor omniscient. Physicians and middlemen are consequently both producers of real wealth. Other prestigious persons performing similar services are lawyers, teachers, and corporation executives.

Markets Create Information

One of the continuing themes of this book is that supply and demand, or the market process of competing bids and offers, create indexes of value for decisionmakers by placing price tags on available resources. The capacity of the market to generate high-quality information at low cost is one of its most important but least appreciated virtues. Middlemen are important participants in this process.

But what, you may ask, is "the market"? That's a good question and not an easy one to answer. The market is clearly not a place, though it may sometimes be closely identified with a particular place. Nor is it anything one can observe in the usual sense of observation. It is finally just a set of interrelationships, or what we have called a "process of competing bids and offers."

Markets are not peculiar to capitalism. They also exist in the most thoroughly socialist of societies. They aren't uniquely associated with business firms or the "private sector" either. Interrelationships characterized by competing bids and offers are also, as we shall see in Chapter 14, important characteristics of the political process and of government organizations. Nor must money change hands for markets to function, even though the use of money enormously facilitates their working. Rush-hour drivers who look for space, fill it up, and thereby continuously shift the relative value of the options that they all perceive exemplify a market. College students looking for courses to take and departments thinking of courses to offer are participating in a market process, too.

Some markets, like stock markets and commodity markets, are "well organized," which means that the bids and offers of prospective buyers and sellers are rather comprehensively assembled, so that a single price for a fairly uniform good tends to be established for all transactions over a wide geographic area. Other markets, like the market that even the least practiced eye can see operating in a singles bar, are much less well organized: the precise good to be exchanged and the terms of the exchange have to be negotiated for each separate transaction. The market for used furniture is relatively unorganized: transactions take place at prices that vary greatly, because buyers and sellers are not in extensive contact. The market for retail groceries, on the other hand, is far along toward the well-organized end of the spectrum, so that hamburger prices will vary much less over a given area than will used furniture prices.

It is sometimes said that stock markets and commodity markets are more nearly "perfect" than retail grocery markets and used furniture markets. This is a misleading way to describe the difference, because it implies that the latter markets ought to be changed (perfection is better than imperfection). Such a recommendation makes sense, however, only if the costs of improving the markets are less than the gains from more efficient exchange made possible by the improvement. It is often the case, however, that we simply don't know of any way to make it worthwhile. Moreover, some efforts to "improve" markets through government action look suspiciously like efforts to promote special interests.

But in every case the relationships between buyers and sellers, whether constant and extensive or sporadic and scattered, generate prices of some sort: terms of trade. Each such

The range of available opportunities expands when restaurants post their menus outside.

price is a piece of potentially valuable information to other people about available opportunities. The more such prices there are, the more clearly and precisely they are stated, and the more widely they are known, the greater will be the range of opportunities available to people in the society. The greater will be their wealth, in short. Is that not what we finally mean by an increase in wealth? It is a wider range of available opportunities, the ability to do more of whatever it is we want to do.

Middlemen, brokers, and professional traders are specialists in the organization of markets and hence in the creation of valuable information. They presumably specialize in this way because they think they have a comparative advantage in information production. Whatever their motives, however, they provide services on which we all depend.

That is one side of the coin. The other side is that we don't realize how important these functions are, largely because we have trouble seeing that information really is scarce. This blind spot frequently leads us to impose legal restrictions on traders. Speculators are frequent victims of just this kind of public misunderstanding.

Varieties of Speculation

The dictionary defines speculation as "trading in the hope of profit from changes in the market price." That's too narrow a definition, but it will do to get us started. The most celebrated (or more accurately, the most vilified) speculator is the "bear" of Wall Street, who "sells short" — that is, sells for future delivery shares of stock not actually owned at the time of sale. This speculator believes that the stock will go down in price, so that when the time comes for delivery of the shares, they can be purchased at a low price and sold at the previously agreed-upon higher price.

A more important speculator is probably the commodity speculator, who may trade in such items as wheat, soybeans, hogs, lumber, sugar, cocoa, or copper. This kind of speculator buys and sells "futures." These are agreements to deliver or to accept, at some specified date in the future, amounts of a commodity at a price determined now.

These are the spectacular speculators whose feats make the financial pages. A less-publicized speculator is you yourself. You are buying education now, partly in the hope that it will increase the value of the labor services you'll be selling in the future. But the future price of your services could turn out to be too low to justify your present investment.

Another familiar speculator is the consumer who reads that the price of sugar is expected to rise and responds by loading the pantry with a two-year supply. If the price of sugar rises far enough, these sugar hoarders gain. If it does not, they lose. Their wealth has been tied up in sugar, cluttering the pantry shelves and blocking the opportunity to purchase more valuable assets — an interest-bearing savings account, for example.

The motorist who fills the gas tank at the sight of a sign advertising gasoline at two cents a gallon less than the usual price is speculating; the price may be four cents lower two blocks ahead. The motorist who drives on an almost empty tank in hope of lower prices up ahead is a notorious speculator. And the motorists who continually "top" their tanks when gasoline supplies are rumored to be short are surely speculators.

But many people, while failing to notice that they themselves are often speculators, heap blame on the "profiteers" who allegedly "take advantage" of special situations and innocent people in pursuit of their own unprincipled profit. Are speculators really the enemies of the people they are so often alleged to be?

Consequences of Speculation

It is often said that speculators exploit natural disasters by driving up prices before the disaster occurs. And sometimes the expected disaster never even materializes. That is true. But it is only one small and misleading part of the truth. Suppose evidence begins to accumulate in early summer that corn-leaf blight is spreading to major corn-producing areas of the Midwest. A significant percentage of the year's corn crop could be wiped out as a result. People who think this is likely to occur will consequently expect a higher price for corn next year. This expectation will induce some people to pull some corn away from current consumption in order to carry it over into the next crop period when, they believe, the price will be higher. That is speculation.

Many different parties engage in such speculation: farmers substitute other livestock feed for corn in order to maintain their corn stocks at a higher level, either to avoid having to buy corn next year at a higher price or to sell it then at the higher price; industrial users increase their inventories now while the price is relatively low; and traders who might not know a bushel of corn from a peck of soybeans try to make a profit from buying cheap now and selling dear later.

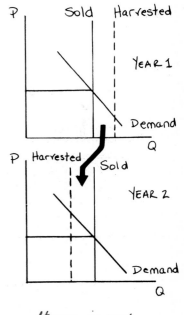

Storage in good year for sale in bad year stabilizes the price.

There are well-organized commodity markets to facilitate this kind of transaction, in which people can buy or sell "futures" — contracts for future delivery of commodities at prices agreed upon now. The effect of all these activities is to reduce the current supply of corn; the price consequently rises. And just as the critic protested, it rises before the disaster occurs.

But that is only a part of the picture. These speculative activities cause corn to be transported *over time* from a period of relative abundance to one of greater scarcity. The price next year, when the blight is expected to have its effects, will therefore be lower than it otherwise would be. Speculators thus even out the flow of commodities into consumption and diminish price fluctuations over time. Since price fluctuations create risks for those who grow or use corn, speculators are actually reducing risk to others. More accurately, they are purchasing risk, in hope of a profit, from others less willing to take risk and willing to pay something in the form of reduced expected returns to avoid it. (Those who choose to sell risk are called *hedgers*.)

A farmer who sells September corn futures when he plants in May is hedging.

A corn chip maker hedges by buying corn futures.

Prophets and Losses

All this assumes, however, that the speculators are correct in their anticipations. What if an unusually large crop appears instead? Then the speculators are transporting corn from a period of lesser to a period of greater abundance and thereby magnifying price fluctuations. This is clearly a misallocation of resources, involving as it does the giving up now of some high-priced corn for the sake of obtaining later an equal amount of low-priced corn. That doesn't help other people.

But neither is it profitable for the speculators! They will sustain losses where they had hoped for gains. We should not expect them, consequently, to behave in this fashion *except as a result of ignorance.* Are speculators likely to be ignorant?

Speculators do make mistakes. (Why would they otherwise be called speculators?) But living as we do in an uncertain world, we have no option but to act in the presence of uncertainty. We can't escape uncertainty and the consequences of ignorance by refusing to act or to think about the future. And if we think we know more than the speculators, we can counter them at a profit by betting against them. It is revealing to note that those who criticize speculators for misreading the future rarely give effective expression to their own supposedly greater insight by entering the market against them. Hindsight, of course, is always in copious supply—and the price is appropriately low.

Speculators provide information. Their offers to buy and sell express their judgments concerning the future in relation to the present. The prices generated by their activities are, like all prices, indexes of value: information for decision-makers on present and future opportunity costs. This information is at least as important to conservatives as it is to gamblers. It is true that the information they provide is "bad" information whenever the speculators are wrong. But harping on this is again a case of comparing one situation with a better but unattainable situation. If we think we can read the future better than the speculators, we are free to express our convictions with money, profit from our insight, and benefit other people in the process.

Meanwhile, those whose ordinary business activities involve them in the use of commodities that are speculatively traded do make effective use of the information generated by the speculators. Farmers consult the prices predicted in the commodity exchanges and so do industrial users. And those who use goods not ordinarily thought of as speculative commodities also take advantage of the information generated by speculators. For we all use prices as information, and prices reflect competing bids and offers inevitably based to a large extent on a (speculative!) reading of the future.

Natural disasters such as droughts, crop diseases, and unseasonable frosts have surprisingly small effects on the price and availability of grain, fruit, and vegetables in the United States. The credit for that must go to speculators, whose foresight acts as an effective buffer between the vagaries of nature and the sturdy dependability of grocers.

The Complex Question of "Insider Trading"

A substantial part of the public's distrust and dislike of speculators is probably grounded in a suspicion that speculators take advantage of information from which they have no right to profit. The problems created by scarce information and consequent uncertainty are often complicated by this sort of disagreement about specific rights and obligations. What do buyers have a right to know? What do suppliers have an obligation to reveal? What constitutes an unfair advantage with respect to information? And who ought to be responsible for acquiring and disseminating important information about products?

The questions are difficult. Lawyers and ethicists were

already arguing in the Middle Ages about the obligations of sellers to reveal to buyers everything they knew when that knowledge might lower prices. If a merchant brought grain to a starving city, was he morally or legally bound to tell his customers that additional grain shipments were on the way? Or could he legitimately keep this knowledge to himself and watch hungry customers bid up the price of his grain?

If you think the merchant had at least a moral obligation in such a case to reveal what he knew (*not* the universal conclusion of medieval ethicists, by the way), would you also say that someone selling corporate stock has an obligation to reveal any unfavorable information he has about the corporation's prospects before he sells? What is the difference between the two cases that might make us decide them differently? Is it the impersonal character of the stock transaction, the fact that sellers don't know who is buying what they sell? Is it the high cost of disseminating information to all prospective buyers? Or is it a lingering uncertainty about the accuracy, reliability, and relevance of the unfavorable information?

While "full disclosure" has an ethically attractive ring, the concept doesn't hold up too well under examination. Sometimes the information people have is wrong; if they have an obligation to reveal what they think they know, do they also have an obligation to compensate people who relied to their detriment on mistaken information? Moreover, information is not a simple matter of words. Telling people doesn't necessarily inform them. They can fail to understand, not believe, not be listening, not care, or not remember. In addressing any large group you will always find that some have forgotten what you said before others have understood, and that some still won't care enough to listen when others have stopped listening out of boredom. Moreover, what is valuable information to one person will often be mere noise to another, and if you try to tell everybody what they want to know, you may generate so much static that no one learns anything from your communication. If you try to avoid deceiving some, you will in the process fail to provide others with information they wanted to have.

The most serious objection to any full-disclosure requirement is that requiring people to reveal everything they know prior to any transaction would destroy much of the incentive to acquire costly but socially valuable information. We don't require inventors or writers to give away their ideas. Why should we require those who discover, sometimes at considerable cost, valuable information that cannot

Is "full disclosure" possible when many are not paying attention?

be patented or copyrighted to make that information freely available to others? While it is surely important that a society's rules of the game endorse honesty and integrity, it is also important that they encourage the search for new knowledge and the willingness to take risks when that knowledge is far from certain.

A high percentage of the "insider trading" cases prominently prosecuted in recent years by the Securities and Exchange Commission involved a violation of what the law calls *fiduciary obligations*, moral and legal duties taken on by contract. When "insider trading" flows from the violation of fiduciary obligations, it can be unambiguously condemned. Suppose the employees of a brokerage or law firm that has been hired to assist in a corporate takeover use the knowledge acquired in the course of their employment to purchase the stock of the target firm before the takeover attempt is announced. Because their actions will raise the price of the target firm and make the takeover more costly, they betray the interests of the firm that hired them. The situation is analogous to that of a county council member who uses his official knowledge to tip off friends about the location of a new highway so they can buy up the land. He would be increasing the cost of the highway project to his constituents, the taxpayers of the county, and his friends' purchases would be properly condemned as "insider trading" because they traded on the basis of information given to them in violation of a fiduciary obligation.

Trading that violates fiduciary obligation is clearly wrong.

It would be absurd to define illegal "insider trading" as all trading that takes place on the basis of information not available to everyone else. Such a definition would implicitly assert that information is not a scarce good and that markets should function like roulette wheels. We clearly do want to prohibit all trading that violates fiduciary obligations. But what about trading that violates no fiduciary obligations yet does take advantage of "insider information"?

Suppose you are a scientist employed by a leading pharmaceutical firm, and you come to the conclusion that the line of research you are pursuing is likely to be very successful: your efforts are going to produce an anti-cancer drug, let's suppose, that is likely to produce huge profits for your employer. It would make good sense for you to purchase stock in the company under these circumstances. If you did so, however, you would clearly be trading on the basis of information not available to others, information only available to persons who are "on the inside" of your research work. Would your purchase be illegal?

When should it be illegal to benefit from "inside" information?

The law on such cases is not clear at the present time. You might want to ask yourself why a scientist should be prevented from investing in her own work? Whom does she harm? The people who sold her the stock, ignorant of the impending discovery that may (*or may not!*) send the stock price higher? Suppose the scientist already owned a large block of her company's stock, was planning to sell it, and changed her mind because her research on the anti-cancer drug suddenly began to look promising. Should she be accused of *nontrading* on the basis of inside information? The people she hurts now are the people who would have benefited from acquiring stock that was going to rise sharply in value. In either case, why do these people deserve special protection? What rights of theirs were violated by the scientist's decision to buy (or not to sell)?

Hostility to "insider trading" is grounded in the sound conviction that no one should have an unfair advantage. The problem lies in the difficulty of deciding what constitutes an *unfair* advantage. It won't do at all to conclude that *every* advantage is unfair. If we are going to acknowledge that information is an inescapably scarce good, we shall have to wrestle continually with the question of when and why particular inside information confers an unfair advantage.

The Liability Question

What should be done about transactions that don't turn out as expected? New appliances that don't work properly, medicines that produce undesired side effects, or airplanes that crash? Who should be held liable for the damages?

One good answer is: Whoever agreed in advance to accept the liability. While it is almost impossible to assign liability in a fair and effective way after the fact, it is usually quite easy to do so prior to the transaction. If buyers want warranties against defects or the promise of monetary compensation in the event of an accident, they can refuse to purchase unless they get the contracts for which they are looking. Sellers will only offer such guarantees when they expect the benefits in additional sales to exceed the expected costs. Sellers will presumably start accepting responsibility for mishaps that they are in a good position to control, while buyers will accept the liabilities that they can bear more cheaply than they can persuade sellers to shoulder them. Sellers and buyers alike will have incentives to search for and use all information which they have a comparative advantage in gathering.

Our courts in recent years have been moving *away from* this approach to the problem of liability, apparently influenced by the belief that some parties have the power to negotiate and enforce unfair contracts. Ordinary consumers are too ignorant, from this perspective, to defend themselves against large corporations or expert professionals who know how to write contracts that will let them behave irresponsibly and get away with it. So the courts have been throwing out prior agreements negotiated by the parties and allowing juries to determine liability — after the fact, of course. Juries are drawn from that same population of ordinary consumers who were previously judged incapable of looking out after their own interests. Asked to resolve complex technical questions, they often fall back on the "deep-pocket" principle: "We don't know who is at fault, but these poor people were hurt and those other parties are rich enough to compensate them."

The fairness of that approach to liability must certainly be questioned. Its long-run consequences are equally disturbing. When liability is arbitrarily assigned to the deepest pocket in the neighborhood, possessors of deep pockets will leave the neighborhood. Many products and services whose use entails substantial risk will not be supplied, regardless of the benefits. Cities will close public parks rather than accept liability for the consequences of every foolish act performed on playground equipment; pharmaceutical manufacturers will no longer produce life-saving vaccines if they must pay enormous sums to the tiny fraction of users who suffer adverse side effects; life will become less safe as firms refuse to introduce new and safer technology because the potential liability costs are too high.

Caveat emptor means: let the buyer beware. It is a legal principle, once widely accepted by the courts, which holds that sellers can be liable only for those qualities of a product that they specifically guarantee. Beyond that, the buyer must pay the consequences of a mistaken purchase. That doctrine has now been almost totally eclipsed by *caveat venditor*, let the seller beware, on the assumption that sellers are always in a better position to anticipate and prevent mistakes and to provide compensation when mistakes occur. Buyers increasingly are receiving the legal right to demand compensation from sellers for any deficiency in the product, including deficiencies of which the seller could not be aware and even some deficiencies created by improper buyer use of the product. The buyer of a rotary lawnmower who cuts off a finger by pulling grass from the mower while it is running may be

"Deep-pocket" liability is attractive to jurors but dangerous for everyone (Is it fair?)

able to extract financial compensation from the manufacturer by arguing that there wasn't an adequate warning, or that the mower should have been designed so that its user couldn't do such a foolish thing.

People respond to the costs that they expect to bear. If sellers must pay for foolish actions by buyers, they will attempt to prevent foolish actions. How? By selling only foolproof products. Should we applaud? The trouble is that foolproof products will be very expensive products. When mattress manufacturers sell only mattresses that cannot be ignited by a lighted cigarette, everyone who buys a new mattress must pay for a quality that is useful only to the small minority that falls asleep while holding lit cigarettes. That helps a few, but harms many more.

Sellers have a cost advantage in the generation of a great deal of information about products and in the creation of many product safeguards; but with other kinds of information and safeguards the comparative advantage will lie with buyers. If *caveat emptor* once compelled buyers to take high-cost actions to protect themselves, *caveat venditor* is now compelling sellers to take some precautions for which buyers could undoubtedly find much less costly substitutes.

Physicians and Malpractice Suits

The furor over malpractice suits against physicians and the rise in the cost of malpractice insurance raises similar questions. Malpractice once meant negligent or improper action by a physician that resulted in death or injury to the patient. Increasingly today it means making a mistake, any mistake at all that results in harm to the patient, even if the physician's diagnosis and treatment satisfied the highest standards of currently acceptable medical procedures. Where will this take us?

If physicians are held liable for malpractice whenever they make a mistake, they will try even harder to avoid making mistakes. Isn't that what we want? Not altogether. We actually *want* physicians to accept the risk of making mistakes when the cost to the patient of avoiding mistakes becomes greater than the cost of committing them. Forget about money costs, which tend to introduce irrelevant emotions into the discussion, and simply set pain against pain and death against death. How many tests should a physician perform before settling on a diagnosis? Each additional test reduces the probability of pain or death from a particular disease but also entails pain and risk of its own. Would you want to submit to a spinal tap to be certain you don't have an obscure but fatal disease never yet found outside the is-land of Madura in the Java Sea?

The common contention that even the smallest risk of death is too great to accept simply makes no sense. It might make sense if risk could always be avoided without incur-ring new risks. That isn't the case, however. It only appears to be the case to those who concentrate on just one risk at a time. The harsh-sounding truth is that some ways of pro-longing life are not worth the cost. The apparent harshness of that statement disappears when we recall that resources used in one way to reduce the number of probable deaths are not available for use in other ways that could possibly prevent an even larger number of premature deaths. It's always a good idea to ask, "What will we do instead?" We might, for example, prevent a few airplane crashes if we prohibited all takeoffs in inclement weather; but we would thereby cause far more travelers to die in accidents. Many people, pre-vented by the safety regulation from taking a commercial airline flight, would substitute a much more dangerous auto-mobile trip.

We can never do only one thing.

It also helps to remember that we're dealing with prob-abilities and uncertainty. If the highway department uses the rest of its budget to straighten out Deadman's Curve, where five people die each year, and consequently leaves uncorrected the Lake Road grade crossing, where three people die each year, the department does *not* thereby "sentence three people to death." No particular persons must die because of the highway department's decision. And any driver who wants to get through that crossing safely has the option to stop, look, and listen. It may in fact be much more productive of "saved lives" in this case to take dollars out of highway improve-ments and put them into warning signs, thereby increasing the responsibility of buyers (drivers) for their own safety and reducing the responsibility of suppliers (highway builders).

Safety is a complex and multifaceted good that can be produced in an endless variety of ways. It tends to be pro-duced most satisfactorily in a society where the rules of the game are clear and stable and people are encouraged to negotiate the arrangements they prefer.

Once Over Lightly

An opportunity of which you're unaware is not a real oppor-tunity. Information is therefore a valuable resource, whose possession enables people to increase their wealth.

Information is a scarce good whose production usually entails costs. The efficient decisionmaker accumulates additional information only as long as the anticipated marginal benefit is greater than the marginal cost.

A great deal of economic activity is best understood as a response to the fact that information is a scarce good. The much-abused "middleman" is in large part a specialist in information production. Just as the real estate broker enables prospective buyers and sellers to locate one another, so the typical retailer provides customers with knowledge of the goods sellers are offering and brings sellers into contact with those who want the sellers' offerings.

The common habit of viewing the middleman as an unproductive bandit on the highway of trade stems from the erroneous assumption that information is a free good.

Everyone who makes a decision in the absence of complete information about the future consequences of all available opportunities is a speculator. So everyone is a speculator.

People who think they know more than others about the relationship between present and future scarcities will want to buy in one time period for sale in the other. If they are correct, they make a profit on their superior insight and also transport goods through time from periods of lesser to greater scarcity. If they're wrong in their predictions, they perversely move goods from periods of greater to lesser scarcity and suffer the penalty of a personal loss on their transactions.

Because prices are summary indicators of scarcity, they are valuable information. Those whose buying and selling activities create prices are generating information that is useful to others.

A person who is able to shift the full cost of mistakes onto others has little incentive to gather information before acting. A person who is compelled to bear the full cost of mistakes committed by others will attempt to keep them from committing mistakes. Avoiding mistakes is also costly, but people will tend to slight the costs that they themselves don't have to bear.

The cost of producing information is not the same for everyone. If a system of appropriate incentives is allowed to evolve, people will specialize in the production of those kinds of information in which they have comparative advantage.

Questions for Discussion

1. Students frequently complain about the low prices the campus bookstore pays for used texts. Why then do they sell to the bookstore? Is it true that they cannot find a buyer on their own? Or is it more true that they are unwilling to go to the trouble (incur the cost) of finding a buyer on their own? What useful service does the college bookstore perform in handling used texts? Can you be sure it's a genuine service and not just a "rip-off"?

2. Evaluate the following paragraph from a newspaper article:

   > One sure way to save money on groceries is to eliminate the middleman by buying directly from farmers and other suppliers. This is what a group of socially motivated and normally hungry people have decided to do by forming a grocery cooperative.

   If it really is possible to save money on groceries by "buying directly," why do so few people do it?

3. If you found that you could reduce your bills for new clothing 10 percent by buying exclusively from catalogs, would you do it? Why would some people be unwilling to take advantage of this "saving"? What do people do when they go "shopping"? How often have you discovered what you were looking for by seeing what sellers were offering?

4. Would you expect prices for goods of similar quality offered in garage sales to vary more than prices for goods offered in regular retail outlets? Why? Do the differences in prices mean that someone is being cheated, or that someone is taking unfair advantage of someone else?

5. A man approaches you in a busy airport terminal, shows you a handsome wristwatch, which he says is worth $135, and offers to let you have it for $25. Would you buy it? Would you be more willing to buy it if you had better information? What do you "know" when you buy a watch from an established local jeweler that you do not know in this situation?

6. Have you ever tested your butcher's scales to be sure they are accurate? How do you know you aren't being consistently short-weighted?

7. Why does a new car lose so much of its value in the first year? Is it because Americans have an irrational attachment to cars that are new rather than used?

   (a) Which year-old car is more likely to be on the used-car market: one that performed handsomely for its owner or one that had to be taken in regularly for repairs during its first year?

   (b) Which set of vehicles being offered for sale will contain a larger percentage of vehicles with defects known to the seller but unknown to the buyer: new cars or year-old cars?

   (c) What does all this imply about the prices sellers are willing to accept and that buyers are willing to offer for year-old cars, relative to what they would be if all buyers and sellers had complete information?

(d) Why do used-car dealers sometimes provide warranties with the cars they sell and at other times advertise "As Is — No Warranties, All Sales Final"?

8. You find out in late December that you can probably make $1000 on a business deal if you can gain the goodwill of a client by getting him two tickets to the Super Bowl game. You manage to buy two well-located seats from a scalper for $250. Were you cheated by the scalper? Or are you glad that scalpers exist? Why do so many people intensely dislike scalpers?

9. The spring graduation exercises at Boston University in 1989 featured both U.S. President George Bush and French President François Mitterand. Each of the 5600 graduates was given four free tickets. An active market for tickets developed, and some were reportedly sold for $100.

    (a) Do you think the students who sold their tickets were behaving unethically? (The transactions were *not* illegal.)
    (b) Were the people who paid $100 for "free" tickets exploited?

10. The Augusta National golf club sells badges that function as tickets to the four-day Masters golf tournament for $90. The event has been a sellout for almost 20 years, and a 5000-name waiting list has been closed since 1978. Augusta National requires badge purchasers to sign a pledge that they will not resell their tickets. *The Wall Street Journal* sports commentator Frederick C. Klein found the going rate for Masters badges in 1989 to be $1500.

    (a) Why doesn't Augusta National raise the price of the badges?
    (b) Why does the golf club want to prevent reselling of badges?

11. Suppose that you are leaving tomorrow for a two-week combined business and vacation trip to a distant location. You'll be traveling by plane.

    (a) In what way are you speculating as you pack your suitcase?
    (b) On which side would you be more inclined to err — taking too many clothes and having to haul heavy suitcases around, or taking too few and finding yourself without an item you want?
    (c) Would your answer to the previous question differ according to whether you were planning to be in a large city or a remote resort?
    (d) Suppose you take only a single pair of dress shoes and accidentally spill ink on one of them just before an important business meeting. You dash out quickly and buy a new pair of shoes. Explain how the shoe seller's willingness to take a risk reduced your risk in taking only a single pair of dress shoes.

12. The June 18, 1979, issue of *Time* magazine contained an article on hoarding in the United States in which a number of social scientists were quoted. A sociologist said that gasoline hoarding was not rational but rather a result of Americans' emotional stake in their cars. A historian said hoarding was an absolutely typical American trait. Some attributed hoarding to a

"shortage psychosis," and others spoke of "panic buying." Another sociologist said that strong leadership was required to stop such "competitive behavior."

(a) How could we decide whether hoarding is irrational, psychotic, a national character trait, a product of emotion and panic, *or* an intelligent response to uncertainty?

(b) What is the difference between hoarding and maintaining an appropriate level of inventory?

(c) Why do both business firms and households maintain inventories? How do they decide on the proper level of inventories for particular goods?

13. Are you speculating when you buy fire insurance on your home? Could you save money by getting together with your friends to form an insurance cooperative, thereby eliminating the necessity of paying something to a middleman (the insurance company)? What kinds of useful information do insurance companies provide?

14. You decide in May that the coming summer's corn crop will be much larger and the fall corn price consequently much lower than most people expect.

(a) To act on your beliefs, should you buy or should you sell December corn futures? (*Futures* are contracts to buy or sell at a future date at a price established now.)

(b) If a substantial number of knowledgeable people come to share your opinion about the size of this summer's crop, what will happen to the price of December corn futures?

(c) What information will this change in the price of corn futures convey to current holders and users of corn?

(d) How will this information affect their decisions about holding corn for future sale or use?

(e) How will these decisions, based on the information provided by the change in the price of December corn futures, affect June consumption?

(f) Can speculators carry a bumper crop *backward in time* from a period of lesser to a period of greater scarcity?

15. *The Wall Street Journal* published two articles in the winter of 1985 on food and famine in Sudan and Ethiopia. One was titled "The Tragedy of Sudan's Spreading Starvation Is That It's Caused by Man's Errors, Not Nature's" (January 22, 1985); the other was headed "Getting Excess U.S. Food to World's Hungry Is Complicated by Politics and Bureaucracy" (March 14, 1985).

(a) The former article said that the government in Sudan "has had to impose credit restrictions to stop banks from financing speculators hoping to profit from the misery." It also quoted a relief specialist working in the Sudan who claimed that assistance always came too late and who called for "a system of advance warning and standby funds." Don't speculators provide a system of advance warning? Do speculators who "profit from . . . misery" create the misery from which they profit or add to it? Or do they alleviate the misery from which they profit?

(b) The article also described wasteful crosshauling of food: trucks taking food from A to B passed other trucks hauling food from B to A. It also said that the United States stopped selling food and began giving it away when British charitable organizations protested that the policy of selling the food was depriving those who needed it most. A U.S. official said that the selling policy was instituted at the urging of local governments "who didn't want local markets disrupted," but the United States agreed nonetheless to change the policy. Do you see a connection between disruption of local markets and wasteful crosshauling or other delays in getting contributed food from dockside to hungry mouths?

(c) Suppose that the U.S. government and all other contributors to famine relief were to distribute among the starving people the money that had been contributed, and let these people purchase food for themselves. Do you think food would more quickly and surely get into the hands of hungry people under such a system than under one in which Western relief organizations try to handle the distribution of the food itself?

(d) Those who condemn shopkeepers and other middlemen as worthless, wasteful, and wicked seem to be saying that the physical distribution of valuable goods is not a difficult social problem to handle once the goods have been produced. The African nations that have instituted capital punishment for those who speculate in food supplies seem to be saying the same thing. The two articles cited suggest otherwise. But would you want to be a merchant participating in a food distribution system when a charge of speculating or profiteering could result in the death penalty?

16. A construction company signs a contract in January with a developer calling for the completion of 100 houses by the end of October at a price fixed in the contract. The construction company wants to protect itself against the possibility of sizable increases in the price of lumber that could wipe out any profit on the transaction. The Chicago Mercantile Exchange offers an opportunity to buy or sell lumber futures, which are contracts calling for the delivery in specified future months of 150,000 board feet of spruce, pine, or fir at a price agreed upon now. A lumber futures contract is available that calls for July delivery.

(a) Would the construction company want to buy or to sell July lumber futures when it signs the construction contract in January?

(b) Suppose that July lumber futures are trading in January at $200 per 1000 board feet. When July arrives, construction lumber has risen in price to $220 per 100 board feet. As a result, the construction company will have to pay 10 percent more for lumber than it expected to pay. How will it use its futures contracts to offset this loss?

(c) Suppose the price of lumber had fallen to $180 instead of rising to $220. Why will this not result in an unexpectedly large profit for the construction company on its contract with the developer?

17. Suppose you are in your car trying to make a left turn across heavy traffic on a busy highway. You plan to turn as soon as the large truck coming toward you has passed. But then you notice that there is a long line of cars following the truck. You make an instant decision and turn in front of the truck.

   Assume you saved 2 minutes by turning at that time rather than waiting for the whole line of traffic to clear, that you value your time at $6 an hour, and there was a probability of .0001 that your car would stall and the truck would be unable to stop so that you would be killed. What was the implicit value that you placed on avoiding the collision when you decided to turn? Would it be correct to say that this is the implicit maximum value you assign to your own life?

18. A letter to the editor of an urban newspaper, criticizing as "foolhardy" a fatal attempt by a Japanese mountain climber to make a solo ascent of Mt. McKinley in the winter, concluded with this sentence: "Safe mountaineering is and always should be the bottom line." What is "safe mountaineering"?

19. My neighbor is an orthopedic surgeon who enjoys building things out of wood. He purchased a power saw to reduce the time he had to spend cutting lumber. But he subsequently decided that he didn't want to risk an accident and sold the saw to me. Since he is a more careful worker than I am, the probability that he would have severed a finger using the saw is less than the probability that I will do so. Nonetheless, I am willing to take the risk while he is not. Use the concept of opportunity cost to explain the difference in our attitudes toward the hazards of using power saws.

20. When a manufacturing firm cuts costs in an overseas plant by adopting occupational safety standards that are more lax than the standards governing its domestic operations, is it exploiting its foreign employees? Why might potential workers in a very poor country be willing, even eager, to accept workplace hazards that workers would not accept in a wealthier country? Who is harmed and therefore most likely to protest the adoption of less-strict workplace safety standards in the operation of overseas plants?

21. Does a policy of protecting people against losses due to their own mistakes make those mistakes more frequent and the losses consequently greater?

   (a) Will insured houses have more fires than uninsured houses, other things being equal? Why?

   (b) Would people take more effective precautions against theft of their automobiles if insurance companies stopped selling policies that offered compensation for losses due to theft?

(c) Why is it so much easier to purchase insurance against loss due to fire than against loss due to being laid off or discharged from one's job?

(d) People who work in jobs covered by unemployment compensation do have some of the benefits of insurance against job loss. Do you think this causes people to be laid off or discharged more often?

22. If the Food and Drug Administration prolongs the testing period for new drugs in order to protect consumers against threats to their life and health from the premature introduction of drugs with unknown but dangerous side effects, will it actually succeed in protecting consumers? What is the threat to life and health that the FDA thereby increases?

23. A commissioner of the Food and Drug Administration said that, although he was willing to weigh health risks against health benefits in formulating commission rulings, he was absolutely opposed to weighing health risks against economic factors. Evaluate this statement.

24. We can reduce the probability that children will die from accidentally swallowing large quantities of drugs by requiring drug dispensers to provide containers with child-resistant caps on request. Can we further reduce that probability by prohibiting the dispensation of drugs except in containers with child-resistant caps? What will drug purchasers do who have difficulty opening these caps, such as people with arthritis, if they are not allowed to purchase prescription drugs in containers with caps that are easy to open?

25. Economists Richard McKenzie and John Warner have estimated that highway deaths would rise by about 150 per year if tighter safety regulations increased air fares by 10 percent. Through what processes would this occur? (McKenzie and Warner conservatively assume that the price elasticity of demand for air travel is only 0.1, and that only 40 percent of those who don't fly because of the higher fares will choose to make their planned trip by car.) The average number of major airline fatalities per year has been *less than* 150 since airline deregulation in 1978. What does this indicate about the desirability of imposing tighter safety regulations on commercial airlines? If new discoveries enable the airlines to increase safety at no cost or a trivial cost, will the airlines adopt the innovations without being legally required to do so? (Data are from a *Wall Street Journal* article of March 7, 1989.)

26. In the autumn of 1981 authorities in the Soviet Union raised the price of vodka in an attempt to reduce alcoholism. Two years later they lowered the price again, reportedly in order to stop the increase in the incidence of alcohol poisoning. What general rule is illustrated by this case, the case of the child-resistant medicine caps, and the case of overly safe airplane travel?

27. A bill introduced in Congress in 1989 would prohibit federal employees from receiving reimbursement if they stayed at hotels that did not have both sprinklers and smoke detectors. The purpose, of course, was to put pressure on hotels to install these safety devices; the round-about method

was chosen because the constitution doesn't grant this regulatory authority to the federal government. Do you think the benefit in enhanced safety is likely to be large enough to justify the cost of installing sprinkler systems in hotels that do not currently have them? Would you agree that the cost is justified even if it saves only one life?

28. In 1977 Seattle passed an ordinance requiring that new multilevel parking garages have barriers at least 18 inches high to stop automobiles from going through the walls. The ordinance was not made retroactive. In 1987 a car broke through a fifth-floor wall in a parking garage that did not have the 18-inch barriers because it had been constructed prior to the ordinance. Three people were killed. A local newspaper editorialized as follows:

> It was a freak, as well as tragic, accident. The odds against a similar occurrence are high. Yet certainly it is possible. The City Council therefore must not hesitate in ordering that all multilevel garages in the city be brought into compliance with what are now ten-year-old safety standards.

(a) What is the flaw in the editorial's argument?

(b) Why does it often make sense to apply more stringent safety standards only to new construction while exempting existing structures? Consider, for example, a proposal to make all housing "earthquake proof."

29. The text asserts that the issue of insider trading is a complex one. You might be able to convince yourself of this by trying to answer the following questions.

(a) An art expert spots a drawing in an antique store that looks to her like a Pablo Picasso. If it is a genuine Picasso, it is worth thousands of dollars. The price tag says $35. Should she say nothing and buy it? Tell the store owner that she suspects the drawing is by Picasso? Buy it and share her profit with the antique store owner if it turns out in fact to be by Picasso? Can she be confident the store owner will in turn share *his* profit with the person who sold it to him?

(b) A print shop employee deduces the identity of a corporation that is about to become a takeover target from documents he is preparing for the corporation planning the takeover. Should he be permitted to use this information to purchase stock in the target company?

(c) An oil company is about to announce that it has discovered a huge new oil field in Brazil. Should employees of the company who already know the good news be permitted to purchase their company's stock prior to the public announcement?

(d) A stockbroker with a long list of clients to whom he gives investment advice learns from a disgruntled employee that a seemingly profitable insurance firm has been fraudulently managed and is about to declare bankruptcy. Should he be permitted to advise his clients to sell their stock in the insurance company before news of its plight gets out? Or must he make the information he has acquired public before he may legally advise his clients to sell?

  (e) The chief executive of a corporation believes she has put together an extremely competent management team that is going to produce much larger profits for the company than it has been accustomed to earning. Should she be permitted to buy large amounts of the company's stock without first publicizing her belief?

  (f) Should people selling their homes be morally obligated to tell potential buyers about all the hidden defects? A basement that floods after extremely heavy rains? Neighbors who have loud all-night parties outdoors in the summer? Squirrels that like to nest in the attic?

30. Does advertising communicate valuable information? Does it inform, persuade, manipulate, or misinform? Consider each of the following instances of advertising.

  (a) The telephone company's Yellow Pages.

  (b) Newspaper want-ads.

  (c) Grocery-store advertisements of "specials" in the newspaper's food section.

  (d) A television commercial showing rich and handsome people getting in and out of the advertiser's automobile.

31. Much advertising conveys little information beyond the name of the product. Is there any way that such advertising could benefit consumers? Does the fact that a seller is willing to spend money publicizing the name of a product indicate anything about the seller's confidence in that product's quality?

32. Walter Wriston, former chairman of Citicorp, argued in an address to the American Society of Newspaper Editors that the government was suppressing information or censoring the news when it tried to prohibit firms from posting higher prices. He argued that firms don't so much raise prices as announce that prices have gone up. In what sense are price controls a form of censorship?

33. Since the Bill of Rights in the U.S. Constitution prohibits government from censoring the promises of political candidates, however absurd or irresponsible, why doesn't it afford the same protection to commercial advertisements? Is it because deceptive commercial claims do more damage to the society and its members than do deceptive political claims? Is it because citizens can more easily and effectively evaluate political claims on their own, but need considerable protection against deceptive claims for commercial products? If neither of these seems an adequate explanation for the difference, what explanation would you suggest?

34. The news media report that a severe frost has done extensive damage to the Florida orange crop and that frozen orange juice will soon be in very short supply. How would you evaluate each of the following actions? Choose one of the options: completely fair, probably fair, probably unfair, totally unfair.

(a) Local grocer raises the price on all frozen orange juice in the store as soon as she hears the news.

(b) Homemaker rushes to the store and buys a three-month supply of frozen orange juice as soon as she hears the news.

(c) Orange grower whose crop was not touched by the frost raises the price for all his oranges as soon as he hears the news.

(d) Orange grower whose crop was severely damaged raises the price for all of her remaining oranges as soon as she hears the news.

(e) Orange juice processors rush to purchase as many oranges as they can as soon as they hear the news.

Are all your answers consistent?

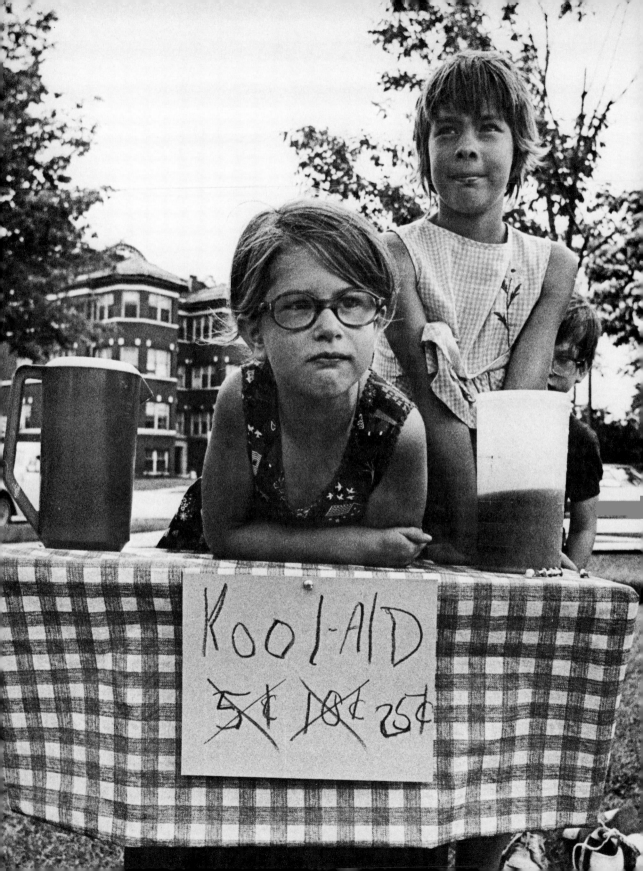

Chapter 8

Price Setting and the Question of Monopoly

The term *administered prices* was first introduced to public discussion in the 1930s in order to make a distinction between prices that were set by supply and demand and prices supposedly set unilaterally by sellers. Since that time the term has been widely used, especially by those who believe that the U.S. economic system is dominated by large corporations. Some critics have accused professional economists of ignoring the role of administered prices in the American economy, and of pretending that prices are all set by supply and demand. According to most of these critics, the American economy is today largely controlled by monopolists and oligopolists, who pay no attention to supply and demand, but instead use their market power to manipulate prices according to their own selfish and narrow interests.

It is impossible to evaluate any of these claims without first obtaining a clearer notion of what is meant by such terms as *administered prices* and *monopolist*. We have consciously steered around these issues as much as we could in the preceding chapters. The tactic that usually enabled us to do so was the implicit assumption that there were so many buyers and sellers in any market at which we were looking that none of them had any power to affect the price through individual action. It is now time to look more closely at issues that have been bypassed.

Who Qualifies as a Monopolist

We begin with the word *monopoly*, the product of two Greek words meaning "one seller." Are there any monopolists in that strict sense of the word? Try to think of something that is sold exclusively by one seller.

Local telephone service suggests itself as a good example. But is it an accurate example? There were many independent sellers of telephone service in the United States, as a matter of fact, even before the breakup of AT&T in 1984. Still, that may be beside the point. For any given buyer there is typically one seller, since telephone companies usually enjoy exclusive selling privileges in particular areas. On the other hand, buyers don't have to live in a given area; they can move to another franchise area if they prefer the product there. Back comes a justifiably impatient snort: "That's irrelevant." But it's not completely irrelevant. Moving your residence may be a prohibitively expensive way to shift your telephone patronage, and it's hard to imagine people actually moving just because they resent the local phone company. But that *is* a way of obtaining a substitute product. And by its absurdity, our example calls attention to the crux of the problem: the availability of substitutes.

Suppose we redefine the commodity sold by telephone companies and call it "communication services." There would be nothing intrinsically misleading about that. After all, that is why anyone wants a telephone: to obtain communication services. But if this is the product being sold, the telephone company is clearly *not* a monopolist, but rather a seller in competition with Western Union, the post office, various messenger and delivery services, loud shouting, fast running, and all sorts of computer communication techniques. The point of all this is simply that, if we define the commodity broadly enough, not a single commodity in the country is sold by a monopolist.

Now let's look at the other side of the coin. Suppose we define the commodity very narrowly. If telegrams are not the same thing as telephone calls, neither is a gallon of milk at the little store next door the same thing as a gallon of milk three blocks away at the supermarket. If you have no car, are rocking a screaming baby who won't stop until fed, and have no one to leave the baby with, the milk three blocks away is a vividly different commodity from the milk at the store next door. Ask any parent of a small baby. Thus, we are forced to conclude that, when the commodity is defined narrowly enough, every seller is a monopolist, since no two sellers will ever be offering completely identical products.

We're trying to convince you that the word *monopoly* is extraordinarily ambiguous. For everyone or no one is a sole seller depending on how we define the commodity being sold. Furthermore, there is no satisfactory way to decide in all cases just how broadly or narrowly the concept of a commodity ought to be defined. The Supreme Court of the United States has sometimes listened to persuasive arguments on both sides of a contested definition and then di-

vided in its decision. Take cellophane, for example. Is it a
separate commodity or should it be put in the category "flexible wrapping materials"? The answer given in cases such as
this may determine whether a manufacturer is convicted
under federal antimonopoly laws.

Alternatives, Elasticity, and Market Power

So let's try another approach. What would be so bad about a
single seller if we found one? The telephone company hints
at the answer when it advertises: "We may be the only
phone company in town, but we try not to act like it." If we
find a case where there really is only one seller, the customer will have no alternatives. No one wants to be without
alternatives. The poorer our alternatives, the weaker our
position and the more easily we can be taken advantage of.

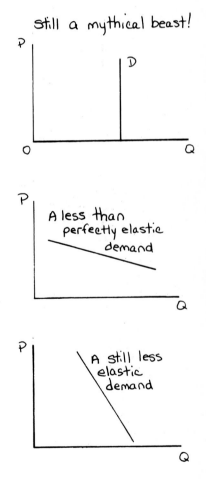

still a mythical beast!

A less than perfectly elastic demand

A still less elastic demand

But we learned in Chapter 2 that there are always some
alternatives. There is a substitute for anything, even the services of the local telephone company. After all, no one
"needs" a telephone. On the other hand, a phone is a valued
convenience for many families and business firms. The concept from economics that suggests itself is price elasticity of
demand.

No seller is a monopolist in the strictest sense of the
word because there is no such thing as a *perfectly* inelastic
demand. No seller has any buyer totally over the barrel. On
the other hand, very few sellers of anything face perfectly
elastic demand curves. Anything less than complete elasticity means that sellers will retain some business when they
raise their price, which in turn implies that sellers have at
least a morsel of market power. Where is the line between a
morsel and monopoly?

There is no clear line of demarcation unless we decide
to draw one arbitrarily. Elasticities of demand reflect the
availability of substitutes; other things remaining equal, the
more good substitutes there are for anything, the more elastic will be the demand for it. Market power is thus seen to
be a matter of degree and to be inversely related to elasticity
of demand. Defined in this way, the term *market power* has
a meaning that we can talk about and use. But we have not
yet found a useful definition for the word *monopoly*.

Privileges and Restrictions

Let's try another approach. In the early nineteenth century
there was often no distinction made in the United States

between a monopoly and a corporation. The reason was that corporations had always been created by special governmental acts. They received, whether from Crown and Parliament before the Revolution or from state and national legislatures afterward, special "patents," as they were called: official documents granting rights and privileges not available to others. Corporate charters were therefore called "grants of monopoly," since they gave to one party a power that was withheld from others. The East India Company was such a "monopoly," and the special privilege of selling tea in the colonies, given to it in 1773, helped bring on the American Revolution.

Here is another and quite different meaning of monopoly, one related to acts of the state. If the state allows some to engage in an activity but prosecutes others for doing so, or if it taxes or restricts some sellers but not others, or if it grants protection or assistance to some while compelling others to make their own way unaided, the state is creating exclusive privileges. This meaning for the word *monopoly* has contemporary relevance as well as historical significance.

Many business organizations operate with monopoly grants of this kind. In the name of all sorts of commendable-sounding goals — public safety, fair competition, stability, national security, efficiency — governments at all levels have imposed restrictions on entry into various industries or trades. The beneficiaries of these restrictions always include the parties who can escape them. These parties will rarely admit that they enjoy a grant of monopoly power. But the effect of the restrictions nonetheless is to prevent some from competing who would otherwise do so.

We are not saying that restrictions on entry into a market are always to be condemned, or that the businesses which benefit necessarily behave badly afterward, or that consumers can never be better off as a consequence of restrictions on competition. We are only concerned that the restrictions be noted so that their consequences can be evaluated. They will often turn out to be different from what most people assume. We could, if we wished, use the word *monopolist* to describe any individual or organization operating with the advantage of special privileges granted by the government. The trouble is that most people no longer use the word in this way. By such a definition, the postal service is a monopolist, as are most public utilities, many liquor stores, morticians, and crop dusters; the American Medical Association, state bar associations, and labor unions; farmers with acreage allotments, licensed barbers, and most taxicab firms. The list is long indeed.

And so we are going to take the heroic step of dropping the word *monopoly* from our working vocabulary. Its meanings are too many and too vague. "'When I use a word,' Humpty Dumpty said in a rather scornful tone, 'it means just what I choose it to mean — neither more nor less.'" *Monopoly* is a favorite of contemporary Humpty Dumpties. And that's why we are not going to employ it. We shall try to use alternative terms that are more likely to communicate the precise situation we have in mind.

Price Takers and Price Searchers

Let's go back now to the phrase with which this chapter began: administered prices. Is there a distinction between administered prices and prices that are set by supply and demand?

It's a free country, as they say, and businesses are usually free to set their own prices. The USX Corporation (formerly United States Steel) has substantial discretion when it prints its price lists, and a wheat farmer from Kansas can feel quite safe from the threat of prosecution if he decides to offer his crop at $5.00 per bushel. But there is obviously an important difference that helps to explain why USX hires people to decide what its prices should be and wheat farmers do not. The differrence, we shall nonetheless insist, is a difference of degree, not kind.

Take the case of the wheat farmer first. If he consults the financial pages of his newspaper or tunes in for the noonday market reports, he will find that number 2 ordinary hard Kansas City wheat opened at $3.43¾ a bushel. That news may disappoint or delight him, but there is almost nothing he can do to change it. If he decides that the price is an excellent one and sells his entire crop for immediate delivery, the market will feel scarcely a ripple. Even if he is one of the biggest wheat farmers in the state, he is still such a small part of the total number of those offering to buy or sell wheat that he cannot affect the price. The difference between what the closing price will be if he sells all his crop and what it will be if he sells only half of it will not be as much as ¼ cent.

Economists therefore call the wheat farmer a *price taker*. He cannot affect the price by his own actions. The price at the local grain elevator is determined by the actions of many buyers and sellers all over the country. If the farmer exer-

Price	Quantity Demanded (of that farmer's wheat)
$3.45	None at all
$3.43	All he has
$3.41	All he has

(when the market price is $3.43¾)

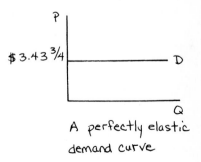

A perfectly elastic demand curve

cises his legal right to put a price tag on his wheat 2 cents higher than the market decrees, he will sell no wheat. And since he can sell all the wheat he has at the going price, he has no incentive to offer to sell any wheat at less than the going price. Price takers face perfectly elastic demand curves, or what for all practical purposes amount to perfectly elastic demand curves. The demand curves are horizontal at the going price.

Most sellers are not in this position. They can raise their prices if they choose, without losing all their sales. And, unlike the farmer, they can't always sell everything they're capable of producing without lowering their prices. At higher prices they will sell less; at lower prices they will be able to sell more. They must choose a price or set of prices. Economists therefore call them *price searchers.* Torn between the desire for higher prices and the desire for larger sales, they must search out the price or set of prices most advantageous to them.

Price searchers include USX, the trustees of a private university weighing a tuition increase, the proprietor of a local grocery store, and the little boy selling lemonade on a hot afternoon. There is a long tradition in economics of referring to all price searchers as monopolists. But this is a technical use of the word that is confusing to everyone except professional economists. Since the little boy selling lemonade does not face a perfectly elastic demand curve, he is not a price taker but a price searcher. It seems silly to anyone not steeped in the history of economics to call him a monopolist. So we shall not do it. The term *price searcher* captures the situation in which we're interested. Price searchers all have some market power, but it is a matter of degree inversely related to the elasticity of the demand the seller faces.

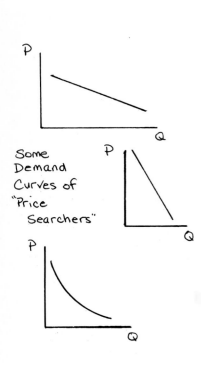

Some Demand Curves of "Price Searchers"

Price Takers' Markets and "Optimal" Resource Allocation

Economists applied the disapproving term *monopolist* to what we shall call *price searcher* in large part because they wanted to emphasize the different consequences of these two types of price setting. Markets in which all buyers and sellers were price takers were graced with the approving term *competitive markets.* We want to point out the advantages they saw in price takers' markets without adopting the misleading monopolistic–competitive distinction, which erroneously implies that price searchers face no competition. To do

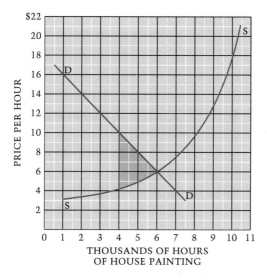

FIGURE 8A   Demand and supply curves for house painting in Pratte Falls

so we shall use the graph of Figure 8A, which shows the demand and supply curves for house painters during a particular summer in the town of Pratte Falls.

The number of house-painting hours that will be demanded and supplied depends on the price per hour of house painters' services. Since people's skills in this area differ considerably, we shall simplify our exposition by assuming that each hour of service shown on the horizontal axis has been adjusted for quality. If Freddie Fumblefingers is only 40 percent as productive in an hour as the average Pratte Falls painter, he will take 2½ hours to supply "one hour" of the good shown on the graph. Betsy Brightbrush, who is three times as good as the average, supplies "one hour" of house painting every 20 tminutes.

The first point to remember is that supply curves are marginal opportunity-cost curves. The curve labeled SS in Figure 8A shows the value of all the opportunities given up as Pratte Fallers provide progressively larger amounts of house-painting services. The people who contribute to the lower-left portions of the curve are people with large comparative advantages in house painting, because they are either extremely adept painters or extraordinarily inept at everything else. The upper-right portion of the the curve, including sections not even shown, depicts the supply responses of those who would have to give up a lucrative law practice to paint, who are subject to attacks of dizziness at heights above seven feet, or who for any other reason must sacrifice a highly valued opportunity in order to supply an hour of house painting. Keep in mind that the marginal-cost curve of any single individual will also eventually slope upward to the right. The value of the opportunities forgone as one devotes more and more time to any particular activity is bound to increase as that activity crowds out alternative activities, simply because people sacrifice their least-valued opportunities first and give up more highly valued opportunities only in response to a stronger inducement.[1]

If the price now settles down at $6 an hour, so that 6000 hours of the good are exchanged over the summer, the heart of many economists will leap with a special kind of joy. Why? Because at the price of $6, given the demand and supply curves, no unit of the good is being produced whose marginal opportunity cost, as represented by the supply curve, exceeds its marginal benefit, as represented by the demand curve. Moreover, every unit of the good whose marginal benefit exceeds its marginal cost is being produced. And how could we do better than that? Economists have traditionally gone so far as to call such an arrangement an *optimal allocation of resources. Optimal* means best, which is surely excessive praise; but let's look a little more closely to see exactly what's happening here.

Suppose that the people supplying those 6000 hours at $6 an hour decide that they deserve larger incomes and somehow persuade the town council to pass a law setting $10 an hour as the minimum price for an hour of house-painting services. We'll suppose further that the law is effectively enforced. What will happen? Only 4000 hours will now be demanded. And since that's all that can be sold, that's all that will *actually* be supplied, even though, as the graph shows, painters will *want* to supply about twice that amount at a price of $10.

Establishment and enforcement of the $10 price will make some people better off and others worse off. Note that some of those who are worse off may be former house pain-

[1]This hypothetical example also illustrates the fundamental similarity of supply and demand. The people who are willing to pay up to $20 per hour to have someone else paint their houses, and who thereby create that portion of the demand curve below $20, may well be among the people who create the supply curve at prices above $20. Example: "I'll pay up to $20 per hour to get my house painted this summer. But if I have to pay more than that, I'll do it myself." Such a person, who stops demanding and starts supplying to himself at some high enough price may, at an even higher price, also begin supplying to others.

ters forced into less desirable occupations by the legislated
price increase. Economists have no satisfactory way of
balancing one person's gain against another person's loss to
decide whether net social well-being will go up or down as
the result of such a change. About all they can really do is
point out that the Pratte Falls law prevents mutually advantageous exchange. The area under the demand curve between
4000 and 6000 hours represents the dollar value of what demanders are willing to give up to obtain those units of the
good. The area under the supply curve represents the dollar
value of what suppliers are willing to give up to provide
those units of service. The difference between the two areas,
shaded in Figure 8A, is a potential gain from trade that the
ordinance effectively removes by prohibiting any exchanges
at less than $10 an hour.

What does all this have to do with price takers' markets
and their superiority, in traditional economic analysis, over
price searchers' markets? It comes to this: prices that are
fixed above marginal cost rule out some mutually advantageous exchange opportunities. In price takers' markets, sellers don't have the power to set and keep the price above
marginal cost. In price searchers' markets, they do.

How serious that problem is and how high the costs of
correcting it might be are two of the questions that will run
through Chapters 9 and 10.

Administered Prices Once Again

It would seem then that price searchers set their own prices,
whereas price takers accept what the market sets. Is this the
distinction between administered prices and those prices
that are set by supply and demand? Not if one thinks about
it carefully. Every seller in the last analysis sets the final
price, though some sellers can do so with little or no real
searching, because they in effect accept the prevailing price
(price takers). A more serious objection is that price searchers are by no means free from the constraints imposed by
supply and demand.

"Big oil" is a favorite target of those who decry administered prices, but whatever the faults or failings of corporations
in the oil industry, their decisions are surely conditioned by
supply and demand. Supply depends on cost, and cost is
taken into account if price searchers hope to find what they
are looking for, which is presumably the most profitable
price to set. Firms in the oil industry may have excessive
market power. Whether or not they do, or which ones do and

which ones do not, or how much market power any firm has — all these questions can best be investigated by looking at marginal-cost curves and demand curves and how they change over time in response to the pressures of competition. We will discover nothing useful if we pretend that there are firms that "administer" prices *in total disregard of supply and demand.*

So we end up with no usable meaning for the term *administered prices* either. *All* prices are administered and *all* prices are set by supply and demand. The term *administered prices* consequently will not be used in subsequent chapters. An examination of its history would reveal that it has more often been used as a polite "bad word" than as a concept to aid analysis or critical discussion. Economic problems are sufficiently complex without complicating them further by using terms that generate much heat and no light.

One other term appeared in the introductory paragraph: *oligopolist.* The dictionary suggests that an oligopolist is "one of a few sellers." The Big Three in automobiles and the major cigarette manufacturers are commonly cited as examples of oligopoly situations. But what about the daily newspapers in a large city? Or do they compete with other newspapers that can be trucked or flown in, with news magazines, billboards, television, the Yellow Pages? What is the commodity that allegedly has only a few sellers? Should it be broadly or narrowly defined? What about gasoline stations? Hardware stores? Automobile dealers? Shops that restring tennis rackets? How few is few? We don't have to multiply examples to discover that all the problems associated with defining a monopolist as a single seller return to haunt us when we define an oligopolist as one of a few sellers.

There is a special market situation to which many economists have chosen to apply the term *oligopoly.* We'll examine and analyze that situation in Chapter 10. But we shall not use the word *oligopoly,* on the grounds that, like administered prices and monopoly, it creates confusion rather than clarity and understanding.

Once Over Lightly

The word *monopoly* means literally one seller. But whether any seller is the only seller depends on how narrowly or broadly we define the product. Under a sufficiently broad definition, there are innumerable sellers of every product. Under a sufficiently narrow definition, however, every seller's product differs from every other's, and all sellers are monopolists. The word *monopoly* is therefore inherently ambiguous and will not be used in subsequent chapters.

The antisocial connotations of the word *monopoly* stem from the belief that the customers of a sole seller have no alternatives and are therefore at the mercy of the seller. Since there are in fact alternatives to every course of action and substitutes for every good, no seller ever has unlimited power over buyers. Market power is always a matter of degree.

The concept of price elasticity of demand provides a useful way of thinking and talking about the degree of market power. Demand elasticities, which can vary between zero and infinity, reflect the availability of substitutes. The more good alternatives buyers have, the more elastic are the demand curves sellers face and the more limited is the power of sellers to establish terms of sale strongly advantageous to themselves.

In the early years of the United States, a monopoly usually meant an organization to which the government had granted some exclusive privilege. The monopolist was often the only legal seller. Although this meaning of the term is no longer common, it does have contemporary relevance since federal, state, and local governments are extensively involved in the granting of special privileges that restrict competition.

A useful distinction to make in trying to understand how prices are established is the distinction between *price takers* and *price searchers.* Price takers must accept the price decreed by the market. Buyers have such excellent substitutes for the product that any attempt to raise the price or otherwise shift the terms of sale will leave the seller with no customers at all. The price searcher, on the other hand, can sell different quantities at different prices and must therefore search for the most advantageous price.

When price is greater than marginal cost, some goods are not going to be produced and sold despite the fact that the monetary value buyers place on acquiring them is higher than the monetary cost to suppliers of making them available. Competition tends to push production in price takers' markets to the point where price and marginal cost are equal.

The concept of *administered prices* is misleading inasmuch as almost all prices are "administered" by sellers — within the constraints imposed by their situation. The important question is whether competition imposes adequate constraints in particular circumstances.

The word *oligopoly* is at least as ambiguous as *mono-*

poly; whether there are just a few or very many sellers depends on how we choose to define the product. And so the word *oligopoly* will also be discarded in favor of terms that are more precisely descriptive.

Questions For Discussions

1. List some commodities or services that are sold by only one seller. Then list some of the close substitutes for these goods. How much market power is possessed by the single sellers you listed?
2. Does a firm have a monopoly if it publishes the only morning newspaper in a particular city? If it publishes the only daily newspaper, morning or afternoon? If it publishes the only daily newspaper and owns the only television channel in the city? What are the various goods that a daily newspaper supplies? With what other goods do they compete?
3. Electric utilities are usually given exclusive franchises by the government to sell electricity in a particular area. Are they in competition with sellers of anything else? Do they compete for sales in any way with electric-utility companies franchised to operate in other areas?
4. Is the U.S. Postal Service a monopoly?

   (a) With whom does the Postal Service compete in its first-class mail service (for correspondence)? Its second-class mail service (for publishers of newspapers and magazines)? Its third-class mail service (for advertisers)? Its parcel service? Its express mail service (guaranteed next-day delivery)?
   (b) If the Postal Service has the power to set its prices without regard to supply and demand, why does it usually operate at a loss? Why doesn't it raise its prices and eliminate those troublesome losses?
   (c) When the Postal Service raised the first-class postage rate by about 13 percent recently (from 22¢ to 25¢), do you think its revenue from first-class mail also rose by 13 percent? What would a 13 percent increase in revenue have implied about the elasticity of demand for first-class mail service?
5. Is AMTRAK a monopolist? If you want to travel by train between cities in the United States, you are likely to find that AMTRAK provides the only such service. Why is it nonetheless misleading to refer to AMTRAK as a monopolist? Is "intercity rail passenger service" a commodity for which there are no good substitutes?
6. The good that the public school systems in American cities supply is one that many persons are required by law to consume. Moreover, competing suppliers, because they are denied the right to finance their activities through taxation, must ordinarily charge much higher prices than the public schools charge. Are public school systems monopolists?

7. It is illegal to market certain agricultural commodities, such as tobacco, unless the product was grown on land which the federal government has licensed for the growing of these commodities. Does this mean tobacco farmers are monopolists? Are they price takers or are they price searchers?

8. If monopolies are undesirable, as almost everyone seems to assume, why do governments so often try to protect particular sellers against the competition that additional entrants to the industry would provide?

   (a) Why does the U.S. government prohibit people from competing with the Postal Service in the delivery of first-class mail?

   (b) Why do cities almost always impose stringent restrictions on those who would like to provide a transportation service to compete directly with the city-owned or -licensed urban bus service?

9. Which are the biggest big businesses in the United States? Here are the ten business corporations with the largest sales in 1988, as listed by *Forbes* magazine in its issue of May 1, 1989:

(1) General Motors	(6) General Electric
(2) Ford Motor	(7) Mobil
(3) Exxon	(8) Chrysler
(4) IBM	(9) AT&T
(5) Sears, Roebuck	(10) Texaco

   Is sales volume really the best sure measure of a corporation's size? The sales volume of a firm positioned at the end of the production–distribution process will include all the value added by those who contributed to earlier stages of the process. For example, Kroger, a grocery retailer, had sales in 1988 of $17.5 billion while Weyerhaeuser, a lumber producer, had sales of $10 billion. Is Kroger 75% larger than Weyerhaeuser? In 1988 the value of the assets owned by Kroger was $4.6 billion, while Weyerhaeuser had assets of $15.4 billion. Here is the *Forbes* ranking for 1988 in terms of the value of assets:

(1) Citicorp	(6) General Electric
(2) General Motors	(7) Chase Manhattan
(3) Ford Motor	(8) BankAmerica
(4) American Express	(9) Salomon
(5) Federal National Mortgage	(10) J.P. Morgan & Co.

   This is obviously another flawed measure of size. Seven of the top ten are financial corporations, whose assets are principally the liabilities of others. Citicorp's assets of $207.7 billion earned $1.7 billion in profits in 1988, a return of only 0.8%. General Motors, second in assets, had a poor year in 1988 but still earned $4.6 billion on its assets of $163.8 billion, a 2.8% return. The net income earned on assets might be a truer indication of corporate size. Here is the *Forbes* list of the ten biggest net income receivers in 1988:

(1)	IBM	(6)	Dow Chemical
(2)	Ford Motor	(7)	E.I. du Pont
(3)	Exxon	(8)	Mobil
(4)	General Motors	(9)	Philip Morris
(5)	General Electric	(10)	Amoco

The *Forbes* ranking by market value shows the ten largest corporations in 1988 as measured by investors' estimates of their worth:

(1)	IBM	(6)	Ford Motor
(2)	Exxon	(7)	Philip Morris
(3)	General Electric	(8)	Merck
(4)	AT&T	(9)	E.I. du Pont
(5)	General Motors	(10)	Amoco

A still different ranking emerges if we measure the size of a corporation by the number of its employees:

(1)	General Motors	(6)	AT&T
(2)	Sears, Roebuck	(7)	General Electric
(3)	IBM	(8)	PepsiCo
(4)	Ford Motor	(9)	Marriott
(5)	K Mart	(10)	Wal-Mart

Do any of these measures provide a reliable indication of relative power or of relative importance to the overall society? Five of the largest 20 corporations measured by sales volume were international oil companies in 1988 (as was the 21st). Does this mean that Big Oil has enormous power? Or does it mean that none of the huge oil companies has a great deal of power because all face stiff competition from others?

10. It has been argued by some that we can measure the extent to which "monopolists and oligopolists" control the U.S. economy by looking at *concentration ratios* in various industries. These ratios, calculated by the Bureau of the Census, show the percentage of the total shipments in various industries that are accounted for by the 4 largest, 8 largest, 20 largest, and 50 largest companies in each industry. Table 8A shows the ratios for selected industries as calculated from the 1982 Census of Manufacturers, the most current data available at this time.

(a) Why does the concentration ratio in motor vehicles and car bodies provide a seriously exaggerated indication of the market power of U.S. automobile manufacturers?

(b) The concentration ratios in meatpacking plants and fluid milk are similar. It is much more costly, however, to ship fluid milk long distances than it is to ship processed meat. What difference does this make if we're trying to infer the degree of market power from an industry's concentration ratio?

(c) Why is the similarity of the concentration ratio in newspapers to that in meatpacking plants probably not very significant?

TABLE 8A Percentage of shipments accounted for by large manufacturing companies in the United States, selected industries

Industry	4 Largest	8 Largest	20 Largest	50 Largest
1. Petroleum refining	28%	48%	76%	93%
2. Motor vehicles and car bodies	92	97	99	99+
3. Blast furnaces and steel mills	42	64	82	95
4. Aircraft	64	81	98	99+
5. Meatpacking plants	20	43	60	75
6. Fluid milk	16	27	48	66
7. Newspapers	22	34	49	66
8. Sawmills and planing mills	17	23	34	46
9. Plastic materials and resins	22	38	64	89
10. Soap and other detergents	60	73	83	90

(d) Do the progressively higher concentration ratios in lumber, plastics, and then soap (the 8th, 9th, and 10th industries listed) indicate a progressively greater degree of market power? How large geographically are the markets for the lumber, plastics, or soap shipped from a particular manufacturing plant?

(e) Petroleum refining is more highly concentrated than petroleum production or distribution. Do the data suggest that the oil companies can set whatever prices they choose?

11. One often reads that there are "only three firms in the industry" (or five firms, or eight firms), and that this is too few for competition to be effective. How would you define an industry? Do firms in different industries (however defined) compete with one another? Are all the firms within a single industry (however defined) in competition with one another?

12. Do steel girders for bridge construction produced in Utah compete at all with girders produced in Maryland? (The phrase "at all" will usually make a statement true.) Can you think of ways in which wood products compete with steel girders?

13. Is the college you're attending a price searcher? How much freedom does it have in setting the tuition rate you will pay? Might a just-enrolled freshman answer the above differently from an about-to-graduate senior? Does your college enjoy any special grants of legal privilege?

14. Those who use the term *administered prices* do not include in this classification the prices charged by grocery stores. Nonetheless, grocers stamping prices on products seem clearly to be "administering" prices. Can you suggest criteria that would enable us to distinguish "administered" from "nonadministered" prices?

15. Adam Smith wrote the following in *The Wealth of Nations:* "The price of monopoly is upon every occasion the highest which can be got ... the highest which can be squeezed out of the buyers, or which, it is supposed, they will consent to give." Does this assertion have any clear and defensible

meaning, or must we conclude that even the founder of economics sometimes reasoned carelessly?

16. It has been argued that the development of the railroad in the middle of the nineteenth century substantially reduced the market power of many American manufacturing firms. Explain.

17. The graph on the left in Figure 8B portrays the market demand for U.S.-grown wheat (D) and the aggregated marginal cost curves of U.S. wheat growers (S) in a given year.

   (a) Draw the demand for the wheat of Ferdinand Elizer, a South Dakota wheat farmer, on the right-hand graph.
   (b) How would the demand curve faced by Ferd Elizer shift if the government offered all wheat farmers a subsidy of $1.50 per bushel?
   (c) What would Ferd Elizer's demand curve look like if the government imposed a tax on wheat, requiring farmers to remit $1 for every bushel they sell?

18. The number of moorage sites for houseboats in Seattle has been limited by law to 440 since the city adopted a Shoreline Management Plan in 1975. All sites are currently occupied by houseboats. Some houseboat owners who do not own their moorage sites asked the city to impose controls on the rents that owners could legally charge. They claimed that, with the vacancy rate at zero, owners had acquired a monopoly and could consequently set rents as high as they pleased.

   (a) The graph in Figure 8C shows an imaginary demand curve for moorage sites, labeled DD. Construct the supply curve from the data provided above. [Assume throughout this problem, until part (i), that the sites are owned by 440 different people.]
   (b) What will happen if owners set the rental rate at $275 per month?
   (c) What will happen if owners set the rental rate at $225 per month?
   (d) Is it true that a zero vacancy rate enables owners to set any rental rate they please? What does a low vacancy rate in residential or office space usually indicate?
   (e) What effect on the rental rate would you predict if houseboat living became much more popular in Seattle? What would happen if houseboat living declined in popularity? What are some factors that might cause such an increase or decrease in the demand for houseboat living?
   (f) What would be the effect on the rental rate if 40 additional moorage sites became available through a modification of the Shoreline Management Plan?
   (g) What would be the effect on rental rates of a $50-per-month increase in the property tax that site owners must pay? Demonstrate your result graphically.
   (h) What would be the effect of a $50-per-month tax on houseboat occupants? Use the graph to answer.

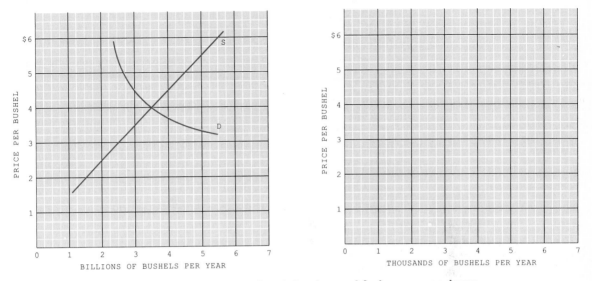

FIGURE 8B   Market demand and the demand facing one producer

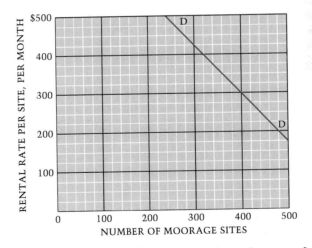

FIGURE 8C   Hypothetical demand and supply curves for houseboat moorage sites in Seattle

(i) Does a zero vacancy rate indicate monopoly power? Suppose all 440 moorage sites were acquired by one party who consequently became the only supplier of moorage sites for houseboats in Seattle. Would this owner now be able to set rents as high as she pleased? What do you think would happen to the vacancy rate if one party became the only seller of moorage space?

(j) Why do you suppose the houseboat owners chose to use the word "monopoly" in asking the city council to regulate rental rates?

19. Market power is not the only kind of power that business firms might have and exercise. Neither market power nor any of these other types of power is necessarily correlated closely with the size of business firms. You might want to think about the nature, sources, and consequences of some of the powers listed below and how they are linked (or not linked) with market power. Power:

(a) as capability, the ability to achieve desired results;
(b) to influence the outcome of elections;
(c) to influence legislation;
(d) to influence regulatory agencies of government;
(e) to manipulate people through advertising;
(f) to pollute the environment; to reduce pollution;
(g) to pursue sexist and racist hiring policies; to institute affirmative action programs;
(h) to intervene in the affairs of other nations;
(i) to shape the basic attitudes and beliefs of people.

What about the power that we sometimes assume others must have simply because we ourselves feel power*less*? Is it true that someone always has power to cause or to prevent undesirable events?

20. Congress has authorized the Federal Communications Commission to monitor the content of radio and television broadcasts and to revoke the licenses of stations that do not adequately serve the public interest. No member of Congress would seriously contemplate exercising such supervision over newspapers, especially in view of the clear prohibition contained in the U.S. Constitution's Bill of Rights. Two justifications are usually offered whenever anyone questions this control over broadcasters' freedom of expression. One is that Congress may regulate radio and television stations because the airwaves belong to the public. The other is that broadcasting frequencies are naturally scarce, and that broadcasters

must be prevented from abusing the power given to them by control of a scarce natural resource.

(a) Why do the airwaves belong to the public? Can you think of a fair and effective way for the public to relinquish its ownership, so that Congress would no longer be obliged to control broadcast content?

(b) There are over 1500 television stations and more than 10,000 radio stations currently broadcasting in the United States. More than 95 percent of U.S. households receive at least five television signals, and cable has enormously expanded these options. Dozens of radio stations are available in major urban areas, and where they are not, it is not because of any scarcity of spectrum space. How much power does the natural scarcity of broadcasting frequencies actually give to broadcasters?

Chapter 9 _____

Price Searching

How do price searchers find what they're looking for, and what happens when they find it? We're going to argue in this chapter that price searchers estimate marginal costs and marginal revenues and then try to set prices that will enable them to sell all those units of their product — and only those units — for which marginal revenue is expected to be greater than marginal cost. Does that sound complicated? It's just the logic of the process for maximizing net revenue, or total revenue minus total cost. But is it the procedure business firms actually use? It sounds much too theoretical, like something an economist might dream up but few real-world sellers would even recognize.

net revenue defined: Total revenue minus total cost.

The Popular Theory of Price Setting

It certainly is not the way most people assume that prices get set. The everyday explanation is a simple cost-plus-markup theory: business firms calculate their unit costs and add on a percentage markup. A large number of price searchers will themselves describe their price-setting practices in terms of the cost-plus-markup theory. Their testimony deserves to be taken seriously, but it isn't conclusive evidence. A lot of people cannot correctly describe a process in which they themselves regularly and successfully engage. Most people who ride bicycles, for example, don't know how they keep the bicycle balanced. And if asked to think about it, they'll conclude that they keep the bicycle from tipping by leaning or shifting their weight slightly each time the bicycle inclines in one direction. If that were the way they actually balanced, they wouldn't make it to the end of the block. In reality they balance by steering, not leaning; they turn the front wheel imperceptibly and allow centrifugal force to counter any tendency to tip. The fact that they don't know what they're doing doesn't keep them from doing it. Although they can balance successfully only by winding along

199

Why are percentage markups so much larger in furniture stores than in grocery stores?

Why do furniture stores often lower their percentage markups for a few days (during sales)?

Why do furniture stores sometimes go bankrupt if their percentage markups are typically so large?

a series of curves whose precise curvature will be inversely proportional to the square of the speed at which they're proceeding, many mathematical illiterates are skillful cyclists.

There are excellent reasons for doubting cost-plus-markup theory. One is that it tells us nothing about the size of the markup. Why choose a 25 rather than a 50 percent markup? Why do different firms mark up their prices by different percentages? Why will the same firm vary its percentage markup at different times, on different products, and even when selling to different people? Why do sellers sometimes set their prices *below* their average unit cost?

Moreover, if firms can always mark up their prices proportionately when their costs rise, why don't they raise their prices *before* their costs rise? Why are they satisfied with a smaller net revenue when they could be earning more? That doesn't square with the perennial complaints of many price setters that they aren't making adequate profits. We all know, too, that firms are sometimes forced out of business by rising costs. That couldn't happen if every firm were able to mark up its prices to cover any increase in costs.

The popular cost-plus-markup theory is obviously inadequate. It just doesn't explain the phenomena with which we're all familiar. We'll return to the question of why so many people, including price searchers themselves, nevertheless hold to the theory. But we can't do that until we've gone through the economist's explanation of the price-searching process.

Introducing Ed Sike

Simple cases are best for illuminating basic principles. We're going to examine the imaginary case of Ed Sike, a sophomore who is supporting himself at Ivy College by working as special-events manager for the College Student Association. One of Ed's tasks is to run a Friday night feature-film series that is open to the college community, and a large part of that job is setting ticket prices.

Let's suppose that Ed has to pay the following bills each time he shows a movie:

Film rental	$1800
Auditorium rental	250
Operator	50
Ticket takers	100
Total:	$2200

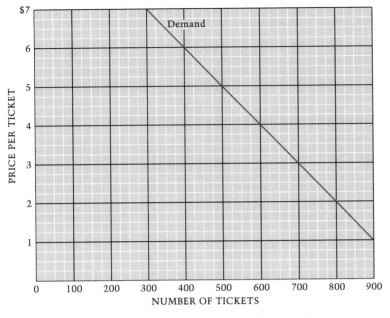

FIGURE 9A   Weekly demand for tickets to films

Ed's budget receives all the revenue from ticket sales. The auditorium seats 700 people. And Ed has somehow discovered the precise demand for the films he shows. (We'll relax that heroic assumption later on.) The demand, which (quite remarkably) doesn't change from film to film, is graphed in Figure 9A. Given this information, what will Ed want to charge for tickets?

We can't answer that question until we know Ed's objectives. If his aim is to fill all the seats without having to turn anyone away, $3 would be the best price to set. That's the price at which the quantity of tickets demanded would equal the number of seats available in the auditorium. One possible objection to a $3 price, however, is that each film showing would lose money. Total costs would be $2200, but total revenue would be only $2100.

That isn't necessarily a compelling objection. The student association may be willing to subsidize the films, perhaps because someone thinks movies make an important contribution to liberal education. If Ed doesn't have to cover costs out of ticket revenue, all sorts of possibilities open up. For example, he might set the price at $2.50. That would cause the quantity demanded to exceed the quantity supplied, but it might also make Ed a very popular man on

Price	Quantity Demanded	Total Revenue	Net Revenue
$3.00	700	$2100	− $100
2.50	750	1750*	−$450

* Remember— there are only
   700 seats.

campus — someone who can get you tickets to a Friday night film even though the film is already "sold out."

We'll come back to that possibility in a later chapter when we look more closely at how "nonprofit" institutions work. Let's assume for now that Ed not only has to get enough revenue from ticket sales to cover all costs, but that he's under orders to earn as much *net* revenue from the series as he can. Under these circumstances, what price will Ed want to charge for a ticket?

The Basic Rule for Maximizing Net Revenue

Look again at the basic rule presented in the first paragraph of this chapter, the rule we said all price searchers try to follow if their goal is to maximize net revenue: set the price or prices that will enable you to sell all those units and only those units for which marginal revenue is expected to be greater than marginal cost.

Marginal cost you've met before. That's the additional cost a seller expects to incur as a result of a contemplated action. In this case the action is *selling another ticket*. Look at the data on Ed Sike's costs. What is the additional cost to him of selling another ticket? Since all $2200 of his costs have to be paid no matter how many tickets he sells, the marginal cost of selling another ticket is zero, under the assumptions we've adopted. If you wanted to draw the marginal cost curve on Figure 9A, it would be a horizontal line running across the graph at $0.

The Concept of Marginal Revenue

But what's marginal revenue? *Marginal revenue is the additional revenue expected from an action under consideration.* For Ed Sike, marginal revenue is the extra revenue received from selling one more ticket.

If you look at the demand curve in Figure 9A, you can see at a glance that Ed Sike's net revenue is going to depend on the price he decides to set. At $3 total revenue would be $2100, and so net revenue would be *minus* $100. At $6 net revenue would be $200: $2400 in total revenue minus $2200 in costs. It would also be $200 if the ticket price was set at $4. At what price would net revenue be maximized, given the data with which we're working?

The answer is $5. If the price is set at $5, then 500 tickets will be sold. Total revenue will be $2500, and net revenue will be $300. Ed can't do any better than that.

How do we know? One way to find the answer is to try out every possible price. A better way, because it clarifies the

To maximize net revenue, set a price that will enable you to sell all those units, but only those units for which marginal revenue is expected to be greater than marginal cost.

Price	Quantity Demanded	Total Revenue
$7	300	$2100
6	400	2400
5	500	2500
4	600	2400
3	700	2100

logic of the process we're trying to explain, is to locate the
quantity at which marginal revenue equals marginal cost and
then find the price at which exactly that quantity can be sold.

The logic is simple. Each of the first 500 tickets that Ed
sells adds more to his revenue than it adds to his costs. (Remember that in this particular case it adds *nothing* to his
costs; marginal cost is zero no matter how many tickets are
being sold.) But each ticket sold beyond 500 adds more to
costs than to revenue. It adds nothing to costs, but it adds
less than nothing to total revenue, because marginal revenue
becomes negative after 500 tickets have been sold.

Why Marginal Revenue Is Less Than Price

It seems at first that this can't be correct. Since Ed is still
taking in money for each ticket he sells beyond 500, the
additional revenue from selling another ticket, or marginal
revenue, looks as if it ought to be positive. But that appearance is in fact false. It ignores something very important. In
order to sell additional tickets, Ed has to lower the price.
And when he does so, he lowers the price not only to the
additional customers he's trying to capture with the price
decrease, but also to all those customers who would have
purchased tickets at the higher price. The additional revenue
he gains from the new customers is offset by revenue lost, or
given up, from the old customers. After he has sold 500 tickets, the revenue lost becomes greater than the revenue
gained, and so marginal revenue becomes negative.

Let's check it out by looking carefully at the graph. Suppose Ed set the price at $5. At that price he would sell 500
tickets, and total revenue would be $2500.

What would happen if he decided to sell 550 tickets? To
do so, he would have to lower the price to $4.50. That would
bring him an additional $4.50 from each of the 50 "new" cus-
tomers, for a total of $225 extra. But it would cost him 50
cents *not* paid now by each of the 500 "old" customers who
were willing to pay $5 until Ed offered to sell them tickets at
$4.50: 500 times 50 cents is $250. That more than offsets the
$225 gained. Ed Sike actually reduced his total revenue by $25
when he decided to expand his ticket sales from 500 to 550.
Marginal revenue is *negative* over this range.

We can be even more precise. Since the additional revenue
from the 50 additional tickets sold is minus $25, we can say
that marginal revenue per ticket is minus 50 cents when Ed
tries to expand sales from 500 to 550. If we want to show that
on Figure 9A, we can plot marginal revenue as minus 50 cents
at 525 tickets, the midpoint between 500 and 550.

*Lowering the
price from A to
B gains some
revenue from
additional sales,
but also loses
some revenue
because all
buyers now
pay the
lowest prices.*

Check your understanding of the basic idea by asking what happens when Ed expands his sales from 450 to 500 tickets. The demand curve shows he could sell 450 tickets for $5.50 each. To sell 500 tickets, he must lower the price to $5. So his total revenue will be $2475 when he sells 450 tickets, and $2500 when he sells 500 tickets. The additional or marginal revenue is 50 cents per extra ticket sold when Ed expands his sales from 450 to 500 tickets. We would therefore plot plus 50 cents as the marginal revenue at 475 tickets.

If we connected these two points with a straight line, the resulting marginal-revenue curve would intersect the marginal-cost curve at precisely 500 tickets. Consequently, we can say that if Ed is content to sell fewer than 500 tickets, he sacrifices potential net revenue by failing to sell some tickets for which marginal revenue is greater than marginal cost. If he sells more than 500 tickets, Ed sacrifices potential net revenue by selling some tickets for which marginal revenue is less than marginal cost. He therefore maximizes net revenue by selling exactly 500 tickets: the quantity at which marginal revenue equals marginal cost. And the demand curve tells us that 500 tickets can be sold by setting the ticket price at $5.

Setting Marginal Revenue to Equal Marginal Cost

You can be sure you've grasped the idea if you're able to figure out what would happen if the film distributor changed the rental fee from a flat $1800 to $800 plus $2 for every ticket sold.

The key difference is that Ed's marginal costs would now rise from zero to $2. Each additional ticket sold would now add $2 to total cost; the marginal-cost curve is a horizontal line at $2. Since to maximize net revenue, Ed must sell all those tickets for which marginal revenue is greater than marginal cost, and no tickets for which marginal cost is greater than marginal revenue, Ed wants to find the price and quantity at which marginal revenue will exactly equal $2.

The marginal-revenue curve has been drawn in Figure 9B. This curve shows by how much the sale of one additional ticket increases total revenue at the various volumes possible. Marginal revenue is $4 when 300 tickets are being sold and falls rapidly as sales increase, becoming negative after 500 tickets are sold. We now see at once that, given the film distributor's new policy, Ed will want to sell 400 tickets. This is the quantity that equates marginal revenue and marginal

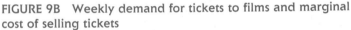

FIGURE 9B   Weekly demand for tickets to films and marginal cost of selling tickets

cost. To sell 400 tickets, Ed should set the price at $6. It turns out that Ed does somewhat better under the film distributor's new policy than he did under the old one. Total revenue is now $2400 and total cost is $2000, for a net revenue of $400.

What About Those Empty Seats?

Under both the old and the new policy, seats were "going to waste." That phrase is in quotation marks because waste, you should recall from Chapter 6, is an evaluative concept. What constitutes waste from the point of view of moviegoers may be efficiency from the point of view of exhibitors like Ed. Still, there does seem to be something wasteful about this situation from everyone's perspective. There are people who want to see the movies, who are willing to pay Ed an amount greater than his marginal cost if he will let them in, but to whom Ed nonetheless denies admission. Movie fans are missing an opportunity for which they're willing to pay the marginal cost; and Ed isn't getting any revenue from those empty seats for which people are willing to pay more than his marginal cost. There seems to be a substantial gain from exchange that isn't being realized. (The situation matches the case of the house painters under a legal minimum wage, as discussed in Chapter 8; it's not an "optimal" arrangement of resources.)

Situations like this are extremely common, of course. At almost every major-league baseball game there will be empty seats inside the stadium, and people outside the stadium who would be happy to pay the team owner for the chance to sit in them. Since letting in another spectator adds nothing to the cost of playing the game, the owner would gain extra net revenue from each additional fan admitted at any ticket price greater than zero. But this will be the case only if the owner can reduce the ticket price to the "new" customers without also reducing the price to those who are willing to pay more to see the game.

The Price Discriminator's Dilemma

There's the catch. It is in fact efficient (from his point of view) for Ed to leave 200 or 300 seats empty, as long as the cost of discriminating among potential ticket buyers is greater than the additional revenue that can be gained through discrimination. Let's see what this means.

Suppose Ed is paying a flat $1800 rental fee, charging $5, selling 500 tickets, and earning $300 per week. One Friday night he looks over the house and says to himself: "I could increase my net revenue by filling those 200 empty seats. All I'd have to do is lower the price to $3, but *only* for those who won't attend if I charge them more than that. I'd get an extra $600 each week, and 200 additional people could enjoy these fine movies."

A brilliant idea? The following week Ed hangs up a new sign at the campus ticket outlet: "$5 per ticket," it says; and then it adds in smaller print: "$3 for those unwilling to pay more." What's going to happen? Almost all the ticket buyers will pay $3, of course, because they're all "unwilling to pay more" if they can get their tickets for $3. Ed will end up with only $2100 in revenue and a loss of $100 from that week's program. It wasn't such a brilliant idea after all.

The flaw, however, was more in the execution than in the idea itself. What Ed must do if he wants to eliminate the "waste" of empty seats and lost revenue is find a sufficiently low-cost procedure for distinguishing among potential buyers. He has to be able to offer low prices to those who otherwise won't buy, without making those low prices available to customers who are willing to purchase tickets at higher prices. Ed might be able to pick up a few hints from the Ivy College administration.

The College as Price Searcher

College administrators often talk about the high costs of providing an education and the need for charitable contributions to make up that 50 percent or so of the cost not covered by tuition. Have you ever wondered why it is, then, that privately owned colleges grant tuition scholarships to needy students? If colleges are so poor that they must ask for charity, why do they simultaneously *dispense* charity? The answer is that they probably don't. Tuition scholarships for needy students may be a partially successful attempt to do what Ed Sike failed to do.

Figure 9C is the demand for admission to Ivy College as estimated by the college administration. We shall assume that the marginal cost of enrolling another student is zero. That isn't accurate, but it's realistic enough for our purposes and it doesn't affect the logic of the argument in any event. Ivy College wants to find the tuition rate that will maximize its receipts.

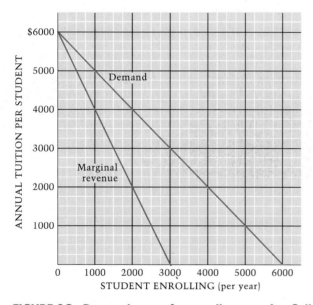

FIGURE 9C   Demand curve for enrollment at Ivy College

Note: There is a simple gimmick you can use to obtain quickly the marginal-revenue curve corresponding to any straight-line demand curve. Draw perpendiculars to the price axis from the demand curve; bisect the perpendiculars; extend a straight line through these midpoints. The marginal revenue corresponding to any point on the demand curve will then be the point on this line (the marginal-revenue curve) directly below the point on the demand curve in which you're interested. Thus the marginal revenue is zero when the price is $3000.

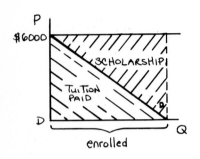

P
$6000
SCHOLARSHIP
TUITION
PAID
D
Q
enrolled

If Ivy restricts itself to a uniform price for all, it will set the tuition at $3000 per year, enroll 3000 students (the enrollment at which marginal revenue equals marginal cost), and gross $9,000,000. But some students whom it would be profitable to enroll are excluded by this tuition rate, and some students who would have been willing to pay more are admitted for only $3000. Ivy's administrators wish they could charge what each student is willing to pay. If they could find out the maximum each student (or the parents) would pay rather than be denied admission to Ivy, they could set the annual tuition at $6000 and then give scholarships (price rebates) to each student. The scholarship would equal the difference between $6000 and the maximum each student is willing to pay.

The problem is how to get information on willingness to pay. Students or their parents will not reveal the full value of Ivy to them if they know that candor will cause them to pay a higher price. But if willingness to pay is correlated with wealth, a partial solution lies at hand. Ivy announces that scholarships are available to needy students. Need must be established by filling out a statement on family wealth and income. Families will complete the forms in order to qualify for scholarship aid and will thereby provide the college with information it can use to discriminate. If the correlation were perfect between income and willingness to pay, and if families filled out the forms honestly, Ivy could discriminate with precision and increase its gross receipts to $18,000,000 (the area under the entire demand curve). Marginal revenue would be equal to price despite the fact that Ivy is a price searcher.

Be careful about condemning Ivy College! Notice some of the consequences of this discriminatory pricing policy. First of all, Ivy earns more income. If you approve of Ivy, why begrudge it a larger income from tuition? Is it better for philanthropists and taxpayers to cover Ivy's annual deficit than for students (or their parents) to do so through being charged the maximum they're willing to pay? Notice, too, that under a perfectly discriminating system of tuition charges, 3000 students who would otherwise be turned away are enabled to enroll at Ivy. They aren't complaining.

Some Strategies for Price Discrimination

Sellers have developed a wide variety of strategies for doing what Ivy College does through its tuition scholarship program. The goal is to find low-cost techniques for distinguishing high-price from low-price buyers and then to offer reduced prices exclusively to those who otherwise won't purchase the product.

For example, grocery stores often offer discounts to customers who present special coupons clipped from newspaper advertisements. Why do they do this? The discounts are designed to attract bargain-hunting shoppers who otherwise wouldn't patronize the store. Customers who fail to present coupons at the checkout counter thereby identify themselves as people who aren't price-conscious bargain-seekers. So they pay higher prices.

If airlines lower their ticket prices, they can fill some empty seats with vacation travelers who would otherwise go by car. But the airlines don't want to lower their prices for business travelers who are willing to pay high fares to save time, and for whom the cost of travel is a tax-deductible expense anyway. How can the airlines distinguish these two classes of travelers and give discounts only to those who won't fly without them? One way is to confine the discount prices to those who buy round-trip tickets and stay more than a week or over a weekend. Business travelers usually can't afford to stay away that long. It's far from an infallible way to discriminate, but it's a low-cost system and it works surprisingly well.

Discount prices are commonly offered for all kinds of entertainment events to children, students, and senior citizens. Is this an act of generosity on the part of those who sponsor the events? It's more likely that they want to attract some additional business from groups that are more sensitive to prices, but without lowering the price to everyone. Potential customers with more elastic demands for the good are prime targets for special price reductions, *if* the seller has a low-cost way to identify the people with more elastic demand curves *and* can prevent them from reselling to people with less elastic demand curves.

Ed Sike Finds a Way

Let's return to the case of Ed Sike. Suppose his data on the demand for tickets enable him to distinguish the student demand from the staff and faculty demand. In Figure 9D we've drawn two demand curves to show these separate student and staff–faculty demands for tickets to the Friday film series. (If you add the curves together — summing the quantities demanded by each group at various prices — you'll get the demand curve presented in Figure 9A.) Our question is: Can Ed, knowing these separate demand curves, increase his net revenue by setting different prices for students and for staff or faculty?

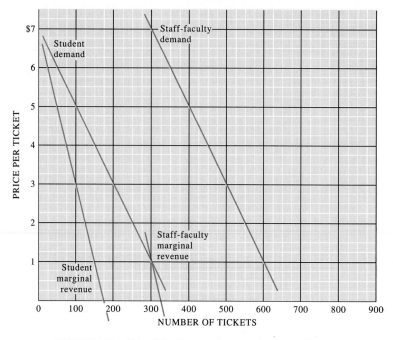

FIGURE 9D   Weekly demand for tickets to films

Intuition suggests it might work. The typical student doesn't have a lot of income and so tends to pay attention to prices. Staff and faculty members who want to see the films are less likely to change their minds because of a modest price increase. It might be that Ed could do better by lowering the price he charges students and raising the price to staff and faculty.

Recall that when marginal cost was zero, Ed maximized net revenue by charging $5 per ticket and selling 500 tickets. Now he wants to set marginal revenue equal to marginal cost *for each group separately.*

Marginal revenue from sales to the students equals zero (marginal cost) at 175 tickets. To sell 175 tickets to students, Ed should charge them $3.50.

Marginal revenue from sales to staff and faculty equals zero at 325 tickets. To sell that number to staff and faculty, Ed should charge them $6.50.

He'll still be selling 500 tickets. But his total revenue will now be $2725 rather than $2500, and his net revenue will increase from $300 to $525.

Why did it work? It worked because the student demand for tickets was much more elastic than was the staff and faculty demand at the common price of $5. By lowering the price to the students, who are more responsive to price changes, and raising the price to staff and faculty members, who are less responsive, Ed does a more effective job of extracting from each group what it's willing to pay.

Note carefully, however, that the entire scheme is crucially dependent on Ed's ability to identify members of each group and prevent them from reselling tickets. It won't do to let students buy tickets for $3.50 and then sell them to members of the staff or faculty. Ed's price-discrimination system would probably work because he could, at low cost, print the tickets in different colors and require that official college I.D. cards be shown when the tickets are presented at the door.

Resentment and Rationale

Of course, Ed would also have to justify his "exploitation" of staff and faculty. That's not likely to be a problem in this case. He could say that $6.50 is what each ticket "really" costs and that the $3.50 price to students is the result of a special subsidy to promote liberal education. Don't underestimate the importance of "justification." Price discrimination of this type increases Ed's net revenue and doesn't compel anyone to pay more than they're willing to pay. But it can arouse fierce indignation on the part of those who aren't offered the discount prices.

As an example, consider the bitter complaints of all those cross-country air travelers who found a few years ago that they had to pay more per mile than people flying between Los Angeles and New York. Why should a round-trip ticket from Seattle to New York, for example, cost more than a similar ticket from Los Angeles to New York, especially when Seattle is closer to New York? The explanation was the fierce competition among the numerous carriers operating between the nation's two largest cities. This competition created excellent substitutes for any one airline's tickets, made the demand curve that each airline faced very elastic, and kept prices close to marginal cost. To Seattle–New York travelers, however, it looked as if they were subsidizing Los Angeles–New York passengers, and they didn't like it.

Lunch and Dinner Prices

Everything we've been talking about is nicely illustrated in the common restaurant practice of charging more for the same food in the evening than at lunch.

The 3 conditions for successful price discrimination: The seller must be able to:
(1) distinguish buyers with different elasticities of demand.
(2) prevent low-price buyers from reselling to high-price buyers.
(3) control resentment.

A more elastic demand lowers the net-revenue-maximizing price.

Why do restaurants catering to both a luncheon and a dinner trade mark up their prices so much more on dinners than on lunches? The theory we've presented looks for the answer in different elasticities of demand. Lunch customers as a class are much more responsive to price increases or decreases than are dinner customers. A 10 percent increase in the price of a luncheon entrée will often lose the restaurant more customers than would a 30 percent increase in the price of the same item on the dinner menu. There are several reasons for this.

One is the fact that lunch customers eat out so much more frequently. People who buy lunch five times a week have many opportunities to gather information on relative prices. And because 50 cents less or more adds up over the course of a month, they have a strong incentive to shop around for the best deal, to stick to it when they think they've found it, and to shift when something better comes along. A dinner out, by contrast, is a much more rare event for most people; they have, as a consequence, less opportunity and less incentive to gather information on relative prices.

Another major reason for the lower price elasticity of demand among dinner patrons is the fact that what they pay for their food is typically only a fraction of what they are paying for the entire event or experience of "dinner out." A couple going out for dinner may pay $10 for a babysitter, $3 for parking, and $15 for cocktails or wine. If they pay $14 each for their dinners, the food is only half of their costs for the evening. And so a 40 percent hike in the menu price comes through to them as only a 20 percent increase in the cost of their evening out.

We should therefore expect to see restaurant managers following low-markup policies at lunch and high-markup policies at dinner. To reduce the chance of indignation and resentment, they will do a little more than merely raise the price of the London broil from $8 at lunch to $14 at dinner. They will also offer the dinner patron both soup *and* salad (the luncheon customers must choose one or the other) and perhaps include coffee in the price of the dinner (but not the lunch). A $6 increase is thus "justified" by an increase in marginal food cost of perhaps 40 cents. The real reason for the different markups, however, is found in the different elasticities of demand characteristic of luncheon and dinner patrons.

Cost Plus Markup Reconsidered

So how do price searchers find what they're looking for? By (1) estimating the marginal cost and marginal revenue, (2) determining the level of output that will enable them to sell all those units of output and only those units for which marginal revenue is greater than marginal cost, and (3) setting their price or prices so that they can just manage to sell the output produced. That sounds complicated, and it is. The logic is simple enough. But the estimates of marginal cost and especially the estimates of demand and marginal revenue are hard to make accurately. That's why price searchers are called "searchers." And why they could sometimes be called price "gropers."

The complexity and uncertainty of the price searcher's task help explain the popularity of the cost-plus-markup theory. Every search has to begin somewhere. Why not begin with the wholesale cost of an item plus a percentage markup adequate to cover overhead costs and yield a reasonable profit? If costs increase, why not assume that competitors' costs have also increased and try passing the higher cost on to customers? Why not begin with the assumption that the future will be like the past and that the procedures which have previously yielded good results will continue to do so? In that case one would try to increase prices roughly in proportion to any cost increases experienced, and one would expect eventually to be forced by competition to lower one's prices roughly in proportion to any lowering of costs.

The cost-plus-markup procedure is in general a rule of thumb for price searchers, offering a place from which to begin looking, a first approximation in the continuing search for an elusive and shifting target. But price searchers engage in cost-plus-markup pricing only as a search technique and only until they discover they are making a mistake. The marginal-cost/marginal-revenue analysis of this chapter explains how price searchers recognize mistakes and what criteria they use in moving from rules of thumb and first approximations toward the most profitable pricing policy.

Once Over Lightly

Price searchers are looking for pricing structures that will enable them to sell all units for which marginal revenue exceeds marginal cost.

The popularity of the cost-plus-markup theory of pricing rests on its usefulness as a search technique and the fact that people often cannot correctly explain processes in which they regularly and successfully engage.

A crucial factor for the price searcher is the ability or inability to discriminate: to charge high prices for units that are in high demand and low prices for units that would not otherwise be purchased, without allowing the sales at lower prices to "spoil the market" for high-price sales.

A rule for successful price searching often quoted by economists is: set marginal revenue equal to marginal cost. This means: continue selling as long as the additional revenue from a sale exceeds the additional cost. Skillful price searchers are people who know this rule (even when they don't fully realize they're using it) and who also have a knack for distinguishing the relevant marginal possibilities. The possibilities are endless, which helps to make price theory a fascinating exploration for people with a penchant for puzzle solving.

Sellers in the real world don't have precisely defined demand curves from which they can derive marginal-revenue curves to compare with marginal-cost curves. Working with such curves is nonetheless good exercise for a student who wants to begin thinking systematically about the ways in which competition affects the choices people make and the choices they confront.

Questions for Discussion

1. The rule for maximizing net revenue (total revenue minus total cost) is: take any action if, but only if, the expected marginal revenue exceeds the expected marginal cost. What is marginal revenue? How is it related to demand? You can test your grasp of this key concept by examining the case of Maureen Supplize, who runs a yacht dealership. She has five potential customers, and she knows how much each would be willing to pay for one of her yachts.

J.P. Morgan	$13 million
J.D. Rockefeller	11 million
J.R. Ewing	9 million
J.C. Penney	7 million
J.P. Kennedy	5 million

(a) Fill in the blanks in the second column on the next page to complete the demand schedule implied by these data.

				Under Perfect Price Discrimination	
Price of Yacht	Quantity Demanded	Total Revenue	Marginal Revenue	Marginal Revenue	Total Revenue
			$	$	
$13 million	$_____	$_____	_____	_____	$_____
11	_____	_____	_____	_____	_____
9	_____	_____	_____	_____	_____
7	_____	_____	_____	_____	_____
5	_____	_____	_____	_____	_____

(b) Fill in the blanks in the third column to show Maureen's total receipts from yacht sales at the various prices listed.

(c) Fill in the blanks in the fourth column to show the extra revenue obtained by Maureen from each additional yacht she manages to sell when she lowers her selling price.

(d) How many yachts will she want to sell if her goal is to maximize *total* revenue? (Don't start thinking yet about selling to different people at different prices. We'll take that up later. Assume for now that she can't get away with charging one buyer more than another.) What price will she want to set?

(e) Now assume that her goal is to maximize *net* revenue and that the marginal cost to her of selling a yacht is $6 million. In other words, each additional yacht she sells adds $6 million to her total costs. How many yachts will she now want to sell? What price will she want to set?

(f) If you have proceeded correctly, you should now be able to experience something of Maureen's frustration. Ewing and Penney are both willing to pay more for a yacht than it costs Maureen to sell one to them. Yet she can't sell to either without reducing her net revenue. Why?

(g) Suppose now that none of her customers is acquainted with any of the others and that she can consequently get away with charging each one the maximum he is willing to pay. Under such an arrangement, which we shall call "perfect" price discrimination, what is Maureen's marginal-revenue schedule? Fill in the blanks in the fifth column.

(h) How many yachts will Maureen now want to sell?

(i) Fill in her *total* revenue schedule under "perfect" price discrimination.

2. "A price searcher should set marginal revenue as far above marginal cost as possible." Explain why this statement is wrong. What is being erroneously assumed by someone who thinks that net receipts will be zero at an output where marginal revenue equals marginal cost?

3. Locate the most profitable uniform price for sellers to set in each of the situations graphed in Figure 9E and the quantity they will want to produce and sell. Then shade the area that represents the net income from that pricing policy. What will happen to net income in each case if the price is raised? If it's lowered? (Caution: What happens if a seller whose marginal-revenue curve is the same as the demand curve raises the price?)

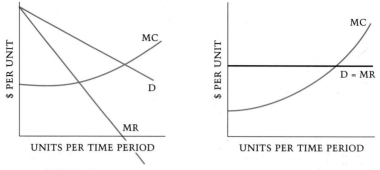

FIGURE 9E   Finding the most profitable selling price

FIGURE 9F   Marginal cost and demand curves for two companies

4. The marginal-cost curves of the Anchorage Aardvark Breeding Company and the Houston Aardvark Breeding Company are identical, but the demand curves they face differ, as shown in Figure 9F.

   (a) What price will each firm want to set?
   (b) Suppose something happens to raise marginal cost for each firm to $20 while nothing else changes. What price will each now set?
   (c) What is the relationship between elasticity of demand and the profit-maximizing percentage markup?

5. Have you ever wondered why otherwise identical books usually sell for so much more in hardcover than in softcover editions?

   (a) Is it because publishers must pay so much more to produce books with hardcovers?

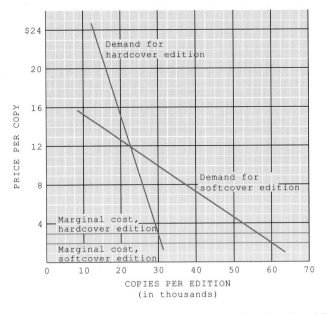

FIGURE 9G   Marginal cost and demand curves for a book publisher

(b) Some potential buyers will have a strong preference for a hardcover edition. They include libraries, purchasers who intend to use the book intensively, and people looking for gift items. Would you expect the price elasticity of demand at any particular price to be greater or less for the hardcover than for the softcover edition?

(c) Figure 9G shows the marginal cost to a publisher of producing and selling hardcover and softcover editions of a particular book and the demand curve for each edition. What prices will the publisher want to set? How much of this reflects cost differences?

6. The graph in Figure 9H presents the daily demand for round-trip tickets on Transcontinental Airlines' flights between Seattle and New York City and between Los Angeles and New York City. Assume that the cost to Transcontinental of carrying an additional passenger is $25 one way, for a round-trip marginal cost of $50.

(a) What specific expenses would enter into Transcontinental's marginal cost (of selling an additional round-trip ticket)?

(b) Construct the marginal-revenue curves that correspond to each of the demand curves shown, using the technique described in Figure 9C.

(c) How many tickets of each kind would Transcontinental want to sell to maximize its net revenue?

(d) What price would it want to set on each route?

(e) Are Seattle customers subsidizing Los Angeles customers? What price would Transcontinental want to set for its Seattle flights if it terminated its Los Angeles operation? For its Los Angeles flights if it terminated

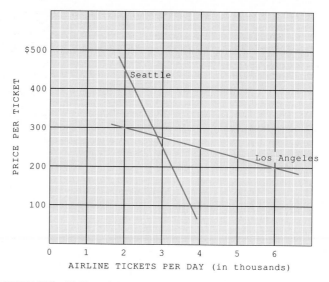

FIGURE 9H   Airline tickets between Seattle and Los Angeles

its Seattle operation? Are Seattle prices higher *because* Los Angeles prices are lower?

(f) Are Seattle prices perhaps *lower* because of Transcontinental's Los Angeles operation? Since Transcontinental is adding to its net revenue by flying Los Angeles passengers, it could well be the case that the Los Angeles operation is enabling it to stay in business. How would this contribute to lower prices for Seattle customers?

7. Many firms use a technique called *target pricing* in trying to decide what prices to set for new products they're introducing. The target price is a price that enables the firm to recover a certain percentage of the product's development and production costs. What, in addition to costs, must the seller know in order to calculate the return a particular price will yield? If earnings from the sale of the product turn out to fall short of the target, should the firm raise the price? If earnings exceed the firm's expectations, should it lower the price?

8. How should the British and French manufacturers of the Concorde supersonic commercial airliner take account of the planes's development costs in determining the prices to charge airline companies? Should they suspend production if they can't obtain a price that will cover development costs?

9. When the university's athletic director announces that football ticket prices are being raised for next year, he is likely to say this unfortunate step has been made necessary by rising costs — perhaps the rising cost of the women's sports program. How does the cost of the women's sports program affect the marginal cost of selling a football ticket? If you are unable to think of any answer to that question, ask yourself how the prospect of a winning season affects the cost of selling a football ticket. Which plays a larger role in determining the most profitable price at which

to sell football tickets: the athletic department's budget for women's sports or an excellent team?

10. On the day of home football games, the University of Washington raises the price of parking on some of its lots from 75 cents to $6 per vehicle. This is done, according to the Committee on Transportation, so that regular parking users do not subsidize the cost of providing parking for football fans. Would regular users be subsidizing football parkers if the rate stayed at 75 cents on football Saturdays?

11. Are advertising costs capable of affecting the net-revenue-maximizing price for the product advertised?

(a) Do beer drinkers have to pay more for the beer they drink because the brewery pays a huge sum of money to advertise it on national television?

(b) When a breakfast-food company pays a celebrity athlete a million dollars for the right to put his picture on the cereal box, will this lead to an increase in the price of the cereal?

12. Can an oil company raise the price of its gasoline to cover the costs of a huge oil spill for which it is liable? What would happen if Exxon, for example, raised the refinery price of gasoline at a time when other refiners were not raising their prices?

13. Do small convenience stores charge higher prices (on average) than large supermarkets charge because the small stores have higher overhead costs per unit of sales? How can a seller induce customers to pay a higher price for a product than they would have to pay elsewhere?

14. Can hog owners raise the prices at which they sell when feed costs go up?

(a) A rise in the price of hog feed increases the cost to hog farmers of continuing to feed the hogs they have. What is the alternative to continuing to feed and fatten hogs? Why might an increase in the price of hog feed lead to a short-run decline in the price of hogs?

(b) By what process will an increase in the price of hog feed eventually produce an increase in the price of hogs?

15. In 1985 Missouri began assessing commercial property for tax purposes at a higher percentage of "fair market value" than residential property. For purposes of this reassessment, apartment buildings of 5 or more units were classified as commercial property; property taxes on such buildings increased sharply, while taxes on apartment buildings with 4 units or fewer did not change.

(a) Would you expect this change to increase the rents paid by people living in large apartment buildings relative to the rents paid by tenants in buildings with fewer than 5 units? Does the tax increase affect either the marginal cost to the landlord of renting or the demand for apartments on the part of tenants?

(b) What effect do you think this tax change will have on the average size of apartment units in existing buildings? What effect will it have on the average size of apartment buildings constructed in the future?

(c) What effect would you predict from this change in assessment methods on the demand for units in buildings of fewer than 5 units and hence on the rental rates tenants will pay for such units?

(d) The president of the St. Louis Apartment Association was quoted as saying that no apartment owners would pay those tax increases, but rather would pass them along in the form of rent increases. If owners can raise rents in this fashion after property taxes rise, why don't they raise them *before* the taxes rise and increase their income? If owners can pass on tax increases, why did some Missouri apartment owners go to the expense of filing a suit to overturn the reassessment?

16. One store sells Wilson Championship extra-duty felt optic-yellow tennis balls at $2.49 for a can of three. Another store in the same shopping center sells Wilson Championship extra-duty felt optic-yellow tennis balls at $1.99 for a can of three. How is this possible? Why would anyone buy balls from the first store? Why do you think we repeated the long description in the second sentence instead of just saying "identical tennis balls"?

17. Why do camera retailers so often sell the cameras themselves at prices very close to their own wholesale cost, while marking up the price of accessories (carrying cases, extra lenses, filters, and so on) by 100 percent or more?

18. Some Manhattan restaurants have experimented with using two breakfast menus. One, with higher printed prices, is handed to entering customers who look like tourists. The other menu, with lower prices, is given to customers in business clothing who look like people on their way to work. How might this two-menu policy raise net revenue for the restaurants using it?

19. A *Wall Street Journal* story (July 25, 1980) reports that tourists in China are charged more than double the price that Chinese pay for movies, taxicabs, and airline or train tickets, and that many manufactured items offered for sale in "friendship" stores can actually be purchased for half as much in retail stores in Hong Kong. Can you explain this?

The Chinese also charge foreign diplomats very high prices for apartments, but often charge lower "friendship" rents to representatives from poor Third World nations. Do the lower rents charged Third World diplomats represent a foreign-policy decision or an attempt to maximize net revenue?

20. Professional sports teams have long sponsored "Ladies' Days," occasions on which women are admitted at reduced prices. Is this a case of discrimination against males, since the teams never have a "Gentlemen's Day"? How would you explain "Ladies' Day"?

21. In a city where most movie theaters charge $5 or more for admission, a few movie theaters, called discount movie houses, may charge as little as $1 or $2 for admission. The discount theaters will often show the same movies as the more expensive theaters, but a few months later.

(a) Do the first-run movie houses have higher costs that necessitate their higher prices?

(b) The studios that provide the movies often charge as much as 90% of the box-office revenue in the first week or two after a major movie has been released, but the percentage then drops steadily. The studio take may be as low as 35% by the time a movie reaches discount houses. Can this fact account for the difference in ticket prices?

(c) Why are the studios able to extract 90% of the gross ticket revenue from first-run movie houses but willing to let discount houses show their films for only 35% of gross?

(d) Movie theaters usually net about 75 cents out of every dollar spent on refreshments. How does this help explain why theaters are willing to give up 90% of their ticket revenue to obtain a first-run showing of a "blockbuster"? (Does this fact make you at all skeptical about signs that prohibit movie goers from bringing food or drink in from outside "for the safety and comfort of our patrons"?)

(e) If studios raise the price they charge discount houses to $1 per ticket or 35% of ticket revenue, whichever is greater, by how much would you expect a discount house currently charging $1 to raise its price?

22. Some theaters presenting live drama have begun experimenting with "Pay-What-You-Can" pricing for certain performances. A theater in San Diego adopted this policy for one Saturday matinee per production. Normal ticket prices run from $18 to $28. Payments for the special matinees ranged from 25 cents to $18.

(a) How do these theaters prevent *everyone* from taking advantage of the lower prices?

(b) Why would anyone pay $18 for a ticket that they could have purchased for 25 cents?

(c) Do you believe that people will really pay what they *can* under such a system? Do you think that wealthier people will on average pay more than poorer people?

(d) Many theaters sell steeply discounted tickets on the day of the performance. How do they keep all their patrons from waiting until the day of the performance to purchase tickets?

23. New York City has an ordinance requiring retailers to post prices for items they sell. In 1988 the Department of Consumer Affairs begain to enforce the ordinance against art galleries. Many gallery owners protested vehemently. Why?

24. An August 1981 newspaper story reported what it called "a mystery." Representatives of the manufacturer and the regional distributor of Head skis tried to buy the entire stock of their own skis being offered for sale at very low prices by a chain of discount stores. At one store the purchasers immediately went outside and broke all the skis in the store parking lot. Can you explain this mystery?

Does the following information provide any clues? The manager of a sporting goods store that regularly carries Head skis said the action was an attempt by the distributor to get defective skis off the market. An executive with the discount store said the skis were not defective but were a standard production model originally destined for shipment out of the country. What were the manufacturer and distributor trying to do and what went wrong?

25. Advice columnist Ann Landers has several times attacked in her column a practice engaged in by some clothing retailers. They will slash or tear items they have been unable to sell and throw them away rather than give them to employees or low-income people. Ann was puzzled by this behavior. The only plausible explanation she could think of was one suggested by a Nebraska reader: Stores are trying to protect themselves against people who will obtain such merchandise at no charge and then bring it back to the store for credit. Can you give her a much more plausible explanation?

26. Would telephone companies earn larger or smaller net revenues if they charged for local service on the basis of the number of calls made? Draw the demand curve of a "typical" customer and compare the possibilities. How well could the phone company do by setting the net-revenue-maximizing price for individual calls? How well could it do by charging the maximum amount a customer is willing to pay rather than do without phone service and then giving customers an unlimited number of "free" local calls? Why is it, do you suppose, that local calls are typically "free" for residential customers while they must pay extra for each long-distance call?

27. The National Collegiate Athletic Association has a rule that sponsors of post-season "bowl" games must pay a minimum of $500,000 to the colleges supplying the football teams. Sometimes the bowl bid will be contingent on the college's willingness to purchase a large number of tickets to the bowl game.

    (a) How much is a college actually being paid for a bowl appearance if it receives $500,000 but obtains the invitation on the condition that it purchase 10,000 twenty-dollar tickets?
    (b) Will a college consent to such an arrangement if it knows it cannot hope to sell more than a hundred or so of the tickets to its fans?

28. The discussion of lunch and dinner prices at the end of the chapter may be leaving out something important. Dinner patrons almost always take more time to eat than do lunch patrons. Doesn't this raise the cost of providing dinner? Under what circumstances would it *not* raise the cost? If lingering over a meal is costly to restaurants, they will presumably try to prevent or limit it. How might they do this without irritating customers? Will restaurants ever want to *encourage* lingering? How might they do this?

29. In 1980 Heublein Inc. raised the price of its Popov brand vodka by 8 percent, in what it called a move to "reposition" the brand. Sales fell only 1 percent in response to the 8 percent price increase.

    (a) Since vodka is colorless, odorless, and tasteless, why do you suppose consumers are willing to pay substantially more for some brands of vodka?

(b) What do you suppose Heublein was trying to do when it "repositioned" its Popov brand?

(c) Marketing people refer to certain goods that are kept on display as "ego-sensitive" merchandise and point out that consumers show a preference for higher prices when it comes to ego-sensitive goods. Does that mean that sellers of such goods can always earn more by raising prices?

30. Suppose you're willing to pay 60 cents for one doughnut with your morning coffee and 30 cents for a second doughnut. The owner of the doughnut shop knows this and also knows that his cost of selling an additional doughnut is 20 cents. Should he charge you 60 cents or 30 cents if he wants to maximize his net revenue? How about 60 cents and two for 90 cents?

31. Why will sellers make offers like this one? "Buy two giant pizzas at regular price and get a third one for only a dollar."

32. If a surgeon charges $1500 to remove the gallbladder of a wealthy patient and $500 to remove another patient's gallbladder, is she exploiting the first patient or giving a discount to the second? How does she prevent the second patient from buying several operations at the lower price and reselling them for a profit to wealthy patients?

33. You want to sell at auction an antique dining-room suite. There are three people who want it, and they're willing to pay $8000, $6000, and $4000, respectively. Your reservation price (the price above which the bidding must go before you sell) is $5000. No one in the room has any information about the value of the suite to anyone else.

(a) At about what price will the suite be sold?

(b) Suppose you run a Dutch auction. The auctioneer announces a price well above what anyone would be willing to pay and then gradually lowers the price until a bid is received. At about what price will the suite be sold?

(c) Why do stores sometimes add to their advertisements: "Available only while supplies last"?

34. You and your fiancée are shopping for wedding rings. After showing you a sample of his wares, the jeweler asks, "What price did you have in mind?"

(a) Why does he ask this question?

(b) If you tell him you don't plan to spend more than $200 on each ring, are you helping him find the rings to sell you or the price to charge for the rings you prefer?

(c) What might be a good technique for finding out the lowest price at which the jeweler is willing to sell the rings you like?

Chapter 10

Competition and Government Policy

Will economic competition disappear unless the government has an active program to preserve it? Or does competition preserve itself, sometimes in the face of diligent efforts by the government to restrict it?

Is the government promoting competition when it prevents larger, more efficient, or perhaps more unscrupulous firms from driving other firms out of business? Or does the protection of competitors entail the suppression of competition?

When the government prohibits mergers, is it preventing competitors from eliminating rivals? Or is it stifling the development of more competitive and efficient organizational forms?

What do we mean by competition and how are we to decide whether the economy or some sector of it is adequately competitive? Is competition in an industry to be measured by the number of competitors, by the practices in which they engage, or by the behavior of prices, costs, and profits and the industry's record with respect to innovation?

Those questions will not be answered conclusively in this chapter. But we hope that, when you've finished thinking about the sources and consequences of competition as well as the origins and effects of government policies, you will have a better sense of what the issues are.

The Pressures of Competition

All sellers facing demand curves that are less than perfectly elastic — tilted downward to the right rather than horizontal — will maximize net revenue by restricting sales or output and keeping the selling price above marginal cost. (Unless they can practice "perfect" price discrimination.) How and why that occurs was the theme of the preceding chapter.

One problem from the seller's viewpoint with prices

higher than marginal cost is that they are a standing invitation to competition. If a piece of apple pie that costs the cafeteria owner 30 cents is selling for 90 cents, the owner is likely to insist that the 60-cent difference isn't profit; it's only a contribution toward meeting all the other costs of running the cafeteria: labor, taxes, rent, equipment maintenance, breakage, theft, and so on. That may be completely true. Nonetheless, each additional piece of pie that is sold for 90 cents contributes a net 60 cents toward the owner's wealth. If the same is true for all the other cafés and cafeterias in town, each owner will be earnestly wishing that more hungry people would abandon the other eating places and buy their apple pie from him.

Wishes like this often prompt action. Pie prices might be slightly reduced after 3 p.m. to induce some afternoon coffee-break customers to allow themselves a little treat. Or a sign could be put up after 3 p.m. announcing free coffee with pie purchases. There are dangers inherent in this strategy. Some lunch customers may simply postpone their dessert at noon and have it at three when it's cheaper. And competing restaurants may undermine the promotional effort by offering their own inducements, so that instead of capturing additional customers each owner ends up selling only as much pie as previously but at lower prices.

We assumed in the last chapter that Ed Sike and some of the other sellers whose policies we were examining somehow knew exactly what the demand was for their product. That assumption was useful in enabling us to present the logic of the simple price-seaching process. In reality, of course, sellers must usually probe for information on the demand for their product and try to stimulate and maintain it by advertising and by offering reliable service. Moreover, when there are several sellers of a product in the market, each seller's demand curve is going to depend on the policies, including the price policies, of those competing sellers. The demand for Ed Sike's film series will shift downward to the left if neighboring theaters show better movies or cut their prices, or if sororities and fraternities pick Friday night to sponsor parties, or if the college basketball team plays home games on Friday nights and hits a winning streak.

The price that any one cafeteria in the downtown area sets for apple pie will affect the demand (curve or schedule) for apple pie at other restaurants. Since each of the restaurants will be using estimates of its own demand to set prices that will, in turn, affect the demand all other restaurants encounter, we have a situation more closely resembling chess or poker than a technical maximization problem. The best price for anyone to set *next* may depend on the price set *last*, as in a game of chess. The neat little world of Chapter 9, with its clearly defined curves, becomes blurry. Unfortunately from an analytic standpoint, though perhaps fortunately from an aesthetic one, the real world is not as neatly outlined as the pages in a coloring book.

Chapter 8 introduced the word *oligopoly*, meaning "few sellers." We decided there that the concept of a few sellers shared all the ambiguities of the concept of a single seller, ambiguities inherent in the problem of deciding just how broadly or narrowly to define the commodity being sold. Some economists have retained the slippery word oligopoly and have assigned it a very special meaning: a situation in which the demand curve of one seller depends on the reactions of identifiable other sellers, sometimes called *rivals.* Whether or not we choose to call this oligopoly — the usage is certainly misleading — situations of that sort, where the demand curves of different sellers are significantly interdependent, are obviously both common and important. It all adds to the competitive pressures of which sellers so commonly complain.

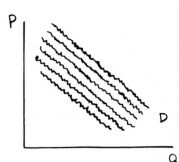

Demand curve as
seller perceives it

Controlling Competition

Then why don't sellers agree not to compete, or to compete less, or to share the market among themselves in some mutually satisfactory way? The answer is that they would very much like to do so and often try, but it isn't as easy as it might seem at first. Agreements between competing sellers to maintain prices and share markets are usually unenforceable in court and are, moreover, illegal under the laws of many states and under federal law where it is applicable. In addition, it's very difficult to devise agreements that everyone will accept, that will cover all the possibilities, and that can be effectively enforced. The incentives to compete are so persistent that soon one or the other party will seek to circumvent the terms of the agreement. On top of all this, successful collusion by the members of a cartel[1] will attract the attention of outsiders, who will begin trying to enter the business in order to enjoy some of the profits that collusion has created.

---

[1] A cartel is an agreement among a group of sellers to regulate prices or output. There are also buyers' cartels, such as the owners of professional basketball teams mentioned in Chapter 3 who want a single league to keep down the cost of hiring players.

Horizontal merger:
Two oil-refining companies.

Conglomerate merger:
An oil-refining company and a steel maker.

Vertical merger:
An oil-refining company and a gasoline-retailing chain.

that the merger will substantially lessen competition in an industry already made up of a relatively few very large firms. But suppose they sell in different geographic areas? Suppose they each specialize in a different line of steel products? Suppose each is on the edge of failure and that the merger will lead to economies that may enable both to survive?

A great deal of dispute has arisen in recent years regarding so-called *conglomerate mergers:* mergers between firms producing widely divergent goods. Does the acquisition of a car-rental firm by an electrical-machinery manufacturer enable the rental firm to compete more effectively against Hertz and Avis? Does it lead to special arrangements between the machinery manufacturer, its suppliers, and the rental firm that tie up a portion of the car-rental business and thus reduce competition? Do conglomerate mergers lead to concentrations of financial power that are dangerous and undesirable regardless of their effects on competition?

What about *vertical mergers*, mergers between firms that previously existed in a supplier–buyer relationship, as when a supermarket chain acquires a food processor? Is this more likely to increase efficiency or to reduce competition by depriving other food processors of opportunities to sell?

What constitutes an illegally unfair trade practice? Is it unfair for a large firm to demand discounts from its suppliers? Is it unfair for suppliers to offer discounts to some purchasers but not to others? What about the whole question of advertising? Do large firms have unfair advantages in advertising, advantages that advertising increases? Must advertising be truthful in order to be fair? Of course it must, almost by definition. But what is the truth, the whole truth, and nothing but the truth? Anyone who thinks about this issue seriously or for very long is forced to admit that the regulation of "deceptive" advertising by the Federal Trade Commission inevitably involves the commission in complex questions of purpose and effect and in a large number of judgments that appear quite arbitrary.

And always we return to the root problem: restrictions on competitors will reduce their ability to compete. Competition is essentially the offering of additional opportunities, and additional opportunities mean a wider range of choices and hence greater wealth. But the manner in which a firm expands the set of opportunities it offers may diminish, over a short or a longer period, the set of opportunities other firms are able to offer. Under what circumstances do we want the government to restrict one firm's competitive efforts for the sake of the larger or long-run competitive situation? It is important to remember that many of the most effective pressures on government policies stem not from consumer but from producer interests. And those policies will too often be shaped by the desire of producers to protect themselves against the rigors of the competitive life.

Vertical Restraints: Competitive or Anticompetitive?

Current controversies over vertical restraints on competition illustrate many of the opposing arguments and conflicting interests that complicate antitrust policy. From 1937 to 1976, as mentioned earlier, federal legislation exempted from the Sherman Act state-endorsed price-fixing agreements between manufacturers and retailers. Congress had no sooner rescinded this exemption, making such agreements automatically illegal once again, than the courts started to carve out exceptions to the principle that manufacturers may not try to control competition at the retail level. Congress subsequently responded by trying to prohibit altogether what it had once encouraged. Legislation has been introduced in both the House and the Senate in recent years that would sharply curtail the power of manufacturers to control the behavior of those who distribute their products.

Is there any way that consumers could benefit from a manufacturer's refusal to sell to a retailer who reduced the resale price below some recommended minimum, or from a decision to limit the number of retail outlets that will be allowed to carry the manufacturer's product in a given geographic area? It would seem that such actions could only produce higher prices and poorer quality service for consumers. That conclusion becomes much less certain, however, when we ask why any manufacturer might want to prevent price discounting by retailers or hold down the number of stores carrying its product.

Manufacturers sometimes conclude that they will be unable to market their product successfully unless consumers are provided with a substantial range of pre- and post-sale services, such as information on ways the product can be utilized profitably, continuing instruction on operating procedures, or fast and dependable maintenance service. Retailers will only want to supply these services if they can increase their own net revenue by doing so, that is, if supplying these services will increase their sales by more than enough to cover the cost of the services.

Such services will not be supplied, and hence the manufacturer's product cannot be successfully marketed,

Why would a manufacturer want retailers to charge more (and consequently sell less)? Why would a manufacturer want fewer retailers selling its products?

whenever retailers are able to "free ride" on the services provided by other retailers. Consider the case of personal computers. These products could not have been introduced into offices and homes as quickly as they were if selling effort had not been accompanied by a whole lot of instructional effort. Instructional effort *was* selling effort, perhaps the most effective kind of selling effort. But did it produce sales for the party providing the instruction? There's the catch. Retailers who incurred the cost of teaching people how to make effective use of one type of personal computer could easily be undermined by competing retailers who provided no instructional services but catered to the demand that others had created.

Manufacturers who set minimum resale prices or limit the number of outlets in an area may be trying to protect cooperating distributors from free-riding distributors. Their interest would be in marketing their product effectively, not in reducing competition. Of course, the manufacturer's actions *would* limit competition. But in the absence of such actions there might be even less competition, as the product could not be effectively marketed at all.

Should manufacturers be allowed to restrict competition at the retail level, then, as part of a reasonable effort to market their product? The courts have been allowing such activities in recent years, on a case-by-case basis, looking at the context, intent, and probable effects of the "vertical" restrictions. That hasn't made everyone happy. Distributors who were cut off or otherwise disciplined by manufacturers have complained to Congress and some members of Congress have responded with bills that would severely limit the rights of manufacturers in this area. Proponents of such bills argue that they want to enhance competition. Opponents reply that the effect will be to reduce competition by seriously curtailing the power of manufacturers and distributors to devise and agree upon effective marketing procedures.

The Range of Opinion

Is the whole body of "antitrust" law perhaps more of a hindrance than a help to competition? There are some who come to that conclusion. There are others — heavily concentrated, it often seems, in the economics profession — who would retain the Sherman Act and the antimerger provisions of the Clayton Act and junk the rest. Some of these defenders claim that the Sherman and Clayton acts have made important contributions to the maintenance of a competitive econ-

omy. Others claim that they could make a much larger contribution if they were seriously enforced. But still others
view them at best as harmless rhetoric, at worst as weapons
that, in the hands of ignorant political appointees, may do a
lot of damage to the economy.

The author is firmly convinced that he doesn't know
who is right. "Antitrust" policy is certainly full of contradictions, of cases where the right hand is doing what the left
hand is undoing. State laws rarely promote competition;
more often they promote the interests of the competitor protectors rather than the competition protectors. Federal enforcement of the Sherman Act and the antimerger provisions
of the Clayton Act often seems to strain at gnats while
swallowing camels. Firms unable to compete effectively by
offering their customers lower prices and better quality
sometimes file complaints under the antitrust laws to see if
they can persuade the courts to raise the prices or reduce the
quality of their competitors' offerings. On the other hand,
the existence of the Sherman Act, with its ringing denuncia-
tion of price-fixing conspiracies, may have retarded the development in this country of the cartel arrangements that
have so often appeared in western Europe and Japan. The
economist George Stigler once suggested that "the ghost of
Senator Sherman is an ex officio member of the board of
directors of every large company." While that statement will
never meet the minimum criteria for empirical scientific
truths, good history is still a long way from being a pure
science.

Toward Evaluation

The conclusions that we shall offer at the end are far more
modest than the questions with which we began. They are
only two in number.

Restrictions on potential competitors reduce the range
and diminish the availability of substitute goods and allow
sellers more room to increase their own wealth by denying
opportunities to others. Competition is a process, not a state
of affairs. To put it another way, competition can be recognized only in motion pictures, not in still photographs. The
fact, for example, that the price of some good is exactly the
same, no matter from which seller you buy, establishes absolutely nothing about whether the industry producing that
good is adequately competitive. The important question is
how those prices all came to be identical. It happens with
surprising frequency that even public figures, who ought to

know better, will infer an absence of competition from the uniformity of price. The quickest antidote to this error is the recollection that wheat farmers all charge the same price.

The other observation is that an inadequate situation must be compared with more desirable situations that are actually attainable. It is a mistake to contrast a less-than-ideal situation with an ideal-but-unattainable situation. There are costs involved in changed market structures, such as the cost of an investigation, prosecution, court order, and compliance under antitrust statutes. Only if these marginal costs are less than the marginal benefits can one maintain that we would be "better off" if we took legal action to reduce the market power of price searchers, to prevent business mergers, or to prohibit practices that might eventually lessen competition.

Once Over Lightly

A gap between the price of a good and the marginal cost of making it available is a source of potential advantage to someone. Competition occurs in the economy as people locate such differentials and try to exploit them by filling that gap with additional goods.

Competition takes more forms than we can list and usually more forms than competitors can anticipate and head off.

Because competition tends to transfer the gains from providing a good to purchasers and to other suppliers, firms frequently try to obtain government assistance in excluding competitors, often displaying remarkable ingenuity and stunning sophistry.

Firms often charge that their competitors, whether domestic or foreign, are "selling below cost" and call for the government to prevent such "predatory" practices. Most such charges make sense only if they include some expenses in per-unit cost that are irrelevant to the particular decisions under attack. They make a different kind of sense when we remember that sellers characteristically prefer less competition.

The notion that government is the Defender of Competition Against Rapacious Monopolists is probably more a hope than a reality. Federal, state, and local governments have created and preserved numerous positions of special privilege whose effect is to restrict competition and reduce the options available to consumers.

An adequate and balanced evaluation of the substantial body of statutes, commission decrees, and judicial holdings that makes up federal antitrust policy has not yet been published.

Competition is a process in which competitors engage. We obviously cannot have competition without competitors. It does not seem as obvious to people that we also cannot have competition if we prohibit competitors from taking actions intended to increase their share of the market.

Questions for Discussion

1. A few years ago a major airline began asking in-flight passengers to complete a lengthy "Passenger Survey." A cover note from the Senior Vice President for Marketing said that passengers who completed the survey would be helping the airline provide "the best possible service." Questions were asked about the purpose of this trip, frequency of flying, type of fare paid, what would have been done had no discount fare been available, how the ticket was purchased, and income of the traveler. What was the airline trying to do?

2. How would you account for the fact that although some observers claim competition is declining in the American economy, every business firm insists that it faces strenuous competition?

3. Consult the technical definition of *oligopoly* presented in the text. Are the manufacturers of cigarettes oligopolists by that definition? Are the owners of the gasoline stations in a small town oligopolists? Name some other sellers who are and are not oligopolists by that definition.

4. If a commercial airline reduces its prices in September, at the end of the vacation season, for tickets purchased two weeks in advance with a stay over a Saturday night, what will happen to the number of tickets it sells? Does it matter whether other airlines match its price cuts? Suppose the airline knows that changes in its fares *will* be matched by all its major competitors. If it nonetheless decides to reduce its fares, will it be causing a change in the demand for its tickets or only a change in the quantity demanded?

5. The attempt by sellers to make their product more attractive to consumers is sometimes called *product differentiation.*

   (a) Is product differentiation a wasteful process, imposing costs on sellers that are greater than the benefits conferred on buyers? Think of cases where it probably is wasteful in this sense and other cases where it is not.

   (b) Evaluate the following argument: "New practices initiated by sellers to differentiate their products are liable to be wasteful from the social point of view because they are liable to entail high marginal costs and low marginal benefits. But this only means that producers have already made use of the low-cost/high-benefit techniques of product differentiation; it does not show that the whole process of product differentiation is wasteful."

6. A 1982 survey by a New York advertising agency found that many consumers thought there were too many different brands available for sale in several product categories. For example, 72 percent of the consumers surveyed thought there were too many brands of dry cereal, and 60 percent thought there were too many brands of bar soap. How many is "too many" from your point of view if you know exactly what you want? How many is "too few" if you can't find what you're looking for? (The survey by Batten, Barton, Durstine, and Osborn was described in the April 22, 1982, issue of *The Wall Street Journal.*)

7. Why must an effective price-fixing agreement between sellers include such restrictions on sales as output limitations or geographic divisions of sales territory?

8. This problem is designed to help you appreciate the joys and tribulations of cartels.

   Let D in Figure 10A be the demand for oil and MC the sum of the marginal cost curves of all oil producers. (Ignore the line labeled H for now.)

   (a) If oil producers are price takers because there are thousands of them and they have no effective cartel, why will the price of oil move toward $9 per barrel? What will occur if the price is much above or below $9?

   (b) Now assume that one party acquires control over all producing oil wells and hence the power to control the price by controlling output. How many millions of barrels per day (mb/d) will be produced if the goal is to maximize net revenue? What price will be set?

   (c) Change the above assumption slightly. The oil wells remain under the ownership and control of the thousands of original owners, but each owner agrees to sell only at the price determined by the Organizer of Prices to Exploit Consumers (OPEC). This is an agent hired by the oil producers to determine and announce the price for oil that will be most advantageous to oil producers collectively. OPEC announces that the price shall be $29 per barrel. What must occur if this price is to hold?

   (d) Why will the individual oil producers want to sell individually a quantity of oil that sums in aggregate to far more than 13 mb/d?

   (e) How can OPEC prevent output from expanding way beyond 13 mb/d and thereby bringing down the price of oil? If OPEC assigns production quotas to each individual oil producer, how can it make sure that all the producers will be satisfied that their quotas are "fair"? How can it make sure that individual producers don't exceed their quotas?

   (f) Is the demand curve for oil that obtains when oil has long been selling at $9 per barrel and is expected to remain at about that level likely to remain unchanged when the price of oil rises to $29 per barrel and is expected to stay at that much higher level for a number of years? What sort of developments are likely to *shift the demand* over time? What effect will this have on the oil producers who created OPEC?

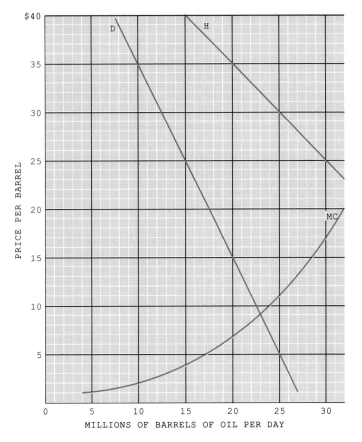

FIGURE 10A   Market demand for oil and combined marginal
cost curves of producers

(g) A serious threat to the wealth of the OPEC oil producers is likely to
come from *new* producers who are attracted into the industry by
OPEC's success in raising the price of oil. In the case of the real-world
OPEC (Organization of Petroleum Exporting Countries), the 13 member
nations saw their sales decline between 1980 and 1985 from over 30
mb/d to fewer than 15 mb/d, with some of the difference reflecting a
reduced total demand but most of it a result of increased production
by non-OPEC members. Suppose that H had been the demand for OPEC
oil in the happy days when the cartel began operating. Compare the
price, output, and total revenue of OPEC's members when the demand
is H with the price, output, and total revenue when the demand is
D — even assuming no "cheating" by cartel members.

9. The analysis in the preceding question raises an interesting issue: Why
did the Organization of Petroleum Exporting Countries succeed so well

for so long in raising the world price of oil? A major part of any answer is contained in the concept of the marginal cost of producing and selling oil. The cost of extracting oil from an established field can be very low indeed, so low as to be almost negligible. But the relevant marginal cost is the cost of extracting *and selling*. In the 1970s, many respected parties were predicting that, because the demand for petroleum products was highly inelastic and the world's reserves were quickly running out, the price per barrel might rise by the end of the century as high as $1000 a barrel. How do expectations of such dramatically higher future prices affect the opportunity cost of selling oil currently? How would such expectations solve OPEC's "cheating" problem? Why did those extravagant expectations, so common in the 1970s, disappear by the mid-1980s?

10. Some states have established legal minimum prices for liquor sold at retail. Do you think this eliminates competition among retail liquor stores? Why do you think retailers in such states often lend glassware without charge to customers planning parties?

11. All the real estate brokers in an area will generally charge the same fee for selling a house, a certain percentage of the sales price established by some association and adhered to by all real estate agents as a matter of "ethical practice."

    (a) Why would it be unethical if a broker offered to accept 5 rather than 6 percent for selling your house? Toward whom would it be unethical?

    (b) How do real estate agents compete with one another?

    (c) Is an industry likely to become overcrowded if it's successful in fixing a high minimum price for its product? Is the real estate profession overcrowded in your judgment? What evidence might be used to answer this question?

12. A survey reported in the *Harvard Business Review* asked businesspeople to describe the unethical practices in their own industry that they would most like to see eliminated. Of those responding, 62 percent mentioned "unfair pricing," "dishonest advertising," "unfair competitive practices," or "cheating customers." How would you interpret these responses? How would you define the practices they condemn?

13. Examine the paragraph in the text recounting the complaint of the nursing-home operator. How many wrong or misleading assertions can you locate in that paragraph?

14. The legislature of a large state recently considered a bill that would require all grocery stores and drugstores selling package liquor to provide separate entrances to their liquor departments. It was maintained by supporters of the bill that this was necessary to prevent minors from entering the liquor department. Who do you think lobbied for this bill? Why?

15. A study several years ago pointed out that 73 percent of the professions licensed by a populous midwestern state required entrants to have "good character." Why? How can good character be determined? Who is best

able to determine whether morticians' characters are sufficiently blameless to entitle them to a license?

16. The Seattle City Council stopped setting taxicab rates in May 1979. Soon thereafter efforts began to compel the city to resume regulation. Are you surprised to learn that those efforts were financed and promoted by the owners of taxicabs? Do you believe their statement: "We're doing it to keep people from being ripped off"?

17. A former chief executive officer of AT&T testified in August 1981, in an antitrust suit, that AT&T had tried to forestall competition to the Bell system in order to safeguard its quality of service rather than to protect its profit. Does that claim surprise you? Do you think it's true?

18. A March 10, 1982, letter to *The Wall Street Journal* argued that "continued economic regulation of the motor carrier industry . . . is in the public interest." The letter, signed by the president of the American Trucking Association, argued that collective rate making and restrictions on entry were necessary to prevent unstable service, industry concentration, loss of service to small communities, predatory pricing, and discrimination against small shippers and small communities. Are you surprised to learn that members of the American Trucking Association *want* to be regulated by government so that they don't act contrary to the public interest?

19. The president of a county medical society in Florida warned doctors there that if they took out even a small ad in the Yellow Pages, they would be "summarily called before the executive committee of the county association to explain their actions." He added his opinion that using boldface type in a standard Yellow Pages listing constituted "unprofessional conduct."

    (a) What kind of doctor is least likely to want to advertise? Which doctors are most likely to want to advertise?

    (b) What is the consumer interest in this matter? Is advertising by physicians likely to lead to better or poorer service for patients?

20. An advocate of state regulation of cosmetologists and barbers in Washington State argued that the state cosmetology agency had taken in $756,805 in revenue in the preceding year while spending only $589,014, thus providing a net benefit to the state. Where would you look to locate some additional costs created by the agency?

21. When the Washington State legislature was debating a bill in 1981 that would allow optometrists to administer certain eyedrops during eye exams, 50 ophthalmologists descended on the Capitol to lobby against the bill. The chairman of the state Academy of Ophthalmology told a reporter: "There is no economic advantage one way or the other." The ophthalmologists' sole concern was that, if the bill became law, "more people will be harmed through inappropriate use of drugs." Do you believe that 50 medical specialists all took a day off from their practices to lobby the legislature exclusively out of concern for the public's health?

22. In 1987 the Washington State Utilities and Transportation Commission began a crackdown on unlicensed movers of household goods.

    (a) The commission's enforcement chief said the crackdown occurred because of consumer complaints about damaged goods and price manipulation and because authorized carriers were complaining about growing competition from unlicensed movers. Which set of complaints do you suppose put the most pressure on the commission? How many consumers do you think know about the existence of the State's Utilities and Transportation Commission? How many licensed movers probably know about the Commission?

    (b) State officials have said that the legislature set strict requirements for entry into the moving industry in the 1930s because legislators were concerned that "unregulated, cutthroat competition would lead to a deterioration in service, safety problems, overly intensive competition in urban areas and a lack of service in rural areas." Do you agree that these problems are likely to arise in the absence of regulation? Does competition *usually* lead to a deterioration in service? When is competition "cutthroat" and "overly intensive"? If you ask this last question of people already in the moving industry, how are they likely to respond?

    (c) There is a "stringent public convenience and necessity test" for any new firm seeking a mover's permit, which places on the applicant firm the burden of proving that its services are needed. Can that be proved?

    (d) The transportation director for the state commission is on record as believing that there are currently "more licensed movers than is necessary—as far as service rather than rates are concerned." What is the relationship between high rates and sufficient service?

    (e) What does the fact that there are dozens of unlicensed movers operating in the state indicate about the transportation director's claim?

23. In January 1983 a U.S. appeals court rejected a lower-court finding that AT&T had engaged in "predatory pricing" against MCI Communications Inc. by setting rates "below cost" on some of its long-distance services. Go back to question 3 in Chapter 5 and examine AT&T's explanation of what a long-distance call "costs." Would you be willing to argue that any price under 68.9 cents for the initial minute is evidence of below-cost pricing? How would you determine whether particular long-distance rates are above or below cost?

24. The Big Three auto makers in the United States asked the Commerce Department in 1988 to "consult" with Japanese manufacturers about alleged "dumping" of compact pickup trucks in the U.S. market. Under trade law, illegal "dumping" occurs when foreign firms sell in the United States at prices below what they sell for in their domestic market *and* thereby cause the profits or employment of U.S. competitors to fall.

    (a) Why would a Japanese firm want to sell pickup trucks in the United States for less than it charges in Japan?

(b) Since the Big Three's truck sales were nearing record levels when the complaint was filed, they could not show a drop in profits or employment. Instead, they argued on the basis of "lost opportunity": 140,000 additional trucks would have been sold had the Japanese not "dumped" vehicles in the United States. If lost opportunity constitutes injury, is there any reason to require a showing of injury to support a dumping complaint?

25. In June 1983 the U.S. Justice Department agreed to drop a consent decree that it had extracted from Safeway 25 years earlier, under which Safeway had been prohibited from selling at prices below its cost of acquiring grocery products or at "unreasonably low prices" that might be above cost. The decree stemmed from a government suit that had accused Safeway of selling below cost in an effort to monopolize the market for retail food in Texas and New Mexico.

(a) How likely is it that Safeway or anyone else would be able to monopolize the market for retail food in two states?
(b) The alleged attempt to monopolize led Safeway to reduce prices to customers. Who do you suppose complained to the Justice Department about Safeway's behavior?
(c) What is the appropriate way to determine the cost of specific grocery items? Is a retailer selling paper bags below cost when it makes them available to customers at no charge? Is the retailer cross-subsidizing paper bags? [For more on cross-subsidies, see question 28 below, especially part (d).]

26. Which of the following products are being sold below cost? With what other products are they competing? Is the competition "unfair"?

(a) Coffee offered by a bank to its customers without charge.
(b) As many cups of coffee after dinner as the diner in an expensive restaurant requests, at no extra charge.
(c) Commercial television programs.
(d) Soft drinks on an airline flight.
(e) A roll of film given to each adult customer during a pizza shop's first week of operation.

27. Three elements that must be present for a firm to be engaged in predatory pricing are pricing (1) below cost, (2) in order to eliminate rivals, and (3) with the intention of raising prices afterward to recoup. What factors would make the last step of the process difficult to complete? Under what kinds of circumstances would it be relatively easy? Can you cite any actual examples?

28. Here is a simplified problem on "predatory pricing" to help you get a clearer grasp of some of the issues.
    The demand for the shipping services of the Midwestern Railroad Company is shown as D in Figure 10B. The marginal cost to Midwestern

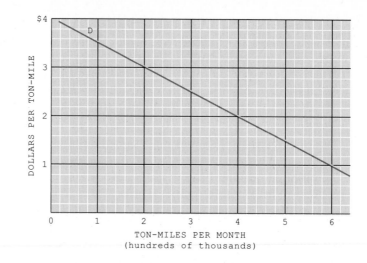

FIGURE 10B   Demand for shipping services of the Midwestern Railroad Company

of carrying freight is $1 per ton-mile. In addition to its marginal costs, Midwestern has monthly expenses of $480,000 covering all those costs that are not affected by the amount of freight the railroad carries: property taxes, mortgage payments on equipment, most wages and salaries, and so on.

(a) If Midwestern sets marginal cost equal to marginal revenue to maximize its net revenue from operation of the railroad, what rate will it set per ton-mile? How many ton-miles of freight will it carry per month? What will be its monthly loss?

(b) Now assume that the demand curve above $2.00 is entirely the demand from coal producers, and that the demand below $2.00 comes entirely from grain shippers. If Midwestern sets different rates for coal and for grain, what rate will it want to set in each case to maximize net revenue? How many ton-miles of coal and of grain, respectively, will Midwestern carry each month? What will now be its total costs and its total revenue?

(c) Suppose that prior to the institution of a separate and lower price for grain, barge companies on the Ohio, Illinois, and Mississippi rivers had been charging $2.00 per ton-mile to carry grain. Why will they be unhappy about Midwestern's two-price policy? If they want to protest that Midwestern is charging a price "below cost," what evidence can they come up with to support their complaint? What is Midwestern's "total cost" per unit for carrying a ton-mile of freight?

(d) If Midwestern is carrying grain "below cost," is it "cross-subsidizing" by using the "excess profits" earned from "exploiting" coal producers? Or is it also carrying coal "below cost"? How can Midwestern earn a positive net revenue by charging rates "below cost" on all the freight it carries? (To clarify the picture, you might want to plot Midwestern's total cost per unit on the graph, and then note the relationship between price and cost under first a single-price and then a dual-price policy.)

(e) If you were a member of a regulatory commission charged with preventing exploitation of shippers as well as predatory pricing aimed at competitors while also preserving the profits of the railroad, would you approve or disapprove Midwestern's dual-price policy?

29. The Staggers Rail Act of 1980 substantially reduced the power of the Interstate Commerce Commission to control the rates that railroads charge shippers.

(a) The president of the National Coal Association has denounced the system of "letting the railroads charge what the traffic will bear" and has called for renewed rate regulation. Many other shippers, however, applaud the extensive deregulation of the railroads. Why might the coal industry favor rate regulation while most shippers oppose it?

(b) One 1983 study of the price elasticity of demand for rail transport of grain in the Corn Belt states calculated an elasticity coefficient of 3.75. What is the nature of the competition that makes the demand elasticity so high?

(c) If the railroads, barge lines, and trucking firms of this country were allowed to set their rates free from government regulation, what do you think would follow: "gouging of customers" (higher prices) or "ruinous price cutting" (lower prices)? Does this happen in other areas of the economy where prices are not regulated by commissions — for example, in the grocery or automobile industries?

30. What is the difference between reducing prices to attract more customers and reducing prices in order to monopolize?

31. In 1989, an airline coach ticket from Frankfurt, West Germany, to Chicago cost $1313. A coach ticket from Athens to Chicago, with a stop in Frankfurt on the way, cost only $839.

(a) Why would the longer flight cost less?

(b) Travelers flying from Frankfurt to Chicago who learned about this price differential began buying tickets for an Athens-to-Chicago flight. They then boarded in Frankfurt and threw away the Athens to Frankfurt portion of the ticket. The airlines countered with a rule that allowed travel agents to sell the bargain tickets only in the country of origin — Greece in this case. The U.S. Transportation Department thereupon issued a formal order objecting to a rule that penalized travelers who buy one-way tickets in this country for travel between two foreign cities, and the airlines backed down (at least temporarily). Do you think the Frankfurt to Chicago travelers who used the Athens ticket were behaving unfairly? Was the rule with which the airlines countered unfair? Was it unfair for the Transportation Department to object? (Keep in mind that the Transportation Department has the power to make the life of airlines much more pleasant or unpleasant.) Was it unfair of the airlines to charge less for a flight from Athens in the first place?

(c) What do you think will be the eventual outcome if the Transportation Department continues to prevent the airlines from enforcing their rule on purchasing in the country of origin?

(d) Which would be the more pro-competition policy for the Transportation Department? To allow the airlines to set their own rules on ticket prices and sales, or to prevent them from adopting a rule that makes it difficult for ineligible persons to purchase discount tickets?

32. A federal judge held in November 1988 that commercial airlines may legally refuse to allow discount travel agencies to handle their tickets. These are agencies that sell tickets below the airlines' published prices to travelers who know exactly what ticket they want, by rebating a portion of their commission. Discount travel agencies do not help travelers plan their trips.

(a) How could travelers who need extensive information nonetheless be able to take advantage of the discount prices?

(b) Why might the airlines be interested in protecting the commissions of full-service travel agencies?

33. Suppose Congress decided to prevent manufacturers from controlling "free-riding" behavior among distributors of their products by branding all such efforts as an illegal conspiracy in restraint of trade.

(a) What option would remain open to manufacturers? (Hint: Can a firm conspire with itself?)

(b) How might government efforts to preserve the independence of distributors in their business relations with manufacturers threaten the continued existence of the distributors?

34. Is it legitimate for government to prevent independent business firms from agreeing among themselves not to sell below a certain price? If you have no misgivings about the legitimacy of this legal restraint, ask yourself whether it is also acceptable for government to prevent business firms from agreeing among themselves not to purchase above a certain price? What about extending the prohibition to customers? Why should it be legal for customers to do what business firms may not do? What about employees who agree not to work below a certain wage? Can you reconcile what appears to be legislative discrimination against business firms with the principle that all citizens ought to be equal before the law?

35. Prior to the deregulation of the commercial airlines, Republic and Northwest Airlines were required by the Civil Aeronautics Board to charge the same fares. After deregulation, they were prohibited from getting together to agree on a common fare schedule. After the two airlines merged, they were free to set fares as their interests dictated. If one of these makes sense, how can the others be defended?

36. In 1984 Congress passed the Cable Communications Policy Act and substantially deregulated the cable-TV industry. Since that time the industry has fought to preserve its unregulated status, generally by claiming that any legal restraints on its behavior will deny Amerian viewers some of the programs they want. The industry has simultaneously tried to persuade cities and the federal government not to allow electrical utilities or telephone companies to build competing systems. They say this will lead to overbuilding and price cutting. Would you conclude from all this that the cable-TV industry is in favor of competition or opposed to it?

37. The Federal Trade Commission staff sought (unsuccessfully) in 1980 to secure approval for "no-fault" antitrust cases. The government would not have to prove, under this approach, that a large firm had acted anticompetitively, only that the firm in fact commands a dominant share of the market. Would this promote or retard competition?

38. Think about this assertion put forward by the economist M.A. Adelman: "A useful if not very precise index of the strength of competition . . . is the resentment of unsuccessful competitors." How would you evaluate the argument by other firms in the office equipment industry that IBM engages in unfair competition?

Chapter 11 _____

Profit

"Perhaps no term or concept in economic discussion is used with a more bewildering variety of well-established meanings than *profit*." That sentence was written about sixty years ago by Frank Knight, a distinguished student of the subject, to introduce an encyclopedia article on profit. The situation has not changed greatly since then. A few years ago *The Wall Street Journal* ran a feature article entitled "Some Plain Truth about Profit." The author listed no fewer than seven distinct definitions of the word *profit* that have been employed by "economic experts," decided none of them was very helpful, and then offered his own. A month later the *Journal* published seven letters of response from its readers; their verdicts on the new definition and accompanying exposition ran from excellent through misleading to ridiculous.

So what shall we do? We shall take the coward's course and assert that *there is no correct definition of profit.* The meaning of any word depends, after all, on the way people use it; and it is an incontrovertible fact that people (including economists) use *profit* in many different senses. We certainly don't want to quibble about mere definitions. But attitudes toward profit and such closely related concepts as cost of production and interest affect economic legislation, and those attitudes depend in large part on what people have in mind when they use the terms. So we're going to expend an unusual amount of effort in this chapter trying to decide what things ought to be called, but only insofar as we must do so to avoid both misleading distinctions and misleading identifications. We don't want to ignore important realities. But neither do we want to be misled by language into seeing things that don't exist.

Profit as "Total Revenue Minus Total Cost"

The most common definition of profit is simply *total revenue minus total cost*. That's almost everyone's intuitive

Profit

$\underline{\text{Total Revenue (P} \times \text{Q)}}$
$\underline{- \text{ Total Cost (av \$} \times \text{Q)}}$
Business Profit
or Economic Profit
↑
(Explicit (Implicit Costs)

253

definition of the term and that's how we've used it until now. A synonym would be *net revenue*. When a business firm has paid all its costs, what it has left over is profit, or net revenue. But before we can agree on the size of profits, defined in this way, we have to agree on what counts as costs.

What Should Be Included in Costs?

Monetary outlays are not the same as costs, at least not from the opportunity-cost perspective. This is clear in the case of an owner-operated business: part of the cost of doing business is the owner's own labor, even though owners may not figure their salaries as part of their regular costs and write no weekly payroll check to themselves. If owners pay rent for the building they use, they'll count the rental payments as part of their costs; but they may fail to do so if they themselves own the building. They ought to do so, however, because they're losing the amount that could be obtained from renting the building to someone else. There is a genuine cost in not having the building available for alternative uses.

Business proprietors may also be using equipment that they bought and now own. If they bought the equipment with a bank loan, they will include the interest on their bank payments in their costs. But suppose they bought the equipment out of previously accumulated savings? Then they gave up interest income that they could have obtained from letting someone else use their savings, and this is certainly part of the opportunity cost of doing business. But they may or may not decide to include the forgone income in their costs. The point is that they should. The income forgone represents a genuine cost for the business.

Corporate profits have a legal definition because corporations must pay taxes on their profits. But the legal definition is unsatisfactory from an opportunity-cost point of view. It begins with the commonsense definition of profit as revenue minus costs. But it excludes from cost the dividend payments made to stockholders of the corporation while including the interest payments made to bondholders. Are these payments that different? Both seem to be payments for the use of borrowed funds. The principal difference is that payments to bondholders are a contractual obligation of a fixed amount, whereas the dividends paid to stockholders are a kind of residual that may vary from year to year or quarter to quarter. Still, the funds loaned by the stockholders are funds not earning income somewhere else, and those funds

The total cost of operating an enterprise is the value of all the opportunities that must be given up in order to operate it.

were loaned only because the stockholders expected to receive a return at least equal in value to their next-best opportunity. Surely some portion of the dividends paid by corporations represents a cost of doing business, no matter how dividends are regarded for purposes of taxation.

Why Is Interest Paid?

But why is interest paid in the first place? For what is it a payment?

The notion that interest is a payment for the use of money, the way that a Hertz or Avis fee is a payment for the use of a car, is quite mistaken. My employer offers me money in return for my services; I hand that money over to grocers, utility companies, and others to secure goods that they supply and I want; they in turn use the money I provide them to pay their employees, and so on. None of us pays any interest for the use of the money that changes hands in this way. Moreover, if I choose to put a pair of $20 bills into my sugar bowl for a rainy day and it doesn't rain for several years, the Federal Reserve Bank that issued those bills doesn't charge me for their use during this period. Contrast that with the probable reaction of Hertz or Avis if I stored one of their cars in my garage for a rainy day.

The usual way to obtain money is to earn it by selling a service to someone. We only pay interest when we *borrow* money. Borrowing is a matter of obtaining money that we have not earned — *yet*. Borrowers want money *now* though they currently have no valuable service to offer in exchange for it. They persuade lenders to give them money now by promising to pay later. The ratio between what is given back later and what is obtained now determines the interest rate.

Interest is thus the price that people pay to obtain resources now rather than wait until they have earned the money with which to buy the resources. The best way to think about interest is to view it as *the premium paid to obtain current command of resources*.

To explain why interest is paid, then, we must explain why present resources are generally more valuable than future resources. That isn't too hard to understand. Having resources now expands one's opportunities. Present command of resources will often enable us to do things that cause our earning capacity to increase over time, so that we will have more resources at some future date than we would otherwise have had. When we see such a prospect, we want to borrow. And we are willing to pay, if we have to, a pre-

We don't pay any rent to Federal Reserve Banks for use of the paper money they have produced and put into circulation.

People pay interest in order to obtain current command over resources.

Present command of resources is generally worth more than future command of the same resources.

mium — interest — as long as the interest is less than what we expect to gain as a result of borrowing.

Suppose that Robinson Crusoe, long a useful character in economists' arguments, keeps himself alive from day to day by digging for clams with his fingernails. Five clams a day is the most he can obtain by digging with his hands during every available hour. And five clams per day is just enough to keep body and soul together, so that Robinson is living on the edge of bare subsistence. If he had a shovel, however, he could triple his daily output to fifteen clams. Unfortunately for Robinson, it would require a month's work to manufacture a suitable shovel, during which time he could not dig for clams and would consequently starve.

How many clams would Robinson Crusoe be willing to give up later in return for 150 clams now, or more accurately, in return for five clams a day on each of the next thirty days while he is all tied up in shovel making? He could *afford* to give up as many as 300 clams at the end of the second month and each month thereafter, because that is how much the loan of 150 clams now would increase his productivity in future months. Presumably he would be *willing* to give up any amount less than that if he had no other way of obtaining a shovel.

Clams now are worth more than clams later if, as in this case, present command of clams enables one to increase the future production of clams. The rate of exchange between present and future clams would be the rate of interest in Robinson Crusoe's world. And it would have no relationship at all to money.

There are very few tasks that cannot be performed more effectively with the appropriate tools, which is to say, with the assistance of *capital*. Capital in economics means *produced goods used to increase the production of future goods*. Examples include Crusoe's shovel, cash registers in retail stores, drill presses in a sheet-metal fabricating shop, the card catalogue in libraries, and all the skills embodied in human beings that enable them to produce more goods than they could produce before they acquired those skills. As long as people believe that they can increase their future productivity by acquiring present command of resources and creating capital from them, they will be willing to pay a premium to obtain resources now rather than wait until they have "earned" them.

Interest is consequently not something unique to capitalist economies, much less a result of the avarice and power of bankers and other moneylenders. Above all, it is not something that could be eliminated just by making more money available. Interest rates are generally talked about as if they were the cost of borrowing money simply because money is the usual means by which people acquire possession of present goods. But interest would exist in an economy that functioned without money, since it's fundamentally the difference in value between present and future goods.

We don't want to leave the impression that it's only the productivity of capital that makes resources now generally more valuable than resources at some future date. Consumers also seem to display what the economist calls *a positive rate of time preference*; that is, people tend to place a higher subjective value on consumption in the near future than on consumption in the more distant future.

You are probably one of those people. Here is a little test you might use to find out whether you are indeed among that overwhelming majority with a positive rate of time preference. Imagine that you have responded to one of those innumerable promotions that come in the mail with large and gaudy announcements on the envelope stating that YOU MAY ALREADY HAVE WON A BRAND NEW $45,000 SPORTSCAR. And to your own utter astonishment, you find out that you have actually won the grand prize! You are very happy, of course. Then you learn that the car won't be delivered to you until about one year from now. You are still happy; but you are probably a lot less happy than you were when you imagined yourself driving that sportscar already next week. In fact, you would most likely be willing to pay a substantial sum of money to get the car now rather than having to wait a year. If all this describes you, then you have a positive rate of time preference.

Some critics have interpreted positive time preference as evidence of shortsightedness, or of inability to imagine the distant future with as much vividness and force as one contemplates the immediate future, or of an innate human tendency to view the future through rose-tinted glasses. Each of these interpretations casts suspicion on the ultimate "rationality" of time preference. Given the facts of human mortality, however, and all the contingencies of life, it isn't necessarily irrational or shortsighted to prefer a bird in the hand to two in the bush. Moreover, if people have reason to believe that their income will increase over time, they could very logically conclude that giving up something now entails a larger subjective sacrifice than giving up quite a bit more of the same thing at a future date when they expect their income to be larger.

If you place the same value on $800 now as on $1000 one year from now, you have a 25 percent rate of time preference.

Whatever the relative importance of each factor, it is clear that people's beliefs about the productivity of capital goods and their preferences for consuming sooner rather than later have combined to produce a premium on present goods over future goods and thus a positive rate of interest in every known society. Interest is paid, then — to answer the question with which we began this section — to induce people to give up present command of resources. It is a payment for the value of the opportunity that lenders forgo, a payment that borrowers are willing to make because of the opportunities that borrowing opens up for them.

The Risk Factor in Interest Rates

The rates charged by banks to corporate borrowers, by department stores to customers with revolving charge accounts, or by individuals lending to savings-and-loan institutions all reflect the net rate of time preference in a particular society. But they also include risk premiums of various sizes plus differences in the cost of negotiating loans. It will ordinarily cost you more per dollar to borrow from a commercial bank than it will cost a large and successful corporation. This doesn't really mean that you're paying a higher rate of interest, however. You are paying for the costs incurred by the bank in investigating your credit standing and doing the bookkeeping entailed by your loan, as well as a kind of insurance premium that the bank collects from the borrower in anticipation of losses through costs of collection and defaults. If the bank could not charge this premium, it would not find it advantageous to make loans to customers in higher-risk categories. So when legislators impose ceilings on the "annual interest" that lenders may legally charge, they don't reduce interest rates so much as they exclude certain categories of borrowers from contracting for loans. Since the borrowers wouldn't contract for the loans unless they deemed them advantageous, it's difficult to discover in what way maximum interest-rate laws benefit low-income borrowers.

This is an important point, and not only because it corrects certain popular but mistaken notions about interest-rate legislation. The return that any lender will demand as a condition of lending depends on what the lender could obtain by lending to a different borrower *plus* the risk assigned to that particular loan. Commercial lenders aren't unique in that respect. Imagine the bonds of two corporations, one of them IBM and the other a shaky corporation teetering on the

edge of bankruptcy. Both sets of bonds have a maturity value
of $1000 and are scheduled to mature one year from now.
At what prices will these bonds be bought and sold on the
market?

Suppose the IBM issue sells at $917. That $917 now will
be worth $1000 at maturity (in one year) at a 9 percent rate
of interest. The $917 price would mean, in effect, that people
are willing to hold IBM bonds if they anticipate a 9 percent
annual return, because $917 times 1.09, the principal plus
the interest, is $1000.

$$\$917 \times 1.09 = \$1000$$

But the bonds of the shaky corporation would sell for far
less even if they were bought by the same people who purchased the IBM bonds. The probability of default is so much
higher in the second case that buyers could be persuaded to
take the risk only if they were offered the possibility of a
very high return. If the second issue sold for $714, buyers
would be demanding the possibility of a 40 percent annual
return.

$$\$714 \times 1.40 = \$1000$$

If all works out well, they'll receive $203 more than
they would have earned from holding an IBM bond. But that
outcome is highly uncertain, and there is also the possibility
they'll lose most or all of the principal. The higher "interest
rate" on the latter bonds should therefore be interpreted as a
risk premium, rather than as pure interest. Perhaps when
legislators contemplate interest-rate ceilings, they should ask
themselves whether they have ever purchased bonds at a
heavy discount.

Real and Nominal Interest Rates

Interest rates include one other component that has been
especially important since the mid-1960s. They include, as
we have seen, the greater value that present command of
resources has over future command of identical resources
and a premium to cover both the lender's cost of negotiating
the loan and the risk of default by the borrower. They also
incorporate an additional amount to compensate the lender
for any expected decrease in the purchasing power of money.

As these words are being written, the U.S. government is
agreeing to pay 7 percent interest to borrow money for one
year. The risk that the federal government will default is negligible, in large part because (as we shall see in later chapters)
the federal government can manufacture money to meet its
obligations. The cost of negotiating loans to the U.S. Treasury is also negligible. Does this mean that present command
of resources is worth about 7 percent more than command of

The real rate of interest is the market rate (the nominal rate) minus the expected rate of inflation.

nominal = rate in name only (market rate)

resources a year from now? Not at all. It means that lenders expect something on the order of 4 percent inflation over the next twelve months. Since they expect to be paid back in dollars whose purchasing power is going to be 4 percent less than the purchasing power of the dollars they are lending, they add 4 percent to the rate of interest they require as a condition of lending. The market rate of interest, the rate actually quoted, is thus the "real" rate *plus* the expected rate of inflation.

Economists sometimes refer to the market rate as the *nominal* rate (the rate in name only), to express the fact that additional interest paid to compensate for inflation is not really interest. Since 1970, the average rate on high-grade corporate bonds (like those of IBM) over the course of the year has varied between 7.21 percent (in 1972) and 14.17 percent (in 1981). This variation results primarily from differences in expected rates of inflation. The same is true for home mortgage rates. Borrowers who paid more than 15 percent to obtain mortgages in 1982, when rates on new-home mortgages averaged 15.14 percent, were not paying anything close to that rate to obtain present command of living space. The real rate they were paying was about 3 percent. Perhaps 2 percent was for loan arrangement costs and the risk of default. The rest reflected the high rate of inflation generally expected at the beginning of the 1980s.

Uncertainty: A Necessary Condition for Profit

Let's summarize the argument now. Total cost is opportunity cost, and so it includes not only a firm's payments to others for commodities and services used, but also the implicit value of any goods — labor, land, capital — that the firm itself supplies. Interest payments are part of the firm's costs, including the portion of its dividends that is about equal to the interest return its shareholders could have received by lending their money elsewhere. When we include all these opportunity costs in our calculations of total costs, there seems to be no reason why any firm would have to earn revenues in excess of costs. Firms could make zero profits and continue in business. They could even be considered successful firms and be able to borrow new funds for expansion — as long as their revenues were adequate to cover all their costs.

In fact, if there were some way for a firm to get into a line of business that *guaranteed* more in revenue than it entailed in cost, wouldn't so many people move into that line of business that competition would reduce the difference between revenue and cost to zero? Remember that cost means all costs, including an actual or implicit payment for getting the business organized and keeping it in operation. The certainty of a return greater than this would surely attract new business firms. Their entry would increase output, reduce the price of the product consistently with the law of demand, and thus reduce the gap between total revenue and total cost. The gap might simultaneously be reduced from the other direction as the new entrants increased the demand and raised the cost for the inputs used in turning out the product. Only when the gap between total revenue and total cost had disappeared, or when profits had been reduced to zero, would there no longer be any incentive for new firms to enter.

In the actual, continually changing, and always uncertain world, it doesn't work that way. People see profits being made in particular lines of business but they aren't sure how to go about cutting themselves in on the profits. In a world of scarce information, the existence of such profits might not even be widely known. And so *profits do exist and continue to exist* without being reduced to zero by competition. But this happens *because of uncertainty,* in the absence of which everything relevant to profit making would be generally known, all opportunities for profit making fully exploited, and profits everywhere consequently equal to zero.

The same argument applies to losses. No one would embark on a business enterprise knowing that the total revenue was going to fall short of the total cost. But the future is uncertain; events don't always work out as investors hope; decisions are made and actions taken that prove to be mistakes; and so losses do occur.

Since there would be no profits or losses in a world without uncertainty, we conclude that profit (or loss) is the consequence of uncertainty. Profit is thus not a payment that has to be made to obtain some resource or another. It is a residual; it is what's left over out of revenue when costs have all been met; it is the result of predicting the future more accurately than most others have predicted it.

The Pursuit of Profit

Let's consider a simple example. Suppose you read an advertisement urging you to invest in Florida real estate because its value increases by 30 percent each year. A 30 percent annual return is more than you can expect to receive from

a "good deal" that is a "sure thing" won't be a good deal any longer when people find out about it.

Scarce information

alternative investments, so you sink $30,000 into an undeveloped lot near Orlando. You plan to sell it in a year for $39,000. But you will probably be disappointed.

If Florida real estate really can be expected to increase in value by 30 percent per year, many people will be eager to buy Florida lots. Their eagerness to purchase will bid up the price of the lots, until the lots are no longer better buys than other available investment opportunities. If there happen to be many investors who uncritically accept the claims of the advertisement, their eagerness to benefit from the promised appreciation in real estate prices could even bid the present price of lots so high that price decreases — rather than increases — will subsequently occur.

No one can make a profit by putting money into an asset or an operation that is *generally expected* to return more than the going rate of interest. For that would be a "good deal." And the demand for a "good deal" bids up the cost of getting in on it, until it's no longer a better deal than other assets or opportunities.

Every investor knows this. The time to buy Xerox or Polaroid was before the word got around. Those who bought stock in these companies after it became widely known that they were going to earn large net revenues from their new products received no profits. About the best they could hope for was the going rate of interest as a return on their investment. The market price of Xerox and Polaroid stock was bid up by people eager to share in those companies' future earnings, until the earnings relative to what had to be paid to share in them were no more attractive than earnings generally available in the market.

The common notion that one can accumulate wealth by investing in profitable companies is therefore seriously misleading. International Business Machines is rightly regarded as a highly profitable corporation, because it has consistently earned large returns for many years on its original investment. But the market value of IBM stock long ago increased to take full account of its expected high future earnings. Consequently, IBM stock is not necessarily a better buy than the stock of many companies with dismal earning records.

The way to accumulate a fortune is to supply something that can be sold for much more than it costs to produce, or to invest in someone else's enterprises that are going to generate huge net revenues by doing this. But it's essential that this outcome be uncertain. And there's the rub. You must know more than others — or be able to read the uncertain future more accurately — if you hope to make large profits.

Or else you rely solely on luck. But if you rely on luck, you have an equal probability of being unlucky and sustaining a large loss. The significant thing about pure luck is that it's pure. Any investors who consistently make profits, defined as net income *beyond the common rate of return from readily available investment opportunities*, must be predicting the uncertain future more successfully than others.

The Entrepreneur

The argument of the preceding section may have left the impression that people make profits simply by forecasting better than others, so that profits are nothing but the consequence of successful speculation. That would be only a half truth; profit making also has a more active and creative side which we must not overlook. People don't just sit around and bet on the outcomes of other people's activity. They also try — or at least some of them do — to organize things differently. Their incentive is the belief that a particular reorganization will return revenues greater than its costs. The term for such people is *entrepreneur*.

The English equivalent is *undertaker*, a nicely descriptive term whose use we have unfortunately lost by surrendering it completely to undertakers of funerals. Entrepreneurs are people who undertake to reorganize a segment of the social world. What makes them the undertakers or entrepreneurs rather than mere participants is that they accept responsibility for the outcome. They say in effect to all the others whose cooperation is required for their project: "I'll pay you an agreed-upon amount if you will perform an agreed-upon service. If my project fails, you won't lose: I'll take the loss. If it succeeds, you will still get only the agreed-upon amount: I'll take the profit." Entrepreneurs receive the residual, what is left over after all prior agreements have been honored. They choose to put themselves in this position because they think they can "pull it off." They have confidence in their own insight and foresight.

Entrepreneurs are society's agents of change. They are the people who perceive gaps between what is and what might be and opportunities to profit from closing those gaps. They acquire control over the resources they must employ to close the gaps by hiring the resources from their owners. The owners surrender control over the resources they own in return for the entrepreneur's payment. The sum of these payments are the entrepreneur's costs. The difference between these costs and the total revenue from the entrepreneur's project is the entrepreneur's profit — or loss, if the entrepreneur's perception was mistaken.

Everyone Is Doing It

We ought to pause a moment to clear the concept of profit (and loss) from the narrow connotations that it may have acquired in the course of this discussion. Profits and losses appear everywhere, for everyone, and not just for business firms or those who invest in financial assets.

Consider the sad case of Giuseppe Vibrato, who attends a music conservatory for three years, planning on a career in opera. At about the time of Vibrato's graduation, the public abandons all interest in opera. So Vibrato sustains a loss. We mustn't exaggerate the loss, for Vibrato may receive a generous return on his educational investment in the form of many years of listening to himself sing Verdi and Wagner. (Education can prepare people to enjoy life as well as provide them with marketable skills.) But to the extent that Vibrato paid tuition and sacrificed earnings for three years in order to earn an income in opera, the unexpected change in public tastes caused him to sustain a loss. Vibrato took the loss because he was the entrepreneur. The music conservatory received all the tuition agreed upon.

In the same way aerospace engineers suffer losses when the federal government cuts back on the space program, college professors receive profits when the federal government decides to spend huge sums on higher education, authors make a profit when they hit on a book that captivates the public, and highly trained astrologers took a loss when people abandoned the belief that the stars shape individual destiny. (But note also that in the last case some of their intellectual descendants have recently made profits from an unexpected return to older persuasions.) Engineers, professors, authors, and astrologers all become entrepreneurs when they undertake reorganizational projects, including projects to reorganize their own knowledge and skills.

All these examples involve monetary income. But profits and losses don't have to entail changes in monetary wealth. The skier who undertakes a trip to the slopes and then finds rain incurs a loss. If he heads for the lodge to drown his sorrows and there meets his future wife, he makes a profit. If she turns out after several years of marriage to be even more pleasant and intelligent than he had thought, his profit increases. And the profit from that rain-drenched ski trip becomes almost exorbitant if they jointly produce a cherubic child who fills their days with cheer. These examples remind us that undeserved profits occur in all aspects of life and — equally important — that they also depend most of the time on the exercise of foresight and discretion. This last point has considerable political importance.

"Windfall" Profits and Losses

One term that's often used to describe these differences between expected and realized outcomes is *windfalls*. Because the differences can be positive or negative, we should speak of *windfall profits* and *windfall losses*. We don't often encounter the term *windfall losses*, however, and it's worthwhile to think about why we don't. The word *windfall* originally referred to fruit that was blown down from a tree. The fruit was not earned through the effort of climbing and picking but was a gift of the wind, which blows unpredictably and beyond anyone's control. The term *windfall profit* implies an origin in luck rather than merit. Windfall profits are thus undeserved profits, because no one *deserves* good luck.

Of course, no one deserves bad luck either. So why don't we speak of windfall losses? The reason would appear to be that people don't go about claiming a *right* to losses, or insisting that society is violating their rights in compensating them for losses sustained. The adjective *windfall* is only attached to *profit* because only in the case of profit do people frequently want to counter the claim that the recipient earned or otherwise deserved what happened.

When we talk about what people do or do not deserve, we're talking about ethics rather than economics. Ethics is such a difficult subject that we would much prefer to go around it. But economists are once again beginning to discover (Adam Smith was fully aware of it two centuries ago!) that supply curves and demand curves — the most basic building blocks of economic analysis — depend on convictions and commitments that are fundamentally ethical in nature. This fact will be dogging our steps throughout this and the next three chapters. We had better turn now and face it squarely.

Property Rights: An Introduction to the Concept

The heart of the matter from the standpoint of the economic analyst is that the decisions people make in any economic system depend in a crucial way on the property rights that are established and accepted in that society. The term *prop-*

erty rights — as we use it in this book — has a much broader connotation than what is usually conjured up in people's minds. Perhaps when you hear the term you picture a rancher with a shotgun saying, "Git off my land," or someone indignantly announcing, "It belongs to me and I can do what I want with it!" We must enlarge the concept far beyond those images if it's to help us understand how economic systems function, how income is distributed, why pollution occurs, or what we can reasonably expect from government. When economists speak of property rights, they have in mind something closely akin to what we have called "the rules of the game." *Property rights are rights to control the way in which particular resources will be used and to assign the resulting costs and benefits.* It is property rights — or what people believe to be the relevant rules of the game — that determine how the processes of supply and demand will work themselves out in a society.

Perhaps the best way to explain is to illustrate, using the notion of "windfall" profits and losses.

Property rights create expectations. Expectations guide decisions.

How Shall We Treat "Windfalls"?

Oil refiners maintain sizable inventories of crude oil in order to assure a smooth and continuous operation of the refinery. If forces beyond their control increase the demand for or reduce the supply of crude petroleum, its price will rise. The value of the refiners' inventories will therefore rise, too. An increase in the value of a firm's inventories is an addition to its wealth, and additions to wealth are what we call income. Any income of business firms in excess of costs we call profit. So oil refiners, in this case, receive a profit from the occurrence of events beyond their control. Almost everyone will (and did) call that a windfall profit. Some go further and argue that it ought to be taxed away, because the refiners have no right to receive windfall profits. They belong by right to . . . whom?

This case illustrates the dependence of actions on expectations and of expectations on established property rights, as well as the significance of ethical convictions in the shaping or reshaping of property rights. The managers of a refinery accumulate inventories in the first place because they expect to be able to use them when and how they please. (That's not quite accurate; the managers know that they would not be allowed to use the inventories as they pleased if it pleased them to pump some onto the city's sidewalks for the fun of seeing pedestrians slip and slide. But they did expect to be allowed to use the inventories for accepted business purposes.) This expectation reflects existing property rights. Under a different set of rights, the managers of the refinery might have chosen to accumulate less inventory or even none at all. They would have chosen to accumulate very little if, according to the accepted rules of the society, anyone who wants some crude is entitled to draw freely on the inventories of anyone else who happens to have some in stock. The refinery managers would also have chosen to carry smaller levels of inventory had they thought that the taxing authorities would appropriate any increase in inventory value due to price increases, without compensating the firm for losses due to price declines and a consequent fall in the value of inventory. People don't normally accept wagers of the form, "Heads I break even, tails I lose." The accepted rules of the society — customs and moral principles as well as laws — affect people's behavior by defining their property rights.

Expectations and Actions

We're focusing on property rights related to the oil inventories of refiners. But you should notice that everything else associated with the operation of the refineries, including the actions of employees, stockholders, motorists, or legislators, can also be viewed as a response to prevailing property rights. People act as they do because of the expectations created by existing property rights. Employees show up for work because they confidently expect to claim a paycheck on Friday. Stockholders purchase and retain shares because they expect to be cut in, as a matter of legal right, for a percentage of the firm's earnings proportionate to the number of shares they own. Motorists buy automobiles because they expect to be able to obtain suitable fuel at acceptable prices. And legislators draft laws that may alter the expectations of everyone else because they themselves expect to be able to win reelection by doing so.

Expectations are always much more complex than any of the capsule summaries above suggest. Oil refiners don't accumulate inventories exclusively in order to smooth the flow of production or to fulfill their contracts with customers. They also look ahead, try to anticipate changes in supply or demand, add to inventories if they predict higher prices in the future, and reduce inventories to some minimum level if they expect prices to fall. To some degree, in short, the inventory managers of an oil refinery function like the speculators described in Chapter 7. *Thy cannot choose not to speculate,* since both holding and not holding large inventories are speculative decisions, either of which could lead to a substantial gain or loss. Which of these eventually appears will depend on the relationship between what the managers expect to happen and what actually happens.

The windfalls that result from the inventory decisions of oil-refinery managers turn out now to be not altogether windfalls after all. Windfalls are, by definition, the product of pure luck. It follows that managers who obtain them for their firms by predicting the future a little bit or a whole lot better than others are not really obtaining windfalls. They *are* obtaining increased profits — of that much we can be sure. The source of these profits is the fact that the managers' decisions predicted the future more accurately than did the predictions of others. That's also clear. Were the profits deserved? That is not as clear. It's at least in part an ethical question, and one on which opinions differ sharply.

Although economic analysis cannot by itself resolve such ethical issues, it can contribute to a resolution of the debate by clarifying the consequences of alternative answers. If people expect to have the profits from correct decisions taken away from them, on the grounds that such profits are undeserved, and if they also expect that the losses that accrue from incorrect decisions will not be fully subsidized, they will attempt to minimize risk. Decisions will converge toward the average. Only short-range projects will be undertaken. Fewer resources will be invested in research. Innovative projects will be explored less often. Problems that could have been avoided through better foresight will be encountered more frequently. Coordination failures will occur more often as individuals try to reduce their private risks.

If profits are confiscated, but losses lie where they fall...

If both the profits and the losses that arise from the inescapable necessity of making decisions in the presence of uncertainty are removed from those who made the decisions and shared by everyone in society, less care will be invested in the making of decisions. Taking care is costly whenever it means, as it usually does, the forgoing of valuable opportunities. That is why people behave "care-lessly" when they themselves have nothing to gain or lose. It is also why students usually read more "care-fully" in a course taken for grade credit than in one they're only auditing. And it explains why people without theft insurance on their automobiles more often take the trouble to roll up all the windows and lock the doors.

If profits are confiscated and losses are fully compensated...

The significance of these consequences can, of course, be debated. To what extent do progress, achievement, creativity, wealth, harmony, happiness, or any other of these hard-to-define goods depend on the willingness to take risks or to take care? But the consequences themselves could be denied only by someone who was prepared to argue that superior knowledge of a legitimate kind does not exist, that everyone is equally well informed or equally ignorant — except insofar as some have unfair advantages. That, too, could probably be argued. All advantages become unfair advantages if one begins with the assumption that no one *ought* to have any kind of advantage over another. But does anyone seriously maintain this? Are we prepared to restrict the game of basketball to people who are 5 feet, 9 inches tall and require Van Cliburn to wear mittens while playing the piano? The issue of merit, of what people deserve, does without question influence our convictions about the rights that people ought to have. But the rights that people believe themselves to have also entail consequences. In order to secure certain consequences that we want, we may be required to concede rights to people without regard to their personal merit. To take an extreme example: if rewards to criminal informants produce very large benefits for the rest of us, then probably such rewards ought to be paid, even though the informants obviously don't deserve them in any moral sense.

The term *windfall profit* is dangerous, because it suggests that such profits ought to be taxed or otherwise taken away. The difficulty with this is that no one knows how to distinguish the profits that are produced by astute forecasting from those profits that are purely the product of luck. Moreover, the potential of profit is an important, perhaps indispensable stimulus to action. The potential of a profit prompts entrepreneurs to search for more efficient ways of combining resources, new products for which there may be a demand, and organizational innovations that promise to increase effectiveness. The potential of profit often persuades people to take pains when they would otherwise prefer not to and to take chances in which the possible benefits to others are associated with the possibility of substantial losses for the one taking the chance. The potential of profit persuades some people (the unusually courageous, or fool-hardy, or adventurous, or greedy, or perceptive, or knowledgeable, or public-spirited — who among us is competent to judge?) to increase the security of others by accepting risks themselves.

Restrictions on Competition

Something important seems to be missing from this analysis of profit. If profit is always the consequence of uncertainty, what were all those special interest groups pursuing in the preceding chapter? When associations of physicians, plumbers, farmers, airline pilots, nursing home operators, or automobile manufacturers urge the government to restrict competition in their trade, what are they after? They surely aren't pursuing uncertainty. On the contrary, they are trying to reduce uncertainty, at least for themselves, by preventing price cutting and keeping out competitors. If they succeed in their efforts, don't they secure for themselves something close to a guaranteed profit? And a guarantee is at the opposite pole from uncertainty.

As we said at the beginning of this chapter, there is little to be gained by arguing about definitions. We do want to take a closer look, however, to see whether restrictions on the ability to compete really do give rise to something we can call a guaranteed profit.

Suppose that you accidentally — with no investment of time, effort, or other resources — discover the way to build a better mousetrap. You snagged the blueprints, let's say, while out fishing. Recognizing the value of your find, you immediately obtain a patent from the government and make plans to go into production. Since the world will beat a path to the door of anyone who builds a better mousetrap, and since the patent prohibits any competitor from duplicating your product for 17 years, you are going to become rich. It's a virtual certainty. And the first year's results confirm your happy prediction: net revenue is $100,000. You can confidently expect another $100,000 for each of the next 16 years. It looks like an annual *and fairly certain* profit of $100,000. But let's pursue the story further.

What is the source of this "profit"? It's your patent, of course, which prevents competition from eroding the difference between your total revenue and your total costs. But have you accurately calculated the cost of producing these superior mousetraps?

Competition on Other Fronts

If ownership of the patent generates a virtually certain $100,000 per year for you in net revenue, wouldn't its ownership generate just as much income for somebody else? In fact, wouldn't the patent be even more valuable — generate more than $100,000 annually — in the hands of someone who had specialized in mousetraps and knew more than you about their production and distribution? So some of those who beat a path to your door when you build a better mousetrap are going to be established mousetrap manufacturers who want to purchase or rent your patent. You will consequently discover that the cost to you of continuing as the exclusive producer of these superior mousetraps has gone up by the value of the opportunity you spurn if you decline to sell or lease your patent.

Suppose a long-established maker of mousetraps offers to buy your patent for $1.5 million. How might the firm arrive at such a figure? It could estimate that your patent will produce at least a $200,000 annual increase in its net revenue. If the going rate of return on relatively risk-free investments, such as U.S. government bonds, is currently 10 percent, your patent is a good investment at a purchase price of $1.5 million; it promises to yield more than 13 percent per year. Of course, the firm would prefer to get that patent for less. At a price of $1.2 million, $200,000 becomes a 16.5 percent annual return on investment. But there are other mousetrap manufacturers; 16.5 percent is too good a deal for them to pass by, and so the winning bid rises to $1.5 million. That's the process by which the market price of your patent would be determined.

What does all this do to your annual "profit" of $100,000? It wipes it out entirely and turns your "profit" into an actual loss. Do you see why and how? When competition among mousetrap makers sets a price of $1.5 million on your patent, the cost to you of continuing to manufacture mousetraps increases by about $150,000 per year, which is the income you will forgo if you decide not to sell your patent and invest the proceeds in government bonds. What has happened is this: When the word got out that ownership of your patent was a virtual guarantee of profit — an annual revenue greater than cost — potential owners began bidding for the patent. Their bids transformed your "profit" into a cost of production: the value of the opportunity you forgo by not selling.

What about the firm that buys your patent? Will it make a profit afterwards? It might. If events turn out as the firm had hoped and its net revenue does increase by $200,000 a year, acquisition of the patent will prove to have been a smart move. Of course, $150,000 of that $200,000 will be a cost of production: the income forgone by investing $1.5 million in the patent rather than in government bonds. The

$200,000 is 13.13 percent of $1,500,000.

$200,000 is 16.7 percent of $1,200,000.

$1,500,000 will yield an income of $150,000 per year at an interest rate of 10 percent. This is the annual cost of continuing to own the patent.

remaining $50,000 could be viewed as a genuine profit, the result of prior uncertainty about the actual value of the patent to the acquiring firm, a return to the firm's entrepreneurial initiatives in obtaining and employing your patent.

Notice, though, that the process of competition just described will resume once the $50,000 becomes relatively "certain." Other firms might renew the bidding for the patent, raising its price above $1.5 million. Should the patent be worth more than $1.5 million *only to this firm*, that would suggest this firm controls some unique complementary resources — a marketing manager, perhaps, with a special talent for designing ads that arouse the fear of mice. In that case, the price of the complementary resources will be bid up as other firms discover what's going on and try to obtain these "profitable" resources for their own use. If the firm is forced to pay the marketing manager a higher salary to retain his services, a part of the "profit" will turn into an addition to its wage and salary costs.

You can watch this happening in all sorts of places once you have learned where to look.

Competition for the Key Resource

When the government tries to increase the income of wheat farmers by guaranteeing them a higher price for their product, land suitable for wheat production becomes more valuable and so its price rises. Tenant farmers subsequently have to pay more for the land they rent and farmers who try to buy land must pay more to get it. The increased "profit" for wheat farmers at which the government policy was aimed produces, as soon as the policy becomes known, an increase in the cost of producing wheat, through a rise in the cost of using land. The beneficiaries will be those who owned land suitable for growing wheat before it became generally known that the government was going to raise the support price of wheat. The profits from the increase in the support price for wheat will go to those lucky enough or foresighted enough to have the relevant property rights at the appropriate time.

When taxicab operators secure legislation restricting the number of cabs that are licensed to operate in a city, ownership of a license becomes more valuable. Competition for the licenses then bids up their price until the cost of operating a cab — including the opportunity cost of acquiring or of retaining ownership of the license — is equal to the revenue from its operation. That doesn't mean taxicab operators don't get any benefit from their lobbying campaign. Those who owned licenses before the legal restrictions were generally anticipated benefit from an increase in the value of their licenses. That increase is their profit, and it's what they were hoping for when they launched their lobbying efforts, when they became political entrepreneurs. But after the lobbying efforts have succeeded it will cost more to operate a cab, because each cab operator will now have to own a costly license in order to do so.

The right to broadcast on a VHF television channel in a large city is a very valuable property right. If the Federal Communications Commission were to assign these rights to the highest bidder, the government would receive a tidy sum and the "profit" from use of the channel would become a cost of doing business to the broadcaster. In fact, however, the FCC has always assigned the right to use a particular channel, without charge, on the basis of obscure criteria having to do with the merit of competing applicants and the promises they make regarding future public service. As a result, applicants compete by hiring lawyers, accountants, and assorted public-relations specialists to influence the FCC's assignment. In this case the critical resource that creates a "profit" is the FCC's decision, and competition among entrepreneurs consequently aims at acquiring control of that decision. The "profit" from receipt of the channel is transformed along the way into the cost of exerting political influence.

Competition and Property Rights

Profits and losses arise from uncertainty and cannot exist in the absence of uncertainty. Where everything relevant to the making of a profit is known for certain, competition to obtain the profit will eliminate it, either by reducing revenue or by raising cost. There's nothing very surprising about that conclusion; it follows logically from the way we have defined cost and profit. What matters, and what this chapter was intended to clarify, are the forms that competition and entrepreneurial activity take in response to the lure of a possible profit and the social consequences that emerge.

Will the pursuit of profit lead people to produce better mousetraps or to prevent others from selling better mousetraps in their territory? Will it yield more wheat or higher-priced wheat land? Better taxi service or an increase in the cost of licenses? Lower prices for consumers or higher in-

. comes for the owners of critical resources? Exploration or retrenchment? Innovations in technology or in social organization? A wider range of choices or more restrictions on choice? The answers will depend on the rules of the game and the system of property rights that they create.

An Appendix: Discounting and Present Values

If the prevailing annual interest rate reflects the greater value that people assign to goods now over goods one year from now, it follows that the value of goods expected to be received a year from now must be discounted by the rate of interest to determine their *present value*. The process of discounting to determine the present value of future goods plays a large part in economic decisionmaking. Mastering this process will equip you better to understand the analysis of subsequent chapters and will acquaint you with procedures widely employed in the business and financial world.

Suppose that Ivy College, that well-managed institution of higher learning introduced in Chapter 9, offers the parents of entering students a Tuition Stabilization Plan. Tuition, currently at $2000, is almost sure to rise each year, they point out, because of continuing inflation. Ivy even announces in advance its intention to increase the annual tuition charge by $200 in each of the next three years. But parents who subscribe to the TSP receive a special deal. They pay $8000 in September of the first year and nothing thereafter. In effect, says Ivy's multicolored brochure, parents who sign up for TSP save $1200 on the cost of their child's education. Ivy may go so far as to call it a 15 percent saving.

But is $8000 paid now really less than $2000 now plus $2200 one year from now, $2400 two years from now, and $2600 three years from now? The last three amounts are amounts due in the future, and future dollars, like any other future goods, must be discounted if we want to assess their present value. What interest rate should we use? The best answer is provided by the opportunity cost to the parents of lending money to Ivy College, since that is in effect what they are doing. They are lending Ivy money by paying the tuition before it is due. Thus $2000 of the sophomore year tuition is lent for one year, $2000 of the junior year tuition is lent for two years, and $2000 of the senior year tuition is lent for three years. What's the alternative opportunity for those amounts?

What a Present Amount Grows To

Suppose the parents sell stock to obtain the money, and their stock investments ordinarily earn an annual return, in dividends plus increased market price, of 12 percent a year. Then the opportunity cost of lending $2000 to Ivy College for one year is $240. That's $240 expended to avoid $200 in increased tuition — not an attractive arrangement. The junior-year loan is an even poorer investment: $2000 grows in two years, at 12 percent per year, to $2000 × 1.12 × 1.12 or $2508.80. The phenomenon of compound interest is at work, and it makes the three-year loan still less appealing. To avoid the $600 in additional tuition due for the senior year, the parents give up $809.86 that they might otherwise have earned from the ownership of stock, since $2000 × 1.12^3 is $2809.86.

Present Value of Future Amounts

We've assessed Ivy's proposal by calculating what a dollar now will grow to, at the appropriate rate of return, in one year, two years, and three years, and comparing those amounts with the tuition that would ordinarily be due in one year, in two years, and in three years. We can reach the same conclusion by working in the other direction. What is the *present value* of the $2200 that will be due in one year? That amounts to asking: What present sum would grow to exactly $2200 in one year if invested at 12 percent? The answer is $2200 divided by 1.12, or $1964.29, which means that in prepaying the sophomore year tuition the parents give up $2000 now to save $36 less than that in present value. The $2400 that would be due in two years has a present value of $2400 divided by (1.12 × 1.12), or $1913.27, which is $87 less than what the parents actually pay. The $2600, when divided by 1.12^3, turns out to have a present value of only $1850.63.

People who make these computations in the course of their everyday business decisions use tables that enable them to calculate quickly the sum to which a present amount will grow or the present value of future amounts. Three such tables are provided on the succeeding pages. You can use the first two, Tables 11A and 11B, to check the conclusions just presented, which is a subtle way of suggesting that you practice with the tables until you're able to obtain the above results. One more problem will be presented to introduce you to the third table, Table 11C.

TABLE 11A Amount to which $1 will grow in the designated number of years when compounded annually at various interest rates

Year	1%	2%	3%	4%	6%	9%	12%	15%	24%	36%
1	1.010	1.020	1.030	1.040	1.060	1.090	1.120	1.150	1.240	1.360
2	1.020	1.040	1.061	1.082	1.124	1.188	1.254	1.322	1.538	1.850
3	1.030	1.061	1.093	1.125	1.191	1.295	1.405	1.521	1.907	2.515
4	1.041	1.082	1.126	1.170	1.262	1.412	1.574	1.749	2.364	3.421
5	1.051	1.104	1.159	1.217	1.338	1.539	1.762	2.011	2.932	4.653
6	1.062	1.126	1.194	1.265	1.419	1.677	1.974	2.313	3.635	6.328
7	1.072	1.149	1.230	1.316	1.504	1.828	2.211	2.660	4.508	8.605
8	1.083	1.172	1.267	1.369	1.594	1.993	2.476	3.059	5.590	11.703
9	1.094	1.195	1.305	1.423	1.689	2.172	2.773	3.518	6.931	15.917
10	1.105	1.219	1.344	1.480	1.791	2.367	3.106	4.046	8.594	21.647
11	1.116	1.243	1.384	1.539	1.898	2.580	3.479	4.652	10.657	29.439
12	1.127	1.268	1.426	1.601	2.012	2.813	3.896	5.350	13.215	40.037
13	1.138	1.294	1.469	1.665	2.133	3.066	4.363	6.153	16.386	54.451
14	1.149	1.319	1.513	1.732	2.261	3.342	4.887	7.076	20.319	74.053
15	1.161	1.346	1.558	1.801	2.397	3.642	5.474	8.137	25.196	100.71
16	1.173	1.373	1.605	1.873	2.540	3.970	6.130	9.358	31.243	136.97
17	1.184	1.400	1.653	1.948	2.693	4.328	6.866	10.761	38.741	186.28
18	1.196	1.428	1.702	2.026	2.854	4.717	7.690	12.375	48.039	253.34
19	1.208	1.457	1.754	2.107	3.026	5.142	8.613	14.232	59.568	344.54
20	1.220	1.486	1.806	2.191	3.207	5.604	9.646	16.367	73.864	468.57
25	1.282	1.641	2.094	2.666	4.292	8.623	17.000	32.919	216.54	2180.1
30	1.348	1.811	2.427	3.243	5.743	13.268	29.960	66.212	634.82	10143
40	1.489	2.208	3.262	4.801	10.286	31.409	93.051	267.86	5455.9	. . .
50	1.645	2.692	4.384	7.107	18.420	74.358	289.00	1083.7	46890	. . .
60	1.817	3.281	5.892	10.520	32.988	176.03	897.60	4384.0	. . .	. . .
70	2.007	4.000	7.918	15.572	59.076	416.73	2787.8	17736	. . .	. . .
80	2.217	4.875	10.641	23.050	105.80	986.55	8658.5	71751	. . .	. . .
90	2.449	5.943	14.300	34.119	189.46	2335.5	26892	. . .	. . .	. . .
100	2.705	7.245	19.219	50.505	339.30	5529.0	83522	. . .	. . .	. . .

Present Value of Annuities

What should a maker of mousetraps be willing to pay for a patent that is expected to produce an additional $200,000 per year for the next 17 years? It is certainly less than 17 times $200,000 or $3.4 million.

   If U.S. government bonds are available that pay 10 percent per year, $3.4 million invested in them will yield $340,000 a year, which is considerably more than $200,000 a

TABLE 11B Present value of $1 at the end of the designated number of years when discounted at various interest rates

Year	1%	2%	3%	4%	6%	9%	12%	15%	24%	36%
1	0.990	0.980	0.971	0.962	0.943	0.917	0.893	0.870	0.806	0.735
2	0.980	0.961	0.943	0.925	0.890	0.842	0.797	0.756	0.650	0.541
3	0.971	0.942	0.915	0.889	0.840	0.772	0.712	0.658	0.524	0.398
4	0.961	0.924	0.888	0.855	0.792	0.708	0.636	0.572	0.423	0.292
5	0.951	0.906	0.863	0.822	0.747	0.650	0.567	0.497	0.341	0.215
6	0.942	0.888	0.837	0.790	0.705	0.596	0.507	0.432	0.275	0.158
7	0.933	0.871	0.813	0.760	0.665	0.547	0.452	0.376	0.222	0.116
8	0.923	0.853	0.789	0.731	0.627	0.502	0.404	0.327	0.179	0.085
9	0.914	0.837	0.766	0.703	0.592	0.460	0.361	0.284	0.144	0.063
10	0.905	0.820	0.744	0.676	0.558	0.422	0.322	0.247	0.116	0.046
11	0.896	0.804	0.722	0.650	0.527	0.388	0.287	0.215	0.094	0.034
12	0.887	0.788	0.701	0.625	0.497	0.356	0.257	0.187	0.076	0.025
13	0.879	0.773	0.681	0.601	0.469	0.326	0.229	0.163	0.061	0.018
14	0.870	0.758	0.661	0.577	0.442	0.299	0.205	0.141	0.049	0.014
15	0.861	0.743	0.642	0.555	0.417	0.275	0.183	0.123	0.040	0.010
16	0.853	0.728	0.623	0.534	0.394	0.252	0.163	0.107	0.032	0.007
17	0.844	0.714	0.605	0.513	0.371	0.231	0.146	0.093	0.026	0.005
18	0.836	0.700	0.587	0.494	0.350	0.212	0.130	0.081	0.021	0.004
19	0.828	0.686	0.570	0.475	0.331	0.194	0.116	0.070	0.017	0.003
20	0.820	0.673	0.554	0.456	0.312	0.178	0.104	0.061	0.014	0.002
25	0.780	0.610	0.478	0.375	0.233	0.116	0.059	0.030	0.005	0.000
30	0.742	0.552	0.412	0.308	0.174	0.075	0.033	0.015	0.002	0.000
40	0.672	0.453	0.307	0.208	0.097	0.032	0.011	0.004	0.000	0.000
50	0.608	0.372	0.228	0.141	0.054	0.013	0.003	0.001	0.000	0.000
60	0.550	0.305	0.170	0.095	0.030	0.006	0.001	0.000	0.000	0.000
70	0.498	0.250	0.126	0.064	0.017	0.002	0.000	0.000	0.000	0.000
80	0.451	0.205	0.094	0.043	0.009	0.001	0.000	0.000	0.000	0.000
90	0.408	0.168	0.070	0.029	0.005	0.000	0.000	0.000	0.000	0.000
100	0.370	0.138	0.052	0.020	0.003	0.000	0.000	0.000	0.000	0.000

year. Moreover, that $340,000 will continue indefinitely, while the $200,000 will end after 17 years. So the mousetrap maker clearly won't be willing to pay $3.4 million for the patent.

The maximum that the firm will be willing to pay is the present value of $200,000 to be received at the end of each of the next 17 years. (We assume that all the income becomes available at the end of the year to simplify our calculations.) We could calculate that by summing the first 17 amounts in

TABLE 11C Annuity table: Present value of $1 received at the end of each year for the designated number of years when discounted at various interest rates

Year	1%	2%	3%	4%	6%	9%	12%	15%	24%	36%
1	0.990	0.980	0.971	0.962	0.943	0.917	0.893	0.870	0.806	0.735
2	1.970	1.942	1.913	1.886	1.833	1.759	1.690	1.626	1.457	1.276
3	2.941	2.884	2.829	2.775	2.673	2.531	2.402	2.283	1.981	1.673
4	3.902	3.808	3.717	3.630	3.465	3.240	3.037	2.855	2.404	1.966
5	4.853	4.713	4.580	4.452	4.212	3.890	3.605	3.352	2.745	2.181
6	5.795	5.601	5.417	5.242	4.917	4.486	4.111	3.784	3.020	2.339
7	6.728	6.472	6.230	6.002	5.582	5.033	4.564	4.160	3.242	2.455
8	7.652	7.325	7.020	6.733	6.210	5.535	4.968	4.487	3.421	2.540
9	8.566	8.162	7.786	7.435	6.802	5.995	5.328	4.772	3.566	2.603
10	9.471	8.983	8.530	8.111	7.360	6.418	5.650	5.019	3.682	2.649
11	10.368	9.787	9.253	8.760	7.887	6.805	5.938	5.234	3.776	2.683
12	11.255	10.575	9.954	9.385	8.384	7.161	6.194	5.421	3.851	2.708
13	12.134	11.348	10.635	9.986	8.853	7.487	6.424	5.583	3.912	2.727
14	13.004	12.106	11.296	10.563	9.295	7.786	6.628	5.724	3.962	2.740
15	13.865	12.849	11.938	11.118	9.712	8.061	6.811	5.847	4.001	2.750
16	14.718	13.578	12.561	11.652	10.106	8.313	6.974	5.954	4.033	2.757
17	15.562	14.292	13.166	12.166	10.477	8.544	7.120	6.047	4.059	2.763
18	16.398	14.992	13.754	12.659	10.828	8.756	7.250	6.128	4.080	2.767
19	17.226	15.678	14.324	13.134	11.158	8.950	7.366	6.198	4.097	2.770
20	18.046	16.351	14.877	13.590	11.470	9.129	7.469	6.259	4.110	2.772
25	22.023	19.523	17.413	15.622	12.783	9.823	7.843	6.464	4.147	2.777
30	25.808	22.396	19.600	17.292	13.765	10.274	8.055	6.566	4.160	2.778
40	32.835	27.355	23.115	19.793	15.046	10.757	8.244	6.642	4.166	2.778
50	39.196	31.424	25.730	21.482	15.762	10.962	8.304	6.661	4.167	2.778
60	44.955	34.761	27.676	22.623	16.161	11.048	8.324	6.665	4.167	2.778
70	50.169	37.499	29.123	23.395	16.385	11.084	8.330	6.666	4.167	2.778
80	54.888	39.745	30.201	23.915	16.509	11.100	8.332	6.667	4.167	2.778
90	59.161	41.587	31.002	24.267	16.579	11.106	8.333	6.667	4.167	2.778
100	63.029	43.098	31.599	24.505	16.618	11.109	8.333	6.667	4.167	2.778

the appropriate column of Table 11B and multiplying by $200,000. Table 11C saves us that effort. The row for 17 years shows the present value of $1 received at the end of *each* of the next 17 years at various interest rates.

But what interest rate should we choose? If a less risky investment, like government bonds, pays 10 percent, then we wouldn't want to choose a rate lower than 10 percent. On the other hand, that 10 percent rate on government bonds is the return on a *fixed dollar* amount. It is therefore a nominal, not a real, rate of return: a return expressed in dollars that can change in value rather than a return expressed in real purchasing power. If the value of the dollar were to fall 4 percent each year, which is to say, if inflation occurred at a 4 percent annual rate, then the real return from a nominal interest rate of 10 percent would be only 6 percent.

The net revenue from manufacturing mousetraps can reasonably be expected to vary right along with the rate of inflation. If the price of everything doubles, the net revenue from mousetrap manufacturing ought to double, too — if other things are equal, as we're assuming. In that case, we would be taking account twice of the effects of inflation if we discounted the expected net revenue from acquiring the patent at a rate of interest incorporating expectations of inflation. A 6 percent or even a 4 percent discount rate seems more appropriate.

Let's try 4 percent. What is the present value of $200,000 to be received at the end of each of the next 17 years when discounted at 4 percent? Table 11C says that $1 for 17 years has a present value of $12.166. The present value of a $200,000 annuity (an annuity is an annual amount) is therefore $2,433,200.

That's a good bit higher than the $1.5 million estimated in the chapter. Unless that $200,000 is highly certain, however, it's surely too much to offer for the patent. If the mousetrap manufacturer plays it safe and offers only $2,095,400, it would be discounting the expected future income at 6 percent.

At a discount rate of 9 percent, $200,000 a year for each of the next 17 years has a present value of $1,708,800.

Use Table 11C to check these results for yourself. The appropriate interest rate will be one that takes account of the patent purchaser's subjective estimate of the risks entailed in the purchase. Will the patent stand up to legal challenges? Will someone else invent an even better mousetrap? Will new technologies for the eradication of mice turn mousetraps into museum relics? The more uncertain the expected income whose present value we want to determine, the higher the interest rate at which we will want to discount it.

One last question: What happens to the present value of the patent if we assume it can be renewed upon expiration for an additional 13 years? If we discount at 9 percent, $200,000 for each of the next 30 years is $2,054,800. Notice that this is only $346,000 more than the value of a 17-year income stream. That shouldn't surprise you. A dollar that isn't due until 18 years from now has a present value of only 21 cents when discounted at 9 percent. And a dollar in 30 years has a present value of only 7½ cents.

Once Over Lightly

Profit is a term with many meanings. The meanings must be sorted out if we want to understand the way in which economic systems function.

Profit can be usefully defined as total revenue minus total cost if we include all opportunity costs in our calculation of total cost.

Interest, which is often confused with profit, is a cost for anyone who pays it. It is the cost of obtaining present command of resources, or the difference in value between present and future goods. It is usually attached to money loans simply because money represents general command over present or future goods.

Quoted interest rates also incorporate the costs of arranging and insuring the loan plus the expected rate of inflation. The real interest rate is the nominal rate minus the expected rate of inflation.

The rate of interest in a society is typically positive because people generally find present goods more valuable than future goods.

Profit arises from uncertainty. In the absence of uncertainty, any differences between total revenue and total cost would be competed away and profits would become zero.

The possibility of a profit encourages entrepreneurial activity. Entrepreneurs undertake to reorganize some part of the social world in the belief that the reorganization will create benefits greater than its costs. The entrepreneur's profit is the residual: whatever is left over after paying all those whose cooperation had to be secured in order to complete the entrepreneur's project.

The entrepreneur's profits disappear when "the truth gets out." Once the entrepreneur's activity has shown how a profit can be made, the revenue available to the entrepreneur or any imitator will decline. If scarcity of a key resource prevents others from imitating the entrepreneur, competition for that resource will raise its price until cost equals revenue.

The forms that competition takes in any society are determined by the relevant rules of the game, or by the property rights that assign the ability to allocate resources and to appropriate the benefits from their use.

Questions for Discussion

1. Chuck Waggin owns and operates a small tax-accounting firm, which he runs out of the basement of his home.

   (a) The basement was just wasted space until Chuck turned it into an office for his business. He says his firm is more profitable than most tax-accounting businesses because he doesn't have to pay any rent. Do you agree that rent is not a cost of production for Chuck?

   (b) Chuck recently turned down an offer to go to work for a larger firm at a salary of $45,000 a year. Chuck's net income from his business runs about $35,000 a year. Would you say that Chuck's firm is profitable?

   (c) Chuck says he likes being his own boss, and that he would be willing to sacrifice at least $25,000 a year in income to avoid working for someone else. Does that information change your answer to part (b)?

   (d) Chuck recently invested $10,000 of his savings in an office computer. How would you include the effects of this investment in his costs?

   (e) Chuck could have earned 12 percent per year on his savings had he not used them to buy the personal computer. If he had not had these savings, he still would have bought the computer, using a loan from the bank at 18 percent annual interest to finance the purchase. Is the opportunity cost of owning the computer really less for Chuck because he had savings of his own from which to buy it? If Chuck had been required to pay 18 percent interest to the bank rather than giving up 12 percent interest, for what would the additional 6 percent have been a payment? Does Chuck reduce his costs by financing the computer purchase himself?

2. Here are the first three sentences from a booklet on "The Arithmetic of Interest Rates" published by the Federal Reserve Bank of New York: "Everything has a price. And money is no exception. Its price – the interest rate – is determined in the marketplace where money is borrowed and lent." Is it correct to speak of interest as the price of money?

   (a) If interest is the price of money in the same way in which 35 cents is the price of an orange, then we should expect an increase in the quantity of money to lead to lower interest rates just as an increase in the quantity of oranges leads to a reduced price for oranges. Why then are interest rates very high in nations that allow their money supplies to increase very rapidly?

   (b) A large increase in the supply of money will indeed have an effect on "the price of money" similar to the effect of a large increase in the supply of oranges on the price of oranges – if by "price" we mean value relative to other goods. The term we use to describe a fall in the value of money relative to other goods is *inflation*. If an increase in the supply of money creates expectations of inflation, what will happen to interest rates?

(c) Interest is the price of something, but not of money. What is the good whose price has gone up when the interest rate rises?

(d) The law of demand says that a higher price for a good causes less of that good to be demanded. What is the good for which the quantity demanded declines when the interest rate rises?

3. What form would the rate of interest take in a society that used no money but depended entirely on barter for the exchange of goods?

4. You purchase for $900 a $1000 government bond maturing one year from the date of purchase. Will you make a profit if you hold the bond to maturity? Will you make a profit if there is a sharp, general increase in prevailing interest rates a week after your purchase? What effect will this have on the price you can obtain from selling your bond in the market?

5. Humbert and Ambler are very different personalities. Humbert likes to eat, drink, be merry, and let the future care for itself. He suspects that the world is going to disintegrate in a few years anyway. Ambler is only 21 but is already planning conscientiously for her retirement years. What would you predict about their respective rates of time preference? How do people of Humbert's type benefit from the existence of people like Ambler, and vice versa?

6. What effect would you expect the rate of technological innovation in a society to have on the level of interest rates? Why?

7. "When lenders extend credit to high-risk borrowers, they must raise the interest rates they charge low-risk borrowers in order to cover their losses from defaults." Do you agree?

8. Suppose that Congress imposes a 10 percent ceiling on the interest rate that may be charged for federally guaranteed mortgages. Lending institutions, meanwhile, find themselves able to obtain all the mortgage business they want at 12 percent interest. Will they lend at 10 percent? How might the interest ceiling be circumvented? If you wanted to purchase a house and were eligible for a federally guaranteed mortgage, would you want Congress to set an interest-rate ceiling on such loans?

9. "A wealthy society has little difficulty paying interest. But in a poor country with almost no capital, economic planners cannot afford to take interest charges into account in their calculations." What's wrong with that argument?

10. If a district-court judge enters a $300-million judgment against a corporation for violation of antitrust statutes, do the owners of that corporation sustain a loss? What form will it take? If you believe that the judge was in error and that his decision will eventually be reversed on appeal, how could you profit from your knowledge?

11. You buy shares of common stock in two corporations. Over the next six months, the price of one falls and the price of the other rises. Which was a better buy? Which would be the better one to sell if you want cash?

12. Evaluate the following argument: "General Motors has taken advantage of its dominant position in the automobile industry and made huge profits

year after year. It would be perfectly just, therefore, to impose a special tax on General Motors as a way of recovering for society some of the exorbitant profits earned in the past." Who would pay that tax?

13. In March 1980, 157 farmers filed a suit against the federal government asking for $18 million in damages incurred as a result of an erroneous prediction by the Bureau of Reclamation. The Bureau had estimated that water for irrigation in 1977 would be only 6 percent of normal because of a severe drought the previous winter. As a result, the 157 suing farmers had dug expensive wells, planted less valuable crops, and in some cases had planted no crops at all. The actual runoff proved to be much higher than the Bureau's predictions, but the truth came too late to do these farmers any good. What caused the farmers' loss? How do they want that loss to be allocated? Do you think they had a legitimate case? Should a carnival operator be able to sue the weather bureau if almost no one comes to the carnival on a fine, sunny day because the weather forecast erroneously predicted thunder-showers?

14. In the spring of 1963 Fidel Castro announced a sugar-production goal for 1970 of 10 million tons. As the target date approached and it began to appear that this much-publicized target might not be attained, the Cuban government transferred labor and other resources in large amounts from the production of alternative goods into the production of sugar. The goal was still missed by a large margin. How do you suppose the consequent loss was distributed? How would the profit have been distributed had this decision turned out better than anticipated?

15. Oil producers immediately objected when President Carter proposed in 1979 that the decontrol of oil prices be accompanied by a "windfall-profits" tax.

(a) The oil producers claimed that the tax would reduce companies' incentives for new exploration and drilling. The press secretary for the late Senator Henry Jackson, then chairman of the Senate Energy Committee, denied this claim in the following words: "As far as increased production is concerned, the oil companies have an enormous cash flow right now. The incentives are already there." Do profits earned in the past (or current cash flow) provide incentives to explore and drill for oil?

(b) The reported net income after taxes in 1978 of 94 leading companies in the petroleum production and refining industry was $14,971 million. Is $15 billion enough money to finance extensive exploration and drilling for new oil? Were those $15 billion an incentive to explore and drill?

(c) The nine largest manufacturers of tobacco products in the United States earned a net income after taxes of $1,313 million in 1978. Would $1.3 billion pay for much oil exploration? Under what circumstances might the profits earned in the tobacco industry be used to explore for oil?

(d) Much of the exploration and drilling for oil that occurred in the United

States in the past was financed by borrowing, not out of the net income from previous production or refining. Under what circumstances can money be borrowed to finance the search for new oil?

(e) Why would any firm in the business of producing or refining oil choose to invest some of its profits in shopping-center development (or anything else) rather than in exploration for oil?

(f) Does the news that the 94 largest firms in the petroleum production and refining industry earned $15 billion in 1978 make *you* eager to (1) explore and drill for oil, or (2) buy stock in oil companies?

(g) What difference would it make to your answers in the preceding part of this question to know any of the following (which all happen to be true)? (1) Oil industry profits rose 12 percent from 1977 to 1978. (2) The average return on stockholders' equity in the oil industry in 1978 was 14.3 percent compared with 14.0 percent in 1977. (3) The average percentage return of leading manufacturing corporations in 1978 was 15.9 percent; it was 14.9 percent in 1977.

(h) Suppose the government imposes a windfall-profits tax on all net income received from the sale of oil already discovered and flowing, but exempts from the tax all oil that is found after the tax is imposed. Will this maintain incentives to explore and drill for oil?

(i) Why do critics of the oil industry rarely distinguish between producers (who bring oil out of the ground) and refiners (who turn it into useful products)?

(j) Senator Jackson popularized the term "obscene profits" in discussing the profits of the oil industry during and immediately after the original OPEC price increases of 1973–74. Assuming that he intended *obscene* to mean repulsive or disgusting, rather than lewd or sexually exciting, explain the circumstances under which one might reasonably describe profits as obscene.

16. Some people consider the spring herring run near Sitka, Alaska, the most profitable fishing opportunity in the world. Fishing boats have occasionally netted $500,000 worth of herring in a three-hour season. It is not the herring so much as their eggs, called roe, that the fishermen are after, because of the enormous Japanese demand. The basic question: Is it really possible to earn enormous profits by fishing for a few hours in the ocean off Sitka?

(a) In order to protect the spawning herring from overexploitation, the state limits the season to a few hours and a small area and allows only licensed boats to participate. The number of permits has been 52 since 1978. Anyone who wants to participate must purchase a license from a current holder. The price is about $300,000. Why? What determines the going price of a license? How does this affect the profitability of herring fishing?

(b) Boat captains hire airplane spotters to increase the likelihood that they will catch some herring during the three-hour season. Spotting is a dangerous occupation with several dozen planes crisscrossing a small area, and pilots can sometimes command $30,000 as herring spotters. Why are boat captains willing to pay such an extraordinary fee?

(c) If a licensed boat's fishing gear malfunctions, the captain may rent a bystander's boat for as much as $100,000. Why would anyone pay such an exorbitant rental fee? Why would there be any bystanders in the area in the first place?

(d) A licensed boat may catch as much as $500,000 worth of herring. Or it may catch nothing. Estimate the annual loss of a licensed captain whose boat catches nothing.

(e) The crew's wages depend on their boat's success. Are they entrepreneurs? Are their wages really wages? Or are they profits (or losses!)?

(f) If a captain who has agreed to pay each of five crewmen 10 percent of the catch and to pay his airplane spotter 20 percent hauls in $100,000 worth of herring, has he earned a profit?

(This question is based on a *Wall Street Journal* feature of May 15, 1987.)

17. The text argues that if an activity is known to be profitable, more people will go into that activity and the profits will disappear. Does that apply to the selling of cocaine?

(a) The costs of selling cocaine include the risk of being arrested and imprisoned. Why is a ten-year sentence not twice as strong a deterrent as a five-year sentence? Why does one chance in five of being imprisoned for ten years translate into *less* than two years imprisonment? Is a cocaine seller likely to use a high or a low discount rate in deciding on the subjective cost of possible imprisonment? Why is the threat of imprisonment more effective in deterring some people than others?

(b) Another cost of selling is the risk of being killed by competitors. This cost will be much lower for some people than for others. Characterize a person for whom this cost will be relatively low.

(c) For whom is the selling of cocaine profitable?

18. About half of all new restaurants fail within a year, and 85 percent close within five years. What do these figures indicate about the profitability of the restaurant business? Why do so many entrepreneurs nonetheless start up new restaurants every year?

19. In June 1979 the provincial legislature of Quebec gave final approval to legislation authorizing the expropriation of Asbestos Corporation, a mining concern with headquarters in Montreal. Asbestos Corporation was at the time a 55 percent-owned subsidiary of General Dynamics Corporation.

(a) General Dynamics had repeatedly insisted that it did not want to sell to the province of Quebec. What do the officers of a corporation usually mean when they say they do not want to sell a subsidiary?

(b) In a voluntary sale the price is set by mutual agreement. In a forced sale some other method must be used to determine the price or compensation to be received for the expropriated property. A study commissioned by the province put the value of Asbestos Corporation at about $42 a share. A valuation done for General Dynamics set the value at almost $100 a share. If you were the arbitrator asked to decide on the *true value*, what data would you consult to find the answer?

(c) Suppose someone suggests that the fair value of the corporation be determined by the going market price of Asbestos Corporation stock. If the stock were widely held by the public, investors would determine the value of a share by what they were willing to pay to own it or had to be paid to surrender ownership. What is the flaw in this proposal? What determines the price of a corporation's stock when that corporation faces imminent nationalization?

(d) Could General Dynamics benefit from nationalization if the compensation received was less than the sum of what was originally paid to purchase the assets of Asbestos Corporation, plus the cost of all subsequent additions and improvements to those assets?

(e) General Dynamics finally agreed to sell in late 1981, under the threat of expropriation. Soon thereafter, mounting concern over the health effects of exposure to asbestos particles led to a massive decline in the demand for asbestos, and the government-owned firm began to incur losses. By 1985, the stock had fallen to $4.50 a share from $37 a share just prior to its acquisition by the Quebec government. Did General Dynamics profit from the nationalization?

20. Everybody knows that laborers receive wages and capitalists receive profits. But is it true?

(a) If employees agree to continue working for an employer who is currently unable to pay them, because they don't want the firm to fail, are they working for wages or for profits?

(b) If you agree to loan your lawnmower to someone who wants to start a lawn-care business, on condition that he pay you $2 each time he borrows it, are you a capitalist? Is your $2 properly called profit? Would your answers differ if he agreed to pay you 20 percent of his gross receipts?

21. Are entrepreneurs necessarily capitalists?

(a) The text defines the entrepreneur as the one who assumes responsibility by guaranteeing all others a fixed amount for their cooperation. When and why do others trust the entrepreneur's guarantee? If this question seems abstract, ask yourself whether you will work hard for someone when you don't expect to see your first paycheck until you have worked three weeks. When and why will you not trust an employer in this way?

(b) Who besides employees typically receives guarantees from the entrepreneur that they must trust if they are to do business with the entrepreneur? What is the basis for their confidence in the entrepreneur's promises?

(c) Why do employees ever agree to let the employer have all the profits?

(d) Why do employers ever agree to guarantee the employee a certain wage, no matter how badly things turn out?

22. You ask your college for permission to set up a lemonade stand at the annual spring commencement, and the college grants permission. After paying your bills for materials (lemons, sugar, cups, and so forth), you clear $250 for an afternoon's work.

(a) Did you make a $250 profit?
(b) Are you likely to be given the lemonade concession again next year? What difference does it make whether or not word gets around about how much you cleared?
(c) If the college next year auctions off the franchise, how much would you be willing to bid? Who will then get the profit from the lemonade stand?

23. Prior to 1980, the Interstate Commerce Commission rarely granted new permits to trucking firms to haul goods interstate, and operating rights were often extremely valuable. They were listed as assets on the books of trucking companies and made up a significant part of the purchase price whenever such companies were sold.

(a) What factors established the market value of such operating rights?
(b) When the Motor Carrier Act of 1980 took effect, allowing much easier entry into interstate trucking, the market value of operating rights fell. Why?
(c) Was this fall a loss?
(d) Losses as well as profits are the consequence of uncertainty. What was the uncertainty that produced this loss for trucking companies in 1980?
(e) What would have happened to the value of operating rights in the 1970s if everyone had known 10 years in advance that Congress was going to ease restrictions on entry into interstate trucking after 1980?
(f) The Motor Carrier Act of 1980 was a change in the rules of the game. Which were the principal property rights affected, and with what consequences?

24. Seats on the New York Stock Exchange have sold in recent years for about $400,000. Why would anyone pay that much to be allowed to trade stocks on the New York Stock Exchange? Does that price prove that one can make large profits by trading on the floor of the NYSE?

25. The average price of farmland in the United States tripled during the 1970s. How would you account for this? Who profited from the increase?

26. In June 1985 the U.S. Department of Agriculture announced its decision to end controls on hops production. In 1966 each hops grower in business at the time had been assigned a share of the total amount of hops that could be sold. Ever since, new hops farmers have had to purchase or lease allotments from existing growers, at a considerable price. The Agriculture Department, in announcing its decision to terminate the system, objected

to the fact that new growers had to pay for an allotment that had been given to the original growers at no charge. Does the Agriculture Department's objection make any sense? If the allotments had *not* acquired any value after 1966, what would this imply about the original decision to restrict hops production?

27. The following paragraph is condensed from a long letter to the editor of a metropolitan newspaper:

> If you want to make money real fast, buy a mobile home park. You can raise the rents to your heart's content, because the tenants usually can't afford to move. And even if they could, there is usually no place to go, since there aren't enough mobile home parks to take care of all the people who own mobile homes.

(a) If the situation is as dire for owners of mobile homes as the letter writer says, what will already have happened to the purchase price of mobile home parks? Do owners of such parks make huge profits from renting space to mobile home owners?

(b) If existing mobile home parks can be operated very profitably or sold for very high prices, why don't entrepreneurs create more such parks?

(c) If the city responds to the complaint of this letter writer and others by putting price controls on the rental rates mobile home parks may charge, what will happen to the price of mobile homes currently occupying rent-controlled sites?

28. Can those who own the stock of a large business corporation prevent the managers from pursuing their own interests rather than the interests of the shareholders? How can they effectively monitor the managers' behavior and persuade the corporation's board of directors to discharge executives whose goal is power, privileges, and "perks" for themselves rather than net revenue for the owners? Can't the managers generally use their positions and the corporation's resources to nominate and secure the election of directors who will be partial to management rather than guardians of the shareholders' interests? (The question that follows continues this line of inquiry, but in a different direction.)

29. Can those who own the stock of a large business corporation prevent the managers from pursuing their own interests rather than the interests of the shareholders?

(a) What happens to the price of a corporation's stock when it is managed for the benefit of the managers rather than the shareholders?

(b) What would happen to the stock price if some individual or group gained voting control over the board of directors and replaced the management with people willing and able to pursue maximum net revenue for shareholders?

(c) How do these facts create incentives for some people to invest resources in monitoring managers' behavior?

(d) How does the prospect of what managers like to call "a hostile takeover" restrain the behavior of managers? Toward whom is a hostile takeover hostile? Toward whom is it friendly?

(e) Are those who specialize in corporate takeovers entrepreneurs?

30. Marxists often used to argue that the owners of capital were not entitled to any income from that ownership because labor produced all value. Today they are more likely to admit that capital contributes to the production of value, but they still deny the right of capitalists to receive a profit on the grounds that the *ownership* of capital is not productive.

(a) Would you be willing to argue that those who own capital *have a right* to whatever income they can obtain from that capital? Is this the same as arguing that they *deserve* the income? Is it the same as saying that they *ought to be allowed* to receive the income?

(b) Does the productivity of resources depend at all on those who manage those resources, or are all individuals and all organizations equally good at managing resources efficiently? Does the ownership of resources have anything to do with who manages those resources? Is it true that the ownership of capital is not productive?

31. Are the profits of entrepreneurs obtained through coercion or through persuasion? (Definition of terms: *coercion* — inducing people to cooperate by reducing their options; *persuasion* — inducing people to cooperate by expanding their options.) If you don't know how to answer the question, try thinking about the adequacy in this context of the proposed definitions for coercion and persuasion.

32. An increased demand for walnut furniture has greatly increased the price of black walnut lumber, prompting some people to plant black walnut trees on their property. If mature walnut trees are worth $500 apiece and take 50 years to grow to a harvestable size, what is the present value of a black walnut tree that has just been planted? Defend your choice of a discount rate. How low will the cost of planting have to be to induce substantial planting at this time? How will substantial planting at this time affect the probable harvest value of the trees? Do you see why it's difficult to profit from planting valuable trees?

33. A *Wall Street Journal* article on fire safety in high-rise buildings contained this argument: "Sprinklers can save on insurance rates by providing added protection. By one estimate the savings over 30 years would pay for the system, but high-rise buildings are often built by speculators who plan to sell them far sooner than that."

(a) Why is the fact that builders typically sell high-rise buildings within a few years irrelevant to the decision about installing sprinkler systems?

(b) If you don't see that it's irrelevant, ask yourself why contractors who build homes that they plan to sell within a year often put on roofing material with a fifteen-year warranty.

(c) Suppose a sprinkler system costs $30,000 to install and produces savings in insurance premiums of $1000 per year. How many years of such savings would be required to justify the expenditure if the interest rate is 1 percent per year? 2 percent? Are you surprised that builders aren't impressed by savings on insurance that takes 30 years to equal the amount spent to obtain those savings?

34. The Army Corps of Engineers estimates that a canal between Tussle and Big Stone would save shippers $500,000 per year. The canal would cost $20 million to construct and $200,000 per year to maintain.

(a) Is it correct to say that the canal is a good investment in the long run because it will save society a net $300,000 per year and eventually that will come to more than the $20 million construction cost?

(b) About how low would the interest rate have to be to make the canal a profitable investment? (The canal would not be profitable if the interest payments plus maintenance costs ate up the saving to shippers.)

(c) "The advantage of having the government build the canal is that government can do things that are in the public interest whereas private enterprise is constrained by narrow considerations of profitability." Evaluate that argument.

35. A company offers retiring employees an option on their pension benefits. They may choose either to receive a designated sum each month for as long as they live or a lump sum at the time of retirement.

(a) How could the firm go about determining the present value of a certain amount each month for life?

(b) How will a rise in interest rates affect the size of the lump-sum option?

(c) What is the present value of a $10,000 annual pension to be received at the end of each of the next 15 years when discounted at 9 percent? When discounted at 12 percent?

(d) Does a rise in interest rates make the lump-sum option less attractive to retiring employees?

36. Many mortgage contracts on residences include a due-on-sale clause, which says that the full amount of the unpaid balance falls due when the residence is sold. This prevents the new buyer from taking over or "assuming" the mortgage of the seller.

(a) If in 1985 the seller still owed $20,000 on a 30-year mortgage taken out in 1965 at 6 percent interest, and current mortgage rates are 12 percent, why will the lending institution *not* want the buyer to assume the existing mortgage?

(b) If the buyer assumes the existing mortgage, she will have to make monthly payments of about $225 to pay off the $20,000 still due to the lending institution. If the buyer has to secure a new loan at 12 percent, the monthly payments would come to about $295 if the $20,000 balance is to be paid off in 10 years. By assuming the mortgage, the borrower is able to save about $840 a year for 10 years. How will the seller be able to capture that saving for himself?

(c) In recent years some state legislatures and occasionally even state courts have decided that due-on-sale clauses in mortgage contracts should not be enforced. This was a change in the rules of the game. How did it affect property rights, and with what consequences for these parties: lending institutions; sellers of houses with low-rate mortgages containing due-on-sale clauses; buyers of such houses; sellers of houses without low-rate mortgages?

37. The state lottery claims that its grand prize is $1 million. The lucky winner will receive $50,000 upon presentation of the winning ticket plus $50,000 at the end of each of the next 19 years. Is that really a $1 million prize? What is it actually worth? Will you want to use a real or a nominal interest rate to discount these future amounts? Why? Suppose the 19 future payments were all to be adjusted for any intervening changes in the value of money. What interest rate would you use then to calculate the present value of the "$1 million" prize? What effect does the decision to "index" future payments to changes in the value of money have on the present value of the prize?

38. "Save it," somebody says. "Don't sell it. It's not worth much now, but in 20 years it will probably be worth five times as much." Should you save it or sell it? What will $1 now be worth in 20 years if invested at the rate of interest currently obtainable from relatively risk-free loans?

39. What is the present value of each of the following when discounted at interest rates of 4 and 15 percent?

(a) A $10,000 prize in a limerick-writing contest, to be received one year from now.

(b) A $10,000 cash legacy from your Aunt Mehitabel, to be received when you reach your 25th birthday. (If you have already passed it, choose some other birthday.)

(c) $10,000 per year for each of the next ten years, beginning one year from now, as first prize for telling in 25 words or less why you like a detergent.

(d) Ownership of an office building from which you expect to receive an annual net income of $10,000 per year for each of the next 30 years, at the end of which time you expect to sell the building and land for $100,000. Assume the annual amounts are all received at the end of each year.

(e) $10,000 in additional income per year from age 25 to age 65 if you're willing to go to school for an extra 5 years when you reach the age of 20.

40. If a gallon of gasoline currently costs $1, and if the price increases in future years at exactly the rate of inflation, what will be the price of gasoline five years, ten years, and twenty years from now if inflation occurs at an annual rate of 2 percent? If it occurs at a 6 percent annual rate? If it occurs at a 12 percent annual rate?

41. The U.S. Constitution prohibits government from taking private property for public use "without just compensation."

(a) In what manner do rent controls "take" private property?

(b) If a city were required to compensate owners for any losses they incurred as a result of rent controls, would cities be less likely to impose such controls?

(c) If a city *abolishes* rent controls that have been in effect for many years, does it "take" property from anyone?

42. When the government takes over privately owned land for a highway and pays compensation to the owners, should that compensation be based on its value in its present use, on its value in the use to which the government will put it, or on the value of the adjoining land that will increase (or decrease) in value because of the highway? What is unfair about each option?

43. Suppose it costs $100,000 a year just to maintain a large, old church building on Manhattan Island in New York City. Membership has declined to about 100, and so the congregation discusses whether it can afford to keep the church open any longer.

(a) What is it costing per member to continue using the building as a church? What major cost component have you left out if your answer is $1000?

(b) If a developer offers $2 million for the site (not an unreasonable price in Manhattan), what is the annual cost to the congregation of continuing to use the building?

(c) If the congregation had 400 members and was quite capable of meeting the regular maintenance costs, could it afford to ignore the developer's offer of $2 million? What would be the real cost, as distinct from the nominal or money cost, of rejecting the offer?

(d) In 1977, a Manhattan synagogue with declining membership sold its building to a Seventh-Day Adventist congregation for $400,000. The rabbi said he was "happy to get rid of it" because of dwindling attendance and high operating costs. But the new owners soon encountered the same problems. When they then put the building up for sale, it was purchased for $2.4 million. Who, if anyone, made a profit from these transactions?

(e) The people who live near an old, attractive church building would usually much prefer to see the building remain than to have it torn down and replaced by an office tower or condominium complex. In New York City, neighbors have sometimes been able to lobby the Landmarks Preservation Commission and have the building officially declared a "landmark." Once that occurs, the building cannot be torn down or substantially altered. Are such neighbors entrepreneurs? How does such an official landmark designation alter property rights? Would a congregation that wants to sell its building profit from removal of a landmark designation?

(f) The executive director of the NYC landmarks commission, when asked to comment on a suit filed by a congregation whose church building had been declared a landmark, said that "a church should be forever." Do you think this is or should be part of the established rules of the game in society: that church buildings are forever?

(g) A former director for the arts of the National Council of Churches commented as follows on the demolition of church buildings in favor of commercial structures: "I don't give a damn what others think. It's a perversion that property is more important than beauty." Has he accurately described the issue in depicting it as a choice between "property" and "beauty"? (This entire question draws extensively upon a *Wall Street Journal* article of September 27, 1982, written by Luis Ubinas.)

Chapter 12_____

The Distribution of Income

Have you ever reflected on the fact that we all obtain our incomes by inducing other people to provide them? We also produce some goods for ourselves directly, of course, and there may even be a few hermits in the country who never use money and never have to depend on other people's cooperation. Except for counterfeiters, however, we all get our money incomes from other people.

We persuade them to hire us, to buy from us, to lend to us, or simply to recognize that our status entitles us to income. That last technique is the one employed by children to extract income from their parents, by retired people to get social security benefits, by people who qualify for unemployment compensation, and by the lucky holders of winning lottery tickets, to mention just a few. Another way to put it is that we supply what other people are willing to pay for. In short, the distribution of income results from supply and demand.

Suppliers and Demanders

We took this roundabout route to get to that very orthodox conclusion in order to underline the fact that income isn't really distributed — regardless of what the title of this chapter asserts. No one actually distributes income in our society in the sense of parceling it out. People's incomes are the outcome of many interacting decisions, decisions ultimately made by different individuals on the basis of the benefits and the costs they expect from their decisions.

Individuals aren't free to decide just anything they please, of course. Few of us can decide to obtain $300,000 per year by getting others to watch us play basketball. People make *constrained* choices. But they do choose. Income is not a fact of nature. Unlike height and (natural) hair color, choice can change it. Income may be more like place of resi-

295

dence. Although few of us can choose to live anywhere, most of us have substantial discretion about where we're going to live, whether Iowa or California, city or suburb, apartment or house. The decisions of other people, from relatives through employers to housing developers, interact with our own preferences to determine the relative costs and advantages of living in one place or another. Places of residence, like incomes, are the outcome of millions of interrelated decisions.

Those decisions, it should be noted, can even be unfair — and often are. Racial prejudices limit people's options with respect both to choosing residence and to securing money income. Suppliers and demanders sometimes perpetrate frauds. People are the victims of poor schooling or destructive environments that limit their options in later life. Sometimes what matters is who you know rather than what you can do. Thus, the claim that income accrues to people as a result of supply and demand is not an endorsement of existing income patterns but a way of thinking about the subject.

Economic theory explains the distribution of income as the product of the supply of and demand for *productive services*. The word *productive* means no more than *demanded*; an activity is productive if it enables people to obtain something for which they're willing to pay. All sorts of thoroughly disreputable persons (you may provide your own list) are thus suppliers of productive services. Nor does the word *service* necessarily mean that effort has been expended. A man who lives entirely on his inheritance is supplying a productive service, in our sense of the term, by giving up some command over current resources. No one would dream of commending him for effort, since he makes none. But a playboy heir who lives off dividends still contributes to current production by the activity of not consuming his capital. The relevant fact for economic analysis is not the merit of the playboy but the demand for the resources whose ownership provides him with regular income.

The demand for productive services will generate no income for a person who owns no resources capable of supplying those services. The distribution of income among individuals or families depends fundamentally, therefore, on the ownership of productive resources.

Sometimes this is expressed by saying that the distribution of income depends on the prior distribution of wealth. That's an acceptable restatement, as long as we don't define wealth too narrowly. The trouble is that most empirical studies of personal wealthholdings, as well as the ordinary connotation of the word, restrict wealth to such assets as cash, stocks, bonds, and real estate. However, most of the income that Americans receive annually does not derive from ownership of wealth in these forms but rather from the ownership of *human capital*.

Capital and Human Resources

We defined the term *capital* in Chapter 11. As economists use the word, it means *produced means of production,* or *goods that can be used to produce future goods.* Machinery is capital, as are industrial and commercial buildings. But so are the knowledge and skills that people accumulate through education, training, or experience and that enable them to supply valuable productive services to others. Only when we include human capital in our definition of wealth is it at all adequate to say that the distribution of income depends on the distribution of wealth.

   Total employee compensation, for example, regularly dwarfs corporate profits in the government's annual calculations of the national income. During the 1980s, "compensation of employees" came to about 15 times the total of dividends plus retained corporation earnings.

   This does not mean that factory operatives and office workers take home the bulk of the nation's income. The human services that produce most of the nation's income include the services of physicians, corporate executives, athletes, actors, and rock stars as well as teachers, typists, and technicians. The point is that, contrary to popular belief, inequality in the distribution of income in the United States today arises primarily from unequal abilities to supply valuable human services. Human capital has to be included in our definition of wealth, because most income is earned in the United States by supplying the services of human resources.

Human Capital and Investment

Is it misleading, though, to refer to these resources as *capital*? Capital means *produced resources.* To what extent are the abilities that enable people to command high incomes *produced* rather than inherited or just stumbled upon? It seems impossible to generalize safely or usefully in response to this question. Perhaps the word *capabilities* would therefore be a more neutral and consequently more satisfactory term.

Most of the income Americans receive derives from ownership of human capital.

People add to their stock of human capital by investing in themselves.

On the other hand, the implication that these capabilities are *produced* does call attention to a fact of some importance. People can and do choose to acquire additional capabilities in the expectation of earning additional income. They invest in themselves by going to school, acquiring special job training, practicing certain skills, or otherwise adding to the value of the services they can supply to others. It makes sense to refer to such investments in oneself as the acquisition of human capital.

We must once again beware of confusing the question of function with the question of merit, a confusion to which we referred earlier in discussing profits — and which seems to crop up in conjunction with any issue of income distribution. The value of a tax accountant's services doesn't depend on the extent to which his or her skills were acquired rather than inherited. But it does depend on the level of those skills, and that level can usually be raised through diligent effort. The expectation of an increased income from the sale of their services induces tax accountants to pore over tedious tax-court rulings when they would rather be playing golf. Pride and a sense of craftsmanship may also be at work. But the prospect of a greater income exercises a constant and steady pressure on people to acquire capabilities that will permit them to supply more valuable services to others. That's a useful social function, even if we were to decide that all differences between people are ultimately matters of good or evil fortune, so that people are never authorized to say that they *deserve* the incomes they receive.

Property Rights and Income

Who then owns productive resources? They're owned by many different people, individually and jointly, through partnerships, corporations, and informal arrangements. The owners acquired these resources by many different means, most of which we can never hope to untangle in retrospect. The resources themselves have an enormous variety of forms, running all the way from ideas and skills to turret lathes and fertile fields. Do not assume, however, that the people who own productive resources are the ones who happen to have possession or who have the title deed in their safe-deposit box. Property rights depend on the reigning rules of the game, not on mere physical facts.

Suppose you "own" your driveway but are unable to prevent people from parking on the street in a way that blocks your entrance. Since you can't expect to park in it yourself or to receive income from renting the space to others, you don't have an effective property right and consequently don't own a parking space. Perhaps what you own is a shuffleboard court or a splendid place to play hopscotch.

Consider the case of a woman who has been expertly trained as a physician but can't obtain a license to practice because she was educated in a foreign country. She owns a human resource of limited value; the only services she can supply will be to her own family and friends.

The owner of an apartment building under rent controls may be unable to set rents high enough to cover taxes and maintenance. In that case, he doesn't actually own the units. The services that the units provide are appropriated by the tenants occupying the apartments, who are thus the effective owners. The proof of the nominal owner's actual non-ownership in such a case would be his inability to sell the units at any price and his willingness simply to abandon them by surrendering legal ownership to the taxing authorities.

Federal law says that the airwaves belong to the public. But the Federal Communications Commission allows the owners of television stations to use assigned channels at no charge. Since the owners of the stations can appropriate the income from supplying television services, they are the actual owners of the channels. A proof of this will be their ability to sell the physical plant and facilities at a price many times greater than the cost of the facilities' reproduction — *if* the purchaser can expect to obtain, along with the station, the right to use the assigned channel.

The mayor of a city doesn't legally own any of the city's facilities. But if she can expect to enjoy the benefits supplied by a spacious office, a large staff, motorcycle escorts for her limousine, and a place at the head table for just about any banquet she chooses to attend, her wealth is much greater than it seems. She cannot sell these property rights, it's true; so they're limited in that respect. But *all* property rights are limited in one respect or another. The ability to sell is an important part of property rights; but it is only one stick in a larger bundle, and its absence limits but doesn't eliminate property rights.

Ownership is a bundle of sticks. Some sticks may be missing from the bundle.

Actual, Legal, and Moral Rights

A useful distinction that can often help us agree on what we're talking about is the distinction between actual and legal or moral property rights. It is people's actual rights that govern their expectations and consequently determine how they will behave. If the city council decrees that dog owners must keep their pets on a leash while they are in city parks and clean up all mementoes that the dogs leave behind, the council thereby grants city residents the *legal* right to stroll barefoot through the parks without fear or trembling. If the police cannot enforce the ordinance, however, and many dog owners simply ignore it, resident's *actual* rights will diverge from their legal rights. What park users see as their actual rights will determine whether or not they take off their shoes. If they leave their shoes on while indignantly insisting that they "have a right" to a park free of dog feces, they are asserting a *moral* right, a right that they believe they *ought* to enjoy.

Because rights are social facts, they depend on acceptance by others of the appropriate obligations. Until dog owners accept the obligation to monitor their pets' behavior — either to avoid legal penalties or to show consideration for others — park users will not enjoy the actual right to frolic fearlessly and will consequently keep their shoes on while strolling in the park.

Expectations and Investment

Every decision about the use of resources is based finally on the expectations of the decisionmaker. Families and individuals decide whether to consume or to invest their income by assessing the relative values of the benefits they expect to receive from each option. And they choose among alternative investments by considering not only the expected rates of return, but also the confidence with which those returns can be expected. People who fear confiscation of their investments will opt for investments that are difficult to confiscate, even though they promise a lower return than more vulnerable investment projects. Dictators who suspect their control is slipping shift into Swiss bank accounts, and ethnic minorities encountering native hostility invest in jewelry or other readily portable wealth. The most readily portable form of wealth is human capital, which may explain why prospering ethnic minorities have so often obtained unusually high levels of education. Of course, even human capital *can* be confiscated; people who are barred from practicing a profession for which they were trained have effectively been deprived of the human resource which that training created.

When you reflect on the fact that the returns from investment decisions are *future* returns, you realize that a person's rate of time preference also affects consumption or investment decisions. Someone who discounts future events at a high rate will be present-oriented, will prefer consumption to investment, and will thereby choose in effect to receive a lower income in future years. On the other hand, people who discount at a low rate of interest will be more willing to give up present consumption for the sake of greater consumption in the future and will consequently invest more heavily while they're young, thereby securing for themselves a higher expected income in later years. The interesting implication of all this is that people choose, to some extent, their lifetime income profiles.

A further implication is that we can't always tell from a simple comparison of two people's current incomes which of them has the higher income. A promising student in the last year of medical school probably has a large *negative* income. But would we really want to say that he or she is poorer than someone the same age who is earning $10,000 a year from a semiskilled job? The relevant comparison is *lifetime* incomes. That was the comparison relevant to the medical student's decision to become a physician, and it's probably the more relevant comparison for anyone who wants to evaluate the equity of a particular income distribution. ·

Data on lifetime incomes are hard to obtain, of course, except long after the fact. That's probably why we continue to exaggerate the poverty of many people who are students and the wealth of many who were students long ago. The two errors don't necessarily cancel out, however. If public policy responds to these opposite exaggerations by transferring income from the older to the younger group, it lowers the expected rate of return and hence the amount of investment that will occur during people's younger years.

LIFETIME INCOME PROFILES

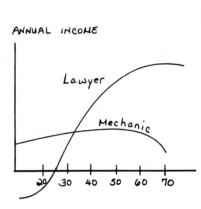

AGE OF INCOME RECIPIENT

The Law of Demand and Productive Services

The demand for the services of productive resources is like all other demand curves: it slopes downward to the right. Other things remaining equal, a larger quantity will be demanded at lower prices and a smaller quantity at higher prices. In the case of productive resources, this relationship may be so well disguised that people won't see it or will refuse to believe it. But the relationship will hold whether it's recognized or not.

The best example is probably the case of labor services demanded by an employer. Employers purchase labor services after estimating the probable contribution those services will make toward the creation of income. They hire when they expect the additional revenue from a hiring decision to be greater than the additional cost which the decision entails. They use the simple rule of Chapter 9: take those actions and only those actions whose expected marginal revenue is greater than their expected marginal cost. The higher the wage rate, the higher the marginal cost of purchasing labor services. Other things remaining equal, therefore, a smaller quantity of labor services will be demanded as the price that must be paid to obtain them goes up.

Why is this so widely and frequently denied? It's denied, for example, by those who insist that opposition to legal minimum wages is evidence of indifference toward the plight of the poor. But do poor people really benefit from legislated increases in the minimum wage? If the legal minimum is no higher than what employers are already paying, it has no effect. It will have an impact only if some covered employers are paying less than the legal minimum. But won't these employers lay some workers off if they're compelled to pay a higher wage, or at least not replace workers who quit?

"They wouldn't have to" isn't a good answer. It's a common answer, because so many people believe that employers pay wages "out of profits" and can therefore refrain from laying workers off when wage rates rise, as long as profits are adequate to cover the increased wages. This seems to imply that the quantity of labor services demanded is a constant, dictated perhaps by technology, so that the only options before employers are either to pay the higher wage rates or to close down the operation. But the demand for labor services is not perfectly inelastic and will at times be highly elastic, because employers can almost always find substitutes, within some range, for labor services of any particular type.

What we have here is a clear example of the Popular Perspective described in Chapter 4. Most voters seem to reason about the minimum wage as if both the number of unskilled persons willing to work and the number of unskilled workers that employers want to hire are constants. Below some low minimum wage ($3 an hour?), no one will be willing to work. Above some maximum ($7 or $8 an hour?), employers who rely on unskilled labor will have to close their doors. Between these limits, both the supply curve and the demand curve for unskilled labor are completely inelastic. Under these circumstances, whoever has the most clout is going to determine the wage for unskilled

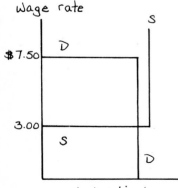

Wage rate

$7.50

3.00

Number hired

labor. Why leave that clout in the hands of employers? When the law steps in and decrees a minimum, employers are compelled to pay at least a decent wage. A modest amount of wealth is thereby transferred from employers (and their customers if employers raise prices in response to the higher legal minimum wage) into the hands a some of the neediest members of society. From the Popular Perspective, the only issue is how we want income to be distributed.

The traditional (some would say notorious) hostility of most economists to a high legal minimum wage is rooted in their conviction that supply curves slope upward to the right and demand curves slope downward. The number of un- skilled persons willing to supply their labor services is not a constant but increases when the wage rate rises, so that more people will be competing for the available jobs when the prevailing wage is higher. And at higher wages, employ- ers of unskilled workers find all sorts of ways to economize on the help they "need."

Consider what the owners of a fast-food franchise might do if an increase in the legal minimum wage forced them to pay a 25 percent higher hourly wage to the teenagers they employ? It simply is not true that it takes a fixed number of workers to operate the franchise; there are many margins on which adjustments might be made that would reduce the number of employees. One is hours of operation; at a low wage rate it might be profitable to open during less busy times of the day; but not at a higher wage rate. Another is quality of service; quick service can be offered at peak times by having surplus employees during slack times; when wage rates rise, economies can be achieved by reducing that surplus and making customers wait a bit longer during peak periods. Of course, that will raise the effective price to cus- tomers and so turn some away; but no sensible business firm wants to serve customers regardless of the cost of doing so. There are all sorts of ways to economize on labor of a par- ticular kind, ways that an outsider won't be able to think of. Some of them will be ways to economize that the owners didn't think of either, until a rise in their labor costs gave them a strong incentive to think harder and longer.

It's true but largely irrelevant that the present federal legal minimum wage won't provide a weekly income suffi- cient to support a family at the level to which most Ameri- cans are accustomed. For one thing, many wage earners don't have families to support or are not the principal source of support for the families to whose incomes they contribute. Nearly one-half of those employed at the minimum wage are members of families with incomes *above* the U.S. average. More crucially, if $150 a week isn't an adequate income, nothing per week is even less adequate. A large increase in the legal minimum wage would produce more income for some; but it would mean less income for a substantial number who could not obtain employment at a significantly higher wage.

It's important to look at the actual numbers when talking about the probable effects of an increase in the legal minimum wage and also at who is exempted. If the minimum is raised to $4.75 an hour at a time when fast-food franchises are offering $5 to starting employees, and if exemptions are written into the law for agricultural workers, employees who receive income from tips, and trainees, the increase would probably have few observable effects. Battles over the minimum wage do sometimes seem to be mostly opportunities for people with different political views to call each other insulting names.

People or Machines?

The strange notion that the demand for labor services of any type is completely inelastic with respect to the wage rate also seems to underlie the widespread belief (or fear) that machines "destroy" jobs because they are so much more productive than people. But what could it mean to say that machines are "more productive" than people? Employers aren't interested in mere physical or technical capabilities; they're interested in the relation between marginal revenues and marginal costs. A machine is more efficient than a person and hence will be substituted for a person only if the marginal revenue from the machine's use *relative to its marginal cost* is greater than the same ratio for a person. That implies, among other things, that wage rates play an important part in shaping the speed and direction of technological change in the economy.

Automatic elevators didn't replace elevator operators in the United States in recent years merely because of improvements in technology. Time, money, and energy were spent to develop automatic elevators — and building owners subsequently installed them — because of benefit-cost estimates they made, not because automatic elevators were new and shiny. In some other society where the wage rates (opportunity costs) of elevator operators are quite low, elevators run by trained operators could still be more efficient than automatic elevators.

The fear that our society or any society may run out of jobs is an odd kind of fear. A job, after all, represents an obstacle to be overcome. A society that has run out of jobs for people to do has come very close to overcoming scarcity; and that would be something to cheer, not fear. We're not in any such fortunate situation. Technological innovations release labor resources from some employments to make them available for others. The automatic or self-service elevator made it possible for people who were formerly employed in transporting passengers up and down to do something else, to make some other and additional contribution to our total output of commodities and services.

The reallocation of labor in response to changed circumstances does lead to a loss of wealth for some people. A rising demand for labor attracted some elevator operators into more remunerative employments and pulled up the wages of the rest; automatic elevators were in part a response to this situation. But as they were introduced, some elevator operators found themselves pushed rather than pulled: deprived of their present jobs and compelled to accept less desirable alternatives, rather than attracted away from their present positions by better opportunities. Such people suffered, at least temporarily, a loss of wealth. They were forced to incur the cost of searching for new employment, and they were not guaranteed that the new job would be better than the old. Resistance to technological change and fear of automation are therefore quite understandable. Even college professors have been known to speak harshly about the introduction of such technological innovations as videotaped lectures and teaching machines.

The Derived Demand for Productive Services

Another factor that may help to conceal the downward-sloping character of the demand curve for productive services is the derived nature of that demand. The demand for productive services is derived from the demand for the goods they produce. When firms announce that they're expanding their hiring or laying some workers off, they almost never attribute the decision to a change in wage rates. Instead, they credit (or blame) the market for their product: "Sales have increased beyond our expectations" or "Inventories of finished goods have grown to unacceptable levels because of disappointing sales." Thus, the quantity of services demanded at any time from carpenters or automobile assemblers will seem to depend on conditions in the housing or automobile market, rather than on the wages of carpenters or automobile assemblers.

But they actually depend on both. The prices of houses and of automobiles and the way they are produced have been influenced by the wage rates that had to be paid to obtain the services of carpenters and of automobile assemblers. In the case of carpenters, fewer new houses are purchased, and hence fewer carpenters are employed, insofar as the cost of obtaining carpenters' services has raised the price of new construction. Moreover, houses are increasingly constructed in ways that economize on carpenters' services, with less elaborate woodwork, for example, and with factory-built cabinets.

Demand Creates Income

Our discussion of the demand for productive services has emphasized the demand as a *constraint:* the income that owners of productive resources can obtain by supplying the services of the resources they own is limited by the demand for those services. The corollary also deserves emphasis: the income that resource owners can receive is *created* by the demand for the services of those resources. Any sheik who owns an oil well provides a vivid illustration.

Whether a country like Kuwait, which each year produces about a thousand barrels of oil per inhabitant, is fabulously wealthy or almost desperately poor depends on the demand for the services of a thick and flammable liquid hydrocarbon that seemed both ugly and useless when it was first discovered. In the absence of that demand, the Organization of Petroleum Exporting Countries (OPEC) would have had less influence over world affairs during the 1970s than the Audubon Society. But given the enormous demand that had developed in this century for the services of petroleum, OPEC became a household word.

Who Competes Against Whom?

When owners of productive resources form organizations like OPEC in an effort to increase their incomes, they often argue that their association will enable them to compete more effectively against the buyers of whatever service they're supplying. Whether we call this argument confused or devious depends on how we want to assess the motives of those who make it. The plain fact is that buyers don't compete against sellers. Buyers compete against one another to obtain what sellers are supplying. Sellers compete against sellers to obtain the custom of buyers. The competition that OPEC was designed to eliminate was competition among the petroleum-exporting countries. OPEC succeeded insofar as it was able to restrict production.

Buyers may try to play the same game. We can refer at this point to an example used earlier: the agreement among owners of professional sports teams not to compete for the services of athletes. To make this agreement effective they had to assign the exclusive right to each athlete's services to a single owner. This is the purpose of the "draft," as developed by owners' associations in major professional sports. When buyers present this kind of unified position, organization on the part of sellers may be an effective way of countering their power. But the objective of the sellers' association in such circumstances would be to *reactivate competition* among the buyers or to *reduce competition* among the sellers and could not be described correctly as an attempt to compete more effectively against the buyers.

Unions and Competition

In the case of labor unions, the basic federal statute regulating union organization and collective bargaining makes the mistake of asserting in its preamble that unorganized workers need unions to help them compete against corporations. But workers compete against workers, corporate employers against corporate employers. And this is the competition that affects wage rates.

Employers can't pay their workers whatever wage their callous hearts suggest for the same reason that Exxon was never able to buy oil from Saudi Arabia for whatever price it chose. Workers have alternative opportunities in the form of other employers, and Saudi Arabia always had alternative opportunities in the form of other refiners. The services of workers are valuable to employers, and so they're willing to bid for them, even though that may raise the going wage. The services of crude oil are valuable to refiners, and so they too are willing to bid, raising its price above $3 a barrel in 1972 before OPEC learned how to restrict production, above $30 a barrel when OPEC mastered the art, and keeping it for a while above $20 a barrel even when OPEC began to disintegrate in the 1980s.

Similarly, workers cannot successfully insist on the wage they think they deserve if other workers are willing to supply very similar services at lower wage rates. Workers

Buyers prefer that sellers have 12 men on the field rather than 11, because buyers don't compete against sellers.

WAGE RATE

S

D

Employment

Employment opportunities are eliminated by enforcement of high wage.

compete against other workers, and unions are in part attempts to control *this* competition. The implication is that unions improve the position of the members they represent by finding ways to restrict competition from those who are not members of the union. They may do this directly, for example, by securing contracts with employers that make union membership a prior condition of employment and then limiting membership. Or they may do it indirectly. Just as a legal minimum wage excludes some people from employment opportunities, so a high wage secured by union contract (perhaps under the threat of a strike or total withdrawal of labor services) excludes those who would be willing to work for less.

The belief that unions arose in the United States to counter the power of large corporations is unsupported by history. Unions first became powerful in this country in industries characterized by small-scale firms: construction, printing, textiles, mining. The railroads are an exception that supports the rule: it was special legislation that enabled unions to become powerful in the railroad industry. The unions that today bargain with the large corporations in steel, automobiles, and electrical machinery were originally missionary projects of the unions that bargained mostly with small employers.

Family Incomes Since World War II

What does it all come to? What's the pattern of the income distribution among people in the United States?

There are many ways to summarize and present the data on income distribution that the Bureau of the Census gathers. The most common is the quintile (by fifths) distribution of family income. The Census Bureau counted a little over 65 million families in the United States in 1987. This includes everyone except individuals living alone or living with persons to whom they were not related by kinship or marriage. Table 12A shows the percentage of total family income received in 1987 and in four earlier years by the 20 percent of these families with the lowest incomes, by the second-lowest fifth, and so on up to the 20 percent who received the highest incomes. If family income were equally distributed, each fifth would receive 20 percent of the total. That obviously isn't the case. The percentage received by the highest 5 percent is also shown in the table.

People who encounter these data for the first time are usually quite surprised. The figures seem to indicate that the

TABLE 12A   Money income of families — percentage of
aggregate income received by each fifth and highest
5 percent

	1950	1960	1970	1980	1987
Lowest fifth	4.5	4.8	5.4	5.1	4.6
Second fifth	12.0	12.2	12.2	11.6	10.8
Middle fifth	17.4	17.8	17.6	17.5	16.9
Fourth fifth	23.4	24.0	23.8	24.3	24.1
Highest fifth	42.7	41.3	40.9	41.6	43.7
Highest 5 percent	17.3	15.9	15.6	15.3	16.9

Source: U.S. Bureau of the Census, *Current Population Reports*, series P-60, No. 162.

distribution of income in the United States hasn't changed
significantly since World War II, despite progressive income
taxes and vastly expanded government programs for transferring income to low-income families and individuals. The
data don't agree with "what everyone knows."

In this case, however, "what everyone knows" may be
more accurate than what the percentages seem to show. To
begin with, these percentages refer to income before the payment of personal taxes. The data also take no account of
in-kind transfers. They do reflect *money transfers*. Thus,
they include income from private pensions, veterans' benefits, social security benefits, the program of Aid to Families
with Dependent Children (AFDC), and all other welfare assistance — *when paid in money*. But they don't include the
value of such in-kind transfers as medical assistance, rent
subsidies, or food stamps — all of which are income even
though they don't involve the exchange of money. Nor are
the data adjusted to take account of differing family sizes.
The top quintile contains 30 percent more persons than the
lowest quintile.[1] When these adjustments are made, the
share of lower-income groups rises and that of upper-income
groups falls. One careful attempt to make these adjustments
for the year 1984 produced the results shown in Table 12B.
The share of the top fifth declines from nine times to five
times that of the bottom fifth.

A Spurious Rigidity

A more fundamental difficulty with data of this sort is that
they don't actually mean what they seem to say. Even the
adjusted data of Table 12B give a misleading picture of the

[1]It's also important to know that families in the top quintile supply four
times as many weeks of work as families in the bottom quintile.

TABLE 12B Percentage of aggregate family income received by each fifth of families in 1984: Census Bureau data and adjusted data

	Money Income as Calculated by Census Bureau	Census Bureau Data Adjusted to Take Account of Taxes, In-kind Transfers, and Family Size
Lowest fifth	4.7%	7.3%
Second fifth	11.0	13.4
Middle fifth	17.0	18.1
Fourth fifth	24.4	24.4
Highest fifth	42.9	36.8

Source: Frank Levy, *Dollars and Dreams* (New York: Norton, 1987) p.195.

actual inequality of the U.S. family-income distribution. We're inclined to assume without thinking about it that the families in the second or fourth quintile in a current year are the same families (or an earlier generation of the same families) who occupied those fifths in some preceding year. This isn't necessarily the case. In fact, it's quite unlikely to be the case for one simple reason: the relative income position of a family depends very much on the age of the family's principal earner.

The data of Table 12C illustrate what we're talking about. They show the median income of all families in 1987 by the age of the householder. (Embarrassed by its use of the term *head*, the Bureau has substituted the term *householder*, defined as the owner of the residence or, in the case of joint ownership, the person whose name appears first on the survey form.) The table demonstrates unmistakably that a substantial amount of the inequality that shows up in a still picture would disappear if we were able to take a moving picture — that is, to compare the incomes of families over the lifetimes of the householders.

When we compare the data of Table 12C with the upper

TABLE 12C Family money incomes in 1987

Age of Householder	Median Income
15 to 24 years	$16,204
25 to 34 years	26,923
35 to 44 years	34,929
45 to 54 years	37,250
55 to 64 years	27,538
65 years and over	14,334

Source: U.S. Bureau of the Census, *Current Population Reports*, series P-60, No. 162.

limits of the various family-income quintiles in 1987, we find that "an average family" would move in its lifetime from the second fifth through the middle fifth into the fourth fifth and descend to near the top of the lowest fifth when the householder retires.[2]

On Redistributing Income

Interest in issues of this sort usually grows out of a belief that too much inequality in the distribution of income is undesirable. Few people pause to think their way carefully through the questions of why inequality is undesirable, how much inequality is acceptable, or why income inequality should be of so much more concern than inequalities of other kinds.

Regardless of how these important questions are answered, programs to reduce the income inequality among U. S. families and individuals will run up against a fundamental difficulty: since income isn't really distributed, it can't actually be redistributed. No one is in a position to apportion shares of the social product. The most that even government can do is alter the rules of the game in the hope of securing a preferred outcome. What happens next will not be exactly what was intended and may be something altogether different.

The simplest and most direct way to reduce income inequality would appear to be a program of taxes on high incomes and cash transfers to people with low incomes. But nothing about economic systems is ever as simple and direct as it seems at first glance. To raise taxes on high incomes, the government must change the rules that relate taxes owed to particular kinds of income received. When it does so, people don't merely pay the higher taxes; they also try to adjust their behavior to minimize the impact of the new rules. Some of these adjustments will be legal tax avoidance; others may be illegal tax evasion; but they all combine to drive a wedge between what was intended when the rules were rewritten and what actually emerges. The revenue that results from the tax increase will be less, and may be much less, than what was hoped for.

In order to supplement the incomes of poor people, government must write new rules controlling eligibility for grants. These rule revisions will also have undesired effects

---

[2]The upper limits of the lowest through the fourth fifth in 1987 were, respectively, $14,450; $25,100; $36,600; and $52,910.

as people adjust their behavior to fit the new criteria. Once again the adjustments will be both legal and illegal; but their combined effect can be substantial, because there are so many margins along which adjustments can be made. The number of people classified as poor may actually increase as a result of efforts to reduce poverty.

Consider the hypothetical but unfortunately not implausible case of a single-parent family with three small children. Suppose the mother is currently receiving $400 a month in cash grants, food stamps worth $100 per month, and subsidized medical care for herself and the children worth $50 a month. Then she obtains a job offer promising $1000 per month. Will she take the job and go off welfare? Would she be better off if she did so?

Her income from welfare is not taxed; but she will have to pay social security and income taxes on her earnings. She will also have to secure day care for the children, buy some additional clothing, and incur transportation expenses if she takes the job. Moreover, she will lose her monthly cash grant and her family's eligibility for food stamps and medicaid. When she adds up all these costs of taking the job, she may find that her earnings are going to be taxed at a marginal rate of 90 percent or more.

Plug in some plausible numbers and check the results for yourself. If the income and social security taxes plus day care, transportation, and clothing expenses take $350 a month from her paycheck, and the loss of welfare reduces her monthly income by $550, she would be giving up $900 in order to earn $1000. That amounts to a 90 percent marginal tax rate, or a 90 percent tax on *additions* to her welfare income — which isn't terribly attractive. No one could accuse a mother in such a situation of laziness or irresponsibility if she decided to turn down the job offer, stay on welfare, and care for her children.

People with yachts are wealthy; people who scrounge through trash barrels and garbage cans are poor. But if we write new rules that obligate every yacht owner to contribute $10,000 a year to a fund for trash and garbage scroungers and grant each scrounger a right to $2000 a year from the fund, the number of recorded yacht owners will rapidly decline and the number of people claiming to be scroungers will show a remarkable increase. That may be an overly dramatic way to summarize the problem, but it makes the essential point. A large society such as the United States cannot allocate tasks and benefits to its citizens the way that loving parents do it in a family: on the basis of abilities

Marginal tax rate:
the percentage of additional income taken by the tax collector.

and needs. Tasks and benefits will inevitably be allocated in response to people's pursuit of their own interests under the perceived rules of the game. What government can achieve by way of income redistribution is pretty well confined to what can be achieved by changing the rules. That will almost certainly turn out to be something less satisfactory than what was hoped for when the rules were changed.

Changing Rules and Social Cooperation

It might be thought that the solution is to change the rules again when the initial change doesn't yield the desired results, and to keep on modifying the rules until the target has been attained. But who has the knowledge that would be required to choose these fine adjustments? Even if the knowledge were available, would anyone have the power to put them into effect in a democratic society? Most important of all, what happens to the complex cooperative processes on which a highly specialized economic system depends if the society is subjected to continuous changes in the rules of the game?

People invest, make sacrifices, and otherwise commit themselves in the belief that established property rights will be respected, that the rules will *not* be changed "in the middle of the game." A rule that says the rules can be changed at any time would destroy the foundation for most social cooperation. Property rights must be reasonably clear and stable if people are to plan for the future and to take long-run consequences into account.

It's also worth observing that when expectations are regularly frustrated by unanticipated changes in the rules of the game, participants stop playing the ordinary game and shift their attention to the game that matters: making the rules.

Once Over Lightly

The distribution of income is the result of the supply of and demand for productive services.

The production of productive resources is investment, or the creation of capital. One important form of capital is human capital, or productive capabilities embodied in human beings. The production of human capital is an important consideration, because monetary income is primarily earned in the United States, even by the wealthy, through supplying the services of human resources.

The amount and nature of the investment that will occur in a society depend on established and accepted property rights, because property rights determine what people can expect from the actions that are open to them.

Lower rates of time preference encourage investment over consumption. Greater uncertainty about future returns from investment will prompt the discounting of future income at higher rates and consequently will lead to less investment.

The demand for productive services of any kind will not be perfectly inelastic. A greater quantity will be demanded at lower prices and a lesser quantity at higher prices, because there are substitutes for any productive service.

Potential users of productive services decide on the amount they will demand by comparing the marginal-benefit/marginal-cost ratios of alternative procedures for achieving their purposes.

The demand for productive services, and hence their price, is partly dependent on the demand for the goods they produce. But the price of productive services also reacts back on the cost and price of producing particular goods and thus on the quantity that will be produced and sold.

Suppliers of productive services don't compete against buyers of those services. Suppliers compete against other suppliers, buyers against other buyers. The quest for higher incomes produces attempts to suppress competition, because what a seller can obtain and what a buyer must pay will depend on the alternative opportunities that competitors are providing.

Census Bureau data on the distribution of family money incomes exaggerate the inequality of income in the United States by neglecting in-kind transfers, personal taxes, differences in family size, and other important factors. They also give an erroneous impression of rigidity by ignoring the extensive circulation of individual families throughout the overall distribution.

Social cooperation on any extensive scale requires relatively stable property rights because it presupposes the ability to predict the consequences of decisions.

Questions for Discussion

1. *Income* is a flow of receipts per unit of time: $240 per week, or $30,000 a year. *Wealth* is a stock of assets: cash, shares of stock, buildings, tools, and so on. How are income and wealth related?

(a) If you own an annuity that will pay you a $10,000 income for each of the next 20 years, what is the present value of that annuity? How much does the annuity contribute to your wealth?

(b) Suppose you own 100 shares of stock in a promising new company that has not yet begun to pay dividends and probably won't do so for several years. The stock is currently exchanging on the New York Stock Exchange for $50 a share. What is your wealth from ownership of this stock? If you wanted to convert this wealth into income, how could you do so? About how much income could you obtain without reducing the amount of your wealth?

(c) Why would the stock referred to above be bought for $50 a share if the company isn't expected to pay any dividends for several years?

(d) A privately owned automobile is wealth. Does it yield income to its owner? In what form?

(e) What determines the market value of a house and thus its contribution to the wealth of the owner? Do the expected benefits from living in the house (income) determine the value of the house (wealth)? Or does the price of the house determine the income received by living in it? Suppose someone happens to detest the house which he owns and occupies because it has such distracting views of the bay and the mountains from every window. Would this idiosyncratic attitude reduce his income from living in the house? Would it reduce his wealth from owning the house? What behavior would this inconsistency between his income and his wealth probably induce?

(f) Is an engineering degree wealth? What determines the value of such a degree? How could an engineer with a freshly minted degree who is just beginning her first job convert some of her wealth into current income in order to buy furniture for her apartment?

(g) A successful and popular physician decides to retire and "sell his practice." What is he actually selling? What will determine its value to a potential buyer?

(h) Is the expectation of future retirement benefits a part of one's wealth? Is the expectation of social security benefits a major part of the wealth of someone 65 years of age?

2. In a widely publicized 1983 case, the ex-wife of a doctor sued to obtain half the value of his medical degree, on the grounds that she had helped put him through medical school and was entitled to half of everything they owned under California's community property law.

(a) The attorney for the doctor insisted that education was not property and so could not be shared because it had no value at the time it was acquired. If the doctor had dropped dead upon receiving his diploma, his wife would not have gotten one cent, the attorney claimed. Do you agree?

(b) Suppose the couple had owned a house which burned down at the time of their divorce. What steps do people take to protect themselves against the accidental destruction or other loss of valuable physical assets? What steps do young physicians usually take to assure their families a large income even if the physician drops dead?

(c) The wife's attorneys asked for $250,000 as her share of the value of her ex-husband's medical training. Suppose the medical degree could be conservatively expected to add $30,000 per year for 30 years to what the doctor would have earned without the degree. Since this amount will presumably rise with any inflation that occurs over the period, a real rather than nominal interest rate should be used to calculate its present value. Would you support the ex-wife's attorneys in their estimate of what she was entitled to? What is one-half the present value of a $30,000 annuity for 30 years when discounted at 4 percent?

(d) The doctor said: "I don't think she is entitled to half of my future." His ex-wife said: "I should get a return on my investment in the partnership." The couple separated after ten years of marriage during which she worked as an accountant while he completed medical school, an internship, and a residency. How would you decide the issue?

3. When the New York Knicks professional basketball team was negotiating a contract with Patrick Ewing, the first player chosen in the 1985 draft, they estimated that his signing would induce twice as many people to purchase season tickets. That would add $3 million to the Knicks' revenue in ticket sales alone. What was the value to the Knicks of Ewing's services? Was this value *human capital*?

4. Alpha and Beta are identical twins. Alpha quit high school at age 15 to take a job because she craves a sporty car. Beta believes her sister is foolish; she intends to go to college, obtain a graduate degree, and make far more money than Alpha will ever see.

(a) Why does the fact that Beta's income will be far larger than Alpha's after ten years not necessarily mean that Alpha made a foolish decision from the standpoint of monetary income?

(b) Use the tables of Chapter 11 to compare (1) the present value at age 15 of $20,000 per year to age 65 with (2) the present value at age 15 of $40,000 per year to age 65 when the latter income doesn't start until age 25. Compare these amounts at discount rates of 12 percent and again at discount rates of 3 percent.

(c) Would it be irrational for Alpha to discount future income at a rate of 12 percent?

5. Should college students be required to pay the full cost of their own education?

(a) Who benefits from a person's obtaining a college education?

(b) If only low-income students are to receive educational subsidies, where would you place the ceiling on low incomes?

(c) If education is an investment designed to secure a higher future income, why don't people who want to acquire years of expensive education simply borrow the money — the way business firms borrow to finance investment?

6. If television channels belong to the public, not to the owners of the television stations who are allowed to use them, why will the sale price of a television station often be more than ten times the cost of replacing all the physical facilities that change hands after the sale? What is the previous owner selling?

7. Who owns national parks? The government? The people? Park Service officials in the Interior Department? What are the implications of a sign that reads: "U.S. Government Property: No Trespassing"?

8. Your airplane boarding pass assigns you seat A, by the window. When you come to your row you find a six-year-old child sitting in your seat. His boarding pass says C. You ask him to move, but he says he wants to look out the window and tells you to take his seat on the aisle. Since you also want to look at the scenery, you call the cabin attendant and explain the situation. The cabin attendant says, "Do you *really* want me to make that little child move away from the window?"

    At this point, who owns seat A? Sort out the actual, legal, and moral property rights in this case.

9. A Santa Monica apartment owner decided to tear down his six-unit apartment building rather than operate under rent controls. The city refused him permission to tear down the building, however, claiming that its interest in preserving rental housing took precedence over his right to demolish his property. The California Supreme Court sustained Santa Monica's refusal to allow the demolition.

    Who owns the building? Sort out the actual, legal, and moral property rights in this case.

10. "Entitlement programs" of the federal government are defined as "programs that provide benefit payments for individuals whose eligibility is determined by law." Because the criteria for eligibility are established by existing law, expenditures are not controlled by the process of congressional appropriation.

    (a) Would you say that the beneficiaries of entitlement programs receive income because of certain property rights?

    (b) The criteria for some entitlement programs are outside the range of the beneficiaries' choice: payments based on age are an example, or veterans' benefits. Other programs use criteria that persons can more or less choose to satisfy. Would you expect the law of demand to affect the rate at which expenditures increase in this second category?

11. Prior to 1977, the national food stamp program gave each participating household a monthly stamp allotment sufficient to purchase a minimally adequate diet. The allotment varied with family size but not with family income. What varied with income was the price the family had to pay for the stamps. This ranged from nothing for the poorest families to about 85 percent of the stamps' value for the eligible families with the highest

incomes. This system was changed in 1977 to one in which allotments did vary with family income but stamps were given away rather than sold. The 1977 reform received strong support from the argument that it was absurd if not downright immoral to make poor people pay for food stamps. Was it absurd? What were the consequences of this policy?

(a) Suppose a family earning $300 a month chooses to spend $150 on housing, $100 on food, and $50 on other goods. Then it is given $100 in food stamps. Why can't we predict how much the family will subsequently spend per month on housing, food, and other goods? What is the range of possibilities?

(b) If government officials want to be sure that the poor family uses its food stamp allotment to double its monthly expenditure on food, how can they constrain the family's choice to the outcome desired by the officials? (Assume that the family does not sell the stamps for money, something that does occur but is illegal.)

(c) Is a family better off if it chooses to use food stamps as a substitute for income previously spent on food, so that it can increase its consumption of other goods? Or should the family be constrained to follow an expenditure pattern dictated by government officials (and presumably based on the recommendations of nutritionists)?

(d) If the government makes large grants to church-owned colleges to support instruction in science but provides no funds to support religious instruction, does the government in reality support science but not religion?

(e) If a donor to a united charity appeal earmarks her contribution for alcoholism counseling, does she thereby increase the funds that will be available for alcoholism counseling in her community?

12. The claim is often made — and also often ridiculed — that taxes on income reduce people's incentives to earn income.

(a) If you were required to pay the government 50 percent of all money income you earn during the summer, would you choose to work more or fewer hours than if your income was not subject to tax? Would you look for ways to raise your income without raising your money income or taxable income?

(b) How does a 50 percent marginal tax rate (additional taxes divided by additional income) affect the cost to a physician of building his own home rather than hiring a contractor?

(c) An unmarried woman with three preschool children has no earned income but is receiving $400 a month in cash welfare assistance, plus food stamps worth $200 a month and government-financed medical care worth $100 a month. She is offered a job that will pay $1000 a month. If she takes the job, she will no longer be eligible for any of the cash or in-kind assistance. What is the marginal tax rate to which her earnings are subject? Would you take the job in her situation?

13. Teachers began encountering serious job shortages in the 1970s after many years of rising demand for their services. An intensified interest in unionization followed. What can unionization accomplish for teachers in a highly unfavorable job market? Who is likely to benefit? Who will be harmed?

14. "Farmers complaining that they can't get field hands now that the bracero program has been curtailed aren't sincere," said an official of the United Packinghouse Workers Union. "About one-third of the unemployed in Los Angeles are former farm workers, and the farmers could get them back if they'd make wages and working conditions attractive enough." Do you think farmers are insincere? Could California farmers get enough workers if they tried harder? Explain.

15. Under a closed-shop arrangement, employers may hire only workers who are already union members. Under a union-shop arrangement, employers may hire whomever they please but the employees must then join the union. What different effects would you expect these alternative arrangements to have on wages? On employment? On discrimination by the union against members of minority races? Why?

16. College professors in the United States have never had an effective union. Then why did their average wage rise spectacularly in the 1960s? How might college professors have used unionization to obtain even larger salary increases over this period? Why might some professors be interested in a law that prohibited anyone without an earned doctorate from teaching in colleges? What consequences would you predict if a few states passed such a law?

17. Do the relative salaries of humanities professors and football coaches at major state universities reflect the relative value of football and humanities? Do they reflect the number of years that professors and coaches must spend acquiring an education? The number of hours they work? The difficulty or unpleasantness of their work? Why do the football coaches usually receive salaries that are so much higher?

18. Until the program was abolished in 1987, the goverment of Holland paid a stipend to artists, based on such factors as marital status and number of children, and took in return a selection of the artists' work deemed equivalent in value. Most of the work so purchased disappeared into warehouses.

    (a) Do you think a program like this raises the average income of artists?
    (b) How might it actually lower the average income of artists?

19. There has been a growing trend in recent years toward two-tier contracts in wage negotiations between employers and unions. Current employees receive one wage; new employees are hired at a much lower wage rate.

    (a) How might such an arrangement benefit each of the following four parties: employers; current employees; union leaders; new employees.
    (b) For which of the above four groups would such a two-tier contract tend to become less satisfactory as time went by?

20. Do high wage rates in such strongly unionized industries as steel and automobiles pull up the general level of wages in nonunionized, lower-wage

industries? If you think they do, what is the process by which this occurs? If contracts that call for high wages reduce employment opportunities in the industries that must pay these wages, where do the excluded workers find employment?

21. A plumbers' local in Fort Lauderdale, Florida, some years ago voluntarily lowered by 45 percent the hourly rate for union workers on low-rise construction projects. The higher rate continued to apply to high-rise construction. The business manager of the union said this was being done to curb inflation and help homeowners. Do you think it might also have been done because nonunion plumbers were available in the area at less than half of union scale? Why do you suppose the union didn't lower the rate on high-rise construction work as well?

22. "If we had no unions with their united strength we would have unlimited hours of work, low wages, child labor wherever possible, speed-up and unsafe and dangerous working conditions. All these evils of the industrial system have been eliminated by workers united into unions and withholding their labor."

   (a) Do you agree with that statement from a newspaper letter?
   (b) Can you think of a way to test the statement or any part of it?

23. A letter to a magazine wonders "how [we will] cope with the growing number of unemployed put out of work by corporate capital-intensive high technology," and asks: "To what end these corporate methodologies that actually impoverish more than they enrich most of us?"

   (a) Can you help the writer find an answer?
   (b) The percentage of Americans 16 and over and not in the armed forces who were employed through the year averaged 57.5 percent in 1968, 59.3 percent in 1978, and 62.3 percent in 1988. Does this trend support the letter writer's argument?

24. A nationally syndicated columnist, in attacking a proposal to reduce the federal minimum wage from $3.35 to $2.50 an hour for teenagers, stated: "Any employer with an eye to the bottom line, would prefer to hire help at 85 cents an hour less, given a choice."

   (a) If the minimum wage for teenagers were lowered by 85 cents, why would some employers "with an eye to the bottom line" choose not to reduce the wage rate paid their teenage employees?
   (b) Why do so many employers pay teenagers (and others) wages that are far above the legal minimum wage—even in the absence of a union contract or any apparent threat of unionization?
   (c) The same columnist denies that lowering the minimum wage for teenagers would increase the number of jobs available to teenagers. "It takes McDonald's X amount of workers to offer its products to the public and that is probably going to be the amount of help hired, regardless of wages." Do you agree? What do you think would happen if

McDonald's had to pay $7.70 an hour to its employees? Would X turn out to be a constant?

25. How would each of the following groups be affected by a large increase in the legal minimum wage?

   (a) Unionized workers
   (b) Teenagers
   (c) Unskilled workers

26. "Comparable worth" is the name of a movement that began in the 1980s to determine the worth of different jobs and then to adjust relative wage rates to the relative worth of those jobs. The movement gains most of its support from the belief that women are unfairly discriminated against in the labor market. The jobs at which most of them work (e.g., secretaries and nurses) are regarded as "women's jobs" and so are allegedly paid less than their "comparable worth." The comparison is with jobs traditionally held by men.

   (a) Can a job have an inherent worth? Can you think of any situation where the worth of a job is not its value to some particular party in a specific situation?
   (b) Imagine a medical clinic with 20 medical doctors, one nurse, and one laboratory technician. Is it plausible to suppose that an additional nurse or lab technician could have more worth to the clinic in such a situation than an additional doctor?
   (c) The worth or value that influences decisions is always *marginal* worth or value. Why is a secretary worth more to the economics department if it employs only one than if it employs eight? Describe a situation in which the worth of a secretary to the economics department would likely be greater than the worth of an economist fully armed with a Ph.D.
   (d) Why will an employer who follows the maximizing rule of Chapter 9 – do more if marginal revenue exceeds marginal cost, less if marginal cost exceeds marginal revenue – want to pay each employee a wage equal to his or her marginal worth? What would be implied by the assertion that an employer was paying employees less than their marginal worth?

27. The graph in Figure 12A depicts the marginal value of nurses and of custodians to the Community General Hospital.

   (a) Why might a nurse be worth as much as $80 an hour to the hospital? Why might a custodian be worth as much as $30 an hour? Do you think a hospital forced to pay $75 an hour for the services of a nurse would ever put the nurse to work emptying bedpans, taking temperatures, or serving meals to patients?
   (b) Now suppose that the custodians are unionized and that the hospital

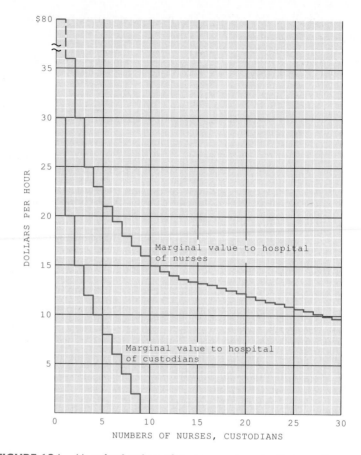

FIGURE 12A Marginal value of nurses and custodians at Community General Hospital

must pay its custodians $19 an hour. How many custodians will the hospital hire? What will be the marginal worth of a custodian?

(c) Assume that the nurses are not unionized and that the hospital is able to obtain as many nurses as it wants to hire at an hourly wage of $10. How many nurses would it want to hire? What would be the marginal worth of a nurse?

(d) What would be the relative worth in this situation of a custodian and a nurse? Would their relative worth reflect the intrinsic importance of their work?

(e) Will hospitals use nurses to empty bedpans if it can hire them for $10 an hour? Will it ask nurses or will it ask custodians to empty wastebaskets if custodians must be paid twice as much as nurses? What hospital tasks do you suppose would be performed by custodians if they had to be paid $29 an hour? Would a custodian's services become worth three times as much as a nurse's services?

28. Why would nurses be willing to work for as little as $10 an hour, as in the preceding question?

(a) What factors determine the supply curve of nurses' services?

(b) Until fairly recently one could become a registered nurse by completing a three-year nurses' training program at a certified hospital. The general rule now is that nurses must acquire a bachelor of science degree and will not be admitted to nursing curricula until they have successfully completed courses in inorganic and organic chemistry, microbiology, mathematics, social science, and language. Do these tougher requirements increase the value of registered nurses to prospective employers? Do they shift the supply curve of nurses? Are they likely to affect the wage rate that must be paid for nurses? Will this affect the marginal worth of nurses?

29. What happens when buyers are not price takers, but price searchers? Suppose you receive $6.25 per 100 for distributing advertising flyers door to door. You have a very large territory so that your business is limited only by your ability to hire help. Your potential help consists exclusively of the teenagers in your neighborhood, each of whom can distribute 100 flyers per hour. They are all willing to work one hour for you, but each insists upon a different minimum wage. Here are their minimum demands:

Alan	$3.00
Betty	3.50
Chuck	4.00
Donna	4.50
Elmer	5.00
Frances	5.50
George	6.00
Hepzibah	6.50

How many of these workers do you want to hire if your goal is to maximize your net revenue and *all employees must be paid at the same wage rate?*

(a) What is your marginal revenue from hiring an additional worker?

(b) What is your marginal cost from hiring an additional worker when you hire Alan? When you hire Betty? When you hire Chuck? Which is the last worker you can hire if you want to keep marginal cost from exceeding marginal revenue?

(c) Suppose a large hospital is in a similar position with respect to nurses. It can hire all the nurses it is likely to want; but it must offer a higher wage to attract additional nurses: some will work for very little, others for a bit more, and so on up to those who will only work if they can obtain a very high wage. Why might such a hospital find itself facing what it perceives as a chronic shortage of nurses? How might it respond? (Hint: What do sellers attempt to do when additional sales would "spoil" their market?)

30. Question 27 above assumed that the custodians' union was able to enforce a wage rate of $19 an hour.

   (a) Is this likely, given what you know about supply and demand for custodians' services?
   (b) What would the union have to do to maintain the wage rate for custodians at $19 an hour?
   (c) Why is it easier for a union of electricians than for a union of custodians to establish a wage of $19 an hour for members?
   (d) Why are so few typists and clerical workers organized into unions?
   (e) Why have skilled workers, who tend to receive higher wages anyway, generally been more successful in forming unions and raising their wages than unskilled workers?

31. Should high-school history and English teachers be paid as much as science and math teachers?

   (a) Suppose that a school district pays all high-school teachers with the same years of experience the same salary, regardless of teaching field, and that this produces a surplus of history and English teachers and a shortage of science and math teachers. Would this create a case for salary differentials?
   (b) How could the problem of concurrent surplus and shortage be solved without paying science and math teachers more than history and English teachers?
   (c) Why has the policy of identical wages in fact produced shortages of science and math teachers along with surpluses of history and English teachers in many school districts? What factors have contributed on the demand side? On the supply side?

32. According to the American Medical Association, physicians in family practice have experienced a decline in their average incomes in recent years while medical specialists' incomes were rising. Surgical specialists have been doing best of all, and their average incomes are now about twice what generalists earn.

   (a) Much of this difference in income arises from long-established differences in the fees paid by insurers for various medical services. The American Society of Internal Medicine claims that insurers' fee schedules are unfair. How would you decide on the validity of such a claim? What is a fair way to determine the relative worth of a successful surgical procedure against that of an accurate diagnosis followed by an effective prescription?
   (b) Surgeons justify their higher incomes by claiming that they spend four more years in school than do general practitioners. Do four additional years in school justify higher fees because it's costly to attend school, or because those extra years in school improve knowledge and skill levels?

33. A survey conducted during the 1980 recession revealed that 118,000 households were dissolved in one month.

   (a) Why would a recession cause households to disappear? What happens to them?
   (b) What happened to average family income as a result?

34. In each of the cases described below, an increase in the family's monetary income puts all members of the original family into families with lower incomes. Explain how this occurs. Does it imply that the individuals involved are worse off? What important questions does it raise about the interpretation of family-income data?

   (a) An elderly couple living with their married son receive an increase in social security benefits that permits the couple to obtain their own apartment.
   (b) Two married people who fight constantly, and stay together only because they can't afford to maintain two homes, separate with great relief when both receive promotions and raises, each taking one of the children.
   (c) The husband of an orthopedic surgeon quits his job to stay home, tend the house, and give the children better care when his wife's practice begins to earn a very large income.

35. How should in-kind transfers be treated in calculating the incomes of people on welfare?

   (a) Does it make sense to count the monetary value of food stamps, rent subsidies, and free school lunches in the income of a family on welfare?
   (b) How would this lead to an overstatement of their income? (Hint: Would you rather have a shopping cart full of items that someone else selected or the money equivalent of those items?)
   (c) Medicare benefits are a major contribution to the well-being of many elderly Americans. If an elderly person receives a $5000 operation, should we calculate that person's income as $5000 higher?

36. We often encounter the phrase "the low-income elderly." How poor are elderly people in the United States?

   (a) Why does the figure in Table 12C seriously understate the average relative income of people over 65?
   (b) In 1982 only 8.5 percent of all elderly persons in families lived below the official poverty line, as compared with 27 percent in 1959. How do you suppose this change came about?
   (c) How many benefits can you think of that accrue to people over 65 but don't affect their money incomes?

37. A substantial number of government programs are specifically intended to improve the relative position of lower-income groups. In addition, government economic policies in other areas are often formulated in ways

designed to avoid harming lower-income groups. Such policies are usually defended on the grounds that they promote greater justice in the distribution of income.

(a) Can you defend the assertion that the distribution of income that emerges from the interactions of demand and supply is just? Can you defend the assertion that it is unjust?

(b) How would you define a just distribution (or an unjust distribution) of income?

(c) If the preceding question is too difficult, perhaps you can define a *more* just (or less unjust) distribution of income.

(d) Two common but very different ways to define justice are in terms of *rules* and in terms of *results*. We usually define a just (or fair) game of any sort in terms of rules: Were the rules clearly stated, known and accepted in advance, and impartially enforced? We do not use the game's final score as a test of its fairness. On the other hand, we are likely to assess the justice with which food, clothing, and other goods are distributed among children in a family in terms of results: Does each child receive an equal share except insofar as differences among the children clearly call for unequal shares? Few would want to define a just distribution of income among children in terms of impartial rules regarding competition for goods.

Which of these provides better criteria for assessing the justice or injustice of the income distribution in a society such as the United States?

38. Almost everyone at one time or another has used the term *a fair wage*. What does it mean? Evaluate each of the following definitions of a fair wage. What insight does it express? What reality does it overlook?

(a) A wage that reflects the social value of the work.

(b) A wage that reflects the danger, difficulty, and general arduousness of the work.

(c) A wage that adequately compensates the employee for the time and trouble spent learning the trade.

(d) A wage that meets the employee's needs.

(e) A wage sufficient to support a family.

(f) A wage that reflects the profitability of the employer's business.

(g) The customary wage.

(h) The wage established through collective bargaining.

(i) The same wage for everyone.

(j) A wage that the employee considers fair.

(k) A wage of which the employer is not ashamed.

(l) The wage that clears the market.

(m) A wage agreed upon by employer and employee when both are adequately informed.

39. Suppose you have an irrational prejudice against non-Polish pickle packers and refuse to purchase any pickles that haven't been packed by Polish people.

(a) How will this prejudice affect the price you must pay for pickles of a given quality?

(b) How does an employer pay for any decision to discriminate in hiring on the basis of criteria unrelated to job performance?

(c) Do employers in general benefit from employment discrimination directed against nonwhites and women? Who does benefit?

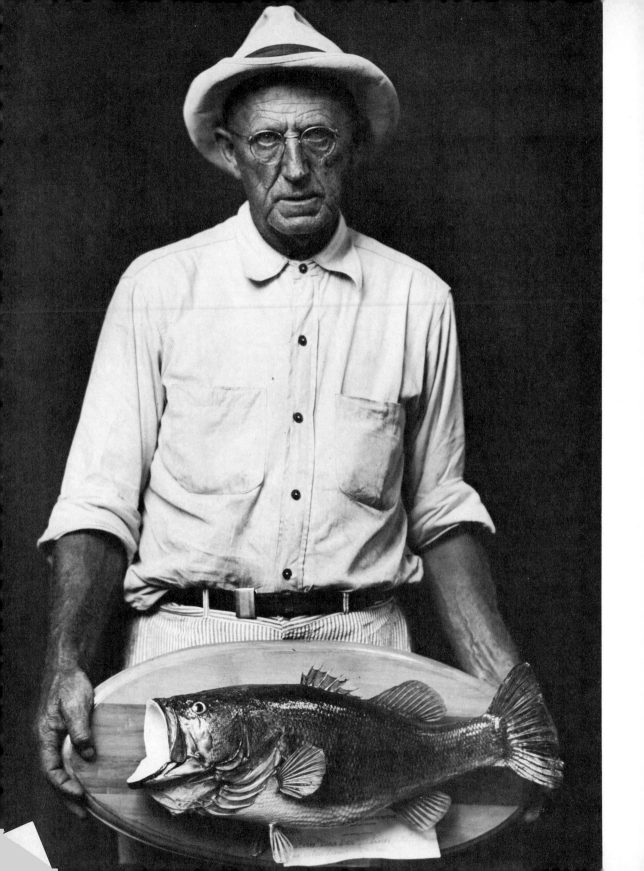

Chapter 13

Pollution and Conflicting Rights

Many people have concluded in recent years that the growing problem of pollution demonstrates the inadequacy of a purely economic point of view. That position is vigorously rejected in this chapter. Ecology and economics are very closely related, as a matter of fact, and in more than the common Greek stem of the words. Ecology in the narrow sense is a branch of biology that deals with the interrelations between organisms and their environment. In the broader meaning of the word, it's a point of view, an informing conviction that everything ultimately depends on everything else. Actions prompt reactions, and the reactions set the stage for all future actions. That is also the point of view of economic theory. Economics and ecology are allies, not competitors or antagonists.

The economist maintains that if pollution is a growing problem in our society, it's because we have allowed or even encouraged people to neglect certain important costs. The problem requires for its solution that we find ways to correct this neglect. If, like Stephen Leacock's Lord Ronald, we fling ourselves on a horse and ride madly off in all directions, we're not likely to find acceptable solutions.

Our first task is to agree on exactly what we mean by pollution. Unfortunately, that's not quite as easy as it might seem.

A Definition of Pollution

It won't do at all to define pollution as damage to the environment. That's much too broad. Everything we do, including walking and breathing, damages some part of the environment. Nor can we salvage this definition by inserting the word *irreversible* before "damage to the environment." That dramatizes the problem but does nothing to clarify it. Most of the damage we do to our environment in the ordinary course of living will in fact never be reversed; but very little damage is irreversible in the sense that it cannot be reversed no matter what people do.

We must begin by recognizing that pollution is a cost, a cost of engaging in valued, productive activities. It is a cost, however, with one distinctive feature: it is borne by people who have not agreed to do so. *Pollution*, in short, refers to *costs imposed on others without their consent.*

Disagreements and Property Rights

The core of the pollution *problem* is what the economist calls *externalities* or *spillovers*. These are *consequences of action that the actors don't take into account and that therefore don't influence their decisions.*

Individuals who behave according to the economic way of thinking engage in activities for the sake of the benefits they expect to receive, after taking into account the associated costs they expect to bear. Most of our costs in obtaining the goods we want are monetary payments to others to induce them to bear the costs of providing what we're after. The costs we bear in the pursuit of our goals turn out to be largely the prices we have to pay to obtain the cooperation of other people.

We all benefit, however, from a great deal of valuable cooperation for which we don't have to pay a cent. The reasons vary. Our collaborators may be generous people who are glad to be of assistance. They may not have noticed how much they're helping us and how large a sum we would be willing to pay if we had to. The cost they bear in cooperating may just be too small for them to bother about. Or they might know that they're providing valuable assistance at considerable cost to themselves but also that there is nothing they can really do about it. It is this last case that generates the *problem* of pollution.

Reflect for a moment on the phenomenon of garbage—ordinary kitchen garbage, like egg shells and potato peelings. Is it pollution? It is certainly a "bad," an undesired by-product of a process that produced something good. But we don't ordinarily think of it as pollution unless it has been put in a place where it doesn't belong. Garbage generates no social problems as long as those who create it leave it only in places where they have permission to leave it. All sorts of "bads" are like that. Obnoxious sounds are "bads"; but the deafening clatter of pots and pans is not "noise pollution" to employees who are being paid to work in the kitchen. Because they have given their consent (for pay, of course), they don't complain and there is consequently no noise pollution problem. Motor oil stains on the coveralls of a mechanic are another familiar "bad" that represents no pollution problem because the mechanic has agreed to let it occur.

The reason it's misleading to think of pollution as a fact of physical nature is that this way of thinking about it obscures the nature of the problem. Pollution *problems* don't arise until someone objects: "You are obtaining your good by imposing this cost on me (or us), and you have no right to do that." A pollution problem reflects a disagreement about property rights. The problem is solved not by eliminating all damage to the environment — an obvious impossibility — but by resolving disagreements over property rights.

Pollution creates a social problem (with which economic theory can deal) when someone objects.

Soot on the Windowsills

Does this make sense? Let's try it out. Why does almost everyone agree that the soot that falls on their windowsills from a nearby factory's smokestacks is pollution? Because they all agree that the factory's managers *have no right* to impose the costs of waste disposal on neighboring home-owners.

Why does almost everyone agree that the oil that washes up on an ocean beach is pollution? Because they all believe that whoever is responsible *had no right* to let an oil spill occur. Somebody chose a method of drilling for oil or flushing tanks or whatever that imposed a large part of the costs on users of the beach who had not agreed to bear it.

Does this seem clear? It shouldn't, because it really isn't.

Suppose the offending smokestack is a low one that drops all its soot within a 500-yard radius. Suppose further that all the land within reach of the smokestack's emissions belongs to the corporation that owns the factory, and that this corporation rents out the houses it built on its own land only after informing prospective tenants that they will have to live with soot on their windowsills. If the home seekers nonetheless decide to move in, the lower rent or other advantages that these houses offer must be enough, in their eyes, to compensate them for the expected cost of living with the factory's soot. They have consented to the soot on their windowsills, and so it creates no pollution *problem*. The soot is still as dark and dirty as it ever was; but it is no longer a cost imposed on others without their consent.

You may go ahead and refer to that soot as pollution if you're absolutely determined to do so; but if you have any respect for consistency you will then have to explain why the egg shells you toss in the garbage can are *not* pollution. The important fact is that the tenants were paid to consent to the soot, just as your garbage collector is paid to clean out the messes you leave in your garbage can. If everyone agrees that all parties are acting within their rights, there can be no pollution *problems*.

Oil on the Beach

Let's use the second case above — the oil-fouled beach — to draw out some more implications of this property-rights approach to the pollution issue. Suppose that the beach in question is a public one near a major port, and that the oil on the beach is a long-term accumulation from the ordinary and legal operations of a multitude of ocean-going ships. Of course, the whole operation *could* be cleaner. If someone were willing to incur the cost, a port operation could be made as antiseptic as a surgical operation. But would the benefit be worth the cost?

To someone who loves the beach but doesn't give a fig for ocean commerce and cares not one whit for the advantages others derive from international trade, the benefit would be greater than the cost — because the cost *to this single-minded individual* would be nothing. The opportunities that would have to be forgone if the port were closed (and no one could afford to operate it with zero contamination of the beach) are opportunities that he does not value. He can logically continue, therefore, to call that oil on the beach *pollution*. In doing so he is asserting that the relevant property rights are wrongly assigned: that he ought to be protected in the enjoyment of an oil-free beach even though that would infringe on the property rights of all those who benefit from continued operation of the port.

It would be a mistake, though, for someone who approved the existing assignment of property rights to complain that the beach is "polluted." To do so would be to concede that our fanatical beach lover should have the right to stop the entire port operation by withholding his consent. But that is precisely the point at issue. The oil on the beach is pollution, in the sense of a "bad" against which one may protest and a problem to be resolved, only for someone who claims that those who put it there had no right to do so.

An Analysis of Airport Noise

Let's try this argument out at the airport. Commercial jets make a lot of noise. Do they generate noise pollution *problems*? Not for the airport baggage handlers, because they

consent to be subjected to the noise. Their consent is secured by the payment of a wage. Is the noise pollution to
families who live near the airport? It is if they bought their
house before the airport was contemplated. The noise of the
jets deprives them of peace and quiet without their consent.

Now change the situation. Suppose the airport authorities buy all the adjacent land at prices that reflect the
land's value before the planning of the airport. Then, after
the airport is finished, the airport authorities resell the land
for whatever price buyers consent to pay. Those who build
or buy homes on this land will hear the noise of the jets, but
the noise will not create a pollution problem for them because they will have consented to bear it. They knew about
the noise when they bought but presumably decided that the
lower price for the land was adequate compensation for the
noise of the jets.

Let's introduce a further change in the situation. The
people who bought their houses after the airport had been
constructed, fully knowing about the noise, may now decide to
lobby the city council for noise-abatement restrictions. If they
succeed and the airlines are required to eliminate all flights
before 7 a.m. and after 10 p.m., the airlines then become, in
an important sense, the victims of pollution. The new noise-
abatement rules impose costs on the airlines without securing their consent. The homeowners are obtaining benefits for
themselves and letting the costs be borne by others.

Conflicting Rights

But should those costs be called pollution? *Silence* pollution?
There is little point in arguing about what we're going to
call something. It is important, however, that we see clearly
what's happening, and that we not suppose we have solved a
problem when we've only created a new one to take its
place. The characteristic of jet noise that we must not overlook is its association with valuable opportunities. Jet noise
isn't created around airports in order to bedevil the neighbors: it is a by-product in the production of the valuable service of rapid transportation. We could without doubt eliminate jet noise by eliminating jet airplanes. But would the
gain in peace and quiet be enough to outweigh the loss to all
those who want to travel quickly between distant points?
That's the question.

We pointed out way back in Chapter 2 that the demand
is never completely inelastic for *any* good, not even for the
good of clean air. With clean air, as with peace and quiet, we

must decide exactly how much we want — in view of the fact that more can be obtained only by giving up increasing amounts of other goods that we also want. The problem is compounded when, as in the present case, those who receive the benefits and those who pay the costs are different people. It would all be much simpler if we had to choose only between the wicked polluters and the virtuous citizens. This kind of choice is so easy and appealing, in fact, that we often succumb to the temptation of defining the problem in exclusively moral terms. *Industry* and *corporations* and *vested interests* want to foul our streams, darken our air, cut down our forests, strip-mine our land, and destroy our heritage for the sake of "their" profits. Who would hesitate a moment in deciding between the conflicting claims of greedy exploiters and "the American people"? But those who pose the issues in this way are either engaging in propaganda or deceiving themselves. Our actual choices are almost always choices between the legitimate expectations of some and the legitimate expectations of others.

Moreover, we have confused the issue for ourselves by identifying pollution with environmental damage. The flaw in this identification is that it fails to indicate when and why pollution is a problem. Everything, including the simple act of breathing, damages the environment, whereas many polluting acts do not damage the biological environment in any accepted sense of that term. Actions that alter the environment don't become problems until they infringe on someone's rights. The infallible sign of a pollution problem is the statement, "You have no right to do that, because it interferes with my right to do this." Pollution problems arise when people's expectations about what they can and may do come into conflict. The problems disappear when disagreements about property rights are resolved — when those who formerly protested the actions of others consent to those actions.[1]

An Impossible Goal

"That's absurd," says the voice from the rear which has been silent through several chapters. "People's expectations will

---

[1]Does this mean that nothing matters except the values and interests of human beings? That wastes discharged into a stream, for example, are not pollution if they damage nothing except wildlife with no commercial or recreational use? Not at all. The analysis implies only that until some human being speaks out against the damage, there is no *social* problem, and hence no problem that economic theory can help us resolve.

always conflict to some extent. People in a large society like ours are bound to disagree about who has which rights. We can't expect everybody to consent to absolutely everything that other people want to do. With your definition of pollution, pollution would be impossible to get rid of."

Precisely. There may be no more important lesson for us to learn about pollution than that pollution so thoroughly permeates our society that we cannot realistically hope to eliminate it. Pollution exists when teenagers play their transistor radios and thereby infringe on the right of other bus passengers to enjoy peace and quiet; pollution still exists, though in a changed form, when the other bus passengers infringe on the teenagers' right to hear music by enforcing their own desire for peace and quiet. Pollution exists when a rose lover cultivates his bushes and thereby infringes on the right of rose-fever victims to breathe easily; the pollution does not disappear but only changes its form when the rose-fever sufferers infringe on the right of the rose lover by uprooting his rose bushes.

Traffic on a residential street imposes costs on the homeowners, which they would like to eliminate. But sealing off one end of the street imposes costs on the drivers who are now compelled to take a less satisfactory route. A coal-burning utility pumping sulfur dioxide into the air is imposing costs on people in the vicinity of the plant. But if those people compel the utility to burn more expensive low-sulfur coal, they are imposing costs on consumers of the utility's electricity. A pollution problem means that rights are in conflict and poses the question: Whose rights ought to prevail?

Reducing Pollution: The First Steps

We want to turn our attention in the rest of this chapter to four procedures for reducing pollution problems or maintaining them within acceptable bounds. The first is the cultivation of the civic virtues of empathy, courtesy, humility, and tolerance among the members of a society. Civilization will simply be impossible among a people who don't possess substantial amounts of these virtues. If people insist on obtaining absolutely everything to which they think they have a right, civilization will give way to warfare. But how to cultivate or renew these virtues where they have withered — that is a question far beyond the scope of this book. We would do well to remember, however, that the other procedures for controlling pollution that we're now going to examine —

negotiation, adjudication, and legislation — presuppose these virtues to some extent, because they presuppose an established society, and they work more effectively the more widely these virtues are practiced.

Reducing Pollution by Negotiation

Our everyday garden-variety procedure for minimizing pollution problems is *negotiation*. We strike bargains with one another. People consent to bear the costs associated with the production of particular goods because other people who want those goods offer compensation that makes it worth their while. That's why baggage handlers don't complain about jet noise or automobile mechanics about the grease on their clothes, and why the owner of a dog kennel will cheerfully let other people's dogs perform the same act that arouses an urban lawn fancier to fury.

"Work it out for yourselves" is sound advice. Because people differ so widely in their tastes, talents, and other circumstances, they will often be able to negotiate an exchange of costs that makes everyone involved better off than before. Moreover, the necessity of working it out for themselves encourages cooperation among those who are in the best position to know the possibilities. When people aren't required to negotiate, they often adopt positions that are costly to others. For example, they demand legislation that would prohibit smoking in restaurants, rather than ask for a table where no smoke will blow. And they point indignantly to minute traces of tobacco smoke in the air, while ignoring the dangerous emissions that they themselves put into the atmosphere by driving to the restaurant.

We would probably have a much greater respect for negotiation as a social procedure for reducing pollution problems if we learned to recognize the myriad ways in which we actually use it. People who hate the noise and dirt of the city move to outlying areas. People who detest the culture of suburbia live in small towns. People who despise the isolation of rural life choose to live in the city. The hard-of-hearing get residential real estate bargains under airport approach lanes. Surfboard riders seek out companions and thereby voluntarily segregate themselves from swimmers who hate to dodge surfboards. The afternoon naptaker pays $1.59 for a box of earplugs and thereafter lives in peace with the neighboring teenager's mufflerless motorcycle. Not everyone is completely satisfied. But voluntary exchange does reduce the total of costs imposed on reluctant bystanders.

Negotiation produces mutual gains from exchange

Negotiation cannot be effective, however, unless property rights are clearly defined. Voluntary exchange of any sort works well only when all involved parties agree on who owns what. In some cases, a clarification of property rights may be all that stands in the way of a mutually satisfactory agreement.

Suppose, for example, that Smith and Brown disagree by two feet on the location of the boundary line dividing their properties. It wouldn't matter much, since both want to plant flowers in the disputed strip, except for the fact that Smith wants to plant zinnias and Brown has his heart set on petunias. Until the question of who has a right to do what is settled, neither one will plant flowers, and both will be living with the inferior alternative of crabgrass.

If they then hire a surveyor who proves that Smith in fact owns the disputed strip, flowers can finally bloom. Nor will the flowers necessarily be zinnias! Once it's clearly established that Smith is the owner and hence has the right to decide what will grow in the boundary strip, Brown may be able to purchase that right. Brown's passion for petunias could be so powerful that he offers Smith $25 a year for the right to grow them between their lots. And if Smith prefers petunias *with* $25 to zinnias without $25, the flowers that bloom will be petunias.

Clearly established property rights provide the basis for negotiation.

Reducing Pollution by Adjudication

In introducing the boundary surveyor, we introduced another important social procedure for reducing pollution problems: *adjudication*, by which we mean a process for deciding who has which rights. People will not be able to improve their positions through the exchange of rights if they aren't sure what rights anyone has to begin with. Clearly defined property rights are not a sufficient condition for successful negotiations, but they do seem to be a necessary condition.

Property rights that might once have been clearly and adequately defined can become vague and uncertain when surrounding circumstances change. The development of low-cost photocopying techniques, to take one example, created an enormous amount of uncertainty about what copyright holders could realistically expect to sell in view of the new capability that photocopy machines gave to every possessor of a book. When evolving circumstances make previously compatible property rights incompatible, adjudication is one way of settling the conflict.

We are using the term *adjudication* to refer specifically

to the kind of resolution that the surveyor provided: a resolution that *discovers* who has which rights. The surveyor answered the question of ownership by investigating, not by choosing. If Smith and Brown had agreed to flip a coin, they would have relied on a procedure that does not discover but rather *creates* property rights. The distinction between the discovery and the creation of property rights is an important one, because *discovery or adjudication aims at maintaining the continuity of expectations*. At the end of Chapter 12 we emphasized the importance of stable expectations in securing effective cooperation among the members of a society. When expectations change radically, supply and demand decisions also change radically. That, in turn, alters in unpredicted ways the relative costs and benefits of all kinds of actions and so induces additional changes in supply and demand. In short, if no one knows what to expect, no one knows what to do or what others will do. The result is chaos. Stable expectations are another of those realities whose importance we haven't learned to recognize, because we don't notice how society is working when it's working well.

Adjudication clarifies property rights.

The Case of the Complaining Homeowner

We can use the airport once more to bring out the importance of adjudication, or the discovery rather than creation of rights, in resolving disputes over property rights. Polly Sigh, who owns a house ten miles from a major airport but directly under the principal approach route, may decide one morning—when her sleep has been interrupted by commercial jets—that she deserves compensation. The airport or the airlines ought to pay her something, she decides, for depriving her of the opportunity to use her bedroom as a place of rest and renewal. She is the victim of pollution, of costs imposed on her without her consent. So she files suit demanding compensation.

Ought she to get it? Is she *likely* to get it? Assume that Polly bought the house before the airport was even thought about, so that no one can say she knew the situation when she bought and has already received her compensation in the form of a lower purchase price. She is consequently, by our definition, the victim of pollution. The noise pollution to which she is subject could be eliminated if she were paid the amount by which the airport reduces the market price of her house. But *should* she be compensated?

The trouble is that there are thousands of homeowners

with equally valid claims. If one receives compensation, all ought to receive compensation. But if all receive compensation, a heavy cost will be imposed on the airport and the airlines and eventually on airline passengers, either through reduced service or higher prices.

At first glance that might seem fair enough. Higher prices will compel airline passengers to pay the costs of the noise that is created as a by-product of their travel. But now a new problem forces itself on our attention. Externalities run throughout society. Shall we correct for them *all*? Shall homeowners receive compensation for the automobile traffic that goes past, the dandelions that their neighbors let go to seed, the passing gifts of dog-walkers and their pets, the noise of the neighborhood children, the sound of power mowers, the spreading chestnut tree next door that blocks their view, or the loss of the shade if their neighbor cuts down the spreading chestnut tree because it blocks *his* view? When we are through with homeowners, we would have to start ordering the compensation of pedestrians, many of whom suffer from the same sorts of uncompensated costs that afflict homeowners. Perhaps we could, in the final stages of our effort to make the world perfect, impose fines on especially dull people in order to compensate those whom they bore.

We just can't do that. There are too many spillovers; the appropriate compensations would be too difficult to determine. Even the direction in which compensation ought to be paid will often be unclear. Wouldn't it be just as much in order, for example, to levy fines on inattentive people to compensate the bores whose sensitivities they offend? Who says bores are worse than boors?

The Importance of Precedents

We are ready for the question: *Should* Polly Sigh, the homeowner ten miles from the airport, be compensated by airline passengers for the inconvenience she suffers as a result of the flights from which they benefit? Our answer: It would be extraordinarily difficult and probably impossible to do so in a way that was both practical and fair.

We originally asked *two* questions, however. The second question asked whether homeowners in such circumstances were *likely* to receive compensation. The answer to this question is almost certainly *no*. The courts would attempt to decide the issue by *discovering* what rights the contending parties have, and homeowners would end up with very little to show on their behalf. The ruling consideration would almost surely be this: that homeowners and those in the business of providing airline transportation have proceeded for a long time on the expectation that no such compensation must be paid. *These expectations indicate the respective property rights of homeowners and airlines.*

We could even prove that homeowners ten miles from the airport don't have a legal right to be compensated for the noise, simply by showing that the market price of homes under the approach route would jump sharply if the court decision held in favor of the homeowner. This would be an *unexpected event* that would create profits for homeowners and losses for holders of airline stock. The appearance of these unexpected changes in values would be conclusive evidence that the affected parties did not believe such compensation was owed, and that the court decision had consequently *created* property rights that had not existed previously.

There's a qualification to this conclusion that further establishes the point we're making. If a judge held for the homeowner in such a case, the price of affected houses might rise very little, because prospective home buyers would probably be advised that the judge had erred and was likely to be reversed on appeal. The concept of error is instructive. There can be no error when the decision *creates* the rights. Error is possible only when the decision seeks to *discover* what the rights are that actually prevail and therefore ought to govern the outcome of the case.

Adjudication, or the attempt to resolve conflicting claims by seeking to discover existing rights, always tries to avoid unexpected decisions or outcomes. It tries to settle disagreements over property rights by supporting and reinforcing *the expectations that are most widely and confidently held.* Adjudication is thus an effort to maintain the continuity of expectations in the presence of changing circumstances. And stable expectations, we remind you once more, are the foundation of effective cooperation in any large, complex society.

The Problem of Radical Change

Adjudication is an evolutionary approach to the problems of pollution. But sometimes changes don't occur at an evolutionary pace. When we're overtaken by events so novel that established principles and practices furnish little guidance in dealing with them, adjudication cannot work very well.

Technological innovations often force rapid changes on us in a wide variety of situations. Snowmobiles, pesticides, radar-assisted whaling ships, antibiotics, and nuclear reactors are just a few of the many examples that could be cited from recent years. When technological innovation radically expands our capacity to inflict costs on others without obtaining their consent, new rules may be required to resolve the problems.

The demand for new definitions of property rights has also been created by rising incomes. Not too may years ago Americans seemed to have had a working consensus that the social advantages from allowing the atmosphere to be used as an industrial dump were greater than the disadvantages. Our laws and customs decreed that the atmosphere belonged to everyone and therefore to no one, so that factory owners were free to use it as a receptacle for industrial wastes. People could move away from factories, or purchase residential space near the factories at a low price if they preferred that saving to the delights of clean air. Meanwhile, factories held their costs down by discharging wastes into the atmosphere, and this meant a greater availability of the goods that factories produced. But the situation has changed. The goods that factories produce are now available in much larger quantities, and many people have begun to place a lower relative valuation on them. When we begin to place a higher relative value on blue skies and clean air, we start to think of them as our _right_. We start to claim a property right in these environmental goods and demand that others stop putting them to uses that are incompatible with our ability to enjoy them. That requires new rules, not just an application of the old rules to new situations.

Reducing Pollution by Legislation

We call the creation of new rules _legislation_. The line between adjudication and legislation is not as clear in practice as all this pretends. But the distinction is important in principle, because legislation creates changes in prevailing property rights, and changing the rules of the game always raises the question of fairness and often compels major adjustments in behavior. The challenge for a society that wants to reduce pollution is to legislate in ways that avoid gross injustices and that minimize the cost of achieving the objectives. We shall focus on the second of those criteria, not because it's more important, but because economic theory has more to say about minimizing costs than about maximizing justice.

Physical Restrictions on Polluters

The legislation of uniform physical restrictions is a popular approach to the problem of pollution. "Command and control" it's called. After some date, no one is allowed to discharge more than so many particles of this or that into the air or the water system. This approach will almost certainly fail to minimize the cost per unit of pollution reduction. It ignores the variety of ways in which a given objective can usually be achieved and, therefore, offers few incentives to people to search for and implement the least costly alternative. We're going to use a very simplified example to illustrate some principles of pollution control that deserve to be better understood and more widely appreciated.

Suppose that everything that fouls the air over the city of Springfield comes from three sources: automobiles, utilities, and factories. The following table shows the quantities of polluting material put into the air of Springfield monthly by each source. It also shows the cost to each polluter of eliminating the objectionable emissions. (You will notice that the analysis treats each of the three sources as a *single decision making unit*, to keep the analysis simple enough to be useful.)

	Units of Obnoxious Material Emitted Monthly	Cost of Eliminating Emissions, per Unit
Automobiles	20,000	$ 5
Utilities	30,000	10
Factories	40,000	20

Now let's suppose that the Environmental Protection Agency (EPA) decides to improve the air quality over Springfield by securing a reduction of monthly emissions from the present total of 90,000 to a tolerable total of 60,000. (We'll pass by the question for now of how the EPA decides that 60,000 is the tolerable level.) There are many ways to reach that objective. The EPA could set 20,000 as the maximum allowable emissions from each source, or require each source to reduce its emissions by 10,000, or order a one-third reduction in emissions by each source. Let's compare the costs of each approach.

Setting a 20,000 unit ceiling on each source would achieve the goal at a total cost of $500,000. Utilities would pay $10 for each of the 10,000 units by which they reduce their emissions, factories would pay $20 for each of the 20,000 units by which they reduce their emissions, and automobiles would escape all costs, because they're already at the target level.

Requiring each source to reduce emissions by 10,000 units would achieve the goal at a total cost of $350,000. Automobiles would pay $50,000, utilities $100,000, and factories $200,000. This is clearly a less costly way to reach the goal.

Ordering a one-third reduction by all sources would result in total costs of $400,000: $33,333 to the automobiles, $100,000 to the utilities, and $266,667 to the factories. From the standpoint of cost minimization, that's better than the first solution but not as good as the second.

There's an even less costly way to go, however. The EPA would minimize the cost of achieving its objective if it ordered a 20,000-unit reduction by automobiles and a 10,000-unit reduction by utilities and left the factories alone. The total cost of getting pollution down from 90,000 to 60,000 units by this method would be $200,000: $100,000 paid by the automobiles and $100,000 paid by the utilities. Would the EPA be likely to choose this approach?

Another Approach: Taxing Emissions

Let's defer that question and examine the problem further. Suppose that the EPA doesn't actually know how much it will cost per unit to reduce pollution from each source. That's much more plausible than our original assumption, for several reasons. The polluters themselves will be in the best position to know the actual costs, but they will also have an incentive to exaggerate their costs in pleadings before the EPA or the public. Moreover, exaggeration will not be wholly dishonest, because one never knows for certain the costs of something that hasn't yet been tried, and it's just ordinary prudence to estimate them high, especially if higher estimates mean the costs are less likely to be imposed. Finally, though costs can usually be reduced through research and experiment, no one can predict the results that research and experiment will produce. What is the least costly solution when the EPA is faced with this kind of information scarcity?

The EPA would gain the applause of many economists if it responded to this situation by imposing a tax per unit of emissions and then allowing each party to respond as it

Cost of uniform ceiling:

To utilities: $10,000 \times \$10 = \$100,000$

To factories: $20,00 \times \$20 = \$400,000$
$$\overline{\$500,000}$$

Cost of uniform quanity reduction:

To automobiles: $10,000 \times \$5 = \$50,000$

To utilities: $10,000 \times \$10 = \$100,000$

To factories: $10,000 \times \$20 = \$200,000$
$$\overline{\$350,000}$$

Cost of uniform percentage reduction:

To automobiles: $\frac{1}{3}(20,000) \times \$5 = \$33,333$

To utilities: $\frac{1}{3}(30,000) \times \$10 = \$100,000$

To factories: $\frac{1}{3}(40,000) \times \$20 = \$266,667$

Least-Cost Solution:

To automobiles: $20,000 \times \$5 = \$100,000$

To utilities: $10,000 \times \$10 = \$100,000$
$$\overline{\$200,000}$$

thought best. If you're willing to grant that pollution is a spillover cost, a cost not borne by its producer, placing a tax on polluting activities makes good sense. If the tax per unit of pollutant can somehow be set equal to the spillover cost per unit, the creator and presumed beneficiary of the costs is made to bear them.

If that makes the polluting activity too costly to continue, it will cease, as it should if its costs are greater than its benefits. If the benefits still outweigh the costs when the tax is being paid, then the polluting activity will continue, though at a lesser rate because it's now more costly. But in that case the tax revenue will be available to compensate — to buy the consent of — those on whom the spillover costs are falling.

In the Springfield case, any tax rate between $5 and $10 will reduce pollution by 20,000 units per month. It will induce the automobiles to avoid the tax by choosing the lesser-cost-alternative of eliminating their obnoxious emissions. Utilities will choose to avoid the tax when it rises above $10 per unit emitted, so that a tax rate of $11 would reduce emissions by 50,000 units per month, while simultaneously garnering $440,000 in revenue with which to compensate the suffering citizens of Springfield for the obnoxious material the factories are continuing to spew into the air.

As we have set up the problem, there is no tax rate that achieves a reduction to exactly 60,000 units: $9.99 would lower pollution to only 70,000 units, and $10.01 would lower it all the way to 40,000 units. In the real world, costs would not be the same for all levels of emission reduction but would be relatively low for small percentage reductions from each source and extremely high as we approached 100 percent. The pursuit of perfection is almost always prohibitively expensive.

But the inability of *any* tax rate to achieve some particular physical target is not so much a criticism of the tax approach to pollution control as a criticism of physical targets. Why aim at 60,000 units? *Every* unit is a "bad," so why not eliminate them all? The answer, as you know by this time, is that there are costs of eliminating those costs that we call pollution. The task for the EPA is to compare the marginal costs of reducing the emissions with the marginal benefits. The use of taxes enables the EPA to acquire information about these costs and benefits by observing what happens when variously estimated pollution costs are assessed against the polluters. It's an approach that lends itself to learning by experimentation. And obtaining reliable informa-

tion about costs and benefits is essential to any program of
environmental protection that is concerned with human
well-being.

The Issue of Fairness

Let's go back now to a question that we asked but deferred
answering. After comparing the costs of four different ways
of reducing Springfield air pollution to 60,000 units per
month, we asked whether the EPA was likely in such a situation to choose the least costly approach. We put off answering in order to argue that physical directives of any sort — the
command-and-control method — were generally inferior to
taxes as a way of controlling pollution. By taxing emissions,
we enlist the aid of the price system in solving our problem.
But the tax approach isn't popular with the public for a
reason that would also make it difficult for the EPA to issue
the least costly set of physical directives. *It doesn't seem
fair.* Taxes on pollution have acquired the derogatory label of
"licenses to pollute," and they're widely rejected because
they supposedly place the whole burden of reducing pollution on the poor while allowing the rich to go right on foul-
ing the environment. Choosing the people who must reduce
their pollution on the basis of the cost to them of doing so,
which is required by the least-cost solution, also seems arbitrary and unjust to many people.

    The "license to pollute" argument, however, is confused
from the outset. If pollution is a cost inflicted on others
without their consent, people who secure consent by paying
the cost are no longer polluting. It's true enough that they
will still be imposing costs on others. But there's nothing at
all wrong with that as long as they compensate them
adequately. If people object that the tax they pay isn't
enough to make up for the costs they create, they are really
saying that the tax rate should be increased, not that such
taxes are a "license to pollute."

Exchange and Efficiency in Pollution Control

An important part of any reply to those who raise the fairness issue, however, is to show that the *efficient* solution
can be achieved while settling the *fairness* issue in different
ways. In other words, we don't necessarily commit ourselves
to place the costs on any particular parties when we select
the most efficient solution. The Springfield case can again
provide our illustration.

Suppose that the EPA wants to impose the entire cost of pollution reduction on the factories, whether because the factories can best afford it, because they have long been the heaviest polluters, because everyone in Springfield dislikes them, or for some reason more closely related to fairness. Whatever the reason, all the EPA need do is tell the factories that they will have to pay a tax of $10.05 for each unit of pollution emitted monthly in excess of 60,000, regardless of the pollution's source. The factories will then look for the least costly way to deal with this situation. If they have all the information that we have, they will offer the automobiles $100,000 to eliminate all their pollution and offer the utilities $100,000 to reduce their pollution by 10,000 units.

The factories will thus reduce the level of pollution in Springfield to 60,000 units. They'll do so to avoid a tax of $301,500. But rather than reduce their own emissions by 30,000 units, which would cost the factories $600,000, they'll pay the most efficient pollution reducers in the city $200,000 to do the job for them.

Pollution reduction is a lot like any other useful activity in that some are more efficient at it than others. Just as we gain from having our food, toys, and cosmetics produced by those with a comparative advantage in their production, so we gain by having additional clean air produced by those with the greatest comparative advantage at the job. But comparative advantages are exploited through exchange. That's why the tax approach to pollution reduction is in general superior to an approach that assigns physical restrictions to particular firms. The tax approach tries to alter relative money costs to reflect new decisions about who has which rights. But it then leaves all parties free to trade on the basis of their own comparative advantages and to secure the new social goals in the most efficient manner.

The Bubble Concept

In 1979 the Environmental Protection Agency took a large step in the direction suggested by this analysis when it issued new regulations to permit and encourage trade-offs among air-pollution sources. Rather than set rigid limits on allowable emissions from each smokestack, enforcement agencies would permit factories to exceed the limits at one point if they could make it up at another point. They could pretend that there was a giant bubble over the entire factory (hence the name for this approach — the bubble concept) and control total emissions into the bubble. Under this policy, firms could lower the cost of achieving a target level of air quality by allowing emissions to rise wherever their control was especially costly and making it up where emissions could be reduced at lower cost.

This approach was challenged in court by environmental groups who claimed that it allowed additional pollution to occur in areas where air quality was already not in compliance with EPA standards. A firm should not be allowed to belch obnoxious substances from smokestack A just because it had reduced the emissions from smokestack B. If the emissions from B could be reduced at low cost, the environmentalists argued, then they should be reduced. But the emissions from A should not be allowed to increase. The environmentalist argument implicitly assumes that there is only one good: clean air.

The Supreme Court rejected this argument in 1984, thereby opening the way for existing plants and factories to expand in areas with air quality problems (without worsening the air quality) and encouraging the EPA to go one step further. If firms and plants were to be allowed to make internal trade-offs in the interest of efficiency, or achieving given goals at the lowest possible cost, why couldn't such trade-offs also be allowed *between* firms? If an electrical utility wanted to build a new generating plant to satisfy its customers' demands, it might be able to do so without worsening air quality by persuading some other firm to reduce its emissions by the amount that the utility was going to expand emissions. In effect, firms would be allowed to buy and sell "rights to pollute."

That did not sit at all well with more ardent environmentalists, who argued that no one owned a "right to pollute" and therefore no one else could buy it. The premise is false, however. Firms do in fact have rights to discharge obnoxious substances into the air, as proved by the fact that they do it openly and are not fined. They have both actual and legal "rights to pollute." By accepting and clarifying those rights, the EPA allowed a market in such rights to evolve, which meant in turn that firms could purchase their pollution control programs from other firms that had a comparative advantage in pollution control. If the EPA allows the purchasing firm to use only some percentage of the rights purchased — to use 100, for example, they have to purchase 130 — it can enlist the expanded bubble concept in the service of progressively cleaner air. Note, too, that those who want the air to be even cleaner than the EPA requires may be able, under this system, to buy up "pollution rights" and retire them.

The system won't work, however, unless the rights are clearly defined and can be counted on. No individual or group will be willing to buy up rights in order to retire them if the regulatory authorities can respond by creating new rights to replace the ones retired. Nor will firms be willing to pay money to purchase rights if they believe they can get the same rights from the regulatory authorities with just a little lobbying. And firms are much more likely to invest resources in discovering and devising ways to reduce their emissions below what they are legally entitled to emit if they know that they can sell the results to someone else.

Cleaning up the air is an especially difficult environmental challenge. The sources of air pollution are numerous and hard to monitor. And the costs of cleaning up the air, in benefits forgone, will often be much higher than we are inclined to suppose when we're thinking exclusively about factories (where other people work) and conveniently forgetting about our own chimneys, automobile exhaust pipes, backyard barbecues, and household sprays. The enormous benefits from cleaner air coupled with the high costs of attaining it ought to make us appreciate any system that can give us more of what we want at a lower cost.

Rights and Efficiency

We don't want to conclude this chapter with an endorsement of efficiency, because inefficiency is not the fundamental problem. Pollution is a problem because people disagree about rights. When people agree on who owns what rights, they begin exchanging rights in ways that expand mutual benefits and reduce mutual costs. If property rights can be clearly established, efficiency will take care of itself.

Once Over Lightly

Pollution problems are the result of spillover costs, or what economists call negative externalities. They are costs that people create in the process of producing goods but which they impose on others who have not consented to bear them.

The first condition for the control of pollution problems is that people understand clearly who has which rights. The existence of pollution problems entails disagreements over property rights, and disagreements must be clarified before they can be resolved.

Pollution problems can be eliminated entirely only if everyone consents freely to everything that others want to do. Perfection is consequently impossible. But the degree to which it can be approached in any society will depend crucially on the extent to which very traditional civic virtues are honored and practiced.

Negotiation is the standard procedure used by members of a society to secure the cooperation and consent of others without imposing unwelcome costs on one another. Negotiation is easier and more effective when property rights are more clearly specified.

Conflicting claims of right can often be resolved by examining established principles and practices. Adjudication in this manner preserves the continuity of people's expectations. Unexpected changes in effective property rights are in general not desirable, because they arbitrarily transfer wealth from one party to another and also make social coordination more difficult by making it harder for anyone to plan with confidence.

Rapid or radical social change may make it so difficult to resolve conflicting claims through adjudication that legislation is called for. Legislation means the creation of new rules to establish and define what people may do with the resources at their command.

New rules will produce lower-cost solutions to pollution problems if they make it easier rather than more difficult for parties to employ their comparative advantages by exchanging rights and obligations.

Rules that place taxes on undesired emissions are usually more effective than detailed physical regulations in resolving pollution problems, because they make greater use of people's detailed knowledge of relevant differences.

Fairness and efficiency can often be partially reconciled in the creation of new rules by allowing those to whom the costs of change are assigned to negotiate an exchange with others who can realize the same objectives at a lower cost.

Questions for Discussion

1. Does it make sense to define pollution as "damage to the environment"?

   (a) Sunshine changes the environment, and the changes are sometimes damaging or even fatal to various living organisms, including human beings. Is sunshine therefore pollution?

   (b) If you are unwilling to think of sunshine as pollution, *why* do you reject the designation? Is it because sunshine cannot be controlled by humans? (It can.) Is it because sunshine occurs naturally? (Do you, I, or the manufacturers of aerosol sprays occur *unnaturally?*)

(c) Why do some people try to acquire dark suntans every summer, despite evidence that extensive exposure to sunshine often causes sunburn, sunstroke, and skin cancer?

(d) If you love sunshine, are the clouds that cover the sun pollution? Is a new high-rise building pollution if it casts a shadow on your home and yard?

2. Here is a question that may help to clarify the text's definition of pollution problems. Why is it that pigeons in downtown parks create no pollution problems whereas people who feed the pigeons do?

3. No one who genuinely cares about the environment would be a litterer. Which of these would you want to call *littering*?

(a) Dumping trash in a farmer's field rather than hauling it to the county dump.

(b) Paying one dollar and then dumping trash in the field of a farmer who has erected a sign: "Dump Site Open to the Public — $1 Per Vehicle." What is the difference?

(c) Tossing a candy wrapper on the sidewalk.

(d) Tossing a candy wrapper under your seat at a major league baseball game. (Why do people who would never toss peanut shells on the sidewalk often toss them on the floor when attending sports events?)

(e) Throwing confetti from an office building during a downtown parade.

4. Does the practice of clearcutting forests damage the environment? Why do you suppose timber companies engage in clearcutting on lands they own if it damages the environment? If the practice of clearcutting results in lower prices for construction lumber, whose environment is improved by clearcutting? Does clearcutting create pollution problems?

5. Are Western ranchers damaging the environment when they kill coyotes? The environment for whom? Whose environment is improved when the coyote population is reduced? Do mousetraps damage the environment?

6. Officials in the suburb of River Edge, New Jersey, passed an ordinance in November 1982 making it illegal for residents to park vehicles with commercial license plates or with signs on the doors in their driveways overnight.

(a) Does this ordinance reduce "visual pollution"?

(b) Does it "protect property values"? Which property values?

7. Do cigarette smokers create pollution problems? Do they create pollution problems if they smoke only in their own homes?

8. Why do people disturb others by talking during movies? Do the talkers and those whom they're disturbing agree about the rights one acquires by purchasing a movie ticket?

9. What are the property-rights claims that are in conflict in each of the cases below? What is the resolution that would best "protect the environment"?

(a) Owners of motorcycles want to remove their mufflers to obtain more efficient engine performance, but the law limits the noise that any motorcycle may emit.

(b) A group wants to prohibit billboards along rural highways, but farmers claim they have a right to erect any kind of sign they want on their own property.

(c) A Missouri state legislator introduced a bill in 1984 making it a crime to blow your nose in a loud or offensive manner in a restaurant.

(d) A Connecticut state legislator proposed a bill in 1985 that would ban the throwing of rice at weddings on the grounds that uncooked rice is unhealthful for birds.

(e) Restaurant owners want to exclude people whose dress doesn't satisfy certain standards. (Should this be legal?)

(f) People who never bathe want to use city buses. People who never brush or comb their hair want to sit and stroll in public parks. (Should the unwashed be barred from the buses? The unkempt, from the parks?)

10. Do we need laws to prevent cropland erosion?

(a) How will farming practices that cause soil erosion affect the present value of farmland?

(b) How will an owner of farmland who wants to maximize the present value of the land decide whether or not to adopt particular soil conservation measures?

(c) Why will a tenant farmer ordinarily adopt fewer and less-effective soil conservation techniques?

(d) Why would landowners ever permit farm tenants to reduce the present value of the land through practices that raise current yields but increase the vulnerability of the land to erosion?

(e) What are some of the consequences of soil erosion that impose costs on people other than landowners? Will even an owner-operator take these costs fully into account in making decisions about whether and how to plow and plant land that is particularly subject to wind or water erosion?

(f) Suppose that people who are farming their own land have trouble earning enough income to pay their mortgages and begin to fear that they will lose ownership of the land to lending institutions. How will this fear affect their decisions about the trade-off between increased yields and reduced soil erosion?

(g) A Montana farmer buys hundreds of thousands of acres of grazing land from longtime ranch operators, then plows up the land and plants wheat. Why did the ranchers sell? Why did the purchasing farmer convert the land from livestock to wheat production? If the farmer knew he would be required to compensate residents of the county for the dust storms that will result when the land is shifted from livestock to wheat, might he find raising livestock more profitable than growing wheat?

(h) Should farmers whose practices aggravate the problem of dust storms be required to compensate others for the additional dust they put into the air? How could such a compensation system be administered?

11. When you bought your house, only 5 commercial planes passed over it daily, on the average. That number has grown slowly and almost imperceptibly over the intervening years and now numbers 150. Is the change from 5 to 150 a drastic or radical change? Is your situation with 150 planes flying over your house each day more tolerable because the number increased slowly and imperceptibly? Would you be more likely to receive compensation of some sort if the changes had occurred over a very short period of time? Does the fact that we can't tell which straw broke the camel's back mean that the addition of more straw to the camel's burden was not the cause of its broken back?

12. Many large urban airports have established programs for buying out those homeowners most seriously affected by airport noise.

(a) Do people who own houses directly under an approach route and within 5000 feet of the runway deserve compensation for the noise made by planes landing or taking off? If you think they do, ask yourself where you will draw the line. What about people whose homes are 15,000 feet from the beginning of the runway or who live very close to but not quite under the approach route?

(b) If the owner is renting the house out, should it be the owner or the tenants who receive compensation? Why?

(c) Are current owners the appropriate people to compensate? Wasn't a current owner compensated in the purchase price if the house was bought within the past few years?

(d) What difference does it make in your answer to the previous question whether it was generally believed when the house changed hands that the airport would buy out those homeowners most severely affected by the noise?

13. If airlines are required to pay landing fees that are adjusted to take account of the level of particular aircraft's noise emissions, the time of day or night when they land, and the density of the residential population in the vicinity of the airport, how will airlines take steps to reduce the impact of their operations on homeowners who live near airports?

(a) A government agency in 1977 calculated for each of 23 airports the decline in the annual rental value of surrounding property due to noise and divided this total by the number of takeoffs and landings during the year. The highest average was $196.67 for New York's La Guardia; the lowest was the Portland, Oregon airport with a cost of $0.82 per takeoff or landing. This means that each takeoff or landing imposed a combined cost of almost $200 on La Guardia's neighbors, but less then a $1 cost on all those living around the Portland airport. Will airlines find it in their interest to use some airports more than they now do and others less if their landing and takeoff fees are increased by these amounts? (Multiply by 2 to convert 1977 dollars roughly into 1990 dollars.)

(b) Will airlines be more likely to install retrofitted noise-control gear or buy new and quieter planes if they must pay higher fees for noisier aircraft? Respond to the argument that "no airline is going to scrap an expensive 707 just to save a few $400 airport surcharges." Is this critic of surcharges thinking marginally?

(c) How would such a system of surcharges induce airlines to fly their noisier planes to Portland and their quieter ones to New York City, or to use Dulles Airport rather than National when flying into Washington, DC? (Dulles, which is far out in the Virginia countryside, showed a cost of $5.64 per operation in the 1977 study.)

14. Each additional vehicle that enters the freeway during the morning rush hour slows all the other automobiles using the freeway. What are the costs considered by each motorist as he or she decides whether or not to use the freeway? What are the costs created for others by this decision? Why is it true – not a joke – that "cars multiply to congest the expressways constructed to eliminate congestion"?

15. What would be the consequences of making the freeway into a tollway? Why might you, as a regular user of the expressway, prefer a toll during the rush hour to not paying any toll? When is it better for a limited-access highway to be a freeway, and when is it better for it to be a tollway?

16. There are two passenger ferries that can be used to cross the river: a tug (large but slow) and a speedboat (small but fast). Every hour, 15 people want to cross the river. Since there is no charge for using either ferry, passengers choose to minimize the time spent in crossing. The tug can carry 1 passenger or 15 passengers across in 21 minutes. The crossing time for the speedboat depends upon the number of passengers:

Number of Passengers	Travel Time in Minutes
1	10
2	12
3	14
4	16
5	18
6	20
7	22

(a) How will the 15 passengers distribute themselves each hour between the two ferries?

(b) What kind of fee system would minimize *total travel time*?

(c) What are the negative externalities present in this problem?

(d) Who would gain and who would lose if fees were charged for crossing in the speedboat?

17. If a tax on downtown parking is used to subsidize and improve the city's bus system, are drivers being taxed to provide benefits that accrue only to nondrivers? If you commuted to work each day in your own car because you had to use the car in your work, why might you want to vote in favor of an increased tax on downtown parking to finance subsidies for bus commuters?

18. History books often lament the destruction of the great herds of bison that roamed the western prairies prior to the arrival of white men.

    (a) Why were so many white men willing to shoot these animals and leave their meat and hide to rot? Wasn't this highly wasteful? Why did so many people apparently place such a high value on a moment of sport as to kill these animals for no other reason than the excitement of it?

    (b) Who bore the costs when a hunter shot a bison or "buffalo" from the window of a passing train?

    (c) Was the near extinction of the buffalo an irreversible act? Or could we bring those huge herds of buffalo back within a few years if the proper incentives existed?

    (d) What is the animal that has replaced the buffalo on the western prairies? Why do the numerous vast herds of cattle that cover the country not suffer the fate of the buffalo? What do you think would happen to the relative size of cattle and buffalo herds if Americans lost their taste for beef and acquired an intense love of buffalo meat?

19. What difference does ownership make?

    (a) What response would you predict from the Sierra Club if an oil company requested a permit to extract natural gas from a wilderness area owned by the federal government?

    (b) What difference do you think it would make to the Sierra Club's decision if the oil company was willing to pay an enormous royalty to the federal government because there was a great deal of natural gas available in that wilderness area?

    (c) What difference do you think it would make if the oil company promised to extract the natural gas in ways that had a very small impact on the environment?

    (d) What difference do you think it would make if the wilderness area, instead of belonging to the federal government, was the property of the Sierra Club?

    (e) Why do you suppose the Audubon Society allows three oil companies to extract natural gas from its 26,800-acre Rainey Wildlife Sanctuary in Louisiana?

    (f) The oil companies in the Rainey Sanctuary pay almost a million dollars per year in royalties to the Audubon Society. Do you think this arrangement promotes the purposes of the Audubon Society? Do you think it promotes the well-being of natural-gas consumers? (The instructive story of the Rainey Sanctuary was told by economists John Baden and Richard Stroup in the July 1981 issue of *Reason* magazine.)

(g) Is it rational for the Audubon Society to allow extraction of natural gas from its own land while opposing it elsewhere?

20. Major construction projects often cannot be undertaken today until an environmental impact statement (EIS) has been filed. Groups that oppose a project can delay its approval by showing that the EIS is incomplete. Is it possible to produce a *complete* description of the impact that any construction project will have on its environment? What effects should the drafters of an EIS be allowed to omit? What effects will opponents of a project agree are irrelevant to the EIS?

21. Four major American cement companies filed environmental lawsuits in 1980 to block the construction of a terminal to receive foreign cement in the small port of Redwood City, California. They claimed that the unloading of cement would put dust into the air that would endanger pelicans, fish, and marine ecosystems. Cement companies also used environmental laws in an effort to block the construction of cement terminals at three other California ports between 1978 and 1983, according to a *Wall Street Journal* article of December 28, 1984. Why do you suppose these companies were willing to spend money in defense of brown pelicans? How can we determine whether someone claiming to defend the environment is sincere? How can we prevent persons from using environmental legislation to advance their own, much narrower interests?

22. Should the socioeconomic effects of a construction project be included in the environmental impact statement written by its promoters? If the effect of a project will be to raise property values in the neighborhood, is this a positive environmental impact? For whom would it be a negative impact on the environment? What methods or criteria should be used to decide whether to authorize a project that improves the environment for some people and worsens it for others?

23. Many towns have begun passing laws that set a limit on the amount of new housing that can be constructed each year. They defend these laws as attempts to protect the environment. What are the effects of such laws? Do they really protect the environment? Do you think they have an effect on the average income of the new people who move to the towns?

24. Should states pass "solar access" laws to prevent people from putting structures on their property that would block solar devices on other buildings? Would this protect property rights or deprive people of property rights? Why are rights to solar access generally poorly defined and uncertain at the present time? How does this uncertainty inhibit the development of solar energy devices?

25. A large mulberry tree in your neighbor's yard provides you with welcome shade but gives her only a lot of inedible and messy mulberries. She wants to cut the tree down.

(a) Does she have the legal right to do so?
(b) You say to her: "I know you hate those messy mulberries, but not nearly as much as I would hate losing the shade." Can you prove your

statement? If you can't prove that you value continued shade more than she values a clean yard, can you induce *her* to place a higher value on *her* benefits from leaving the tree than on *her* benefits from cutting it down? (Hint: How do you induce the sewer cleaner to decide he would rather clear your sewer line on a Sunday afternoon than watch his favorite football team?)

(c) An alternative route for you is to challenge her legal right to cut down the tree. You might try to have the tree declared a historic landmark, or go to court to demand that she file an environmental impact statement before being allowed to remove the tree. What is the danger to you in this tactic? (Hint: If you think you may be prevented in the future from exercising a right you now possess, will you wait to see what becomes of your right or will you exercise it while you still clearly have it?)

26. Two children are quarreling about who gets to choose the program that will be watched on the family's single television set. This is a case of conflicting property rights.

(a) Should the parents tell them to work it out for themselves? Under what circumstances is this likely to produce a satisfactory resolution of the conflict?

(b) How do poorly defined property rights make it more difficult in such a case to achieve a satisfactory resolution through negotiation?

(c) Show how the parents might contribute to a resolution of the conflict first by offering adjudication, then by providing legislation.

27. "I'd pay almost anything if I could get all my classes scheduled before 11:30 so that I can take this great job I've got lined up for the afternoons." Why will it be difficult for the speaker to get what he wants despite his willingness to pay a high price for it?

28. A *Wall Street Journal* article (September 16, 1981) on business attitudes toward regulatory standards under the Reagan administration reported that many corporate executives say that they have adjusted quite well to existing regulations and see no big need for a rollback.

(a) Why might a company that has been compelled by law to reduce its emission of air pollutants *not* want to see the law relaxed?

(b) Why is it important that regulations governing air pollution by industry not be changed frequently?

29. Here is a quotation from *A Treatise of Human Nature* by David Hume. The words were written around 1740.

Our property is nothing but those goods, whose constant possession is established by the laws of society; that is, by the laws of justice. . . .

No one can doubt, that the convention for the distinction of property, and for the stability of possession, is of all circumstances the most necessary to the establishment of human society, and that after the agreement

for the fixing and observing of this rule, there remains little or nothing to
be done towards settling a perfect harmony and concord.

Has Hume exaggerated the importance of clearly defined and stable property rights?

30. Surveys by the Michigan Highway Department showed that beverage-con-
tainer litter decreased 82 percent and total litter decreased 32 percent when
the state adopted a mandatory-deposit law for beer and soft-drink containers. According to one estimate of the effect of the law on prices, Michigan
consumers were paying an extra $300 million per year for beer and soft
drinks as a result of the law.

(a) If these figures are correct, is the mandatory-deposit law "cost effective"
in your judgment? How could you decide?

(b) Suppose we knew that Michigan citizens actually value the reduction
in litter at more than $300 million per year. Would this demonstrate
the cost effectiveness of the mandatory-deposit law?

(c) How many people could be hired full time to walk around picking up
litter for $300 million per year? Assume that litter-lifters receive $5
an hour, which works out to $10,000 a year for 50 weeks of 40 hours
each. Do you think such an army of full-time litter-lifters could reduce
total litter by considerably more than 32 percent?

31. Some EPA officials began wondering aloud in 1989 whether it was really
worthwhile to control ozone as stringently as the Clean Air Act requires.
The ozone standard was set at a level that would prevent any adverse
health effects on people who exercise in an area with high ozone concentrations.

(a) Is there any scientific way to decide whether the benefits from a stringent ozone standard are greater than its costs?

(b) According to a *New York Times* article of April 3, 1989, 51 percent of
the annual emissions of volatile organic compounds that produce ozone
at ground level come from the operation of motor vehicles. So we could
protect our health either by prohibiting so much driving or by exercising
less in those urban areas where, on a few days in the year, ozone levels
exceed the standard. Which is the more efficient way to protect our
health?

(c) Industrial solvents create 4 percent of the emissions and household
solvents create 5 percent of them. If we pass legislation to reduce the
use of solvents, is the legislation more likely to restrict industrial or
household use? Would a restriction on industrial use show that people
are more important than profits?

32. In 1987 a Tacoma, Washington electrical utility purchased from a manufacturing firm, for $265,000, the right to add 60 tons of "particulate
matter" to the air each year. The manufacturer had reduced its annual
emissions by 69 tons a few years earlier through modernizing its plant.

The representative of an environmental organization objected that the practice of selling rights to pollute simply meant that "as soon as one air polluter drops out of the ring, there will be a ready substitute."

(a) What benefits of the system does this criticism ignore?
(b) The utility used the credits to renovate and operate a generating plant that would burn garbage as well as other fuels, thus reducing solid waste disposal problems. Is it better for the environment to bury or to incinerate garbage?

33. Suppose that government environmental agencies decide exactly how much of each kind of industrial pollutant they will allow within a given airshed and sell the rights to discharge these quantities of pollutants to the highest bidder.

(a) Which firms would offer the highest bids?
(b) How could citizens interested in cleaner air than the environmental agency had ordered use this system to obtain what they want?

34. "Taxes can't control pollution. They'll just drive the little firms out of business while the big firms, who can afford to pay, go right on polluting." Do you agree?

35. Assume that the graph in Figure 13A shows how much it costs per year per car to reduce undesirable automobile emissions by various percentages through mandatory exhaust-control devices.

(a) Why does the curve rise slowly at first and increase more rapidly as emission levels decline? Is this a peculiar characteristic of automobile exhaust-control systems, or is it a more general relationship?

FIGURE 13A Costs of reducing automobile emissions

(b) Does this curve tell us how much emissions ought to be reduced? Does it provide any guidance at all to those who make public policy in this area?

(c) If you think of this curve as the marginal cost of supplying cleaner air, what kind of data would you want in order to construct the demand for cleaner air? What would be the significance of the intersection between these two curves?

(d) Suppose you want to find out how much people in your area value cleaner air. So you commission a survey in which people are asked how much they *would be willing to pay* in order to obtain various levels of reduction in the amount of noxious automobile emissions in their community. Can you generally count on them to tell the truth? Remember that they know they won't be held to their valuation — that is, they won't actually be required to pay what they say they would be willing to pay. What are the major sources of bias in such a survey procedure?

(e) Suppose that your survey is done for the government and that the people whom you ask know they will actually be required to pay an annual tax equal to the amount they say they are willing to pay for whatever level of reductions is finally decided on and enforced. What sort of bias will this introduce into your measurement of the community demand for cleaner air?

(f) "No cost is too great to pay to reduce the smog level." Do you think that people who make such statements expect to be among those who actually pay the costs of reducing the smog level?

36. Here is a paragraph from a letter to *The Wall Street Journal* (September 20, 1982) written by the Chairman of the House Subcommittee on Health and the Environment:

> The cheapest and best way to clean air is to make sure that new industrial facilities are built clean. It is far easier to build a new coke oven or blast furnace clean than to try to retrofit an old facility with pollution controls. Just as replacing old, dirty cars with new, clean cars will lessen automotive pollution, so too will turning over America's capital stock clean the air.

A law that requires new cars or new industrial facilities to be "clean" raises the cost of producing new cars or new facilities and hence their price. How will that encourage longer use of old and "dirty" cars and facilities? Show how a law could result in *dirtier* air by setting excessively stringent and costly controls on new cars or industrial facilities.

37. Where is the best place to dispose of solid waste? The most common answer is NIMBY — Not In My Back Yard.

(a) How does a city discriminate unfairly against some people whenever it chooses a new waste disposal site?

(b) What makes people willing to let others dispose of solid waste in their "back yard"?

(c) What would happen if a city "awarded" its new waste disposal site to the community that was most willing to accept it? How might such willingness be obtained and measured?

38. Milk trucks traveling from the dairy farms of Pushpin to the bottling plants in Poetrie must travel an additional 18 miles each day because the bridge is out over the Bentham River. The county road commissioners ask you to do a benefit-cost study to determine whether a new bridge should be built.

(a) What would you want to include in benefits and in costs?
(b) Would you want to know the total benefits from milk drinking in the county or the total cost of driving milk trucks?
(c) How is this related to comparisons of the total benefits and total costs of pollution-control programs?
(d) If appendectomies have saved far more lives than they have cost over the years, should you have your healthy appendix removed by a welder? (The point of this absurd question is that the net benefits from appendectomies do not justify removing *every* appendix by *any* means.)

39. A political cartoon shows a man in a gas mask wheezing and gasping his way to the bank to deposit a sack of money. The caption reads: "News item: The Environmental Protection Agency has decided federal smog standards are too costly for cities and industry."

(a) How does the use of the money sack in the cartoon misrepresent the issue? What are some of the *real* costs of strict smog standards?
(b) Why does the assertion that current smog standards are too costly *not* necessarily mean that smog should be allowed to increase? (Hint: There are many different ways to improve air quality. Current standards actually require specific actions; they do not simply establish a target in terms of air quality.)

40. Bombast City allows motor vehicles to be operated without mufflers if they carry a current noise license, which costs $20 per month. In Tranquil Heights it is illegal to operate a motor vehicle without a muffler, and the fine for violation is $100. Motorists who choose to violate the ordinance are caught and fined about once every 5 months. In other words, Bombast City permits noisy vehicles upon payment of a fee and Tranquil Heights prohibits them and fines violators. The fee and the fine are monetarily equivalent when we multiply the fine by the probability of .2 that it will have to be paid in any month.

(a) Given this monetary equivalence, what is the difference between the approaches of Bombast City and Tranquil Heights to the problem of mufflers and noisy motor vehicles?
(b) It's clear that people who drive without mufflers in Bombast City are licensed to make noise. Do the people who drive without mufflers in Tranquil Heights acquire a license when they pay their fines? Would

the legislators of Tranquil Heights agree that payment of the fine authorizes one to drive without a muffler?

(c) One difference between "you may make noise if you pay" and "you may not make noise and you'll pay if you do" is that in the latter case but not the former the party who makes noise does something that the society condemns as *wrong*. Does this fact exercise its own effect on behavior? How do societies usually respond when individuals *persist* in behavior that has been legally condemned as wrong? Does the penalty remain constant, as it does in the case of a fee for permitted behavior?

(d) Does this distinction aid us in understanding what lies behind some of the objections to pollution fees? When people protest that fees based on emissions into the air or water constitute a "license to pollute," are they perhaps objecting to the law's *authorization* of the emissions? Do they want the emitters to bear moral blame as well as higher monetary costs? Why might people who are intensely interested in cleaner air or water want the issue to be a moral one?

(e) When would it be desirable to treat discharges into the air or the water as costs imposed on others that will be allowed upon payment of a fee, and when would it be better to treat them as crimes punishable by fines?

41. The industrialized nations of Europe and North America have been eager in recent years to secure international agreements to restrict industrial practices that threaten to cause deterioration in the quality of the environment. The less-industrialized countries of the world have been far less eager for such agreements. How would you explain this? Why are people more likely to become concerned about the quality of the environment as their incomes rise?

42. Here is a multiple-choice question for you to think about.

The buildings and grounds at Ivy College are far more littered than the buildings and grounds at the Ivyville Shopping Mall because: (1) students are slobs by nature; (2) more people use the Ivy College campus than use the shopping mall; (3) customers at the shopping mall have less opportunity to litter because they don't smoke or purchase take-out food; (4) customers at the mall have less incentive to litter because they are proud to be "Ivyville Mallers" and so take good care of their "campus"; (5) there are people at the mall but not on the Ivy College campus who expect to receive substantial financial benefits from keeping the buildings and grounds litter-free.

Chapter 14

Markets and Government

What should we leave to the market and what are appropriate tasks for government? It's difficult to answer that question unless we know what we mean by *the market* and by *government*. To choose intelligently we must know what the options are, and the choice between market and government is by no means as clear as our public-policy debates often make it seem.

Private Versus Public?

Most of the standard contrasts between the market system and government don't hold up very well under close examination. To begin with, the market is usually characterized as the *private* sector, with government agencies and officials occupying the *public* sector. But what can this possibly mean? It surely doesn't mean that consumers and the managers of business firms pursue private interests, whereas everyone who works for government pursues the public interest. The senator who claims that "the public interest" guides all his decisions is in fact guided by a personal interpretation of the public interest, filtered through all sorts of private interests: reelection, influence with colleagues, relations with the press, popular image, and place in the history books. Senators *may* be less interested than business executives in maximizing their private monetary income, but they're probably more interested on average in acquiring prestige and power.

The same kind of analysis applies to any employee of a government agency, whether it's a high appointed official on a regulatory commission or someone just starting a job at the lowest civil-service rank. However lofty, noble, or impartial the stated objectives of a government agency, its day-to-day activities will be the consequence of decisions made by ordinary mortals, subject to the pull and push of incentives remarkably similar to those that operate in the private sector. Moreover, in recent years a special devotion to "the public interest" has been claimed for themselves by many executives in leading business corporations, eager to persuade us that the ultimate touchstone for their policies is not the maximization of net revenue but the fulfillment of their social responsibilities. We would be well advised to discount *all* the rhetoric about public versus private interests and to look for the incentives that actually shape the decisions that people make.

Competition and Individualism

Some other common contrasts between the market and the government also grow more indistinct the longer we look at them. The market sector is often called the *competitive* sector. But there is competition in government, too, as every election year demonstrates. Within any government agency, competition for promotion exists among employees. Competition also occurs between government agencies vying for a larger share of appropriations. The two major political parties are continually competing. The executive branch competes with the legislative, members of Congress compete for committee assignments, even district judges compete with one another in the hope of an eventual appointment to a higher court. Do Supreme Court justices, holding appointments for life at the pinnacle of their profession, compete for reputation among editorial writers and law-school professors?

Sometimes we're told that *individualism* is the distinguishing characteristic of the market sector. But what constitutes "individualism"? Many of those who enter the market sector go to work for large corporations right after leaving school and continue as employees until retirement. Is there any significant difference between working in Baltimore as an employee of the Social Security Administration and working in Hartford as an employee of an insurance company? When Britain experimented after World War II with nationalizing, denationalizing, and renationalizing its steel industry, most of the employees (and lots of other people, too) had trouble discerning any difference. Some of the characters who frequent the halls of Congress seem far more individualistic (or at least more idiosyncratic) than the people who pass through the corridors of business.

Economic Theory and Government Action

Economic theory attempts to explain the workings of society on the assumption that all participants want to advance their own interests and try to do so in a rational way. The marginal-cost/marginal-revenue rule that we introduced explicitly in Chapter 9, but have in fact been using throughout the book, is merely a formal expression of these assumptions: the way to advance one's interests is to expand each activity whose marginal revenue exceeds its marginal cost and to contract any activity whose marginal cost is greater than its marginal revenue. The economist does not assume, as we've pointed out before, that money or material goods are the only costs and revenues (or benefits) that consumers and producers care about, or that the interests people pursue are narrow and selfish ones. Economic theory can throw light on the social consequences of every kind of human interest.[1] Why shouldn't that apply to the human purposes and the social processes that control the course of government activities?

RE-ELECTION PROSPECTS

Marginal Benefit

Marginal Cost

NUMBER OF BABIES KISSED

Our answer is that it *does* apply. The principles of social interaction that guide production of *Time* or *Newsweek* are not as different from those that guide production of the *Federal Reserve Bulletin* as people commonly suppose. Governments as well as privately owned firms produce commodities and services. Governments, too, can do that only by obtaining productive resources whose opportunity cost is the value of what they would have produced in their next most valuable employment. Governments as well as privately owned firms therefore must bid for the resources they want and offer the owners of those resources adequate incentives. You'll want to note (we'll come back to it) that the government can use negative as well as positive incentives: the threat of imprisonment, for example, may be a major incentive as some people decide what portion of their income to offer the Internal Revenue Service each spring. United Way can't use that inducement. Governments even face the problem of marketing their output and of price searching, though monetary prices play a much smaller role in the distribution of government products. But there can be no doubt that demand curves exist for government-provided goods and that, since these goods are characteristically scarce, they must be rationed by means of some discriminatory criteria. And the people with a demand for government goods will consequently compete to satisfy those criteria, to pay the established price.

[1]An interest in chaos might be the one exception. In a society where people did not value rationality, but celebrated instead the rule of caprice, accident, and purposeless action, economic theory would have almost no predictive power. Its predictive power is correspondingly greatest in those areas of social life most marked by foresight and premeditated action.

The main advantage of looking at government in this way is that it counters the tendency to think of government as a deus ex machina: a heaven-sent power that can resolve difficulties as magically as a playwright does in the final act of every farce. It makes our expectations of government more realistic. It encourages us to ask about the conditions that enable government to act effectively in any given circumstance and not just to suppose that government always gets what it wants or catches what it chases. This way of looking at government also reminds us that the immediately preceding sentence was misleading in its suggestion that government is an "it"; for government is *many different people interacting on the basis of prevailing property rights.*

If you're wondering what property rights can possibly have to do with the behavior of government, you may have forgotten momentarily that economists use the concept of property rights to describe the rules of the game. Every participant in the processes of government, from voters through civil-service employees to the president, has certain expectations about what voters or civil servants or the president can and may do. Those expectations reflect *property rights.* Maybe it would help if we substituted for *property rights* the phrase *what people think they can get away with.* Unfortunately, that has connotations of conniving and unethical behavior that we don't intend at all. But the phrase does convey the force of the property-rights concept; the actions that people take will depend on their expectations about the consequences of those actions, on the anticipated marginal benefits and marginal costs to themselves of the decisions they're weighing. That's as true in the Senate Office Building as it is on the floor of the New York Stock Exchange. The key to understanding each of those worlds is a grasp of the very different property rights of senators and of stockbrokers.

The Right to Use Coercion

There is one significant difference between government and nongovernment that doesn't grow indistinct or disappear as we inspect it more carefully. *Government possesses a generally conceded and exclusive right to coerce adults.* The right is *generally* conceded, but not universally; thoroughgoing anarchists don't grant it, and neither do those who accept government in principle but reject as illegitimate the authority of the particular government under which they live. It's an *exclusive* right because, as we say, "people don't have the right to take the law into their own hands"; everyone is supposed to appeal to officers of government (police, judges, legislators) when coercion seems called for. And it's the right to coerce *adults* that uniquely distinguishes government, because parents are generally conceded the right to coerce children under certain circumstances.

What does it mean to coerce? We smuggled our definition of coercion into a discussion question in Chapter 11. *To coerce means to induce cooperation by reducing people's options.* Coercion should be contrasted with the other way of obtaining cooperation from people, which is persuasion. *To persuade means to induce cooperation by offering people additional options.*

In a few cases we may not be able to agree whether particular actions constitute coercion or persuasion. These cases will often turn out to involve real or alleged deception, so that our disagreement turns on the issue of what people actually thought their options were when they were induced by others to cooperate. Or we might be disagreeing about the rights that we think people *ought* to have. But this definition will usually allow us to distinguish coercive from noncoercive efforts to influence the behavior of others. It is only to government that we grant the right to secure cooperation by withdrawing options, reducing people's freedom, taking away some of their rights.

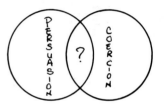

Coercion has a bad reputation, because most of us believe (or think we believe) that people should generally be allowed to do what they want to do. In addition, coercion implies authority, and many of us react with automatic hostility to claims of authority. But the traffic laws that tell us we must drive on the right and stop when the light turns red simultaneously coerce us and expand our freedom. The reason they expand our freedom is that they also coerce others. We all get where we're going faster and more safely, because we accept the coercion of traffic laws. This is the traditional defense of government and its right to coerce: we may all be able to achieve greater freedom and expanded options if we all accept some limitations on our freedom and some reduction in our options.

Is Government Necessary?

But do we have to use coercion? Couldn't we get equally good results by relying on voluntary cooperation? We have seen throughout this book that voluntary exchange is the principal mechanism of coordination in our society. Why couldn't voluntary exchange become the *only* means through which we induce cooperation? By asking this question seriously and pushing for an answer, we can gain some important insights into the capabilities and limitations of the various ways in which we try to get things done.

One way to get at the issue is to ask what would happen if there were no government at all in our society. What problems would arise? Would important tasks cease to be performed? Couldn't people resolve those problems and accomplish those tasks either through individual action or by forming voluntary associations? A good example with which to begin sorting out the issues is the case of police protection. Would there be no police if there were no government? That can't be the case, since private police forces exist at the present time. But these forces supplement a basic, given level of government police protection, providing additional protection for those who want it and are willing to pay for it. Could we obtain that basic protection in the absence of government?

Excluding Nonpayers

Why not? If there were no government, people who wanted police protection could simply purchase it from private security agencies — much as those people do who aren't satisfied with the service that government provides now. Wouldn't that system even be more fair than the one we actually have? People with lots of property to protect and little time, inclination, or ability to protect it themselves would have to pay for the service. Those who own little property or are in a good position to guard it themselves wouldn't have to pay taxes for police protection that doesn't really benefit them. We make people pay for their own food, rather than providing it out of tax revenues, because we know that people want vastly different quantities and qualities. Why not use the same system for police protection?

The correct answer is *not* that police protection is a "basic necessity"; food is even more basic and necessary. The difference is that food can be supplied exclusively to those who pay for it and denied entirely to those who refuse to pay. And that's not altogether the case with police protection. The patrol officers whom my neighbors hire to guard their houses provide a measure of security also to my house, as a spillover benefit, when they patrol our street. Potential burglars won't realize that I haven't subscribed to the neighborhood security service and that they're consequently safe from apprehension if they break into my house. In fact, the burglars may *not* be altogether safe if they do that. The patrol officers might decide that they can most effectively protect their customers' property by arresting *all* the burglars they discover, regardless of whose property is being burglarized. That gives me protection for which I didn't pay.

In much the same way, firefighters hired to protect my neighbors' houses might choose to put out a grass fire in my yard or a blaze in my attic just to keep it from spreading to their customers' property. And when they extinguish fires on their customers' property, they diminish the chance that the property of adjacent nonsubscribers will catch fire. In both cases someone who doesn't pay nonetheless acquires a benefit from production of the good. The key feature is the inability of the producers — the police officers or the firefighters — to exclude nonpayers.

Who will have an incentive to supply a good if people can obtain it without paying for it?

The Free-Rider Problem

When people can obtain a good whether they pay for it or not, they have less incentive to pay. They're tempted to become *free riders: people who accept benefits without paying their share of the cost of providing those benefits.* But if no one has an incentive to pay the costs, no one will have an incentive to provide the benefits. As a result, goods won't be produced, despite the fact that everyone values them more than the cost of producing them.

The free-rider concept describes one of the most frustrating problems in the study of social organization. It especially frustrates those who don't understand why the problem exists and who therefore keep insisting that it *ought* to go away:

"We can lick the energy problem if each of us will only. . . . "

"There would be no litter on our highways if each of us would only. . . . "

"If each of us studies the issues and goes to the polls on election day. . . . "

"If every nation would only renounce forever the use of force as a means of resolving international disagreements. . . . "

Those who plead so plaintively in all these and dozens of similar cases recognize correctly that we could all gain "if each of us would only." They are frustrated by the persistent failure of people to do what would clearly and by everyone's admission make them all better off.

The free-rider problem frustrates economists, too, because economists encounter so much resistance when they try to persuade people that each *will not do what is in the*

If all wheat farmers reduced their planting by 50 percent, all would earn a larger net revenue.

But . . . If all other wheat farmers reduce their planting by 50 percent, any one wheat farmer could make a fortune by increasing his planting by 50 percent.

What would you predict?

interest of all unless it is in the interest of each. People's actions are guided by the costs they expect to bear and the benefits they expect to receive *as a result of those actions.* If the benefits accruing to Jane Marcet will be exactly the same for all practical purposes whether or not she takes a particular action – but she will incur significant costs by taking it – she will not take the action.

If Jane is noble and generous, she will derive a great deal of benefit from helping others, while thinking lightly of the sacrifices she makes to do so. Consequently, she will take some actions that others will not take. That must be stressed, because the free-rider concept definitely does not assert that people are completely selfish or that altruism plays no part in social life. Quite to the contrary, no society could continue to exist in which people were *completely* selfish. We asserted in Chapter 13 – and will remind you again here – that some amount of genuine concern for the well-being of others is essential if any social cooperation at all is to occur. Neither markets nor governments could exist among people with no ability to empathize, to internalize at least some of what others experience.

✳ Positive Externalities and Free Riders

In stressing the significance of the free-rider concept, the economist is insisting only that people have *limited* concepts of self-interest, that they do not by and large entertain the inner feelings of others, especially more distant others, with as much vividness and force as they experience costs and benefits that impinge on them more directly. The economist who calls attention to the free-rider problem is saying that positive externalities exist as well as negative ones, and that these externalities encourage people to behave as free riders. *Positive externalities are benefits that decisionmakers ignore because they accrue to people other than those who created the benefits.* They raise this question: Will anyone have an adequate incentive to create those benefits, or will everyone wait and hope to receive them as a spillover benefit from the actions of others?

Positive externalities or spillover benefits are probably even more widespread in modern societies than are spillover costs, the negative externalities that give rise to complaints about pollution. Homeowners who maintain beautiful lawns produce spillover benefits for neighbors and passers-by. People with engaging smiles distribute spillover benefits to everyone they encounter. Citizens who take the trouble to

inform themselves on community issues improve the quality
of public decisions and thereby benefit everyone. Moreover,
ordinary producers and sellers regularly and as a matter of
course provide benefits to customers considerably greater
than what the customers are required to pay for them.
Eliminating all spillover benefits would be as absurdly impossible as eliminating all pollution. Nonetheless, spillover
benefits and the free-riding tendencies they encourage do
create some serious social problems. Coercion through the
agency of government is a way of dealing with these problems.

Transaction Costs and Coercion

We get a useful handle on the issue when we recognize that
voluntary exchange always entails some *transaction costs.*
These are simply *the costs of negotiating and monitoring
agreements to exchange.* Every commercial sale entails some
transaction costs: buyer and seller must find each other,
agree on what they're willing to offer and want to receive,
and make reasonably sure that they're actually getting what
they expected to get. Sellers in particular must incur transaction costs to be sure that nonpayers don't obtain the goods
that they're supplying. Long-established business operations
keep down transaction costs by reducing them to routine,
thereby enabling all parties to derive larger net benefits from
exchange. When transaction costs are so high, however, that
they exceed the benefits from exchange, exchange won't
occur and the potential benefits will be lost. Government
can be viewed as an institution for reducing transaction
costs through the use of coercion.

The amount of mutually advantageous exchange that occurs in a society is limited by transaction costs.

Law and Order

Let's take a look at some traditional functions of government to see how much this approach explains. We begin
with the problem of "law and order." We can now summarize the argument of the last few pages: high transaction
costs make it difficult to exclude nonpayers from the benefits of police patrols. To prevent free riders from destroying
the incentive to supply police protection, government employs coercion. It supplies the service to everyone and pays
for it with involuntary contributions called taxes.

A judicial system for resolving disputes that arise between citizens could perhaps be created through voluntary
efforts somewhat more easily than a police force, as is suggested by the existence of numerous arbitration systems fi-

nanced by voluntary efforts. But everyone benefits when the people occupying a common territory are all subject to the same system of laws and judicial rulings. Uniform and consistently enforced rules that are binding on all, whether or not they consent, make it much easier for everyone to plan with confidence. And the ability to plan confidently is what distinguishes a cooperating society from a chaotic mob. Since a system of laws and courts confers substantial benefits on people whether or not they choose to help pay for it and to be bound by it, societies use coercion to create and operate systems of justice.

National Defense

National defense is a very traditional function of government, and it provides the classic example of a benefit that can't be provided, except at prohibitive cost, exclusively to those who pay for it. Because free-rider problems would make it practically impossible to rely on voluntary contributions to finance a system of national defense, societies resort to coercion, collecting the funds through taxation.

How can a supplier of national defense make it available exclusively to those who have paid their defense subscription fee?

Note carefully, however, because the point is easily overlooked, that government does not have to rely entirely on coercion to produce the good called national defense. And no government does. The taxes used to finance a military force are coercive levies. But when the funds are used to hire people for the armed forces and to purchase equipment from suppliers, government is relying on persuasion and voluntary cooperation, just as it does in supplying police officers and judges. This raises an interesting question. Why will a government sometimes use coercion to achieve its objectives when it would appear that persuasion would work just as well or even better? Why will a government choose to draft people into the armed forces (and onto juries) rather than rely on volunteers? Most people who work for government are persuaded, not compelled to do so. Why are some coerced? The dangers to which military personnel are subject cannot be the whole answer, since people are attracted into far more dangerous occupations without conscription. We'll suggest an explanation a little further on.

Roads and Schools

What about roads? Would we enjoy an adequate system of streets and highways if we didn't use coercion to finance them? Be careful; an adequate system doesn't necessarily mean the quantity and quality we now have. Roads are over-supplied if the benefits from particular additions are less than the costs of making those additions, and that can surely occur. But is there any reason to expect a systematic under-supply of streets and highways if their provision is left en-tirely to voluntary efforts? The transaction costs could be rather staggering if all streets and highways were owned and operated by people who had to rely entirely on tolls for the collection of revenue. The benefits, moreover, don't accrue exclusively to those who drive. People who live along a dusty gravel road receive benefits from the paving of that road even if they never drive. The experience of those who have built roads in remote areas or in private developments without using coercion suggests both that it can be done and that the costs of securing cooperation by exclusively volun-tary means can be quite high.

What is the case for using coercion to finance education? The argument here is that people will acquire education only up to the point at which the marginal cost to themselves equals the marginal benefit to themselves. But education supposedly generates substantial externalities, benefits that accrue to people other than the person acquiring the educa-tion. Thus, everyone in a democracy benefits when citizens learn to read and to think. Because we don't take account of the benefits to others in deciding how much education to obtain, we obtain less than the optimal amount. By using taxes to subsidize education, the government lowers its cost to potential students and induces them to acquire more than they otherwise would. The question arises, as it does with roads, whether the use of coercion to prevent undersupply does not lead in practice to oversupply. We'll return to that question.

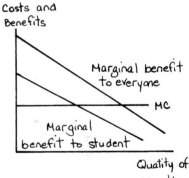

Income Redistribution

Another important category of government action is the pro-vision of special benefits — money grants, food stamps, medi-cal care, housing subsidies, and a variety of social services — to impoverished or disabled people. Why does this kind of activity require the use of coercion? Why don't we leave it to voluntary philanthropy, rather than compel people to con-tribute through the tax system? One part of the answer is that charity is subject to the free-rider problem. Assume that all citizens are charitably disposed and want to see more income made available to especially poor and unfortunate people. Although some citizens derive satisfaction from contributing to a charitable cause, most would prefer that problems be solved and suffering be relieved at a minimum cost to themselves. They want to see poor people helped, but they also want to see others do the helping. And so they tend to behave like free riders. They hold back somewhat on their contributions in the hope that others will contribute enough to take care of the problem. But with everyone waiting for others to contribute, contributions fall short of the amount that everyone would prefer to see raised. Under such circumstances taxation can make people want to contribute more by assuring them that others are also doing their share.

The Regulation of Voluntary Exchange

What about the extensive list of government activities that fall under the category of regulation? Why do federal, state, and local governments regulate so many of the activities of citizens, using coercion to control the terms on which people may engage in voluntary exchange? Putting it in just that way — using coercion to control voluntary exchange — may prompt us to think a little harder and longer about all the things that government does in the name of regulation.

Part of the answer is the widely held belief that the powerful and unscrupulous will take unfair advantage of the weak and the innocent unless the government regulates certain kinds of voluntary exchange. This is the parentalistic argument[2], which no doubt has some merit but which has also often been abused by special interests precisely to take unfair advantage of the weak and the innocent.

Transaction costs provide another part of the answer. It would be very costly for all of us to carry our own scales to check the accuracy of the ones that butchers use and our own gallon cans to be sure the gasoline pumps aren't cheating us. When physicians must be licensed and new drugs approved by the Food and Drug Administration before they can be marketed, buyers are spared the cost of evaluating goods whose quality most of them would be unable to assess for themselves — except at prohibitive costs. By compelling sellers to obtain certification, government agencies can enable us all to make satisfactory exchanges at lower cost. A substantial amount of government regulation can be viewed as coercion designed to reduce the cost of acquiring information.

[2]Most people would say *paternalistic*. But *parentalistic* is a more accurate and less sexist term.

The glaring flaw in this defense of regulation, however, is that it fails to account for the enthusiasm with which sellers so often support regulation. Those who have studied the matter know very well that the demand for government regulation of sellers more often originates with the sellers than with their customers. We saw in Chapter 10 why this occurs: sellers are eager to restrict competition, and government regulation in the name of consumer protection is a technique of proved effectiveness for eliminating competition. But why do the victims cooperate? Why does government employ coercion to promote special interests when it's supposed to be the responsibility of government to promote the public interest?

Government and the Public Interest

The basic answer suggested by economic theory brings us back in a surprising way to the problem with which we began this chapter. The coercive actions taken by government to compensate for the limitations inherent in purely voluntary cooperation are themselves subject to the same limitations. The reason for this is that coercion itself depends on voluntary cooperation. Persuasion always precedes coercion, because government will not act until particular people have been persuaded to act. Government is not the genie in Aladdin's lamp. Government is people interacting, paying attention to the expected costs and benefits of the alternatives that they perceive. The disconcerting part of all this is that the problems created by transaction costs, externalities, and free riders are particularly acute in the political life of democracies.

A surprising number of people assume without thinking about it that "government acts in the public interest." But does it really? Does it always do so? Why do we think so? Do citizens become more virtuous when they move from the line in the supermarket to the line at the polling place? Do people's characters change when they give up a post in industry or academia to take a position with the government? Suppose we define the public interest as what everyone would want if everyone were adequately informed and impartial. Does economic theory have anything useful to say about the likelihood that government actions will proceed from adequate information and an impartial viewpoint?

Those whose decisions make up the sum of government actions will pay attention to the information actually available to them and the incentives that actually confront them. Economic theory predicts that this information and these incentives will tend to be both limited and biased.

Information and Democratic Governments

We can begin with citizen voters. None of us knows enough to cast an adequately intelligent vote. To persuade yourself that this is so, conduct a little mental experiment. Suppose you know that your vote, whether on a candidate or a ballot proposition, would determine the outcome of the election; your vote and your vote alone will decide the question. How much information would you gather before casting that crucial vote? A lot would depend, of course, on the importance of the office or the issue. But you would surely invest far more time and energy in acquiring information than you do when you're just one voter among 50 thousand or 50 million. As it is, most citizens, including intelligent, well-read, and public-spirited citizens, step into the polling place on election day equipped only with a lot of prejudices, a few hunches, some poorly tested bits of information, and vast areas of total ignorance. We do this because it's rational to do so! Given the actual importance of our one vote in 50 thousand or 50 million, it would be an almost unconscionable waste of time for us to learn enough to cast an adequately informed vote. The issue is not simply one of selfishness or lack of dedication to the well-being of society. A voter who wanted to make a personal sacrifice for the good of the commonwealth could do far more per hour, per dollar, or per calorie in social-service volunteer work than by gathering enough information to cast an adequately informed vote.

"But if everybody thought that way," goes the standard objection, "democracy wouldn't work." This objection is another instance of the argument that the free-rider phenomenon doesn't exist because the world would be a more satisfactory place if it did not exist. Those who are committed to democracy had better concern themselves with ways to make it work when citizen voters are uninformed and misinformed, and not pretend that voters have knowledge they obviously don't have.

Some defenders of democracy aren't overly discouraged by the incompetence of citizen voters. They rely on elected representatives to acquire the information that must be available if decisions are to be made in the public interest.

Rational ignorance: when it's not worthwhile to learn.

Their confidence has a reasonable foundation in reality. Because the vote of each legislator has a far greater probability of affecting the outcome, because legislators can use the information they acquire to influence others in significant ways, because legislators are provided with staff and other information-gathering resources, because many people will have a strong interest in making relevant information available to legislators, because legislators' votes are monitored and must be defended—for all these reasons and more, elected representatives are far more likely to be adequately informed about the issues on which they vote than are ordinary citizens.

The Interests of Elected Officials

But even if we can assume that legislators' votes are adequately informed, are we entitled to assume that they will be votes in the public interest? Are elected representatives impartial? Another way of asking the same question is to ask whether they will always vote in the way that the information available to them tells them they ought to vote. Economic theory assumes that people act in their own interest, not that they act in the public interest. Sometimes it will be in a legislator's interest to pursue the public interest. But finding ways to produce such harmony is the major issue in the design of political institutions; we can't simply *assume* this advantageous concord without asking whether the institutions under which we live are likely to produce it. Because an interest in reelection is a common and healthy interest among most elected officials, we'll focus our analysis on this one particular private interest. Is an interest in being reelected likely to lead elected officials to vote and act in the public interest?

Let's begin by noticing how it limits their planning horizons. Elected officials can't afford to look too far ahead. Results must be available by the next election or the incumbent could be replaced by someone who offers better promises. We shall see in the last part of this book how an emphasis on the short run makes it difficult for governments to deal effectively with recessions and inflations. But the same will be true for any policy that requires current sacrifices for the sake of future benefits. Elected officials will tend to discount heavily the value of all future benefits that aren't expected until after the election. Their interest in reelection will thus keep them from fully using their own

Paying $2000 one year from now for $1,000 in benefits right now is worthwhile to someone who wouldn't otherwise be around one year from now.

superior knowledge about the consequences of particular policies.

In listing some of the reasons why legislators are likely to be well informed, we mentioned two that also explain why legislators will not always vote in the way that their information tells them they ought to vote. These were the last two reasons cited: many people have a strong interest in making relevant information available to legislators, and legislators' votes are monitored and must be defended. The problem is that the interest in providing information (or lobbying) and in holding legislators accountable for their actions is concentrated in special-interest groups. The positive externalities associated with the political process makes this almost inevitable.

Conflict in recent years over deregulation in the transportation industry illustrates the problem and also shows how the special interests can sometimes be defeated. The commercial airlines were essentially deregulated in 1978 and the regulatory authority, the Civil Aeronautics Board, went out of business completely in 1982. This occurred despite the airlines' predictions that service quality would decline, the pilot union's warnings about safety, the objection of smaller cities that they would be deprived of service, and the determined resistance of many members of Congress who knew how to earn political points with the special interests among their constituencies by leaning on the CAB. The interests of passengers in more flights and lower prices were effectively championed in this case by a handful of legislators who seem to have read some economics and who were aided by the tide of disillusionment with government that rose in the 1970s and crested in the 1980s.

The continuing struggle to deregulate the trucking industry shows how special interests can sometimes defeat other special interests. Regulation by the Interstate Commerce Commission over the years had produced wasteful practices and higher prices to shippers that ultimately showed up as higher prices for just about everything we buy. But there were people who benefited from all this. By restricting competition, regulation created privileged positions for the trucking firms that owned operating rights and for members of the Teamsters Union. These groups expected deregulation to reduce their wealth substantially. They were therefore extremely active in lobbying members of Congress, in making campaign contributions, and in threatening retaliation against elected officials who might vote to "throw the trucking industry open to the chaos of competition."

The dollar benefits to the rest of us from lower transportation costs would almost surely be greater in the aggregate than the losses that the trucking firms and the drivers expected to suffer from deregulation. Nonetheless we did not see any significant amount of lobbying effort, campaign contributions, or demonstrations on the part of ordinary consumers directed at getting Congress to vote for deregulation. The individual interest that each of us has in deregulation is simply not great enough to induce any of us to involve ourselves actively in the fight. The political pressure for deregulation that persuaded Congress came from shippers. Because they stood to gain large benefits from deregulation, shippers organized the political opposition that led to partial deregulation of the motor carrier industry in 1980. They received a powerful assist from the same political tide that helped abolish the CAB.

Similar stories can be told about the railroad industry. The maritime industry, on the other hand, still uses "national security" arguments to retain the benefits of government regulation that has produced absurd wastes but also huge financial benefits for a favored few.

The process is always the same. The few who have much to gain invest vast resources in trying to influence the legislature. The many with more to gain in total but less to gain individually invest nothing. Legislators respond to this sort of pressure, because a substantial number of them find that doing so serves their interest in being reelected. It seems rather futile to fault them for this; an *ex*-legislator with untarnished principles is a less effective public servant than a legislator who has bent a few principles to survive and fight another day. The fault lies with the externalities that prompt most of us to behave like free riders, hoping that someone else will assume the costs of lobbying for the measures from which we would all benefit.

Positive Externalities and Government Policies

Our conclusion should come as no surprise. Government policies will tend to be dominated by special interests. Government will lean toward actions that harm many people just a little bit, rather than actions that displease a few people very much. Government policies will be guided not so much by the public interest as by an endless succession of extremely partial interests. This is why consumer interests win the oratorical contests, but producer interests control policy. The interests of producers are simply more concentrated, more sharply focused. Producers know that their action or inaction can make a significant difference to their own welfare, and so it's in their interest to act. But no individual consumer can expect more than a small benefit from political action, so none of them has an incentive to accept the costs.

Is this why the use of coercion to prevent an undersupply of roads often leads to an oversupply? The taxpayers' general interest in economy doesn't fare well when it goes head to head with a small group's intense interest in having a road or building a road. The same analysis applies to schooling. Those who produce schooling (the author's own vested interest, let it be noted) can make life difficult for legislators who try to save taxpayers money by reducing expenditures on education or research. Here is an explanation for the otherwise puzzling behavior of legislatures that approve larger and larger expenditures — even when every member favors reduced expenditures. There is no way to cut a budget without cutting specific projects. With every special interest organized to make certain that the cuts occur in someone else's project, expenditures cannot be reduced.

Why did we long have a military draft in this country, and what is the probability that Congress will restore it? Military conscription, as we noted earlier, extends the use of coercion into areas where persuasion is quite capable of securing the cooperation we want (at least in peacetime). The draft probably persisted as long as it did because the military establishment had a strong and sharply focused interest in maintaining a ready flow of personnel for the armed forces, whereas most of those who were adversely affected by the draft had a stronger incentive to find a personal escape route than to attack the whole system. It is interesting to note how many current advocates of reinstating the draft are now talking about *universal* conscription of young people for short-term service of some kind. Will this tactic (assuming that it is a tactic) increase the number of those who are opposed to the draft? Or will it reduce the expected cost to each draftee below that critical point at which he or she would be willing to do political battle to prevent reestablishment of the draft?

What can we say about government actions to relieve poverty? We can predict that legislators will be slow to replace in-kind transfers with money transfers. Farmers benefit from the food-stamp program, the building trades benefit from housing subsidies, the medical-care industry expands with health-care assistance, teachers benefit from educational subsidies for the poor, and social workers know that giving money to the poor will never be as advantageous as hiring more members of the "helping professions." The political influence of these groups makes it easier for legislatures to support in-kind transfers to the poor than to support money transfers. There may be other and better grounds for rejecting money transfers, but this alternative would get more respectful attention in Congress if money were produced and sold by a money industry.

How Do People Identify the Public Interest?

None of this implies that farmers, hospital administrators, or social workers have no regard for the public interest. It implies only that they all have *some* regard for their own interests. And even those who work for government agencies charged specifically to protect the public interest define it with reference to their own special interests.

Consider, for example, a member of the Food and Drug Administration (FDA), responsible for preventing the introduction of new drugs without adequate testing. What is adequate testing? It's testing that makes sure we know all the side effects of a new drug before we allow it on the market. But we can *never* be sure. All we can do is acquire additional information and thus reduce the risk that someone will be killed or seriously harmed by an unanticipated side effect. How far should we reduce the risk? Not *too* far, because there are costs as well as benefits attached to additional testing. A major cost will be the lives lost and the suffering not relieved because the drug isn't available while it's being tested.

How will an FDA commissioner evaluate these two costs: the lives lost through premature introduction and the lives lost through excessive delay in introduction of new drugs? People will blame the FDA if an approved drug turns out to have disastrous side effects, and they will applaud the FDA if it refuses to approve a drug that subsequently turns out to have disastrous side effects in other countries. But almost no one condemns the FDA for lives lost while a drug is being tested or applauds the FDA for cutting the testing period short in order to get a new drug on the market. The conclusion is obvious. FDA commissioners will find it in the public interest to test drugs beyond the point at which the marginal benefit equals the marginal cost to patients.

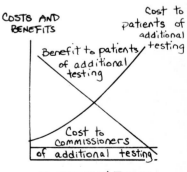

If all this is unsettling to those for whom it is an article of faith that the government takes care of the public interest, it may be time to question this article of faith. Perhaps it stems from the habit of equating "government" with "nation" and extending to the former the reverence felt for the latter. Or it may be a result of our belief that government is the last resort and therefore must be an effective resort, since we don't like to admit to any unsolvable problems. There's a popular bit of deductive reasoning that also leads toward this conclusion. It asserts that all social problems are the result of human behavior, that human behavior can be altered by law, and that government makes the laws, from which the argument concludes that government can solve all social problems.

Alexis de Tocqueville offered a more realistic view in *Democracy in America* (Book I, Chapter VIII): "There is no country in which everything can be provided for by the laws, or in which political institutions can prove a substitute for common sense and public morality."

Once Over Lightly

Economic theory assumes that the actions of government follow from the decisions of citizens and government officials who are paying attention to the marginal costs and marginal benefits to themselves of alternative courses of action.

The distinguishing characteristic of government is its generally conceded and exclusive right to use coercion. To coerce means to induce cooperation by reducing people's options. Voluntary cooperation relies exclusively on persuasion, which secures desired behavior by offering additional options.

Coercion is useful to the members of a society, because it can sometimes secure the production of goods that everyone values at more than the cost of supplying them, but which would not be supplied through purely voluntary cooperation.

A supply failure of this sort is likely to occur when there is no low-cost way of confining supply of a good to those who pay for it, or of preventing demanders from becoming free riders.

Coercion may be able to secure the supply of such goods by lowering transaction costs. These are deadweight costs incurred in the process of carrying through an exchange.

The traditional activities of government turn out on examination to be largely actions aimed at reducing transaction costs and overcoming free-rider problems.

The coercive activities of government presuppose voluntary cooperation. Persuasion precedes coercion because, in the last analysis, citizens and government officials must be persuaded to employ coercion in particular ways. This implies that the limits on the effectiveness of voluntary cooperation that justify coercive action by government are limitations also on the effectiveness of the government's coercive action.

Positive externalities thoroughly permeate the political process in a democratic government. They make it unlikely that citizen voters will be adequately informed or that elected or appointed officials will consistently act in the way that the information available to them tells them they ought to act.

Questions for Discussion

1. In what general, systematic way do the interests pursued by officials in government differ from the interests pursued by people in the private sector? Consider the following cases:

   (a) The president of a state-owned university and the president of a privately owned university.
   (b) A member of the U.S. House of Representatives who aspires to a seat in the Senate and a traveling sales representative for a large business corporation who wants a job as sales manager at one of the firm's plants.
   (c) A prominent political figure who wants to become president of the United States and a prominent actor who wants to receive an Academy Award.
   (d) An urban police officer and a uniformed guard employed by a private security firm.
   (e) A grant-awarding official in the Small Business Administration and a loan officer in a bank.

2. In each of the following examples, what are the significant differences between government-owned and nongovernment-owned enterprises? Why do you think the government owns the enterprises mentioned? What different forms does competition take in the case of government-owned enterprises? In what different ways do they operate because of their government ownership?

   (a) Investor-owned utilities and utilities owned by states or municipalities.
   (b) State colleges and private colleges.

22. Why do some people who drink alcoholic beverages vote in favor of legal prohibition?

23. Here is the opening sentence of a newspaper editorial lamenting the tiny turnout for a public hearing on improving the high schools in a large U.S. city: "Given the number of people who complain about public education, it's amazing how few attend meetings to tell the schools how to do better." Is it really surprising that many complain but few attend meetings?

    (a) What is the cost of complaining? What is the cost of attending a meeting?

    (b) What is the probability that a concerned citizen who spends an evening at a public hearing will actually be able to influence policies in a large urban school district?

    (c) The relative benefit-cost ratios of complaining and attending would seem to provide an adequate explanation for the facts lamented by the newspaper editorialist. But how can we explain the behavior of "activists," those few people who seem always willing to turn out for meetings on even the most inopportune occasions? Are there satisfactions other than that of actually affecting public policy that people can obtain through political participation?

24. Most parent-teacher associations have a hard time getting people to attend meetings and do other work for the associations.

    (a) Why does this not imply either that parents don't care about their children's education or that they don't think the PTA accomplishes anything?

    (b) Why is attendance usually better among teachers than among parents?

    (c) Why do a few parents choose to be very actively involved in the PTA?

25. Hospitals often find it not worth their while to hold down their costs, because reductions in costs produce lower reimbursement payments from government as well as a lower quality of patient care. A letter to *The Wall Street Journal* (February 24, 1982) complains about this attitude on the part of hospital administrators:

    > [E]very health care provider looks no further than his own checkbook. . . .
    > If all providers would look to the size of the jar rather than the one jelly
    > bean they have plucked from it, there would be bigger and better beans
    > for everyone.

    How does this illustrate both the free-rider problem and the "if each of us would only" fallacy?

26. Largely in order to keep its streets free of traffic congestion, Singapore levies taxes on automobiles that raise their price about 150 percent.

    (a) Is it possible that car owners in Singapore are better off with the tax than they would be without it?

(b) Assume that all car owners in Singapore believe that the benefit to themselves from reduced congestion due to the tax is worth more than the tax they must pay. Does it follow that each car owner will voluntarily pay the tax?

(c) What would be a better tax than a tax on automobile ownership if the goal is to reduce traffic congestion?

27. Each of the ten families on a suburban block is likely to have its own power lawn mower. Why don't families more often share a single lawn mower? Try to enumerate the principal transaction costs that stand in the way of such a cooperative arrangement.

28. It's difficult for entertainers to supply their services exclusively to those television viewers who are willing to pay for the entertainment.

(a) How do entertainers nonetheless manage to secure payment for providing their services to television viewers? Think through the way in which the free-rider problem is handled in network television. To whom do entertainers sell their services? Through what sequence of transactions do viewers receive the entertainment? How is the free-rider problem handled at each stage?

(b) Some homeowners today try to get cable-television programs without subscribing by picking up the signal from satellites, using their own receiving dishes. How does the use of scramblers and decoders by pay-television companies illustrate the acceptance of transaction costs to eliminate free riders?

29. If running laps around the football field improves the conditioning of athletes and makes them more effective players, why do so many players try to get away with running fewer laps than the coach orders? Who receives the benefits and who bears the cost of such conditioning activities? Are coaches likely to order their players to run a more-than-optimal number of laps?

30. When a government agency requires households or businesses to submit detailed reports on their activities, the costs are borne by those who must prepare the reports and the benefits (in the form of additional information) are received entirely by the agency.

(a) How does this explain the expansion of government-required paperwork despite a general consensus that such paperwork is already excessive?

(b) Do you think the requirements would decline if agencies were required to use funds from their budget allocations to compensate those who must submit the forms?

(c) Should teachers be required to read and comment on all papers that they require their students to write?

3

Chapter 15

Inflation, Recession, Unemployment: An Introduction

There is one responsibility of government that receives about as much attention these days from the press and public as all the others put together: the responsibility of the federal government to prevent, cure, or otherwise control inflations and recessions. Except for an incidental mention, Chapter 14 ignored this responsibility in examining the functions of government. We'll make up for that omission now. The remainder of this book will be devoted almost entirely to the issue of aggregate economic fluctuations and government stabilization policies.

Why do we regard periods of inflation and recession as *problems?* Some readers will be thinking at this point that anyone who has to ask a question like that is too stupid to understand the answer. Inflation means a rise in the cost of living, and anything that makes it more costly for people to live is obviously a problem. As for recessions, they cause a loss of income and of jobs, and no one has to be told why both of those are problems. But matters are not that simple.

Dollar Prices and Real Costs

In the case of inflation, matters are not that way at all. *Inflation is not a rise in the cost of living. Inflation is basically a fall in the value or purchasing power of money.* Looking at it in another way, we can say that inflation is a rise in the money price of goods. You may even, if you wish, speak of inflation as a rise in the money cost of living. But the key word is *money*. A $2 hamburger this year really costs no more than a $1 hamburger last year if the cost of obtaining a dollar has been cut in half since last year.

The cost of obtaining anything is the value of what must be given up to obtain it. We get so into the habit of expressing the value of sacrificed opportunities in the common denominator of money that we sometimes forget to check on whether the value of the common denominator has changed. But that is precisely what inflation is. It's not an increase in the height of everything we're measuring — it's a decrease in the length of the yardstick that we're using to do our measuring.

Of course, everything is finally relative to everything else. It's logically possible to insist that money has maintained a constant value in recent years and everything else has gone up. But that would be as sensible as arguing that the price of a barrel of crude oil remained unchanged through the 1970s, when OPEC succeeded in reducing world oil production, while the value of everything else declined by about 75 percent. When we find oil prices moving relative to everything else, common sense tells us to look for the explanation in changes that have occurred in the conditions of supply or demand for oil — not for "everything else." When we see money prices moving relative to everything else, common sense ought to dictate the same course of inquiry.

Perhaps we would be more likely to see the essential link between money and inflation if we stopped to realize that *inflation simply could not occur in the absence of money.* If all exchanges occurred through barter, there would be absolutely no way in which we could experience inflation. You may have to think about it for a moment to convince yourself. But inflation is a logical impossibility in a society in which goods are exchanged directly for other goods without any use of money.

In a barter economy (where no money was used), it would be logically impossible for all prices to rise.

Uncertainty About the Future Value of Money

If inflation does not actually raise the cost of living, why is it a problem? Why does everyone worry so much about it? *The problems that inflation creates are caused almost entirely by uncertainty.* It is not the fact that the value of money is falling that creates problems, but the fact that the future value of money cannot be predicted. A high but steady rate of inflation on which everyone could confidently depend would cause fewer problems than a lower but less predictable rate of inflation.

Deflation, which is *a rise in the value or purchasing power of money,* is just as much of a problem for society as is inflation, insofar as it also introduces uncertainty into the calculations of planners. The same is even true of disinflation, something experienced in the United States in 1982 and 1983. *Disinflation is a slowing down of the inflation rate;* it also creates serious difficulties for those who fail to anticipate it correctly when making long-term plans.

The Real Costs of Inflation

Consider what happened to financial institutions that loaned money in 1965 on 15-year mortgages at a 6 percent annual interest rate, the standard rate in that year on mortgage loans for new homes. The lenders presumably expected a continuation of the inflation rate that they had experienced over the preceding decade, a rate of less than 2 percent per year. That would have left them with a 4 percent per year *real* return on their mortgage loans: the nominal rate of 6 percent minus the 2 percent per year decline in the value of money. But unexpected inflation played havoc with their expectations. From 1965 to 1980, the dollar declined in value an average of 6 percent per year. That left the lenders with a zero rate of return for the period, which was hardly enough to cover their costs. Lending institutions sustained large losses as a direct result of their failure to predict future changes in the value of money, and many went out of business.

When the value of money is expected to fall rapidly, it pays to take on debt. And anyone who wants to save had better be sure to put those savings into something whose dollar value will keep up with the inflation rate — something like real estate, for example. So when Americans concluded in the 1970s that inflation rates of 5 or even 10 percent per year were going to be the rule, not the exception, the demand to own real estate increased substantially. The purchase price of land and houses consequently rose. Mortgage rates on new homes also rose, to 10 percent in 1978 and on up to more than 15 percent in 1982. People were paying high prices for homes and financing them at high interest rates in the first few years of the 1980s because they had been experiencing 10 percent per year inflation and expected it to continue or even accelerate. But it did not. The inflation rate unexpectedly fell below 7 percent in 1982 and below 4 percent in 1983. Home buyers suddenly found that they had paid too much for the houses they owned and that, with their incomes no longer increasing by 10 or 15 percent per year, they could not keep up the monthly payments for which they had contracted.

The uncertainty about future prices that inflation generates leads to arbitrary redistributions of wealth, to costly efforts by people to protect themselves against losses in

Inflation, deflation, disinflation, — all cause problems by making the future more uncertain.

wealth, and — perhaps most serious of all — to mounting levels of resentment that can eventually cripple a society's capacity to maintain cooperation among its members.

Redistributions of Wealth

Inflation generates profits for some and losses for others because people fail to anticipate it correctly. Moreover, everyone isn't equally able to act appropriately once the truth about inflation comes to be known. Some sellers' prices are set for only short periods of time and can move up quickly in response to increased demand. Examples are the prices of farm products and many of the raw materials used in industrial production. Others respond much less quickly to changed circumstances. Commercial and residential rents are usually set by contract and often cannot be changed for long periods. There are ways for landlords to compel reopenings of contracts in order to negotiate higher rentals, but these procedures entail additional costs to the landlord. Wages and salaries are typically established by agreements that are supposed to extend over longer periods of time. These agreements can also be renegotiated during the contract period, and some will even contain formal clauses calling for renegotiation if certain conditions change. Wages and salaries, however, tend to be less quickly responsive to changed conditions than are the prices of most goods.

Many prices cannot be raised quickly because to do so requires the consent of a regulatory body that may move with glacial speed: gas and electric utilities and telephone companies often complain of their inability to respond quickly enough to higher costs. Then there are those creditors who made long-term loans and can't raise the payments they receive for that service until the loan matures — which might be 25 years in the future. On the other hand, consider the happy position of the federal government prior to 1985 when the income tax was indexed so that personal exemptions, the standard deduction, and tax brackets all increased with inflation. Prior to indexing, the federal government was able to sell us national defense and a variety of social services and charge a price (the personal income tax) that not only increased but increased at a progressive rate as we all spent and took in more money because the value of money had fallen.

The net result of everything described above is that inflation redistributes income extensively and almost capriciously.

Prices that respond more slowly don't necessarily increase less; they just take longer to get where they're going. But that still means income is redistributed during the transitional period so that some people will have lost out even after they have caught up. The redistributive effects of inflation depend heavily on how rapidly the inflation occurs, because this affects the ability of different people to anticipate and adjust to it. From 1967 to 1973, for example, the consumer price index rose 41 percent, while the mean hourly wage of production workers in private industry rose 46 percent. So wages more than kept pace. But when the price level spurted up 16 percent from January 1973 to July 1974, the mean hourly wage increased only 12 percent, so that the real hourly wage declined.

People learn to protect themselves against slow, steady inflation.

These redistributions of wealth are hardly enough to account for the public's hostility toward inflation. The strength of the popular pressure on government to control inflation (or at least to seem to be controlling it) can be appreciated only if one understands why the beneficiaries of inflation so often join the victims in denouncing it. The principal reason is that they mistakenly think they are victims, too.

There is no better example than residential rents. At the outset of any period of rapid inflation, rents will lag well behind the rate of increase in other prices, including the "price" of labor as measured by average hourly wage rates. The result is that inflation redistributes wealth from landlords to tenants. But tenants don't realize this. They notice the increases in their rents. They don't notice that their rent is increasing at a lower percentage rate than the prices of everything else, including their own incomes. So they conclude they're being hurt by inflation, when in fact they are its beneficiaries.

Many of us are also inclined to exaggerate somewhat our own merit and the value of our contribution to the welfare of the world. So when we look back and notice that our annual income has gone up 120 percent over the last decade, we regard that as a 120 percent increase in the world's appreciation of our worth. When someone points out that the official index of consumer prices shows a 100 percent increase over the same period, we don't deflate that generous estimate of our own improvement. We still think we earned a 120 percent increase in our income, and we resent the fact that we have to pay twice as much nowadays for the things we buy.

Protection Costs

Illusion thus plays a major role in making inflation unpopular and creating pressure on governments to do something about it. But the costs of inflation to a society as a whole are not completely illusory. Imagine a situation in which the various state governments controlled the standards for weights and measures. Suppose that the only way to effect a shift to the metric system was to be sneaky about it — to expand the inch gradually until it measured $\frac{1}{36}$ of a meter. So at periodic but unpredictable intervals over the next ten years, the officials of various states announced to their jurisdictions an official increase in the length of the inch — "never enough to notice," as they were fond of saying, but enough to increase the inch from its former length of 0.0254 meters to the desired length of 0.027⅑ meters.

Where would the costs of such a procedure show up? They would appear in resources devoted to guessing the timing and rate of changes and ensuring against the consequences of mistakes; in resources spent on translating measurements when goods produced in one state are used in another; in resources employed to fit tools conforming to older specifications to products made to newer specifications; in resources wasted on the correction of mistakes arising from the increased uncertainty and from the complexity of the coordinating task.

The real costs of inflation to a society are like the costs just described. We suggested a few paragraphs back that inflation is a change in the length of the measuring instrument. That doesn't mean inflation has no real costs. An elastic measuring instrument is a serious problem whenever decisions have to be coordinated over space and time. A large real cost of inflation is the effort and other resources that people devote to "beating" it. As evidence, thumb through a few of the unbelievable number of paperback books published in recent years telling people how to come out ahead or at least stay even during periods of inflation.

Inflation and Social Conflict

The most serious cost of inflation to a society such as ours, however, may be the damage it does to our resources of mutual trust and goodwill. We have tried to call your attention on several occasions to a fact that was well appreciated by Adam Smith, but which his modern successors in the economics profession too often slight. The cooperation that is the essence of society and of civilization presupposes a substantial amount of self-restraint on the part of its members, or a willingness to include the interests of others in the conception of one's own interests. If people come to believe that they're being defrauded, they will more readily throw off the constraints of ethics and do unto others what they think is being done unto them. When the illusory losses of inflation are added to the actual redistributions of wealth that inflation causes, the aggregate sense of injustice may rise to a critical level.

If people then organize into groups to secure a redress of their grievances through coercion, they feed the anger and resentment of others. School teachers striking in protest against salaries that don't keep pace with inflation add to citizen dissatisfaction with the school system and the taxes required to support it. The inflation that convinces tenants they are the victims of landlord exploitation – but which actually reduces the relative price of renting – creates low vacancy rates. This makes it appear that higher prices do not produce more rental housing and so accomplish nothing except the enrichment of landlords. Meanwhile, the net revenue of landlords will actually be falling, bringing with it the predictable consequences for maintenance and the state of landlord–tenant feelings. Political demands become more strident when people believe they are being victimized, and the total of claims that groups start to insist on as their right climbs well above 100 percent of the society's output. These demands become concentrated on government because government is increasingly thought to have the duty and the power to set all things right. Elected officials will find themselves under pressure to do something, even if that something provides only short-term symptomatic relief and worsens the problem in the long run. Every action taken by government in response to mounting levels of citizen discontent creates a reason for doing more, either in response to the next interest group or to remedy the unanticipated problems caused by the last response. When the sum of the expectations by far exceeds the sum of what is available to satisfy them – and people begin using coercion to satisfy their expectations – something must give way. It could too easily be the consensus on which the society itself is founded.

What Happens in a Recession?

Recession is related to *recede,* which means to withdraw or retreat. A recession is a retreat from earlier rates of growth in the total output of the economy. By a general consent earned over many years, the National Bureau of Economic Research, a private, nonprofit research organization, has the privilege of deciding officially when a slowdown in growth has become a recession. But would every substantial slowdown in growth have to be a recession? Is perpetual growth the only possible norm?

That implication is avoided when we realize that *the costs of a recession are largely the costs of disappointed expectations.* The point is fundamental. If we lose sight of the relationship between recession and disappointment, we'll find ourselves unable to distinguish between unemployment and leisure, or between changes that leave people worse off than before and changes that add to human welfare. We may also miss seeing the crucial role that uncertainty plays in causing recessions and thereby conclude that recessions can be cured with remedies that are more likely to aggravate the disease.

If a recession were merely a slowdown in the rate of economic growth, recessions would be popular with advocates of zero economic growth and all those who think we should reduce our emphasis on the production of marketable goods. But recessions aren't popular with these groups or anyone else, because they entail *unintended and therefore disruptive slowdowns* in the rate of economic growth. Bare statistics on aggregate output, like the data on gross national product that we'll be looking at in the next chapter, are incapable of revealing disappointed expectations. We may be able to infer widespread disappointment from such statistics, but aggregate data could truly measure a recession only if they could somehow measure the gaps between the output that people have counted on producing and what they finally decided to produce.

Producers' expectations are frustrated every day, of course. But every day some other producers are delighted to discover that events have turned out *better* than they had expected. A recession occurs when, for some reason, the number and depth of the disappointments increase without any compensating increase in the quantity and quality of delightful surprises. Why that occurs and what can be done about it will be a major question in the chapters ahead.

We described the phenomenon of recession just now by referring to output or production. The costs and causes of recessions, however, may better be described in terms of income. It is the lost income that finally disappoints producers, and it is declining income that induces producers to cut back on the rate of output. The owners or managers of business firms count on selling some quantity of their product at some anticipated price. But when sales prove disappointing, inventories of unsold goods pile up, costs run ahead of revenues, and so production is slowed down or stopped altogether for a while. Net income is the criterion that guides these decisions.

When business firms reduce their rate of production below what they had intended earlier, they often lay workers off and thereby create unemployment. This is the problem that first comes to mind when we think about recessions: a rising rate of unemployment. But what exactly is the problem? Once again we must ask for patience from the reader who thinks the question is stupid because the answer is obvious. The answer is obvious only until we begin thinking about it carefully.

When Is Unemployment a Problem?

Recessions do indeed cause unemployment to increase. But it doesn't increase from zero, and it doesn't fall back to zero when the recession is over. Even in the year 1944, 1.2 percent of the labor force was classified as unemployed, at a time when one-sixth of the entire labor force was in the armed forces, and people were being urged to leave school to take jobs, to come out of retirement, and to work six- or seven-day weeks. No one who lived through those labor-hungry years would believe that 1.2 percent of the labor force could not find jobs in 1944.

There is some amount of unemployment that no one worries about because it isn't a problem. How much is that? What is an acceptable unemployment rate? How can we distinguish problem unemployment from nonproblem unemployment? The distinction is important, because when unemployment reaches a "problem level," political pressure to do something about it begins to build. What the federal government does in response to these pressures will definitely have costs and may have other undesirable consequences, especially if unemployment is, in reality, not above the critical "problem level." But where is that level and how do we recognize it?

In some circles it is still common practice to duck the whole question by saying something like this: unemployment becomes a problem when it rises above the level of purely "frictional" unemployment. And "frictional" unemployment is the amount of unemployment that poses no problem because it represents ordinary labor-market turn-over. This might be a satisfactory procedure if we had reason to believe that "ordinary labor-market turnover" was some identifiable constant over time. Quite to the contrary, how-ever, we have excellent reasons for supposing that "ordinary labor-market turnover" is a variable, rather than a constant, and that it changes in response to a variety of factors that have shifted substantially in recent years.

What we would really like to do is find some way to distinguish clearly between those who are *unemployed* and those who are merely *not employed*. The extreme cases are easy to distinguish. Some people would do almost anything to find satisfactory employment, whereas there is almost nothing that would persuade others to accept a job. But did you spot the fudge factors in that preceding sentence? People who would describe themselves as "desperate" for work will nonetheless decline *some* job opportunities in the expecta-tion of finding something better. And very few of those who say they "absolutely" don't want a job would decline *every* offer that might come their way. People who say they "can't find a job" mean they can't find a job at which they're will-ing to work. Those who say they "don't want to work" mean that they don't want to work at any job they can find. In some cases, the difference between those two situations isn't going to be discernible to an outside observer.

Employed, Not Employed, and Unemployed

The outside observers on whom we depend to make this distinction for us are some highly trained employees of the U.S. government. The official data on U.S. unemployment are published by the Bureau of Labor Statistics (BLS), an agency in the U.S. Department of Labor. The source of the data is the *Current Population Survey*, a sample survey of households which the Census Bureau conducts on behalf of the BLS. The sample consists of about 55,800 households, selected to represent the entire population and interviewed monthly. (The data are *not* derived, contrary to what many people think, from claims for unemployment compensation.)

In order to be included at all in the BLS report, a person must first be in *the noninstitutional population*. This is *the total of those who are 16 years of age or older, and not re-siding in an institution* such as a prison or a hospital.

Each person in the noninstitutional population is then classified as either employed, unemployed, or not in the labor force. Deciding who is employed presents no serious

Total population
−under 16 or
institutionalized
=noninstitutional-
ized population
−not in the
* labor force*
=labor force
−employed
=unemployed

problems. But what is the distinction between someone who is *unemployed* and someone who is "not in the labor force" and therefore merely *not employed*? The BLS has developed precise criteria for distinguishing between these two groups and measures the size of each with considerable confidence. Measurement is not the problem. The problem is the significance of the distinction, especially in light of the highly diverse and changing costs to particular people of being "not in the labor force" or being officially unemployed.

Let's look more closely. To be classified in the household survey as unemployed, an individual must (1) be in the noninstitutional population; (2) have been without employment during the survey week; (3) have made specific efforts to find employment sometime during the preceding four weeks; and (4) be presently available for work. (Persons who are on layoff or are waiting to start a new job within 30 days are counted as unemployed without meeting the third criterion above, which requires that they be actively looking for employment.) The unemployed divided by the labor force yields the official unemployment rate, which makes the newspapers and the newscasts when the BLS publishes it each month.[1]

Details of this sort don't make very exciting reading. But it is crucial that we know what people must do or not do in order to meet the BLS criteria for being unemployed. There is simply no way to understand the significance of unemployment or the nature of the problem it presents unless we know something about the cost of being unemployed to those who make choices that lead to their being unemployed.

Labor-Market Decisions

The concept of choice is important, because economic theory tries to explain *all* behavior as the consequence of choice — under constraints, of course. Insofar as people have no discernible or significant amount of choice in a situation, economic theory has nothing useful to say about their behavior. In assuming that unemployment results from the choices people make, we are not assuming that everyone has good choices, much less that unemployed people enjoy their

---

[1]Data on the number of people employed or unemployed in any quarter or month are *seasonally adjusted* by the BLS. This means that they have been corrected to eliminate the effects of variations caused entirely by seasonal factors — the closing of schools in June, extra hiring in December, major holidays, and so on. Seasonal adjustment lets us detect trends that would otherwise be concealed or exaggerated by purely seasonal fluctuations.

condition. To choose simply means to select the best available alternative, on the basis of one's expectations regarding relative costs and benefits. The economic way of thinking urges us to explain changes in social phenomena, including changes in unemployment rates, as consequences of changes in perceived costs and benefits.

The BLS definition makes quite clear the specific choices that produce the status called "unemployed": (1) a decision to look actively for employment and (2) a decision not to accept the employment opportunities offered. Both clearly are choices people make. The first decision stands at the fork that leads either to being unemployed or to being out of the labor force. The second decision marks the fork that leads to employment or to continued unemployment. For large numbers of people, the anticipated benefits and costs of particular decisions at those forks have changed considerably in recent years. As a result, particular unemployment rates don't mean what they meant 25 years ago or even ten years ago.

Unemployment Rates and Employment Rates

Table 15A summarizes labor force activity in the United States from 1950 through 1989. The unemployment rates for each year appear under "Unemployed" in the column headed "Percentage of Labor Force." If you run your eye down that column, you will notice that the unemployment rate rises and falls. The sudden increases usually mark the appearance of recessions, while the subsequent (and slower) declines in the rate reflect recovery from the recessions.

The column reveals something else: a strong upward drift in the unemployment rate since 1970. While the rate did decline steadily in the 1980s after reaching its recession-induced peaks in 1982 and 1983, it was still at 6.9 percent in 1986, long after the recession had ended and recovery had begun. That 6.9 percent is higher than the unemployment rates experienced in recessions during the 1950s and 1960s.

Why has this occurred? What's been happening since 1970? Why has the unemployment rate gotten "stuck" at such high levels in recent years?

A lot of answers commonly given to that question are demonstrably wrong. The rising unemployment rates of recent years can't be blamed on automation or foreign competition or any other factor that might have slowed down job creation, because jobs were in fact created in the U.S. economy even faster after 1970 than in the preceding two decades. The column labeled "Total Employed" tells the story. From 1970 to 1985, the number of persons employed increased 35 percent, whereas in the fifteen years prior to 1970 total employment had increased by less than 25 percent.

The last column of the table reveals that the upward drift in the unemployment rate since 1970 has been accompanied by a significant rise in the *employment* rate. That's not the logical impossibility it appears to be. The employment rate compares employment with population. It shows that a higher percentage of working-age Americans were actually employed in 1986, when the unemployment rate was 6.9 percent, than had been employed in 1969, when the unemployment rate was only 3.4 percent. The basic reason for this surprising fact is that many more people *wanted* to work in 1986 than in 1969. The labor force participation rate, shown in the fourth column, has risen remarkably over the last two decades.

The principal cause, as you might suspect, was the decision of so many more women to enter the labor force. There was actually a decline in the rate of labor force participation by males during this period, but the flow of females into the labor force more than made up for it. Whereas 373 of every 1000 employed civilians in the United States were female in 1969, 452 of every 1000 were female in 1989.

The Unemployment Puzzle

These data on employment ought to relieve any fears that the rising unemployment rate of recent years reflects some kind of breakdown in the economic system's capacity to create jobs. A puzzle nonetheless remains. Why are so many more job seekers today failing to find what they're looking for? Why has the percentage of those who want jobs but don't have them approximately doubled since the 1960s? Some will suppose that the higher rate of labor force participation itself supplies the answer: any time more are looking for something, a smaller percentage will succeed in finding it. But this belief reflects the common fallacy that jobs are scarce goods. They really are not. As long as our wants for producible goods remain unsatisfied, we should not run out of useful tasks for people to perform. A rise in the unemployment rate reflects not a growing scarcity of jobs but rather a change in the expected costs and benefits of looking for and accepting employment.

The key question: Why do some people who say they want a job but who don't have one not make stronger efforts to find employment?

TABLE 15A Employment status of the noninstitutional population 16 years and over, 1950 to 1989 (numbers in thousands)

| Year | Noninstitutional Population | Number in Labor Force | Percentage of Noninstitutional Population in Labor Force | Labor Force | | | | | Not in Labor Force | Employed as Percentage of Noninstitutional Population |
| | | | | Employed | | | Unemployed | | | |
				Total Employed	Resident Armed Forces	Civilian Employment	Number Unemployed	Percentage of Labor Force		
1950	106,164	63,377	59.7	60,087	1,169	58,918	3,288	5.2	42,787	56.6
1951	106,764	64,160	60.1	62,104	2,143	59,961	2,055	3.2	42,604	58.2
1952	107,617	64,524	60.0	62,636	2,386	60,250	1,883	2.9	43,093	58.2
1953	109,287	65,246	59.7	63,410	2,231	61,179	1,834	2.8	44,041	58.0
1954	110,463	65,785	59.6	62,251	2,142	60,109	3,532	5.4	44,678	56.4
1955	111,747	67,087	60.0	64,234	2,064	62,170	2,852	4.3	44,660	57.5
1956	112,919	68,517	60.7	65,764	1,965	63,799	2,750	4.0	44,402	58.2
1957	114,213	68,877	60.3	66,019	1,948	64,071	2,859	4.2	45,336	57.8
1958	115,574	69,486	60.1	64,883	1,847	63,036	4,602	6.6	46,088	56.1
1959	117,117	70,157	59.9	66,418	1,788	64,630	3,740	5.3	46,960	56.7
1960	119,106	71,489	60.0	67,639	1,861	65,778	3,852	5.4	47,617	56.8
1961	120,671	72,359	60.0	67,646	1,900	65,746	4,714	6.5	48,312	56.1
1962	122,214	72,675	59.5	68,763	2,061	66,702	3,911	5.4	49,539	56.3
1963	124,422	73,839	59.3	69,768	2,006	67,762	4,070	5.5	50,583	56.1
1964	126,503	75,109	59.4	71,323	2,018	69,305	3,786	5.0	51,394	56.4
1965	128,459	76,401	59.5	73,034	1,946	71,088	3,366	4.4	52,058	56.9
1966	130,180	77,892	59.8	75,017	2,122	72,895	2,875	3.7	52,288	57.6

1967	132,092	79,565	60.2	76,590	2,218	74,372	2,975	3.7	52,527	58.0
1968	134,281	80,990	60.3	78,173	2,253	75,920	2,817	3.5	53,291	58.2
1969	136,573	82,972	60.8	80,140	2,238	77,902	2,832	3.4	53,602	58.7
1970	139,203	84,889	61.0	80,796	2,118	78,678	4,093	4.8	54,315	58.0
1971	142,189	86,355	60.7	81,340	1,973	79,367	5,016	5.8	55,834	57.2
1972	145,939	88,847	60.9	83,966	1,813	82,153	4,882	5.5	57,091	57.5
1973	148,870	91,203	61.3	86,838	1,774	85,064	4,365	4.8	57,667	58.3
1974	151,841	93,670	61.7	88,515	1,721	86,794	5,156	5.5	58,171	58.3
1975	154,831	95,453	61.6	87,524	1,678	85,846	7,929	8.3	59,377	56.5
1976	157,818	97,826	62.0	90,420	1,668	88,752	7,406	7.6	59,991	57.3
1977	160,689	100,665	62.6	93,673	1,656	92,017	6,991	6.9	60,025	58.3
1978	163,541	103,882	63.5	97,679	1,631	96,048	6,202	6.0	59,659	59.8
1979	166,460	106,559	64.0	100,421	1,597	98,824	6,137	5.8	59,900	60.3
1980	169,349	108,544	64.1	100,907	1,604	99,303	7,637	7.0	60,806	59.6
1981	171,775	110,315	64.2	102,042	1,645	100,397	8,273	7.5	61,460	59.4
1982	173,939	111,872	64.3	101,194	1,668	99,526	10,678	9.5	62,067	58.2
1983	175,891	113,226	64.4	102,510	1,676	100,834	10,717	9.5	62,665	58.3
1984	178,080	115,241	64.7	106,702	1,697	105,005	8,539	7.4	62,839	59.9
1985	179,912	117,167	65.1	108,856	1,706	107,150	8,312	7.1	62,744	60.5
1986	182,293	119,540	65.6	111,303	1,706	109,597	8,237	6.9	62,752	61.1
1987	184,490	121,602	65.9	114,177	1,737	112,440	7,425	6.1	62,888	61.9
1988	186,322	123,378	66.2	116,677	1,709	114,968	6,701	5.4	62,944	62.6
1989	188,081	125,557	66.8	119,030	1,688	117,342	6,528	5.2	62,523	63.3

Source: Bureau of Labor Statistics.

Costs and Decisions

We must beware of aggregation. Both the cost of taking a job and the cost of not taking one will differ considerably from one person to another, depending on such factors as skill, experience, age, family responsibilities, other sources of income, and even the values and attitudes of those whose opinions the person respects.

Consider the situation of teenagers living with their families. They often want jobs and may actively seek them in ways that qualify them for inclusion in the ranks of the officially unemployed. But if they're currently attending school, they are "presently available" for a very limited number of jobs. If they're on summer vacation, employers won't want to hire them for jobs that require a lot of training, so they aren't really "available" for these jobs either. If they're out of high school but trying to make up their minds about college, they'll be reluctant to accept any job that requires a commitment. Moreover, the job opportunities available to them will tend to be relatively unattractive, because employers don't want to pay much to teenagers, who tend to be unskilled and who quit before the employer has recovered the cost of training them.

But someone receiving free room and board from parents can afford to search for a long time, or to quit a job that proves unsatisfactory and start looking again. Any job will begin to seem unsatisfactory to teenagers who discover that they must work while their friends are partying. When we put all this together, we see that the cost of taking and keeping a job is high and rising for most teenagers, and that the cost of continuing to look is relatively low. Should we be either surprised or disturbed, then, to discover that the unemployment rate among people 16 to 19 years old averaged more than 18 percent in the 1980s?

Since lost income is usually the main cost of being unemployed, anything that promises to maintain people's incomes while they're not working is likely to increase the unemployment rate. Thus, the sizable expansion since the 1960s in government welfare grants has undoubtedly contributed to the increase in unemployment.

Since the 1960s, we have offered unemployment insurance to more workers, extended the duration of benefits, and generally loosened the criteria for eligibility. Of course, this won't induce people with well-paid and highly satisfying jobs to get themselves fired so they can. start drawing unemployment compensation. At the margin, however, more generous unemployment benefits do make people less determined to hang on to current jobs and less eager to accept new ones, thus raising the unemployment rate. In Holland, where unemployment benefits replace, for extended periods, from 75 to 99 percent of the net income from working, and where eligibility criteria are not very strict, the unemployment rate in the 1980s averaged more than 12 percent. The wonder is that it wasn't higher.

The rise since the 1960s in the number of multi-earner families must have had the same kind of effect. When we consider the impact of income and social security taxes on earnings plus all the other costs associated with working, the financial incentive for a second earner to find a new job when an old one has been lost diminishes dramatically. It will sometimes even be negative until eligibility for unemployment compensation has been exhausted.

Expectations and Reality

Remember, too, that economic decisions depend on expectations. People enter the labor force because they *expect* to find satisfactory employment. If for some reason the expectations of many labor force entrants are unrealistically high, the result will be an increase in the unemployment rate. Suppose, for example, that more opportunities open up in the business world for women who want to enter management. These improved prospects will induce more women to enter or remain in the labor force. It's quite possible that the expectation of more and better career opportunities for women could pull so many additional women into the labor force that the female unemployment rate would actually rise. Unemployment would remain high until expectations adjusted to reality — or reality caught up with expectations.

Similarly, if recent college graduates or freshly minted lawyers hold exaggerated views about the value of their degrees in the labor market, the unemployment rate among them will rise. Steelworkers who are accustomed to wage rates about double the average of the wages usually paid in manufacturing will be slow to accept employment at lower wages when the steel companies for which they've been working go out of business. They aren't very different from homeowners who refuse to believe that the house they are trying to sell won't move at the price they're asking; "for sale" signs consequently multiply and stay up longer in a declining real estate market.

A slowing in the rate of inflation will have a similar

effect on the unemployment rate through the wedge that it opens between expected and actual wage offers. If a protracted period of high inflation has accustomed employees to large annual wage increases, they may find employers' wage offers inadequate once the inflation rate slows down. Employees who expect a higher wage than they are offered will more readily give up existing jobs and will prolong their searches for new jobs, which is going to raise the unemployment rate.

A Summing Up

We don't want to point out so many trees that you lose sight of the forest. The principal thesis we've been trying to establish is that unemployment is not simply something that happens *to* people, like being hit by lightning. In a recession, the demand for labor decreases, and this causes unemployment to rise. The recovery after a recession increases the demand for labor, and unemployment falls. But it doesn't follow from this that all unemployment is the result of an inadequate demand for labor. Unemployment rates are the product of complex decisions by both demanders and suppliers of labor, all of whom pay attention to the expected opportunity costs of their decisions to supply or to demand.

Moreover, the costs of unemployment don't fall with equal severity on every unemployed person and don't take the same form from one person to another. For some, the lost income is the principal cost of unemployment. For others, the cost of unemployment will be the loss of some goods that they value even more highly than money income: a sense of contributing, a daily discipline, workplace associations, challenge and variety. For some people the sum of these costs will be crushing; for others the costs will be negligible; and for a few who receive unemployment compensation and live in families with more than one earner, the costs can even be negative.

There is no undifferentiated mass called *the unemployed*, on whom the burdens of unemployment fall. There is no constant number above which unemployment first begins to be a problem. There is no single policy suitable for reducing all unemployment. There is no clear line that divides the unemployed from those who happen to be only "not employed." In the last analysis, the distinction between suffering unemployment and enjoying leisure can be made only by the person who calculates the relative net advantages of taking and of not taking a job.

None of these explanations of unemployment, however, tells us why recessions occur, pushing unemployment substantially higher for prolonged periods. We must turn our attention now to the causes and consequences of fluctuations in the overall or aggregate level of economic activity.

Once Over Lightly

Inflation is an increase in the average money price of goods. It is not an increase in the cost of living but a decrease in the purchasing power of money.

Inflation does impose real burdens on a society. It redistributes wealth, induces people to spend resources trying to anticipate its effects, and stimulates dissatisfaction and conflict among people who believe, rightly or wrongly, that they're being harmed by inflation. All these are effects of the increased uncertainty that inflation introduces into people's estimates of future prices.

A recession is an unanticipated and disruptive slowdown in the rate of increase in total output and income.

Recessions add to unemployment by causing the demand for some goods — and hence for the labor of those who produce the goods — to fall short of expectations.

The level of unemployment depends on the supply of labor as well as the demand. The Bureau of Labor Statistics counts as unemployed all those who are not currently employed *and* are actively seeking employment. Both the decision to enter the labor force and the decision not to accept particular job offers will depend on people's estimates of the relative advantages of alternative opportunities.

Different unemployment rates for different population groups do not merely reflect differences in the demand for the labor services of the people in those groups. They also reflect variations in the cost to different people of searching for, accepting, and retaining employment.

Unemployment rates were high in the 1970s and 1980s in comparison with unemployment rates in the 1950s and 1960s. But labor force participation rates and employment rates also rose to record-high levels in the 1980s.

Higher unemployment rates coupled with rising employment rates suggest that the expected benefits and costs both of entering the labor force and of remaining unemployed have been changing in recent years for many members of the noninstitutional population.

Questions for Discussion

1. Was the "cost of living" in the United States higher or lower in 1985 than it had been in 1955?

   (a) The following data are adapted from the consumer price index:

   - The amount of food that could be purchased for a dollar in 1985 cost only 26¢ in 1955.
   - A dollar's worth of housing in 1985 could have been rented in 1955 for 32¢.
   - The clothing that a dollar bought in 1985 was available for 45¢ in 1955.
   - A dollar's worth of medical care in 1985 cost only 16¢ in 1955.

   Why do these data give us no answer to the question above?

   (b) Here are some additional data that might help you answer the question: the average hourly earnings of workers employed in the private sector outside agriculture were about $1.70 in 1955 and $8.60 in 1985.

   (c) The data above suggest that one hour's wage of an average worker purchased considerably more food, shelter, and clothing in 1985 than it had done in 1955, but somewhat less medical care. Can you think of some good reasons for believing that the data on medical care are misleading? (Hint: The good that we are after when we purchase medical care is *health*. Did the medical services available in 1955 produce better health as effectively as medical services did in 1985?)

2. The text asserts that a society which did not make use of money but conducted all exchange by barter logically could not experience inflation. If you doubt this, ask yourself what form inflation could take in a bartering society. What would it mean to say that the average price of all goods in such a society had risen 10 percent?

3. Figure 15A compares the annual inflation rate in the United States from 1955 to 1985 with the average annual rate of return received by holders of home mortgages over this same period.

   (a) What was the approximate real rate of return on mortgage loans in 1955? In 1970? In 1975? In 1980? In 1985?

   (b) How did the negative rate of return in 1975 and 1980 contribute to the very high rate of return after 1983?

   (c) The inflation rate after 1983 fell to approximately what it had been from 1956 to 1958. Mortgage rates rose very little in response to the accelerated inflation of the late 1950s. Why were they so slow to fall in response to the disinflation of the early 1980s?

4. Numerous public-opinion surveys in the 1970s showed that the majority of Americans regarded inflation as a more serious threat than unemployment.

   (a) Did this imply that the majority of Americans would rather be un-

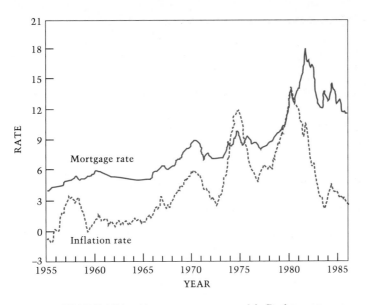

FIGURE 15A   Mortgage rates and inflation rates

employed in a period of stable prices than employed in a time of rising prices?

(b) If the management of a firm allowed employees to vote on whether the firm should lay off 10 percent of the employees or reduce wage rates by 5 percent, how do you think they would vote? Do you think the outcome of the vote would depend on whether the employees knew in advance exactly who would be laid off?

5. If inflation redistributes income and wealth, there will be gainers as well as losers. Which classes and categories of people are most likely to gain and lose from an inflation? What difference does it make how well the inflation is anticipated?

6. Professor Plato received an annual salary of $12,000 in 1965 and $35,000 in 1985. The price level increased about 250 percent between 1965 and 1985.

(a) How did his real income change from 1965 to 1985?

(b) Is Professor Plato likely to think that his additional experience entitled him to a much larger salary in 1985?

(c) Do you think it was inflation or changed conditions of supply and demand that caused Professor Plato's real income to fall between 1965 and 1985?

(d) Professor Plato's college classmate, Rock Igneous, was also earning $12,000 a year in 1965, working as a mining engineer. In 1985 Rock's salary was $60,000. Why do you suppose that he fared so much better than Professor Plato in this inflationary period?

(e) Do you think it would have been easier or harder for the college to reduce Plato's salary from $12,000 to $10,000 in a period of stable prices than to raise it from $12,000 to $35,000 in a period when prices rose 250 percent? Why?

7. A letter to the editor of *The Wall Street Journal* (October 15, 1985) complained that it was "not only a fallacy but a fraud" for the Bureau of Labor Statistics to claim that the price level had risen only 3.5 percent during the past year. As evidence the writer cited the following price increases during the preceding twelve-month period: first-class postage, 20¢ to 22¢; the Sunday *New York Times*, $1 to $1.25; *The Wall Street Journal*, 40¢ to 50¢; "some" coinbox telephone calls, 10¢ to 25¢.

An accompanying letter told an opposite story: "The orange juice I buy is $1.99 a quart; a year ago it was $2.49. My 'jug wine' is $4.09, as opposed to $4.49 a year ago. Instant coffee is $3.19, up from $2.99, but has been running a 30-cent coupon offer all summer."

Is it possible for the price level to rise at different rates for different people?

8. Why do you suppose it costs over 40 percent more to maintain a living standard in Oakland, California, than it costs to maintain a comparable standard in El Paso, Texas? Would it be correct to say that the cost of living is higher in Oakland?

9. A *Wall Street Journal* article of August 13, 1985, describes the effects of runaway inflation on daily life in Bolivia, where prices were rising at an annual rate of 8000 percent.

   (a) If prices rise by 9 percent per week, by what percentage will they increase in the course of a year? (You can use Table 11A to find the answer.)
   (b) What is the present value of one dollar in wages to be received at the end of a four-week pay period when inflation is running at a rate of 9 percent per week? (Use Table 11B.)
   (c) Why do you suppose that Bolivians try to convert their wages into either goods or U.S. dollars immediately upon receipt?
   (d) If peso prices for goods are rising in Bolivia while U.S. dollar prices being quoted for the same goods are stable, is Bolivia experiencing inflation or is it not? How does this example illustrate the point that inflation is a fall in the value of money?
   (e) The *Journal* quotes a Bolivian as saying, "We don't produce anything. We are all currency speculators." How can the people of a country survive if they are all currency speculators?
   (f) The same Bolivian commented: "People don't know what's good and bad anymore. We have become an amoral society." A prominent politician said: "We've learned you must be an idiot to do things by the rules." In what manner does runaway inflation undermine social morality?

10. In Switzerland, an unemployment rate of 1 percent has long been considered *high*. When recession hit Switzerland in the mid-1970s, the official unemployment rate stayed below 1 percent even when total manufacturing

employment declined by more than 15 percent over a two-year period. How do you suppose the Swiss manage to maintain such a low unemployment rate even in the face of rapidly declining employment opportunities? (It may help you to know that about 10 percent of the Swiss population is made up of foreign workers, mostly Italians, Spanish, Portuguese, and Yugoslavs, who are not allowed to stay in Switzerland without jobs.)

11. At least prior to *perestroika*, unemployment did not exist by definition in the Soviet Union, where any unemployment at all was held to be inconsistent with socialism. It was not just a matter of definition, however. There were so many jobs relative to workers that *Pravda*, the Communist Party newspaper, urged the passage of laws that would prohibit job-quitting without adequate cause and would subject able-bodied workers to arrest if they were out of work for more than two weeks. How do you suppose the Soviet Union maintained a surplus of jobs while the United States seems to have had a surplus of workers?

12. The unemployment rates in West Germany, France, and Italy in 1989 were about 9 percent, 11 percent, and 12 percent, respectively. Why do you think they were so much higher than in the USSR?

13. Determine the missing numbers for the following set of imaginary U.S. data, using the definitions provided in the text:

Noninstitutional population	180,000,000
Resident armed forces	2,000,000
Civilian employment	106,000,000
Not in the labor force	64,000,000
Labor force	_____
Unemployed	_____
Unemployment rate	_____
Employment rate	_____

14. Can there be "overfull" employment?

   (a) Suppose that the vacancy rate on apartments in a large city is less than 1 percent. What undesirable consequences might be associated with such a full level of apartment employment? Would you enjoy moving to a city with such a low vacancy rate?

   (b) If you are driving on only 80 percent of the automobile tires you own, is the spare tire unemployed? Would you like to be driving with your tires at "full employment"? Across the Great Salt Lake Desert?

15. Jones is a tool and die maker earning $20 an hour. He is suddenly laid off.

   (a) He frequents employment agencies, reads want ads, and follows up leads on tool-and-die-making jobs for two weeks. Is he unemployed during this time, as the BLS measures unemployment?

   (b) At the end of two weeks he is offered a job driving a bread truck that pays $4.50 an hour. He turns it down. Is he unemployed?

(c) He receives an offer of a job as a tool and die maker in a city 125 miles away. He turns it down because his teenage children don't want to change high schools. Is he unemployed?

(d) After three months of searching, Jones becomes discouraged and quits looking. Is he unemployed?

16. A woman is laid off from her job and goes to work for herself (becomes self-employed) "producing" information about alternative job opportunities. How long she will remain self-employed in this way depends on her "productivity" (i.e., whether she is generating what she considers valuable information) and the opportunity cost of this self-employment (which she'll want to continue as long as her anticipated marginal revenue exceeds anticipated marginal cost). How will the duration of measured unemployment be affected by:

(a) unemployment compensation?

(b) food-stamp programs?

(c) persistent rumors that many large firms are beginning to hire?

(d) a spirit of confidence and optimism?

17. Should the hypothetical individuals who made each of the following statements be classified as unemployed or as not in the labor force? Which of them is voluntarily rather than involuntarily unemployed?

(a) "I quit my job and I'm going to remain unemployed until I find a job that pays $1000 for 10 hours' work a week."

(b) "I was laid off last month. 1 had a great job as marketing consultant to a franchising chain. They paid me $1000 a week for about 10 hours of work. I'm going to keep looking until I find another job like that one."

(c) "I decided I could no longer be a part of the military–industrial complex, so I quit my job. I'm looking now for an engineer's position that doesn't require me to participate in murder, pollution, and mind-raping."

(d) "When they laid me off, I figured I could easily find another job in teaching. But now I don't care. I'll take any job at all that pays what I used to get."

(e) "I've been out of work for six months, and I'm pretty desperate. I'll do anything that's legal to get food for my family. But I have an invalid wife and five small children, so I can't take any job that pays less than $500 a week."

(f) "I could get any one of a dozen jobs tomorrow. But I don't want to. I'm eligible for three more months of unemployment compensation, so I'm just going to take it easy until the checks run out. Oh, if something really good turned up, I'd take it, of course."

(g) "I could get any one of a dozen jobs tomorrow. But I don't want to. I'm eligible for three more months of unemployment compensation, so I'm just going to spend my time really looking. I'm going to use those three months to find the very best job I can possibly get."

18. According to Polson and Company, a Minneapolis executive-search firm, the higher the salary the longer it takes for a job seeker to obtain a new position. The rule of thumb is one additional month of searching for every $10,000 in annual compensation. Is a month spent in searching rather than earning income a good investment if it pays $10,000 per year? (Data are from a *Wall Street Journal* article of December 15, 1989.)

Chapter 16

Production, Prices and Aggregate Fluctuations

How do we measure changes in the value of money or the price level? How do we measure changes in the rate at which we are producing total output? And what do those measures tell us about the performance of the U.S. economy in recent years?

Gross National Product

The experience of the Great Depression in the 1930s gave encouragement to efforts that had begun around 1920 to compile reliable data on the overall performance of the U.S. economy. The best-known statistical series evolving out of these efforts is the national income and product accounts, compiled by the Bureau of Economic Analysis in the U.S. Department of Commerce. If you read only the front page of the daily newspaper, you will have encountered the gross national product. This is the most comprehensive item in the Department of Commerce accounts and the one most frequently cited. Some people watch the behavior of GNP, as it is familiarly known, with the intensity of children listening to the weather report on the morning of a picnic.

The gross national product is the market value of all the final goods produced in the entire country in the course of a year. Only the value of final goods is calculated in order to minimize overcounting. If the Bureau of Economic Analysis added the value of all the sheet metal to the value of all the automobiles produced in a year, it would have counted some of the sheet metal twice: once when it was sold by the steel companies to automobile manufacturers, and once more as a component in the final price of the cars. To reduce the amount of such double counting, the value of intermediate goods is assumed to be incorporated into the market price of final goods.

423

Another way to think of and measure total output is to regard it as the sum of all the successive *value added* at each stage of the production process. In the case of bread, for example, it's the value added successively by the wheat farmer, the miller, the baker, the distributor, and the retailer as the loaf wends its way toward the customer's shopping cart. The price of the final good is then the summed value of all these successive contributions to output.

As the name of the accounts suggests, GNP can also be thought of and calculated as the value of the national income. The national income is the sum of all the payments made in the course of the production process to those who did the producing: the owners of labor, capital, and other resources. The value of the national output must necessarily equal the value of the national income, when properly calculated, because every dollar paid for output becomes income for someone. An apparent exception would be the amount of tax, such as sales tax, paid on a purchase. But this is income, too; it's income for government, which uses it to pay for the resources that government employs in the process of producing goods.

Another question might arise about unsold goods. They are part of the year's output, but since they aren't sold, they don't seem to generate income for anyone. This is handled in the accounts by assuming that the business firm that produced the goods also bought them. It surely had to pay to get them produced. And while it may not have intended to buy them itself, goods produced and not sold are indeed added, however reluctantly, to the inventories of the firm that produced them.

Thus, we can actually measure GNP in *three* ways, all of which would yield the same total if we made no errors in counting: (1) the value added by each producer in the course of contributing to the year's total output of final goods; (2) the total income received, in the form of wages and salaries, interest, rent, and profits, by those who contributed the resources used to produce the year's total output; (3) the total purchases of final goods by households, business firms, and government, plus the purchases of foreigners in excess of what the foreigners sold us in return. When unsold goods are counted as additions to inventory and added to the total purchases of business firms, the sum of household, business, government, and (net) foreign expenditures on final goods must add up exactly to the total value of the goods produced.

Gross national product is
—the sum of all the value added by producers at each stage of the production process,

or

—the total income received by those producers,

or

the total purchase of newly produced final goods.

Some Limitations of National Income Accounting

Never make the mistake of confusing the gross national product with gross national well-being. The concept of GNP is based on so many conventions, with so many essentially arbitrary inclusions and omissions, that it should never be used to compare the well-being of different nations. The most it can do is indicate whether we're going faster or slowing down. And even there it gives misleading indications if we try to make comparisons over a long period of time.

Two examples may be enough to teach you caution. Among the services not counted by the Department of Commerce statisticians in the calculation of GNP are the services of the spouse who maintains the home. It is too difficult to evaluate these services, despite their enormous importance, so they are completely excluded from the accounts. But the value of hired housekeepers' services can be measured, by the payments made to obtain them; hence they do enter into the accounts. As a result, GNP will tend to decline as a direct consequence of marriages and increase with a rising divorce rate. It is doubtful that real welfare moves in the same direction. Also, as more women enter the labor force, the GNP expands by the amount of their contribution to total output, as measured by their earnings. Since there is no deduction, however, for the value of the work they are no longer doing at home, the increase in GNP exaggerates the increase in the value of total output — unless their housework had no value.

A second example to teach caution: when a coal-burning station generates electricity, its output enters GNP. When people are hired to clean and paint as a consequence of the sooty fallout from the generating plant, GNP rises once more. Overcounting obviously occurs in this case. It would make sense, if we were interested in welfare, to deduct the cost of the cleaning from the value of the electricity generated. If Chapter 13 did not put you sufficiently on guard, then be warned once more: the consequences for human welfare of particular economic decisions are not always what they seem at first glance. Systems for keeping score are useful, but they inevitably harbor deficiencies that must be kept in mind by those who use them. And the good life is far more than the simple sum of the values that enter into the national income and product accounts.

Nominal and Real Gross National Product

Can we use the gross national product to represent the total output of goods? We clearly cannot, because GNP is the product of prices as well as quantities. Consider the decade of the 1970s, when the gross national product rose from $1 trillion to $2.5 trillion. Only a small part of this represented an increase in the quantity of goods produced; most of it was a fictitious or purely nominal increase attributable to the rapid inflation that occurred in the 1970s.

The Bureau of Economic Analysis comes to our aid at this point by calculating for each period the value that GNP would have had if prices had remained unchanged. The technique they use is to figure the value of the current period's output in terms of the prices of an earlier year, chosen for reference purposes. The reference year is currently 1982. Let's see how the Bureau adjusts the nominal measure of GNP to arrive at a real measure of the quantity of goods produced.

Nominal GNP, or GNP in current dollars, was $2,508.2 billion in 1979. If all the goods produced in 1979 were valued at base-year prices, the prices that prevailed for those goods in 1982, the GNP would have been $3,192.3 billion.

Nominal GNP in 1970 was $1,015.5 billion. Measured in the prices that those goods came to command in 1982, however, the value of 1970 GNP was $2,416.2 billion.

Now we can calculate the real increase in gross national product during the 1970s. Total output or the aggregate quantity of goods produced rose 32 percent from 1970 to 1979. That's far less than the almost 150 percent increase in nominal gross national product during the decade.

Real gross national product is the value of all final goods produced in a year stated *in unchanging prices*, specifically, the prices that held in the base year, which is presently 1982. It is our most comprehensive measure of changes in the rate at which goods are being produced.

The Implicit GNP Deflator

We also now have at hand a measure of changes in the overall price level or the value of money. Since nominal GNP was $2,508.2 billion and real GNP was $3,192.3 billion in 1979, the average price of GNP goods in 1979 must have been 78.6 percent of what they were in the base year of 1982. Nominal GNP divided by real GNP is the *implicit GNP deflator*. It is implicit in the definitions of real and

1979 GNP:

$2,508 billion in
1979 prices
$3,192 billion in
1982 prices
1970 GNP:
$1,016 billion in
1970 prices
$2,416 billion in
1982 prices

$$2416\overline{)3192} \quad 1.32$$

$$\frac{\$2,508}{\$3,192} = .786$$

nominal GNP. It is called the deflator because it can be used to deflate (or inflate) current-dollar calculations in order to arrive at a measure of real changes in output. It functions as a price index, with prices in the year 1982 set equal to 100 (percent).

The GNP deflator is our most comprehensive measure of changes in the price level or the purchasing power of money and the one that was used in Chapter 15 to discuss changing rates of inflation. It is not the best-known measure, however. That distinction belongs to the consumer price index, a measure of changes in the money price of goods that enter into the budgets of typical urban consumers. The Bureau of Labor Statistics surveys consumer prices each month and publishes the results toward the end of the succeeding month. The GNP deflator, by contrast, is much more difficult to calculate and only appears at quarterly intervals and after a lengthy time lag. So while the GNP deflator is more comprehensive, the consumer price index is more timely. It's the index that makes the front page of newspapers each month whenever there is substantial public concern about inflation.

Recessions and Inflations Since 1950

Table 16A presents nominal gross national product, real gross national product, and the implicit GNP deflator for each year from 1950 to 1989. It also shows the percentage changes from the preceding year for real GNP and the price level as measured by the GNP deflator.

The recessions sustained by the U.S. economy since 1950 show up fairly clearly in the fourth column, as prolonged slowdowns or actual declines in the rate of real GNP growth. They aren't completely clear, because the National Bureau of Economic Research has no hard criteria for infallibly distinguishing a recession from something slightly less serious. There were officially designated recessions in each of the years in which real GNP declined — 1954, 1958, 1970, 1974–75, 1980, and 1982; but the National Bureau also decided that a recession occurred in 1960.

Another portrayal of the history of recessions in the United States is provided in Figure 16A. This figure charts quarterly rates of change in real GNP from 1950 to 1989. Real GNP declined during each quarter in which the line dips below the zero-change baseline.

Just below Figure 16A is Figure 16B, showing the official BLS unemployment rates over the same period. Notice that

TABLE 16A Gross national product (in billions of dollars) and the price level, 1950 to 1989 (minor inconsistencies are due to errors introduced by rounding)

Year	Nominal Gross National Product	Real Gross National Product, in 1982 Prices	Percentage Change from Preceding Year	Implicit GNP Deflator (1982 = 100)	Percentage Change from Preceding Year
1950	$288	$1,204	8.5	23.9	2.0
1951	333	1,328	10.3	25.1	4.8
1952	352	1,380	3.9	25.5	1.5
1953	372	1,435	4.0	25.9	1.6
1954	373	1,416	−1.3	26.3	1.6
1955	406	1,495	5.6	27.2	3.2
1956	428	1,526	2.1	28.1	3.4
1957	451	1,551	1.7	29.1	3.6
1958	457	1,539	−0.8	29.7	2.1
1959	496	1,629	5.8	30.4	2.4
1960	515	1,665	2.2	30.9	1.6
1961	534	1,709	2.6	31.2	1.0
1962	575	1,799	5.3	31.9	2.2
1963	607	1,873	4.1	32.4	1.6
1964	650	1,973	5.3	32.9	1.5
1965	705	2,088	5.8	33.8	2.7
1966	772	2,208	5.8	35.0	3.6
1967	816	2,271	2.9	35.9	2.6
1968	893	2,366	4.1	37.7	5.0
1969	964	2,423	2.4	39.8	5.6
1970	1,016	2,416	−0.3	42.0	5.5
1971	1,103	2,485	2.8	44.4	5.7
1972	1,213	2,609	5.0	46.5	4.7
1973	1,359	2,744	5.2	49.5	6.5
1974	1,473	2,729	−0.5	54.0	9.1
1975	1,598	2,695	−1.3	59.3	9.8
1976	1,783	2,827	4.9	63.1	6.4
1977	1,991	2,959	4.7	67.3	6.7
1978	2,250	3,115	5.3	72.2	7.3
1979	2,508	3,192	2.5	78.6	8.9
1980	2,732	3,187	−0.2	85.7	9.0
1981	3,053	3,249	1.9	94.0	9.7
1982	3,166	3,166	−2.5	100.0	6.4
1983	3,406	3,279	3.6	103.9	3.9
1984	3,772	3,501	6.8	107.7	3.7
1985	4,015	3,619	3.4	110.9	3.0
1986	4,232	3,718	2.7	113.8	2.6
1987	4,524	3,854	3.7	117.4	3.2
1988	4,881	4,024	4.4	121.3	3.3
1989	5,234	4,144	3.0	126.3	4.1

Source: Bureau of Economic Analysis.

FIGURE 16A   Quarterly changes in real gross national product (Source: Bureau of Economic Analysis)

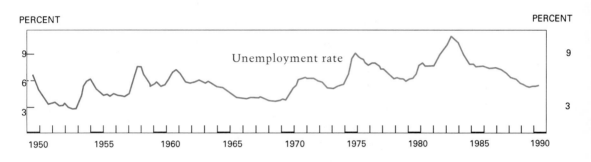

FIGURE 16B   Unemployed as percent of labor force (Source: Bureau of Labor Statistics)

unemployment rises as a result of recessions, but with a lag; it falls when the recovery occurs, but again with a distinct lag. Moreover, the base level of unemployment to which the economy returns afterward has tended to rise after each recession, with the exception of the decade following the 1960–61 recession. And since 1970, as was pointed out in the preceding chapter, the unemployment rate has been "sticking" at levels that it never reached even in recessions during the 1950s and 1960s. Despite the long economic recovery that occurred after 1982, the unemployment rate did not fall below 6 percent until 1988.

The last column in Table 16A shows that inflation also became a more serious problem in the 1970s than it had been in the preceding two decades. Inflation averaged about 2½ percent per year in the 1950s and 1960s. From 1970 to 1981, however, it ran at an average annual rate above 7 percent. The years 1974 and 1975 are especially disturbing. A severe recession in those years produced sharply higher unemployment (see Figures 16A and 16B) while at the same time the price level was shooting up at rates unknown in the United States except in conjunction with major wars. The word began to spread in the 1970s, aided powerfully by television and newspaper commentators, that an unprecedented malady had seized the economy, one that economists were powerless to explain: recession coupled with inflation.

These rumors were incorrect. Inflation had occurred previously during recessions, most recently in the recessions of 1958 and 1960 — though the inflation in those years had been considerably less rapid. Nor were economists completely at a loss for an explanation. On the other hand, some oversimplified notions about the causes of recession and inflation, notions that economists had helped create, were very definitely called into question by the experiences of the 1970s. The severe recession of 1974–75 at a time when prices were rising at a 10 percent annual rate made it abundantly clear that recession and inflation were not "opposites."

What Causes Aggregate Fluctuations?

What causes the sharp fluctuations revealed in Figure 16A in the rate at which aggregate production increases? What could make the real gross national product grow at an annual rate of 9 percent in the second quarter of 1978, decline at an annual rate of 9½ percent in the second quarter of 1980, and then increase once more in the first quarter of 1981 at an annual rate of 9 percent? Why has the GNP deflator, our most comprehensive measure of the overall price level, risen in every year since World War II, as shown in Table 16A? Why does it rise at such varying rates?

One answer is: Why not? Change and chance rule the social universe. Production and prices are bound to be affected by the shocks of wars, new discoveries, revolutions, or natural disasters. It is stability, not fluctuations, that would require explanation. A look at the data for almost any commodity we might name will not reveal stability over time in either output levels or prices. Why then should we expect stability in aggregate output or the average of all prices?

That argument is pertinent but not altogether satisfactory. Large changes in production and price levels for individual goods — agricultural commodities, automobiles, personal computers, movie admissions — are easier to understand than are large changes in overall production and the average level of money prices. A lot of the changes and chances that shift the demand or the supply for individual goods ought to cancel each other out, in accordance with "the law of large numbers." Why doesn't this law produce a much more steady rate of growth in real GNP and a more stable price level?

Part of the explanation is that economic systems transmit viruses. A setback or an unexpected bit of good fortune in one sector of the economy generates setbacks or good fortune for other sectors with which it is linked. A bad month for automobile sales, for example, triggered by a spell of unusually cold and snowy weather, could lead to production cutbacks and layoffs in automobile assembly plants, which might in turn produce reduced orders at steel plants that specialize in sheet metal and reduced business for the stores and shops that cater heavily to assembly plant workers, resulting eventually in layoffs in steel plants and retail establishments and thus setting off further ripple effects.

Economists have developed a variety of models and metaphors to describe the ways in which relatively small initial disturbances might be transmitted through the economic system to produce large aggregate effects. They all rely on some kind of circular-flow mechanism to show how an economic system can transform small events into the boom-and-bust patterns that have been known to characterize market-coordinated economic systems for at least 200 years. Because everyone's spending becomes income for someone else and income in turn determines how much people will be able to spend, the decision to spend a little more or a little less, prompted perhaps by a slight change in the public's confidence about the future, can produce a spiraling effect.

Demand-Side and Supply-Side Economics

As national income and product accounting reminds us, the total income available for the purchase of newly produced goods is always and necessarily equal to the price paid for those goods. This is an important truth — at least to begin with. It counters the strange but widespread and persistent fear that total output might increase too fast for total demand to keep up, so that the economic system collapses as a result of overproduction. Total income is always going to increase at precisely the same rate as total output, for the simple reason that they are the same phenomenon viewed from opposite sides.

That can be granted, however, without conceding that total demand will necessarily equal total output. What if people choose not to spend some of their income? Won't the decision to save a portion of the income received reduce aggregate demand below the level of total output? And might this not cause overproduction and economic collapse?

The answer depends on what people do with the income they save. Except in the rare and unimportant case of misers and similar cranks, people invest what they save. That at least was the consensus view of the original supply-side economists, which included the great majority of economists up until the 1930s. People don't tuck their savings under their mattresses or into their cookie jars. They put their savings to work. If they themselves don't purchase capital goods with the income they save, then they purchase financial assets of some kind (bonds, stocks, savings accounts) and thereby turn their savings over to someone else who is going to purchase capital goods. Adam Smith put the doctrine concisely when he said: "What is annually saved is as regularly consumed as what is annually spent, and nearly in the same time too; but it is consumed by a different set of people."

Smith thought that people would have to be "perfectly crazy" (his term) not to invest everything they chose to save, at least where there was "tolerable security." The fear of overproduction or underconsumption was therefore groundless. In the opinion of Smith and most of his successors worrying that aggregate demand might be insufficient was evidence that one had not understood the basic working of economic systems. Overproduction was not a problem; the challenge was to increase production, so that people might be supplied with more of the "necessaries and conveniencies" of life. Government's job in the economic system was not to stimulate demand but to preserve incentives, principally by maintaining the security of property. If this were done, people's natural desire to better their condition would lead them to produce, to save, to invest, and thereby to promote a continually rising rate of output. Consumption — the demand side — would take care of itself.

The Great Depression laid this optimistic belief firmly to rest. It became obvious in the 1930s that aggregate demand did not always "take care of itself." The result was the rise of new economic theories and policies concerned with the care and nurture of aggregate demand.

Demand-side economics flourished for many years, until the experiences of the 1970s revealed some of its more glaring limitations. Then we saw renewed interest in the contribution of supply-side factors to economic growth and price stability.

Where do we go from here? Back to basics. We had better begin by talking about that interesting social institution known as *money*.

Once Over Lightly

The gross national product is the market value of all the final goods produced in a year. It can be thought of either as the sum of all the value added by producers, as the total income earned by owners of productive resources, or as the sum of expenditures for new goods by households, business firms, government, and foreigners.

Gross national product in current dollars is the nominal GNP. Real GNP is calculated by determining what the value of nominal GNP would be if measured in the prices of a reference or base year.

Dividing nominal GNP for any year by real GNP yields a comprehensive price index known as the implicit GNP deflator. A better known though less comprehensive measure of price level changes is available monthly in the consumer price index.

The dominant view among economists prior to the 1930s was that total spending or aggregate demand will always be adequate, and that genuine economic problems represent malfunctions on the side of supply. The Great Depression of the 1930s provided persuasive evidence that aggregate demand could generate serious problems for an economic system and inaugurated an age of "demand-side" economics.

Questions for Discussion

1. This question tries to make you think carefully about the relationship between income and output.

   (a) Can your personal income exceed the value of your personal output, at least for a limited time? How is this possible? Is it possible without gifts or loans from others?

   (b) Can the total income of all the members of a society, such as the United States, exceed the total value of all their output? How would this be possible?

   (c) If we learned that a particular society's total output had increased by 10 percent while its total income had increased by only 6 percent, what would we conclude must have happened?

2. How much do the following activities collectively contribute to the gross national product? Jack Lumber fells a tree and sells it for $10 to Saul Mill, who cuts it into boards that he sells for $25 to Lum Yard, who sells them

at retail for $50 to Paul Thumbs, who uses them to build bookcases for his den that he thinks are lovely and that he wouldn't sell for less than $100. Be sure that you avoid double counting in making your calculations.

3. People who want to call attention to the huge size of certain business corporations will often compare the corporations' gross revenue from sales with the gross national product of some smaller nations. The implication is that General Motors, for example, is bigger than Sweden in some relevant economic sense because its gross revenue exceeds Sweden's gross national product. Why is this a misleading comparison? If we added together the gross revenue of all business firms in the United States, why would it be much larger than the U.S. gross national product? What must we subtract from a corporation's gross revenue to obtain the amount of its contribution to the gross national product?

4. List some ways in which increased inefficiency could cause GNP to rise. Are there any goods contributing to the total GNP whose rising output clearly reflects reduced welfare? What about home-security systems that protect against burglars?

5. If it could be shown that a rising GNP is associated with a rising level of anxiety, tension, and conflict in the population, would you favor deducting these psychological costs to obtain the true value of gross national product? How would you do so? How would you place a dollar value on increased anxiety?

6. Would you favor including the services of homemakers in the calculation of gross national product? What arguments could be given for doing so? Are there any good reasons for continuing to exclude these services from the calculation of GNP? Do you think the exclusion reflects sexist attitudes, and that if more men were homemakers, the Bureau of Economic Analysis would change its ways? Why doesn't the Bureau count the value of a husband's work as a backyard barbecue chef, when it does count the very same sort of work done for pay by someone in a barbecued-rib outlet?

7. As an economy industrializes, a larger percentage of its population tends to enter the labor force as conventionally measured. Fewer goods intended for use in the home are produced in the home, and a larger proportion of total product passes through the marketplace. What does this imply about the validity of GNP data in industrializing societies? Will estimates of per-capita income derived from GNP data tend to overstate or understate improvement over time?

8. To be certain that you understand the relationship between nominal GNP, real GNP, and the GNP deflator, fill in the following table.

Year	Nominal GNP	Real GNP	GNP Deflator
1	$3960 billion	$3600 billion	_____
2	_____	$3800 billion	115
3	$4800 billion	_____	120

9. You might want to familiarize yourself in a general way with the history of the U.S. economy in the post-World War II era, as it is summarized in Table 16A and Figures 16A and 16B.

   (a) Nominal GNP increased almost 18 fold from 1950 to 1989. By how much did real GNP increase over this period?

   (b) At which column in Table 16A would you look to find the years dominated by recessions? What years were they? Don't overlook 1960, which contained an official recession that might easily be missed; Figure 16A provides a more detailed and clearer picture. Which of the seven recessions since 1950 – the National Bureau of Economic Research made a sometimes-disputed decision to count the 1980 and 1982 recessions separately instead of as a single, long recession – was the most severe?

   (c) There was a great deal of public concern in early 1958 about the inflation that the nation had been experiencing for the previous three years, and some talk about the desirability of imposing price controls to stop it. In 1986, by contrast, there was enormous public satisfaction with our success in stopping inflation over the preceding three years. How would you explain these very different reactions to very similar inflation rates?

   (d) Using Figures 16A and 16B, estimate how long it takes after the bottom of a recession is reached for the unemployment rate to hit its peak and start declining. About how long does it seem to take for the unemployment rate to fall back down after a recession has ended and recovery has begun?

10. *The General Theory of Employment, Interest and Money*, published in 1936 by the British economist John Maynard Keynes, did a great deal to shift economists' attention away from supply-side factors in their thinking about recession and inflation. In Chapter 19, Keynes summarizes his theory, beginning with what he takes as "given."

> We take as given the existing skill and quantity of available labour, the existing quality and quantity of available equipment, the existing technique, the degree of competition, the tastes and habits of the consumer, the disutility of different intensities of labour and of the activities of supervision and organisation, as well as the social structure. . . .

Can you think of any factors other than the ones listed (and excluded from consideration) by Keynes that might influence the supply side of economic activity?

Chapter 17

The Supply of Money

Some economists believe that both inflation and recession are primarily caused by changes in the quantity of money held by the public, and that stabilizing the growth rate of the money stock is the most important contribution that government can make to stabilizing the economy. Other economists assign money a less dominant role in causing instability and propose a considerably larger role for government in controlling inflation and recession. All would agree, however, that the monetary system is closely linked to the problems of inflation and recession. We must therefore find out what money is and how and why the quantity of money held by the public changes over time.

Money as a Unit of Accounting

You probably didn't even notice that we have come this far without discussing money. The previous chapters, after all, were full of dollar signs, and dollars are money. But the dollars referred to so far were simply conventional units for discussing values—a common denominator that enabled us to compare and add apples and oranges, convenient transportation and unpolluted air, goods in the hand and goods in the bush, the services of engineers and the gains from exchange.

One important function of money in a social system is to provide such a unit for accounting. We might have used any other common denominator, such as bread or human labor. We could have stated the values of gasoline and sugar in terms of the number of standard loaves for which a gallon of one and a pound of the other will exchange. Or we could have expressed the gross national product as the equivalent of so many hours of "average" labor time. But we're all accustomed to thinking and talking about values in terms of dollars because we have had a lot of practice in translating the values of diverse commodities and services into dollar

437

terms. Money functions effectively as a unit of accounting because of all the experience we've had with its more important function as a medium of exchange.

Money as a Medium of Exchange

A "medium of exchange" is just what the words say: a middle-thing used in the process of exchanging one good for another. The alternative to employing a medium of exchange is barter: exchanging the goods at our command directly for the goods we want to obtain. What do we use in the United States as our medium of exchange?

Most people who think about money think immediately of green pieces of paper, called Federal Reserve notes, and coins in various sizes and colors. Economists lump these all together and call it the currency component of the money supply. But what else do we use as a medium of exchange?

The most widely used medium of exchange is not currency but deposit credits in commercial banks, usually called checking accounts, but officially known as *demand deposits*, because they are deposits that can be withdrawn or transferred on demand.

Students often have trouble at first in seeing that demand deposits really are money. They themselves may handle all their transactions by means of currency, and when they receive a check, they cash it; that is, they obtain currency for the check and spend the currency. But student habits are in no way typical of the transaction procedures employed by business firms, government units, and households. The overwhelming majority of exchanges, measured in dollar value, employ demand deposits as the medium of exchange. Purchasers instruct their banks to transfer ownership of a portion of the purchasers' deposits to sellers: they write a check, in other words. Sellers typically deposit the checks rather than cash them, thereby instructing their own banks to collect the ownership whose transfer was ordered by the check writer. No currency at all changes hands. The bank in which the check is deposited makes an entry in its books; the bank on which the check is written makes an equal but opposite entry in its books.

It isn't hard to imagine a situation in which demand deposits are the only medium of exchange. As credit cards become more common, people will carry less currency and pay for more of their purchases with monthly checks. Couldn't all transactions be handled in this way? It would be possible, even though inconvenient in some cases. But currency could disappear entirely without any reduction in our use of money as a medium of exchange.

Currency plus demand deposits. Is that all? Suppose someone asks, "How much money do you have?" You would calculate the currency in your possession. Having read this far you would then add the balance in your checking account. Should you also add what you have in your savings account? You can get it out quickly or transfer it to your checking account. It's available for spending, even though savings accounts can't be used directly as a medium of exchange. But then what of the deposit you have in a savings-and-loan institution? You could also convert that amount into "ready cash." And why not also the government bonds you own? They can be cashed too. How far shall we go in calculating how much money you have? Your automobile could also be converted into currency or a demand deposit. Is it therefore money?

Money as Liquidity

Notice what we've done now. We have shifted the definition of money from "the commonly employed medium of exchange" to "assets that can be exchanged in order to obtain other goods." But any asset at all, under the right circumstances, can be exchanged for other goods. Is every good therefore to be included in the money supply?

The distinguishing characteristic of money is its *liquidity*. Money is a liquid asset. The more liquid something is, the more moneylike it is. When an asset is completely liquid, it has attained the zenith of moneyness.

What do we mean by liquidity? *The liquidity of an asset refers to the cost of exchanging it for other assets.* An asset that can be exchanged for any other asset at a zero cost is a completely liquid asset. The Federal Reserve note in your wallet is an excellent example. It's an asset you can give in exchange for a great variety of other things you might want; sellers of every sort are willing to accept it without question *and without discounting it.* An asset that cannot be exchanged at all, because no one else would be willing to give anything in exchange for it, would be a completely illiquid asset. (Your toothbrush?) If you own a government savings bond, you can exchange it for other assets; but first you'll have to incur the cost of a trip to the bank where you exchange the bond for currency. So government savings bonds

We accept
Federal Reserve Notes
(eagerly)

No
Personal Toothbrushes
Accepted

are liquid assets but they're not as liquid as Federal Reserve notes. Are they money? Just how liquid does an asset have to be to qualify as money? That turns out to be a difficult question on which competent people disagree. In this world of continuous variables and every shade of gray, assets will rarely hit either end of the liquid-illiquid continuum. Most assets are somewhat liquid. The point to remember is that an asset becomes more moneylike as it becomes more liquid, as the cost of exchanging it for other assets approaches zero.

The concept of liquidity is important in the economist's way of looking at the world. To possess liquid assets is to have a greater range of choices, better opportunities, and hence more wealth. Your wealth, by which we mean the range of options available to you, will depend among other things on the precise forms in which you're currently holding the goods you own, or in the useful jargon of finance, on the *composition of your asset portfolio*. Suppose, for example, that you're in a strange city with a checkbook but no currency, and you're hungry. The restaurant signs "No Checks Accepted" establish that you are at the moment not as wealthy as you would be with $20 less in your checking account and a $20 bill in your wallet. You may also be driving an expensive sports car. But exchanging it for a meal (plus other assets) would almost certainly entail a substantial loss of wealth, because sports cars are not fully liquid assets.

How Money Creates Wealth

The advantages of using money rather than employing a barter system are enormous. The cost of exchanging would be far greater, and social wealth as a consequence far less, if there were no money to facilitate the process. In an economic system limited to barter, people would have to spend an inordinate amount of time searching for others with whom they could advantageously exchange. A violin maker would have to find a grocer, a haberdasher, an electrical utility, and a glue supplier, among many others, all willing to accept violins in return for the goods they sell. All that time devoted to searching would be time not available for violin making, and the production of violins would fall. Aware of the high costs of exchanging, people would increasingly try to produce goods for their own use, thus avoiding the necessity of searching out others from whom they can buy and to whom they can sell. Specialization would decline dramatically in a society confined to barter. And that means, of course, that people would lose the benefits that accrue from the systematic and widespread exploitation of comparative advantage. The evolution of some kind of money system in almost every known society, even when conditions were extremely unfavorable for it, is eloquent testimony to the advantages of having a generally accepted medium of exchange.

Defining the Money Stock

So the moneyness of particular assets is a matter of degree. How then are we going to define the money supply in the United States? The answer is: *somewhat arbitrarily*. There just is no completely satisfactory way to decide what should be counted in the money supply and what should be excluded. Some economists, known as monetarists, believe that changes in the rate at which the money supply grows make up the most important single factor causing recessions and inflations. Their contention is difficult to prove or dis-prove because they can't agree completely on what counts as money. That isn't because they're a disputatious lot. The appropriate definition of money is a function of financial institutions and social practices that evolve over time, usu-ally very slowly, but sometimes with dramatic suddenness. You might even say that scholars can't agree on the best definition of money because the public, whose practices make something money, does not itself know what it will be using next year as a medium of exchange.

If we adhered strictly to the definition of money as the common medium of exchange, we would want to define the money supply in the United States as the total of currency in circulation plus checkable deposits (deposits at financial institutions that can be transferred by writing a check) plus travelers checks. That's what we use to pay for almost all our transactions. To avoid double counting we must include only the currency that is in circulation, or outside the bank-ing system. Thus, when someone deposits a $20 bill in a checking account, the money supply doesn't change. The demand-deposit component rises by $20, but currency in circulation falls by $20. If we continued to count as money the currency now in the bank's possession, we would falsely conclude that deposits or withdrawals of currency from checking accounts change the quantity of the exchange medium held by the community. But they obviously don't; they change only the *form* in which it's held. After you've

The narrowly-defined money supply (M1): currency in circulation, checkable deposits, and travelers' checks.

written a check for "cash," you have exactly as much money as before, and so does everyone else.

But do we want to define money strictly as that which actually functions as the common medium of exchange? What we're really after is insight into the determinants of total monetary expenditures for other goods, or aggregate demand. That will partially depend, as we shall see, on the amount of money people are holding relative to the quantities of other goods that they own or would like to acquire. The more money people possess, other things being equal, the more likely are they to surrender some portion of it in exchange for an alternate good when an attractive opportunity presents itself. Now it is quite clear that most people don't just look at their present stock of currency and demand deposits in deciding how much money they have. Savings held in commercial banks or in nonbank thrift institutions, such as savings-and-loan associations, would be regarded by most people as "available cash." So shouldn't we include these deposits in our working definition of the money supply?

The broadly-defined money supply (M2): currency in circulation, checkable deposits, travelers' checks, and non-checkable deposits.

The central bank of the United States, called the Federal Reserve, calculates the money supply in two principal ways and publishes the figures as M1 and M2. M1 attempts to measure the actual medium of exchange and is therefore sometimes referred to as the *narrowly defined* money supply. M1 is the sum of currency in circulation, demand deposits, other checkable deposits, and travelers checks. M2, the *broadly defined* money supply, is the sum of M1 plus savings deposits, time deposits in denominations of less than $100,000, money-market mutual-fund shares, and a couple of other relatively minor components that you don't even want to know about. M2 is an attempt to measure the stock of highly liquid assets that the public is holding.

Table 17A gives you some notion of the magnitude of each of these measures of the money stock. Since the quantity of money can and does fluctuate considerably from day to day, figures are usually expressed as averages over some period of time. The numbers provided here are in billions of dollars and give the averages of daily figures in December of each year. Also shown is the percentage by which each measure of the money stock increased from the preceding year.

The stock of money, no matter in which of the two ways we measure it, has increased substantially since 1960. The average annual rate of increase from 1960 to 1989 was about 6 percent for M1 and 8 percent for M2. Moreover, the percentage rates of increase varied considerably, both be-

TABLE 17A   Stock of money (in billions of dollars) and annual 7A percentage increases

Year	M1	Percentage Increase	M2	Percentage Increase
1960	$141	0.5	$ 312	4.9
1961	145	3.2	336	7.4
1962	148	1.9	363	8.1
1963	153	3.7	393	8.4
1964	160	4.6	425	8.0
1965	168	4.7	459	8.1
1966	172	2.5	480	4.5
1967	183	6.5	524	9.2
1968	198	7.7	566	8.0
1969	204	3.3	590	4.1
1970	215	5.1	628	6.5
1971	228	6.5	713	13.5
1972	249	9.2	805	13.0
1973	263	5.5	861	6.9
1974	274	4.3	909	5.5
1975	288	4.8	1,023	12.6
1976	307	6.6	1,164	13.7
1977	332	8.2	1,287	10.6
1978	359	8.2	1,389	8.0
1979	386	7.6	1,500	8.0
1980	412	6.8	1,633	8.9
1981	439	6.5	1,796	10.0
1982	476	8.5	1,955	8.8
1983	522	9.6	2,186	11.8
1984	552	5.7	2,367	8.3
1985	621	12.4	2,567	8.5
1986	726	17.0	2,811	9.5
1987	752	3.6	2,910	3.5
1988	790	5.1	3,070	5.5
1989	797	0.9	3,216	4.8

Source: Board of Governors of the Federal Reserve System

tween the two measures of the money stock and from year to year within each measure. Why? How has this come about? Where did all this additional money come from?

Commercial Bank Lending and the Creation of Money

The basic answer is that it came about through a net expansion of commercial bank loans. *The money stock increases when commercial banks make loans to their customers and decreases when customers repay the loans obtained from*

COMMERCIAL BANK

ASSETS	LIABILITIES
+Your $500 IOU	+$500 Demand deposit

COMMERCIAL BANK

ASSETS	LIABILITIES
−$500 Currency from vault	−$500 Demand deposit

COMMERCIAL BANK

ASSETS	LIABILITIES
−Your $500 IOU +$500 Currency from your cookie jar	

COMMERCIAL BANK

ASSETS	LIABILITIES
−Your $500 IOU	−$500 Demand deposit

commercial banks. That's the short of the story. The long of it is a bit more complicated but not really difficult to grasp.

Suppose your application for a loan of $500 from the First National Bank is approved. The lending officer will make out a deposit slip in your name for $500, initial it, and hand it to a teller who will then credit your checking account with an additional $500. Demand deposits will have risen by $500. The money stock will be larger by that amount.

Where did the $500 come from? The bank *created* the $500 to lend you. Out of thin air? Not really. But the raw material isn't as important at this point as the fact that the bank really did create new money in making you a loan.

But what if you don't have a checking account at First National? Then the bank can open one and start you off with a $500 balance. But what if you don't want a demand deposit: you want the money? Slips! A demand deposit *is* money. You can use it to buy whatever it is you borrowed for. All right, but what if you decide to withdraw your $500 right away in $20 bills? Fine. The teller will accommodate you. The total of demand deposits will fall by $500, but the total of currency in circulation will increase by $500. The bank takes the currency from its vault, where it is not money, and gives it to you, whereupon it becomes currency held by the nonbank public or currency in circulation and hence *is* money.

Does it all seem too simple? Why don't banks keep on doing that indefinitely? It seems just like having your own money machine in the basement. We'll see in a moment that banks are limited in their ability to make loans and thus add to the money stock. But first let's see how the stock of money is decreased.

One year later your note comes due. In the interim you've built up your money balance to be able to pay off the loan on time. You have $500 (plus the interest due, which we neglect for present purposes) either in your checking account or your cookie jar. If it's in the cookie jar, you turn it over to the bank on the due date and money in circulation drops by $500. Note again that currency counts as money when and only when it's held outside the banking system.

If, as is more likely, you have the $500 in your checking account, you write a check for that amount to the bank. The bank subtracts $500 from your demand-deposit balance. The money stock goes down by $500.

If you've grasped this simple process, you understand how money, defined as M1, is created and destroyed.

Changes in the size of M2 are the consequence of the public's preferences regarding the form in which it wants to hold its stock of money assets. If you transferred the $500 you had borrowed out of your checking account and into a savings account at the bank where you borrowed, M1 would fall by $500. But M2 would be unchanged, because M2 includes everything in M1; the $500 contributes just as much to the total of M2 when it's in a checking account as when it's in the savings account. In short, commercial-bank lending increases M1. The public's desire to hold more or less of its assets in demand deposits or savings accounts will determine the different rates of growth between M1 and M2.

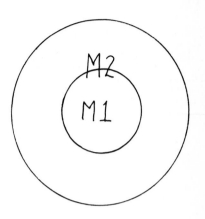

The Central Bank

But you must be wondering what has been left out. Surely private, commercial bankers can't create money without constraint. And you're right; they can't. First, the bankers must find people willing to borrow on the terms at which the banks are willing to lend. Second, each bank must operate within the constraint imposed by its reserves. That's the constraint which government authorities use in their efforts to exercise control over bank lending and hence over the process of money creation. Every bank is legally required to hold reserves in forms specified by law. A bank may make new loans, and thus create money, only when it has free reserves — that is, reserves greater than the minimum amount it's legally obligated to hold. And the Fed (the common name for the managers of the Federal Reserve) has the power to increase or decrease the reserves of the banking system.

The Federal Reserve is the central bank of the United States, created by an act of Congress in 1913. Although technically owned by the commercial banks that are its members, the Fed is in practical fact a government agency. Its board of governors in Washington is appointed by the president of the United States, with the consent of the Senate. And the board effectively controls the policies of the twelve banks that make up the system. We seem to have twelve central banks, but this is only an appearance, a legacy from the days when much of the country harbored a populist suspicion of Easterners, Wall Streeters, and men in striped pants with cutaway coats. These suspicions were allayed by scattering banks around the country. But the Fed has actually been a single bank (with branches) at least since the legislative changes enacted by Congress in the 1930s. The power of any one of the twelve branch banks depends pretty much on the amount of influence it's able to exert on policy formation through its executive officers and research staff.

Bank Reserves as Constraints on Money Creation

Because of its power to fix legal reserve requirements for banks (within wide limits set by Congress) and its power to expand or contract the dollar volume of reserves, the Fed controls the lending activities of the commercial banking system and thus the process of money creation. Reserve requirements differ for savings deposits and demand deposits; moreover, the legal reserve requirement on demand deposits currently varies between 3 and 12 percent, depending on the size of a particular bank's demand-deposit liabilities. (Note that demand deposits are bank *liabilities:* your bank owes you the amount in your checking account.) The Fed also decides what may count as legal reserves — since 1960 it has been the banks' vault cash plus the deposits the commercial banks themselves have at the Federal Reserve Bank of their district. To see what all this has to do with changes in the money stock, we'll come in for a close-up look at the First National Bank of Anywhere.

Suppose that First National Bank is holding $10 million in vault cash, has $30 million on deposit with the Federal Reserve Bank, and is required by law to hold $38 million in reserves against its outstanding liabilities. That $38 million will be the sum and product of a lot of complex calculations involving different percentage reserve requirements for different liabilities. But we don't have to get into all the arithmetic, because it's irrelevant to our purposes. All we have to know is that First National Bank has $2 million in *excess reserves*. At least they're excess from the legal point of view. If First National has a reason of its own for holding $2 million more in reserves than it's legally required to hold, those won't really be excess reserves — any more than the amount in your checking account is an excess reserve because you aren't *legally* required to hold anything in your checking account.

But we're going to assume that First National has no desire to hold more reserves than the law says it must. So First National is indeed holding $2 million in excess reserves. Banks make use of excess reserves by lending them. First National can make new loans totaling $2 million if it can find acceptable borrowers. Let's assume it finds them and watch what happens as a result.

First National makes the loans by creating new demand

deposits for its borrowers. The moment it does so, the stock of money increases by $2 million. All participants are happier than before. First National has additional income earning assets in the form of the borrowers' IOUs, and the borrowers have the money that they wanted badly enough to pay interest for it.

    The story doesn't end here, however. The bank loans transformed $2 million of excess reserves into a $2 million addition to the stock of M1. But what will now happen to the $2 million in the checking accounts of the borrowers? Since people usually borrow in order to spend, we'll assume that's what these borrowers do, too. They write checks totaling $2 million.

FIRST NATIONAL BANK	
ASSETS	LIABILITIES
+$2 Million in IOUs	+$2 Million in demand deposits

The Dispersion of Excess Reserves

When the payees receive the checks, they deposit them in their own banks. Run the process through in your mind to convince yourself that no money is created or destroyed in this process. If borrower A writes a $100 check to the order of payee B, and B deposits that check in Second National Bank, Second National will add $100 to B's checking account and send the check to the Federal Reserve Bank for clearing. The Federal Reserve Bank will credit Second National with an additional $100 in its reserve account, will subtract $100 from the amount it has credited on its books to the reserve account of First National, and will send the check to First National. First National will subtract $100 from A's checking account. At the end of the process, the $100 of recently created money will be in B's checking account, and $100 of First National's excess reserves will have been added to the reserves of Second National.

    But now Second National will have excess reserves! It acquired $100 in new liabilities and $100 in new reserves. But, under our fractional reserve system, *at least* $88 of those new reserves will be excess reserves, because the *maximum* reserve requirement is 12 percent. So Second National will have an additional $88 more to lend.

    All around the commercial banking system, wherever the checks sent out by the borrowers are being deposited by payees, new additions are being made in this manner to the excess reserves of commercial banks. Some reserves will probably even find their way right back into First National, because some of the payees are almost certain to be depositors of First National Bank. All these new excess reserves permit further loans, which in turn create more M1. And when these further additions to the stock of M1 are spent by the borrowers and redeposited by payees, still more additions are made to the excess reserves of the commercial banking system.

The conclusion of the matter is this: *a dollar of original excess reserves can create several dollars in additional money* as banks use their excess reserves to acquire interest-paying assets. Exactly how many dollars of additional money will be generated from one additional dollar of excess reserves? We don't know. The ratio of new money to new reserves will depend on the legal reserve requirements in force, the public's preferences about the form in which it wants to hold money, the lending policies and practices of banks, cash-management procedures of the federal government, the balance between exports and imports, and even the monetary policies of foreign central banks. The most important thing to know about this ratio may just be that it varies a good bit and is highly unpredictable, especially over short periods of time — such as a few months.

We know at least that the commercial banks can't continue indefinitely to create new money out of a given quantity of new reserves. Additional lending creates additional liabilities against which reserves must be held, so that continual lending will eventually "use up" the excess reserves on which the lending was based. Moreover, the public will tend to withdraw larger quantities of money from the banking system as the stock of money increases, and every dollar of currency that moves into circulation reduces bank reserves by a dollar.

The discussion has been carried on in terms of excess reserves, additional loans, and more money. The process also works in reverse. When a bank's reserves fall below the legal minimum, it reduces its rate of new loans below the rate at which old loans are being repaid, in order to acquire the additional required reserves. If the entire banking system is doing this, the result is a net contraction of loans and hence a reduction in the money stock. Eventually, through the acquisition by the commercial banks of additional currency formerly in the hands of the public and the reduction of demand deposits as the public repays loans, the legal minimum reserve-to-deposit ratio will be reached. The process of contraction will stop.

It should be clear from all this that excess reserves plus a demand for bank loans on the part of eligible borrowers are the two factors jointly controlling the expansion of the money stock. The Fed can therefore influence the growth of the money stock either by changing the legal reserve requirements or by somehow changing the dollar volume of bank reserves. The latter is in fact the Fed's regular operating lever in money management.

The Tools Used by the Fed

How does the Fed actually go at the job of expanding or contracting the money supply? The most powerful tool and the one that sets the stage for the rest is the authority to establish legal reserve requirements. Changes in reserve requirements are generally viewed by Fed officials as a blunt weapon, not suitable for the delicate surgery that monetary management usually requires. They prefer to take the reserve requirements as the framework and alter the volume of reserves.

How is that done? The briefest explanation is that the Fed creates and destroys reserves in the same way that commercial banks create and destroy money: by extending and contracting loans.

The Fed can extend a loan to a commercial bank directly. It does so by crediting the bank's reserve account and taking in return the bank's IOU or someone else's IOU (*e.g.,* a government bond) that happens to be in the bank's portfolio — just as a commercial bank lends to its customers by creating a deposit balance in return for an IOU. The interest rate at which such loans are made is called the *discount rate.* It's a financial-page celebrity, because many people look on it as a sign of current Fed policy. It probably is more of a symbol than a genuine rationing device, since the Fed is selective about the banks to which it will lend. Official Fed policy is to accommodate special circumstances, rather than lend to any bank willing to pay the rate, and to behave more like a stern uncle than a profit-seeking lender. But that's what most people look for from a central bank.

The principal technique that the Fed employs is the purchase and sale of United States government bonds in what are called *open market operations.* The Fed currently holds a portfolio of government bonds worth more than $200 billion. When it increases its holdings by purchasing securities through dealers in government bonds, it writes checks for the amount of the purchases on its own credit. These checks are deposited in commercial banks. When the banks forward the checks to their Federal Reserve Bank, they are credited with additions to their reserve balances.

In short, the acquisition by the Federal Reserve Banks of new earning assets, which is the same thing as the extension of credit to someone, whether the government or banks, increases commercial-bank reserves by that amount. And that,

FEDERAL RESERVE BANKS

ASSETS	LIABILITIES
+ Government bonds	+ Commercial bank reserves

COMMERCIAL BANKS

ASSETS	LIABILITIES
+ Reserve accounts	+ Demand deposits

as we have seen, enables commercial banks to increase their own loans and thereby the money stock.

The entire process is reversible. The Fed can withdraw credit from member banks or sell some of the government bonds already in its asset portfolio. This results in a reduction of commercial-bank reserves. For example, when the Fed sells a $1000 government bond, the bond winds up in the hands of someone who pays the bond dealer with a check. But the dealer in turn pays the Fed with a check, and the amount of the check is deducted from the reserve account of the bank on which it is drawn. That wipes out a portion of the total reserves of the banking system.

Who Is Really in Charge?

Open market operations, as we said, are the principal working tool of monetary management. A special committee, made up of the seven members of the board of governors and five of the twelve Reserve Bank presidents, sits as the Open Market Committee and continuously determines the direction of monetary policy. The question of the effectiveness with which the Open Market Committee manages the money supply has long been debated by friends and critics of the Fed, among both economists and politicians.

There are two main questions. One is the determination of policy: Does the Fed set appropriate goals? Does it try to do what it ought to be doing? The other is the execution of policy: Does the Fed do an effective job of achieving the goals it sets for itself? The questions are related, of course, because intelligent policy formulation presupposes a realistic assessment of technical capabilities. The football coach who orders a passing strategy when his team is two touchdowns behind in the fourth quarter is making a poor policy decision if the quarterback has a rubber arm and all the receivers have butterfingers. Beware of textbook accounts which, like football plays on the blackboard, gloss over problems of execution and assume that the opposition isn't doing any planning of its own. It's a gross oversimplification to suppose that the Fed has a monetary brake and a monetary accelerator with which it adjusts the money stock as quickly and surely as you slow down and speed up your car in traffic. Monetary management may be more like driving a balky mule train that sometimes won't stop going even when firmly ordered to halt. To make matters worse, there's a bunch of bickering backseat drivers on the wagon, and some of them aren't above shouting their own instructions or even trying to grab the reins from the driver. We'll return to these problems in later chapters when we examine monetary policy.

Why Should Banks Hold Reserves?

Throughout our description of money and the banking system, we have treated reserves as constraints on the power of banks to make loans and thus to expand the money supply. That seems to have little or nothing to do with the concept of a reserve fund, something that can be drawn on in an emergency. But legal reserves do not in fact perform a significant reserve function. The reserve requirement is today primarily a limitation on the ability of the commercial banking system to expand the money stock.

But isn't it necessary for the banks to hold reserves against the possibility of a "run" by depositors? If a lot of depositors suddenly lost confidence in a bank for some reason and tried to withdraw their deposits in currency, the bank would be unable to honor those withdrawals. And if that happened, the loss of confidence might spread to other banks and bring down a large part of the banking system.

There actually hasn't been a financial panic like that in the United States for over fifty years. The reason, however, has little to do with the level of bank reserves. Bank customers no longer rush to withdraw their deposits on every rumor of financial trouble because their deposits are now insured by the Federal Deposit Insurance Corporation (FDIC). If a bank closes, for whatever reason, its depositors can expect reimbursement within a few days. Some critics argued when the FDIC was created in 1933 that the premiums it charged banks to insure their deposits were far too low, and that the FDIC would go broke trying to pay off depositors when banks closed their doors. But the very existence of the FDIC ended the phenomenon of bank runs; and in the absence of runs, banks no longer failed the way they formerly did. The FDIC premiums have thus proved more than adequate.[1] And

---

[1]If it's a good idea for the government to insure depositors in commercial banks against loss, it must also be a good idea for the federal government to insure depositors in savings and loan institutions against loss. Right? The trouble with such insurance is that it gives depositors no incentive to monitor the behavior of the institutions in which they place their deposits. Depositor indifference combined with lax oversight by the regulatory authorities (the latter often prompted by members of Congress seeking to do favors for generous constituents) created the enormous losses in the savings and loan industry that American taxpayers will be paying for into the 21st century. "We" agreed to do so when "we" promised that the Federal Savings and Loan Insurance Corporation would cover any losses that depositors in S&Ls might suffer.

the institution of the FDIC may well be the single most stabilizing reform enacted in the 1930s.

Some credit must also go to improved Federal Reserve procedures since the 1930s. The Fed now understands clearly that it has the responsibility to provide short-term liquidity to the banking system, without regard to the amounts banks happen to be holding as reserves. Thus, a bank today can meet any demand for currency, however large, by securing additional currency from the Fed. If the bank were to use up its entire reserve balance, the Federal Reserve Bank would simply lend the bank additional reserves, taking as collateral some of the IOUs in the asset portfolio of the borrowing bank. Banks are granted access to this "discount privilege" whenever they have a legitimate demand for additional reserves, and this has made the whole banking and monetary system more flexible in response to changing conditions as well as more resistant to crises and temporary dislocations.

What About Gold?

But hasn't something important still been left out of all this? If reserves aren't really reserves, what is it that provides backing for money? Doesn't money have to have some kind of backing? And where does gold fit into the picture?

The conviction that money must have "backing" if it is to have value raises an interesting question. What stands behind the backing to give *it* value? And behind the backing of the backing? But the whole set of questions is misdirected. In economics, value is the consequence of scarcity. And scarcity is the result of demand plus limited availability. It's clear enough why there exists a demand for money: it can be used to obtain all sorts of other things that people want, which is to say that it's accepted as a medium of exchange. The other part of the picture, limited availability, is taken care of, more or less effectively, by the monetary managers. No "backing" is required. If this makes you nervous or causes you to doubt the value of your currency or checking account, you can easily shore up your faith by "selling" your money to others. You'll find that they're willing to take it and to give you other valuable assets in exchange.

The critical factor in preserving the value of money is limited availability and confidence that the supply will continue to be limited. Nature has made gold relatively rare. It's up to the Fed to keep Federal Reserve notes and demand deposits relatively rare. But many people have far more confidence in the reliability of nature than in the reliability of central banks and governments. That's why some intelligent and well-informed people would like to see us return to a genuine gold standard, under which currency could be exchanged for gold at some fixed ratio. It's not because they think that money must have backing, but because they distrust government money managers. If the government were required to maintain the convertibility of demand deposits into currency and currency into gold at predetermined exchange ratios, the limited availability of gold would severely restrict the power to increase the money stock.

As a matter of fact, governments are often tempted, especially in wartime, to create additional money as a way of financing expenditures without the painful necessity of openly levying taxes. And they haven't always resisted the temptation. The consequence has usually been inflation, a more concealed but hardly a more equitable way for the government to finance its expenditures. Urging a return to the gold standard would seem to be a counsel of despair, however. A government so irresponsible that it must be reined in by gold would be most unlikely to adopt a gold standard and even more unlikely to respond to the pressure of such a rein. The problem of irresponsible government is a weighty one; but it's hard to believe that the problem could be solved through a return to the gold standard. In any event, the United States seems unlikely to adopt the gold standard in the near future. We will probably have to be satisfied with making the present system work.

Once Over Lightly

Money is a social institution that increases wealth by lowering costs of exchange, thereby enabling people to specialize more fully in accordance with their own comparative advantages.

The moneyness of any asset is a matter of degree. An asset is money insofar as it is liquid. An asset is completely liquid when it can be exchanged for other goods at no cost. Whatever assets everyone freely accepts as a medium of exchange make up a society's stock of money.

In the United States today the stock of money is primarily the total of currency held outside the banking system plus the demand-deposit liabilities of commercial banks. But other assets, such as savings deposits, which can be converted into currency or demand deposits at negligible cost, also contribute to overall liquidity and are therefore included in more comprehensive measurements of the money stock.

The money stock increases or decreases primarily as commercial banks expand or contract their lending.

The managers of the Federal Reserve System have the responsibility for regulating the size of the money stock. The Fed does so by controlling bank lending through its power to set the legal ratio between commercial-bank liabilities and reserves and to expand or contract those reserves through loans to commercial banks and through open-market operations.

The idea that money must have "backing" to have value is not correct. Money must only be acceptable as a medium of exchange to have value. Limited availability is a necessary condition for continued acceptability of any functioning medium of exchange.

Questions for Discussion

1. Do we ever use human labor rather than money as our "unit of accounting"? Have you ever encountered a comparison of international living standards which refers to the number of hours an average person must work in each country to earn the price of a loaf of bread, a pair of shoes, or a refrigerator? Why is this done?

2. Would your existence be more or less secure if we had a barter economy?

   (a) Why would we all be poorer if we had to rely entirely on barter to exchange goods?
   (b) Why might people's incomes fluctuate less in a society that did not use money?
   (c) Is a very poor family subject to 10 percent fluctuations in its income more or less secure than a wealthy family that experiences 50 percent fluctuations in its income?.
   (d) We are much wealthier than we would be if our society did not use money, but our incomes are probably somewhat more uncertain than they would be if we relied entirely on barter. Can you think of any other important social consequences that emerge from the use of money?

3. Adam Smith complained in *The Wealth of Nations* that many people confused money with wealth. Is this a confusion?

   (a) Doesn't everyone's wealth increase when they acquire more money?
   (b) If any one person's wealth increases when he or she acquires more money, doesn't it follow logically that more money for everyone means more wealth for everyone?
   (c) What would happen if the government of India tackled the problem of poverty by printing more rupees and distributing them generously to the poorest people in the country?

4. If someone asked how much money you have, how would you go about calculating the answer?

   (a) Wouldn't you want to know why the person was asking? If you were out shopping and the other person wanted to borrow money from you to make a purchase, would you include the amount in your checking account as well as the currency in your wallet? When would you and when would you not? Is it ever appropriate to answer, "I have my credit card with me"?

   (b) If you were to ask people how much money they have in the bank, most would probably not distinguish in answering between their checking-account and savings-account balances. Why might economists want to distinguish between the two? Why might this distinction have become less important in recent years as banks have made it easier for people to transfer deposits between savings accounts and checking accounts?

5. What is the value of *liquidity?*

6. Shares of common stock listed on a major exchange can be sold quickly — that is, exchanged for other assets. Is stock as liquid as money? Why might people hold part of their wealth in common stocks and part in money? Why might they shift the composition of their portfolios in order to hold more of one asset and less of the other?

7. People usually cannot spend the deposits they hold in commercial-bank savings accounts or savings-and-loan institutions without first withdrawing the funds — that is, converting them into currency or demand deposits. But since they're able to do that at almost no cost, these deposits are assets almost as liquid as checking-account balances.

   (a) Would you expect total spending to be more closely correlated with M1 or with M2?

   (b) Will your answer change if savings-and-loan institutions allow customers to pay bills through telephone transfers of their deposits to the accounts of others?

8. At any moment some already-printed Federal Reserve notes will be in (a) the wallets of the public, (b) the vaults and tills of commercial banks, (c) the vaults of Federal Reserve Banks. How does each enter into or otherwise affect the total money supply?

9. How does a withdrawal of currency from checking accounts affect the money stock? How does it affect a bank's reserves? How does it affect excess reserves? What effect might this withdrawal subsequently have on the money stock?

10. A good technique for getting a handle on the way in which commercial bank and central bank activities affect the stock of money is to trace the effects of their actions on assets and liabilities. The basic rule is that any change in assets must be matched by a corresponding change in liabilities

or an off-setting change in other assets, so that total assets always equal total liabilities.

Set up four columns for yourself, with the headings given below, and trace through the effects of the actions described. The first one has been completed for you.

Federal Reserve Banks		Commercial Bank System	
Assets	Liabilities	Assets	Liabilities
(1) +$10,000 govt. bonds	(4) +$10,000 reserve account	(3) +$10,000 reserve account	(2) +$10,000 checking account

(a) Paying by means of check, a Federal Reserve Bank purchases $10,000 worth of government bonds from a member of the public, who deposits the check in a commercial bank, which then sends the check to the Federal Reserve Bank for credit to its reserve account.
(b) A commercial bank extends a $5000 loan to a customer.
(c) A customer uses a $5000 loan to pay for a new car, writing a check to a car dealer, who deposits the check in a commercial bank.
(d) A car dealer withdraws $2000 in currency from a commercial bank, which then obtains more currency from a Federal Reserve Bank by drawing down its reserve account.

11. Many people worry about the size of the national debt. Suppose the Federal Reserve Banks bought up all outstanding marketable securities, so that – in a sense – the government only owed the debt to itself. How could this be done? What would happen as a result?
12. You're the manager of a commercial bank and you want to increase your bank's free reserves. Perhaps you currently have *negative* excess reserves – in which case your bank is borrowing from the Fed and the Fed may be putting pressure on you to remove that debt. Or you may simply believe that your bank would be in a more advantageous position with a somewhat higher level of free reserves. What policies could you pursue to reach your objective? What effects would these policies have on the banking and monetary system?
13. Why does the Fed use open-market operations as its principal tool of monetary management, rather than changes in legal-reserve requirements? What are the differences in the effects that each technique would have on individual banks, on the commercial banking system as a whole, and on the money supply?
14. Why might the Fed find it significantly easier to expand the money stock in a period of prosperity than in a period of recession? What must the Fed be able to do if it wants the quantity of money in the hands of the public to increase?
15. The narrowly defined money stock in the United States grew at an average annual rate of 4.1 percent during the 1960s, while nominal gross national

product was growing at an average rate of 7.1 percent. In the 1970s, the growth rate of M1 was 6.7 percent per year and the growth rate of nominal GNP was 10.4 percent.

(a) This question anticipates the analysis of the next two chapters – but do you think there is a causal connection between the higher growth rates of both M1 and nominal GNP in the 1970s?

(b) In the 1960s real GNP increased at an average annual rate of 4.3 percent; in the 1970s, at the rate of 3.5 percent. Is a higher rate of growth in nominal GNP desirable if it doesn't produce faster growth in real GNP?

16. The table below shows the average annual growth rates in the stock of money, nominal GNP, and real GNP in the 1960s and in the 1970s for five major nations.

(a) Are faster rates of money growth generally associated with faster rates of growth in nominal GNP?

(b) Are faster rates of growth in nominal GNP generally associated with faster rates of growth in real GNP?

	1960s			1970s		
	Money Stock	Nominal GNP	Real GNP	Money Stock	Nominal GNP	Real GNP
Canada	6.1%	8.5%	5.5%	10.8%	13.2%	4.4%
France	10.6	10.2	5.8	11.6	13.5	3.9
Japan	18.1	16.6	11.1	15.3	13.0	4.9
United Kingdom	3.0	6.4	3.0	12.6	15.9	2.3
West Germany	7.3	7.8	4.6	10.0	8.4	2.9

17. Commercial banks create money by extending loans. It's important that you see exactly why they can do this, and why money is ordinarily *not* created by the lending activities of other institutions.

(a) What is the advantage possessed by commercial banks that enables them to create money when they make loans? Credit unions and consumer credit companies do not have this advantage, and consequently do not create money when they extend loans to their customers. What do they lack that commercial banks have?

(b) Would you like to be able to make loans to your friends at will, simply by creating the money you lend them? You could help your friends, increase your popularity, and even earn a little interest if you could learn how to do this. What is the secret?

(c) Suppose everyone in town knows you, knows your signature, and trusts you completely. When a friend asks to borrow $10, you simply write a note saying, "I'll pay $10 to the holder of this note," sign it, and hand it to the friend. Will the friend be able to spend your note, that is, use it as money? Will the merchant who receives the note be able to spend it in turn, perhaps by giving it out in changing a $20 bill? Will you have succeeded in creating money? Would this differ from a situation in which a check you had written, payable to "Cash," circulated from hand to hand without being deposited?

(d) The narrowly defined money stock, or M1, is made up of Federal Reserve notes, checkable deposits, and travelers checks. All of these are liabilities of trusted financial institutions. What does a person or institution have to do to be able to create money?

(e) In February of 1983 the State of California made plans to begin paying some of its bills with IOUs, because the governor and the legislature were unable to agree on a budget. Could a state IOU function as money? Suppose you were a supplier to the state or someone due a tax refund, and you received in the mail an IOU instead of a check. Could you spend it? What might you do if you were desperate for cash and didn't want to wait for the governor and legislature to resolve their differences?

18. An article by Art Pine in *The Wall Street Journal* of March 29, 1984 described the giant stones used for almost 2000 years as money on the island of Yap in Micronesia.

(a) Because the stones are worthless when broken, people leave the larger ones where they are and simply take note of the fact that ownership has changed. How is this similar to paying by check?

(b) Some of the stones are propped up in rows in village "banks." Suppose that the person who lives next door to the "bank" is entrusted with the responsibility of keeping track of who owns what portion of each stone. How could this person use his position to make loans and thus expand the quantity of money?

19. Suppose you are in the grain exporting business and you sell $10,000 worth of wheat to Switzerland. The dollar-franc exchange rate is $1 for 1.5 francs, so the purchaser pays by writing you a check for 15,000 Swiss francs. How could you spend those francs without converting them into dollars and without leaving the United States? Under what circumstances might someone to whom you owe money prefer to be paid in Swiss francs rather than dollars? If Americans begin paying their bills with foreign currencies, do those currencies become part of the money stock in the United States?

20. *Fiat* is a Latin word meaning *let it become*. The term *fiat money* is sometimes used to describe paper money that is not backed by gold or anything else and that consequently has value merely because some authority has declared, "Let it become money."

(a) Is fiat money any less money than gold coins are? What kind of "authority" does it take to turn a "worthless piece of paper" into money?

(b) Are U.S. dollars money in Canada? Are Canadian dollars money in the United States? Why are U.S. dollars warmly welcomed by retailers in many countries of the world? Can you think of circumstances in which the people of a country would refuse to accept their own national currency in payment but would welcome payments made in U.S. dollars? What does all this indicate about the "authority" of governments that try to create fiat money?

21. If it is *not* essential that money have "backing" of some kind, why do so many people believe otherwise?
22. "Nature has made gold rare, but people have made it scarce." Explain.
23. Money gets a lot of attention but tends to have a bad press. Are the authors of the following statements talking about money as we have defined it? Or are they using money as a synonym or symbol for something else? What is that "something else" in each case where you conclude that money is not really the subject of discussion?

   (a) "The love of money is the root of all evil." (Often misquoted as "Money is the root of all evil.")
   (b) "Health is . . . a blessing that money cannot buy."
   (c) "If this be not love, it is madness, and then it is pardonable. Nay, yet a more certain sign than all this: I give thee my money."
   (d) "Wine maketh merry; but money answereth all things."
   (e) "Words are the tokens current and accepted for conceits, as moneys are for values."
   (f) "Money speaks sense in a language all nations understand."
   (g) "Americans are too interested in money."
   (h) "Protecting our natural environment is more important than making money."

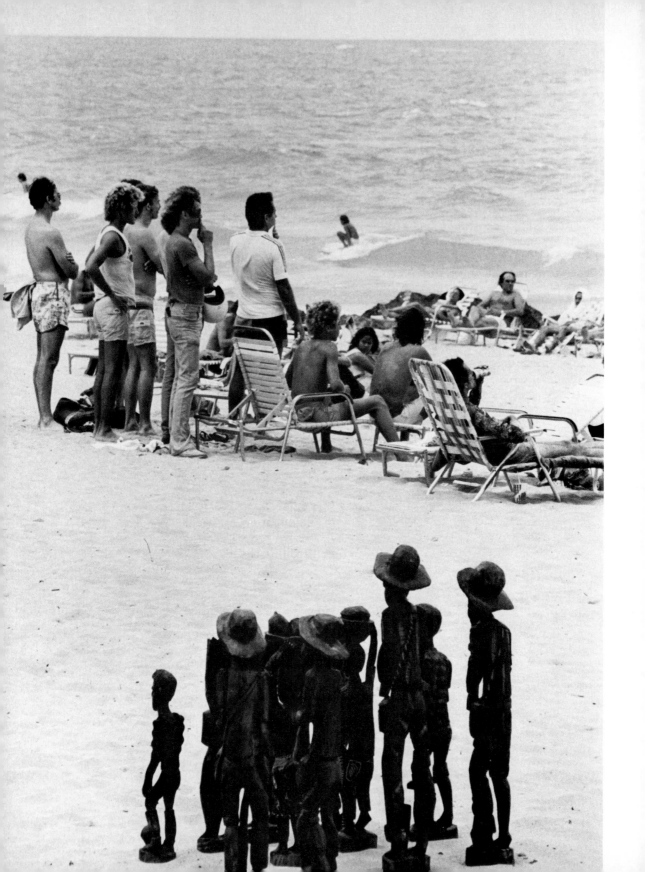

Chapter 18———————

Demand-Side Economics: Monetarist and Keynesian Perspectives

What happens when the quantity of money in the hands of the public increases or decreases? Do people increase their spending as they acquire larger money balances? Do they reduce their spending when the quantity of money available to them declines? How quickly do they respond? And what difference does it all make? These are questions that *monetarists* are inclined to ask, because they maintain that changes in the quantity of money, through their effect on total spending, or aggregate demand, are the principal cause of instability both in the price level and in total output.

Not all economists agree with that position. In the 1930s, largely as an outgrowth of ideas advanced by John Maynard Keynes, many economists adopted the view that aggregate demand could and did behave in a highly de-stabilizing manner without any prior change in the quantity of money. Keynesian economists consequently assigned much less importance than do monetarists to controlling the size of the money stock. They located the roots of instability elsewhere and expected less by way of control or cure from those responsible for managing the money supply.

Both monetarists and Keynesians, it should be noted, lay primary stress on aggregate demand. Because they find the key to stability in the control of aggregate demand, we can group them together as *demand-side economists*. In this chapter, our aim is to clarify the principal points of agreement and disagreement among demand-side economists. We begin with the monetarists.

The Monetarist Perspective: The Demand for Money

The key proposition in the monetarist position is *stability in the demand for money*. The phrase "demand for money" strikes most people as a little odd when they first hear it. The demand for anything, such as raspberry jam, usually

461

refers to the quantities people will want to purchase during a specified time period at various prices. At higher prices, people will shift toward substitutes for raspberry jam; at lower prices, they'll substitute raspberry jam more frequently for other goods. But what sense do those sentences make if we insert "money" in place of "raspberry jam"?.

They make excellent and important sense if we remember two things: (1) money is not the same as income; and (2) although demand for raspberry jam is a demand to acquire and consume, the demand for money is a demand to *hold* an asset, not to "consume" it.

Distinguishing Stocks from Flows

You will never understand the important concept of the demand for money if you identify money with money income. *Money income is a flow* and so must always be stated with reference to some time period: $4 per hour, $800 per month, $12,000 per year. But *money itself is a stock;* it is a certain amount in existence at some time. Because the size of the stock varies from day to day, we can measure it only with respect to some point in time. But it is *at a point* in time that we try to measure the size of a stock; we measure the size of a flow *during a period* of time.

Thus, an employee who says, "I'm going in to see the boss this afternoon and demand more money," really means that he or she is going to insist on more money income: a larger flow of money per month. That is *not* what we're talking about here. The amount of money that people hold (as a stock) will usually be related closely to the amount of money income they receive regularly (as a flow). But it's certainly possible for one to go up while the other is going down.

The way to understand this is to think it through. How much money, defined as M1, are you currently holding? In other words, what is the sum of your checking-account balance and the currency plus coin that you have in your pocket, purse, billfold, and bureau drawer? Whatever it is, what must you do in order to increase or decrease this amount? To decrease it, you must exchange money for other assets (we'll assume you don't lose it or throw it away). These assets could be anything from food for immediate consumption to shares of stock in AT&T. To increase the amount of M1 you're currently holding, you must give up other assets in exchange for currency or an addition to your checking-account balance (we'll rule out finding money or stealing it).

Now let's suppose you've been working 20 hours a week

for $4 an hour. You've been exchanging 20 hours of your time each week for $80, yielding a money income of $80 per week. Then you decide to spend more time studying, so you cut your work hours to 15 per week and your income to $60 per week. If at the same time you reduce your expenditures by more than $20 per week (you eliminate a lot of recreation activities, let's say, in order to increase your study time), you will be adding to the stock of money you hold, even though your income has decreased.

It all seems too obvious to summarize. But we're going to use these basic relationships, and they should be clear in your mind. People add to the stock of money they hold, to their money balances, by reducing their expenditures below their income or by exchanging other assets for money. They reduce their money balances by raising their expenditures above their income or exchanging money for other assets.

Why Do People Hold Money Balances?

The demand for money, we said, is a demand to *hold* money, not to consume it. Money isn't unique in this respect. Lots of goods yield services by being held: fine art, shares of stock, and houses are examples. The demand for all of them should be understood, therefore, as a demand to hold the good in question, not to "use it up." It's clear how paintings, corporate stock, and houses yield services by being held or owned. But isn't it true that money provides a service only when it's spent?

It is *not* true. Money does provide services when it's spent, which is why people want to hold money in the first place. They're looking forward to the enjoyment of what they expect the money to buy them. But money also provides a service while it is being held. If it did not, no one would hold it, because holding money is costly. While holding money we're sacrificing the valuable current services that other goods would yield us if we bought them with the money: the interest on a government bond, the pleasure of a Woody Allen movie, a comfortable armchair in which to relax. Since present goods are more valuable than future goods, why don't people immediately spend their money income when they receive it and maintain their stock of money balances at zero? They obviously don't do this. And that implies, correctly, that holding money yields a valuable service, a service valuable enough in comparison with the cost of holding money to persuade people to hold those amounts that they do hold.

Meat eaten per year is a flow. Meat in the freezer is a stock. The stock can be increased by purchasing more than is eaten for a time.

The desire to hold more meat in the freezer does not necessarily imply a desire to eat more meat per year.

That service, quite simply, is flexibility. By holding money rather than some other asset, you increase your freedom to maneuver. You make it easier for yourself to buy what you want when you want it, to take advantage of opportunities that you don't know about yet, or to escape from an unexpected misfortune. Moreover, you make these things possible for yourself without the trouble and expense of first taking a trip to the bank or making a visit to your stockbroker. A synonym for flexibility is *liquidity*, a concept introduced in the preceding chapter to describe money. An asset that can be exchanged at any time at its full value for any other asset is a completely liquid asset. Money is, by definition, the most liquid asset in a society. The demand for money is the demand for liquidity.

Actual and Preferred Money Balances

M is the quantity of money supplied and the quantity being held. Quantity actually held must equal M. Quantity public would prefer to hold may be greater or less than M.

Whatever the quantity of money the public *prefers* to hold, the quantity it *actually* holds will be the quantity supplied. This is a simple but important point to keep in mind. The size of the money stock at any time, however measured, will necessarily be equal to the quantity of money balances the public is holding at that time. But *actual money balances may not be equal to preferred money balances.* If the stock of money increased at a time when the public was satisfied with its current money holdings, some people would have to find themselves holding larger money balances than they preferred to hold. And so they would take steps to reduce their money balances back to the preferred level. If the money stock declined when people were holding their preferred amounts of money, they would try to raise their balances back up to the previous level. They would make these adjustments in the way we've already described, by changing the relationship between their incomes and their expenditures, or by changing the composition of their assets — exchanging corporate stock for money, perhaps, or money for government bonds.

When additional money is supplied to a public that is already holding the amount it prefers to hold, the public will attempt to exchange that additional money for other goods. This will increase the aggregate demand for goods other than money, including those newly produced goods that make up the gross national product. This increased demand will produce some combination of higher prices and larger output. Gross national product can thus be expected to increase in response to an increase in demand for new goods that was prompted in turn by an increase in the quantity of money supplied to a public already holding its preferred amount of money balances. GNP will continue to rise in this way as long as spending for new goods keeps increasing. And spending will continue to increase as long as people are still holding more money than they want to hold.

Notice that the attempt by individuals to reduce their money holdings by increasing their expenditures adds to the money holdings of others; it doesn't reduce the money stock. The public's attempt to reduce its money balances can't succeed, because all the money that's supplied must be held by someone. What happens instead is that the attempt to reduce actual money balances to the level of preferred money balances causes total income to rise, until the public prefers to hold money balances equal to the quantity that has been supplied.

This way of putting it is somewhat misleading, because it suggests that people are *coerced* into holding the quantity of money that the monetary authorities, in conjunction with the banking system, supply. That's not true, of course. The money supply increases when commercial banks increase their loans. More loans mean people who *wanted to borrow* now have the ready money they were looking for. Surely they didn't borrow money and agree to pay interest on it in order to let that money sit idly in their bank accounts. They'll spend it, for whatever they had in mind when they borrowed.

Let's suppose it's a couple that borrowed in order to buy new living-room furniture. When they make the purchase, they transfer the amount that the bank had credited to their checking account to the owners of the furniture store. What do the furniture retailers do in turn? They *don't* say: "Drat! Here we were happily holding the quantity of money we preferred to hold. Then that inconsiderate couple stuck us with this extra money. Now we're going to have to waste our time figuring out a way to get rid of it. Do we know anybody we can dump it on?" Instead they say: "Great! We sold a couch and two chairs. Business is good. Our furniture inventory is down, however, so we'd better use this new money to replenish our stock." And so they (joyfully!) pass the money on to their suppliers, who accept it, also joyfully, and repeat the thinking of the furniture retailers.

The logic of it all is quite simple and really rather obvious once you think it through. More money produces more spending, which produces rising incomes until people become willing to hold that additional amount of money. At

The attempt to exchange money for other assets increases nominal GNP. The quantity of money the public wants to hold increases when nominal GNP increases. Nominal GNP increases until the public is willing to hold the quantity of money supplied by the Fed.

that point, GNP stops increasing. *The key assumption* that makes it all work is that *the quantity of money the public prefers to hold and will attempt to hold is some stable fraction of money income or expenditures.*

Why the Demand for Money May Change

Monetarists don't claim that the demand for money never changes. They readily admit that it will change in response to changing financial practices, such as greater use of credit cards or telephone transfer systems that make it easy to switch funds from one kind of bank deposit to another. But financial practices usually evolve somewhat slowly, as a result of which changes in the public's preferences with respect to money balances also occur slowly. That's still consistent with a *stable* demand for money.

Monetarists also don't claim that the quantity of money the public wants to hold is completely inelastic with respect to the rate of return on financial assets. If the rate of return one can obtain on safe and liquid financial assets rises, the opportunity cost of holding cash rather than some of these other assets goes up. And when the cost of holding money increases, people will want to hold somewhat less. It follows, then, that if the Fed brought down interest rates by making more credit available to commercial banks and the public, the quantity of money balances the public would want to hold would increase. Monetarists concede this. They simply don't believe that this is a major influence on the fraction of income and expenditures the public will want to hold in money balances. It doesn't invalidate their basic working assumption that the public wants to hold money balances equal to some stable fraction of nominal gross national product.

Monetarists certainly do not claim that the demand for money will remain stable in the face of any and all changes in the behavior of the monetary authorities. If a lot more money is suddenly supplied to the public, the value or purchasing power of money is eventually going to fall. People know that. At least many of them do. And when people expect the value of any asset they're holding to take a large tumble, they try to unload the asset before that happens. In short, people will become less willing to hold money balances when they anticipate an increase in the inflation rate. Conversely, they will want to hold larger balances if they decide the inflation rate is going to decrease significantly.

The implication of all this is that the public will try to

The demand for money depends upon its expected value.

If people expect its value to decline rapidly, they will not want to hold money.

hold money balances equal to some fairly stable fraction of nominal gross national product as long as those who control the supply of money behave in a moderate and responsible way. The monetarist thesis, in short, is that when the aggregate demand (for goods) changes in some drastic and destabilizing way, the suppliers of money, not the demanders, are responsible.

The villains in the monetarist drama are the suppliers of the money.

How Stable Is the Demand for Money?

How accurate is this thesis? That turns out to be one of the main issues separating monetarists from Keynesians. Unfortunately, it's not an easy question to settle. If the demand for money is basically stable, as monetarists aver, then aggregate demand will be stable as long as the monetary authorities prevent the money supply from behaving in a destabilizing fashion. The task of the monetary authorities then becomes to maintain a steady, modest, and predictable rate of growth in bank reserves and the money supply.

If, however, the demand for money is subject to sudden and sizable shifts, then the economy may be inherently unstable. Aggregate demand will be subject to large, unpredictable changes, and both the price level and real output are likely to bounce about in damaging ways. On this view the government may be called on to exercise a substantial role in offsetting destabilizing changes in aggregate demand that originate in the private sector.

If we were to find that the money stock, however measured, is always the same fraction of nominal GNP, from month to month and year to year, the monetarist case would be pretty well established. We could safely assume that the demand for money is stable and we could begin looking elsewhere to find an explanation for observed fluctuations in the price level and in output. In actual fact, the measured ratio of the money stock to GNP has not been constant, over the short run or the long run. And in the 1930s, it rose suddenly and substantially, as aggregate spending collapsed, the price level fell, and real GNP tumbled. Was this rise in the demand for money the cause of the Great Depression?

The Great Depression

It was the Great Depression of the 1930s that decisively turned the attention of economists and policymakers toward the problem of aggregate demand. Half a century later, much of our thinking about recession, unemployment, and even inflation is still shaped by the experiences of the Great Depression. Anyone who lived through the 1930s will readily understand how the events of a single decade could have such an enduring impact.

For four successive years, beginning in 1930, real output and income declined. It declined by huge amounts: 9 percent in 1930, 8 percent in 1931, 14 percent in 1932, and another 2 percent in 1933. Compare that record with the performance of the U.S. economy since World War II as summarized in Table 16A. On only one occasion has total output declined in two successive years: it fell in 1974 and again in 1975. But the percentage declines were only 0.5 percent and 1.3 percent, almost unnoticeable by the standards of the Great Depression.

Moreover, a full recovery never occurred in the 1930s. In the three years after the 1974–75 recession, output increased by about 5 percent per year, quickly making up the ground lost during the recession. But six years after the trough of the Great Depression was finally reached in 1933, total output and income were only 1.5 percent above what they had been in 1929. With a larger population in 1939 than in 1929, that tiny increase in output and income over the decade was far below what would have been required just to restore predepression levels of prosperity. The per-capita after-tax income of Americans actually fell by 7 percent from 1929 to 1939. (It had fallen by almost 30 percent from 1929 to 1933.) The Great Depression even featured a recession within a depression, as real output and income dropped 4 percent from 1937 to 1938.

The most vividly remembered experience of those who lived through the 1930s, however, is the experience of massive, stubborn unemployment. If we leave out 1930, when unemployment was still growing, the unemployment rates of the 1930s averaged more than 19 percent. That is almost one out of every five members of the labor force. At the bottom of the recession, in 1933, 25 percent of the labor force was officially counted as unemployed.

The depth of the recession from 1929 to 1933 was unprecedented in U.S. history. Just as unsettling, however, was the persistent failure of the economy to recover fully after the decline ended. Economists had long known about recessions. They had even made some progress toward understanding why they occurred and what might be done to reduce their severity. But a basic assumption in all theorizing about recessions was that they were temporary disturbances. Recessions were the consequence of mistaken decisions based on misleading or erroneous expectations, and they quickly ran their course as those mistakes were corrected. When the corrections had been made, recovery was supposed to begin and carry total output and income to new heights. Recessions were viewed as temporary interruptions within an overall pattern of long-term growth. The experience of the 1930s raised grave doubts, for obvious reasons, about the adequacy of that analysis.

Keynes and *The General Theory*

One man did so much to crystallize economists' rethinking of recessions during and after the 1930s that his name was attached to the "new economics" that emerged. John Maynard Keynes (rhymes with *gains*) was a British economist who lived from 1883 to 1946. He enjoyed a brilliant and diversified career as investor, editor, teacher, writer, government servant, and architect of systems for the reconstructing of international finance. But he is chiefly remembered today as the author of a book published at the beginning of 1936, entitled *The General Theory of Employment, Interest and Money*.

The General Theory, to give it the abbreviated title by which it's usually known, is by common agreement an obscure and badly organized book. "What *The General Theory* Means" was a topic for innumerable essays and symposia in the years immediately following its publication, evidence that its message was deemed important, but that no one quite knew what the essential message was. Books and articles about what Keynes *really* meant continue to appear today, more than half a century after the publication of *The General Theory*. But consensus at least exists on this much: Keynes believed that the traditional approach of economists to the question of recession came close to assuming the problem away, and that modern industrial economies such as those of Great Britain or the United States did not incline automatically toward full employment.

Order and Disorder in Economic Systems

One of the characteristics of economic theory about which Keynes had misgivings was its tendency to be *a theory of orderly coordination*. But if recessions resulted from a breakdown of the coordinative mechanism, no satisfactory explanation or remedy for recessions would be obtained from a theory which *assumed* that the mechanism was working adequately.

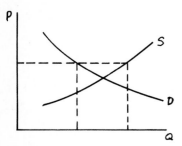

Traditional economic analysis looked on recessions as periods of temporary surplus, for that seems to be what we observe in a recession. Workers are unable to find jobs and products cannot be sold; the quantities of labor and produced goods being supplied are greater than the quantities currently demanded. The economist's ordinary solution to a surplus is a lower price. If workers can't find jobs, it's because they're holding out for a wage that's above their value to employers; at some lower wage all those who want work will be able to find it. If producers can't sell their entire output, it's again because they're asking too high a price; useful goods can always be sold at a sufficiently low price. It's a matter of supply and demand. A recession is simply a temporary disequilibrium. It will come to an end when prices and wages move to their equilibrium or market-clearing levels.

But how long will this take? It only happens instantaneously on the supply and demand graphs of economists. In the real world, market-clearing prices must be searched for, and that process may take weeks, months, or even longer. In the interim the world doesn't stand still. Unemployed workers reduce their spending because they're no longer receiving income, which further reduces the demand for goods. Producers who find themselves with unwanted additions to their inventories cut back production, laying off more workers and reducing the demand for the other goods they use as inputs. Might not an excess supply of labor and produced goods cause a downward spiral in income and demand before prices had fallen far enough to eliminate the surpluses? In that case, prices would have to fall still further to close the gap between supply and demand. Don't recessions, in fact, display just such a cumulative pattern of declining production, reduced income, further declines in production, and further reduced income?

The timeless equilibrium analysis of the traditional economics in which Keynes had been trained did not examine the groping process by which new equilibrium positions are found. It assumed, in effect, an instantaneous leap to a new equilibrium whenever an old equilibrium was disturbed. But if the causes of recessions are to be found in what happens while the economy is out of equilibrium, then the traditional analysis had indeed assumed the problem away.

The importance of expectations in shaping economic decisions also impressed Keynes very strongly. An emphasis on expectations meant an emphasis on the uncertainty of decision making, the frequency of mistakes, the need for time in which to adjust to unanticipated events, and the disorder of economic systems. None of this was captured in the timeless, orderly, errorless world of traditional equilibrium analysis. In *The General Theory* Keynes sought to explain the phenomenon of recession by taking into account the consequences of uncertainty and the processes of adjustment over time. That led him to focus on aggregate demand.

The Unstable Force: Investment Spending

The initiating cause of aggregate fluctuations in output and income, in the Keynesian framework, is a change in the desired rate of investment expenditure.

Recall what investment means. To invest is to purchase a good for the sake of the future income it is expected to yield. A business firm is investing, therefore, when it purchases machinery, just as you would be investing if you purchased corporate stock. But we must distinguish between those two kinds of investment, because we're interested now in investment as a process of adding to the demand for new goods, for gross national product. Your purchase of corporate stock would merely be a transfer of financial assets. Even if you bought *new* stock, issued so that the corporation could purchase additional machinery, your surrender of money to acquire stock would be a financial transfer only. The real investment would occur when the new machinery was produced and sold to the corporation that you supplied with funds. Investment in this sense is one of the four components of total expenditures on gross national product — along with household consumption expenditures, government purchases of new commodities and services, and net exports.

Investment is extremely important for the understanding of recessions, in the Keynesian analysis, because investment spending is far less stable than consumption spending. There's no mystery about why that should be the case. It's usually easier to postpone the purchase of capital goods than to postpone the purchase of consumer goods. People are therefore likely to maintain consumption spending at a fairly steady rate, but to "bunch" investment spending at what they consider appropriate times. Moreover, the purchase of any good that's expected to yield its services over a long period of time entails additional uncertainty. Will the stream of services turn out to be as large as it's currently expected to be? Will some new method of securing these services appear soon and make this investment obsolete? Will a more opportune time come along later, perhaps a time when funds can be borrowed more cheaply or when capital-goods producers are offering lower prices? Continually changing conditions can act on the uncertain expectations of investors to produce waves of postponed or accelerated investment expenditures.

Are Fluctuations Self-Correcting?

There was nothing unusual in 1936 about focusing on investment decisions as the principal trigger of economic fluctuations. The big question was and still is: What happens next? *Does the economic system moderate or does it magnify the initial effects* of the change in investment expenditures? Most economists up to the time of Keynes believed that the economic system operated to check and reverse destabilizing decisions. Keynes found it more probable, at least in mature industrial economies, that the system would magnify disturbances and would demonstrate little capacity to generate a recovery from recessions. Which view is correct?

Almost anyone looking back from 1939 at the performance of the American economy over the previous decade would incline toward the Keynesian view. Whatever forces were supposed to arrest a decline in output and income certainly didn't seem to be working from 1929 to 1933. And if a recession was indeed a time for correcting mistakes, after which growth could resume again on a sounder basis, the payoff seemed terribly slow in coming.

Let's look at some of the stabilizing forces that were supposed to dampen recessions and initiate recoveries, then at Keynes' reasons for doubting their effectiveness. One such force was falling prices. Recessions had historically meant a falling price level, or a rising value for money. When people *expect* prices to fall, they become more eager to hold money. But once prices *have* fallen, the real value of the public's money balances is larger. Moreover, prices that have already fallen will be more widely expected to rise than to fall further. These two situations brought about by a recession — larger money holdings in terms of purchasing power and an increased expectation of rising prices — should prompt people to begin reducing their money balances by increasing their rate of expenditures above their incomes. This will bring about recovery.

But suppose the recession produces a sizable fall in output with very little change in prices? The public will still find its stock of money balances growing, relative to income and expenditures. At some point the public will decide it's holding all the money it wants to hold, in view of the lower

If prices will fall, postpone purchases until goods are cheaper.

If prices have fallen, purchase now while goods are cheap.

gross national product, and will begin exchanging money for other goods. This will launch a recovery.

A decline in investment spending also implies less demand for loans, which in turn implies a decrease in the cost of borrowing. But as the cost of borrowing falls, the incentive to invest increases. Some investment projects that had been postponed will now be undertaken in response to better credit terms, and aggregate investment will revive. This will promote recovery.

The idle resources that begin to appear in a recession also provide opportunities for entrepreneurs who were waiting for the right location, a favorable lease, or more advantageous terms from suppliers. Thus, the recession itself encourages new initiatives, increased production, and additional investment. All this works to slow down the decline in a recession and generate a recovery.

Keynesian Doubts

Keynes had reasons for suspecting that none of these countering forces would be sufficient, especially in a wealthy, industrialized economy. To begin with, prices might not fall in response to decreased demand. The market power of larger sellers, the wage-fixing practices of labor unions, and the existence of long-term contracts all tend to put a floor under the existing level of prices. With prices rigid in a downward direction, decreases in aggregate demand would not raise the purchasing power of money. Decreases in demand would operate almost exclusively to reduce total output.

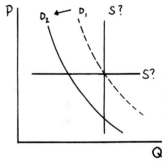

Another objection: although it is true that the public's money holdings increase when its expenditures decrease, that assumes other things remain equal. But they don't remain equal if income falls as fast as expenditures. And a reduction in total output entails a simultaneous reduction in total income, since people receive their income from the sale of what they produce.

If the stock of money doesn't change while gross national product is falling, the ratio between the public's cash balances and its income will rise, of course. But this doesn't necessarily mean the public will find itself holding larger money balances than it *prefers* to hold. Here is another Keynesian reason to doubt the self-stabilizing process: the demand for money might increase substantially because of the public's apprehension about the coming recession and the expectation that the value of money is going to increase.

The lower interest rates and other reduced costs that

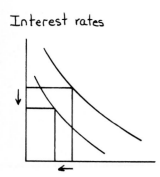

Interest rates

Investment expenditures

Will interest rates fall far enough and fast enough in a recession to compensate for the collapse of investors' confidence?

recessions usually bring in their wake do indeed tend to spur investment and production. But will their combined effect be enough to offset the gloomy expectations that recession creates? How much stimulus is a one-point reduction in the interest rate to entrepreneurs who fear that there will be no demand for their output?

Some of the most interesting passages in *The General Theory* present Keynes' thoughts (usually quite unsystematic) on the importance of expectations. It is expectations, as you know by now, that guide economic decisions. The relevant expectations will not be based exclusively on the decisionmakers' appraisals of their own particular prospects. Larger and more vague considerations will also enter in, such as the state of the economy, the political climate, the social milieu, and even (as Keynes suggests in one place) the nerves, hysteria, digestions, and reactions to the weather of potential investors.

Expectations and the state of confidence were especially important to Keynes' interpretation of the role that money played (or failed to play) in restraining a recession and promoting a recovery. Remember that the monetary authorities can increase the excess reserves of the banking system but cannot compel the commercial banks to extend loans and thereby turn those reserves into money. Moreover, the creation of a larger money stock will not produce an increase in spending if the public responds simply by building up its money balances.

In a recession, everyone tends to become more pessimistic and more cautious. Banks scrutinize potential borrowers more rigorously before extending loans and refuse to renew some loans that come due. Borrowers are less eager to apply for loans because short-term profit prospects seem unfavorable. People look for ways to increase their liquidity as a precautionary move. The expectation of declining prices also adds to the public's preference for holding money rather than assets whose value relative to money is likely to fall. In short, a recession can create a crisis of confidence that worsens the recession by prompting a sharp increase in the demand for money. The monetary authorities may find it difficult to satisfy this demand or to induce people to begin spending their idle balances. In these circumstances, efforts by the central bank to halt a recession or to spur a recovery will be like pushing on a string. "Pushing on a string" became, in fact, a common way of characterizing the impotence of monetary authorities in dealing with recessions.

The conclusions seemed rather clear to most observers by the end of the 1930s. Relatively small changes in demand can trigger substantial changes in output and employment. The cumulative interaction of expenditures, output, income, and expectations can transform minor disturbances into major disruptions, because the economic system does not contain stabilizing forces of sufficient strength. The adjustments of consumers, investors, and producers to changed circumstances don't necessarily push the economy back toward full employment when it begins to slip toward recession. On the contrary, the economy can settle down indefinitely at a rate of output far below capacity and with high unemployment.

The radical departure in the Keynesian way of looking at the world lies in the specific assumptions that were made, not always explicitly, by those who adopted the Keynesian framework. Almost all these assumptions touch on the issue of *coordination*. Does the market economy transmit information smoothly and quickly enough to limit and dampen the effects of destabilizing decisions? Or does it aggravate the effects of such decisions by sending out signals that induce people to make things worse for others in an effort to make things better for themselves, with the eventual consequence that things are worse for almost everyone? The Keynesian attitude toward saving provides perhaps the best example of such a contrast in basic presuppositions.

Saving and Economic Growth

Keynes himself liked to emphasize his theory's implications for the way we regard the act of saving, of refraining from the consumption of income. In the Keynesian perspective, saving is not the unmixed blessing that economists have traditionally assumed it to be. If intended investment falls, the attempt by savers to continue their current rate of saving will prevent consumption expenditure from picking up the slack. The result will be unsold goods, reduced output, and reduced incomes — until savers have been compelled by falling income to scale down their rate of saving to what investors want to spend. This comes close to reversing the traditional argument that high rates of saving are necessary to permit high rates of investment.

It has long been a fundamental tenet of economics that a nation's income and wealth grow roughly in proportion to the growth in its stock of capital. Investment is the process that adds to the capital stock. A higher rate of investment therefore means a faster rate of economic growth, a more rapid rise in national income, and a speedier improvement in living levels. But what determines the rate of investment? The classical answer was: the rate of saving. There is no way for a society to produce capital goods except by withdrawing some of its resources from the production of consumer goods. Those who save abstain from current consumption and either purchase capital goods themselves or turn their income over to others who purchase capital goods. Without saving there can be no investment. (If investment is financed by borrowing from abroad, foreigners must do the saving.) The incentive to save must therefore be preserved and extended, according to the classical argument; it is the root cause of social progress.

Keynes suspected that this line of reasoning might be altogether inapplicable to societies in advanced stages of economic growth. Economic growth, Keynes believed, had two effects that jointly made the practice of thrift an increasingly doubtful virtue. On the one hand, the accumulation of capital in the course of economic growth meant that the most profitable investment opportunities were steadily used up. Further additions to the capital stock had to go toward projects with lower expected rates of return for investors. The incentive to invest consequently tended to fall as economic growth proceeded. (Little thought was given to the possibility that *new* investment opportunities might appear, an omission that reflects the static and pessimistic outlook dominant in the 1930s.)

On the other hand, the incentive to save tended to become stronger. Saving, Keynes maintained, depends primarily on income. People will tend to save more as their income rises and will in fact tend to save a higher proportion of their income as that income increases. Because economic growth increases people's incomes, therefore, it increases the amounts that they desire to save relative to their income.

The implication is that in wealthy, industrialized economies the desire to save will be continually pushing out ahead of the desire to invest. But if people wish to save a larger amount than investors are willing to spend, the savers can't succeed. Their purpose will be frustrated by an insufficient aggregate demand, which will lead to lower output and higher unemployment, until the reduced incomes of savers finally persuade them to save no more than investors are willing to spend.

Demand-Side and Supply-Side Analysis

The classical argument on this issue has been revived in recent years under the title "supply-side economics," a title intended as a criticism of the Keynesian emphasis on aggregate demand. Both sides agree that higher real incomes and more employment opportunities depend on adequate rates of investment. But after that, they diverge. "Supply-siders" insist that the way to get increased investment spending is to enhance the incentive to save. Keynes, by contrast, argued that saving would take care of itself if only the level of investment spending could be maintained. And for that purpose, enhanced incentives to save were worse than useless. The solution lay in maintaining the demand for goods so that investors would want to purchase capital equipment.

From the Keynesian perspective, a chronic tendency toward insufficient demand, created by persistent efforts to save more than investors want to spend, might so damage the "state of confidence" that the aggregate desire to invest actually decreased. Here would be a strange outcome indeed, one that came to be known as the "paradox of thrift" among those who thought that the 1930s had shown it to be a genuine threat to prosperity. An increased desire to save so damages the incentive to invest that output and income fall below the level at which savers can even maintain their previously desired rate of saving. The attempt to save more results in less actual saving. The public would actually succeed in increasing the amount it saves if it determined to save less — and thus spent more.

This would not mean, it's important to note, that anyone can save more by spending more. And that's what counts. A household or business firm that wants to increase its rate of saving will not achieve that end by reducing its rate of saving. The paradox of thrift applies to the actions of savers and investors as a whole. But saving and investment decisions are not made by "wholes." They are made by persons who don't assume — and quite correctly don't assume — that their own actions will induce others to behave in the same way.

The Coordination Problem Once Again

That brings us back to the question of *coordination*. When you think about it for a moment, you realize that almost every single action within an economic system depends for

Keynes: Demand will create supply:

"Supply-siders": Supply will create demand.

The traditional perspective:

INCOME → CONSUMPTION
INCOME → SAVINGS
SAVINGS → INVESTMENT
INVESTMENT → HIGHER OUTPUT AND INCOME

The Keynesian perspective:

INCOME → CONSUMPTION
INCOME → SAVINGS
SAVINGS → LESS DEMAND
LESS DEMAND → LOWER OUTPUT AND INCOME

its success on cooperative behavior on the part of other people. There's no earthly point to an author's struggling to explain Keynesian economics unless many, many other people completely unknown to him are going to cooperate later: editors, printers, sales representatives, postal clerks, professors, bookstores, and students, to mention just a few. Moreover, an author knows that his own efforts will not, by themselves, induce the required cooperation. Nonetheless, he sits at his desk struggling with words, when he would much rather be out playing tennis, because he believes that the system will work. The right people will somehow get the appropriate signals and the book will eventually be produced, marketed, and — here belief becomes hope — purchased in gratifying quantities.

Keynes feared that the system would *not* "work" when it came to the task of coordinating the decisions of savers and the decisions of investors. He feared that aggregate demand might be chronically insufficient in advanced industrial economies, with high levels of unemployment as the consequence. But he offered more than a gloomy diagnosis. He also offered suggestions for a cure. If the private sector was unwilling to invest enough to maintain full employment, government could take steps to close the gap.

That leads us to the consideration of monetary and fiscal policy, the topic for Chapter 19. In the course of the chapter, we will also examine the monetarists' "counterrevolution" and their case for the essential stability of the demand for money.

Once Over Lightly

Economists who emphasize the importance of controlling aggregate demand as a way of achieving high employment with price stability may be usefully divided into monetarists and Keynesians.

Monetarists claim that, because the demand for money is basically stable, the key to a stable economy is stability in the rate at which money is supplied to the economy.

Given a stable demand for money, increases in the quantity of money raise the aggregate demand for goods, and decreases in the quantity of money reduce aggregate demand.

These changes in aggregate demand are the principal cause of fluctuations in output, employment, and the price level, according to the monetarists.

Keynesians point to the Great Depression as evidence that the economy is not inherently stable in the absence of disturbing changes in the money supply. In the Keynesian perspective, disturbances arise from the inherent instability of private-sector spending decisions, especially decisions affecting investment expenditures.

These disturbances are magnified by the functioning of markets, producing large cyclical swings in economic activity and the possibility of semipermanent economic collapse.

In the Keynesian view, aggregate demand may be chronically insufficient to maintain high levels of output and employment. In such circumstances, acts of saving will retard economic growth by removing some demand-side stimulus. This view directly contradicts the classical position, according to which aggregate demand is always adequate and saving accelerates economic growth by allowing further investment in productivity-enhancing capital goods.

Questions for Discussion

1. Analogies must be used with care. But this one may help you visualize the major relationships between the two flows of income and of expenditures and the stock of money. Imagine a lake formed by a dammed-up river. Let the lake represent the stock of money someone is holding. The river above the lake represents income, the river below the lake represents expenditures.

   (a) What must be done to raise or to lower the lake level?
   (b) How could the lake level be raised, even though the flow above the lake is declining? How could the lake level be lowered, even though the flow above the lake is increasing?
   (c) If the dam operator anticipates a late-summer drought and wants to prevent the lake from falling below some desired level, what might be done during the spring?

2. What is the good that people want to obtain more of when they decide to increase the quantity of money they are going to hold?

   (a) What are the major factors you consider in deciding how large you want your stock of money balances to be? What sorts of events would induce you to increase or decrease your preferred stock of money balances?
   (b) What other assets function for you as partial substitutes for money balances?
   (c) What are some of the assets that business firms might choose to hold as partial substitutes for money balances?
   (d) Is a good credit rating an asset that someone might use as a substitute for money balances? Is that what people do when they start off on a

trip carrying little currency but a credit card with a large credit limit and a small current balance?

3. You want to buy a used sailboat if the right one comes along at the right price. You think you'll be able to get a better deal if you can offer the seller immediate cash. What are some good options for you to consider as alternatives to holding M1 while you're searching for the sailboat?

4. Some people think that consumers could stop inflation if they launched a consumer strike against higher prices.

   (a) What would happen to your stock of money balances if you decided to do your part in fighting inflation by reducing your expenditures?
   (b) How likely is it that large numbers of people will choose their preferred level of money balances by neglecting their personal interests and considering instead the contribution they might make to stopping inflation?
   (c) What would happen to the value of your stock of money balances if you did this and inflation continued?

5. Would money function as a medium of exchange if people were unwilling to hold it, even for very short periods of time? Is there any difference between a barter economy and an economy in which people hold no money balances?

6. What effect would you expect each of the following to have on the average size of the checking account balances that business firms and households want to hold?

   (a) An unusually high rate of expenditures is anticipated in the near future.
   (b) The rate of interest on savings accounts rises.
   (c) Banks offer to provide checking account services at no fee on accounts that maintain a $400 minimum balance during any month.
   (d) Banks pay interest on checking accounts.
   (e) The monetary authorities increase the quantity of money rapidly over an extended period of time and the public begins to anticipate a high rate of inflation.

7. We describe the demand for most goods by referring to prices and the number of units that would be demanded at those prices. But economists describe the demand for money by referring to the price (or cost) of holding money and *some percentage of income.*

   (a) Why is the quantity demanded expressed as a percentage in the case of money, rather than as a number of units?
   (b) Would you be willing to say that someone's demand for money had not changed if that person held the same quantity of dollars when his money income had doubled and the purchasing power of dollars had fallen 50 percent?

8. Suppose that every household and business firm decided to spend on Tuesday every dollar it was holding.

  (a) What would be the effect on the stock of money balances held on Wednesday by households and business firms?

  (b) What other effects would you predict from such a mass decision to unload money balances?

  (c) Suppose this decision resulted from a sudden conviction that money was going to be worthless by the end of the week. What do you think would happen?

9. Assume that the public wants to hold money balances, in the form of M1, equal to one-sixth of nominal gross national product.

  (a) How large will GNP have to be to persuade the public to hold $800 billion of M1?

  (b) If M1 rises by $10 billion, by how much will GNP have to rise to induce the public to hold this additional amount of money?

  (c) Will this increase in GNP mean greater prosperity?

10. Anyone who reads extensively in economic history will encounter periodic complaints from merchants about a *scarcity of money* in the hands of the public.

  (a) What observations by a merchant might prompt such a complaint?

  (b) What might cause a widespread increase in the incidence of such complaints from merchants?

  (c) Why do you suppose it is that so many merchants throughout history have associated an abundance of money with prosperity and a scarcity of it with hard times?

  (d) If more money in the possession of a particular merchant's customers will produce prosperity for that merchant, will more money in everyone's hands produce greater prosperity for all merchants?

11. What effect does inflation have on the value of people's money balances? What will happen if the monetary authorities, in an effort to maintain the real value of the public's money holdings, increase the stock of money when inflation occurs?

12. What caused the recession that began in the United States in 1929? Why did the decline continue for four years? Why did the decline occur at such a steep rate? Why did real output not regain its 1929 level until 1939? Why did the unemployment rate remain so extraordinarily high throughout the 1930s? Why has no recession or depression of even remotely comparable severity occurred since World War II? (Substantial disagreement still exists among economic theorists and economic historians on how these questions are to be answered. How one evaluates the long-run importance of Keynes's contribution to economic theory will depend largely on the answers given to these questions.)

13. Can an economy be in equilibrium if much of its industrial capacity is standing idle and a large percentage of its labor force is unemployed? Is that a question about fact or a disguised argument about the proper way to use the concept of equilibrium?

14. Suppose that consumer demand for the following goods turns out to be less than the producers anticipated, so that the goods already produced cannot all be sold at current prices. What consequences would you predict in the case of each good? Would prices or production levels be likely to fall first? How long will the sequence of adjustments take?

    (a) Automobiles.
    (b) Beef cattle.
    (c) Secondary-school teachers.

15. How long must a recession continue or a recovery be delayed before we're justified in assuming that recessions are not *temporary* disturbances?

16. If total expenditures on new goods fall below total income, so that aggregate saving increases, what happens to these savings?

17. Consumer expenditures on durable goods fluctuate far more from year to year than do consumer expenditures on nondurable commodities or services. How does this support the contention that investment expenditures are less stable than consumption expenditures?

18. Do fluctuations in spending for particular goods necessarily cause fluctuations in the output of those goods? Do you think that production rates in the toy industry fluctuate as much as consumer expenditures for toys fluctuate? Under what circumstances can a smooth flow of production be reconciled with variations in expenditure on that output? When are reductions in expenditure most likely to cause production cutbacks and unemployment in a particular firm or industry?

19. The following questions all deal with the relationship between investment and interest rates.

    (a) How do interest rates affect investment spending?
    (b) How do higher interest rates affect residential construction?
    (c) "Shall we maintain production and allow our inventories of unsold goods to rise or should we shut down production until we've managed to sell off most of the finished goods now in the warehouses?" How might the level of interest rates enter into this decision?
    (d) An electric utility postpones construction of a new generating plant because the market price of its bonds is disappointingly low. How does this illustrate the relationship between investment and the interest rate?
    (e) A corporation plans to begin a huge capital expansion program, using proceeds from a sale of new stock. But common-stock prices decline and the firm postpones the stock sale and the investment program it was intended to finance. Does that have anything to do with interest rates?
    (f) "Higher interest rates don't deter any business firm that has a profitable use for the money. If we can make 30 percent on an investment, we're going to invest whether we can borrow at 3 percent or have to pay 12 percent." Evaluate this statement.

(g) "The higher the interest rate I can get, the more I'm going to invest. Investment increases as interest rates rise." Is that a correct argument?

(h) "Interest rates tend to be higher in booms than in recessions. But investment spending is usually greater in booms than in recessions. This implies that high interest rates encourage investment spending and low interest rates discourage it." Criticize that argument.

20. Does investment depend on saving? Can investment occur if there has been no saving? What are the real differences between the older view that investment could be maintained only by maintaining saving and Keynes' view that a high rate of investment might be a precondition for a high rate of saving?

21. Does the "paradox of thrift" imply that saving is an antisocial act and consumption an act that benefits society?

22. Congress cut tax rates substantially in 1964. A long period of rising output and falling unemployment followed. Did the tax cuts work by stimulating consumer spending — the "demand-side" claim? Or did they work by offering investors better after-tax returns — the "supply-side" claim?

23. In the following passage from Adam Smith's *The Wealth of Nations*, the word *stock* refers either to a stock of goods or to a stock of money that can be used to acquire goods.

> In all countries where there is tolerable security, every man of common understanding will endeavor to employ whatever stock he can command, in procuring either present enjoyment or future profit. . . . A man must be perfectly crazy who, where there is tolerable security, does not employ all the stock which he commands [in one of these ways].

(a) Does this passage imply that all income will be either consumed or invested?

(b) Is this passage compatible with Keynes' analysis of the saving–investment relationship?

Chapter 19

Fiscal and
Monetary Policy

It all seems quite simple and straightforward when you first begin to think about it. Government can stop recessions and prevent inflations by using its power to affect the flow of total spending. Surely everyone agrees that government has that power. And if it has the power, it ought to use it. Why should people suffer from unemployment or rising prices when government knows how to prevent them?

It's all so clear and obvious *until* you begin thinking about it more carefully and concretely. Then uncertainties, problems, and contradictions start to appear and multiply rapidly, until in the end you may find yourself suspecting that government actually has very little power to prevent inflation or recession but an enormous capacity to create or aggravate these problems.

Aggregate-Demand Management

The topic of this chapter is *aggregate-demand management by government*. The government has two sets of tools with which it can affect aggregate demand: fiscal policy and monetary policy. Fiscal policy means budget policy. In the context of our discussion, *fiscal policy is policy aimed at controlling undesired changes in aggregate demand through planned changes in government expenditures and taxes.*

Monetary policy is policy aimed at controlling undesired fluctuations in aggregate demand through planned changes in commercial-bank reserves or legal reserve requirements, as explained in Chapter 17.

Economists have changed their minds several times in this century about the relative effectiveness of fiscal and monetary policy. The impotence of monetary policy as a means of restoring prosperity seemed to have been adequately demonstrated in the Great Depression, when the Fed pursued an "easy money" policy but could not stir a

485

*The Great
Depression*

World War II

*Post-war
inflation*

revival of bank lending and private spending. Keynesians and other critics of monetary policy argued that it was ineffective because the demand for money was unpredictable. Increases in the size of the money stock could be canceled out by simultaneous increases in the amount of money the public wanted to hold, perhaps in response to heightened misgivings about the future course of the economy that made people want to build up their reserves of liquid assets.

The power of fiscal policy, on the other hand, seemed to have been demonstrated by the "fiscal experiment" of 1940–1944. After a decade of depression caused by low levels of consumer and investment spending and timid government responses, World War II practically compelled the government to run huge budget deficits. Government expenditures shot up much faster than taxes could be raised, and the economy revived spectacularly. Once they had been restored by a massive injection of government spending, consumption and investment were able to take up the slack when government expenditures fell sharply again after the war. That at least was the story Keynesians told.

Monetary policy inched its way back into esteem after World War II through a concurrence of events. One was the unexpected mildness of recessions in the postwar period and the persistence of inflation. Inflation was a problem against which monetary policy might be more effective than it supposedly was against recession. *Increases* in the money supply might be canceled out by increases in the demand for money; but that did not necessarily mean that *decreases* in the money supply would be equally ineffective. In the metaphor mentioned earlier, one could pull a balloon down with a string even though pushing on the string would not make it rise. As a practical matter, it was also politically much easier to tighten up on money growth when aggregate demand was expanding too rapidly than it was to get tax increases or spending reductions through Congress. So the monetary managers were able to practice their stabilization skills to some extent by trying to control inflation. These experiments in turn persuaded many observers that monetary policy, though perhaps impotent at the depth of a severe depression, might well be effective as an expansionary tool in *mild* recessions.

Meanwhile, economists who weren't satisfied with the Keynesian diagnosis and the prescriptions of fiscal policy were doing research on the critical question of the stability of the demand for money. They argued that the Fed had made enormous mistakes in the 1930s, first in allowing the banking system and the money supply to collapse after 1929, then in failing to provide for a stable monetary expansion. Small wonder that consumer and investor confidence had collapsed, and that the public was inclined to build up liquid reserves in the 1930s whenever it got the chance.

Moreover, the demand for money was showing a great deal of stability in the years after World War II. The public was definitely not hoarding money in response to expansionary Fed policies and increased commercial-bank lending. On the contrary, the public seemed able and eager to use any new credit it could find. Private-sector borrowing grew faster than GNP, to finance business investment, residential construction, and consumer-goods purchases. Under these conditions, monetary policy might be a potent weapon even when used to expand aggregate demand. Monetarists even started to argue that it was fiscal policy rather than monetary policy that was powerless to affect aggregate demand.

Financing Deficits

Suppose the government decided to use fiscal policy to increase aggregate demand, electing to expand government expenditures while reducing taxes. That would create a budget deficit that would have to be financed by borrowing the difference between government expenditures and government tax revenues. Where could the Treasury go to do its borrowing?

from whom is the government borrowing when it runs a budget deficit?

One possibility, if it's permitted by law, is to borrow directly from the Federal Reserve. The Fed simply credits the Treasury with additional deposits in exchange for government bonds. When the Treasury then spends those deposits, they flow into the bank accounts or currency holdings of defense contractors, welfare recipients, government employees, or whoever is on the receiving end of the expenditures. The money stock consequently increases.

These new deposits are also new reserves for the commercial banking system. Banks will therefore find their lending power increased. If they can locate eligible borrowers, the commercial banks will, by expanding their loans, create a further addition to the money stock.

It follows that the money stock could increase by the entire amount of the deficit even though the Fed directly financed only a portion of the deficit. A $50-billion deficit, for example, could be handled through some combination like a Fed purchase of $15 billion in new government securities and commercial-bank purchases of $35 billion. The Fed purchase, by supplying new reserves to the banking system, enables the commercial banks to acquire additional government bonds by creating new demand deposits.

That all looks suspiciously close to Treasury financing of government deficits through the creation of new money. If Congress tries to prevent that by prohibiting the Fed from buying new Treasury bonds, the Fed can simply buy old ones through its ordinary open-market operations. The effect will be, for all practical purposes, precisely the same: government bonds will be added to the Fed's portfolio and additional reserves will flow into the commercial banking system. The only difference is that the Fed will be taking previously issued bonds out of the portfolios of commercial banks, thereby enabling the banks to buy all the newly issued Treasury bonds. That's a difference that doesn't make a difference. The effect is still to increase the stock of money by the amount of the government budget deficit.

Will the lenders create the money they provide to finance the budget deficit?

The "Crowding-Out" Effects of Deficits

Is there then no way for the government to finance a deficit without increasing the stock of money in the process? There is a way. The Treasury must borrow neither from the Fed nor from commercial banks but from nonbank lenders. Instead of getting the banking system to create new money equal to the amount of its deficit, the Treasury must compete with other prospective borrowers for the available supply of loanable funds. But unless there are idle funds around, the Treasury is going to crowd out other borrowers when it goes this route. Interest rates will rise as the Treasury adds its demand to the private-sector demand for credit, and the higher price of credit will have the effect that higher prices always have. It will persuade some borrowers to give up their projects and withdraw from the credit market. The upshot is that the government's deficit spending will simply have displaced some private spending. Government expenditures will rise, but the sum of private-sector consumption and investment expenditures will fall by an equal amount, leaving no effect on aggregate demand. In a remarkable turnabout, it is fiscal policy rather than monetary policy that proves itself incapable of expanding aggregate demand. That at least is the story monetarists tell.

There's one other possibility, however. Suppose the public is holding large money balances because consumers and investors are fearful of the future and don't want to spend. People might be persuaded to exchange those balances for government bonds. That would give the Treasury the money it wants without an increase in the money stock. More spending would then occur with no increase in the money supply, because the government would be spending previously idle balances that the public had been persuaded to exchange for government bonds.

But is that very likely except in a period of deep depression? Perhaps in the 1930s public confidence was so low that deficit spending could tap large idle money balances. But that doesn't seem to describe the situation at any time in the United States since World War II.

Are there idle funds in the hands of the public that can be used to finance the budget deficit?

Links Between Fiscal and Monetary Policy

The conclusion is a simple one. Deficit spending by the government affects the monetary sector. It results in some combination of an enlarged money stock and higher interest rates.[1] Insofar as the Fed tries to prevent government expenditures from crowding out private expenditures by making more reserves available to the banking system when the Treasury is borrowing, it causes a growth in the money stock. If the Fed tries to prevent such an increase, it will force private borrowers to bid against the Treasury for the limited supply of credit. Fiscal policy is therefore inseparable from monetary policy.

Monetary policy, on the other hand, can be conducted independently of fiscal policy. Government spending uses money, but more money can be created and spent independently of any changes in the government budget. It doesn't follow, however, that fiscal policy cannot be a useful aid to monetary policy. Remember that the Fed doesn't control the size of the money stock directly. It can increase the available reserves of the banking system, but it can't force anyone to borrow and thereby convert free reserves into money. Government borrowing and expenditure is therefore one way to increase the money stock and to increase it rapidly. In a period of low confidence, when consumers and investors don't want to borrow, fiscal policy might be the only way to make monetary policy effective. The 1930s come immediately to mind.

All this suggests that the Keynesians might well have

---

[1]What if the federal government borrows from foreigners? To keep the analysis simple, we are assuming for now that the economic system of the United States is isolated from other economic systems. The important complications and qualifications that international exchange introduces will be discussed in Chapter 21.

been correct in the 1930s without being correct today. Those who warned against government budget deficits in the 1930s on the grounds that the deficits would only crowd out private-sector spending and thereby delay the recovery seem rather absurd in retrospect. Of course, it is no less absurd to make policy for the 1990s on the assumption that the times we're living in are basically like those of the 1930s.

The Necessity of Good Timing

Timing is absolutely crucial if aggregate-demand management is to be an effective stabilizing tool. But good timing proves extraordinarily difficult to achieve when it comes to fiscal or monetary policy, and for several reasons.

Time lags:
1. recognizing the problem.

In the first place, we never know until long afterward whether aggregate demand was rising or falling. The economy doesn't come equipped with a speedometer that tells us how fast it's running at any moment. We find out what GNP is doing during the current quarter only at the end of the quarter. Even then the figures provided by the Bureau of Economic Analysis are highly tentative and subject to sizable revisions as more accurate data become available a month and more after the quarter has ended.

What's worse, even if we could know exactly where we are at any time, that wouldn't be enough. Those who conduct fiscal and monetary policy have to know where we're *going to be*, because today's action must aim at compensating for tomorrow's deficiency or excess in aggregate demand. Stabilization policy is necessarily based on forecasting, and short-term economic forecasting, far from being an exact science, isn't even a respectable art.

Particularly troubling is our inability to predict how much time it will take for a fiscal or monetary policy action to have its effects. Estimates of the length of these lags range from a few months to several years, and diligent research efforts designed to nail down the time distribution of the effects haven't produced a workable consensus. The lags may even turn out to vary in ways we can't predict, in which case economists would be trying to measure something that actually has no standard length.

There are good reasons for supposing that the time lags between fiscal or monetary policy actions and their effects are not some constant that can be measured and then relied on. The effects of these actions will depend, after all, on how producers and consumers read their own uncertain individual futures. Government actions reduce some uncertainties, but they add others; they certainly don't enable people to start planning with complete confidence about what the future holds. Meanwhile, the operating procedures of commercial banks, the payment practices of business firms, the perceptions of households and corporations with respect to the advantages of holding assets in one form or another, international monetary transactions, and even the public's efforts to anticipate the effects of government actions will all play a part in determining the distribution over time of any policy's impact on total spending. These factors will be changing continuously. And they are especially likely to change in response to any improvement in our ability to forecast them! It is a case in which forecasts falsify themselves by altering the stock of information that had to be assumed in order to make the forecast. Here's a simple example: if we knew with confidence the pattern that some stock's market price would trace over the coming year, it wouldn't trace that pattern. This is the paradox with which sciences of human behavior must live. Predicting the future changes the future, because the people whose actions create the future read the predictions.

Time lags:
2. from decision
to impact.

The Federal Budget as a Policy Tool

When we turn specifically to fiscal policy, an additional difficulty emerges. There is a touch of comedy in the belief that the federal government can use its budget as a stabilization tool when almost all observers agree that Congress no longer has effective control over the budget. The spending programs of the federal government are so many and so complex that no one can even begin to evaluate all of them for the purpose of determining annual appropriations. As a result, next year's budget begins by taking this year's budget for granted and adding on. Once a program gets in, it's almost impossible to dislodge, because its beneficiaries form a knowledgeable and determined lobby for its continuance, and no one on Capitol Hill has the time, energy, and interest to accumulate the evidence that could justify its removal.

Fiscal policy is not something under the control of the Council of Economic Advisers. A change in government expenditures or in federal taxes requires action by the House of Representatives and then the Senate, with committee meetings before and often after, and a presidential signature at the end. That takes time — and timing is crucial in aggregate demand management. The discussions will be complicated and prolonged by the fact that, even if Congress were to agree quickly on the desirability of a change in expenditures or taxes of a particular amount, it would still have to decide whose taxes will be changed and which expenditures. Conflicting interests will be involved as well as alternative theories about the expansionary or contractionary effects of particular actions. Is it better to cut the taxes of low-income people or to give tax credits for investment? Which will have a greater impact on employment? And are we talking about the long run or the short run? Meanwhile, some members of Congress will certainly decide that an important tax or expenditure bill provides an opportunity to eliminate the depletion allowance for oil producers, give a bonus to retired people on social security, prop up the housing industry through a special subsidy, or take a slap at multinational corporations — to mention only some of the concerns that managed to achieve expression in the March 1975 "antirecessionary" tax bill.

Time lags:
3. deciding
exactly what
to do.

The more in a hurry Congress and the president are, the more likely they are to produce fiscal-policy actions that few competent and impartial observers will be able to defend. The imperative of haste tends to enhance the power of those who are willing to enforce their demands by threatening to block any action at all. But due deliberation, the careful assessment of alternatives, and the weighing of the probable short- and long-term outcomes may require so much time that the moment for action passes before any action is taken. The 1974–75 recession began late in 1973. Congress passed an antirecessionary tax-cut bill at the end of March 1975. Even at that late date, the bill contained evidence of haste. And it came too late to counter the recession but just in time, perhaps, to help fuel the next round of inflation.

Advocates of stabilization through fiscal policy have long been aware of these difficulties. They know that the protracted discussions that precede any congressional action on taxes and expenditures could easily make fiscal policy unworkable: action might not be possible until the time for it has passed. They have consequently looked around for ways to speed up the process. One proposal recommended by some economists and urged by President John F. Kennedy was that Congress authorize unilateral action by the president. Appropriations for particular projects could be approved by Congress and then put on the shelf, to be taken off whenever the president and his advisers decided that the stimulus of increased government expenditures was called for. Congress could also authorize the president to increase or decrease tax rates within narrow limits when aggregate demand seemed excessive or inadequate.

If you're wondering why Congress never acted on such a "sensible" recommendation, think for a moment about the political power that a president would command if he could unilaterally determine the timing of tax decreases and the placement of expenditure projects. Congress isn't likely to grant that kind of power to any president, not even to a trusted president who is a member of the same political party as the majority in both houses of Congress. Some senators and representatives will be deterred by the constitutional principle of a balance of power among the branches of government, some by respect for Lord Acton's maxim that absolute power corrupts absolutely. But all will know that such power in the hands of a president substantially diminishes their own power and influence. The conclusion, therefore, is that fiscal policy *at best* will continue to be a stabilization tool that doesn't become available until the appropriate time for its use has passed.

But isn't this negative verdict on fiscal policy inconsistent with the historical record? Hasn't fiscal policy actually been used effectively to fight recessions?

Stabilization Versus Stimulus

The rather common belief that fiscal policy has proved its effectiveness as a stabilization tool seems to be based largely on a failure to distinguish between the ability to stabilize aggregate demand and the ability to change it. But stabilization requires more than the power to change aggregate demand; it presupposes the power to control it by fairly precise amounts and with close timing. We do have evidence that increased government spending with no increase in taxes, or reduced taxes with no reductions in government spending, can, under the right circumstances, stimulate total spending. World War II seems to be the clearest demonstration of fiscal policy's potency. The Great Depression finally ended when the federal government, responding to the imperatives of wartime, threw fiscal caution aside and began running huge deficits. Federal government expenditures increased 105 percent from 1940 to 1941, by an additional 175 percent in 1942, and by yet another 50 percent in 1943. In 1944 federal government expenditures, after adjustment for changes in the price level, were six and one-half times what they had been in 1940. The federal budget deficit, measured in 1982 dollars, grew from about $5½ billion in 1940 to almost $340 billion in 1944.

The economy responded to this stimulus much as Keynesian analysis suggested that it would. Jolted out of the doldrums of the Great Depression by the massive fiscal stimulus of wartime expenditures, the economy produced almost as much real output in 1944 just for the government sector as it had produced for the combined private and government sectors in 1939. The total real output of the economy in 1944 was more than 75 percent greater than it had been in 1939.

In this colossal but undesigned test of fiscal policy's *stimulative* capabilities, there was no real test of its effectiveness for *stabilization* purposes. Nor could there be any such test until at least a majority in Congress and the president were persuaded to make the experiment. That situation certainly did not exit before 1964. In that year Congress enacted and the president signed a tax-reduction bill that had been argued for largely on Keynesian grounds. Lower taxes without any accompanying reduction in federal government expenditures were supposed to stimulate the economy and reduce the high unemployment rate that had developed and persisted since 1958.

Unemployment did decline after the 1964 tax cut. But even if we could be certain that it declined because the tax cut stimulated aggregate demand, we would once again have evidence for no more than the stimulative potential of fiscal policy. The economy was not in a recession in 1964 and consequently could not be pulled out of one by a compensatory federal budget deficit. The 1964 tax cut actually supports the point we're making, that fiscal policy cannot be used effectively to counter fluctuations in private spending because of the long time lags associated with its use. The Keynesian argument for a tax cut that culminated in the tax reduction of 1964 *began to be made in the recession of 1960.*

Nondiscretionary Fiscal Policy

We've been arguing that the federal government did not, in fact, use changes in tax rates or expenditures as a *stabilization* tool — at least not before the year 1964. We now want to suggest that the fiscal policy of the federal government after World War II may nonetheless have contributed to economic stabilization. The second statement doesn't contradict the first, because a stabilizing fiscal policy doesn't necessarily require legislated changes in tax rates or expenditures. Fiscal policy can be automatic as well as discretionary. Only discretionary fiscal policy is incapacitated by the severe time lags associated with its use.

When an economic downturn begins, tax receipts fall automatically as corporate and personal incomes decline. Because the applicable rates on these two principal sources of federal revenue are progressive, taking a higher percentage of higher incomes, a decline in income actually leads to an even faster decline in taxes. The government also puts some additional income into the hands of the public during a recession whenever the economic decline leads to an automatic increase in unemployment compensation and welfare benefits. These automatic responses to a recession presumably function as stabilizers, dampening fluctuations in income and thereby reducing fluctuations in private spending.

Allowing budget deficits or surpluses to appear and deciding to do nothing about them is also fiscal policy. It must be distinguished from another view that was widely advocated before the 1930s and the publication of Keynes' *General Theory*. The older position held that government should retrench in a recession, deliberately cutting its expenditures and increasing tax rates if necessary in order to preserve a balanced budget. Such a policy, if adopted, would be the exact reverse of what Keynes recommended. But it would be a discretionary fiscal policy, not an automatic one, and it would be subject as a result to the same problems of timing that make any discretionary fiscal policy an inappropriate instrument for stabilization.

Automatic fiscal policy was clearly at work, whether by design or by inadvertence, in the 1958 recession. The federal government's 1957 budget surplus of $5 billion (in 1982 dollars) turned into a $42-billion deficit in 1958. This happened not because Congress and the president chose to cut taxes or increase expenditures, but because federal tax receipts fell in response to the recession, while federal expenditures continued on their previously targeted course.

What contribution did this kind of passive fiscal policy make toward the relative stability of the economy in the years after World War II? We really have no good way of knowing. It can be argued that automatic fiscal policy is bound to increase stability, because it diminishes the impact that changes in investment expenditure have on the income of consumers. With consumer income buffered to some extent against fluctuations in output, the cumulative effect of destabilizing events is reduced. Automatic fiscal policy provides shock absorbers for the economy and may deserve part

Nondiscretionary fiscal policy: do not alter tax rates but let tax receipts fall in a recession.

Pre-Keynesian policy: raise tax rates in a recession to make up for falling receipts.

Keynesian policy: lower tax rates in a recession to expand the deficit.

of the credit for the smoother "ride" of the years after World War II.

The Timing of Monetary Policy

Monetary policy does have one advantage over fiscal policy with respect to timing—unless it turns out to be a *dis*advantage. The monetary authorities aren't immune from the problems created by the fact that we can't predict the future accurately, don't know exactly where we are at the moment, and have no reliable information on the timing of the inevitable lags between policy actions and their ultimate effects on aggregate demand. But the Open Market Committee of the Fed can at least make quick decisions. Its members meet regularly and can confer by telephone between meetings. Moreover, being more insulated from political pressures than Congress or the executive branch, Fed officials can presumably do what they think the situation calls for without catering to the distracting demands of special interests.

But can we be sure that this is an advantage from the standpoint of stabilization? The speed with which the Open Market Committee can act enables it also to make more frequent mistakes. Of course, it can quickly reverse direction when it learns it made an error. But sharp reversals of direction by an institution as powerful as the Open Market Committee can themselves be a destabilizing force.

Disagreement About the Conduct of Monetary Policy

The members of the Open Market Committee do not fully agree among themselves on the definition of a restrictive (tight) or expansionary (easy) monetary policy. The question of the proper target for monetary policy has been a controversial one for a long time. Monetarists hold that the monetary managers should pay attention exclusively to monetary aggregates: measures of the money stock such as M1, M2, or the total of currency in circulation plus commercial-bank reserves, known as the monetary base. The money supply is tight or easy according to the rate at which these aggregates are changing. Another view, to be discussed in the next chapter because it is associated with supply-side economists, is that movements in commodity prices are the appropriate measure of monetary tightness or ease. A third view, long advocated by Keynesians, is that the monetary managers should concentrate on interest rates, using some such measure as the federal funds rate, which is the rate of interest paid by commercial banks to borrow one another's reserves. This group holds that the money supply is tight or easy according to whether interest rates are high or low.

The disagreement between monetarists and Keynesians is complicated by the apparently widespread belief that interest rates reflect the scarcity of money, so that rates can be made to fall by increasing the money stock fast enough. We must think carefully about the relationship between monetary policy and interest rates if we are to avoid the error of assuming that high interest rates are conclusive evidence of tight money. When the Fed increases the stock of money, the demand remaining constant, elementary supply and demand analysis tells us that the price of money will fall. But interest is not the price of money! Interest rates can be thought of as the price of credit, but the price of money is the value of money or its purchasing power. (This was discussed in Chapter 11.)

How *does* monetary policy affect interest rates? When the Fed increases bank reserves as part of an easier money policy, banks are enabled to expand their lending. Credit becomes easier to obtain and interest rates consequently tend to move downward. Easier money leads to lower interest rates — at least temporarily.

But we must push the analysis further. What happens to the new money that is created when the Fed adds to bank reserves and the banks make additional loans? The increase in the stock of money will tend to increase aggregate demand. If the demand for credit from consumers, investors, and government expands when aggregate demand grows, that will tend to pull interest rates back up. The net effect after a longer period of time can't be predicted easily, because monetary policy finally influences both the supply and the demand for credit and pushes them both in the same direction.

Nominal Versus Real Interest Rates

Most importantly, if the expansionary monetary policy leads to an excessive rate of increase in aggregate demand, prices will start to rise. And the expectation of rising prices will cause interest rates to rise. Why? Because if prices are expected to increase by 10 percent per year, lenders will demand an additional 10 percent in interest as compensation for the anticipated decrease in the value or purchasing power of money. And borrowers with the same expectations of in-

Effects of
expansionary
monetary policy:
1. Increased
   supply of credit
2. (?) Increased
   demand for
   credit (?)
3. Increased
   expenditure
4. (?) Accelerated
   inflation (?)
5. Higher nominal
   interest rates
   reflecting
   inflationary
   expectations.

flation will consent to pay the additional 10 percent because they anticipate repaying the loan with depreciated dollars. The *nominal* interest rate – the rate quoted and charged – will then exceed the real rate by 10 percent (or more, if interest income is taxable while interest payments are deductible items!).

The policy dilemma this poses for the Fed becomes exceptionally sharp when critics begin calling for a faster rate of growth in the money stock to get interest rates down. Will faster monetary growth lower or raise interest rates? If Fed watchers following the weekly reports on the money supply come to the conclusion that the Fed is pursuing an inflationary monetary policy, market interest rates may rise to reflect heightened inflationary expectations.

Popular Opinion and Interest Rates

The published reports of the Open Market Committee's policy directives in recent years reveal continuing uncertainty about the proper target at which to aim. But there is very little question about the target at which the general public looks in assessing monetary policy. It looks at interest rates. Moreover, the public looks primarily at nominal interest rates, the only interest rates that anyone publishes, and sees high interest rates as bad almost without qualification. High interest rates allegedly cause inflation (a rise in interest rates does push up the consumer price index) and recession (a rise in *real* interest rates does tend to reduce investment spending). High real interest rates also make it harder for home-buyers to obtain mortgages. High interest rates allegedly "starve" the economy for credit, "choke off" expansion, "pinch" households and business firms, and perpetrate similar violence. The only people thought to benefit from high interest rates are bankers. And who loves bankers?

The majority of the public believes that the Fed can control interest rates and that it has an obligation to keep them at "reasonably" low levels. It can do this, supposedly, by expanding bank reserves whenever interest rates threaten to rise above some "reasonable" level. The upshot of it all is that the Fed runs into enormous public hostility if it tries to tighten its monetary policy at a time when the public is expecting fairly rapid inflation, because those expectations will produce high nominal interest rates that the public will regard as evidence of an excessively restrictive monetary policy. That's exactly what happened, for example, in the last half of 1979. Nominal interest rates were very high by historic standards in 1979, pulled up by the general expectation of rapid inflation in the immediate future. But newspaper articles and financial commentators rarely pointed out that a 12 percent interest rate when inflation was running at a 13 percent annual rate (as it did for a while in 1979) was a very low and in fact negative *real* rate of interest. Nor did they notice that Ml had been growing through the first three quarters of 1979 at a 10 percent annual rate, hardly evidence of a restrictive monetary policy.

The published policy directives of the Open Market Committee do little to clarify the situation. These directives regularly speak of maintaining the federal funds rate within some targeted range, as if the Fed had the power to set that rate independently of what was happening to nominal interest rates in the credit market. Remember, however, that the Fed exercises its influence on the federal funds rate, the interest rate at which banks exchange reserves, through buying and selling government bonds and thereby adding to or subtracting from commercial-bank reserves. If the federal funds rate is rising, it is because rising interest rates are inducing banks to bid more in order to obtain additional reserves that they can lend. To counter this movement, the Fed must supply additional reserves. But could the Fed have pumped large volumes of new reserves into the commercial banking system in mid-1979 without stirring expectations of still more rapid inflation and further stimulating the demand to borrow? No action by the Fed can lower interest rates if that action increases the demand for federal funds by even more than it increases the supply.

This fundamental uncertainty about the effect that open market operations will have on interest rates is what has persuaded many economists, led by the monetarists, that the Fed should ignore interest rates and concentrate on monetary aggregates. The attempt to stabilize interest rates, these economists argue, causes the Fed to lose control over the growth rate of the money stock. And it is the rate at which the money stock grows that in the long run determines the rate at which aggregate demand and hence the nominal gross national product will grow.

Is It Better to Have Tried and Failed?

It has become increasingly obvious in recent years that we don't have the knowledge that would be required to "fine-tune" aggregate demand, to steer the economy on a steady course of full employment with price stability. But are we better off than we would have been if we hadn't tried? Most economists now agree that "fine-tuning" has been oversold, that we have been too optimistic about our ability to reduce fluctuations through aggregate-demand management. A smaller number go further: they argue that the attempt to stabilize has increased both unemployment and inflation.

How could this occur? The key element in the argument is the relationship between recessions and uncertainty. Recessions occur largely because mistakes are made and subsequently have to be corrected. It follows that anything which increases the probability of mistakes, of decisions based on a faulty anticipation of future events, will aggravate the recession problem. The question then becomes: Has the behavior of the federal budget and of the money supply in recent years made the future more predictable? Or has it increased the uncertainties confronting economic decision makers?

Stabilizing Factors

We can't jump from the fact that there have been no major recessions since the 1930s to the conclusion that the net effect of government stabilization efforts was greater stability. Other factors have been at work. In Chapter 17 we mentioned the importance of the Federal Deposit Insurance Corporation in eliminating the phenomenon of bank runs and also the supporting role of the Fed as the guarantor of short-run liquidity to the banking system. Between them they have eliminated the panics that once swept regularly through the financial sector; and with financial panics a thing of the past, the economy has not again had to go through anything even remotely approaching the 25 percent contraction in the money stock experienced between 1929 and 1933.

Another stabilizing factor seems to have been the tendency for personal consumption expenditures after World War II to maintain their own steady rate of increase, with relative disregard for fluctuations in income. Some of this should probably be attributed to relatively high wealth levels, which enable people to maintain their spending during periods of temporarily reduced income. Some of it can also be credited, perhaps, to our system of progressive taxes on personal and corporate income that cushion income against fluctuations in gross national product. The fact that government transfer payments, such as unemployment compensation, move inversely to GNP has an added cushioning effect on aggregate consumption spending.

Destabilizing Factors

If personal-consumption expenditures have been a steady and stabilizing component of aggregate demand, investment expenditures have not. But did fiscal and monetary policy compensate for this instability, or were they a major *cause* of the instability? The construction component of investment is sensitive to monetary policy shifts, and changing monetary policies do seem to have destabilized the building industry. What about the policy of shifting between tax surcharges to dampen inflation and special tax credits for investment spending to promote employment? Since there is usually considerable discretion about the timing of investment expenditures, couldn't government policy reversals be largely responsible for the large fluctuations from year to year in private investment? It's true that policymakers intended to reduce fluctuations through shifting tax policies; but it wouldn't be the only time a tax program hit something other than its target.

What have been the overall effects of government programs? Remember that an unanticipated change in the *composition* of spending will cause unemployment even though *total* spending doesn't change. When the government makes a decision to send people to the moon, to produce a particular military plane, to restrict oil imports, to subsidize a giant railroad system, to enforce high standards of job safety in industry, to become self-sufficient in energy, to encourage home ownership through government-subsidized loans, to enlarge steel-making capacity by granting special tax refunds for investment — when the government does any of these things, it signals labor and other resources to move in specific directions. It tells people to change their places of residence, to acquire particular knowledge and skills, to sink resources into specific projects. *Any subsequent slackening of government intentions or shift in emphases announces that these resource movements were partly mistaken and thereby creates unemployment.* These changing signals from government may also trigger surges of investment spending by industries trying to make rapid adjustments to revised government policies. How sure can we be that private economic decisions are the unstable factor for which government decisions must compensate?

The Benefits and Costs of Aggregative Theories

It's difficult to discuss the problem of recession and unemployment without using large aggregates such as consumption expenditure, investment expenditure, government expenditure, tax revenues, total demand, national output, and national income. But there is an important sense in which these data conceal the very nature of the problem with which we're trying to deal. Total output is the sum of the outputs of several million firms producing different goods under constantly changing conditions, including conditions of both cost and demand that can change in different directions and at different rates for each separate firm. It is these differences and the uncertainties associated with them that produce the phenomenon of recession in the first place.

Remember that a recession is not a mere slowdown in the rate of economic growth. It is an unintended and therefore disruptive slowdown for a large number of producers (but never all producers!) who discover that their revenue expectations relative to their cost expectations were too optimistic. Recessions begin because imbalances have developed and accumulated over a period of time. Recessions can perhaps be measured with highly aggregative concepts. But they cannot be adequately understood or controlled without paying attention to the changing structure of costs and demand from one industry to another, one region of the country to another, and even one firm to another.

Attempting to counter recessions by stimulating aggregate demand assumes more uniformity and homogeneity within recessions than is actually the case. The enlarged demand must be a demand for the right goods if it's going to check the decline in output *in particular firms and industries*, which is the essence of the recession. It's true that in a recession most industries and perhaps most firms will experience disappointing revenue-cost outcomes. But they won't all do so, and among those who do encounter disappointment, the called-for adjustments will range from minor through major all the way to bankruptcy and reorganization. What can we expect to happen, then, if government responds to a recession by expanding aggregate demand?

Won't the result depend on how this policy affects the relative demand for the inputs and for the outputs of particular firms? Doesn't increased demand produce higher costs as well as higher revenues? Remember, too, that inputs are not some stockpile of perfectly substitutable resources that can quickly stop producing X and start producing Y when the demand for X goes down and the demand for Y goes up. Won't a policy of stimulating total demand in response to a recession make life easier for some firms but harder for others?

How will increased government spending on airplanes manufactured in Missouri affect unemployment among Oregon loggers?

The massive economic breakdown of the Great Depression led to the construction of highly aggregative theories of economic fluctuations. That was certainly understandable. Only a highly aggregative theory is likely to suggest a cure sufficiently simple to be workable. And what was above all desired in the 1930s was a workable solution, something that could quickly be put into practice. Part of the tragedy of the Great Depression may have been the timidity that prevented national governments from taking the heroic measures to expand aggregate demand that the events of the 1930s seemed to require: 1929 to 1933 was no "normal" recession. Whatever the circumstances that produced or aggravated the long and deep decline into the depression of the 1930s, there was abundant evidence by 1933 that bold actions by government to stimulate recovery carried a low risk and a high potential benefit.

But if policymakers in the 1930s were guilty of failure to recognize an economic breakdown and to react appropriately, policymakers today may be guilty of responding in equally inappropriate ways by treating every recession as if it were a breakdown. The continuing confidence that many public officials and much of the electorate have in discretionary fiscal and monetary policy — despite the record of their performance — is hard to explain on any other grounds.

It wasn't until the mid-1960s that the United States acquired both a president and a majority in Congress who believed in the effectiveness and desirability of using discretionary fiscal policy along with monetary policy as stabilization techniques. Is the increased instability of the years since then a mere coincidence, to be blamed on external forces beyond the control of policymakers, such as the OPEC cartel and worldwide agricultural failures? That's certainly possible. And those who want to continue advocating discretionary aggregate-demand management, especially in response to recessions, will find in those events a plausible explanation for the fact that increased use of these stabilizing techniques has been accompanied by increased instability. Whether you decide it's consequence or coincidence, the fact remains that our most rapid inflation and highest unemployment rates since World War II appeared *after* both major political parties had committed themselves to fine-tuning of the economy through aggregate-demand management.

Perhaps we have been traumatized by the experiences of the Great Depression into paying altogether too much attention to aggregate demand. What is there that might be done on the supply side to improve the performance of the economy? That will be the question running through Chapter 20.

Once Over Lightly

Fiscal policy and monetary policy are the principal techniques of aggregate-demand management available to officials of the federal government. Fiscal policy aims at controlling fluctuations in aggregate demand through compensatory budget deficits or surpluses. Monetary policy works toward the same goal through control over commercial-bank reserves and legal reserve requirements.

The Keynesian conviction that monetary policy was impotent, a conviction nurtured in the 1930s, gradually gave way after World War II to the realization that monetary policy was important in the control of inflation and might even have some capability of countering mild recessions.

Monetarists have tried to show not only that monetary policy is a powerful weapon, but also that the supposed effects of fiscal policy are actually the result of accompanying monetary policy.

Depending on the circumstances, government deficits might crowd out private spending rather than supplement it. In very different circumstances, such as a deep and prolonged depression in economic activity, government deficits might be a supplement necessary to make expansionary monetary policy effective.

Timing is crucial in any effective stabilization policy. The time lags that inevitably occur between the appearance and the recognition of a problem, the recognition and the decision to take a particular action, and the action and its ultimate effects combine to make aggregate-demand management less stabilizing in practice than on paper.

Attempts to stabilize aggregate demand through fiscal or monetary policy must entail accurate prediction if they are to be successful. But economic forecasting is an undeveloped art. It is made especially hazardous by the fact that the people whose behavior is to be controlled try to anticipate and adjust for the controls.

The political delays inevitably associated with its use create especially acute timing problems for fiscal policy.

Although there is little evidence for the position that discretionary fiscal policy is an effective stabilization tool, a strong case can be made for its power to change aggregate demand under appropriate circumstances.

Nondiscretionary fiscal policy, operating through changes in taxes or government outlays that occur automatically in response to changing levels of output and income, may have contributed significantly to the post-World War II stability of the U.S. economy.

Monetary policy shares with discretionary fiscal policy a better-demonstrated capacity to change than to stabilize aggregate demand.

The successful conduct of monetary policy has been made more difficult by high-level disagreement on the proper targets for control: monetary aggregates, commodity prices, or interest rates.

Monetary expansion may lower interest rates by increasing the availability of credit; but the same policy may subsequently raise them by contributing to an increase in the demand for credit. Moreover, nominal interest rates will rise if monetary expansion creates expectations of more rapid inflation. These difficulties in the control of interest rates make interest-rate management an unreliable and even dangerous policy tool for the monetary managers to use.

There is no convincing evidence that government efforts since World War II to manipulate aggregate demand have actually resulted in lower unemployment rates and less inflation than we would have experienced in the absence of such efforts.

There is considerable evidence to suggest that activities of the federal government, including some of its stabilization efforts, have been seriously destabilizing in their consequences.

Questions for Discussion

1. How does fiscal policy affect monetary policy?

    (a) Under what circumstances could the federal government run a large budget deficit without thereby producing an increase in the size of the money stock?

    (b) Suppose the Fed determined to run a "tight" monetary policy, allowing no growth in commercial-bank reserves, at a time when the federal government was trying to borrow to finance a large budget deficit. What would happen?

    (c) Suppose the federal government began running a large budget surplus, and used the surplus to reduce the size of the national debt. Think through the effects this would be likely to have on the demand for loans from commercial banks. How might this affect the size of the money stock?

2. How will a large federal government budget deficit affect interest rates?

    (a) Assuming that interest rates are set by the demand for and supply of loanable funds, how could a large increase in federal government borrowing *not* produce higher interest rates?

(b) Suppose the Fed tries to prevent the increased government demand for loanable funds from raising interest rates, by increasing the supply of loanable funds through an expansion of commercial bank loans. Will this Fed policy succeed in preventing interest rates from rising? At what point will the Fed's expansionary policy step up the inflation rate? How will the expectation of a higher rate of inflation cause interest rates to rise?

3. Suppose that the federal government begins to run a large budget deficit at a time when many productive resources are idle — factories are operating far below capacity in most industries, and there are surplus supplies of labor in almost every area of the economy.

(a) How might the existence of all these idle resources prevent even a very large increase in government borrowing from leading to an increase in interest rates?

(b) If you found part (a) hard to answer, ask yourself whether an expansionary monetary policy would be likely to cause inflation under the circumstances described. Remember that it is primarily expectations of more rapid inflation that cause interest rates to rise when monetary policy becomes highly expansionary.

4. "An increase or decrease in government spending will usually entail an off-setting decrease or increase in private spending." Under what circumstances would you expect that statement to be true? Why? Under what circumstances would you expect that statement to be false? Why?

5. The late Senator Hubert Humphrey said shortly after the March 1975 tax cuts that "common sense" told him federal borrowing would not raise interest rates and crowd out private borrowers. "To a large extent this credit-market question takes care of itself," he said. "Private demands for credit go down when unemployment is high. This makes room in the credit market for government demand which goes up." Do you agree?

6. If Congress wants to use fiscal policy to counter recessions, should it cut taxes when the recession is a suspicion, when it's a widespread conviction, or when it's officially announced?

7. Assume that Congress and the president want to cut taxes by $5 billion to stimulate the economy in a period of recession. Does it matter whether they cut personal income taxes or corporate income taxes? Whether the cuts in personal income taxes are concentrated among low-income groups or more widely distributed? What difference does it make and to whom does it make a difference?

8. During the depression of the 1930s, increases in federal government expenditures were often accompanied by promises (threats?) of future tax increases to hold down the size of the budget deficit. Do you think this policy had any effect on investment spending? How does the prospect of higher tax rates in the future affect investment decisions?

9. Would you favor the proposal, mentioned in the text, to give the president

authority to change tax rates or authorize expenditures on his own (within congressionally designated limits) as a way of making fiscal policy more flexible? Why or why not?

10. If tax cuts stimulate aggregate demand, is it possible that they also stimulate aggregate supply? How could a reduction in corporate or personal income tax rates affect the supply curves of goods?

11. A budget is essentially a forecast: "This is what revenues are expected to be, this is what expenditures are expected to be."

   (a) How can uncertainty turn a balanced budget into an actual deficit or surplus?

   (b) Do Congress and the president have the ability to produce the relationship between government revenue and expenditures that they want to produce?

   (c) Would government be stabilizing or destabilizing the economy if Congress and the president made frequent changes in tax rates or in spending authorizations in an effort to keep the flow of government spending exactly equal to the flow of its tax receipts?

   (d) If the federal government ought to balance its budget, over what time period ought it to do so? Over what time period do households and business firms balance their budgets?

12. The text mentions three different criteria of a restrictive or expansionary monetary policy.

   (a) Keynesians tend to look at the level of interest rates for evidence on the tightness or ease of current monetary policy. How good an indicator is this? The prime rate (the basic interest rate banks charge their most secure customers) averaged 5.25 percent in 1972, 8 percent in 1973, and 10.8 percent in 1974. Was monetary policy restrictive or expansionary during these years? After falling to 6.8 percent in 1977, the prime rate rose to 9.1 percent, 12.7 percent, 15.3 percent, and 18.9 percent in the next four years. Was monetary policy restrictive from 1977 to 1981?

   (b) Monetarists maintain that the best test of monetary ease or tightness is the rate of growth in measures of the total stock of money. From 1972 to 1974, M1 grew by an annual average rate of 6.2 percent. From 1977 to 1981, M1 increased at an average annual rate of 7.3 percent. For comparison purposes, you might want to know that the average annual rate of increase in M1 over the two decades from 1965 to 1985 was about 6.7 percent. By the monetarist measure, does monetary policy from 1972 to 1974 and 1977 to 1981 look restrictive or expansionary?

   (c) Supply-side economists, whose views will be given more attention in the next chapter, believe that the best test of monetary ease or tightness is what happens to prices. From 1972 to 1974, the producer price index of finished goods rose at an average annual rate of 12.2 percent. Was monetary policy easy or tight by this measure? Before deciding definitely on your answer, you might want to note that 1973 and 1974 were the years in which OPEC first made its mark on petroleum prices. From 1977 to 1981, the average annual increase in the index of prices for finished producer goods was 10.4 percent.

(d) In 1985, the producer price index rose by 1.8 percent while M1 rose 11.9 percent and the prime rate fell from 10.5 to 9.5 percent. Was monetary policy expansionary or restrictive in 1985?

(e) A major reason that these various indicators seem to tell conflicting stories about the ease or tightness of monetary policy is that we are ignoring other relevant factors, such as the effect of expectations on interest rates, or the time lags between changes in the growth rate of monetary aggregates and price level effects. Economists can continue to hold a lot of conflicting opinions in this area because the relationships in which we're interested are not only complex and uncertain but probably also variable over time. When experts disagree, how should citizen-voters decide?

13. The real rate of interest *ex ante* (before the loan is made) is the market or nominal rate minus the *expected* rate of inflation. To the extent that expectations are wrong, the *ex post* (after-the-fact) real rate of interest will be higher or lower than the *ex ante* real rate. Why were *ex post* real interest rates so low in the 1970s and so high in the early 1980s?

14. Evaluate the following assertion: "When aggregate demand is greater than the aggregate capacity of the economy, we get inflation. When it is less, we get recession."

(a) Do firms ever lay off workers when the average price level is rising?

(b) Do firms ever raise their prices during a recession?

(c) How would we know whether the economy was operating at full capacity? Is the aggregate capacity of a single firm ever some definite quantity of output per time period? Think of the college you attend. What would be occurring if it were operating at 100 percent of capacity? Extend the question to an entire industry (e.g., the education industry). Then extend it again to the entire economy.

15. Is aggregate demand inadequate if there is a shortage of automotive mechanics and a surplus of secondary-school teachers? Can substantial unemployment exist at a time when listed job vacancies exceed total unemployment? Why will you find help-wanted ads in newspapers even during recessions?

16. "There is no danger that a government deficit will cause inflation when unemployment stands at 8 percent of the civilian labor force." Do you agree?

17. Suppose the unemployment rate is 8 percent, and economic statisticians tell the government that 2 of those 8 percentage points are a direct result of sharply reduced purchases of new automobiles. Discuss the advantages and disadvantages in such a situation of offering a tax rebate to purchasers of new automobiles equal to 10 percent of the manufacturers' suggested

retail price. Is a dollar of tax reduction offered in this way likely to reduce unemployment more than a dollar of personal income-tax reduction? Are the long-run effects on unemployment likely to be different from the short-run effects?

18. If the government decreased spending on highways by $5 billion and simultaneously increased spending on energy development by $5 billion, what effects, if any, would you predict on the level of unemployment?

19. "The basic cause of an excessively high unemployment rate is uncertainty." Explain whether you agree or disagree with that statement and why.

Chapter 20

Supply-Side Perspectives

The conflict between supply-side and demand-side economics goes back at least to the eighteenth century, even though the terms only came into use in the 1970s. The predecessors of Adam Smith were largely demand-siders, concerned to maintain a flourishing demand for domestic production through policies that restricted foreign competition and kept a large quantity of money in circulation. Smith, by contrast, was a consistent supply-sider, concerned about incentives to producers, convinced that a nation would always have as much money as it could use, and persuaded that additional saving would automatically generate additional investment, never a deficiency of aggregate-demand.

Supply-Side Economics: Its Varied Forms

The term "supply-side economics" was coined in the 1970s to describe a set of analyses and policy recommendations aimed at accelerating economic growth and employment through improving incentives to producers. A more favorable tax and regulatory environment for business was the principal recommendation of those who began to call themselves supply-side economists. In this chapter, however, we are going to use the term "supply-side economics" more broadly, to characterize all those economic analyses that emphasize the ineffectiveness of aggregate-demand management in bringing about high employment with price stability, and that recommend greater attention to factors on the supply side.

We shall find supply-side economists, as we are using the term, on both ends of the political spectrum. Some will claim that because markets do not work adequately, government must take a more active role in controlling prices and incomes if we are to have any chance of controlling both inflation and recession. Others will argue almost the reverse: that markets work so well, they render aggregate demand management powerless to affect output and employment, and that the only way for the government to spur economic expansion is to improve the profit prospects of business firms.

The Popularity of Direct Controls

The general public has never had much trouble believing that inflation is the result of irresponsible behavior on the part of suppliers, whether of labor or products. The public looks for villains when things go wrong and seems to find them in the business firms that announce price increases and the union leaders that call for wage hikes. An excessive rate of increase in aggregate demand is a force too abstract and impersonal to be a good candidate for villain, so that corporations and unions tend to be blamed for inflation even when wages and prices are clearly being pulled up by excess demand, not being pushed up by market power. That's why the imposition of wage and price controls during a period of inflation usually encounters an overwhelmingly favorable response from the public, at least initially.

The popularity of wage and price controls as a way of dealing with inflation makes it all the more urgent that the public understand the mechanisms of inflation. If wages and prices rise after the fiscal or monetary authorities have expanded aggregate demand faster than real output can keep up, or after some disaster (war, oil embargoes, crop failures) has reduced the level of real output, controls are worse than useless. For they suspend the rationing system through which scarce goods get allocated among competing claimants. This means that the goods will have to be allocated by other criteria: buyers will get in line early, cultivate contacts, try to negotiate special agreements, or offer illegal monetary inducements to get around the maximum price. The incentive to hoard goods will increase, because goods are undervalued at their legal prices and because buyers cannot be sure of obtaining supplies in the future. This further aggravates the scarcity.

Producers will also have less incentive to expand output and maintain quality. Production will fall further as manufacturers find themselves unable to obtain particular inputs that have suddenly disappeared from suppliers' inventories; they may even have to suspend production and lay workers off. Export controls will be instituted to keep other countries from taking advantage of the controlled prices. Bartering will creep into the supply system, not only decreasing efficiency but also stirring up cries of inequity from those producers

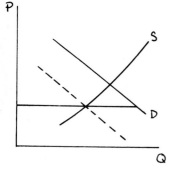

Freezing prices after demand has increased interferes with society's allocation system.

who have nothing of value to offer their suppliers. Items will unexpectedly disappear from retail shelves — paper bags, shoe heels, plastic syringes, fertilizer — as shortages multiply and breed further shortages. Relative prices will not be able to change in response to changing relative scarcities, and so the structure of prices will start to give misleading signals to resource users. In short, suppression of the price system suspends the mechanism of economic coordination, leading to inequities, inefficiencies, and disruptions of production that only worsen the imbalance between demand and supply.

Imposing price controls in the face of an inflation caused by too many dollars chasing too few goods aggravates the problem by reducing the supply of goods and diminishing the incentive of demanders to economize in their use. And this is true whether the imbalance was caused by an excessive creation of dollars or a deficient creation of goods. Moreover, it diverts the attention of the public from the actual causes of the inflation and the proper remedies. Of course, a government whose fiscal and monetary policies have fueled an inflation will be only too happy to encourage the public's belief that private avarice is the root of the problem, that public-spirited self-restraint on the part of citizens is the ultimate answer, and that the rascals who have no public spirit must be controlled by law. Congress will rarely admit that its own spending habits are the cause of any ills, and presidents never locate the cause of inflation in their own earlier policies.

The wage and price controls of World War II are sometimes brought forward as evidence that controls can in fact be effective in preventing excess demand from pulling up prices. But this argument ignores some important facts. It overlooks the public's willingness to put up with shortages and tolerate inequities when they are viewed as temporary necessities. It overlooks the alternative rationing system created by the federal government during World War II to allocate scarce goods among competing claimants: the complex point system, the books of ration stamps, the special gasoline coupons, the priority allocations, and the army of controllers required to make the system work even as well as it did. It overlooks the role of wartime patriotism in securing the voluntary cooperation that kept the system functioning for several years, as well as the illegal and semilegal evasions that sometimes helped the system work by enabling people to circumvent it. And it overlooks the fact that, when the controls were removed, as they eventually had to be, the excess demand dammed up behind them poured out to raise the price level 40 percent between 1945 and 1948.

Price controls may be able to postpone price increases --but at what cost?

Cost-Push Inflation? The Case of OPEC

It is worse than useless to impose price or wage controls
when expansionary fiscal and monetary policies have created
a demand for goods that can't be satisfied at prevailing
prices. Suppressed inflation creates more inequities and inefficiencies than open inflation. But are inflations always the
result of overly expansionary fiscal and monetary policies?
Are all inflations caused by the pull of excessive demand?
Are they never caused by pressure from the supply side? Is
there no such thing as cost-push inflation?

It would be hard to convince any user of petroleum
products that OPEC, for example, played no part in causing
the U.S. inflation of the 1970s. The OPEC cartel used its
market power to reduce the supply of oil and thereby raise
the price of oil substantially to users. Oil and its products
enter into the budgets of consumers, directly and indirectly,
at innumerable points; every good's production cost was
pushed up to some extent by the rise in energy costs. The
only question, it would seem, is what portion of the price
rises from 1973 to 1981 can be attributed to OPEC.

We said way back in Chapter 15 that inflation is a fall in
the price of money, and that its causes must therefore be
sought in the forces affecting the supply of and demand for
money. Is that necessarily the case? If the supply of some
good is reduced through the action of a cartel, or a drought,
or a strike, or any other event, the relative price of that good
will rise. The relative prices of goods that use it as an input
will consequently also tend to rise. Since oil enters in some
fashion as an input into the production of every good, it
would then seem to follow that OPEC has the power to raise
the relative prices of *all* goods and thus to cause inflation.
Money isn't involved.

But the argument is nonsense. The *relative* prices of *all*
goods cannot rise, because nothing would be left relative to
which they could rise. An increase in the relative price of
goods with large inputs of oil in their production processes
logically entails a decrease in the relative price of goods with
smaller inputs of oil in their production processes. To deny
this would be like trying to see whether major-league baseball players are better today than they were a generation ago
by checking on whether major-league clubs win a higher percentage of their games today than they did a generation ago.

Of course, the relative price of all goods *other than
money* can rise; that's not a logical impossibility. And OPEC
could conceivably be responsible for causing an increase in

the price of everything *relative to money*. But don't you find it somewhat odd to focus entirely on oil and to ignore money altogether when the price of *everything* has changed *relative to money*?

Clear the cobwebs for yourself by thinking about the consequences of OPEC's actions in a world without money, where all trade is conducted by barter. OPEC's actions in such a case would have compelled other countries to export more commodities and services per barrel of oil imported. Oil consumers would have had to choose between consuming less oil or sacrificing larger quantities of other goods. With the opportunity cost of acquiring a barrel of oil higher than before, producers would also look for ways to economize. They would produce relatively fewer of any goods that use lots of oil, thereby reducing the supply of these goods and causing an increase in their relative price. What would happen, in summary, is that the relative prices of goods that use lots of oil would rise, and the quantities of them produced and purchased would undergo a relative decline. This necessarily means that the relative prices of goods using very little oil would fall, while the quantities of these goods both produced and purchased would increase.

This is what actually happened after 1973. It happened in the United States in very clumsy and costly ways, because the U.S. government chose to interfere with the movements of relative prices by which these complex processes of reallocation are ordinarily guided. But much of this was camouflaged by changes in the value of money. We fail to see that the relative prices of some goods *fell* as a consequence of OPEC's successes, because our attention is riveted on the price of everything relative to money. The price of everything (or *almost* everything) relative to money rose substantially after 1973. But this occurred because the supply of money increased faster than the demand for money.

From 1973 to 1980 (in the U.S.): the price of heating fuel rose 170% the price of clothing rose 40% the consumer price index rose 85%

Supply-Side Shock and Demand-Side Response

Are we saying, then, that OPEC played no part in causing the U.S. or world inflation of the 1970s? Not at all. We are rather trying to find out exactly what that part might have been. And we're getting close. Suppose that the Fed had held the money supply constant between 1973 and 1980. What would have occurred? The most probable consequence would have been a sharp recession. The United States actually did have a recession that began right at the end of 1973 and continued into 1975. But if the Fed had followed a policy of no growth in the stock of money, or even of substantially slower growth, the recession would almost surely have been more severe.

The reason is that OPEC's actions necessitated large and rapid increases in the relative prices of petroleum-using products. That meant large and rapid *decreases* in the relative prices of other goods. But prices do not always change smoothly and quickly in response to altered conditions of supply and demand. Above all, they do not *fall* smoothly and quickly. The more immediate effect is accumulating inventories, which lead to reduced orders, production cutbacks, and increased unemployment — to recession, in other words. This increased unemployment of labor and other resources continues until relative prices have adjusted to the new circumstances and resources have been reallocated.

The extensive shock that OPEC administered to the U.S. economy in 1973 undoubtedly contributed to the 1974–75 recession. Remember that recessions result from accumulated mistakes; in 1973 OPEC turned a lot of decisions very suddenly into mistakes. In 1973 OPEC unexpectedly compelled an extensive reallocation of resources in the United States, a reallocation that had to be directed by changes in relative prices. The Fed probably made those relative price adjustments easier and the reallocation process consequently quicker by increasing the stock of money. The increased stock of money permitted the necessary price adjustments to occur without any price having to fall in money terms, because all price adjustments could be upward. The goods whose relative prices were supposed to decrease simply rose, in money terms, less than the average. The Fed promoted inflation in response to OPEC's price increases; but it did so in an effort to counter the reduced output and employment caused by OPEC's unexpected success in cartelization.

Market Power, Unemployment, and Inflation

Here may be a major source of pressure on the Fed to pursue inflationary monetary policies. We gave so much space to the question of OPEC's role in the U.S. inflation of the 1970s because the issue illuminates a more general problem. Suppose that a significant number of wage rates are set by collective bargaining and that unions have the ability to obtain wage increases in excess of productivity increases. That would mean that unions (or some unions) can obtain for their members a wage that is above the value of the marginal worker's net contribution to the employer's revenue.

Employers adjust to such a situation by reducing the number of workers they hire. They may not actually lay anyone off; instead they will just refrain from replacing workers as they retire or quit. The result is a reduction in the number of jobs available and an increase in measured unemployment. It makes no difference if we assume that employers can raise their prices and recover the higher labor costs without reducing employment. At higher prices they won't be able to sell as much, and the reduced sales will eventually lead to employment cutbacks. Even if union members realize that higher wages will mean fewer jobs, a majority may vote for the wage increase in the belief that they themselves will be protected by seniority; they are risking the jobs of others.

Rising unemployment caused by this kind of market power puts the Fed under pressure to adopt an expansionary monetary policy. When it does so, prices rise generally. The rise in the price of everything else reduces the relative price of the good whose sales had fallen, its sales expand once more, and employment in that industry is restored. If employers lack the market power to pass the wage increase along to buyers, the increase in the price of all goods does the job for them. The real wage is consequently reduced, and employment is restored to its initial level. The upshot of the matter is that the use of excessive market power creates unemployment problems, and that to deal with the unemployment problems the Fed may be forced to cause inflation.

Many economists who believe that the key to a stable price level is monetary and fiscal restraint on the part of government have nonetheless come to the conclusion that it isn't enough to control aggregate demand. Labor and product markets may no longer function well enough to let fiscal and monetary policy be effective. If strong unions and business firms with substantial market power are able to raise wages and prices in the absence of any increase in demand, monetary and fiscal authorities may have to choose between causing unemployment by refusing to expand aggregate demand or causing inflation by underwriting the wage and price increases.

Supply-Side Controls

An alternative is for government to lay aside the tools of aggregate-demand management and go after the supply-side forces that make price stability incompatible with the maintenance of high employment. If the problem is created by powerful unions, business firms selling in insufficiently competitive markets, and innumerable government regulations that tolerate, encourage, and even require practices that raise costs and reduce efficiency, the solution would appear to be structural reforms directed toward increasing competition and thereby making wages and prices more responsive to changing demand conditions.

Some economic analysts would carry such supply-side policies even further. Because they believe that organized interest groups today have the power simply to set the prices they choose for the goods or services they supply, without regard to the public interest, they want the government to assert an extensive control over economic decisions. In their view, inflation is the product of a struggle among such groups for a larger share of the gross national product. Unless the government establishes some kind of "incomes policy" to contain this struggle, it will face a perpetual choice between expansionary fiscal-monetary policies that allow all parties to obtain what they demand, thus producing inflation, or noninflationary fiscal-monetary policies that produce high unemployment and chronic stagnation.

If that line of argument is essentially correct and the processes of supply and demand are as thoroughly under the control of dominating interest groups as the advocates of "incomes policy" maintain, then this entire book has been much ado about very little. We are obviously not going to grant such a premise. Competition in something very much like its traditional sense is alive and well in the U.S. economy today, subject though it may be to frequent fractures and even occasional bouts of serious illness.

Moreover, if the situation were as serious as the advocates of "incomes policy" say it is, then their "solution" would be little more than wishful thinking. How could a democratic government, after all, create legislation to rein in interest groups that were themselves so firmly in control of the society and its economic life? It must be noted that governments have long been working actively to shore up the interest groups that they are now being called on to put down or control. Is it realistic to expect them suddenly to reverse direction and begin undoing their own work? Even if markets were functioning in a wholly intolerable fashion, that fact would in no way demonstrate any capacity on the part of government to improve the situation. A moment's reflection even suggests that gross malfunctioning of the economy is very likely to be a result of failure on the part of government — failure to perform its essential function of clarifying and enforcing the rules of the game. We'll return to this theme in Chapter 22.

Expectations and Supply

The supply-side economics we have discussed so far grows out of the belief that markets do not work well enough to let demand-side policies be effective. Another version of supply-side economics takes just the opposite tack: markets work too well for demand-side policies to be effective.

Supply-side economists of this persuasion start off by asking why changes in aggregate demand should ever be expected to affect real output at all. People who make production and price decisions don't respond to *aggregate* demand. They pay attention to the demand for their own product. And they mostly learn about the demand for what they themselves are selling by watching their own sales. Automobile dealers, for example, don't increase their purchases from the factory or raise their selling prices because they read that new-car sales are up 4 percent nationally, much less because they hear on the radio that M1 increased over the past four weeks at a 12 percent annual rate. They order more cars when sales deplete their inventories. They raise their prices (probably by reducing discounts, offering less for trade-ins, charging more for accessories) when they find that they can do so and still move cars in an acceptable volume.

Now if aggregate demand increases as a result, let us say, of expansionary monetary policy, automobile dealers will presumably get a share of the increased spending. Sales will improve and the dealers' inventories will decline. Prices may "firm" somewhat as dealers find they can sell cars without offering such generous trade-in allowances; but the principal effect at first is likely to be a greater volume of sales and so additional orders placed with the manufacturers. When the manufacturers respond by increasing production, real GNP will increase. An increase in the money supply will have caused an increase in output and employment.

Remember, however, that the automobile dealers were experiencing only their share of an economywide, general increase in spending. That means increased competition among buyers for resources of every sort. Won't that in turn cause a general increase in costs? The automobile dealers (and everyone else) will find to their dismay that business hasn't really improved. The increase in the money supply has merely produced a proportionate increase in the price level. Once everyone learns what has happened, sales and production will fall back to their original level.

The common belief that an increase in aggregate demand will lead to a permanent increase in output rests on the implicit assumption that producers are supplying less than they're willing to supply *at existing price and cost ratios*. It implies that suppliers aren't acting in their own best interest.

Alternatively, it implies that suppliers are permanently fooled by the increase in aggregate demand. A temporary spurt in production is quite likely in response to an increase in aggregate demand, as long as suppliers don't realize that what they're experiencing is a larger demand for everything and not just for what they themselves are selling. But they will eventually learn that their response was a mistake. When the mistake is recognized and corrected, the rate of real output will again decline and we'll be left with nothing but a higher price level.

The Phillips Curve: Use and Abuse

In 1958 an economist named A. W. Phillips published a study on "The Relationship between Unemployment and the Rate of Change of Money Wage Rates in the United Kingdom, 1861–1957" and invented the "Phillips curve." Phillips showed that there was a stable relationship during the period he studied between the unemployment rate and the rate at which the average money wage increased. Unemployment was greater when money wage rates were increasing more slowly and fell in periods when money wage rates were rising rapidly. That seems thoroughly plausible. During periods of high demand for labor, employers will tend to bid up wage rates to obtain and keep the employees they want. In periods of high unemployment, employers will not have to bid so energetically for labor, and wage rates will increase less.

But the argument was subsequently extended to suggest that unemployment might be reduced by allowing an inflationary rate of increase in money wages and, by extension, in the average of all prices. The Phillips curve of this latter argument purports to show that there is a general trade-off between inflation and unemployment, so that less of one can be obtained by accepting more of the other. But the conclusion doesn't follow either from A. W. Phillips' data or from reflection on the causes of inflation and unemployment. And the notion that government policymakers can reduce the rate of unemployment by deliberately causing inflation is an extremely hazardous one.

It is probably true that prices and wages will be more likely to drift upward when the economy is close to "full" employment. The economic system always contains a great deal of internal movement: industries grow, others decline,

firms rise and fall, new production techniques are introduced, the composition of demand changes, people enter and
exit the labor force. Resources must therefore be attracted
continuously into particular employments through the offer
of acceptable employment terms. But employers and employees don't have perfect information. They must search for
what they want and incur the costs of that search.

In a period of low unemployment, the cost of finding a
new job will, on the average, be lower for employees than
during a period of high unemployment. Employees will
therefore be more ready to give up a job when they think the
wage is unsatisfactory and begin searching for another. So
employers will find it difficult to reduce wages.

Search costs for employers are higher in periods of full
employment. And so employers will offer higher wages than
they might otherwise be willing to offer in order to avoid
making an extensive and costly search for the new employees they want and to reduce the risk of losing present employees, who would be expensive to replace.

The same argument applies to prices in product markets.
When the economy is operating close to capacity, excess
supplies are generally hard to find, and buyers will pay
higher prices rather than search for alternative sources of
supply. In a period of high unemployment and substantial
excess capacity, sellers will be shaving prices, because buyers
are hard to find.

The identical conclusion emerges whichever way we
look at it. "Full" employment fosters an upward creep in
prices and wages; substantial unemployment and excess capacity encourage a downward drift in prices and wages.

The basic argument asserts that the direction of drift in
price and wage movements is a response to tightness or
slackness in markets. In other words, the level of employment is the cause and price–wage movement the effect. But
we can't assume that because full employment causes inflation, inflation will bring about full employment. When
there's a big crowd at the basketball game, the gymnasium
temperature rises because of body heat; but the athletic department can't make a crowd come to watch a losing basketball team by overheating the gymnasium.

Reducing Unemployment by Illusion

Nonetheless, the policy of deliberately stepping up inflation
probably would lower the unemployment rate — temporarily.
People are unemployed because they don't find the job opportunities of which they're aware sufficiently attractive. A

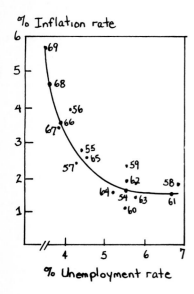

a "well-behaved"
Phillips curve:
U.S., 1954-69

% Inflation rate

policy of deliberate inflation makes job opportunities *seem* more attractive by raising the money wage rate offers of employers. And this is how inflation might reduce unemployment. But the higher wage rate offers are only seemingly more attractive. As long as potential employees don't realize that the job opportunities they're now accepting are in reality no better than the opportunities they previously rejected, employment will indeed rise. But it will subsequently fall back down to its previous level when employees discover what's happening: that inflation is creating the illusion of more attractive wage offers. No permanent reduction in unemployment will have occurred, but the economy will be undergoing more rapid inflation.

A deliberate policy of pursuing lower unemployment by accepting a higher rate of inflation calls, then, for continuously increasing the inflation rate *so that workers always expect less than the actual rate of inflation.* In that way they can be made to overestimate continuously the real value of the money wages they're being offered. Or else the policy assumes that employees pay exclusive attention to money wage rates, never to real wage rates. This is a superficially plausible assumption, since we know that few employees consult the most recent changes in the consumer price index before deciding whether a wage offer is adequate. They look at *money* wage rates, in other words. But they also learn after a while that their wages buy less and adjust their perception of the wage rate's real value. An extreme example will make the point. In 1960 workers stood in line for jobs in manufacturing offering $3 an hour. Manufacturers can find almost no one who will accept employment at that wage today. Employees do know, even if they've never heard of price indexes, that $3 is a much lower hourly wage today than it was a generation ago.

Policy cannot be constructed on the assumption that workers will be permanently fooled, for people learn from experience. And the simultaneous existence of high unemployment with very rapid inflation in the 1970s ought to be sufficient evidence that people have learned. When they begin to take continued inflation for granted, they no longer suffer from the illusion that money wages and real wages are the same thing.

But suppose a government tried this approach to the unemployment problem, found that it couldn't actually lower unemployment, and decided to abandon the policy. Suppose the government had been causing inflation by applying fiscal and monetary stimulus, and now it eases up. After a lag of some length, total spending will stop increasing so rapidly, and producers will be unable to sell at the prices they had anticipated; so inventories will mount, production will be curtailed, and unemployment will rise. Eventually sellers will learn not to expect such a rapid rise in prices. They will adjust downward the prices they ask and the prices they offer to pay for inputs, sales will revive, inventories will decline, production will start up again, and unemployment will fall. But that won't all happen within a week or even a month. The higher unemployment that will result from an attempt to slow down the rate of inflation will be temporary; but temporary can be a long time for those who are laid off.

What it all comes to is that government policies designed to raise output and lower unemployment by increasing aggregate demand will only work if they succeed in creating erroneous expectations on the part of the public. That probably occurred in the latter half of the 1960s. Expansionary fiscal and monetary policies raised output and lowered unemployment, because the public did not know what was happening and consistently underestimated the rate at which costs and prices were going to rise as a result of current policies. But eventually people figured out what was happening and adjusted both their expectations and their behavior. In the 1970s and early 1980s, even more expansionary aggregate-demand policies produced more rapid inflation, but accompanied this time by high rates of unemployment. Once the public caught on, expansionary aggregate-demand policies produced little more than a faster rate of inflation.

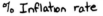

a "not-so-well-behaved" Phillips curve: U.S., 1970-81

Supply-Side Incentives

What policies can government adopt, then, to increase the rate of growth in real GNP and in employment? It must stick to supply-side policies: policies that improve the incentives perceived by those whose decisions might lead to more output and more jobs.

Supply-side economists of this persuasion have consequently laid great emphasis on tax cuts that would increase the after-tax return to labor, innovation, saving, and investment. Some have even argued that total tax receipts might well rise as a result of a reduction in tax rates. This would happen if the lower rates gave such a boost to productive activity that the percentage increase in real GNP exceeded the percentage decline in the rate of taxation; the government would collect more revenue by taking a lower percentage of substantially higher corporate and personal incomes. A supplementary boost to tax revenues, of uncertain but potentially substantial size, would result if portions of the "underground economy" came to the surface as a consequence of lower tax rates. People now taking payment in cash and not reporting it on their tax forms might be induced by lower rates of taxation to pay more tax in return for less guilt and anxiety.

Higher tax revenues as a consequence of lower tax rates is a marvelous promise to anyone prepared to believe it. It was a promise doubly welcome in the late 1970s to those who were concerned not only about high rates of taxation but also about large and growing federal budget deficits.

A Digression on the National Debt

The size of the national debt is a topic that has long been able to arouse hysteria among a large percentage of otherwise thoughtful Americans. People wonder how we will ever pay it off, and while some worry about what might happen if we *cannot* pay it off, others worry about what will ensue if we *do* pay it off. Many probably worry simultaneously about both possibilities. The first step in thinking about federal budget deficits is to see exactly why the national debt does not ever have to be paid off.

The individuals, households, banks, insurance companies, industrial corporations, nonprofit organizations, and government agencies, both in the United States and abroad, to whom the debt is owed are not holding government bonds because they feel sorry for this country. They regard government bonds as good investments. When they no longer do so, they sell what they own to someone else. If lots of people become less willing to hold government bonds, the price of the bonds will fall — just as happens when people become less willing to hold Edward Hopper paintings or urban real estate. As the market price of the bonds declines, the rate of return to someone who purchases them must rise. (Since the dollar return is a set amount, the rate of return always varies inversely with the price paid for the bond.) As the rate of return rises, people become more willing to hold government bonds. Since the U.S. government is not going to default on its debts — it could, if it had to, simply create new money to meet its obligations — there is some price at which people will be willing to hold all the bonds the government has issued.

What happens, however, when these bonds come due? Many of them have very short maturities. If you're seeking cause for alarm, ponder the fact that about 20 percent of the national debt is always due and payable less than one year from the present. This poses no problem, as it turns out. The Treasury Department simply sells new bonds to acquire the funds with which to pay off the old ones; it "rolls the debt over," as the expression goes. As long as the Treasury offers a high enough rate of return, it will be able to roll over as much debt as it cares to. And it can even add to its total indebtedness at the rate of $200 billion per year, as it did for a while in the 1980s, if it is willing to provide lenders with a rate of return that is more attractive than what they can earn elsewhere, taking liquidity and security into account.

The Crowding-Out Problem

And right there is the most important problem created by federal budget deficits. Treasury bond sales put the federal government into competition with every other potential borrower for the available flow of loanable funds. If the monetary authorities do not increase the flow by expanding the money stock, then the federal government is competing with households and businesses for the available flow of savings; and private-sector borrowing and investment will be crowded out as a consequence. If the monetary authorities increase bank reserves to prevent such a "credit crunch," the result will be inflation. Crowding out will still occur; it's just that interest rates will now have to rise far enough to compensate for expected inflation as well as to squeeze out private-sector borrowers.

 Thus, a rapidly rising national debt is undesirable because it reflects large government budget deficits, which raise interest rates and crowd out private borrowing and investment.[1]

Are Tax-Rate Hikes the Solution or the Problem?

Now the standard response to an objectionable deficit is a decrease in expenditures, an increase in revenue, or some combination of the two. Let's assume for purposes of argument that government expenditures cannot be reduced. (We'll see in Chapter 22 why that might be a realistic assumption.) How do we increase government revenues? By raising tax rates? Not necessarily. If the extremely optimistic version of the supply-side argument is correct, lower tax rates will generate larger revenues.

---

[1] We are still pretending that the United States is a closed economic system. As we shall see in the next chapter, foreigners have been helping us out by lending extensively in the United States.

Suppose we agree, however, that this is too optimistic, and that higher tax rates will in fact increase total tax revenue. It doesn't follow that tax rates should be increased to close a deficit. In the first place, the long-run effect of a change in tax rates may be different from the short-run effect. If a 10 percent tax-rate reduction were to raise the annual growth rate of taxable income by 2 percent, the tax cut would be "paying for itself" within five years. In addition, it is surely not a national goal to maximize tax revenues. Deficits are undesirable insofar as they have undesirable effects on the economy. The probable effects of cuts or hikes in tax rates must be set against the probable effects of deficits. An increase from 2 to 4 percent in the annual growth rate would produce a doubling of real output within 18 years. If such an increase in real growth could be obtained by accepting larger federal budget deficits, what reason would be left for objecting to larger deficits?

Of course, opponents of supply-side tax cuts argue that no such positive effect, or at least no positive effect of such dimensions, is going to follow from cutting tax rates at a time when the federal government's budget deficits are shattering records. They may be right; but it still would not follow that we ought to raise rather than lower tax rates. Remember that the deficit does its damage by sopping up too large a percentage of the flow of savings. The question arises, therefore, as to what effect higher or lower tax rates will have on the supply of savings as well as on the demand for them. It's true that the government's credit demands will shrink as it obtains more revenue from taxation. But how will this increase in tax revenue affect the supply of savings? If higher tax rates were to reduce the government deficit by $50 billion and private-sector saving by $100 billion, the tax increase would have aggravated rather than alleviated the crowding-out problem.

Further Complications

Some supply-side economists complain that their policies were denied an opportunity to prove themselves in the first years of the Reagan administration because the supply-side tax cuts were instituted too slowly, too cautiously, and with too many threats of reversal. The failure of Congress to demonstrate enthusiasm for tax-cutting policies darkened investor expectations and so dampened incentives.

Supply-siders also complain that the Fed sabotaged their program with an overly restrictive monetary policy. As evidence they cite the sudden and sharp disinflation of 1982 and 1983. Many economists of the supply-side persuasion have grave doubts about the basic monetarist assumption, stability in the demand for money. They are consequently unwilling to trust the monetary policy preferred by the monetarists — namely, a steady and modest rate of growth in the money stock. If the demand for money were to rise significantly, for any of a number of possible reasons, a modest rate of money growth might be insufficient, they argue, to finance the combined spending plans of consumers, investors, and government. Supply-siders therefore want the Fed to keep its eye on commodity prices when setting monetary policy. Their argument is that the best definition of "enough and not too much" when it comes to monetary policy is whatever produces expectations of stable prices over the long run. They suggest commodity prices, and especially the price of gold, as the best available indicator of long-run price expectations. The Fed failed them, many supply-side economists claim, when it allowed the dollar price of gold to fall about 40 percent from 1980 to 1982. A larger supply of dollars would have prevented this huge and depressing decline in long-run price expectations.

There are so many possibilities to consider that it's easy to see why such a large number of fundamental issues remain unsettled. When there is so little consensus on the appropriate theoretical approach, it is hard to achieve agreement on issues of fact. And in the absence of agreement on the underlying facts, it is hard to decide which competing theoretical framework is most adequate. The truth is sometimes hard to discern even when everyone is pursuing a common objective. And that raises a still more troublesome question.

We have been assuming throughout our discussion of these matters that all parties share a common concern for price stability, economic growth, and low unemployment. No doubt they do. But those are not the only goals of citizens or government officials. We all entertain and pursue a variety of objectives, and we characteristically trade them off against one another on the basis of their anticipated costs and benefits. When we introduce political factors into our discussion of stabilization policy, some serious new problems arise.

We shall consider some of these problems in Chapter 22. But first we must repair a major omission. The U.S. economy is linked with other economies through an extensive network of international exchange. We must therefore try to take the international setting into account before attempting any final conclusions.

Once Over Lightly

Many economists have become dissatisfied with the amount of attention given to demand in the search for the causes and cures of aggregate instability and have begun urging more attention to supply-side forces and factors.

Price and wage increases initiated by groups with substantial market power could make it impossible to achieve high employment and price stability through the management of aggregate demand.

Do direct government controls on prices and wages or efforts by government to reduce the market power of powerful interest groups have the potential for securing high employment levels with low inflation rates? Anyone who thinks they do must explain how democratic governments will be able to impose and manage such programs.

Much of the popularity of demand-side economics stemmed from the belief that government-induced increases in aggregate demand would accelerate the rate of economic growth and cause employment to rise. This result is less likely if producers know what policies the government is following and are consequently not fooled into supposing that the increased demand they observe is a real increase in the demand for their products or services.

In the absence of illusion, some supply-side economists argue, increases in aggregate demand will produce nothing but inflation. They propose tax cuts and other policies to improve incentives to suppliers as more appropriate policies for stimulating economic growth.

The effect of reductions in tax rates on government revenues depends on the extent to which the reductions stimulate effort, innovation, saving, investment, and thus the base on which the taxes are levied.

Whether tax cuts can be expected to increase or reduce government budget deficits (in the long run or the short run?), it should be noted that the deficits are significant largely to the extent to which they crowd out private-sector investment.

The national debt does not ever have to be "paid off." It can be and is "rolled over" as it matures.

Opponents of supply-side policies contend that the policies have been tried and found wanting; advocates say the policies have basically proved themselves despite their not having received a fair trial.

Questions for Discussion

1. What is the difference between a cost-push and a demand-pull inflation?

   (a) The formal definitions are easy enough. But at what evidence could we look to decide whether a particular inflationary surge had been caused by increases in costs or by an overly rapid growth in demand?

   (b) What is wrong with this argument? "If we observe that wage rates have increased faster than productivity has increased during a period of inflation, we may reasonably conclude that wage increases have pushed up prices."

   (c) If union-won wage increases lead to an increase in unemployment and the Fed then expands the money supply in an effort to stimulate economic expansion and lower the unemployment rate, would any inflation that results be more accurately described as cost-push or demand-pull?

2. If OPEC were basically responsible for the surge of inflation that affected the United States between 1973 and 1981, the inflation rate ought to have been even higher during those years in nations more dependent on imported oil than the United States. Here are the average annual rates of increase in the price level from 1973 to 1981 for the United States and six other countries.

	Annual Rate of Increase in Prices 1973 to 1981
United States	8.0%
United Kingdom	15.9
Switzerland	4.0
Mexico	22.6
Japan	6.5
Italy	17.7
Germany	4.6

   (a) Why do you suppose that Switzerland, Japan, and Germany had much lower inflation in these OPEC years than the United Kingdom, even though the United Kingdom was a major oil producer and the other three countries were not?

   (b) Here are the average annual rates of increase in the stock of money in the United States and the six other countries from 1973 to 1981.

	Annual Rate of Increase in Money Supply, 1973 to 1981
United States	6.5%
United Kingdom	11.7
Switzerland	3.4
Mexico	28.8
Japan	8.7
Italy	17.4
Germany	7.8

(c) If you wanted to guess how much inflation a particular nation had experienced from 1973 to 1981, and the only information you could obtain about the nation was *either* the degree of its dependence on imported oil *or* the rate of increase in its money supply, which would you prefer?

3. If a government allows the stock of money to grow at a 25 percent annual rate for several years and sets firm legal ceilings on prices, will inflation occur? What will happen if, at legally enforced prices, the quantity demanded of almost every good is substantially greater than the quantity supplied?

4. How does inflation ease the process of making relative price and wage adjustments?

   (a) Supply and demand conditions in the market for college professors changed markedly from the 1960s to the 1970s. Is it easy for college administrators to lower salaries when supply increases and demand decreases?

   (b) What reaction would you expect from professors who were told that market conditions call for a 7 percent reduction in their annual salary?

   (c) What reaction would you expect from them if they were told that the budget will not allow for any salary increases this year — although the consumer price index has risen 14 percent since last year?

5. Is it possible to control inflation by having a panel of experts pass on all proposed wage or price increases?

   (a) Should such panels include an equal number of business, labor, and consumer representatives?

   (b) How will the members of the panel decide whether a particular increase is "justified" or not?

6. Is it unfair for money wage rates to rise more slowly than prices? Is it unfair for some money wage rates to rise faster and others more slowly than prices? Can you think of some wage and salary rates that ought to rise less rapidly than prices? On what basis would you answer this question?

7. "A teacher of chemistry should not be paid more than a teacher of history simply because the demand for chemistry teachers is greater relative to the supply. Teachers are not commodities. They are professional persons with family responsibilities who are providing essential public services." Do you agree with that statement? If a school district has a serious shortage of science teachers and is prohibited by law from raising wage rates, what can it do? Are there ways to make employment offers more attractive without increasing the official wage rate?

8. If it is true, as some advocates of "incomes policy" maintain, that powerful interest groups prevent the market from working adequately, won't those interest groups be powerful enough to prevent government from passing laws to control them?

9. Suppose the federal government and the Fed jointly announced a decision to double the money supply over the course of the coming year, beginning next week.

   (a) How would you expect this announcement to affect the planning and decisions of suppliers? Would you expect many of them to increase their production or their purchases in anticipation of larger sales? Would you expect many of them to increase their prices after hearing the announcement, without waiting for the money supply or total spending to increase?
   (b) Would you expect suppliers to behave differently if the federal government and the Fed pursued the same policy but did so without announcing it, and even tried to keep secret what they were doing as long as possible?

10. Why is the price level likely to be rising more rapidly when the unemployment rate is low than when it is high?
11. Suppose that a corporation opened a factory employing 5000 workers in a town of 10,000 people. Why would you expect to observe low unemployment, rising wage rates, and rising prices for locally produced goods such as housing and services? What is the causal connection in this case between the town's unemployment rate and its rate of inflation?
12. In the situation described in the preceding question, would you expect prices to start declining if the factory laid off half its labor force? What difference would it make whether the layoff was thought to be temporary or permanent? How much time would it take for a layoff to start bringing down the prices of housing and services in the town?
13. You decide to live in an apartment when you return to campus in the fall. Everyone tells you that apartments are extremely hard to find, so you arrive on campus to start searching a week before school begins.

   (a) If you find something you like but consider it somewhat overpriced, are you likely to take it or to continue looking?
   (b) Is the owner likely to hold it for you for several days, while you continue your search, without a nonrefundable deposit?
   (c) How would the behavior of tenants and owners be different if recent construction had created a surplus of apartment units near the campus?

14. Can inflation reduce unemployment?

   (a) The "help wanted" column of an urban newspaper has been advertising for airport skycaps every day for the past six months. The only job requirements listed are a friendly attitude, a driver's license, and the ability to lift large suitcases. Does the continuous running of this advertisement for six months prove that all the truly unemployed people in the city lack either a friendly attitude, a driver's license, or physical strength?

(b) How could the firm running this advertisement obtain all the qualified skycaps it wants, plus a pool of substitutes and eager apprentices?

(c) How might a sudden, rapid surge of inflation provide this firm with all the applicants it wants?

(d) When and why would the firm again find itself forced to advertise in the "help wanted" column?

15. How large is the national debt of the United States?

(a) The national debt was about $3 trillion at the end of the 1980s. In 1946, as a result of wartime deficits, the debt had reached a record-breaking $270 billion. Why is a simple comparison of these totals seriously misleading?

(b) If we state the 1946 debt in dollars of 1989 purchasing power, it becomes almost $1,700 billion, which is a little more than half the size of the 1989 debt. What is still misleading about this comparison?

(c) The 1946 debt was almost 130 percent of 1946 gross national product; the 1989 debt was about 60 percent of 1989 GNP. Is this the best way to compare the national debt in these two years?

16. The table below shows the size of the gross federal debt at the end of each fiscal year from 1977 to 1982, along with the net interest paid by the government in each year.

Year	Gross Federal Debt (billions of dollars)	Net Interest Paid (billions of dollars)
1977	709.1	28.5
1978	780.4	33.5
1979	833.8	40.7
1980	914.3	50.8
1981	1,003.9	66.7
1982	1,147.0	82.2

(a) Why did the interest paid increase almost 190 percent when the debt increased by only about 60 percent?

(b) If question (a) has you stumped, you might consider what happened to interest rates during this period. The average interest rate on three month loans to the government (ninety day bills) was 5¼ percent in 1977 and 14 percent in 1981. Why did interest rates rise so spectacularly during this period?

17. Will government budget deficits grow or shrink in response to tax cuts? The numbers below are purely hypothetical and consequently provide no answer to that question. The exercise is designed to help you see why people disagree on the answer. Supply-siders forecast a 10 percent annual growth rate if taxes are reduced; non-supply-siders forecast only a 5 percent annual rate of growth. The numbers represent billions of dollars.

Year	Tax Rate	GNP: Supply-Siders' Forecast	GNP: Non-Supply-Siders' Forecast	Govern-ment Expen-ditures	Tax Revenue: Supply-Siders' Forecast	Tax Revenue: Non-Supply-Siders' Forecast
1	11%	$4,000	$4,000	$500	$440	$440
2	10	4,400	4,200	510	_____	_____
3	10	4,840	4,410	521	_____	_____
4	10	5,324	4,631	533	_____	_____

18. In 1988, private saving in the United States was about $730 billion: $145 billion in personal saving and $585 billion in saving by business. Private investment by Americans (in the United States) came to about $765 billion. The federal government ran a deficit in 1988 of close to $140 billion.

(a) From whom could the federal government borrow $140 billion if private savers were not even saving enough to finance private investment? What are the other possibilities?

(b) While the federal government ran a huge deficit in 1988, state and local governments were spending about $55 billion less than they took in. How did that help close the gap?

(c) By how much did total domestic spending in the United States exceed total domestic income in 1988? From where did the difference have to come?

19. While American households were saving about $145 billion in 1988, they were spending approximately $3,225 billion for personal consumption items. Suppose that the prospect of a higher after-tax return on income saved and invested induced the "average" household to reduce its consumption expenditures by 5 percent. How large a contribution would this make to the alleviation of "crowding out" by the federal deficit?

Chapter 21

National Policies and International Exchange

The movement of goods and monetary payments across national boundaries is both a problem and an opportunity for government officials charged with stabilizing their domestic economies. That's why this chapter on international exchange comes before the concluding chapter on national policies for dealing with recession and inflation.

Perhaps the insertion of this chapter *within* the chapters on national policies can also serve as a reminder that international economic policies are constructed by national states. There is no "international government" today with the will and the capacity to establish rules for the governance of international exchange. We often hear that nationalism is obsolete in the era of jet planes, rockets, space exploration, satellite communication, and nuclear weapons. But that's the statement of an ideal, not a description of reality. The present reality is that any actual international economic order will be produced by the interactions of people whose allegiance is *not* to "the community of nations." And no international economic system will get the support of a nation unless that support is seen to be in the best interest of those who control the nation's government.

Accounting for International Transactions

Balance-of-payments accounting provides a useful but potentially misleading way to think about the effects of international transactions on national economies. You can usually avoid being misled if you keep one simple truth in mind: *the balance of payments always balances.* Let's see why that's so and what it means.

In a simplified summary of a nation's balance of payments, all transactions can be assigned to one of four categories: exchange of merchandise, exchange of services, exchange of IOUs, and unilateral transfers.

Exchange of merchandise is self-explanatory. Exchange of services may be less clear. The services exchanged internationally include transportation services, insurance services, and the many kinds of services that tourists purchase when traveling abroad. But internationally-traded services are not only and not even primarily labor services; the most important service that people in one country provide to people in another is the service of capital goods. Investors are providing a very important service when they make capital available to other countries. For this service they receive investment income in return, and income from foreign investments is the largest part of the "services" item in the balance of payments.

The third category, exchange of IOUs, includes evidences of indebtedness of every kind: shares of stock, corporation or government bonds, mortgages, promissory notes, deposits in financial institutions (which are liabilities of the institutions, you will recall from Chapter 17), and paper currency (which is also a liability of the institution that issued it). Unilateral transfers is a fancy term for one-way transactions: payments for nothing at all, such as gifts, or for services rendered in some earlier period, such as pension benefits.

Transactions in each category produce either payments into or payments out of the nation. Exports generate payments into a nation and so are put in the credits column. Imports and other transactions that generate payments out of the nation are assigned to the debits column. Thus, when General Motors sells a Buick to an Italian, payment is made to someone in the United States and the transaction is recorded as a credit item in the U.S. balance of payments. If a British museum sells a Turner painting to an American collector, the American makes a payment abroad and the transaction is a debit in the U.S. balance of payments. The United States gave up a Buick and Britain lost a Turner; but the balance of payments looks at payments, not at the goods for which the payments are made. So those transactions are credit items respectively in the U.S. and British balance of payments. This should put you on guard. A nation that decided to sell all its art treasures to foreigners would be accumulating credits on its balance of payments as it denuded its museums and galleries. *Credit* is clearly not a synonym for *good thing*.

Why does the balance of payments always balance? We shall use the official data from the 1987 U. S. balance of payments to explain and illustrate. Listed below are the totals in each of our four categories, in billions of dollars. Credits and debits are not listed separately for transfers; the number in the debits column says that transfer payments out of the United States exceeded transfers into the United States by $16 billion in 1987.

		Credits		Debits
Merchandise	Exports	$250	Imports	$410
Services	Exports	116	Imports	94
IOUs	Exports	212	Imports	76
Transfers (net)		—		16
Statistical discrepancy		18		
Totals		$596		$596

If the data gatherers who construct the balance of payments had a complete and accurate record of every international transaction, the sum of the items in the credits column would exactly equal the sum of the items in the debits column. In 1987 (and every other year) the records were far from complete and so the sums were not equal. The record keepers rise to each occasion. They add the difference to the smaller total, label it "statistical discrepancy," and thereby *compel* credits to equal debits.

The difference between recorded credits and recorded debits is by definition a statistical discrepancy.

Why Credits Must Equal Debits

Credits must always exactly equal debits because every international transaction necessarily entails another transaction that precisely offsets it. The case of a simple gift probably shows the process most clearly. Suppose that Henry Higgins, who now resides and works in New York, decides to give $100 to his old friend back in London, Eliza Doolittle. Eliza once told Professor Higgins that the balance of payments always balances; but he did not believe it for a moment, and now he wants to vindicate his skepticism while simultaneously demonstrating his affection and esteem for Eliza. "This is a pure gift," he trumpets triumphantly as he drops his $100 check into the envelope and addresses it to Eliza. "I'm getting nothing in return. So debits will rise by $100 while credits will not change. I shall have unbalanced the balance of payments!"

But Henry is mistaken. While the gift is a debit, the check that Eliza acquires is a financial claim on Henry's New York bank. When Eliza holds the check in the air and says, "Hah hah hah, Henry Higgins," she is the proud owner of an American IOU: $100 of demand deposits in a New York bank. Henry overlooked the fact that in making his gift to Eliza he enabled foreigners to increase by $100 the amount of U.S. IOUs that they hold. As long as Eliza keeps the check, she is a foreigner with an investment in the United States. This $100 increase in foreign investment exactly balances the $100 unilateral transfer that Henry Higgins thought had unbalanced the balance of payments.

When Eliza goes to her bank to cash the check and obtain British pounds for it, her bank becomes the owner of the IOU. When the bank sells that deposit to a British importer, the importer owns the IOU. When he in turn uses the $100 to pay for merchandise imported from the United States, the deposit moves back into U.S. ownership and so becomes a debit item in the U.S. balance of payments, because the United States has now imported — repatriated, you might say — an IOU. The balancing item for this debit will be the $100 worth of merchandise that was exported to England, necessitating a payment into the United States and so creating a credit item in the U.S. balance of payments.

The easiest way to understand how the balance of payments remains in continuous balance is to focus on the international exchange of IOUs. If everyone in the United States — households, business firms, and government — imports merchandise and services over some period of time whose value is greater than the value of merchandise and services exported during this time, and if the difference is not made up by unilateral transfers, then Americans must owe the difference to foreigners. That means Americans have exported IOUs to foreigners, which amounts to saying that foreigners have increased their investments in the United States by the exact amount required to close the gap.

Equilibrium and Disequilibrium

If there cannot be a surplus or a deficit in a nation's balance of payments, what is bothering all those people who worry aloud about "the trade deficit" and warn that disaster is imminent if we don't reduce the deficit? Would their anxieties disappear if they learned that credits always equal debits? Probably not. They are worried about something else, something that should properly be called a *disequilibrium* in the balance of payments.

A disequilibrium in economic theory is a discrepancy between what is happening and what people want to happen, between reality and intention. A disequilibrium price for wheat, for example, doesn't show up as a difference between actual sales and purchases, which are necessarily identical, but as a difference between the *intentions* of sellers and purchasers. The quantity that farmers *want* to sell is greater or less than the quantity that consumers *want* to buy.

Another example would be the gap analyzed in Chapter 18 between the quantity of money supplied and the quantity of money demanded. The quantity of money *actually* held by the public has to be the same as the quantity supplied by the monetary system. But the public can *want* to hold more or less. When that's the case, a disequilibrium exists.

The implication of a disequilibrium is that matters will not continue the way they are, adjustments are going to occur, because some relevant parties are not realizing their intentions. The price of wheat will rise, for example, because consumers are unable to buy as much as they want to buy and they are going to bid the price up. Or durable goods inventories are going to begin increasing because the public wants to hold larger money balances than it's currently holding, and that means people will be postponing durable goods purchases.

It follows from all this that we cannot use the concept of equilibrium or disequilibrium unless we can specify the intentions that are currently being frustrated. Those who worry or complain about disequilibrium in the balance of payments never do identify the people who are not succeeding in carrying out their plans. That shouldn't surprise us. The concept of a balance-of-payments disequilibrium is so extraordinarily ambiguous that we would probably be better off if we discarded the notion altogether. There are just too many intentions of too many different kinds entering into the aggregate of international transactions for anyone to assert that intended credits are larger or smaller than intended debits — which is the meaning of a disequilibrium. In general, the larger the universe to which we try to apply the equilibrium concept, the more vague and uncertain is its meaning — and the more likely it is to obscure rather than clarify the problems at which we're looking.

To claim that the U.S. balance of payments is in disequilibrium is really to claim that something undesired is occurring. But from whose point of view is this claim made? Didn't the importers want to purchase whatever they purchased? Didn't banks want to lend whatever they lent? Didn't governments, corporations, or individuals want to

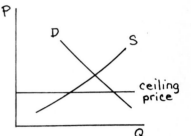

The quantity demanders *want* to purchase is greater than the quantity suppliers *want* to sell.

A "disequilibrium" implies that something will change.

Which of the transactions in the balance of payments accounts was not intended ??

offer the gifts or grants they sent abroad? Who were the people for whom the results of international trade turned out to be inconsistent with what they had intended?

A simple little question should always be addressed to anyone who claims that the balance of payments is in disequilibrium: "How do you know that?" The answer, if followed up properly, will tell you what is worrying the speaker.

The Ambiguities of International Disequilibrium

Suppose we find someone who is concerned about the U.S. trade balance and ask exactly what is disturbing her. If she is well-informed, she may point to the fact that since 1976 the United States has each year imported more merchandise, in value terms, than it exported. The proper reply is to ask why she ignores exports of services and IOUs. Merchandise, services, and IOUs are *all* valuable to the people who receive them. They want them. They give up other goods of value to get them. What is there to worry about?

She may point in reply to the fact that, since 1983, U.S. imports of merchandise *and services* have been greater than our exports of merchandise and services, and that we haven't made up the difference through unilateral transfers. (We have run net debits in unilateral transfers for as long as the records go back.) But once again we must ask why this should be an occasion for concern. It means that Americans in the aggregate are borrowing more from foreigners than foreigners are borrowing from Americans. It does not imply a disequilibrium.

Is it nonetheless reason to worry? A great deal of concern, verging occasionally on hysteria, arose in the 1980s over the huge deficits in the U.S. balance on merchandise trade. The merchandise deficit was not being made up by the balance on services and transfers, with the inevitable consequence that foreigners were increasing substantially their holdings of U.S. IOUs. A lot of people reacted to this with panic, as if foreigners were in a position to foreclose on our mortgage and eager to do so. That's absurd. Lenders don't foreclose when the borrowers are keeping up their payments. Foreigners have been eagerly investing in the IOUs of Americans because they regard investments in the United States as a better deal than the other investments they could make. They like our prospects so they want to own our IOUs. They are happy to be our creditors because they expect it to be profitable for themselves.

Perhaps our hypothetical worrier is concerned about all

Foreigners were not "forced" to lend to us because we were importing more than we were exporting, anymore than we were "forced" to import more than we exported so that foreigners could invest in the U.S.

the interest we will have to pay on those loans. But "we" won't be paying the interest. That will be the obligation of those who did the borrowing. If they were sensible folk, they borrowed intelligently, after calculating that the benefits of the loans would probably exceed the interest costs. If our worrywart thinks they were foolish borrowers, how did she come by this insight? People certainly do borrow foolishly at times. But lenders usually monitor this fairly well.

Disequilibrium as a Disguised Policy Judgment

We have probably gotten very close to the basic anxiety afflicting many of those who began to fret in the 1980s about the U.S. balance of payments: they were worried about the spendthrift ways of Americans as consumers and taxpayers. The sum of what we are currently willing to save and to pay in taxes seems to be considerably less than the sum of what we want to spend on investment projects and government programs. Our growing foreign indebtedness is evidence, according to these people, of our shortsightedness, our self-ishness, our self-indulgence, our want of self-discipline and lack of the ability to govern ourselves.

All that might be true. But none of it constitutes a dis-equilibrium in the balance of payments. The balance of pay-ments is equilibrating nicely to our shortsightedness, selfish-ness, and so on. The balance of payments reflects our situa-tion; it does not cause it. If we are in fact suffering from some sort of national malaise, we will not find any remedy in the balance of payments. The eagerness of foreigners to invest in the United States in the 1980s was in fact an enor-mous advantage to us. With the federal government running deficits as large as $200 billion in a single year, someone had to come up with a lot of loanable funds. Foreigners did what American households and business firms were unwilling to do: save an extra $200 billion to finance the federal budget deficit. Without their assistance, interest rates would have been higher and the U.S. capital stock would have grown more slowly.

On the other hand, if foreigners stopped lending to us so liberally, we would begin to feel some of the consequences of our alleged vices. And maybe we would reform our ways!

A substantial amount of the informed concern in recent years about the deficit on merchandise and services in the U.S. balance of payments seems to be a disguised concern about the federal government's persistent budget deficits and the low current saving rate of U.S. households. But using the concept of international disequilibrium to disguise domestic policy judgments has some unfortunate policy consequences of its own. It muddies discussion, of course, and makes it that much harder to deal responsibly with domestic policy problems. It also opens the door to all those special interests that would welcome a "public interest" justification for special interest policies. If patriotism is the last refuge of scoundrels, as Samuel Johnson suggested, the balance of payments is very often the last refuge of pretending patriots.

The balance of payments has been used to justify tariffs and quotas on imports, restrictions on the relocation of manufacturing plants, subsidies to research and development projects, exemptions from the antitrust laws, threats against foreign governments, taxpayer loans to exporters, and a long list of other government favors to special interests. Some of these might be wise and prudent policies. If they are, however, they ought to be defended openly and clearly, not advocated in the name of a nonexistent balance-of-payments problem.

But Will It Go on Forever?

A claim of disequilibrium, if it's not a disguised policy judgment, is a prediction that things are going to change. The price of wheat will rise, durable goods inventories will increase, and so on. What is being predicted by someone who contends that a nation's foreign trade is in disequilibrium? What is it that cannot be expected to continue as it is?

This is an excellent question with which to pester anyone still determined to employ the concept of disequilibrium when talking about problems of international trade. Those who are worried about the current U.S. "disequilibrium" would most likely point to the willingness of foreigners to increase their holdings of American IOUs. "They won't go on lending to us forever." That may not be true, since there is no definite limit to the ability of U.S. borrowers to pay a satisfactory return to their creditors. But what if it were true, as it surely is for smaller, less prosperous, and less stable nations of the world? Would this be a problem? Or would it be the solution to a problem?

When lenders decide that a potential borrower may be in over his head, some withdraw further credit, some demand better collateral, some scrutinize projects more carefully, some insist on a higher rate of interest. Whenever U.S. borrowers start to make foreign lenders nervous, foreign lenders will behave in ways that make it harder for Americans to borrow. There is no single response that all lenders will make simultaneously, and consequently no reason to expect a crisis. Excessive borrowing creates its own corrective.

In the case of international borrowing, or borrowing and lending between parties with different domestic currencies, the rate of exchange between the currencies is an additional factor of substantial importance.

Foreign-Exchange Rates and Purchasing-Power Parity

Foreign-exchange rates, most simply, are relative prices that tie together *sets* of relative prices. The existing exchange rate between two currencies at any time will roughly express the relative purchasing power of the two currencies. If it takes 50 cents to buy a German mark but only ½ cent to buy a Japanese yen, you can assume, as a first approximation, that 1 dollar, 2 marks, and 200 yen will all buy roughly the same amount of goods in the United States, Germany, and Japan, respectively. Thus, exchange rates, to begin with, adjust to create *purchasing-power parity* among national currencies.

The simplest way to see why this is so is to think about what will happen if it's *not* so. If 1 dollar exchanges for 200 yen, but 200 yen buy appreciably more goods in Japan than 1 dollar buys in the United States, then dollar holders will want to buy yen with dollars in order to get more for their money. That increased demand for yen on the part of dollar holders will not be matched by an increased supply of yen, because yen holders will not be willing to give up 200 yen in return for just 1 dollar. The dollar price of the yen will consequently rise. Dollar holders will have to start offering $1.05 to obtain 200 yen. Viewing the same event from the other side, yen holders will now be able to purchase 1 dollar for about 190 yen.

Purchasing-power parity is only a first approximation, however, as we seek to find out why national currencies exchange for one another at the rates they do. Exchange rates can never exactly equate the purchasing power of two currencies because no two currencies will ever purchase exactly the same array of goods. Some goods, such as a vacation near Mt. Fujiyama, just aren't available for purchase with dollars in the United States or with marks in Germany. Moreover, exchange rates are more responsive to the relative prices of internationally traded goods (farm commodities, machinery, petroleum, automobiles) than to the relative prices of those goods that are rarely exported or imported (housing, most services).

Expectations and Exchange Rates

The expectation that an asset will increase in value causes its value to increase now.

More importantly, however, foreign-exchange rates won't express the *current* purchasing power of currencies when their relative purchasing power is expected to change. A belief that the United States will experience more rapid inflation than Germany in the coming year is a belief that the German mark will lose less value than the U.S. dollar during the year. That belief increases the present demand for marks, relative to the demand for dollars, and causes the current value of the mark to rise relative to the value of the dollar. That explains a great deal that is otherwise inexplicable about movements in exchange rates.

Consider the complaints about the "overvalued dollar" that became chronic in the first half of the 1980s as the value of the U.S. dollar relative to most foreign currencies rose by more than 50 percent from 1980 to 1985. It's not hard to understand why some people were upset. A 50 percent appreciation in the foreign-exchange value of the dollar makes U.S. exports 50 percent more expensive to foreigners. That's not good news for American firms trying to sell in overseas markets. That 50 percent appreciation of the dollar simultaneously reduced the average price of foreign goods in the United States by one-third, a development not welcomed by U.S. firms selling in competition with imports. (It was pointed out less frequently and much less vociferously that those Americans who bought foreign goods at one-third lower prices benefited from doing so; the interests of consumers usually receive less attention than the complaints of producers.)

What caused this steep rise in the foreign-exchange value of the dollar? The first thing to notice is that the dollar had an extremely *low* value in 1980. Through the 1970s the value of the dollar had slid downward in the foreign-exchange markets, until in 1980 it stood at about 70 percent of its value in the 1960s.[1] So most of the appreciation after 1980 was merely a return of the dollar to its earlier value. The first question to ask, then, is why the dollar depreciated in the 1970s.

The Downs and Ups of the Dollar

The answer is the inflation that occurred in the United States in the 1970s. Prior to the 1970s, the United States was

[1]These comparisons refer to the average value of the dollar relative to the currencies of the principal nations with which the United States trades, with the importance of each currency weighted, in calculation of the average, by the volume of trade with that country.

generally expected to run substantially lower inflation rates
than other countries. We were expected to do this because
we had in fact done so since World War II, and our political
institutions seemed generally capable of resisting the inflationary pressures that besieged other governments. With the
dollar expected to maintain its value better than most other
currencies, foreigners chose to hold a substantial amount of
wealth in dollar-denominated assets.

When the 1970s gradually revealed that the United
States was not immune to inflation, and U.S. inflation rates
climbed toward or even above those of other major economic
powers, investors abandoned their confidence in the dollar.
Since they expected it to lose value in the future, they became willing to hold dollars only when they could acquire
them at a lower price. The value of the dollar in foreign exchange consequently declined, until it reached a level at
which foreigners were willing to hold all the dollars supplied
to them.

Then in 1980 evidence mounted that the United States
was again going to bring its rate of inflation under control.
The Fed had declared its determination to control the
rate at which the stock of dollars would grow, and a new
administration with conservative credentials prepared to
take office vowing to end the spendthrift practices that had
supposedly been responsible for the high inflation of the
1970s. It is expectations that control foreign-exchange rates.
The change in expectations raised the value of the dollar
even before the U.S. inflation rate actually declined in 1982
and 1983.

There is more to the story than this, as there always is.
In an introductory account, however, too many details will
obscure the essential picture. And the essential point is that
the desire by foreigners to hold dollars, relative to the quantity of dollars being supplied to them through the international transactions of Americans, determines the foreign-exchange value of the dollar. When foreigners increase their
demand for dollars while other things remain equal, the dollar appreciates. They increase their demand for dollars when
they conclude that the dollar is going to hold its value in the
future better than they previously thought, or that investments in the United States are more attractive than they
seemed to be earlier.

All this causes foreign-exchange rates to move up and
down in ways that make international transactions riskier
than they would otherwise be. Uncertainty of this kind
makes it more difficult for producers to anticipate future
demands for their product; even when they don't sell for

export, they may have to compete with imported products whose prices relative to their own can change suddenly and substantially due to an exchange rate movement. Costly mistakes are consequently made more often, and recessions, which are ultimately rooted in mistaken predictions, tend to become more frequent and more severe. It would seem to be far better if exchange rates were fixed and stable.

The Bretton Woods System

It was largely in order to create a system of stable foreign-exchange rates that the Western nations established the International Monetary Fund (IMF) after World War II. The IMF was supposed to assist any member nation whose currency was tending to depreciate and to advise on devaluation when it appeared that existing exchange rates seriously overstated the currency's value. With varying rates of economic growth from country to country and different rates of domestic inflation, exchange rates might have to be altered occasionally. But the objective of the Bretton Woods System (named after the town in New Hampshire where the international monetary agreements were negotiated in 1944) was fixed exchange rates. Each nation was supposed to buy and sell its currency in order to keep it pegged at the officially established rate of exchange. (Other currencies were pegged to the dollar, and the dollar was pegged to gold.) Out of all this, it was hoped, would develop an expansion of international trade.

If 5 francs = 1 dollar and 1 dollar = 1/35 ounce of gold, then 1 franc = 1/175 ounce of gold

The system wasn't a failure. International trade did expand under the Bretton Woods System, at roughly twice the rate of increase in domestic production. And the advantages of international specialization contributed substantially to rising levels of real income. But an international monetary system with fixed exchange rates is difficult to maintain among governments pursuing divergent domestic policies. Those policies inevitably produced different patterns of growth in industrial and agricultural production, different movements in the structure of relative prices between countries, different rates of inflation, and consequently large fluctuations in the international demand for different countries' currencies. To prevent depreciation or appreciation under these circumstances, governments were often required to intervene heavily and continuously in the foreign-exchange markets.

The governments whose currency was tending to appreciate had to buy foreign currencies. But they paid for foreign currencies with their own currencies, which meant that they were pumping additional money into their domestic economies and causing inflation. A noninflationary monetary policy was difficult if not impossible to pursue for a central bank required to keep its currency from rising in the foreign-exchange markets. The currency would be tending to appreciate because it was undervalued at the fixed exchange rate, which usually meant that the central bank had been doing a better job than other central banks of holding down the rate of domestic inflation. What it all came to was that countries that controlled inflation through domestic policies were put under international pressure to accelerate their rate of inflation.

Governments whose currency was tending to depreciate, usually because of higher-than-average inflation rates, were required under the Bretton Woods System to purchase their own currency to keep its price from falling. But purchase it *with what!* The very situation that caused the depreciation, a high rate of inflation, made it difficult for that nation to sell enough goods to acquire enough foreign exchange to continue buying its own currency. Borrowing from the IMF could only be a stopgap measure. Without a change in the domestic policies that were producing the pressure for depreciation, devaluation was inevitable. Usually those policies consisted of government expenditures in excess of tax revenues, financed through the creation of new money, with inflation as the eventual result. When the IMF extended loans, it was always with the proviso that the government reduce its budget deficit and slow down its creation of new money. But this was largely empty counsel. The domestic pressures that were creating the budget deficits weren't going to disappear because the International Monetary Fund said that deficits were naughty.

Unplanned Consequences

Unfortunately, governments confronting a depreciating currency have another set of options. They can announce that their problems are the result of a "deficit in the balance of payments" and slap controls on imports to "reduce the deficit." A depreciating currency thus gives government officials another public-interest argument with which to camouflage their surrender to producer lobbies always interested in keeping out import competition. The U.S. government frequently played this game in the 1960s. At various times during that final decade of the Bretton Woods System, we raised the cost to American tourists of bringing back foreign merchandise, placed a tax on money borrowed by foreign corporations from U.S. sources, restricted foreign lending by U.S. banks, imposed first voluntary and later mandatory controls on direct investment abroad by U.S. corporations, recalled the dependents of American military personnel stationed overseas, threatened to impose quotas unless particular countries "voluntarily" curtailed their exports to us, and in an endless variety of smaller ways tried to discourage imports and encourage exports. All this was done to "protect the dollar" against the balance-of-payments "deficits" that supposedly threatened the international monetary order. The irony is that we claimed to be doing all this in order to preserve the international monetary order and the system of free trade!

In 1971 the United States essentially abandoned its efforts to keep the dollar's value fixed in terms of gold, and other countries more or less reluctantly gave up their commitments to maintain a fixed rate of exchange between their currencies and the dollar. Exchange rates were turned loose and were allowed to *float*, as the jargon has it, in response to the changing expectations of suppliers and demanders. Some experts immediately announced the breakdown of the international monetary system and the onset of a world monetary crisis. Central bankers around the world called for emergency conferences to create a new system that would restore order before the flow of trade and exchange broke down in chaos.

Fixed or Floating Exchange Rates?

Outside academic circles, and especially among the economists working for central banks, floating exchange rates were regarded as unworkable if desirable, and undesirable if workable. They would increase uncertainty for foreign traders and investors, it was argued. But they would also create additional uncertainty for domestic producers and investors, because a change in exchange rates could quickly and radically change the potential profitability of industries producing import-competitive goods, as well as goods that might be exported. Moreover, governments weren't likely to remain passive when a sudden depreciation in the currency of a major trading country led to an unexpected surge of imports or threatened established export markets. Governments would far more likely retaliate with trade and investment controls that could eventually lead to a breakdown of international exchange.

Nonetheless, the advocates of floating rates have generally had their way since 1971. This was more by default than by design: conflicting national interests simply prevented governments from agreeing on the structure of a new fixed-exchange-rate system. Most countries today don't allow their currencies to float freely but try to keep them in some loose relationship with another major currency or set of currencies. A variety of limited international agreements, such as the European Monetary System that was launched in 1979, have aimed at reducing fluctuations in exchange rates—at least among countries that trade extensively with each other. And some small nations whose international trade is predominantly with a much larger economy have tried to maintain a rigidly fixed rate of exchange between their currency and the currency of the dominant trading partner. The system that has evolved since 1971 has its faults and its localized crises, but it does work. Floating exchange rates have not turned out to be the disaster that the central bankers forecast.

Perhaps the fairest judgment we can make is to say that the advocates of fixed foreign-exchange rates and the advocates of floating rates are *both* correct. The ideal system is one of fixed exchange rates. Just try to imagine what would happen if the dollar had a different and constantly changing value in each of the fifty American states. Do you see how many additional costs and how much new uncertainty that would create for business firms? Our national wealth is in large part a consequence of the extensive specialization that we have been able to practice because low-cost, low-uncertainty trade was possible throughout our vast territory. Fixed exchange rates between the states—the dollar of a Maine film fan always exchanges for exactly one dollar of California-produced films—plays an enormous even if unappreciated part in facilitating that specialization and trade.

But the advocates of floating exchange rates are correct, too. The nations of the world are unlike the states of the United States in two critical ways: they are *not* prohibited by any constitution from restricting the free movement of merchandise, services, financial assets, and people across borders, and they *do* have the ability to run independent monetary policies. The governments of our states lack the power to create the conditions that would permit dollars in Alabama or Alaska to change in value relative to the dollars used in Hawaii and New Hampshire. The governments of nation-states do have that power as well as political incentives to use it in ways that are almost inevitably going to

Fixed exchange rates are the ideal system with ideal governments.

Floating exchange rates may be the best system given the way governments actually behave.

cause the purchasing power of their currencies to change at divergent rates. Trying to maintain fixed exchange rates in a world of radically diverse national economic policies will almost certainly do more harm than good. It will encourage and sometimes even require governments to interfere with international trade, as the only way in which they can reconcile politically opportune domestic policies with predetermined foreign-exchange rates.

Private Interests, National Interests, Public Interests

All this will suggest to some people that there is no longer any international economic order. That might be true for those who equate order with legislated systems and international order with negotiated treaties. But it would not be true for those who see order simply in the continuation and extension of international exchange. It sometimes happens that we become so absorbed in our search for solutions that we forget what the problem was. Is it our goal that consumers, investors, producers, tourists, and bagpipe players—people, in short—be enabled to cooperate more freely across the barriers that national boundaries raise? Or is that the problem—namely, that people are engaging in international transactions that interfere with the goals of national governments?

It is certainly possible that the interests of the larger public might require some restrictions on international exchange. But a thoughtful person will wonder why the national interest seems so regularly to require that more be given away than is received in return; that jobs be preferred to goods; that efficient producers be hobbled to prevent them from using their advantage to the detriment of less-efficient producers; and that in general people be prevented from increasing their wealth by exchanging freely. The skeptic should be pardoned for concluding that the public interest may be something quite different from the national interest, at least as the national interest is usually defined by those who shape international economic policy.

Comparative Advantage Under Attack

The principle of comparative advantage received its first explicit statement in the early nineteenth century as an explanation of the gains to be obtained from international trade. But the principle has never fared well in the area where it originated. "Everyone knows" that imports hurt domestic firms and destroy jobs, whereas exports generate profits for domestic producers and create additional jobs. Policies aimed at restricting imports and subsidizing exports have consequently had a strong political appeal for centuries, and never more so than when a recession is cutting into sales and adding to the level of unemployment.

The argument that imports destroy jobs has the seductive appeal of a half-truth. When Americans buy Japanese radios, they don't buy as many domestically made radios. An increase in radio imports can therefore lead to production cutbacks and layoffs in the domestic radio industry. So the owners and employees of radio-manufacturing firms have an obvious interest in restricting imports. And when they go to Congress to request taxes or quotas on radio imports, they have a handy slogan with which to claim that such protection is good for the country: it protects American jobs. But the argument is misleading.

In the first place, jobs are created by the production of export goods as well as by the production of goods that compete with imports. And American firms can't continue indefinitely to sell abroad if foreigners aren't allowed to sell in the United States. Trade is a two-way street.

Moreover, jobs should not automatically be treated as goods. Some jobs no doubt are intrinsically satisfying and worth doing for themselves without regard to the commodities or services that result. But that's certainly rare. The justification for jobs generally is the income they provide for workers and the corresponding benefit to others in the form of useful goods. The "protect American jobs" argument ignores the gains in real income that come from specialization. If the Japanese can make better radios and sell them at lower prices than American manufacturers can, Americans ought to produce other products and buy their radios from Japan. The attempt to justify the protection of less-efficient producers on the grounds that this will preserve jobs runs quickly into absurdity. Why not push the argument further and produce domestically all the coffee we consume? American soil, climate, and geography are not as well suited for the production of coffee trees as are large areas of Brazil and Colombia. But think of all the jobs we could create by building and operating huge greenhouses in which we try to duplicate the favorable growing conditions in those countries! And why stop with goods currently imported? Think of how many new jobs we could create by outlawing the use of automated equipment in the telephone industry!

Producer Interests and the National Interest

For two centuries, economists have been arguing along these lines against the proponents of restrictions on imports, but not with great success. A French pamphleteer-economist named Frederic Bastiat (1801–1850) wrote a witty satire in 1845 in the form of a petition by the French candlemakers for protection against the unfair competition of the sun. Their request to the Chamber of Deputies for legislation that would protect the jobs of candlemakers by prohibiting windows brilliantly exposes the absurdity of protectionist logic. Bastiat's satire has been reprinted numerous times, but the arguments he ridiculed don't disappear.

Part of the explanation must be found in the resistance of special-interest groups to mere logic. People are readily persuaded by arguments in which they want to believe and have difficulty understanding arguments that run counter to their interests. More importantly, however, the political process almost guarantees that those who stand to benefit from restrictions on international trade will have a louder voice in policy formation than will the larger group that stands to lose. Transaction costs prevent radio purchasers from organizing effectively to oppose domestic producers; and the foreign producers obviously have little influence on domestic policy. The externalities of the political process in a democracy make it almost certain that when government officials come to the point of choosing between the interests of American buyers of radios and American producers of radios, they will be surrounded by the clamor of producers but will hear almost nothing from consumers. Officials who wish to survive in their jobs pay attention to that kind of pressure.

A limited but legitimate argument for protection against imports can be constructed from the costs of change. The closing down of an industry unable to meet foreign competition entails losses for its owners and employees. The more narrowly specialized the displaced resources, the greater the losses. There may be a case for protection in such circumstances. Notice, however, that the argument can be applied to the case of an industry hurt by domestic competition as well as foreign. Domestic competitors have political influence, of course, and are therefore harder to exclude by special legislation. Nonetheless, if resources were attracted to an industry because of government restrictions on imports, it may be unfair to jerk that protection away suddenly.

So there is a case for the maintenance of prior and long-continued restrictions on imports, or at least for their reduction at a slow rate. Equity considerations along with political realities may also suggest a policy of transitional subsidies, designed to reduce the loss to workers and owners or to help them find new opportunities. But this argument cannot be used to support the introduction of new or additional restrictions against imports.

There is no limit to the number of bad arguments that can be constructed in support of import restrictions, and it would be an exercise in futility to attempt to anticipate and refute each one. The fact that there is a kernel of validity in most such arguments complicates the task of their analysis. The valid reasoning must be winnowed from the chaff that surrounds it before the limitations of its applicability can be shown. Nothing would contribute more toward raising the quality of public discussion in this area than a firm grasp of the principle of comparative advantage.

The principle of comparative advantage shows why and how exchange creates wealth. It keeps insisting that the cost of a transaction is the value of what is given up and the benefit is the value of what is obtained, so that it is nonsense to claim that a country can grow wealthy by exporting more than it imports. The principle of comparative advantage undercuts the claim that one country may be more efficient than another in the production of everything: the logical impossibility of that is apparent from the very definition of efficiency as a ratio between the value of what is produced and what is consequently not produced, between the goods obtained and the goods that had to be sacrificed because production entails genuine opportunity costs. By focusing on the real factors involved in production and trade, the principle of comparative advantage dispels the confusion that so easily arises when trade policy is discussed exclusively in monetary terms.

Unfortunately, there are many parties who hope to gain from fostering this sort of confusion, because they know that they have no real chance to obtain the special-interest legislation they're after unless they can obscure what's going on. These are the people who invent deficits in the trade balance, who claim to find evidence for overvalued or undervalued exchange rates, and who regularly discover that their foreign competitors are engaging in unfair trade practices. In the world of political economy, such arguments have weight. That is the central problem for Chapter 22.

Once Over Lightly

The movement of goods across international boundaries can either frustrate or promote the domestic policies of national governments. Government stabilization policies have particularly close interconnections with international trade policies.

The total credits in a nation's balance of international payments must always exactly equal the total of its debits; any discrepancy reflects errors in record keeping.

A disequilibrium in the balance of payments implies that desired credits and desired debits (desired by whom?) are not equal. To assert that the balance of payments is in deficit is to imply that some credit items were unintended, or cannot be expected to continue, or should not have been allowed to occur. The assertion of a balance-of-payments disequilibrium is thus a complex policy judgment disguised as a simple statement of obvious fact.

Foreign-exchange rates are prices that link the sets of relative prices existing in nations with separate currencies. The movement of these rates is an important factor in the coordination of international transactions and payments.

Exchange rates between national currencies reflect the forces of supply and demand, which are in turn guided by the relative domestic purchasing power of the currencies, modified by expectations with regard to the *future* value of holding various currencies or assets exchangeable for them.

Exchange rates can be set arbitrarily only by governments able to enforce arbitrary prohibitions on international exchange.

Fixed exchange rates promote trade and thus create wealth by reducing uncertainty. But fixed exchange rates between currencies presuppose coordinated domestic economic policies.

In a world of uncoordinated domestic economic policies, floating exchange rates probably produce less uncertainty and more trade than do fixed exchange rates, which in practice are frequently revised.

Most arguments in favor of restrictions on international trade ignore the fundamental principle of comparative advantage, a principle that has not fared well in the area of international trade against well-organized producer groups exploiting public ignorance and nationalist sentiments.

Questions for Discussion

1. Suppose you established an accounting system to keep track of your personal "balance of payments" with your trading partners (i.e., everybody else).

   (a) If you "import" a new television set, you must "export" something else to pay for it. What would you have "exported" if you paid cash to the store at which you bought the set? If you traded in your old set and paid cash for the balance? If you wrote a check to cover the purchase? If you put the purchase on a bank credit card? If you simply promised the store owner that you would pay when you got some money this summer?

   (b) Could you have a balance-of-payments deficit or surplus?

   (c) How would you handle the transaction if your Uncle Miltie gave the set to you as a birthday present?

   (d) If you put a lot of large purchases on your bank credit card over several months while making only minimum payments on the account, are you running a deficit of any sort? Why isn't it proper to call it a deficit in your balance of payments? What will happen to prevent this deficit from continuing indefinitely?

2. An American sends $100 in the form of five crisp twenties as a gift to a relative in Vienna. This action counts as a debit in the U.S. balance of payments. Where does the balancing credit item appear as the following events unfold?

   (a) The Austrian relative exchanges the dollars for schillings at a Vienna bank. The bank holds the dollars, because it has customers who frequently want to buy dollars with schillings.

   (b) The Vienna bank sells the dollars to the Austrian central bank in exchange for schillings.

   (c) The Austrian central bank gives the dollars to the German central bank in exchange for schillings that the German central bank had been holding.

   (d) The German central bank sells the dollars to the Volkswagen Company in exchange for marks.

   (e) The Volkswagen Company gives the dollars as expense money to a company executive who is taking a business trip to Pennsylvania. He spends them at a motel in Scranton.

   (f) If the dollars had remained permanently in Europe, would this imply that the United States had a deficit in its balance of international payments?

3. Is it better for a country to export more merchandise and services than it imports, or to import more than it exports? If you're in doubt, ask the same question about a single household, such as yourself. Which is better

for you: a surplus or a deficit in your personal exporting and importing of goods and services?

4. What are the consequences of heavy net investment in the United States by foreigners?

   (a) Does this mean foreigners are obtaining control of our economy?
   (b) What advantages does the United States receive from net investment by foreigners at a time when the federal government is running large budget deficits?
   (c) If foreigners invest in U.S. agricultural land, do they acquire the power to control our food supply? If they buy stock in U.S. corporations, do they acquire the power to use these corporations in ways that run counter to the security interests of the United States?
   (d) Who benefits and who loses if foreign nationals start acquiring large amounts of prime farming land in the Midwest? Who would want to see the price of such land raised and who would not?

5. Canadian firms trying to attract tourists from the United States will sometimes claim in their advertising that U.S. tourists can benefit from the low price of the Canadian dollar.

   (a) Does the U.S. dollar buy more goods in Canada when one Canadian dollar exchanges for 80 U.S. cents than when one Canadian dollar exchanges for one U.S. dollar?
   (b) If the exchange rate of one Canadian dollar for 80 U.S. cents reflects purchasing-power parity, how much should Americans expect to pay, in Canadian dollars, for a hotel room that would cost $40 in the United States? Why might hotel rooms cost considerably more or less than this even though the exchange rate reflects purchasing-power parity?
   (c) Suppose you are a Canadian retailer of some sort, and you're interested in making as much money as possible from the tourist trade. Would it pay you to place this sign in your shop window: "U.S. dollars exchanged for $1.35 Canadian on all purchases"?

6. For many years Mexico maintained the price of its peso at 8 U.S. cents.

   (a) Could Mexico have succeeded in doing this if the Mexican inflation rate had been much faster or slower than the U.S. inflation rate over a number of years?
   (b) From 1963 to 1972, the rate of inflation in Mexico averaged 5 percent per year; in the United States, over the same period, the inflation rate averaged about 4 percent. From 1972 to 1975, however, the U.S. inflation rate ran at 8 percent while the rate in Mexico leaped to 17 percent. Was there any way the Mexican government could have maintained the 8 cents per peso exchange rate after 1975?
   (c) After a series of devaluations, beginning in 1976, the Mexican government in 1982 abandoned all attempts to fix the rate of exchange between

pesos and dollars. Throughout this period the supply of pesos was growing at annual rates in the vicinity of 30 percent. The peso tumbled steeply when the "peg" was abandoned. For a few months thereafter, Americans found Mexican goods remarkably cheap. Why did Mexican goods become major bargains for Americans in 1982? Why didn't the bargain prices last very long?

7. What do people mean when they say that a currency is *overvalued?* The U.S. dollar, for example, was said by many to be overvalued relative to the yen in 1985 when one dollar was exchanging for 250 yen.

   (a) If people think the dollar is worth less than the price it's currently commanding in the foreign-exchange markets, how can they profit from this knowledge? What will happen to them if they turn out to be wrong?

   (b) What is the test of whether they are right or wrong? Where do we look to discover the true value of one currency relative to others?

8. In 1986 the Japanese began complaining that the yen was overvalued, at a time when a dollar could be purchased for 160 yen.

   (a) On what grounds do you suppose the Japanese were making their complaint?

   (b) If the yen is overvalued relative to the dollar, must the dollar necessarily be undervalued relative to the yen?

9. What do you suppose happened to the price of Japanese cars in the United States when the yen appreciated in 1985 and 1986 from 250 to 160 per dollar?

10. How do large changes in foreign-exchange rates, such as the sharp swing from 1985 to 1986 in the dollar–yen exchange rate, affect business firms engaging in extensive international exchange? Who puts political pressure on a government, and what do they ask for, when that government's currency appreciates substantially?

11. From 1980 to 1985, the U.S. dollar appreciated over 50 percent relative to the weighted average of other currencies. How did this affect the following groups?

   (a) Americans interested in buying foreign automobiles.
   (b) Americans interested in buying U.S.-made automobiles.
   (c) American automobile manufacturers and their employees.
   (d) Americans planning foreign travel.
   (e) Americans operating businesses that cater extensively to foreign tourists.
   (f) American firms that export extensively.
   (g) American firms that manufacture items with a lot of imported materials and parts.
   (h) American firms that fit both of the two preceding descriptions.

12. Under a system of fixed exchange rates, every nation must experience approximately the same rate of inflation as every other.

    (a) Why is this so?
    (b) How can a country determined to have both a low inflation rate and a fixed rate of exchange between its own and other nations' currencies go about achieving these two objectives if other countries choose high inflation rates?

13. "Floating exchange rates free a nation to pursue the domestic policies it prefers." Is that true? Is it *desirable* that governments be able to pursue whatever monetary and fiscal policies they wish, free from any constraints that might be imposed by the system of international exchange? From whose point of view might such "freedom" be highly undesirable?

14. What is the difference between exchange rates that are free to fluctuate in response to conditions of supply and demand, and exchange rates that are fixed but are periodically altered in accordance with changed conditions of supply and demand?

15. Why can't one country have a comparative advantage over another country in the production of everything if the first country has excellent natural resources, a huge capital stock, a highly skilled labor force, and ingenious technicians and managers, while the second country is poor in all four areas?

16. What evidence exists to support the view that Japan has a comparative advantage with respect to the United States in the production of small automobiles? How would you account for this comparative advantage? How would you explain the fact that the United States in general seems to have a comparative advantage in the production of large automobiles but a comparative disadvantage in the production of smaller ones?

17. How does the theory of "free riders" help explain the generally greater legislative influence of producers than of consumers?

18. Estimates published in 1972 predicted that the Concorde SST, the French and British supersonic commercial plane, would not repay its development costs, would create environmental problems, and would not generate sufficient additional revenue to cover the associated costs for the airlines that purchased them. These were essentially the objections that led to cancellation of government financing for an American supersonic commercial plane. A counterargument in both cases was that these planes would provide many additional jobs, help the balance of payments, and prevent other countries from gaining an advantage. How would you evaluate these counterarguments?

19. Everyone will agree that *some* policies that would create more jobs for Americans are nonetheless not in the national interest. For example, no one recommends that we build highways without using heavy machinery, even though many more jobs would be created if highways were built entirely with hand tools. When is the job-creation argument actually used? Are there any circumstances in which it's a defensible argument?

20. In order to take advantage of lower production costs, a Massachusetts textile manufacturer builds a factory in North Carolina, and a U.S. television-manufacturing firm opens an assembly plant in Mexico.

(a) In what ways is the action by the television firm different from the action by the textile firm?

(b) Is either action contrary to the national interest?

(c) Is either action likely to encounter effective political opposition?

Chapter 22

Inflation, Recession, and Political Economy

If all the interrelationships that we've been discussing since Chapter 15 were clearly and confidently understood, so that economists could explain cause and effect as precisely as chemists do in their laboratories, government stabilization policies might be set in the public interest. But the theories of economists in this area are much less precise and far more subject to debate than are the theories of chemists. That leaves considerable room for policymakers to talk persuasively about the public interest while actually responding to the pressure of much narrower interests. The net result of such policies could well be less stability rather than more.

The Political Setting

Government is not like Aladdin's marvelous genie, who always obeyed commands and always succeeded in accomplishing what he was told to do. The agencies of government, for all their power and importance, are staffed entirely by human beings. Moreover, even if government is "of the people, by the people, for the people," in Abraham Lincoln's immortal phrase, government is not necessarily going to do what the majority wants. As Chapter 14 tried to show, the policies of government will reflect the interests of those people who are in a position to extract benefits for themselves from the political process at low cost. Government may be unable to prevent inflation or moderate recessions because the people in control of government policies don't actually want to. This is not to suggest that any policymaker prefers inflation to price stability, or frequent and deep recessions to steady levels of production and employment. It suggests only that policymakers may not find it in their interest to do what must be done if periods of recession and inflation are to be avoided.

The economic theory of government predicts that

Government officials have short time horizons.

Governments officials pay attention to those who are paying attention to them.

elected and appointed officials will pay attention to their own interests in choosing policies and carrying them out. Elected officials, with their gaze fixed on the next election, will prefer policies that pay benefits before election day and don't present their costs until after the voters have made their choice. Policies with short-term benefits and long-term costs thus have a strong advantage under the democratic political process. That fact has serious implications for the conduct of stabilization policies.

Moreover, appointed as well as elected officials won't weigh each citizen's interests equally in making their decisions. They'll be partial to the pressures and pleadings of those who make their preferences known precisely, and who care enough to monitor the decisions that government officials finally make. The squeaking wheel gets the grease. Few sugar consumers know or care very strongly how their legislative representative votes on a bill to raise sugar support prices or exclude sugar imports; but you can be certain that U.S. sugar producers know and care, and that your legislator in turn knows and cares who knows and cares — and who does not much care and so isn't paying attention. That is also going to make it more difficult for government to stabilize the economy, for reasons we shall explore.

Time Horizons and the Sequence of Effects

When we look carefully at the way in which changes in fiscal and monetary policy are likely to affect economic activity, we discover how important are the time horizons of those who construct such policy.

Suppose that the government finances an increase in its expenditures by borrowing from commercial banks, thereby increasing the money supply. This will increase the aggregate demand for newly produced goods. We cannot be sure how the resulting effect on GNP will be distributed between larger output and higher prices; but we do have good grounds for believing that any effect on output and employment will appear *before* the effect on prices. The reason is that sellers interpret increased sales as an increased *relative* demand for what they are selling and consequently try to expand output. It takes more time for all these efforts to manifest themselves as an increased demand for resources generally, and to produce an increase in costs and prices. So the "good stuff" arrives first: a rise in real GNP and a fall in the unemployment rate. The "bad stuff," a higher rate of inflation, is delayed. If politicians are contemplating an imminent election—and in the United States every member of the House of Representatives is on average only one year from the next election—the temptation will be strong to pursue short-run "good stuff" and let someone else worry later about the "bad stuff."

Contractionary policies will also produce their effects on output and employment more quickly than they affect the rate of change in the price level. In this case, however, the "bad stuff" arrives before the "good stuff." Any attempt to lower the rate of inflation by narrowing the government deficit and reducing the growth rate of the money supply will threaten to produce increased inventories and hence reduced output and employment. The disinflationary impact will be delayed until the reduced demand for resources has had a chance to exert downward pressure on costs and prices. In short, an attempt to slow down the inflation rate by initiating less-expansionary fiscal and monetary policies is very likely to produce a recession before it succeeds in its aim of reducing inflation.

Changes in aggregate demand affect output and employment before they affect prices.

Destabilization Through Stabilization Policies

What predictions follow? Elected officials will be quick to approve expansionary fiscal and monetary policies, opting for expansion whenever they are in doubt. This course will further commend itself to them because expansionary fiscal and monetary policies would generally be attractive to voters even if they had no effect at all on aggregate demand. Lower taxes and increased expenditures on behalf of interested parties make good campaign material for incumbents. Increased monetary ease tends to lower interest rates, at least momentarily; and that is also looked on approvingly by voters.

Contractionary policies by contrast inflict pain. Higher taxes and reduced expenditures will antagonize voters, as will any higher interest rates that result from tightening the supply of credit. Unless economic decisionmakers understand exactly what is going on and immediately lower their prices when aggregate demand falls, contractionary policies will produce a business slump and a rise in unemployment. The ensuing complaints will be listened to attentively by those who are contemplating an imminent election. They will be sorely tempted to withdraw the painful medicine and substitute the soothing tonic of expansionary policies.

All this suggests that democratic political processes will tend to produce jerky aggregate-demand policies with a bias toward expansion. When expansionary policies produce (eventually) an intolerable rate of inflation, the contractionary brakes will be applied. Unless disinflation comes quickly, however, the resulting recession and unemployment will create pressure to let up on the brakes and step once more on the accelerator. Such "go-stop-go" policies make the future more uncertain and result in more mistakes, which are the basic underlying cause of recessions. More frequent and severe recessions along with a rising rate of inflation could easily become the standard pattern in democratically governed societies.

Deficits Unlimited

Governments that must pay attention to popular opinion have long been tempted to spend more than they collect in taxes. You don't have to study economics to learn that it's easier for a legislator to support tax reductions than tax increases, and to support enlarged expenditures rather than reduced expenditures. As a result, even if every member of the legislature wanted a budget surplus, a surplus wouldn't necessarily emerge. While a large majority of voters may want a decrease in government expenditures, they will also want increased expenditures, or at least no reductions, for the tiny part of the total budget that constitutes their own sliver of the pie. And when that particular sliver is being sliced, each little special-interest group lets the legislators know that a cut at this point will have repercussions on campaign contributions and votes. There's no way to reduce the total budget while expanding each individual item in it. That's why government expenditures rise even though each and every legislator wants them to decline.

Reducing expenditures means reducing some people's benefits.

If this analysis is to account for chronic government budget deficits, however, it has to explain why state and local governments don't produce such deficits, and why the federal government didn't regularly do so before 1970.

First of all, state and local governments differ from the federal government in one crucial respect. Only the federal government has control over the ultimate means for the payment of debts. State and local governments are like you: they can't borrow, and so can't run deficits, unless they can convince potential lenders that today's deficit is a temporary shortfall that will be compensated for by a surplus tomorrow. Chronic, persistent deficits are ruled out by the fact that lenders won't extend credit to a government unless they believe that government will be able to repay its debts in full

and on time. This fact imposes no constraint on the federal
government, however, because lenders know that the federal
government can always *create* the money it needs to meet
its obligations. Although money creation of this sort means
that lenders will be repaid in dollars of decreased value, it
also means that all creditors, not just creditors of the federal
government, will be repaid in depreciated currency. Consequently, no one worries about lending to the federal
government.

That might explain why the federal government runs
continuous and growing budget deficits if we could also explain why the federal government did *not* run chronic deficits before 1970. The answer may be the strong public prejudice against government deficits, a prejudice that used to
view such deficits as immoral, evidence of an irresponsible
failure on the part of government to live within its means.
Moral convictions that are strongly and widely held do operate as an effective check on legislators, especially when a
majority of the legislators themselves adhere to that moral
conviction.

That brings us to the last link in the chain of explanation. Americans are no longer as firmly persuaded as they
once were that deficits are immoral. The public today
vaguely "knows" that a budget deficit can be a means for
promoting prosperity. The lesson supposedly taught by
Keynesian analysis was that budgets don't have to be balanced from year to year; they need only to be balanced over
the course of the business cycle, with surpluses in periods of
prosperity making up for deficits in periods of slump. This
new doctrine was widely used to argue that deficits in the
1960s and 1970s were good for the economy, and that anyone insisting on a balanced federal budget just did not understand "modern economics." Most people are willing to be
convinced of something they would like to be true.

The trouble with this new doctrine is that its effect is to
permit perennial deficits. There is no fiscal period that can
be identified with "the course of the business cycle." As a
result, the surplus that is supposed to balance the deficit
never has to be budgeted; it can always be promised for next
year or the year after. With the last effective pressure toward
a balanced budget thereby eliminated, the bias of the democratic political process takes over and produces a long and
perhaps endless succession of deficits. As the deficit years
continue and the national debt increases but the sky does
not fall, the conviction that the government's budget really
ought to be balanced is bound to lose its hold.

Creditors love to lend to anyone who can create the means of repayments.

Deficits aren't "immoral" if they are policy tools.

The Political Economy of Monetary Policy

We've been paying attention primarily to fiscal policy in the course of arguing that government demand-management policies are likely to be go-stop-go with an expansionary bias. What about monetary policy? Couldn't the monetary authorities refuse to finance government deficits? Suppose that the Fed allowed the money stock to grow by only 4 percent per year. What would happen? Could large and continuing government budget deficits lead to inflation if the monetary authorities withheld their cooperation? And in the absence of accelerating inflation, disruptive changes in policy direction could be less frequent.

These are particularly important questions because the monetary managers are not subject to the political pressures that constrain elected officials. The people who created the Federal Reserve System in 1913 were aware that popular politics exerts pressure on governments to pursue inflationary policies, and so they put control of the monetary system in the hands of an independent agency of the federal government. Members of the Board of Governors are appointed by law for fourteen-year terms, so that they can act independently of Congress and the administration. What would happen if the Fed exercised its statutory independence to the extent of directly opposing the government's fiscal policies?

The Fed would lose in an all-out confrontation, because Congress can, finally, take away the independence that it has granted. On the other hand, Congress would be reluctant to take such dramatic steps or to precipitate a public debate in which members of Congress might be seen as advocates of inflation. So the Fed probably could, up to a point, pursue monetary policies designed to neutralize the impact of federal deficits. Nonetheless, it is doubtful that the Fed would persist for very long in any such policy. The reasons are rooted in uncertainties about the way in which monetary policy works, in the mounting public hostility toward the Fed that such a course would almost surely nurture, and perhaps also in the bureaucratic conservatism that almost inevitably dominates a central bank.

We can at least be sure of this: it will be politically difficult for the Fed to counter inflationary fiscal policies until the public acquires a better understanding of interest rates — how they function to allocate scarce resources among competing claimants and between present and future; how inflationary expectations raise nominal but not real interest rates; how monetary policy actually influences interest rates;

and how limited is the ability of the monetary authorities to control interest rates. We can also be sure that no effective campaign to educate the public on the significance of interest rates will be possible as long as disagreement on the subject exists even among high-ranking officials in the Federal Reserve System.

Why is it, someone might be wondering at this point, that Fed officials have so much trouble deciding at what targets they ought to aim and how best to hit them? Can't they learn from experience? The Federal Reserve has extensive freedom to experiment and enormous resources in people, money, and data with which to carry out experiments on the effectiveness of monetary policy procedures. Moreover, the system's managers have possessed roughly their present powers for forty years now. Why haven't they learned more than they claim to know about the conduct of monetary policy? Is it possible that the Fed suffers from a severe case of bureaucratic inertia?

A vast and powerful organization, insulated from competitive pressures and from effective political control, could easily develop a strong interest in maintaining the status quo. Monetary policy in this country might be a bit of a muddle because the nation's monetary authorities like it that way. It makes them the managers and guardians of important and mysterious processes that no one fully understands.

Discretion and Rules

There is considerable evidence that the use of discretionary fiscal and monetary policy to stabilize the economy has actually increased its instability, at least since the late 1960s. This judgment, which cannot be conclusively demonstrated, will be strenuously resisted by those who want to believe that we do possess the knowledge and skills required to achieve milder recessions and greater price stability through aggregate-demand management. The fact that stabilization policy obviously failed in the 1970s won't discourage anyone who thinks it failed only because the right people weren't in charge. But institutions should not be evaluated on the assumption that angels will run them. It is far more likely that government policies will be controlled by politicians than by angels, and that monetary and especially fiscal policies will be formulated in the same political context that produces decisions on import tariffs, flood-control projects, and the location of military bases.

The alternative to discretionary fiscal and monetary policies is not *no* policy but policy based on firm commitments to known rules. Sometimes this is called *automatic* or *nondiscretionary* fiscal and monetary policy. But there is actually nothing automatic about adhering to clearly enunciated rules, and continuing to do so in the face of strong temptations to relax the rules is certainly a discretionary act. The issue is not whether discretion is better than the absence of discretion. The question, rather, is whether anyone can in fact increase the stability of the economy by deliberately moving the government budget between surplus and deficit and deliberately changing bank reserves or reserve requirements. The alternative view is that efforts to stabilize in these ways will actually be destabilizing, because no one has the knowledge and other capabilities, technical and political, to manipulate aggregate demand with the necessary precision. A sufficiently graceful elephant could stabilize a sailboat in rough weather by shifting its weight with delicacy and perfect timing. But the sailing companions of an elephant without these gifts would probably prefer that it remain quietly in the center of the boat.

The critics of discretionary-demand management also want monetary policy to enunciate a course and stick to it. They want the Fed to maintain a steady hand on the stock of money, either holding it constant or allowing it to increase by some definite, known, uniform, and moderate rate, perhaps one equal to the long-term average growth rate of real output. There are automatic monetary stabilizers as well as automatic fiscal stabilizers in the economic system. A

Those economists who believe that fiscal and monetary policies have aggravated recession and fostered inflation over the last two decades offer two recommendations. With respect to fiscal policy, they want the level of expenditures determined without reference to stabilization imperatives, and tax rates set so as to balance the budget over a normal period. In recessions, tax receipts will fall and the budget will be in deficit. In a period of boom or when a recovery is well along, tax receipts will be high and will generate a surplus. These recurring deficits and surpluses will function as self-regulating governors, dampening oscillations in the economy. Any additional discretionary-policy actions are more likely to aggravate than to reduce instability, because discretionary actions are hard to time appropriately and because anticipation of them creates additional uncertainty for private decisionmakers.

boom will eventually run against rising interest rates and credit rationing if the monetary managers don't feed the boom by pumping new reserves into the banking system. And during a period of economic decline, lending terms will tend to improve as the demand for credit slackens, thus encouraging some potential investors. More management than this, as in the case of fiscal policy, is much more likely to increase than to diminish instability.

Who Is at the Controls?

The drive for a constitutional amendment to require a balanced federal budget rests basically on the belief that political control of the economy must itself be subject to control. That's an important insight. But if such an amendment were to be enacted and ratified, balancing the budget would still be a difficult task. Achieving an annual balance between expenditures and receipts might well produce some highly destabilizing actions on the part of the federal government. And in the last analysis, it wouldn't prevent the timing and allocation of transfer payments, government purchases, or tax-law changes in ways that destabilize the economy but improve the reelection prospects of incumbents.

Although we mustn't expect mortals to be angels, we also mustn't expect miracles from formulas. The Greek physicist Archimedes supposedly said that he could move the earth itself if given one firm spot on which to stand. The thought of such an Archimedean vantage point is alluring to those who worry about economic problems. "There *has* to be a solution. If the economy doesn't work properly, we'll have the government fix it. If the government doesn't work properly, we'll amend the Constitution. If we can't get the Constitution amended, we'll launch a vast educational campaign. If education doesn't work, we'll transform the whole school system. . . . " There just isn't any firm spot on which an Archimedes can set his fulcrum and lever society into the proper position.

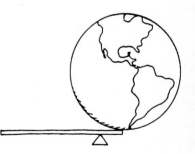

The functioning of the economy, along with the functioning of government and every other social institution, depends finally on our mutual ability to secure cooperation. We noted on the first page of Chapter 1 how difficult it is for most of us even to recognize the many extraordinary ways in which we successfully cooperate every day. As with an automobile engine, it is only failure that attracts our attention. When the engine is performing well, we don't think about it;

we give our attention to the scenery or the road ahead. But because we don't look at our mechanisms of social coordination when they're functioning well, we often fail to discover either how they work or how dependent we are on their continued smooth performance. And we often conclude erroneously that some simple bit of tinkering will make them function even better.

Wealthy, industrialized economic systems have always experienced periodic fluctuations in production and employment. Is instability an inherent characteristic of an economic system operating without government intervention? That's very probably the case. But *how much* instability will exist in the absence of government intervention to stabilize aggregate demand? How deep will recessions be? How much time will ordinarily elapse before recovery begins? What will be the costs of recessions? On whom will they fall? Those are important questions.

But so are these. How much instability will exist in the *presence* of government intervention to stabilize aggregate demand? Does anyone really know enough to compensate for fluctuations in private spending? Who will actually be in charge? What interests will guide their decisions? How often will long-term stability be sacrificed for the sake of a short-term performance that improves reelection prospects?

All these are in large part questions about how well market systems work. How smoothly and quickly do prices adjust to changing conditions of demand or supply? How smoothly and quickly do resources move about in response to the new information that changing prices present? While we can hope that continuing empirical and theoretical inquiry will improve our understanding of these matters, big-picture questions of this sort are notoriously hard to answer to everyone's satisfaction. Fact and fancy, logic and longing get mixed up with each other in the course of such inquiries. Our judgments about what is possible are subtly colored by our visions of what is desirable.

We would probably find it easier to agree on how the economy works if we were all agreed on how we *want* the economy to work. In the absence of such a consensus, however, we might just have to go on discussing the issues without ever being certain that we have found the best solutions.

Once Over Lightly

Government stabilization policies are controlled not by impartial — much less omniscient — experts, but by political processes. Those who make policy do so in the light of their own interests and in response to the incentives they perceive.

Stabilization policies in a democratic society are significantly affected by the relatively short time horizons of government officials, who will be under pressure to ignore the long-run costs of programs that produce short-run benefits.

An unanticipated change in the rate of growth of aggregate demand will affect output and employment before it affects costs and prices. The benefits therefore precede the costs when policy takes an expansionary turn, but the costs precede the benefits when policy turns contractionary. Political officials looking toward imminent elections will consequently find expansionary policies in their interest and contractionary policies contrary to their interest. This will tend to produce go-stop-go policies with an inflationary bias.

The democratic political process also tends to produce chronic federal government budget deficits, which in turn put pressure on the monetary authorities to expand the money supply.

Because the federal government ultimately controls the means of payment, it can always borrow successfully. In the absence of any overriding imperative to achieve a long-run budget balance, democratic political processes may produce an indefinite sequence of budget deficits.

Political pressures on the Fed make the control of inflation through monetary policy a difficult task. Effective monetary policy has also been made more difficult by the inability or unwillingness of the monetary managers to improve the techniques of monetary control.

Government might make its greatest contribution to economic stability by trying to do less. Government policies that were more stable and predictable would introduce less uncertainty into the economic system.

The argument between advocates of discretionary stabilization policy and those who want policy to be governed by fixed rules known in advance turns largely on the issue of how equitably and efficiently markets work.

Questions for Discussion

1. Unanticipated changes in the growth rate of aggregate demand tend to affect production and employment *before* they affect prices.

   (a) Why do the output and employment effects tend to precede the price effects?

    (b) Why does this give elected officials an incentive both to approve expansionary policies and not to persist in contractionary policies?

    (c) Why would a president serving a second term and hence ineligible for reelection still be under pressure to pursue policies with quick benefits and deferred costs? Who would apply the pressure?

2. If the members of Congress genuinely believe that large government budget deficits are a threat to prosperity, why don't they reduce the deficits?

3. Suppose a member of Congress votes against a bill to allocate $100 million in taxpayers' money to an irrigation canal that will provide about $10 million in benefits to a few hundred ranchers. Why might this action cause the legislator a net loss in both votes and campaign contributions?

4. Why do so many members of Congress believe that the federal government should subsidize local projects, such as improvements in bus or subway systems in major cities?

    (a) Who would benefit from construction of a subway system in a large city?

    (b) Can you think of a *public interest* argument for having taxpayers across the country pay for a local subway system?

    (c) If you knew that your taxes were going to go up $10 a year in order to finance a subway in some distant city, would you write a letter of protest to your legislator?

    (d) If your city was being considered for a large federal grant to subsidize an improvement in the local public transportation system, would you expect your local government officials to go to Washington and lobby actively for it? Would you expect your congressional representatives to support it? Would you form a more favorable opinion of local officials and congressional representatives if your city proved successful in its grant application?

5. If you favor reduced government expenditures, do you also favor reducing government financial assistance to programs that benefit you?

6. New York City teetered on the edge of bankruptcy some years ago because it had accumulated large debts through deficit spending and seemed unable either to raise taxes or to cut expenditures sufficiently to balance its budget. Lenders refused to extend additional credit unless the federal government guaranteed that it would pay New York City's debts in the event of a default.

    (a) How did New York City get into such a situation?

    (b) Of what use to lenders was a federal government guarantee when the federal government was in fact running much larger deficits than New York City and had even poorer prospects for balancing its budget?

    (c) What consequences would you predict if the federal government committed itself to paying off all creditors who might otherwise be hurt through the financial default of municipal or state governments?

7. In every year throughout the 1970s and the first half of the 1980s, the combined budgets of state and local governments showed a surplus, whereas the federal government budget was in deficit. How would you account for this dramatic difference?

8. Voters who don't want their taxes increased impose obvious constraints on any democratic government's ability to raise additional revenue. But there are other constraints as well.

    (a) How can people legally avoid a state income or sales tax?
    (b) Voters don't seem to be terribly hostile toward increased taxes on business. Why can't state and local governments collect all the revenue they want simply by raising taxes on businesses?
    (c) Why don't these constraints bind the federal government as effectively as they bind state and local governments?

9. When a state or city government starts borrowing to finance current expenditures (as distinct from capital expenditures for highways, schools, public buildings, and the like), its bond rating usually falls. A lower bond rating indicates a riskier investment.

    (a) Why does the bond rating fall?
    (b) What will happen to the price of bonds whose rating is lowered?
    (c) What does this do to the cost of borrowing?
    (d) How does this constrain state and local governments from borrowing to finance current expenditures?
    (e) What must a state or local government do if it is determined not to borrow to finance current expenditures?
    (f) Why doesn't any of this happen to the federal government when it finances current expenditures through borrowing rather than taxation?

10. When a corporation successfully sells additional bonds or a new issue of common stock, it goes deeply into debt.

    (a) Is this evidence that the corporation is failing or that it's succeeding?
    (b) How well or poorly does an analogy from the area of business indebtedness apply to questions of government indebtedness?
    (c) Suppose the government borrows to construct a dam. How is such borrowing similar to or different from business borrowing for investment?

11. Do you think that people who "live beyond their means" display a character flaw? What about a government that fails to confine its expenditures to the amount of its tax receipts?

12. Suppose the Treasury borrowed $20 billion in September of the presidential election year in order to increase the benefits to be paid on October 1 to recipients of social security benefits, welfare grants, and unemployment compensation. What would be the effects on the money supply? On consumer spending in October? On the unemployment rate? On the price level? On the election? When would you expect these various effects?

13. The Federal Reserve was created to be an independent agency of the federal government — independent, that is, of the immediate political pressures that are felt by elected officials and appointed officials whom the elected officials can demote or discharge.

    (a) Is it "undemocratic" to have an organization as powerful as the Fed that isn't answerable to the voters?
    (b) If Fed officials had to answer to elected officials, would that make them answerable to the voters?
    (c) Under which of these three circumstances do you think it is most likely and under which do you think it is least likely that monetary policy would promote the public interest: the present system; a system under which presidents could dismiss Fed officials the way they can now dismiss cabinet members; a referendum system under which the Fed's policies would have to be periodically approved by a majority vote of the electorate?

14. How independent is the independent Fed? Fed officials and Treasury officials regularly cooperate to smooth the financing and refinancing activities of the federal government as it borrows the vast sums required to cover current deficits and refund the huge national debt.

    (a) Don't people who work cooperatively usually come to see their problems in similar or at least compatible ways? Isn't the Fed more likely to conclude that a particular monetary policy is the best policy if it also happens to ease the financing problems of the Treasury?
    (b) The Treasury would like to keep down the costs of its borrowing and refunding. How could the Fed help achieve this laudable objective?
    (c) If the Fed tries to provide enough reserves to the banking system to make sure that borrowing costs don't rise during large Treasury borrowing operations, what must it do? Why might a succession of such cooperative moves by the Fed eventually cause interest rates and Treasury borrowing costs to rise steeply?

15. Would you expect to find a relationship between an informed person's attitude toward attempts at fine-tuning and his or her reactions to the following judgments? Explain why.

    (a) "Fiscal and monetary managers have better information than business decisionmakers because they have access to statistical data on the overall performance of the economy and don't have to concern themselves with details."
    (b) "The government must establish procedures for national economic planning if we are to avoid the kinds of economic crises experienced in the 1970s."
    (c) "The market does not work as it used to. Competition no longer sets prices or allocates resources in the U.S. economy. Most of that is done by organized interest groups with substantial market power."

(d) "The U.S. economy displays an absurd social imbalance. Privately purchased goods are produced in abundance while public-sector goods such as education must be content with the leavings."

(e) "Power tends to corrupt, and absolute power corrupts absolutely."

Chapter 23

The Limitations of Economics

The possibility of civilization depends largely on how well societies work. What does the economic way of thinking reveal about the working of society? Is there anything of importance that it conceals?

If you can bring yourself to return to the first chapter of this book, you will find a brief discussion of the biases of economic theory. You might want to read that section again, now that you've completed the book. Are those really biases? Or are they something more like useful working hypotheses?

What Economists Know

The economic way of thinking employs such concepts as demand, opportunity cost, marginal effects, and comparative advantage to order familiar phenomena. The economist knows very little about the real world that is not better known by business executives, artisans, engineers, and others who make things happen. What economists do know is *how things fit together*. The concepts of economics enable us to make better sense out of what we observe, to think more consistently and coherently about a wide range of complex social interactions.

This turns out in practice to be a largely negative kind of knowledge about mostly impersonal transactions. The economic way of thinking, as you may have noticed, contributes relatively little to our understanding of relationships within the family or other small groups where people can know one another well enough to cooperate on a personal basis. Economics mostly explains how cooperation occurs among people who don't know one another at all, but who nonetheless manage to work together with extraordinary effectiveness. Perhaps you also detected, as you read through the chapters of this book, a greater emphasis on what *should not* be done than on what *should* be done. But negative conclusions are important. The economist Frank Knight used to defend the heavily negative character of economic reasoning with a quotation: "It ain't ignorance that does the most damage; it's knowin' so derned much that ain't so."

Too many people "know" how to solve pressing social problems. Their mental picture of the economic universe is a simple one, in which intentions can easily be realized and the only obstacle to a better society is therefore a lack of good intentions. But social actions have consequences that run far beyond those that can be easily predicted or foreseen. Restricting textile imports into the United States, for example, does, for the present at least, protect the jobs and income of textile producers; that's clear enough. But it takes a tutored eye to notice that this will shift even more income away from other Americans, by raising textile prices, reducing American export opportunities, and in general inhibiting the exploitation of comparative advantage. Again, it is easy to see that rent controls hold down the money payments that tenants must make to landlords. But how many advocates of such controls are aware of the alternative payments that tenants will have to make, of the new forms of discrimination that will replace discrimination on the basis of money price, and of the short- and long-run effects on the supply of rental housing?

Nonetheless, people easily become impatient with those who warn against the inadvisability of actions that will make matters worse without proposing solutions of their own. And in a society such as ours, accustomed to the almost miraculous accomplishments of science and technology, the demand for "doing something" tends to exceed by a wide margin the supply of genuine solutions to social problems. We have probably erred in assuming that social problems can be handled in the same way that we manage technological problems. We admit that conflicting interests create hard problems for social policymakers. But we still underestimate the difficulties in the way of bringing about planned social change, largely because we underestimate the complexity of social systems, of the networks of interaction through which behavior is coordinated in a society and people are induced to cooperate in the achievement of their goals.

Perhaps that's why economic theory often treats proposals for reform of the economic system so unkindly. It's not that economists are themselves uninterested in reform, much less that they're the paid lackeys of the privileged classes. But economic theory, by revealing the interdependence of decisions, calls attention to the unexamined consequences of proposals for change. "It won't work out that way" is the economist's standard response to many well-intentioned policy proposals. Realism is not necessarily conservatism, but it often looks quite similar. And there is a sense in which knowledge does promote conservatism. Even physicists have been accused of hopeless conservatism by would-be inventors of perpetual-motion machines.

Beyond Mere Economics

John Maynard Keynes once proposed a toast to economists, "the keepers of the possibility of civilization." The *possibility* of civilization — that is all. The efficient allocation of resources enlarges the realm of possibility, but it does not by itself guarantee the progress of civilization. A well-coordinated and smoothly functioning society gives individuals more opportunity to choose; it does not guarantee that they will choose well. The economic way of thinking, especially in a democracy, is an important preliminary. But it is no more than that.

Economists are for the most part prepared to admit that the concepts they employ sometimes distort the reality they study. And they are willing to submit their analysis and conclusions to the test of rational criticism. But some point of view is indispensable to any inquiry, in the physical sciences as well as the social sciences. If the economic way of thinking sometimes leads to distortions, to misplaced emphasis, or even to outright error, the appropriate corrective is rational criticism. The application of that corrective has frequently altered the conclusions of economics in the past. It will probably continue to do so in the future.

Glossary

Definitions or explanations of the terms listed below may be found on the pages whose numbers are printed in the index after these items in **bold type.**

Adjudication
Automatic versus discretionary stabilization policy
Balance of international payments
Capital
Cartels
Coercion
Comparative advantage
Competition
Cost-push inflation
Deadweight costs
Demand, concept of
Demand, law of
Demand, price elasticity of
Demand deposits
Demand for money
Demand-side economics
Discount rate
Economic way of thinking
Efficiency
Entrepreneur
Externalities (spillovers)
Federal funds rate
Federal Reserve
Fiscal policy
Foreign exchange rates
Free riders

Futures (contracts)
Government
Gross national product
Hedgers
Human capital
Implicit GNP deflator
Income and wealth
"Incomes policy"
Inflation
Interest rates
Investment
Keynesianism
Liquidity
Marginal analysis
Marginal cost
Marginal revenue
Markets
Monetarism
Monetary base
Monetary policy
Money
Monopoly
Net revenue
Nominal versus real gross national product
Nominal versus real interest rates
Noninstitutional population

Oligopoly
Open market operations
Opportunity cost
Persuasion
Phillips curve
Pollution
Positive externalities (spillover benefits)
Predatory pricing
Price searchers
Price takers
Profit
Property rights
Public interest
Rationing
Recession
Rules of the game
Saving
Scarcity
Shortage
Speculation
Sunk costs
Supply, price elasticity of
Supply and demand
Supply-side economics
Surplus
Transaction costs
Unemployed versus "not employed"

Index